PRACTICAL UNIX® PROGRAMMING

A Guide to Concurrency, Communication, and Multithreading

Kay A. Robbins and Steven Robbins

The University of Texas at San Antonio

For book and bookstore information

http://www.prenhall.com

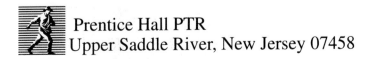

Prentice Hall PTR
Upper Saddle River, New Jersey 07458

Library of Congress Cataloging-in-Publication Data

Robbins, Kay A.
    Practical UNIX programming: a guide to concurrency,
  communication, and multithreading / Kay A. Robbins, Steven Robbins.
        p.   cm.
    Includes bibliographical references and index.
    ISBN 0-13-443706-3 (alk. paper)
    1. UNIX (Computer file) 2. Microcomputers--Programming.
I. Robbins, Steven.   II. Title.
QA76.76.063R615 1996   95-39618
005.4'2--dc20   CIP

Editorial/production supervision: *Jane Bonnell*
Cover design director: *Jerry Votta*
Cover design: *Lundgren Graphics, Ltd.*
Manufacturing manager: *Alexis R. Heydt*
Acquisitions editor: *Gregory G. Doench*
Editorial assistant: *Meg Cowen*

 © 1996 by Prentice Hall PTR
Prentice-Hall, Inc.
A Simon & Schuster Company
Upper Saddle River, New Jersey 07458

The publisher offers discounts on this book when ordered in bulk quantities. For more information, contact Corporate Sales Department, Prentice Hall PTR, One Lake Street, Upper Saddle River, NJ 07458. Phone: 800-382-3419; FAX: 201- 236-7141; E-mail: corpsales@prenhall.com

Linda is a registered trademark of Scientific Computing Associates. MS-DOS is a registered trademark of Microsoft Corporation. NFS, ONC, and Solaris are trademarks or registered trademarks of Sun Microsystems, Inc. SPARCstation is a trademark of SPARC International, Inc., licensed exclusively to Sun Microsystems, Inc. Products bearing SPARC trademarks are based upon an architecture developed by Sun Microsystems, Inc. UNIX is a registered trademark in the United States and other countries licensed exclusively through X/Open Company Ltd. X Window System is a trademark of the Massachusetts Institute of Technology.

Printed in the United States of America
10 9 8 7 6 5 4 3

ISBN 0-13-443706-3

Prentice-Hall International (UK) Limited, *London*
Prentice-Hall of Australia Pty. Limited, *Sydney*
Prentice-Hall Canada Inc., *Toronto*
Prentice-Hall Hispanoamericana, S.A., *Mexico*
Prentice-Hall of India Private Limited, *New Delhi*
Prentice-Hall of Japan, Inc., *Tokyo*
Simon & Schuster Asia Pte. Ltd., *Singapore*
Editora Prentice-Hall do Brasil, Ltda., *Rio de Janeiro*

To our students

Contents

Preface

Computer systems are evolving rapidly from large single-processor mainframes accessed by terminals toward networks of multiprocessor workstations. Ideas such as concurrency, communication, and multithreading have moved out of the research community and into the commercial world. The applications programmer must understand these concepts, and this book is designed to make the concepts accessible at a detailed level.

The book uses a hands-on approach in a nontraditional sense. In the traditional "hands-on" approach to operating systems, programmers implement a simple operating system or modify an existing operating system to add functionality. The hands-on approach provides an in-depth understanding of basic operating system design, but it is hard for programmers to pursue independently in the field. When this approach is used at the average university, instructors spend considerable class time covering implementation details—leaving less time to cover a full range of topics. Also, the traditional hands-on approach usually does not provide practical programming experience with advanced synchronization and communication constructs. An alternative to the hands-on approach is a theoretical presentation. Such a "hands-off" course covers more material but does not give the reader an in-depth understanding of the concepts in practice.

Practical UNIX Programming: A Guide to Concurrency, Communication, and Multithreading bridges the gap between the hands-on and hands-off approaches to operating systems by covering programming under standard UNIX. The professional programmer can use the book independently or as a companion to a reference book such as Stevens' *Advanced Programming in the UNIX Environment* [86] and thereby obtain a better understanding of operating systems and of systems programming. A student can use this book as a companion to a traditional textbook, such as Silbershatz and Galvin's *Operating Systems Concepts* [80] or Tanenbaum's *Modern Operating Systems* [92], to learn about operating systems by doing.

The exercises and projects make this book unique. In fact, the book began as a project workbook. It became clear after preliminary development that the material needed to do the projects was scattered in many places—often found in reference books that provide many details but little conceptual overview. The book has since evolved into a self-contained reference which relies on the latest UNIX standards.

The book is organized into four parts, each of which contains topic chapters and project chapters. A topic chapter covers the specified material in a work-along fashion. The topic chapters have many examples and short exercises of the form "try this" or "what happens if." The topic chapters close with one or more exercise sections. The book provides programming exercises for many fundamental concepts in process management, concurrency, and communication. These programming exercises satisfy the same need as do laboratory experiments in a traditional science course. It is necessary to use the concepts in order to understand them fully. Exercises are specified for step-by-step development and most can be implemented in under 100 lines of code.

Project chapters integrate material from several topic chapters by developing a more extensive application. The projects work on two levels. In addition to illustrating the programming ideas, the projects lead to an understanding of an advanced topic related to the application. These projects are designed in stages and most full implementations are a few hundred lines long. Since a large amount of code does not need to be written, the programmer can concentrate on understanding concepts rather than debugging code. In order to simplify the programming, we make libraries available for network communication.

The table below summarizes the organization of the book—fifteen chapters grouped into four parts. The nine topic chapters do not rely on the six project chapters, and a reader can skip the projects on the first pass through the book.

Part	Topic Chapter	#	Project Chapter	#
I **Fundamentals**	Concurrency	1		
	Processes	2		
	Files	3		
			The Token Ring	4
II **Asynchronous** **Events**	Signals	5		
			Timers	6
			Cracking Shells	7
III **Concurrency**	Semaphores	8		
	POSIX Threads	9		
	Thread Synch	10		
			Virtual Machine	11
IV **Communication**	Client-Server	12		
			Internet Radio	13
	RPCs	14		
			Tuple Space	15

There are many paths through this book. The three topic chapters in Part I are prerequisite for the rest of the book. Readers can cover Parts II through IV in any order after the topic chapters of Part I. The exception is the discussion at the end of later chapters about interactions (e.g., how threads interact with signals).

We have assumed that the readers of this book are good C programmers though not necessarily UNIX C programmers. The reader should be familiar with C programming and basic data structures. Appendix A covers the bare essentials of program development for readers who are new to UNIX. UNIX programmers probably know much of the material found in Chapters 2 and 3, but the coverage here is detailed and later projects rely heavily on it.

A reader should not assume that reading a chapter bestows understanding unless he or she has successfully developed some programs that use the concepts. For a professional programmer, the exercises at the end of the topic chapters provide a minimal hands-on introduction to the material. Typically, an instructor using this text for an operating systems course would select several exercises plus one of the major projects for implementation during a semester course. Each project has a number of variations, so the projects can be used in multiple semesters.

This book includes a synopsis for many of the standard functions. The relevant standards that specify the function appear in the lower right corner of the synopsis box. In general, ISO C is a subset of POSIX.1 and Spec 1170. In some cases the list of required header files differs between standards, with some of the header files being optional for some standards. In these cases the synopsis box lists all relevant header files.

A book like this is never done, but we had to stop somewhere. We welcome your comments and suggestions. You can send email to us at pup@vip.cs.utsa.edu. Information on the book is available on WWW site http://vip.cs.utsa.edu/pup. All of the code included in the book can be obtained from the WWW site or by anonymous ftp to vip.cs.utsa.edu in the directory pub/pup.

Acknowledgments

Our foremost acknowledgment goes to Neal Wagner—friend, colleague, and policeman of the passive voice. Neal was responsible more than anyone else for our writing this book. After all, he argued, since we already had the projects, how much more work could writing the book be? He followed up with lots of support—endless reading and critiquing drafts that greatly improved the book.

Our second acknowledgment goes to the dozen or so undergraduate and graduate operating systems classes we taught in the years from 1988 and 1995 when we were developing this material. We are grateful to the students in these courses for suffering through drafts in various stages of development and for field-testing emerging projects. Their program bugs, comments, complaints, and suggestions made the book a lot better and gave us insight into how these topics interrelate.

We would also like to acknowledge many other people who read the book and made suggestions for improvement or correction or helped in other ways. Dennis Cadena read an entire draft and made many suggestions. Other people who have commented or helped include Jeff Adamek, Laura Connor, Sandy Dykes, Richard Hatch, Philip Helsel, Robert Hiromoto, Clint Jeffery, George Leach, C. Ed Nicol, Richard Rybacki, Robert Shenk, Devang Shah, Dennis Wenzel, and Andrea Whitlock.

We are grateful to Greg Doench, our editor at Prentice Hall, and Meg Cowen, his assistant, for guiding us through the process. They helped us improve the book by gentle suggestions and support without pressure. We would also like to thank Jane Bonnell, our production editor, for all of her help in bringing the book to publication. It was a pleasure to work with these professionals. A number of anonymous reviewers made excellent suggestions which greatly helped in our revision for final publication. We typeset the book using LATEX 2_ε, and we would like to express our appreciation to its producers for making this software freely available.

Special thanks go to our spouses and children for enduring with us the arduous trek that preparing this book turned out to be. Finally, we would like to acknowledge the National Science Foundation for providing support through the NSF-ILI grant USE-0950497 to build a laboratory so that we had the opportunity to develop the original curriculum upon which this book is based.

Part I

Fundamentals

Chapter 1

What Is Concurrency?

Concurrency refers to the sharing of resources in the same time frame. That usually means that several processes share the same CPU (that is, they execute concurrently) or share memory or an I/O device. Incorrect handling of concurrency can lead to programs that fail for no apparent reason, even with the same input for which they previously seemed to work perfectly. Operating systems manage shared resources, and in the past programmers could allow the operating system to handle all aspects of concurrency. That is no longer the case for today's complex programs, which need to run efficiently and robustly on modern computers. Multiprocessor desktop machines and distributed systems are examples of architectures in which concurrency control takes on new and important meaning for systems designers. This chapter introduces the subject of concurrency and provides guidelines for programming on UNIX systems in a concurrent environment.

Computer power has increased geometrically for nearly fifty years [60] in many areas including computational speed, memory and mass-storage capacity, circuit complexity, hardware reliability, and I/O bandwidth. The growth has continued in the past decade, along with sophisticated instruction pipelines on single CPUs, placement of multiple CPUs on a desktop, and an explosion in network connectivity.

The dramatic increases in communication and computing power have triggered fundamental changes in commercial software. Large database and other business applications, which formerly executed on a mainframe connected to terminals, are now distributed over smaller, less expensive machines. Terminals have given way to desktop workstations with graphical user interfaces and multimedia capabilities. At the other end of the spectrum, standalone personal computer applications have evolved to use network communication. A spreadsheet application is no longer an isolated program supporting a single user because an update of the spreadsheet may cause an automatic update of other linked applications which, for example, graph the data or perform sales projections. Applications such as cooperative editing, conferencing, and common whiteboards facilitate group work and interactions. The computing trends are toward sophisticated data sharing, realtime interaction of applications, intelligent graphical user interfaces, and complex data streams which include audio and video as well as text.

All of these developments rely on communication and concurrency. *Communication* is the conveying of information by one entity to another. *Concurrency* is the sharing of resources in the same time frame. When two programs execute on the same system so that their execution is interleaved in time, they are sharing a processor resource. Programs can also share data, code, and devices. The concurrent entities can be threads of execution within programs or within other abstract objects. Concurrency can occur in a system with a single, simple CPU. In fact, a major job of a modern operating system is to manage the concurrent operations of a computer system.

Dealing with concurrency is not easy: Concurrent programs do not always behave as expected, and typical concurrent program bugs do not show up on a regular basis. (The problem may show up only once somewhere in a set of a million executions.) There is no substitute for practical experience with these concepts. This chapter describes examples of concurrency starting with the simplest situations in which concurrency can occur. The remainder of the book amplifies these ideas and provides specific examples.

1.1 Multiprogramming and Multitasking

Operating systems manage system resources—processors, memory, and I/O devices including keyboards, monitors, printers, mice, disks, tapes, CD ROMs, and network interfaces. The convoluted way operating systems appear to work is a consequence of the characteristics of peripheral devices, particularly their speed relative to the CPU or processor. Table 1.1 gives typical processor, memory, and peripheral speeds in nanoseconds. The third column shows these speeds slowed down by a factor of 100 million to give the time scaled in human terms. The scaled time of one operation per second is roughly the rate of the old mechanical calculators of fifty years ago. The cited speeds are a moving target, but the trend is that processor speeds are increasing exponentially causing an increasing performance gap between processors and peripherals.

Disk drives have improved in speed of access, but their rotating mechanical nature limits their performance and disk access times have not improved exponentially. The

Item	Time		Scaled Time in Human Terms (100 million times slower)
Processor Cycle	10 ns	(100 MHz)	1 second
Cache Access	30 ns		3 seconds
Memory Access	200 ns		20 seconds
Context Switch	10, 000 ns	(100 μs)	166 minutes
Disk Access	10, 000, 000 ns	(10 ms)	11 days
Quantum	100, 000, 000 ns	(100 ms)	116 days

Table 1.1: Typical times for components of a computer system. One nanosecond (ns) is 10^{-9} seconds, one microsecond (μs) is 10^{-6} seconds, and one millisecond (ms) is 10^{-3} seconds.

disparity between processor times and disk access times continues to grow, until now the ratio is roughly 1 to $1, 000, 000$ for a 100-MHz processor.

A *process* is an instance of a program in execution. Chapter 2 discusses the mechanism by which a program becomes a process. The *context switch time* is the time it takes to switch from executing one process to another. The *quantum* is roughly the amount of CPU time allocated to a process before it has to let another process run. In a sense, a user at a keyboard is a peripheral device. A fast typist can type a keystroke every 100 milliseconds. This time is the same order of magnitude as the process scheduling quantum, and it is no coincidence that these numbers are comparable for interactive timesharing systems.

Exercise 1.1
A modem is a device that permits a computer to communicate with another computer over a phone line. Typical speeds for modems are 2400 bps, 9600 bps, $14, 400$ bps, and $28, 800$ bps, where bps means "bits per second." Assuming it takes 8 bits to transmit a byte, estimate the time needed to transmit enough characters to fill a computer screen with 25 lines of 80 characters at each bit rate. Now consider a graphics display that consists of an array of 1024 by 768 pixels. Each pixel has a color value which can be one of 256 possible colors. Assume such a pixel value can be transmitted via modem in 8 bits. Estimate the actual time it takes to transmit enough pixels to fill the graphics display at each bit rate assuming that no compression is used. What compression ratio is necessary for a 14.4-Kbps modem to be able to fill a screen of graphics as fast as a 2400-bps modem can fill a screen with text?

bps	Text Time (seconds)	Graphics Time (seconds)
2, 400	6.67	2621
9, 600	1.67	655
14, 400	1.11	437
28, 800	0.56	218

Table 1.2: Comparison of time estimates for filling a screen with text versus graphics over a modem link of a specified speed.

Answer:

The text display has $80 \times 25 = 2000$ characters so $16,000$ bits must be transmitted. The graphics display has $1024 \times 768 = 786,432$ pixels so $6,291,456$ bits must be transmitted. Table 1.2 gives the times. A compression ratio of better than 65 is necessary! The estimates in Table 1.2 do not account for compression or for communication protocol overhead.

Observe from Table 1.1 that a process that performs disk I/O is not using the CPU very efficiently: 10 nanoseconds versus 10 milliseconds, or in human terms, 1 second versus 11 days. Because of that time disparity, most modern operating systems do multi-programming. *Multiprogramming* means that more than one process can be ready to execute. The operating system chooses one of these ready processes for execution. When that process needs to wait for a resource (say a keystroke or a disk access), the operating system saves all of the information needed to resume that process where it left off and chooses another ready process to execute. It is simple to see how that might work since a resource request (such as `read` or `write`) results in an operating system request (a system call), and during the system call the operating system can execute the code to switch to another process.

UNIX not only does multiprogramming, but also *timesharing*. The idea is that the operating system seems to be executing several processes simultaneously. If there is only one CPU, only one instruction from only one process can be executing at any particular time. Since the human time scale is millions (if not billions) of times slower than that of modern computers, the operating system can rapidly switch between processes to give the appearance of several processes executing at the same time.

Consider the following analogy. Suppose a grocery store has several checkout counters (the processes) but only one checker (the CPU). The checker checks one item from a customer (the instruction) and then does the next item for that same customer. Checking continues until a price check (a resource request) is needed. Instead of waiting for the price check and doing nothing, the checker moves to another checkout counter and checks items from another customer. The checker (CPU) is always busy as long as there are customers (processes) ready to check out. This is multiprogramming. The checker is efficient, but customers probably would not want to shop at such a store because of the long wait when there is a large order with no price checks (a CPU-bound process).

Now suppose that the checker checks items for one customer for a maximum of 30 seconds (the quantum). When the checker starts with a customer, a 30-second timer is started. If the timer expires the checker moves to another customer even if no price check is needed. This is timesharing. If the checker is sufficiently fast, the situation is almost equivalent to having one slower checker at each checkout stand. Consider making a video of such a checkout stand, and playing it back at 100 times its normal speed. It would look as if the checker were handling several customers simultaneously.

Exercise 1.2

Suppose that the checker can check one item per second corresponding to a one-second processor cycle time in Table 1.1. According to this table, what would be the maximum time the checker would spend with one customer before moving to a waiting customer?

Answer:

The time is the quantum which is scaled in the table to 116 days. A program may execute billions of instructions in a quantum—a bit more than the number of grocery items the average customer purchases.

If the time to move from one customer to another (the context-switch time) is small compared to the time between switches (the CPU burst time), the checker handles customers efficiently. A drawback of timesharing is the time it wastes switching between customers, but it has the advantage of not wasting the checker's time during a price check, and customers with small orders are not postponed for long periods waiting for customers with large orders.

The analogy would be closer to what happens in an operating system if instead of several checkout counters, there were only one, with the customers crowded around the checker. In order to switch from customer A to customer B, the checker saves the contents of the register tape (the context) and restores it to what it was when it last processed customer B. The context-switch time can be reduced if the cash register has several tapes and can hold the contents of several customers' orders simultaneously. In fact, some computer systems have special hardware to hold many contexts at the same time.

Multiprocessor systems have several processors accessing a shared memory. In the checkout analogy for a multiprocessor system, each customer has an individual register tape and there are multiple checkers who rove the checkout stands working on the orders for unserved customers. Many grocery stores have packers who do this.

1.2 Concurrency at the Applications Level

Concurrency occurs at both the hardware and software level. Concurrency occurs at the hardware level because multiple devices operate at the same time, processors have internal parallelism and work on several instructions simultaneously, systems have multiple processors, and systems interact through network communication. Concurrency occurs at the applications level in signal handling, in the overlap of I/O and processing, in communication, and in the sharing of resources between processes or among threads in the same process. The applications described in this chapter rely on these basic types of concurrency. This section provides an overview of concurrency from the hardware level up.

1.2.1 Interrupts

The execution of a single instruction in a program at the *conventional machine level* is the result of the processor instruction cycle. At any particular time, the processor executes the program whose address is in the program counter. (Modern processors have internal parallelism such as pipelines to reduce execution time, but this discussion does not consider that complication.) Concurrency arises at the conventional machine level because in addition to performing the instruction cycle, the processor controls peripheral devices. A peripheral can generate an electrical signal called an *interrupt* to set a hardware flag within the processor. The detection of an interrupt is part of the instruction cycle itself. On each instruction cycle the processor checks hardware flags to see if any peripheral devices need attention. If the processor detects that an interrupt has occurred, it saves the current value of the program counter and loads a new value which is the address of a special function called an *interrupt service routine*.

An event is *asynchronous* to an entity if the time at which it occurs is not determined by that entity. The interrupts generated by external hardware devices are generally *asynchronous* to programs executing on the system. The interrupts do not always occur at the same point in a program's execution, so a program must give the same result regardless of where it is interrupted. In contrast, an error event such as division by zero is *synchronous* in the sense that it always occurs during the execution of a particular instruction if the same data is presented to the instruction.

Although the interrupt service routine may be part of the program that is interrupted, the processing of an interrupt service routine is a distinct entity with respect to concurrency because interrupts are asynchronous to the process. Operating-system routines called *device drivers* usually handle the interrupts generated by peripheral devices. These drivers then notify the relevant processes that an event has occurred.

Operating systems use interrupts to implement timesharing. Most machines have a device called a *timer* which can generate an interrupt after a specified interval of time. The operating system starts the timer before setting the program counter to execute a user program. When the timer expires, it generates an interrupt causing the CPU to execute the timer interrupt service routine. The interrupt service routine writes the address of the operating system code into the program counter, and the operating system is back in control. When a process loses the CPU in the manner just described, its quantum is said to have *expired*. The operating system puts the process in a queue of processes that are ready to run, and there the process waits for another turn to execute.

1.2.2 Signals

A *signal* is the software notification of a event. Often a signal is a response of the operating system to an interrupt (a hardware event). For example, a keystroke such as `ctrl-c` generates an interrupt for the device driver handling the keyboard. The driver notifies the appropriate processes by sending a signal. The operating system may also send a signal to a process to notify it of a completed I/O operation or an error.

A signal is *generated* when the event that causes the signal occurs. When a signal is generated, the operating system sets a flag corresponding to that signal for the process. Signals can be generated either synchronously or asynchronously. A signal is generated synchronously if it is generated by the process or thread that receives it. The execution of an illegal instruction or a divide-by-zero may generate a synchronous signal. A `ctrl-c` on the keyboard generates an asynchronous signal. Signals (Chapter 5) can be used for timers (Chapter 6), terminating programs (Section 7.5), job control (Section 7.7), asynchronous I/O (Sections 5.9 and 9.1.2), or program monitoring (Section 5.11).

A signal is *caught* if the process which receives the signal executes a handler for the signal. A program that catches a signal has at least two concurrent parts, the main program and the signal handler. The potential concurrency restricts what can be done inside a signal handler (Section 5.6). If the signal handler modifies external variables that the program can modify elsewhere, then proper execution requires that those variables be protected or a problem may occur.

1.2.3 Input and Output

A challenge for operating systems is to coordinate resources that have greatly differing characteristic times of operation. An application may have to handle this problem directly to ensure efficient execution. While a program is waiting for a disk access to complete, the processor can perform millions of other operations. In a timesharing environment, the operating system normally chooses another process to run while the current process waits for the I/O request to complete. The process can itself do other work while it is waiting by using asynchronous I/O (Sections 5.9 and 9.1.2) or dedicated threads (Chapter 9) instead of ordinary blocking I/O. The tradeoff is between the additional performance and the extra programming overhead in using concurrency.

A similar problem occurs when an application monitors two or more input channels such as input from different sources on a network. If standard blocking I/O is used, the application waits for input when it initiates a read from one of the input sources, so it cannot handle input from another source even if it is available. Chapter 9 presents five methods of handling the multiple-source problem. The methods are a) polling with non-blocking I/O, b) asynchronous I/O, c) `select`, d) `poll` (which in spite of its name does not use polling), and e) threads.

1.2.4 Threads and the Sharing of Resources

A traditional method for achieving concurrent execution in UNIX is for the user to create multiple processes using the `fork` system call. The processes usually need to coordinate their operation in some way. In the simplest instance they may only need to coordinate their termination. Even the termination problem is more difficult than it might seem. Chapter 2 addresses process structure and management and introduces the UNIX `fork`, `exec`, and `wait` system calls. Sections 10.2 and 10.3 address subtler issues of process termination.

Processes that have a common ancestor can communicate using a simple mechanism called *pipes* (Chapter 3). Processes without a common ancestor can communicate using signals (Chapter 5), FIFOs (Section 3.9), semaphores (Section 8.2), shared address space (Chapter 9), or messages (Chapter 12).

Multiple threads of execution can provide concurrency within a process. When a program executes, the CPU uses the program counter to determine which instruction to execute next. The resulting stream of instructions is called the program's thread of execution. It is the flow of control for the process. If two distinct threads of execution share a resource within a time frame, care must be taken so that these threads do not interfere with each other. Multiprocessor systems expand the opportunity for concurrency and sharing between applications and within applications. When a multithreaded application has more than one thread of execution concurrently active on a multiprocessor system, multiple instructions from the same process may be executed at the same time.

Until recently there has not been a standard for using threads, and programmers have been reluctant to use threads because each vendor's thread package was different. A thread package might undergo changes with each new operating system release. A thread standard has recently been incorporated into the POSIX.1 standard. Chapters 9 and 10 discuss this new standard.

1.2.5 The Network as the Computer

Another important trend is the distribution of computation over a network. Concurrency and communication meet to form new applications. The most widely used model of distributed computation is the *client-server* model. The basic entities in this model are server processes which manage resources and client processes which require access to shared resources. (A process can be both a server and a client.) A client process shares a resource by sending a request to a server. The server performs the request on behalf of the client and sends a reply to the client. Examples of applications based on the client-server model include file transfer (`ftp`), electronic mail, and file servers. Development of client-server applications requires an understanding of concurrency and communication. A natural mechanism for implementing the client-server model is the remote procedure call or RPC discussed in Chapters 14 and 15.

The *object-based model* is another model for distributed computation. Each resource in the system is viewed as an object with a message-handling interface. All shared resources are accessed in a uniform way. The object-based model shares the advantages of object-oriented programming [60] in that they both allow for controlled incremental development and code reuse. Object frameworks define interactions between code modules. The object model naturally expresses notions of protection. Many of the experimental distributed operating systems, including Argus [62], Amoeba [91], Mach [1], Arjuna [78], Clouds [24] and Emerald [9] are object-based. Object-based models require object managers which track the location of the objects in the system.

An alternative to a truly distributed operating system is to provide application layers which run on top of common standalone operating systems to exploit parallelism on the network. The Parallel Virtual Machine (PVM) is a software package [7] which allows a collection of heterogeneous UNIX workstations to function as a parallel computer for solving large computational problems. PVM manages and monitors tasks which are distributed on various workstations across the network. Chapter 11 develops a dispatcher for a simplified version of PVM, while Chapter 15 develops a tuple space implementation for a simplified version of Linda, a commercial distributed programming language.

1.3 UNIX Standards

The system-level differences in the UNIX operating systems produced by various vendors is confusing. This text follows three important standards—ANSI C, POSIX, and Spec 1170. The C language has been standardized by the American National Standards Institute (ANSI) and the International Standards Organization (ISO) [2, 41].

At the system level, the Institute of Electrical and Electronics Engineers (IEEE) has developed a collection of standards called POSIX [52, 53, 55], which stands for Portable

Operating System Interface. POSIX specifies the interface between the operating system and the user in a standard way so that application programs are portable across platforms. The POSIX standards are also called IEEE Std. 1003. Table 1.3 summarizes the different members of the POSIX standards collection. For example, the standard covering the System Application Program Interface (API) is called IEEE Std. 1003.1 or POSIX.1.

Standard	Date	Description
POSIX.1	1990	System Application Program Interface (API) [C Language]
POSIX.1b	1993	API Amendment 1: Realtime Extension [C Language] (Formerly known as POSIX.4)
POSIX.1c	1995	API Amendment 2: Threads Extension
POSIX.2	1992	Shells and Utilities
POSIX.3	1991	Test methods for POSIX conformance
POSIX.3.1	1992	Test methods for POSIX.1 conformance
POSIX.4	1993	Now called POSIX.1b
POSIX.5	1992	POSIX.1 [ADA Language]
POSIX.6	working	Security
POSIX.7	working	System administration
POSIX.7.1	working	Printing administration
POSIX.7.2	working	Software installation and management
POSIX.7.3	working	User/group management
POSIX.8	working	Transparent file access
POSIX.9	1992	POSIX.1 [FORTRAN Language]
POSIX.12	working	Network services

Table 1.3: Some POSIX standards of interest to systems programmers.

A POSIX-compliant implementation must support the POSIX.1 base standard. Many of the interesting aspects of POSIX.1 are not part of the base standard but rather are defined as extensions to the base standard. An implementation supports a particular extension if the corresponding symbol is defined in that implementation's `unistd.h` header file. Table 1.4 lists the symbols and their corresponding POSIX extension.

POSIX is meant to encompass other operating systems besides UNIX. Even on the UNIX side there are complications. There are two major families of UNIX implementations: System V and BSD. System V evolved from the original AT&T UNIX. BSD UNIX was developed at the University of California at Berkeley with a goal of providing an open system with sophisticated networking support. (See Leffler et al. [59] for a historical overview.) It appears that most commercial versions of UNIX are standard-

Symbol	POSIX.1 Extension
_POSIX_ASYNCHRONOUS_IO	Asynchronous input and output
_POSIX_FSYNC	File synchronization
_POSIX_JOB_CONTROL	Job control
_POSIX_MAPPED_FILES	Memory mapped files
_POSIX_MEMLOCK	Process memory locking
_POSIX_MEMLOCK_RANGE	Range memory locking
_POSIX_MEMORY_PROTECTION	Memory protection
_POSIX_MESSAGE_PASSING	Message passing
_POSIX_PRIORITIZED_IO	Prioritized input and output
_POSIX_PRIORITY_SCHEDULING	Processing scheduling
_POSIX_REALTIME_SIGNALS	Realtime signals
_POSIX_SAVED_IDS	Process has saved set-user-ID
_POSIX_SEMAPHORES	Semaphores
_POSIX_SHARED_MEMORY_OBJECTS	Shared memory objects
_POSIX_SYNCHRONIZED_IO	Synchronized input and output
_POSIX_TIMERS	Timers
_POSIX_VERSION	199309L for conforming implementations

Table 1.4: POSIX.1 compile-time symbolic constants. If the constant is defined in `unistd.h`, the system supports the corresponding POSIX.1 extension.

izing on System V Release 4 and an emerging standard called Spec 1170 developed by the X/Open Foundation [96, 97, 98, 99]. This book emphasizes POSIX, Spec 1170, and System V Release 4. For items such as networking services which are not covered by a POSIX standard, the text follows Spec 1170. For items not covered by either standard, the book uses System V Release 4.

1.4 Programming in UNIX

One approach for learning concurrency is to implement programs in a language designed specifically to support concurrency. Instead, this book uses standard C and UNIX programming to explore the ideas. This section gives brief guidelines for developing system programs under UNIX. Appendix A reviews some basics of UNIX for systems programmers.

Programs request operating services such as input and output by invoking an appropriate *system call*. A system call is an entry point directly into the kernel. The *kernel* is the collection of software modules that run in privileged mode—meaning they have full access to system resources. The system calls are an intrinsic part of the operating system kernel. (Sometimes the terms operating system and kernel are used interchangeably.)

Many general-purpose C library functions are also available. The library functions may or may not invoke system calls. It is not always possible to determine from its definition whether a given function is a library function or a system call. Traditionally, the system calls are described in section 2 of the UNIX manual and the library functions in section 3. The online version of the UNIX manual is called the *man pages*. (Appendix A.1 discusses the man pages.)

When using a system call or a library call, be sure to consult the UNIX man pages to find the proper header or prototype for the call. The man page synopsis identifies the header files to be included when invoking a system call or library function in a program.

Example 1.1

The man page synopsis for the open *system call mentions three header files.*

```
#include <sys/types.h>
#include <sys/stat.h>
#include <fcntl.h>

int open(const char *path, int  oflag,  /*  mode_t  mode  */
         ...);
```

The header files in Example 1.1 contain the prototype for open as well as definitions of various flags that can be used as parameters to the call. Be sure to include these header files in any program that calls open.

What happens when a system call or library call encounters an error? A program usually does not abort—at least not directly. Instead the call returns a value indicating an error condition, and it is up to the program to check for the error and handle it. Typically a return error value is negative if the call return type is int or a NULL if the return type is a pointer.

The man page states that open returns an integer file descriptor on success. On failure, open returns −1 and sets errno to the appropriate error code. The system calls and many library functions return −1 to indicate an error. When an error occurs, these functions also set the external variable errno to an error code. The errno variable is not necessarily overwritten by a subsequent system or library call unless the call generates an error. Before using errno be sure to check the function return value for an error. The man pages specify symbolic names for various errors, and the program can compare errno to these values to determine which type of error occurred. Include the errno.h header file in order to access the symbolic error names associated with errno.

Example 1.2

The following C code segment opens the file my.file *for reading.*

```
#include <stdio.h>
#include <sys/types.h>
#include <sys/stat.h>
#include <fcntl.h>
int fd;

if ((fd = open("my.file", O_RDONLY)) == -1)
    perror("Unsuccessful open of my.file");
```

The C library function perror outputs a message string to standard error followed by the error message from the last system or library call that produced an error. (The last error message might not have anything to do with the last call if the last call did not produce an error.)

```
SYNOPSIS

  #include <stdio.h>

  void perror(const char *s);
                                              ISO C, POSIX.1, Spec 1170
```

Example 1.3

The following output might be produced by Example 1.2 if my.file *does not exist.*

```
Unsuccessful open of my.file: No such file or directory
```

The open call can fail for a variety of reasons, and the man page lists many symbolic error names associated with open. One of the error names is EAGAIN which indicates that the file is locked.

Example 1.4

The following loop retries the open *if the call fails because of locking.*

```
#include <stdio.h>
#include <sys/types.h>
#include <sys/stat.h>
#include <fcntl.h>
#include <errno.h>
int fd;

while (((fd = open("my.file", O_RDONLY)) == -1) && (errno == EAGAIN))
    ;
if (fd == -1)
    perror("Unsuccessful open of my.file");
```

Remember to test `errno` only if the call returns an error. The test in Example 1.4 works because C guarantees that the second operand of `&&` is not evaluated unless the first operand is true.

The C string function `strerror` returns a pointer to an error message.

```
SYNOPSIS

   #include <string.h>

   char *strerror(int errnum);
```
                                                                    ISO C, POSIX.1, Spec 1170

The `errnum` is the value of `errno` associated with the error message. Use `strerror` instead of `perror` to format a message that contains variable values.

Example 1.5

The following C code segment uses `strerror` *to print a system-dependent error message.*

```
#include <string.h>
#include <stdio.h>
#include <sys/types.h>
#include <sys/stat.h>
#include <fcntl.h>
#include <errno.h>
int fd;

if ((fd = open(argv[1], O_RDONLY)) == -1)
    fprintf(stderr, "Could not open file %s: %s\n",
        argv[1], strerror(errno));
```

The filename in Example 1.5 is taken from the first command-line argument, `argv[1]`. The error message includes the filename as well as the system error message.

Most UNIX system calls and C library functions provide good models for implementing functions. Here are guidelines to follow:

- Make use of return values to communicate information and to make error trapping easy for the calling program.

- Do not exit from functions. Instead, return an error value to allow the calling program flexibility in handling the error.

- Make functions general but usable. (Sometimes these are conflicting goals.)

- Do not make unnecessary assumptions about sizes of buffers. (This is often hard to implement.)

- When it is necessary to use limits, use standard, system-defined limits rather than arbitrary constants.
- Do not re-invent the wheel—use standard library functions when possible.
- Do not modify input parameter values unless it makes sense to do so.
- Do not use static variables or dynamic memory allocation if automatic allocation will do just as well.
- Analyze all of the calls to the `malloc` family to make sure the program frees the memory that was allocated.
- Consider whether a function will ever be called recursively, or from a signal handler, or from a thread. Reentrant functions are not self-modifying, so there can be simultaneous invocations active without interference. In contrast, functions with local static or external variables are nonreentrant and may not behave in the desired way when called recursively. (The `errno` causes a big problem here.)
- Analyze the consequences of interruptions by signals.
- Carefully consider how the entire program will terminate.

As an illustration of these principles consider the problem of constructing argument arrays such those as used to pass command-line arguments to C programs. Argument arrays are arrays of pointers to strings.

A UNIX command line consists of tokens (the arguments) which are separated by blanks, tabs, or a backslash(\) just before a newline character. Each token is a string of characters. When a user enters a command corresponding to a C executable program, the shell parses the command line and passes the result to the program in the form of an argument array. (Several later exercises and projects use argument arrays when they create processes to perform various tasks.)

Example 1.6

The following command line contains the four tokens: `mine`, `-c`, `10`, *and* `2.0`.

```
mine -c 10 2.0
```

The first token on a command line is the name of the command or executable. Figure 1.1 shows the argument array for the command line of Example 1.6.

Example 1.7

The `mine` *main program referred to in Example 1.6 might start with the following line.*

```
int main(int argc, char *argv[])
```

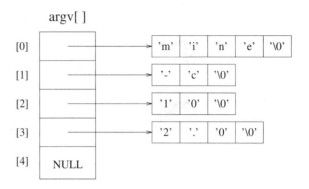

Figure 1.1: The `argv` array for the call `mine -c 10 2.0`.

In Example 1.7, the `argc` parameter contains the number of command-line to-kens (four for Example 1.6), and `argv` is the array of pointers to the command-line tokens. Argument arrays are useful for handling a variable number of arguments in calls to `execvp`. (Refer to Section 2.7 for an example of their application.)

Example 1.8

The following prototype for the `makeargv` *function indicates that the function creates an argument array from a string of tokens.*

```
char **makeargv(char *s);
```

The `makeargv` of Example 1.8 has a string input parameter and returns a pointer to an `argv` array. If the call fails, it returns a `NULL` pointer.

Example 1.9

The following code segment illustrates how the `makeargv` *function of Example 1.8 might be invoked.*

```
#include <stdio.h>
int i;
char **myargv;
char mytest[] = "This is a test";

if ((myargv = makeargv(mytest)) == NULL)
    fprintf(stderr, "Could not construct an argument array\n");
else
    for (i = 0; myargv[i] != NULL; i++)
        printf("%i: %s\n", i, myargv[i]);
```

Example 1.10

The following alternative prototype specifies that `makeargv` *should pass the argument array as a parameter. The alternative version of* `makeargv` *returns an integer giving the number of tokens in the input string. In this case different negative values indicate errors.*

```
int makeargv(char *s, char ***argvp);
```

Example 1.11

The following code segment calls the `makeargv` *defined in Example 1.10.*

```
#include <stdio.h>
int i;
char **myargv;
char mytest[] = "This is a test";
int numtokens;

if ((numtokens = makeargv(mytest, &myargv)) < 0)
    fprintf(stderr, "Could not construct an argument array\n");
else
    for (i = 0; i < numtokens; i++)
        printf("%i: %s\n", i, myargv[i]);
```

Example 1.11 shows one more level of indirection (*) when the address of `myargv` is passed because C uses call-by-value parameter passing. A more general version of `makeargv` allows an extra parameter that represents the set of delimiters to use in parsing the string.

Example 1.12

The following prototype shows a `makeargv` *function that has a delimiter set parameter.*

```
int makeargv(char *s, char *delims, char ***argvp);
```

Program 1.1 calls the `makeargv` function of Example 1.12 to create an argument array from a string passed on the command line. The program checks that it has exactly one command-line argument and outputs a usage message if that is not the case. If `makeargv` encounters an error, it does not exit but returns an error to the calling program. The main program calls `exit(1)` if it fails and `exit(0)` if it completes successfully. The call to `makeargv` uses blank and tab as delimiters. The shell also uses the same delimiters, so be sure to enclose the string in double quotes.

Program 1.1: The `argtest` program takes a single command-line argument which is
a string and calls `makeargv` to create an argument array.

```c
#include <stdio.h>
#include <stdlib.h>
int makeargv(char *s, char *delimiters, char ***argvp);

void main(int argc, char *argv[])
{
   char **myargv;
   char delim[] = " \t";
   int i;
   int numtokens;

   if (argc != 2) {
      fprintf(stderr, "Usage: %s string\n", argv[0]);
      exit(1);
   }
   if ((numtokens = makeargv(argv[1], delim, &myargv)) < 0) {
      fprintf(stderr,
          "Could not construct argument array for %s\n", argv[1]);
      exit(1);
   } else {
      printf("The argument array contains:\n");
      for (i = 0; i < numtokens; i++)
          printf("[%d]:%s\n", i, myargv[i]);
   }
   exit(0);
}
```

─────────────────────────── **Program 1.1** ───────────────────────────

Example 1.13

> *If the executable for Program 1.1 is called* `argtest`, *the following command*
> *creates and prints an argument array for* `This is a test`.

> `argtest "This is a test"`

The implementation of `makeargv` discussed here uses the C library function
`strtok` to split a string into tokens.

SYNOPSIS

```c
   #include <string.h>

   char *strtok(char *s1, const char *s2);
```
                                                          ISO C, POSIX.1, Spec 1170

Use the starting address of the string to parse for s1 on the first call to strtok and a NULL for s1 on the remaining calls. Successive calls return the start of the next token and put a '\0' at the end of the token. The string s2 contains the allowed token delimiters. The strtok function returns NULL when it reaches the end of s1.

It is important not to impose any unnecessary a priori limitations on the size of the array by using buffers of predefined sizes. Although the system-defined constant MAX_CANON is a reasonable buffer size for handling command-line arguments, the makeargv function might be called to make an environment list or from applications that take input from a file. This implementation of makeargv allocates all buffers dynamically by calling calloc. In order to preserve the input string s, makeargv does not apply strtok directly to s, but instead it creates a scratch area of the same size pointed to by t and copies s into it. The overall strategy is

- Allocate space for the tokens instead of modifying s itself. Rather than doing a calloc for each token, allocate a new string t which is the same size as the original string s as shown in Figure 1.2.

- Make a pass through the string t using strtok to count the tokens.

- Use the count (numtokens) to allocate an argv array.

- Use strtok to obtain pointers to the individual tokens, modifying t in the process. (Figure 1.3 shows the method for parsing the tokens in place.)

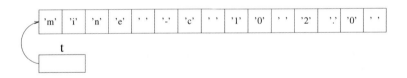

Figure 1.2: The makeargv makes a working copy of the string s so that it does not modify that input parameter.

Program 1.2 shows an implementation of makeargv. Since strtok allows the caller to specify which delimiters to use for separating tokens, the implementation includes a delimiters string as a parameter. The program begins by using strspn to skip over leading delimiters. This ensures that **argvp, which points to the first token, also points to the start of the scratch buffer called t in the program. If an error occurs, this scratch buffer is explicitly freed. Otherwise, the calling program can free this buffer. The free may not be important for most programs, but if makeargv is called frequently from a shell or a long-running communication program, the unfreed space from failed calls to makeargv can accumulate. When using calloc or a related call, analyze whether to free the memory if an error occurs or when the function returns.

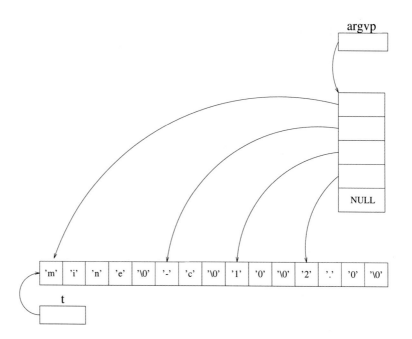

Figure 1.3: The use of `strtok` to allocate strings in place for `makeargv`.

Program 1.2: An implementation of `makeargv`.

```c
#include <string.h>
#include <stdlib.h>
/*
 * Make argv array (*arvp) for tokens in s which are separated by
 * delimiters.   Return -1 on error or the number of tokens otherwise.
 */
int makeargv(char *s, char *delimiters, char ***argvp)
{
    char *t;
    char *snew;
    int numtokens;
    int i;
     /* snew is real start of string after skipping leading delimiters */
    snew = s + strspn(s, delimiters);
                              /* create space for a copy of snew in t */
    if ((t = calloc(strlen(snew) + 1, sizeof(char))) == NULL) {
       *argvp = NULL;
       numtokens = -1;
```

```
   } else {                       /* count the number of tokens in snew */
      strcpy(t, snew);
      if (strtok(t, delimiters) == NULL)
         numtokens = 0;
      else
         for (numtokens = 1; strtok(NULL, delimiters) != NULL;
              numtokens++)
            ;
                  /* create an argument array to contain ptrs to tokens */
      if ((*argvp = calloc(numtokens + 1, sizeof(char *))) == NULL) {
         free(t);
         numtokens = -1;
      } else {                /* insert pointers to tokens into the array */
         if (numtokens > 0) {
            strcpy(t, snew);
            **argvp = strtok(t, delimiters);
            for (i = 1; i < numtokens + 1; i++)
               *((*argvp) + i) = strtok(NULL, delimiters);
         } else {
            **argvp = NULL;
            free(t);
         }
      }
   }
   return numtokens;
}
```

_____ **Program 1.2** _____

1.5 Making Functions Safe

The strtok function is a good example of a function not to emulate because it is non-reentrant. One call to strtok can modify the behavior of future calls because the function keeps track of its position in the string between successive calls. Using strtok safely in a concurrent environment, such as with signals or threads, is not straightforward.

Suppose a program uses strtok in a signal handler. If the signal is delivered between successive calls to strtok elsewhere in the program, the strtok becomes confused. It uses the position from the last call to strtok in the signal handler rather than in the main part of the program.

Remember that signals can be asynchronous, that is, the time at which they occur cannot be determined in advance. If the signal is caught before the first or after the last call to strtok in the main part of the program, all is well. However, if the signal is caught between calls to strtok, the program may fail. The program itself does not have any control over such behavior and may work 99.99% of the time. A similar problem occurs when using threads.

There are two aspects to making functions safe. A function is called *thread-safe* if it can be safely invoked concurrently by multiple threads. A function is called *async-signal safe* if that function can be called without restriction from a signal handler. These terms replace the older notion of a *reentrant function*.

The POSIX.1c standard [54] includes threads and the modifications necessary to the base standard to support their correct execution. The goal is to make most functions defined by POSIX thread-safe. Async-signal safety is more difficult, and Table 5.3 gives a complete list of those functions that are guaranteed to be async-signal safe according to the adopted POSIX.1 standard [52]. Conformance to the POSIX standards is not complete even for operating systems that claim compliance. Check the man pages to determine the safety of a given function in a given version of an operating system.

In the revised POSIX.1 standard all functions except for a short list are thread-safe. Some functions (such as `strtok`) are beyond hope because their definition guarantees that they are nonreentrant. For each of these, POSIX defines a substitute function which has a suffix of `_r`. The thread-safe version of `strtok` is `strtok_r`.

SYNOPSIS

```
#include <string.h>

char *strtok_r(char *s, const char *sep, char **lasts);
```
POSIX.1c

This function behaves similarly to `strtok` except that the parameter `lasts` is a user-provided pointer to a location which is used to save the position in the string needed for the next call to `strtok_r`.

It is possible that all of the nonreentrant versions of similar functions will eventually be removed from the standard. Avoid using them if possible. Unfortunately, many of the standard system calls and C library functions are nonreentrant by definition because they return error information in an external variable, `errno`. The POSIX standards committee decided that all new functions would not use `errno` and would instead return an error number directly as a function return value. The problem of what to do with the functions that already exist remains. Consider `read`, which returns the number of bytes read or −1 if an error occurs. If `read` returns −1, it sets `errno` to indicate the type of error.

SYNOPSIS

```
#include <unistd.h>

ssize_t read(int filedes, void *buf, size_t nbyte);
```
POSIX.1, Spec 1170

Here are alternatives for handling errors, some of which were considered by the standards committee.

- Use the following instead of `read`:

  ```
  int read_r(int filedes, void *buf, size_t nbyte,
             ssize_t *bytesread);
  ```

  which returns an error number or 0 if no error occurs. The last parameter provides a place to store the number of bytes actually read.
- Use the following instead of `read`:

  ```
  ssize_t read_r(int filedes, void *buf, size_t nbyte,
                 int *status);
  ```

  which uses the last parameter to store an error number.
- Implement `errno` as a variable that is local to each thread.
- Implement `errno` as a service that can access a per-thread error number. This means that `errno` would be a macro that invokes a function to get the error number for the currently running thread.
- Change `read` so that it generates a language exception (a signal) if an error occurs.

All of the approaches have serious drawbacks. The first two and the last require programs to be rewritten to use the new `read` function. The third option preserves compatibility, but it requires special support from the linker, compiler, and virtual memory system. The fourth option preserves source code compatibility, since the macro can be defined in `errno.h` which is included when `errno` is used. Unfortunately, application programs that explicitly assign a value to `errno` have to be rewritten if `errno` is a macro. The third and fourth options make the function thread-safe but still cause problems if the function is called from inside a signal handler. The fifth option requires that the program install signal handlers or terminate by default.

1.6 Exercise: Argument Arrays

- Test the `makeargv` function defined in Program 1.2 by using the main program of Program 1.1. Put the `makeargv` function in a separate file called `argvlib.c`. Use a `makefile` with the `make` utility to compile the programs. (Refer to Appendix A.3 for a brief introduction to `make`.) Test the function on a variety of inputs.
- Write a `freeargv` function for `argvlib.c` which has the prototype

  ```
  void freeargv(char ***argvp);
  ```

The `freeargv` function frees the argument array pointed to by `*argvp` and sets `*argvp` to `NULL`.

- Write a complete man page for `makeargv`. (Refer to Appendix A.1 for a discussion of man pages.)

- Write a new version of `strtok` called `estrtok` which treats the occurrence of consecutive delimiters as an empty token rather than as no token. The prototype for `estrtok` is

```
char *estrtok(char *s1, const char *s2);
```

  The `estrtok` might be used by the shell to parse the `PATH` environment variable. The `PATH` variable consists of path prefixes separated by colons (`:`). An empty path prefix is treated as the current working directory. A leading colon is an empty path prefix. When executing a command that does not start with a `'/'`, the shell looks for the executable by appending the command name to each path prefix in turn until it finds the file. For example, if the shell executes the `ls` command and the `PATH` variable has value `/bin:/usr/bin:/usr/local/bin::`, the shell tries to locate the executable by searching successively for `/bin/ls`, `/usr/bin/ls`, `/usr/local/bin/ls` and `./ls`. It stops when it finds the file or exhausts the list of possibilities.

- Rewrite the `makeargv` function of Program 1.2 so that it has the prototype

```
int makeargv(char *s, char *delimiters, int flags,
             char ***argvp);
```

  The `flags` variable specifies conversion options. Define the following options in an include file for `makeargv`:

```
#define EMPTYTOKENS 1   /* Token for consecutive delims */
#define NOTOKENS 0   /* No token for consecutive delims */
```

  When `flags` is `EMPTYTOKENS`, successive delimiters surround an empty token (e.g., `::` in `PATH`). When `flags` is `NOTOKENS`, successive delimiters are skipped over as in the standard `strtok`.

- The standard implementation of `strtok` keeps a static pointer to the start of the next part of the string. Static pointers present problems if there are multiple threads of execution within the same program. Read the man page for `strtok` on your system and see if an alternative is provided. If so, use that alternative. If not, write a `strtok_r` function as described in Section 1.5. The prototype for `strtok_r` is

```
char *strtok_r(char *s1, const char *s2, char **lasts);
```

- Write a reentrant form of `estrtok` called `estrtok_r`.

1.7 Additional Reading

Most general operating systems books present an overview and history of operating systems. Recommended introductions include Chapter 1 of *Modern Operating Systems* by Tanenbaum [92] or Chapters 1 to 3 of *Operating Systems Concepts* by Silberschatz and Galvin [80]. Chapters 1 and 2 of *Distributed Systems: Concepts and Design* by Coulouris, Dollimore, and Kindberg discuss design issues for distributed systems [21]. *Distributed Operating Systems* by Tanenbaum [93] also has a good overview of distributed systems issues, but it provides fewer details about specific distributed systems than [21].

The requisite programming background includes a general knowledge of C and UNIX. *The C Programming Language*, 2nd ed. by Kernighan and Ritchie [58] is a standard C language reference. *C: A Reference Manual*, 4th ed. by Harbison and Steele [37] is an up-to-date C language reference. *UNIX in a Nutshell: A Desktop Quick Reference for System V* published by O'Reilly & Associates is a good UNIX user's reference [68]. *A Practical Guide to the UNIX System*, 3rd ed. by Mark Sobell [82] gives an overview of UNIX and its utilities from the user perspective.

Advanced Programming in the UNIX Environment by Stevens [86] is a key technical reference on the UNIX interface to use in conjunction with this book. Serious systems programmers should acquire the *POSIX Std. 1003.1b System Application Program Interface (API) Amendment 1: Realtime Extension* [53]. The standard is surprisingly readable and thorough. The rationale sections at the end of the standard provide a great deal of insight into the serious issues involved. Finally, *Standard C Library* by Plauger is an interesting, but ultimately detailed, look at C library function implementation [70]. It gives a model for writing good systems-level C code.

Chapter 2

Programs and Processes

A *process* is the basic active entity in most operating system models. One popular definition of a process is an instance of a program whose execution has started but has not yet terminated. This chapter discusses the differences between programs and processes and how the former are transformed into the latter. In addition to covering the process model, process creation, daemon processes, and critical sections, the chapter addresses issues in program layout and object-oriented design.

To write a C source program, a programmer creates disk files containing C statements which are organized into functions. An individual C source file may also contain variable and function declarations, type definitions (e.g., `typedef`), and preprocessor commands (e.g., `#ifdef`, `#include`, `#define`). The source program contains exactly one `main` function. Traditionally C source files have filenames with a `.c` extension. Header files usually contain only type definitions, defined constants, and function declarations and have a `.h` extension.

The C compiler translates each source file into an object file. The compiler then links the individual object files together to produce an *executable module*. A *program* is a file containing an executable module. When a program is run, the operating system copies the executable module into a *program image* in main memory. A *process* is an instance of a program that is executing. Each instance has its own address space and execution state.

When does a program become a process? The operating system reads the program into memory. The allocation of memory for the program image is not enough to make the program a process. The process must have an ID (the *process ID*) so that the operating system can distinguish among individual processes. The *process state* indicates the execution status of an individual process. The operating system keeps track of the process IDs and corresponding process states and uses the information to allocate and manage resources for the system. The operating system also keeps track of the memory occupied by the processes and of the memory available for allocation (the *memory manager*).

When the operating system has added the appropriate information in the kernel data structures and has allocated the necessary resources to run the program code, the program has become a process. Some people call the process defined here a *heavyweight process* because of the work needed to start such a process in contrast to *lightweight processes* (also called threads) discussed in Chapters 9 and 10.

The next two sections discuss program layout and organization. The remaining sections of the chapter address other aspects of process management including identification, creation, inheritance, and termination.

2.1 Layout of a Program Executable

C programs may contain static and automatic variables. The *static* storage class refers to variables that, once allocated, persist throughout the execution of the program. External variables, those defined outside any function, are always static.

The *automatic* storage class refers to variables that come into existence when the block in which they are declared is executed and are discarded when their defining block exits. Variables declared inside a function are automatic unless explicitly declared static. Automatic variables are typically allocated on the program stack so that multiple incarnations of the same variable can exist (in recursion).

Unfortunately, the keyword `static` has two meanings in C. In some cases, it modifies the storage class as defined above and in others it modifies the *linkage class*. Variables and functions can have either *internal linkage* or *external linkage*. The linkage class determines whether they can be accessed in other files that are linked together.

By default, variables declared outside any function and all function name identifiers can be referenced in other files. (They have external linkage by default.) The `static` keyword specifies internal linkage for these identifiers. In this case the `static` keyword modifies the linkage class, because variables that are declared outside a function always have the static storage class. External variables and function identifiers that are modified by the `static` keyword may only be referenced inside the file in which they are defined.

Variables declared inside a function always have internal linkage since they can only be referenced inside that function. By default variables declared inside a function have the automatic storage class. The `static` keyword specifies the static storage class. If a variable declaration has a `static` keyword modifier, the variable has static storage class. Once allocated, it persists until the program terminates. Table 2.1 summarizes this information.

Object	Where Declared	`static` Modifies	`static` Applied?	Storage Class	Linkage Class
variable	inside a function	storage class	yes	static	internal
variable	inside a function	storage class	no	automatic	internal
variable	outside any function	linkage class	yes	static	internal
variable	outside any function	linkage class	no	static	external
function	outside any function	linkage class	yes	static	internal
function	outside any function	linkage class	no	static	external

Table 2.1: Effect of using the `static` keyword modifier in a C program.

Figure 2.1 gives a sample layout of a program image in memory [86]. The program appears to occupy a contiguous block of memory. In practice, the operating system maps the contiguous logical address space of the program executable into physical memory. A common mapping divides the program into equal size pieces called *pages*. The individual pages are located anywhere in memory, and a lookup occurs at each memory reference. This mapping allows a large logical address space for the stack and heap without actually using physical memory unless it is needed. The existence of such an underlying mapping is hidden by the operating system, so the programmer can view the program as logically contiguous.

The program image has several distinct sections. The program text or code is shown in low-order memory. The static initialized and uninitialized variables have their own sections in the image. Other sections include the heap, stack, and environment.

The automatic variables are usually part of the activation record for the function call in which they are created. An *activation record* is a block of memory allocated on the top of the stack to hold the execution context of a function when it is called. The activation record contains the return address, the parameters (whose values are copied from the corresponding arguments in C), status information, and a copy of the CPU register values at the time of the call so that these values can be restored on return. The activation record also contains automatic variables allocated within the function. The particular format for an activation record depends on the hardware and on the compiler. Each function call creates a new activation record on the stack. The activation record is removed from the stack when the function returns, providing the last-called-first-returned order for nested function calls.

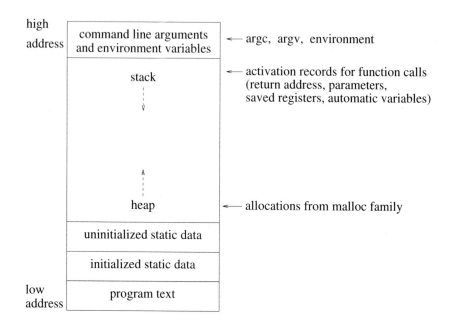

Figure 2.1: A sample layout for a program in main memory.

In addition to the static and automatic variables, the program image contains space for `argc` and `argv` and for allocations by `malloc`. The `malloc` family of functions allocates storage from a free pool called the *heap*. Storage allocated on the heap persists until it is freed or the program exits. If a function calls `malloc`, the storage remains allocated after the return. The program cannot access the storage after the return unless it has a pointer to the storage that is accessible after the function return.

Static variables that are not explicitly initialized in their declarations are initialized to 0 at run time. Notice that the static initialized variables and the static uninitialized variables occupy different sections in the program image. Typically the initialized static variables are part of the executable module on disk, but the uninitialized static variables are not. Of course the automatic variables are not part of the executable module but are allocated on the runtime stack. The initial values of automatic variables are undetermined unless the program explicitly initializes them.

Exercise 2.1

Use `ls -l` to compare the sizes of the executable modules for the following two C programs.

Version 1:

```
int myarray[50000] = {1, 2, 3, 4};
void main(int argc, char *argv[])
{
    myarray[0] = 3;
}
```

Version 2:

```
int myarray[50000];
void main(int argc, char *argv[])
{
    myarray[0] = 3;
}
```

Answer:

The executable module for Version 1 should be about $200,000$ bytes larger than that of Version 2 because the `myarray` of Version 1 is initialized static data and is therefore part of the executable module. The `myarray` of Version 2 is not allocated until the program is loaded in memory, and the array elements are initialized to 0 at that time.

Static variables can make a program unsafe for threaded execution. For example, the C library function `readdir` and its relatives described in Section 3.1.1 use static variables to hold return values. The static return value strategy is also used by client and server stubs for marshaling and unmarshaling arguments for remote procedure calls described in Chapters 14 and 15. Neither situation is thread-safe. External static variables also make code more difficult to debug because of unexpected interactions among functions that use them. For these reasons avoid using static variables except under controlled circumstances.

2.2 Static Objects

One situation in which static variables are commonly used is in the C implementation of a data structure as an object. The data structure and all of the functions that access it are in a single source file, and the data structures are defined outside of any function. The data structure has the `static` attribute, giving it internal linkage: it is private to that source file. Any references to the data structure outside the file are made through the access functions (methods in C++ terminology) defined within the file. The actual details of the data structure should be invisible to the outside world so that a change in the internal implementation does not require a change to the outside references. An implementer can make the object access thread-safe by placing locking mechanisms in the access functions within that file without affecting outside callers.

This section develops an implementation of a list object with the type of static structures just described. The list object is then used by an application that executes commands and keeps a history of the commands it executes. Figure 2.2 shows the schematic of a list represented as an object. The object has three access functions: `add_data`, `get_data`, and `rewind_list`. The data structures for the object and the code for the access functions are in a single file. Several later projects use such a list object including the `newsbiff` program developed in Section 2.15.

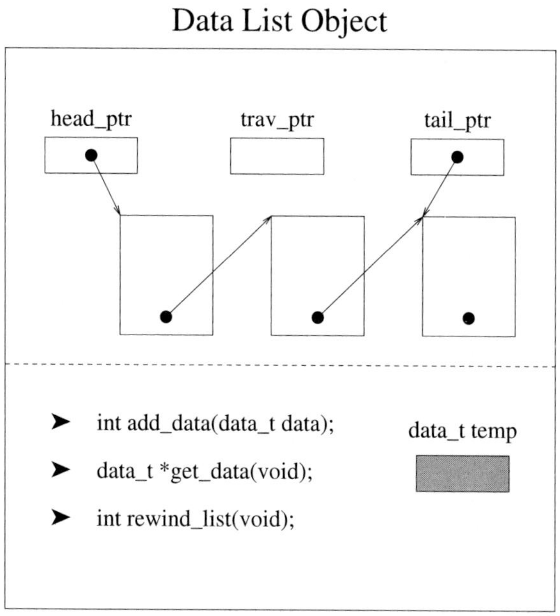

Data List Object

Figure 2.2: A list object with three access functions. The `temp` variable holds the return value for `get_data`.

In an object representation, outside callers do not have access to the internal representation of the object (e.g., they should not be aware that the object is a linked list rather than an array or other representation of the abstract data structure). Program 2.1 shows the header file `list.h` which a calling program includes in order to access the list. The program is aware of the structure of the data but not of the underlying list.

The data items defined in `data_t` consist of a `time_t` value (time) and a char-

acter string of undetermined length (string). Program 2.2 shows an implementation
of the list object depicted in Figure 2.2. The implementation is complicated by the assumption of no upper bound on the length of string.

Program 2.1: The header file list.h.

```
/*                      list.h                            */
#include <sys/types.h>
#include <time.h>

typedef struct data_struct {
     time_t time;
     char *string;
} data_t;

int add_data(data_t data);
data_t *get_data(void);
int rewind_list(void);
```
_____ **Program 2.1** _____

Program 2.2: A list object implementation.

```
#include <stdlib.h>
#include <string.h>
#include "list.h"

typedef struct list_struct {
     data_t item;
     struct list_struct *next;
} list_t;

static list_t *head_ptr = NULL;
static list_t *tail_ptr = NULL;
static list_t **trav_ptr = &head_ptr;
static data_t temp;

/* Allocate a node to hold data and add to end of list.
 * Return 0 if successful or -1 if unsuccessful.
 */
int add_data(data_t data)
{
   list_t *newnode;

   if ((newnode = (list_t *)(malloc(sizeof(list_t) +
                      strlen(data.string) + 1))) == NULL)
      return -1;
```

```
    newnode->item.time = data.time;
    newnode->item.string = (char *)(newnode + sizeof(list_t));
    strcpy(newnode->item.string, data.string);
    newnode->next = NULL;
    if (head_ptr == NULL)
        head_ptr = newnode;
    else tail_ptr->next = newnode;
    tail_ptr = newnode;
    return 0;
}


 /* Return a pointer in temp that has a copy of the data contained
  * in the current node *trav_ptr.   If at the end of the list
  * return NULL.   In any case, update trav_ptr.
  */
data_t *get_data(void)
{
    list_t *t;

    t = *trav_ptr;
    if (t == NULL)
        return NULL;
    if (temp.string != NULL)
        free (temp.string);
    if ( (temp.string =
        (char *) malloc(strlen(t->item.string) + 1)) == NULL)
        return NULL;
    temp.time = t->item.time;
    strcpy(temp.string, t->item.string);
    trav_ptr = &(t->next);
    return &temp;
}


/* Set trav_ptr to contain the address of head_ptr.
 * If head_ptr is NULL, return -1 indicating an empty list.
 * Otherwise return 0.
 */
int rewind_list(void)
{
    trav_ptr = &head_ptr;
    if (head_ptr == NULL)
        return -1;
    else
        return 0;
}
```

———————————————————————— **Program 2.2** ————————————————————————

The `add_data` function appends a node containing `data` to its internal list structure. The `add_data` returns 0 if it is successful and −1 if it is unsuccessful. The `malloc` allocates space for both the `list_t` and its string data in a contiguous block. The only way that `add_data` can fail is if the `malloc` fails. In that case `add_data` returns −1 and `errno` has the value set by the `malloc` since there are no intervening calls.

The `get_data` function returns a pointer to a temporary location (`temp` of Figure 2.2) containing the data from the next item in the list. Successive `get_data` calls overwrite the data. If at the end of the list, `get_data` returns a `NULL` pointer. The list object keeps an internal `trav_ptr` which contains the address of a pointer to the next item to be accessed by `get_data`. Each call to `get_data` moves the `trav_ptr` to point to the next item.

Exercise 2.2
Why is the `trav_ptr` a `list_t **` rather than a `list_t *`?
Answer:
Suppose `trav_ptr` is a `list_t *`. When `get_data` processes the last node in the list, it sets `trav_ptr` to `NULL`. If the program calls `add_data` before calling `get_data` again, the `trav_ptr` misses the item just added.

The `rewind_list` function resets the `trav_ptr` to the address of the `head_ptr`. It returns 0 if the list is nonempty and −1 if the list is empty.

Program 2.3 is an application which executes commands and keeps an internal history using the list data object of Program 2.2. The program inputs commands from standard input and keeps an internal history of these commands and the times at which they were executed. The program takes an optional command-line argument, `history`, which if present causes the program to output a history of commands run so far when the program reads the string `"history"` from standard input. The program uses `fgets` instead of `gets` to prevent a buffer overrun on input.

Program 2.3 calls `runproc` to run the command and `showhistory` to display the history of commands run. `MAX_CANON` is a POSIX-defined constant specifying the maximum number of bytes in a terminal input line. If `MAX_CANON` is not defined in `limits.h`, the maximum line length depends on the particular device and the program sets the value to 8192 bytes.

The `runproc` function calls the `system` function to execute a command.

SYNOPSIS

```
#include <stdlib.h>

int system(const char *string);
```
ISO C, Spec 1170

The system function executes a fork, and the child exec's a shell to execute the given command. The system function returns −1 if the fork or exec fails.

Program 2.4 shows the source file containing the runproc and showhistory functions. The runproc and showhistory functions access the history object. When runproc successfully executes a command, it adds a node to the history list by calling add_data. The showhistory function displays the contents of each node in the list by calling the get_data function.

Program 2.3: The main program which is contained in the source file keeplog.c.

```c
#include <stdio.h>
#include <stdlib.h>
#include <limits.h>
#include <string.h>

#ifndef MAX_CANON
#define MAX_CANON 8192
#endif

void showhistory(FILE *f);
int runproc(char *cmd);

void main(int argc, char *argv[])
{
    char cmd[MAX_CANON];
    int history = 1;

    if (argc == 1)
        history = 0;
    else if ((argc > 2) || strcmp(argv[1], "history")) {
        fprintf(stderr, "Usage: %s [history]\n", argv[0]);
        exit(1);
    }
    while(fgets(cmd, MAX_CANON, stdin) != NULL) {
        if (*(cmd + strlen(cmd) - 1) == '\n')
            *(cmd + strlen(cmd) - 1) = 0;
        if (history && !strcmp(cmd, "history"))
            showhistory(stdout);
        else if (runproc(cmd))
            break;
    }
    printf("\n\n>>>>>>The list of commands executed is:\n");
    showhistory(stdout);
    exit(0);
}
```

Program 2.3 ————————

Program 2.4: The file `keeploglib.c`.

```
#include <stdio.h>
#include <stdlib.h>
#include "list.h"

 /* Execute cmd and store cmd and time of execution in history list. */
int runproc(char *cmd)
{
    data_t execute;

    time(&(execute.time));
    execute.string = cmd;
    if (system(cmd) == -1)
        return -1;
    return add_data(execute);
}

/* Output the history list of the file f */
void showhistory(FILE *f)
{
    data_t *infop;

    rewind_list();
    while ((infop = get_data()) != NULL)
        fprintf(f, "Command: %s\nTime: %s\n", infop->string,
                ctime(&(infop->time)));
    return;
}
```
_____ **Program 2.4** _____

2.3 The Process ID

UNIX identifies processes using a unique integer called the *process ID*. The process that executes the request for creation of a process is called the *parent* of that process, and the created process is called the *child*. The parent process ID identifies the parent of the process. Use `getpid` and `getppid` to determine these IDs.

SYNOPSIS

```
    #include <sys/types.h>
    #include <unistd.h>

    pid_t getpid(void);
    pid_t getppid(void);
```
                                                         POSIX.1, Spec 1170

UNIX associates each process with a particular user called the *owner* of the process. The owner has certain privileges with respect to the process. Each user has a unique identification number called the *user ID*. A process can determine its owner's user ID by calling `getuid`. The owner is the user who executes the program. The process also has an *effective user ID*, which determines the privileges that a process has for accessing resources such as files. The effective user ID can change during the execution of a process. A process can determine its effective user ID by calling `geteuid`.

SYNOPSIS

```
#include <sys/types.h>
#include <unistd.h>

uid_t getuid(void);
uid_t geteuid(void);
```
                                                              POSIX.1, Spec 1170

Example 2.1

The following program prints out its process ID, its parent process ID, and its owner user ID.

```
#include <stdio.h>
#include <sys/types.h>
#include <unistd.h>

void main(void)
{
    printf("Process ID: %ld\n", (long)getpid());
    printf("Parent process ID: %ld\n", (long)getppid());
    printf("Owner user ID: %ld\n", (long)getuid());
}
```

Under POSIX, `getpid` returns a value of type `pid_t` which may be either an `int` or a `long`. To be on the safe side, cast the return value of `getpid` to `long`.

2.4 The Process State

The *state* of a process indicates its status at a particular time. Most operating systems allow some form of the states given in Table 2.2. A *state diagram* is a graphical representation of the allowed states of a process and the allowed transitions between states. Figure 2.3 shows such a diagram. The nodes of the graph represent the possible states, and the edges represent possible transitions. A directed arc from state **A** to state **B** means a process can go directly from state **A** to state **B**. The labels on the arcs indicate the conditions that cause the transitions between states to occur.

State	Meaning
new	process is being created
running	process instructions are being executed
blocked	process is waiting for an event such as I/O
ready	process is waiting to be assigned to a processor
done	process has finished and its resources are deallocated

Table 2.2: Common Process States.

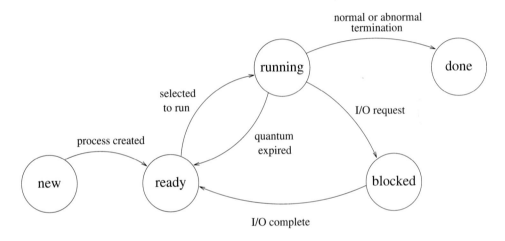

Figure 2.3: A state diagram for a simple operating system.

While a program undergoes the transformation into an active process, it is said to be in the *new* state. When the transformation completes, the operating system puts the process in a queue of processes that are ready to run. The process is then in the *ready* state. Eventually the process scheduler selects the process to run. The process is in the *running* state when it is actually executing on the CPU.

A process in the blocked state is waiting for an event and is not considered to be eligible for execution by the process scheduler. A process can voluntarily move to the *blocked* state by executing a call such as `sleep`. More commonly a process moves to the *blocked* state when it performs an I/O request. Input and output can be thousands of times slower than ordinary instructions. I/O is handled by the operating system, and a process performs I/O by requesting the service through a *system call*. The operating system regains control and can move the process to the blocked state until the operation completes.

The act of removing one process from the running state and replacing it with another is known as a *context switch*. The *context* of a process is the information that is needed about the process and its environment in order to restart it after a context switch. Clearly the executable, stack, registers, and program counter are part of the context, as is the memory used for static and dynamically allocated variables. In order to be able to restart a process in a transparent manner, the operating system also keeps track of the process state, the status of program I/O, user and process identification, privileges, scheduling and accounting information, and memory management information. If a process is waiting for an event or has caught a signal, that information is part of the context too. The context also contains information about other resources such as locks held by the process.

The `ps` utility displays information about processes.

SYNOPSIS

```
ps [-aA] [-G grouplist] [-o format]...[-p proclist]
   [-t termlist] [-U userlist]
```

                                                                        POSIX.2

By default `ps` displays information about processes associated with the user. The `-a` option displays information for processes associated with terminals, while the `-A` option displays information for all processes. The `-o` option specifies the format of the output.

The Spec 1170 specification is slightly different from the POSIX one.

SYNOPSIS

```
ps [-aA] [-defl] [-G grouplist] [-o format]...[-p proclist]
   [-t termlist] [-U userlist] [-g grouplist] [-n namelist]
   [-u userlist]
```

                                                                     Spec 1170

Many vendor implementations of `ps` do not conform exactly to either the POSIX or Spec 1170 specification. Sun Solaris 2, for example, uses `-e` rather than `-A` for the option to get information about all processes. The Sun version with no arguments outputs information about processes associated with the controlling terminal rather than with the user. Controlling terminals are discussed in Section 7.5.

Example 2.2

An execution of `ps -l` *under Sun Solaris 2 produced the following output.*

F	S	UID	PID	PPID	C	PRI	NI	ADDR	SZ	WCHAN	TTY	TIME	COMD
8	S	512	4509	4502	80	40	20	fc579000	205	fc5791c8	pts/13	0:00	csh
8	O	512	4627	4509	13	60	20	fc5b1800	151		pts/13	0:00	ps

The long form of the Sun `ps` in Example 2.2 shows many items of interest for processes associated with the current controlling terminal (with device name `pts/13`). Table 2.3 summarizes the meaning of the various fields.

Header	Meaning
F	flags associated with the process
S	the process state
UID	the user ID of the process owner
PID	the process ID
PPID	the parent process ID
C	the processor utilization used for scheduling
PRI	the priority of the process
NI	the nice value
ADDR	the memory address of the process
SZ	the size of the process image
WCHAN	the address of the event if the process is sleeping
TTY	the controlling terminal
TIME	cumulative execution time
COMMAND	command name

Table 2.3: Fields reported by the long form of the Sun Solaris `ps` command.

2.5 Process Creation and the UNIX `fork`

UNIX creates processes through the `fork` system call by copying the parent's memory image. The new process receives a copy of the address space of the parent. Both processes continue execution at the instruction after the `fork`.

```
SYNOPSIS

   #include <sys/types.h>
   #include <unistd.h>

   pid_t fork(void);
                                        POSIX.1, Spec 1170
```

Creation of two completely identical processes would not be very useful. The `fork` return value is the critical distinguishing characteristic that allows the parent and the child to execute different code. The `fork` returns 0 to the child and returns the child's process ID to the parent.

Example 2.3

In the following code both parent and child execute the x = 1 *assignment statement after returning from the* fork. *There is one process and a single* x *variable before the fork is executed.*

```
#include <sys/types.h>
#include <unistd.h>


x = 0;
fork();
x = 1;
```

After the fork in Example 2.3, there are two independent processes. Each process has its own copy of the x variable. Since the parent and child processes execute independently, they do not execute the code in lock step or modify the same memory location. The parent and child processes are not distinguishable because the fork return value is not tested.

Example 2.4

After the fork in the following code segment, the parent and child output their process IDs.

```
#include <stdio.h>
#include <sys/types.h>
#include <unistd.h>

if ((childpid = fork()) == 0) {
   fprintf(stderr, "I am the child, ID = %ld\n", (long)getpid());
      /*   child code goes here   */
} else if (childpid > 0) {
   fprintf(stderr, "I am the parent, ID = %ld\n", (long)getpid());
      /*  parent code goes here */
}
```

The original process in Example 2.4 has a nonzero value of the childpid variable, so it executes the second fprintf statement. The child process has a zero value of childpid and executes the first fprintf statement. The fprintf output can appear in either order.

Example 2.5

The following code segment creates a chain of n *processes.*

```
#include <stdio.h>
#include <sys/types.h>
#include <unistd.h>
```

```
int i;
int n;
pid_t childpid;
for (i = 1; i < n;   ++i)
   if (childpid = fork())
      break;
fprintf(stderr,"This is process %ld with parent %ld\n",
         (long)getpid(), (long)getppid());
```

On each execution of `fork` in Example 2.5, the parent process has a nonzero `childpid` and hence breaks out of the loop. The child process has a zero value of `childpid` and becomes a parent in the next loop iteration. In case of an error on the `fork`, the return value is −1 and the calling process breaks out of the loop. The exercises in Section 2.12 build on this example.

Figure 2.4 shows a graph representing the chain of processes generated for Example 2.5 when n is 4. Each circle represents a process and is labeled by the value of i that the corresponding process has when it leaves the loop. The edges represent the "is a parent" relationship. $A \rightarrow B$ means process A is the parent of process B.

Figure 2.4: A chain of processes generated by the code segment of Example 2.5 when n is 4.

Example 2.6

The following code segment creates a fan of processes.

```
#include <stdio.h>
#include <sys/types.h>
#include <unistd.h>
```

```
int i;
int n;
pid_t childpid;

for (i = 1; i < n;   ++i)
   if ((childpid = fork()) <= 0)
      break;
fprintf(stderr, "This is process %ld with parent %ld\n",
         (long)getpid(), (long)getppid());
```

Figure 2.5 shows the process fan generated by Example 2.6 when n is 4. The processes in the figure are labeled by the values of i they have when they leave the loop of Example 2.6. The original process creates n - 1 children. The exercises in Section 2.13 build on this example.

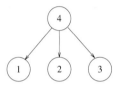

Figure 2.5: A fan of processes generated by the code segment of Example 2.6 when n is 4.

Example 2.7

The following code segment produces a tree of processes.

```
#include <stdio.h>
#include <sys/types.h>
#include <unistd.h>

int i;
int n;
pid_t childpid;

for (i = 1; i < n;   i++)
   if ((childpid = fork()) == -1)
      break;
fprintf(stderr, "This is process %ld with parent %ld\n",
         (long)getpid(), (long)getppid());
```

Figure 2.6 shows the tree of processes generated for Example 2.7 when n is 4. Each process is represented by a circle and labeled by the i value at the time it was created.

The original process is labeled 0. The lowercase letters distinguish processes that were created with the same value of `i`. While this code appears to be similar to that of Example 2.5, it does not distinguish between parent and child on the `fork`. Both the parent and child processes go on to create children on the next iteration of the loop, hence the population explosion.

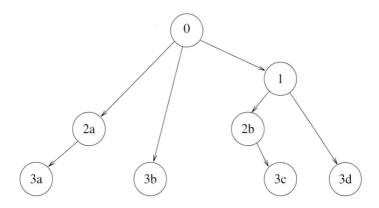

Figure 2.6: A tree of processes produced from a `fork` loop.

The `fork` creates a new process by making a copy of the parent's image in memory. The child *inherits* most of the parent's attributes including environment and privileges. The child also inherits some of the parent's resources such as open files and devices. The implications of inheritance are more complicated than might first appear. Section 3.3 and Chapter 4 explore the issue of file inheritance.

Not every parent attribute or resource is inherited by the child. The child has a new process ID and of course a different parent ID. The child's times for CPU usage are reset to 0. The child does not get locks that the parent holds. If the parent has set an alarm, the child does not receive notification when it expires. The child starts with no pending signals, even if the parent had signals pending at the time of the `fork`.

Although a child inherits its parent's priority and scheduling attributes, it competes for processor time with other processes as a separate entity. A user running on a crowded time-sharing system can obtain a greater share of the CPU time by creating more processes. In contrast, the VAX VMS operating system allows a type of process creation in which all of the processes created by a single user share the CPU time slice that would be allocated to that user. A system manager on a crowded academic UNIX system might restrict process creation to prevent a user from creating processes to get a bigger share of the resources.

2.6 The `wait` System Call

What happens to the parent process after it creates a child? Both parent and child proceed with execution from the point of the `fork`. If a parent wants to wait until the child finishes, it executes `wait` or `waitpid`.

```
SYNOPSIS

   #include <sys/types.h>
   #include <sys/wait.h>

   pid_t wait(int *stat_loc);
   pid_t waitpid(pid_t pid, int *stat_loc, int options);
                                                 POSIX.1, Spec 1170
```

The `wait` causes the caller to pause until a child terminates or stops or until the caller receives a signal. The `wait` returns right away if the process has no children or if a child terminates or stops but has not yet been waited for. If the `wait` returns because a child terminated, the return value is positive and is the process ID of that child. Otherwise, `wait` returns -1 and sets `errno`. An `errno` of `ECHILD` indicates that there were no unwaited-for child processes, and an `errno` value of `EINTR` indicates that the call was interrupted by a signal. The `stat_loc` is a pointer to an integer variable. If the caller passes something other than `NULL`, the `wait` stores the return status of the child. POSIX specifies the macros `WIFEXITED`, `WEXITSTUS`, `WIFSIGNALED`, `WTERMSIG`, `WIFSTOPPED`, and `WSTOPSIG` for testing the child's return status stored in `*stat_loc`. The child returns its status by calling `exit`, `_exit`, or `return`.

Example 2.8
In the following code segment a parent determines the exit status of a child.

```
#include <sys/types.h>
#include <sys/wait.h>
#include <errno.h>

pid_t child;
int status;

while((((child = wait(&status)) == -1) && (errno == EINTR))
   ;
if (child == -1)
   perror("Could not wait for child");
else if (!status)
   printf("Child %ld terminated normally, return status is zero\n",
          (long)child);
else if (WIFEXITED(status))
   printf("Child %ld terminated normally, return status is %d\n",
          (long)child, WEXITSTATUS(status));
```

```
        else if (WIFSIGNALED(status))
            printf("Child %ld terminated due to signal not caught\n",
                   (long)child);
```

Program 2.5 illustrates the `wait` system call. The process has only one child; so if the return value is not the process ID of that child, the `wait` must have returned because of a signal.

Program 2.5: A simple program illustrating the use of `wait`.

```
#include <sys/types.h>
#include <sys/wait.h>
#include <unistd.h>
#include <stdio.h>

void main (void)
{
   pid_t childpid;
   int   status;

   if ((childpid = fork()) == -1) {
      perror("The fork failed");
      exit(1);
   } else if (childpid == 0)
      fprintf(stderr,
         "I am the child with pid = %ld\n", (long)getpid());
   else if (wait(&status) != childpid)
      fprintf(stderr, "A signal must have interrupted the wait\n");
   else
      fprintf(stderr,
         "I am the parent with pid = %ld and child pid = %ld\n",
         (long)getpid(), (long)childpid);
   exit(0);
}
```
_____ **Program 2.5** _____

Exercise 2.3

What are the possible forms of the output from Program 2.5?

Answer:

There are several possibilities.

- If the `fork` fails (unlikely unless the program generates a runaway tree of processes), the `"fork failed"` message appears. Otherwise if there are no signals, something similar to the following appears:

```
I am the child with pid = 3427
I am the parent with pid = 3426 and child pid = 3427
```

- If a signal comes in after the child does the `fprintf` but before the `exit`, the following appears:

```
I am the child with pid = 3427
A signal must have interrupted the wait
```

- If a signal comes in after the child exits and the `wait` returns, the following appears:

```
I am the child with pid = 3427
I am the parent with pid = 3426 and child pid = 3427
```

- If the signal comes in after the child exits, but before the `wait` returns, either of the previous two results is possible depending on when the signal arrives.

- If a signal comes in before the child does the `fprintf` and if the parent gets to its `fprintf` first, the following appears:

```
A signal must have interrupted the wait
I am the child with pid = 3427
```

- Finally, if the signal comes in before the child does the `fprintf` and the child gets to its `fprintf` first, the following appears:

```
I am the child with pid = 3427
A signal must have interrupted the wait
```

In order for the child of Program 2.5 always to print its message first, the parent must `wait` repeatedly until the child exits before printing its own message.

Example 2.9

The following code segment restarts a `wait` *until a particular child finishes.*

```
#include <sys/types.h>
#include <sys/wait.h>
int status;
pid_t childpid;

while(childpid != wait(&status))
   ;
```

The `wait` of Example 2.9 can fail to return the `childpid` because it encounters an error. The way to distinguish a failure because of a signal from other errors is to test `errno`. When `wait` fails, it returns −1 and sets the `errno`. An `errno` value of `EINTR` indicates interruption by a signal.

Example 2.10

   The following code segment loops until the child with process ID `childpid`
   completes or until there is an error.

```
#include <sys/types.h>
#include <sys/wait.h>
#include <errno.h>

int status;
pid_t childpid;

while(childpid != wait(&status))
   if ((childpid == -1) && (errno != EINTR))
      break;
```

The `waitpid` system call provides more flexible methods of waiting for children.
A process can wait for a particular child without waiting for all children. This feature
is useful for tracing a particular child without interference by other terminated children.
The `waitpid` also has a nonblocking form, so a process can periodically check for
unwaited for children without hanging indefinitely.

   The `waitpid` function call takes three parameters: a `pid`, a pointer to location for
returning the status, and option flags. If `pid` is −1, `waitpid` waits for any process.
If `pid` is positive, the `waitpid` waits for the specific child whose process ID is `pid`.
The `WNOHANG` option causes `waitpid` to return even if the status of a child is not
immediately available. Check the man page on `waitpid` for a complete specification
of its parameters.

Example 2.11

   The following code segment waits for any child, avoiding the block if there are
   no children whose status is available. It restarts if the `waitpid` *is interrupted*
   by a signal.

```
#include <sys/types.h>
#include <sys/wait.h>
#include <errno.h>
int status;
pid_t waitreturnpid;

while(waitreturnpid = waitpid(-1, &status, WNOHANG))
   if ((waitreturnpid == -1) && (errno != EINTR))
      break;
```

When `waitpid` returns 0, it means that there are still children to be waited for,
but none of them are ready. What happens to a process whose parent does not wait for
it? It becomes a *zombie* in UNIX terminology. Zombies stay in the system until they
are waited for. If a parent terminates without waiting for a child, the child becomes an

orphan and is adopted by the system `init` process which has process ID equal to 1. The `init` process periodically waits for children so eventually orphan zombies are removed.

Exercise 2.4

The following code segment creates a process fan. All of the forked processes are children of the original process. How are the output messages ordered?

```
#include <stdio.h>
#include <sys/types.h>
#include <sys/wait.h>
#include <unistd.h>
#include <errno.h>

int i;
int n;
pid_t childpid;
int status;

for (i = 1; i < n;  ++i)
    if ((childpid = fork()) <= 0)
        break;
for( ; ; ) {
    childpid = wait(&status);
    if ((childpid == -1) && (errno != EINTR))
        break;
}
fprintf(stderr, "I am process %ld, my parent is %ld\n",
                (long)getpid(), (long)getppid());
```

Answer:

Because none of the forked children are parents, their `wait` returns -1 and sets errno to `ECHILD`. They are not blocked by the second `for` loop. Their identification messages can come out in any order. The message from the original process comes out at the very end after it has waited for all of its children.

Exercise 2.5

The following code segment creates a process chain. Only one forked process is a child of the original process. How are the output messages ordered?

```
#include <stdio.h>
#include <sys/types.h>
#include <sys/wait.h>
#include <unistd.h>
#include <errno.h>

int i;
int n;
pid_t childpid;
```

```
    int status;
    pid_t waitreturn;

    for (i = 1; i < n;   ++i)
       if (childpid = fork())
          break;
    while(childpid != (waitreturn = wait(&status)))
       if ((waitreturn == -1) && (errno != EINTR))
          break;
    fprintf(stderr, "I am process %ld, my parent is %ld\n",
                    (long)getpid(), (long)getppid());
```

Answer:

Each forked child waits for its own child to complete before outputting a message. The messages appear in reverse order of creation.

2.7 The exec System Call

The fork system call creates a copy of the calling process. Many applications require the child process to execute code different from the parent's. The exec family of system calls provides a facility for overlaying the calling process with a new executable module. The traditional way to use the fork–exec combination is to have the child exec the new program while the parent continues to execute the original code.

The six variations of the exec system call are distinguishable by the way command-line arguments and environment are passed and by whether a full pathname has to be given for the executable. The execl calls (execl, execlp, and execle) pass the command-line arguments as a list and are useful if the number of command-line arguments is known at compile time.The execv calls (execv, execvp, and execve) pass the command-line arguments in an argument array.

The code in Program 2.6 calls the ls command with a command-line argument of -1. The program assumes that ls is located in the /usr/bin directory.

Program 2.6: A program that creates a process to run ls -1.

```
#include <sys/types.h>
#include <sys/wait.h>
#include <unistd.h>
#include <stdio.h>
#include <stdlib.h>

void main(void)
{
    pid_t childpid;
```

```
    int status;

    if ((childpid = fork()) == -1)  {
        perror("Error in the fork");
        exit(1);
    } else  if (childpid == 0) {                        /* child code */
        if (execl("/usr/bin/ls", "ls", "-l", NULL) < 0) {
            perror("Exec of ls failed");
            exit(1);
        }
    } else if (childpid != wait(&status))    /* parent code */
        perror("A signal occurred before the child exited");
    exit(0);
}
```

_____ **Program 2.6** _____

```
SYNOPSIS

    #include <unistd.h>

    int execl(const char *path, const char *arg0, ...,
            const char *argn, char * /*NULL*/);
    int execle (const char *path,char *const arg0[], ... ,
            const char *argn, char * /*NULL*/,
            char *const envp[]);
    int execlp (const char *file, const char *arg0, ...,
            const char *argn, char * /*NULL*/);
                                                    POSIX.1, Spec 1170
```

The path parameter to execl is the pathname of the program specified either as a fully-qualified pathname or relative to the current directory. The individual command-line arguments are then listed followed by a NULL pointer. The list of character-string parameters corresponds to the argv array for the exec'd command. Since argv[0] is the program name, it is the second argument of the execl.

An alternative form is execlp which has the same parameters as execl but uses the PATH environment variable to search for the executable. In a similar way, the shell tries to locate the executable file in one of the directories specified by the PATH variable when a user enters a command.

A third form of execl is execle which is like execl except that it takes an additional parameter representing the new environment of the exec'd program. For the other forms of execl, the new program inherits the environment of the parent.

The execv takes exactly two parameters, a pathname for the executable and an argument array. (The makeargv function of Program 1.2 is useful here.) The execvp constructs a full pathname from the file parameter by using path prefixes found in the

PATH environment variable. The execve form requires a third parameter, the envp argument array, specifying the environment for the created process.

```
SYNOPSIS

   #include <unistd.h>

   int execv(const char *path, char *const argv[]);
   int execvp (const char *file, char *const argv[]);
   int execve (const char *path, char *const argv[],
        char *const envp[]);
                                          POSIX.1, Spec 1170
```

Program 2.7 uses execvp to execute a command passed on the command line. Suppose the executable for Program 2.7 is myexec. The original process forks a child and then waits for the child to terminate. The child process calls execvp with the argument array formed by command-line arguments for the original program.

Example 2.12

The following command line causes myexec *to create a new process to execute the* ls -l *command.*

```
myexec ls -l
```

The original argv array produced in Example 2.12 contains pointers to three tokens: myexec, ls, and -1. The argument array for the execvp starts at &argv[1] and contains pointers to the two tokens ls and -1. The parent waits for the child. If the wait is interrupted by a signal, errno is equal to EINTR and the parent restarts its wait.

Program 2.7: A program that creates a process to execute a command passed as command-line arguments.

```c
#include <sys/types.h>
#include <sys/wait.h>
#include <unistd.h>
#include <stdio.h>
#include <errno.h>

void main(int argc, char *argv[])
{
   pid_t childpid;
   int status;

   if ((childpid = fork()) == -1) {
      perror("The fork failed");
```

```
        exit(1);
    } else if (childpid == 0) {                /* child code */
        if (execvp(argv[1], &argv[1]) < 0) {
            perror("The exec of command failed");
            exit(1);
        }
    } else                                     /* parent code */
        while(childpid != wait(&status))
            if ((childpid == -1) && (errno != EINTR))
                break;
    exit(0);
}
```

_____ **Program 2.7** _____

Exercise 2.6

Execute `myexec` of Program 2.7 with the command line `myexec ls -1 *.c`.
How big is the argument array passed as the second argument to `execvp`?

Answer:

It depends on the number of `.c` files in the directory because the shell expands
`*.c` before passing the command line to `myexec`.

The program in Program 2.8 calls `makeargv` of Program 1.2 to create an argument
array from the string passed as its first command-line argument. It then does an `execvp`
of the command represented by that string. Pass a string containing multiple tokens by
placing the string in double quotes (e.g., `myexec "ls -l"`).

Notice that the `makeargv` function is only called by the child process in Program 2.8. If the parent calls `makeargv` before the `fork`, the parent has an unused
argument array allocated in its heap. A single call to `makeargv` does not present a
problem. However, in a shell where the allocation step might be repeated hundreds of
times, the memory cleanup can be a problem.

_____

Program 2.8: A program that creates a process to execute a command passed as the
first command-line argument. Program 1.2 shows an implementation of the `makeargv`
function.

```
#include <sys/types.h>
#include <sys/wait.h>
#include <unistd.h>
#include <stdio.h>
#include <stdlib.h>
#include <errno.h>
```

```
int makeargv(char *s, char *delimiters, char ***argvp);

void main(int argc, char *argv[]) {
    char **myargv;
    char delim[] = " \t";
    pid_t childpid;
    int status;

    if (argc != 2) {
        fprintf(stderr, "Usage: %s string\n", argv[0]);
        exit(1);
    }
    if ((childpid = fork()) == -1) {
        perror("The fork failed");
        exit(1);
    } else if (childpid == 0) {                          /* child code */
        if (makeargv(argv[1], delim, &myargv) < 0) {
            fprintf(stderr, "Argument array could not be constructed\n");
            exit(1);
        } else if (execvp(myargv[0], &myargv[0]) < 0) {
            perror("The exec of command failed");
            exit(1);
        }
    } else                                               /* parent code */
        while(childpid != wait(&status))
            if ((childpid == -1) && (errno != EINTR))
                break;
    exit(0);
}
```
_____ **Program 2.8** _____

The exec copies a new executable into the process image. Exactly what is preserved from the original process is not obvious. The program text, variables, stack, and
heap are overwritten. The new process inherits the environment (meaning the list of
environment variables and their associated values), unless the original process called
execle or execve. Files that are open before the exec are usually still open afterwards (as explained in Chapter 3.3). Chapter 5 discusses the effects of exec on signals
and locks.

Table 2.4 summarizes the attributes that are inherited by the exec'd process. The
second column of the table gives system calls related to the items. The IDs associated
with the process are intact after the exec. If a process sets an alarm before calling exec,
the alarm still generates a signal when it expires. Pending signals are also carried over
on exec in contrast to the fork. The process creates files with the same permissions
as before the exec, and accounting of CPU time continues without being reinitialized.

Attribute	Relevant System Call
process ID	getpid()
parent process ID	getppid()
process group ID	getpgid()
session membership	getsid()
real user ID	getuid()
real group ID	getgid()
supplementary group IDs	getgroups()
time left on an alarm signal	alarm()
current working directory	getcwd()
root directory	
file mode creation mask	umask()
process signal mask	sigprocmask()
pending signals	sigpending()
time used so far	times()

Table 2.4: Attributes that are preserved after calls to exec. The second column gives system calls relevant to these attributes.

2.8 Background Processes and Daemons

The shell is a command interpreter which prompts for commands, reads the commands from standard input, forks children to execute the commands, and waits for the children to finish. When standard input and output come from a terminal-type device, a user can terminate an executing command by entering the interrupt character. (The interrupt character is settable, but often it is ctrl-c.)

Exercise 2.7
   Change to a directory that has a lot of files (e.g., /etc), and execute the following command.

   ls -l

   What happens? Now execute the ls -l command again but enter a ctrl-c as soon as the listing starts to display. Compare the results to the first case.

Answer:
   In the first case the prompt prints out after the directory listing is complete because the shell waits for the child before continuing. In the second case the ctrl-c terminates the ls.

Most shells interpret a line ending with & as a command that should be executed by a background process. When a shell creates a background process, it does not wait for the process to complete before issuing a prompt and accepting additional commands. Furthermore, a ctrl-c from the keyboard does not terminate a background process. (Chapter 7 presents a more technical discussion of background processes.)

Exercise 2.8

Compare the results of Exercise 2.7 with the results of executing the following command.

```
ls -l  &
```

Reenter the ls -l & command and try to terminate it by entering ctrl-c.

Answer:

In the first case the prompt appears before the listing completes. The ctrl-c does not affect background processes, so the second case behaves in the same way as the first.

A *daemon* is a background process that normally runs indefinitely. The UNIX operating system relies on many daemon processes to perform routine (and not so routine) tasks. Under Solaris 2, the pageout daemon handles paging for memory management. The in.rlogind handles remote login requests. Other daemons handle mail, ftp, statistics, and printer requests, to name just a few. A daemon is spun off and does not retain a history of where it came from.

The runback program in Program 2.9 executes its first command-line argument as a background process. The child calls setsid so that it does not get any ctrl-c type interrupts from a controlling terminal.

Program 2.9: The runback program creates a process to execute a command string in the background.

```c
#include <sys/types.h>
#include <sys/wait.h>
#include <unistd.h>
#include <stdio.h>
#include <stdlib.h>
int makeargv(char *s, char *delimiters, char ***argvp);

void main(int argc, char *argv[]) {
   char **myargv;
   char delim[] = " \t";
   pid_t childpid;

   if (argc != 2) {
```

```
        fprintf(stderr, "Usage: %s string\n", argv[0]);
        exit(1);
    }

    if ((childpid = fork()) == -1) {
        perror("The fork failed");
        exit(1);
    } else if (childpid == 0) { /* child becomes a background process */
        if (setsid() == -1)
            perror("Could not become a session leader");
        else if (makeargv(argv[1], delim, &myargv) < 0)
            fprintf(stderr, "Argument array could not be constructed\n");
        else if (execvp(myargv[0], &myargv[0]) < 0)
            perror("The exec of command failed");
        exit(1);                                /* child should never return */
    }
    exit(0);                                           /* parent exits */
}
```

_____ **Program 2.9** _____

The `runback` program of Program 2.9 uses `setsid` to create a new session that does not have a controlling terminal. The session ID determines whether the process has a controlling terminal (so it can receive a signal from `ctrl-c`). Chapter 7 explores these issues in much more detail.

Example 2.13

The following command is similar to entering `ls -l &` *directly from the shell.*

```
runback "ls -l"
```

Some systems have a facility called `biff` which enables mail notification. When a user who is logged in receives mail, `biff` notifies the user in some way, such as beeping at the terminal or displaying a message. (UNIX folklore has it that `biff`'s original author had a dog named Biff who barked at mail carriers.) Program 2.10 shows the code for a C program called `simplebiff.c` which beeps at the terminal at regular intervals if the user `oshacker` has pending mail.

The program notifies the user of mail by sending a `ctrl-g` (ASCII 7) character to standard error. Most terminals handle the receipt of `ctrl-g` by producing a short beep. The program continues beeping every 10 seconds until it is killed or until the mail file is removed.

Example 2.14

The following command starts `simplebiff`.

```
simplebiff &
```

Program 2.10: A simple program to notify `oshacker` of pending mail.

```
#include <stdio.h>
#include <sys/types.h>
#include <sys/stat.h>
#include <fcntl.h>
#include <unistd.h>
#define MAILFILE "/var/mail/oshacker"
#define SLEEPTIME 10

void main(void)
{
   int mailfd;

   for( ; ; ) {
      if ( (mailfd = open(MAILFILE, O_RDONLY)) != -1) {
         fprintf(stderr,"%s", "\007");
         close(mailfd);
      }
      sleep(SLEEPTIME);
   }
}
```

——————————————— **Program 2.10** ———————————————

Program 2.10 illustrates how a daemon process might work. Mail is usually stored in a file in the `/var/mail` or `/var/spool/mail` directory. A file in that directory with the same name as the user's login name contains all unread mail for that user. If `oshacker` has mail, an `open` of `/var/mail/oshacker` succeeds, otherwise the `open` fails. If the file exists, the user has unread mail and the program beeps. In any case the program sleeps and then repeats the process indefinitely.

Program 2.10 is not very general because the user name, mail directory, and sleep time are hardcoded. The POSIX-approved way of getting the user name is to call `getuid` to find out the user ID and then `getpwuid` to find out the login name. The `stat` system call provides more information about a file without the overhead of `open`.

The directory structure for mail varies from system to system, so the user must determine the location of the system mail files in order to use `simplebiff`. The program should allow the user to specify a directory on the command line or to rely on system-specific information communicated by environment variables if this information is available. The POSIX standard specifies several relevant environment variables such as `MAIL`, `MAILCHECK`, `MAILDIR`, and `MAILPATH`. The program should use information from these variables if they have been set. Section 2.9 discusses program access to environment variables and how these variables can communicate system-specific infor-

mation. Section 2.14 discusses a better `biff`. Section 5.5 modifies the `biff` program
to use signals for turning notification on or off.

2.9 The Process Environment

The `biff` of Program 2.10 illustrates the importance of using system-dependent information in an implementation-independent way. No polite programmer would distribute
a program that requires users to change hardcoded directory paths before it works. *Environment variables* provide a mechanism for using system-specific or user-specific information in setting defaults within a program.

An *environment list* consists of an array of pointers to strings of the form *name =
value*. The *name* specifies an environment variable. The *value* specifies a string value.
Each application interprets the environment list in an application-specific way. POSIX.2
specifies the meaning of the environment variables listed in Table 2.5.

Variable	Meaning
HOME	user's initial working directory
LANG	locale when not specified by LC_ALL or LC_*
LC_ALL	overriding name of locale
LC_COLLATE	name of locale for collating information
LC_CTYPE	name of locale for character classification
LC_MONETARY	name of locale for monetary editing
LC_NUMERIC	name of locale for numeric editing
LC_TIME	name of locale for date/time information
LOGNAME	login name associated with a process
PATH	path prefixes for finding the executable
TERM	terminal type for output
TZ	time zone information

Table 2.5: POSIX.2 environment variables and their meanings.

The external variable `environ` points to the process environment list when the
process begins executing. The `environ` variable is defined by

```
extern char **environ
```

The strings in the environment list can appear in any order. If the process is initiated by
`execl`, `execlp`, `execv`, or `execvp`, the process inherits the environment list of
the process just prior to the execution of the `exec`. The `execle` and `execve` calls
specifically set the environment list.

Example 2.15

The following C program outputs the contents of its environment list and exits.

```
#include <stdio.h>
#include <stdlib.h>

extern char **environ;

void main(int argc, char *argv[])
{
   int i;

   printf("The environment list for %s is\n", argv[0]);
   for(i = 0; environ[i] != NULL; i++)
      printf("environ[%d]: %s\n", i, environ[i]);
   exit(0);
}
```

Use `getenv` to determine whether a specific environment variable is defined.

```
SYNOPSIS

   #include <stdlib.h>

   char *getenv(const char *name);
                                              POSIX.1, Spec 1170
```

Pass the name of the environment variable as a string. The `getenv` function returns NULL if the specified variable is not defined. If the variable has a value, `getenv` returns a pointer to the string containing that value. Be careful about calling `getenv` more than once without copying the first return string into a buffer. Some implementations of `getenv` use a static buffer for the return strings and overwrite the buffer on each call.

POSIX.2 specifies that the shell `sh` should use the environment variable MAIL as the pathname of the mailbox for purposes of incoming mail provided that the MAILPATH variable is not set. (See Section 2.14 for more information on MAIL and MAILPATH.)

Example 2.16

The following code segment sets `mailp` *to the value of* MAIL *if it is defined and* MAILPATH *is not defined. Otherwise, it sets* `mailp` *to a default value.*

```
#include <stdlib.h>
#define MAILDEFAULT "/var/mail"
char *mailp = NULL;

if (getenv("MAILPATH") == NULL)
   mailp = getenv("MAIL");
if (mailp == NULL)
   mailp = MAILDEFAULT;
```

The first call to `getenv` in Example 2.16 merely checks for the existence of
`MAILPATH,` so it is not necessary to copy the return value to a separate buffer before
calling `getenv` again.

Do not confuse environment variables with predefined constants like `MAX_CANON`.
The predefined constants are defined in header files with `#define`. Their values are
constants and known at compile time. To see whether a definition of such a constant
exists, use the `#ifndef` compiler directive as in Program 2.3. In contrast, environment
variables are dynamic and their values are not known until runtime.

POSIX.2 specifies an `env` utility for examining the environment and modifying it
for the purposes of executing another command.

SYNOPSIS

```
    env [-i] [name=value] ... [utility [argument ...]]
```
POSIX.2, Spec 1170

When called without arguments, the `env` command shows the current environment.
The optional arguments `[name=value]` specify environment variables to be modified. The optional `utility` argument specifies the command to be executed under
the modified environment. The optional `-i` argument indicates that the environment
specified by the arguments should replace the current environment for the purposes of
executing `utility`. The `env` utility does not modify the environment of the shell that
is executing it.

Example 2.17

In the following output from an execution of `env` *on a machine running Sun
Solaris 2.3, a dash (-) indicates the continuation of a long line.*

```
DISPLAY=:0.0
FONTPATH=/home/robbins/vttool/crttool-2.0/fonts:-
/usr/local/lib/font/85dpi
HELPPATH=/usr/openwin/lib/locale:/usr/openwin/lib/help
HOME=/data1/robbins
HZ=100
LD_LIBRARY_PATH=/usr/openwin/lib:/opt/tex/lib
LOGNAME=robbins
MAIL=/var/mail/robbins
MANPATH=/usr/openwin/share/man:/opt/SUNWspro/man:/usr/man
OPENWINHOME=/usr/openwin
PATH=/usr/openwin/bin:/opt/SUNWspro/bin:/usr/bin:/usr/sbin:-
/usr/ccs/bin:/usr/bin/X11:/opt/gnu/bin:/opt/tex/bin:-
/opt/bin:/data1/robbins/bin:/usr/local/bin:/usr/ccs/lib:.
PROCDIR=/usr/local/bin
PWD=/data1/robbins
SHELL=/bin/csh
TERM=sun-cmd
```

```
TEXFONTS=.:/usr/local/tex/fonts/tfm:/usr/local/src/dvips/PStfms:-
/usr/local/src/dlx/benchmarks/tex/latex:
/data/src/tex/unix3.0/ams/amsfonts/pk/pk300
TZ=US/Central
USER=robbins
XDVIFONTS=/usr/local/tex/fonts/pk
XENVIRONMENT=/data1/robbins/.Xdefaults
XFILESEARCHPATH=/usr/openwin/lib/locale/%L/%T/%N%S:-
/usr/openwin/lib/%T/%N%S
WINDOW_TERMIOS=
TERMCAP=sun-cmd:te=\E[>4h:ti=\E[>4l:tc=sun:
```

2.10 Process Termination in UNIX

When a process terminates, the operating system deallocates the resources held by the terminated process, updates the appropriate statistics, and notifies other processes of the demise. The termination can either be *normal* or *abnormal*. The activities performed during process termination include canceling pending timers and signals, releasing virtual memory resources, releasing other process-held system resources such as locks, and closing open files. The operating system records the process status and resource usage and notifies the parent in response to a `wait` system call. When a process exits, its orphaned children are adopted by the `init` process, the process whose process ID is 1. If its parent process is not waiting for it when it terminates, the process becomes a *zombie*. The `init` process periodically waits for children to get rid of the orphaned zombies.

   A normal termination occurs if there was a `return` from main, an implicit return from main (the main procedure falls off the end), a call to the C function `exit`, or a call to the `_exit` system call. The `exit` C function calls user-defined exit handlers and may provide additional cleanup before it invokes the `_exit` system call.

SYNOPSIS

```
#include <unistd.h>

void _exit(int status);
```
                                                                  POSIX.1, Spec 1170

SYNOPSIS

```
#include <stdlib.h>

void exit(int status);
```
                                                             ISO C, POSIX.1, Spec 1170

Both exit and _exit take an integer parameter, status, indicating the termination status of the program. Use a status value of 0 to indicate a normal termination. Programmer-defined nonzero values of status indicate errors. Example 2.8 on page 48 illustrates how a parent can determine the value of status when it waits for the child. The value is returned by a call to exit or _exit anywhere in the program or by using a return in the main program. The exit and _exit return a value to the parent even if the main program is declared to return void.

The atexit C function installs a user-defined exit handler. Exit handlers are executed on a last-installed-first-executed basis when exit is called. Use multiple calls to atexit to install several handlers. On normal termination, the process calls the handlers as part of the termination, with the first handler installed being the last one executed.

Program 2.11 has an exit handler called show_times which causes statistics about the time used by the program and its children to be output to standard error before the program terminates. The times function returns timing information in the form of the number of clock ticks. The show_times function converts the time to seconds by dividing by the number of clock ticks per second found by calling sysconf. (Chapter 6 gives a more complete discussion of time in UNIX.)

Program 2.11: A program with an exit handler that outputs CPU usage.

```
#include <stdio.h>
#include <stdlib.h>
#include <unistd.h>
#include <sys/times.h>
#include <limits.h>

static void show_times(void)
{
   struct tms times_info;
   double ticks;

   if ((ticks = (double) sysconf(_SC_CLK_TCK)) < 0)
      perror("Cannot determine clock ticks per second");
   else if (times(&times_info) < 0)
      perror("Cannot get times information");
   else {
      fprintf(stderr, "User time:               %8.3f seconds\n",
         times_info.tms_utime/ticks);
      fprintf(stderr, "System time:             %8.3f seconds\n",
         times_info.tms_stime/ticks);
      fprintf(stderr, "Children's user time:    %8.3f seconds\n",
         times_info.tms_cutime/ticks);
```

```
        fprintf(stderr, "Children's system time: %8.3f seconds\n",
            times_info.tms_cstime/ticks);
    }
}

void main(void)
{

    if (atexit(show_times))  {
        fprintf(stderr, "Cannot install show_times exit handler\n");
        exit(1);
    }

    /*  rest of main program goes here */
}
```
_____ **Program 2.11** _____

A process can also terminate abnormally either by calling `abort` or by processing a signal that causes termination. The signal may be generated by an external event (like `ctrl-c` from the keyboard) or by an internal error such as an attempt to access an illegal memory location. If a process aborts abnormally, a core dump may be produced, and user-installed exit handlers are not called.

2.11 Critical Sections

Imagine the following scenario. Suppose that a computer system has a printer that is directly accessible by all of the processes in the system. Each time a process wanted to print something, it would do a `write` to the printer device. How would the printed output look if more than one process tried to write to the printer at the same time? Since the individual processes are allowed only a fixed quantum of processor time, a process starts writing, but if there is a lot to write, its quantum expires and another process is chosen. The resulting printout would have the output from the processes interspersed— an undesirable feature.

The problem with the previous scenario is that the processes are simultaneously attempting to access a shared resource—a resource that should be used only by one process at a time. That is, the printer requires *exclusive access* by the processes in the system. The portion of code in which each process tries to access such a shared resource is called a *critical section*. Something must be done to assure *mutual exclusion* of processes while they are executing within their critical sections.

One method of providing mutual exclusion employs a locking mechanism in which a process acquires a lock that excludes all other processes before entering its critical section. When the process finishes the critical section, it releases the lock. Another approach is to encapsulate shared resources in a manner that ensures exclusive access. Printers are usually handled by having only one process (the printer daemon) access the actual printer. When another process wishes to print, it makes a request to the printer daemon by sending a message. The printer daemon puts the request in a queue and processes one message at a time.

There are many shared resources besides devices, files, and shared variables. Tables and other information in the kernel are shared among processes managing the system. A large operating system has many diverse parts with possibly overlapping critical sections. When one of these parts is modified, it is difficult to determine whether the modification adversely affects other parts without understanding the entire operating system. To reduce the complexity of internal interactions, some operating systems use an *object-oriented* design. Shared tables and other resources are encapsulated as objects with well-defined access functions. The only way to access such a table is through these functions, which have exclusive access built in. In a distributed system, the object interface uses messages. Changes to other modules in an object-oriented system do not have the same impact as they do for uncontrolled access.

On the surface the object-oriented approach appears to be similar to the daemons described in Section 2.8, but structurally these approaches can be very different. There is no requirement that daemons encapsulate resources. They can fight over shared data structures in an uncontrolled way. The object-oriented approach requires that data structures be encapsulated and accessed only through carefully controlled interfaces. Daemons can be implemented using an object-oriented design, but they do not have to be.

2.12 Exercise: Process Chains

This section expands on the process chains of Example 2.5. The chain is a vehicle for experimenting with `wait` and with sharing of devices. In this exercise, the processes share standard error and have critical sections when they output to standard error. Later chapters extend this exercise to critical sections involving other devices (Chapter 3) and a token-ring simulation (Chapter 4).

Program 2.12 creates a chain of processes. It takes a single command-line argument that specifies the number of processes to create. Before exiting, each process outputs its i value, its process ID, its parent process ID, and its child's process ID. There is no `wait`, so a parent process may exit before its child, causing the child process to be adopted by the `init` process (which has process ID of 1). As a result, some of the processes may indicate a parent process ID of 1.

Program 2.12: A simple program for generating a chain of processes.

```c
#include <stdio.h>
#include <stdlib.h>
#include <sys/types.h>
#include <unistd.h>
/*
 *      Sample C program for generating a chain of processes.
 *      Invoke this program with a command-line argument indicating the
 *      number of processes in the chain.  After the chain is created,
 *      each process identifies itself with its process ID,
 *      the process ID of its parent, and the process ID of its child.
 *      Each process then exits.
 */

void main  (int argc, char *argv[])
{
    int     i;
    pid_t   childpid;                   /* process ID of the forked child  */
    int     n;                /* total number of processes in the chain */

                    /* check for valid number of command-line arguments */
    if (argc != 2){
        fprintf (stderr, "Usage: %s processes\n", argv[0]);
        exit(1);
    }
    n = atoi(argv[1]);

    childpid = 0;
    for (i = 1; i < n;   ++i)
        if (childpid = fork())
            break;
    if (childpid == -1) {
        perror("The fork failed");
        exit(1);
    }

    fprintf(stderr,
        "i:%d  process ID:%ld  parent ID:%ld   child ID:%ld\n",
        i, (long)getpid(), (long)getppid(), (long)childpid);
    exit (0);
}
```

Program 2.12 _____

All of the processes in the chain created by Program 2.12 have the same standard input, standard output, and standard error. The `fprintf` to standard error is a program critical section. This exercise explores some implications of critical sections.

- Run Program 2.12 and observe the results for different numbers of processes.

- Fill in the actual process IDs of the processes in the diagram of Figure 2.4 for a run with command-line argument value of 4.

- Experiment with different values for the command-line argument to find out the largest number of processes that the program can generate. Observe the fraction that are adopted.

- Place a `sleep(10)` directly before the final `fprintf` statement in Program 2.12. What is the maximum number of processes generated in this case?

- Put a loop around the final `fprintf` in Program 2.12. Have the loop execute `k` times. Put a `sleep(m)` inside this loop after the `fprintf`. Pass `k` and `m` on the command line. Run the program for several values of `n`, `k`, and `m` and observe the results.

- Modify Program 2.12 by putting a `wait` system call before the final `fprintf` statement. How does this affect the output of the program?

- Modify Program 2.12 by replacing the final `fprintf` statement with a loop that reads `nchars` characters from standard input, one character at a time, and puts them in an array called `mybuf`. The values of `n` and `nchars` should be passed as command-line arguments. After the loop, put a `'\0'` character in entry `nchars` of the array so that it contains a null-terminated string. Output to standard error in a single `fprintf` the process ID followed by a colon followed by the string in `mybuf`. Run the program for several values of `n` and `nchars` and observe the results. Continue typing at the keyboard until all of the processes have exited.

2.13 Exercise: Process Fans

The exercises in this section expand on the fan structure of Example 2.6 through the development of a simple batch processing facility. Modifications in Section 8.8 lead to a license manager for an application program. The batch processing executable is called `runsim`. Write a test program called `testsim` to test the facility.

2.13.1 Specification of `runsim`

The `runsim` program runs up to `pr_limit` processes at a time. The `runsim` program takes exactly one command-line argument specifying the maximum number of simultaneous executions. Follow the outline below for implementing `runsim`. Suggested library functions and system system calls appear in parentheses.

- Check for the appropriate command-line argument and output a usage message if the command line is incorrect.

- Initialize `pr_limit` from the command line. The `pr_limit` variable specifies the maximum number of children allowed to execute at a time.

- The `pr_count` variable holds the number of active children. Initialize it to 0.

- Execute the following main loop until the end-of-file is reached on standard input:

  * If `pr_count` is `pr_limit`, wait for a child to finish (`wait`) and decrement `pr_count`.

  * Read a line from standard input (`fgets`) of up to `MAX_CANON` characters and execute a program corresponding to that command line by forking a child (`fork`, `makeargv`, `execvp`).

  * Increment `pr_count` to track the number of active children.

  * Check to see if any of the children have finished (`waitpid` with the `WNOHANG` option). Decrement `pr_count` for each child that has completed.

- After encountering an end-of-file on standard input, wait for all of the remaining children to finish (`wait`) and then exit.

2.13.2 Testing the `runsim` program

Write a test program called `testsim` that takes two command-line arguments: the sleep time and the repeat factor. The `testsim` program loops repeat factor times. In the loop, `testim` sleeps for the specified sleep time and then outputs a message with its process ID to standard error. Use `runsim` to run multiple copies of the `testsim` program.

Create a test file called `testing.data` that contains commands to run. For example, the file might contain

```
testsim 5 10
testsim 8 10
testsim 4 10
testsim 13 6
testsim 1 12
```

Run the program by entering a command such as

```
runsim 2 < testing.data
```

2.14 Exercise: Simple `biff`

These exercises assume a system with a standard UNIX mail facility rather than a more sophisticated mail system.

- Find out where mail is stored and change the mail directory specification for the `MAILDIR` environment variable to refer to your own mail file. (If unfamiliar with environment variables, refer to Section A.7 for an overview.)
- Change the `MAILFILE` value in Program 2.10 to the pathname of your mail file.
- Compile the source program of Program 2.10 into an executable called `mybiff`.
- Run `mybiff` as a background process by entering `mybiff &`.
- Send yourself some mail and confirm that you are notified.
- Modify `mybiff` so that it uses `stat` to determine whether new mail has arrived.
- Beware that `mybiff` may still running after log-off since it was started in the background. Execute `ps -a` to determine `mybiff`'s process ID. Kill the `mybiff` process by entering the command `kill -KILL pid`. Make sure `mybiff` is gone by doing another `ps -a`.
- Modify the `mybiff` program to determine the user by calling `getuid` followed by `getpwuid`. Test to see that `mybiff` still works.
- Modify the `mybiff` program so that it has the following synopsis:

    ```
    mybiff [-s n]   [-p pathname]
    ```

  The `[ ]` in the synopsis indicates optional command-line arguments. The first command-line argument specifies a sleep interval. If the `-s n` is not provided on the command line, use the value of `SLEEPTIME` as a default. The `-p pathname` gives a pathname for the system mail directory. If this option is not specified on the command line, use the `MAIL` environment variable value as a default value. Use `getopt` to parse the command-line arguments.
- POSIX.2 defines three environment variables for handling mail: `MAIL`, `MAILCHECK`, and `MAILPATH`. Change the `mybiff` program so that it uses these environment variables as defaults if they are defined. Abbreviated versions of the POSIX.2 definitions are the following:

MAIL is the pathname of the mailbox file of the user for purposes of incoming mail notification. A user is informed of incoming mail only if MAIL is set and MAILPATH is not set.

MAILCHECK is a decimal integer specifying how often (in seconds) the shell checks for the arrival of mail in the files specified by MAILPATH or MAIL variables. The default value is 600 seconds.

MAILPATH is a list of pathnames and optional messages separated by colons. If this variable is set, the shell informs the user if any of the files named by the variable are created or any of their modification times change. Each pathname can be followed by %, and a string that will be written to standard error when the modification time changes. If a % character in the pathname is preceded by a backslash, it is treated as a literal % in the pathname.

Modify biff so that it uses MAIL, MAILCHECK, and MAILPATH in a manner consistent with the way the shell interprets these variables. If a sleeptime value or pathname value are given as command-line arguments, these values override those given by the environment variables.

2.15 Exercise: News `biff`

The biff program informs the user of incoming mail. A user might also want to be informed of changes in other files such as the Internet News files. If a system is a news server, it probably organizes articles as individual files whose pathname contains the newsgroup name.

Example 2.18
A system keeps its news files in the directory /var/spool/news. *Article* 1034 *in newsgroup* comp.os.research *is located in the following file.*

```
/var/spool/news/comp/os/research/1034
```

The following exercises develop a facility for biffing when any file in a list of files is changed.

2.15.1 Biffing a Single File

- Write a function called lastmod that returns the time at which a file was last modified. The prototype for lastmod is

  ```
  time_t lastmod(char *pathname);
  ```

Use `stat` to determine the last access time. The `time_t` is time in seconds since 00:00:00 UTC, January 1, 1970. The `lastmod` function returns −1 if there is an error and sets `errno` to the error number for `stat`. Be careful here. POSIX allows `errno` to be a macro, so a program should not set `errno` directly.

● Write a main program that takes a pathname as a command-line argument and calls `lastmod` to determine the time of last modification of the corresponding file. Use `ctime` to print out the `time_t` value in a readable form. Compare the results with those obtained from `ls -l`.

● Write a function called `convertnews` that converts a newsgroup name to a fully-qualified pathname. The prototype of `convertnews` is

```
char *convertnews(char *newsgroup);
```

If the environment variable `NEWSDIR` is defined, use it to determine the path. Otherwise, use `/var/spool/news` as the default. (Call `getenv` to determine whether the environment variable is defined.) For example, if the newsgroup is `comp.os.research` and `NEWSDIR` is not defined, the pathname is

```
/var/spool/news/comp/os/research
```

The `convertnews` function allocates space to hold the converted string and returns a pointer to that space. (A common error is to return a pointer to an automatic variable defined within `convertnews`.) Do not modify `newsgroup` in `convertnews`. The `convertnews` returns a `NULL` pointer if there was an error.

● Write a program that takes a `newsgroup` name and a `sleeptime` value as command-line arguments. Print the time of the last modification of the `newsgroup` and then loop as follows:
  * Sleep for `sleeptime`.

  * Test to see whether the `newsgroup` has been modified.

  * If the `newsgroup` directory has been modified, print out a message with the `newsgroup` name and the time of modification.

Test the program on several newsgroups. Post news to a local newsgroup to verify that the program is working. The `newsgroup` directory can be modified both by news arrival and by expiration. Most systems expire news in the middle of the night.

2.15.2 Creation of a List Object

Create a linked list object to hold the newsgroup pathnames and times of last modification. The list should be singly linked and similar to the one developed in Section 2.2. Keep a head pointer, a tail pointer, and a traverse pointer for the list. The traverse pointer is a pointer to a location containing the current position in the list. Support the following operations on the list:

> `add_data` inserts a node at the end of the list. Pass the pathname, the monitoring name, and modification time. Use `malloc` to allocate space for the node. The prototype for `add_data` is

> ```
> int add_data(char *pathname, *char monitorname,
>             time_t mtime);
> ```

The `pathname` is the actual fully-qualified pathname of the newsgroup. For the newsgroup `comp.os.research` it would be

```
/var/spool/news/comp/os/research
```

The `monitorname` is the newsgroup name that the user provides (e.g., `comp.os.research`). The `mtime` is the time of last modification of the file corresponding to `pathname`. The `add_data` returns 0 if successful and −1 on failure.

> `rewind_list` sets the traverse pointer to the first node in the list. The prototype for `rewind_list` is

> ```
> int rewind_list(void);
> ```

The `rewind_list` returns 0 if the list is not empty and −1 if the list is empty.

> `update_list` checks the modification time of the newsgroup in the node designated by traverse pointer. The prototype for `update_list` is

> ```
> int update_list(char *modifyname, time_t *modtime);
> ```

The `modifyname` is the name that the user uses to identify the particular newsgroup (e.g., `comp.os.research`), and `*modtime` contains the time of last modification. The caller must provide space for the variables pointed to by `modifyname` and `modtime`. If the file has been modified after the time stored in the node, update the node time and return 1. If the file has not been modified return 0. Return −1 if the entry is not in the list.

Write a test program that proves that the list object is working before implementing the `newsbiff`.

Write a main program that takes two command-line arguments: a filename and a `sleeptime` value. The file contains a list of newsgroups to be monitored. Add each newsgroup to the list object. Go into a loop and do the following:

- Sleep for `sleeptime` seconds.
- Call `update_list` in a loop until the entire list object has been traversed. If a newsgroup has been modified, print out a message with the name and date of modification and ring the bell.

2.16 Additional Reading

The book *The Design of the UNIX Operating System* by Bach [6] discusses process implementation under System V. *The Design and Implementation of the 4.3BSD UNIX Operating System* by Leffler et al. [59] discusses process implementation for BSD UNIX. Both of these books are excellent and detailed examinations of how real operating systems are implemented. *Operating Systems: Design and Implementation* by Tanenbaum [89] develops a full implementation of a UNIX-like operating system called MINIX. Unfortunately all of these books are based on older versions of UNIX and are not specifically applicable to POSIX.

Most general operating systems books such as *Operating Systems Concepts*, 4th ed. by Silberschatz and Galvin [80] and *Modern Operating Systems* by Tanenbaum [92] address the process model. Both of these references have case studies on UNIX and on Mach, a well-known microkernel operating system. Making a comparison of these two systems would be useful at this point. *P.S. to Operating Systems* by Dowdy and Lowery [26] focuses on performance issues and analytical models.

Chapter 3

Files

Perhaps the best feature of UNIX is its device independence. The
uniform device interface through file descriptors allows the same
I/O calls to be used for terminals, disks, tapes, audio, and even
network communication. This chapter explores UNIX device-
independent I/O, blocking and nonblocking I/O, and special files
such as pipes. The chapter also covers filters, pipelines, redirection, directory traversal, and descriptor inheritance.

A *peripheral device* is piece of hardware connected to a computer system. Common peripheral devices include disks, tapes, CD ROMs, screens, keyboards, printers,
mice, and network interfaces. User programs perform control and I/O to these devices
by making system calls to operating system programs called *device drivers*. A device
driver hides the details of device operation and protects the device from unauthorized
use. Devices of the same type vary substantially in their operation, so even a single-
user machine needs device drivers to make it usable. Some operating systems provide
pseudodevice drivers to simulate devices such as terminals. Pseudoterminal devices, for
example, simplify the handling of remote login to computer systems over a network or
a modem line.

Some operating systems provide specific system calls for each type of supported device. A systems programmer must learn a complex set of calls for device control and
must rewrite programs to use different devices. UNIX has greatly simplified the programmer device interface by providing uniform access to most devices through five system calls—open, close, read, write, and ioctl. All devices are represented by
files called *special files* that are located in the /dev directory. Thus, disk files and other
devices are named and accessed in the same way. A *regular file* is just an ordinary data

file on disk. A *block special file* represents a device with characteristics similar to a disk. The device driver transfers information from a block special device in blocks or chunks, and usually such devices support the capability of retrieving a block from anywhere on the device. A *character special file* represents a device with characteristics similar to a keyboard. The device appears to represent stream of bytes that must be accessed in sequential order.

Sections 3.1 and 3.2 cover basic UNIX file organization and representation. Section 3.3 explains the differences between file pointers and file descriptors and illustrates how programs use these handles to access open files. Section 3.4 shows how a program can use redirection to change the meaning of a particular file descriptor handle during execution. Section 3.5 introduces pipes for interprocess communication. Section 3.6 discusses blocking `read` and `write` system calls, and Section 3.7 examines situations in which nonblocking calls improve efficiency. Section 3.8 covers the `select` system call for monitoring multiple file descriptors. Section 3.9 discusses FIFOs, and Section 3.10 introduces the audio device to illustrate the use of `ioctl`. The chapter closes with four exercise sections that illustrate different aspects of device access and control.

3.1 Directories and Paths

Data and programs are organized into *files* for permanent storage on disk. Instead of specifying the location of each file on the disk, a user gives a filename and the operating system makes a translation to the location of the physical file. The operating system keeps the association of filenames with locations in *directories*.

When disks were small, a simple table of filename versus position was a sufficient representation for the directory. Larger disks require a more flexible organization, and most systems now use tree-structured directories. This representation arises quite naturally when the directories themselves are files. Figure 3.1 shows a tree-structured organization called a *filesystem*. The square nodes in this tree are directories, and the / designates the *root directory* of the filesystem. The root directory is at the very top of the filesystem tree, and everything else is under it.

The directory marked `dirA` in Figure 3.1 contains the files `my1.dat`, `my2.dat`, and `dirB`. The `dirB` file is called a *subdirectory* of `dirA` because `dirB` is below `dirA` in the filesystem tree. Notice that `dirB` also contains a file named `my1.dat`.

Clearly the filename is not enough to specify a file uniquely since the name `my1.dat` appears more than once in the filesystem. The *absolute* or *fully-qualified pathname* uniquely specifies a file. The absolute pathname specifies all of the nodes in the directory tree on the path from the root to the file itself. UNIX uses / to separate the directory names along the path. (Unfortunately MS-DOS uses \ to separate directory names,

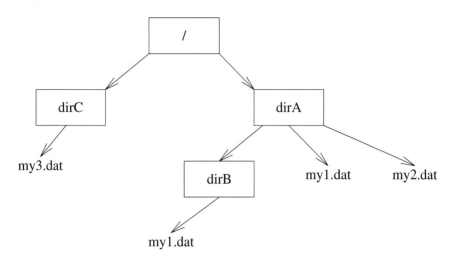

Figure 3.1: Tree structure of a filesystem.

so this is confusing for people who use both operating systems.) The file `my1.dat` in `dirA` in Figure 3.1 has fully-qualified pathname `/dirA/my1.dat`, while `my1.dat` in `dirB` has fully-qualified pathname `/dirA/dirB/my1.dat`.

A program is not required to give fully-qualified pathnames in all cases. At each point in time, every process has an associated directory called the *current working directory* which is used for pathname resolution. If a pathname does not start with `/`, the path is assumed to start with the path to the current working directory. Hence pathnames that do not begin with `/` are sometimes called *relative pathnames*. A dot (`.`) specifies the current directory, and a dot-dot (`..`) specifies the directory above the current one. The root directory has both dot and dot-dot pointing to itself. The current working directory associated with a user's login shell is called the user's *home directory*.

Example 3.1

After the following command is executed, the current working directory for the shell process is `/dirA/dirB`.

```
cd /dirA/dirB
```

If the current working directory is `/dirA/dirB`, the file `my1.dat` of Figure 3.1 in directory `dirA` can be referred to as `../my1.dat`, while the file `my1.dat` in directory `dirB` can be referred to as `my1.dat`, `./my1.dat`, or as `../dirB/my1.dat`. The file `my3.dat` in `dirC` can be referred to as `../../dirC/my3.dat`.

The `getcwd` C library function returns the pathname of the current working directory.

SYNOPSIS

```
#include <unistd.h>

extern char *getcwd(char *buf, size_t size);
```
                                                                        POSIX.1, Spec 1170

The `size` parameter specifies the maximum length pathname that the caller can accommodate. If the current directory pathname is longer than this maximum, `getcwd`
returns −1 and sets `errno` to ERANGE. If `buf` is not NULL, `getcwd` copies the
name into `buf`. If `buf` is NULL, POSIX.1 states that the behavior of `getcwd` is
undefined. In some implementations, `getcwd` uses `malloc` to create a buffer to hold
the pathname. The program can later call `free` to deallocate the space. In any case,
`getcwd` returns a pointer to the name if it is successful.

Example 3.2
The following program outputs the pathname of the current working directory.

```
#include <stdlib.h>
#include <stdio.h>
#include <unistd.h>
#include <limits.h>
#ifndef PATH_MAX
#define PATH_MAX 255
#endif

void main(void)
{
    char mycwd[PATH_MAX + 1];
    if (getcwd(mycwd, PATH_MAX) == NULL) {
        perror("Could not get current working directory");
        exit(1);
    }
    printf("Current working directory: %s\n", mycwd);
    exit(0);
}
```

The PATH_MAX is an optional POSIX.1 constant specifying the maximum length
of a pathname for the implementation. PATH_MAX may or may not be defined in
`limits.h`. The optional POSIX.1 constants can be omitted from `limits.h` if their
values are indeterminate but larger than the required POSIX minimum. For MAX_PATH,
the _POSIX_PATH_MAX constant specifies that an implementation must accommodate
pathname lengths of at least 255. A vendor might allow PATH_MAX to depend on the

amount of available memory space on a specific instance of a specific implementation. The `pathconf` function provides the real value for PATH_MAX.

Example 3.3

The following program outputs the current working directory after determining the implementation's maximum pathname length relative to the root directory.

```
#include <stdio.h>
#include <stdlib.h>
#include <unistd.h>

void main(void)
{
    char *mycwdp;
    long maxpath;
    if ((maxpath= pathconf("/", _PC_PATH_MAX)) == -1) {
        perror("Could not determine maximum pathname length");
        exit(1);
    } else if ((mycwdp = (char *) malloc(maxpath+1)) == NULL) {
        perror("Could not allocate space for directory pathname");
        exit(1);
    } else if (getcwd(mycwdp, maxpath) == NULL) {
        perror("Could not get current working directory");
        exit(1);
    }
    printf("Current working directory: %s\n", mycwdp);
    exit(0);
}
```

There are three functions that determine implementation-specific information.

SYNOPSIS

```
#include <unistd.h>

long sysconf(int name);
long pathconf(const char *path, int name);
long fpathconf(int fildes, int name);
```

POSIX.1, Spec 1170

The `sysconf` function returns values of systemwide limits such as the number of clock ticks per second (_SC_CLK_TCK) or the maximum number of processes allowed per user (_SC_CHILD_MAX). Program 2.11 uses `sysconf` to calculate the number of seconds that a program runs. The `pathconf` and `fpathconf` functions report limits associated with a particular file or directory. Use `fpathconf` for an open file. Example 3.3 uses `pathconf` to find the maximum pathname length starting with the root directory.

3.1.1 Reading Directories

The tree structure of the filesystem hides the files and directories that occur at lower levels in the tree. To locate a specific file or group of files on a system, execute the find utility from the shell.

```
SYNOPSIS

    find path ... [operand_expression]
                                                              POSIX.2, Spec 1170
```

The operand_expression can be quite complicated. Consult the man pages for complete details.

Example 3.4

The following command outputs a list of all files with a .c extension in the current directory or below that are larger than 10 blocks of 512 bytes.

```
find . -name "*.c" -size +10 -print
```

The search only occurs on directories with the appropriate permissions. The *.c *specification has quotes so that the shell does not expand it.*

Use readdir and related calls to access directory information from a C program.

```
SYNOPSIS

    #include <sys/types.h>
    #include <dirent.h>

    DIR *opendir(const char *filename);
    struct dirent *readdir(DIR *dirp);
    void rewinddir(DIR *dirp);
    int closedir(DIR *dirp);
                                                              POSIX.1, Spec 1170
```

```
SYNOPSIS

    #include <sys/types.h>
    #include <dirent.h>

    long telldir(DIR *dirp);
    void seekdir(DIR *dirp, long loc);
                                                                      Spec 1170
```

The opendir function provides a handle to the directory for the other directory functions. Each subsequent call to readdir returns a pointer to a structure containing information about the next directory entry. The readdir returns NULL when it reaches the end of the directory. Use `rewinddir` to start over or `closedir` if finished. The `telldir` returns the offset within the directory of the current entry, while `seekdir` resets the current directory entry to be the one specified by `loc`. To go back to a particular entry, use `telldir` to save its offset and then later issue a `seekdir`. (This approach works as long as the directory is not reorganized to consolidate free space between calls to these functions.) The `telldir` and `seekdir` are not part of POSIX. If needed, their capability can usually be accomplished by saving a filename, using `rewinddir` and executing `readdir` in a loop until the needed file is found.

Program 3.1 displays the filenames contained in the directory whose pathname is passed as a command-line argument. To traverse a directory tree as in `find`, use `stat` to determine which files are directories. Section 3.11 develops a program to traverse a directory tree.

Program 3.1: A program to list files in a directory.

```
#include <stdio.h>
#include <stdlib.h>
#include <string.h>
#include <dirent.h>
#include <errno.h>

void main(int argc, char *argv[])
{
    DIR *dirp;
    struct dirent *direntp;

    if (argc != 2) {
        fprintf(stderr,"Usage: %s directory_name\n", argv[0]);
        exit(1);
    }

    if ((dirp = opendir(argv[1])) == NULL) {
        fprintf(stderr, "Could not open %s directory: %s\n",
                argv[1], strerror(errno));
        exit(1);
    }
    while ( (direntp = readdir( dirp )) != NULL )
        printf("%s\n", direntp->d_name );

    closedir(dirp);
    exit(0);
}
```

_____ **Program 3.1** _____

Program 3.1 does not allocate a `struct dirent` variable to hold the directory information. Rather, `readdir` keeps a static `struct dirent` structure internally and returns a pointer to it. This return structure implies that `readdir` is not thread-safe. POSIX.1c proposes `readdir_r` as an alternative, thread-safe version to support POSIX threads.

Directory entries are not of fixed size, and the `struct dirent` structure is designed to accommodate these variable-length entries. The `struct dirent` structure includes the member

```
char     d_name[];
```

which is a null-terminated character string no longer than NAME_MAX characters. An implementation might make other members of the `struct dirent` structure (such as the inode number) visible to the user. Note that the `struct dirent` structure does not reflect how directory entries are actually represented on disk, but only the structure that `readdir` uses to hold the entry it has retrieved.

3.1.2 Search Paths

In UNIX, a user executes a program by typing the pathname of the file containing the executable. Most of the commonly used programs and utilities are not in the user's current working directory (e.g., `vi`, `cc`). Imagine how inconvenient it would be if users actually had to know the location of all system executables in order to execute them. Fortunately UNIX has a method of looking for executables in a systematic way. It searches all possible directories listed in the PATH environment variable for the executable by using each of the listed directories in turn as the current working directory. PATH contains the fully-qualified pathnames of important directories separated by colons.

Example 3.5

The following is a typical value of the PATH environment variable.

```
/usr/bin:/etc:/usr/local/bin:/usr/ccs/bin:/home/robbins/bin:.
```

The specification of Example 3.5 says that when a command is executed, `/usr/bin` is searched first. If the command is not found, the `/etc` directory is examined next and so on.

Remember that no subdirectories of directories in the PATH are searched unless they are also explicitly specified in the PATH. If in doubt about which version of a particular program is actually being executed, use `which` to get the fully-qualified pathname of the executable.

Exercise 3.1

After the installation of a new operating system, a programmer would like to start using the new ANSI C compiler rather than the non-ANSI compiler previously used. However the compiler does not seem to be accepting function prototypes. What approach should be used to resolve this problem?

Answer:

Execute `which cc` to find out the fully-qualified pathname of the default C compiler. For example, a standard place for the Sun ANSI compiler on a Sun system running Solaris 2 is `/opt/SUNWspro/bin`, but the old style compiler might be kept around in `/usr/ucb`. If `/usr/ucb` comes before `/opt/SUNWspro/bin` in the PATH environment variable definition, `cc` refers to the old BSD compiler. (Note: `which` may not be available on some systems.) Execute `find` to look for the `cc` executables starting from the root:

```
find / -name "cc" -print
```

Do not try this on a system with a lot of disk space as it may take a long time and produce many *permission denied* messages.

It is common for programmers to create a `bin` directory as a subdirectory of their home directories for executables. The directory `/home/robbins/bin` in the PATH of Example 3.5 is an example of such a `bin` directory. The `bin` directory appears before dot (`.`), the current directory, in the search path leading to the problem discussed in the next exercise.

Exercise 3.2

A user develops a program called `calhit` in the subdirectory `progs` of his or her home directory and puts a copy of the executable in the `bin` directory of the same account. The user later modifies `calhit` in the `progs` directory without copying it to the `bin` directory. What happens?

Answer:

The result depends on the value of the PATH environment variable. If the user's PATH is set up in the usual way, the shell searches the `bin` directory first and executes the old version of the program.

Resist the temptation to put the dot (`.`) at the beginning of the PATH in spite of the problem mentioned in Exercise 3.2. Such a PATH specification is regarded as a security risk and may lead to strange results when local programs are executed instead of the standard system programs of the same name.

3.1.3 The UNIX Filesystem

Disk formatting divides a physical disk into regions called *partitions*. Each partition may have a filesystem associated with it. A filesystem consists of a directory tree. A particular filesystem can be mounted at any node in the directory tree of another filesystem. The topmost node in a filesystem is called the *root* of the filesystem. The *root directory* of a process (denoted by /) is the topmost directory that the process can access. All fully-qualified paths in UNIX start from the root directory /. Figure 3.2 shows a typical root filesystem tree.

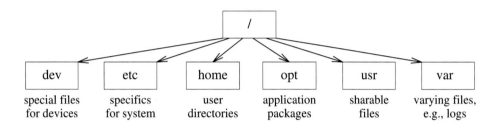

Figure 3.2: Structure of a typical UNIX filesystem

There are some standard directories that appear in the root filesystem. The /dev directory gives specifications for the devices (special files) on the system. The /etc directory holds files containing information regarding the network, accounts, and other databases that are specific to the machine. The /home directory is the default directory for user accounts. The /opt directory is a standard location for applications in System V Release 4. Look for include files in the /usr/include directory. The /var directory contains system files that vary and can grow arbitrarily large (e.g., log files or mail when it arrives, but before it has been read).

3.2 UNIX File Representation

A UNIX file has a description which is stored in a structure called an *inode*. The inode contains information about the file size, its location, the owner of the file, the time of creation, time of last access, time of last modification, permissions, and so on. Most user files are *ordinary files*. Directories are also represented as files and have an associated inode. Devices are represented by *special files*. *Character special files* are used to represent devices such as terminals, while *block special files* are used for disk devices. The *FIFO special files* are used for interprocess communication.

Figure 3.3 shows the inode structure for a typical file. In addition to descriptive information about the file, the inode contains pointers to the first few data blocks of the file. If the file is large, the indirect pointer contains a pointer to a block of pointers to additional data blocks. If the file is still larger, the double indirect pointer contains a pointer to a block of indirect pointers to blocks of direct pointers to the data blocks after the indirect data blocks. If the file is really huge, the triple indirect pointer contains a pointer to a block of double indirect pointers. The word *block* can mean different things (even within UNIX). In this context a block is typically 8K. The number of bytes in a block is always a power of 2.

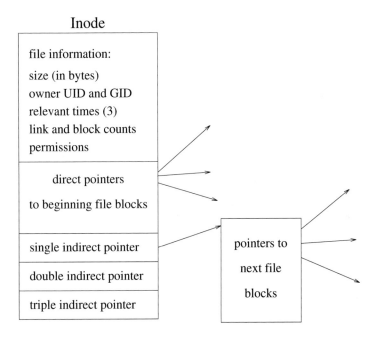

Figure 3.3: Schematic structure of a UNIX file.

Exercise 3.3

Suppose that an inode is 128 bytes, pointers are 4 bytes long, and the status information takes up 68 bytes. Assume a block size of 8K. How much room is there for pointers in the inode? How big a file can be represented with direct pointers? Indirect? Double indirect? Triple indirect?

Answer:

The single, double, and triple indirect pointers take 4 bytes each, so $128 - 68 - 12 = 48$ bytes are available for 12 direct pointers. The size of the inode and the block size are system-dependent. A file as large as $8192 \times 12 = 98,304$ bytes can be represented solely with direct pointers. If the block size is 8K, the single indirect pointer addresses an 8K block which can hold $8192 \div 4 = 2048$ pointers to data blocks. Thus, the single indirect pointer provides the capability of addressing an additional $2048 \times 8192 = 16,777,216$ bytes or 16 megabytes of information. Double indirect addressing provides 2048×2048 pointers with the capability of addressing an additional 32 gigabytes. Triple indirect addressing provides $2048 \times 2048 \times 2048$ pointers with the capability of addressing an additional 64 terabytes (which should be enough for the near future `:-)`).

To retrieve the information contained in the inode of a particular file, use the `stat` system call.

```
SYNOPSIS

    #include <sys/types.h>
    #include <sys/stat.h>

    int stat(const char *path, struct stat *buf);
    int fstat(int fildes, struct stat *buf);
                                                   POSIX.1, Spec 1170
```

```
SYNOPSIS

    #include <sys/stat.h>

    int lstat(const char *path, struct stat *buf);
                                                              Spec 1170
```

Use `fstat` instead of `stat` for open files. The `lstat` call retrieves information for symbolic links which are described in Section 3.2.2. Since symbolic links are not yet part of POSIX, the `lstat` function is not part of POSIX. The `struct stat` structure contains the following members:

```
    mode_t    st_mode;     /* File mode (see mknod(2)) */
    ino_t     st_ino;      /* Inode number */
    dev_t     st_dev;      /* ID of device containing */
                           /* a directory entry for this file */
    dev_t     st_rdev;     /* ID of device */
                           /* This entry is defined only for */
                           /* char special or block special files */
    nlink_t   st_nlink;    /* Number of links */
    uid_t     st_uid;      /* User ID of the file's owner */
    gid_t     st_gid;      /* Group ID of the file's group */
    off_t     st_size;     /* File size in bytes */
    time_t    st_atime;    /* Time of last access */
    time_t    st_mtime;    /* Time of last data modification */
    time_t    st_ctime;    /* Time of last file status change */
                           /* Times measured in seconds since */
                           /* 00:00:00 UTC, Jan. 1, 1970 */
    long      st_blksize;  /* Preferred I/O block size */
    long      st_blocks;   /* Number st_blksize blocks allocated */
```

Example 3.6

The following program uses stat *to determine whether a filename passed on the command line is a directory. If the filename is a directory, it also outputs the time at which the directory was last modified.*

```c
#include <stdio.h>
#include <stdlib.h>
#include <string.h>
#include <errno.h>
#include <time.h>
#include <sys/types.h>
#include <sys/stat.h>

void main(int argc, char *argv[])
{
    struct stat statbuf;

    if (argc != 2) {
        fprintf(stderr, "Usage: %s filename\n", argv[0]);
        exit(1);
    }
    if (stat(argv[1], &statbuf) == -1) {
        fprintf(stderr, "Could not get stat on file %s: %s\n",
                argv[1], strerror(errno));
        exit(1);
    }
    if (statbuf.st_mode & S_IFDIR) {
        printf("%s is a directory: ", argv[1]);
        printf("last modified at %s\n", ctime(&statbuf.st_mtime));
    } else
        printf("%s is not a directory\n", argv[1]);
    exit(0);
}
```

The tree-structured representation of files is fairly efficient for small files and is also flexible if the size of the file changes. When a file is created, the operating system finds free blocks on the disk in which to place the data. Performance considerations dictate that the blocks should be located close to one another on the disk to reduce the seek time. It takes about twenty times as long to read a 16-megabyte file where the data blocks are randomly placed than one in which the data blocks are contiguous.

3.2.1 Directory Representation

A UNIX *directory* is a file containing a correspondence between filenames and inodes. The inode itself does not contain the filename. When a program references a file by path-name, the operating system traverses the filesystem tree to find the filename and inode number in the appropriate directory. Once it has the inode number, the operating system can determine other information about the file by accessing the inode. (For performance reasons, this is not as simple as it seems because the operating system caches both directory entries and inode entries in main memory.)

A directory representation that contains only names and inode numbers has a number of advantages:

- Changing the name of a file requires only changing the directory entry. A file can be moved from one directory to another just by moving the directory entry as long as the move keeps the file on the same partition or slice. The mv command uses this technique for moving files to locations within the same filesystem. Since a directory entry refers to an inode on the same partition as the directory entry itself, mv cannot use this approach to move files between different partitions.
- Only one physical copy of the file needs to exist on disk, but the file may have several names, or the same name in different directories. Again, all of these references must be on the same physical partition.
- Directory entries are of variable length because the filename is of variable length. Directory entries are small, since most of the information is kept in the inode. Manipulating small variable-length structures can be done efficiently. The larger inode structures are of fixed length.

3.2.2 Links

A *link* is an association between a filename and an inode. UNIX has two types of links— hard and symbolic (also called soft). Directory entries are called *hard links* because they directly link filenames to inodes. Soft links or *symbolic links* use the file as a pointer to another filename. The difference between hard links and soft links is not exactly obvious.

A directory entry corresponds to a single hard link, but an inode may have several of these links. Each inode contains the count of the number of hard links to the inode, that is, the total number of directory entries that contain the inode number. The operating system makes a new directory entry and assigns an inode to each newly-created file. Users can create additional hard links to a file with the ln command or the link system call. An additional hard link allocates only a directory entry but uses no other disk space. The new hard link causes the link count entry in the inode to be incremented. Remember a hard link is just a directory entry. Hard links are sometimes just called links.

When a user deletes a file with the rm command or the unlink system call, the operating system deletes the corresponding directory entry and decrements the link count in the inode. It does not free the inode and the corresponding data blocks unless the link count in the inode is decremented to 0.

Figure 3.4 shows a directory entry for a file called `name1` in the directory `/dirA`. The file uses inode 12345. The inode has one link, and the first data block is block 23567. All of the file data is contained in this one block which is represented by the short text in the figure.

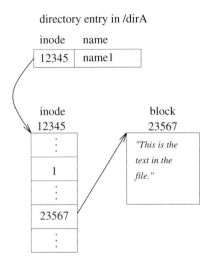

Figure 3.4: A directory, inode, and data block for a simple file.

Example 3.7

The following command creates an entry in `dirB` *containing a pointer to the same inode as* `/dirA/name1`.

```
ln /dirA/name1 /dirB/name2
```

Figure 3.4 shows the directories before the `ln` command of Example 3.7 is executed, and Figure 3.5 shows the directories afterwards. The `ln` creates a link (directory entry) that refers to the same inode as `dirA/name1`. No additional disk space is required, except possibly if the new directory entry increases the number of data blocks needed to hold the directory information. The inode now has two links.

Exercise 3.4

What happens if a user invokes an editor to make a small change to the `/dirA/name1` file of Figure 3.5? How are the files `/dirA/name1` and `/dirB/name2` related?

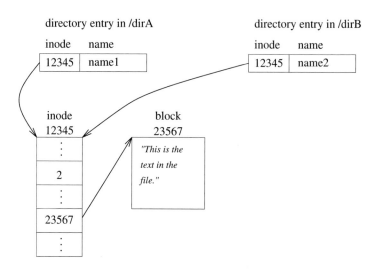

Figure 3.5: Two hard links to the same file as shown in Figure 3.4.

Answer:

The result depends on how the editor works. Most versions of `vi` do not change the inode and so Figure 3.5 still applies. When some editors modify `/dirA/name1`, they copy the file into memory, modify the memory image, and write the memory image to disk with the name `/dirA/name1`. The editor can do this by first unlinking `/dirA/name1` and then creating a new file associated with the name `/dirA/name1`. Thus `/dirA/name1` refers to the new file, and `/dirB/name2` refers to the old one. There are two different inodes, each with one link as illustrated in Figure 3.6. Some editors use `rename` (which is like `mv`) to make a backup copy of the file being edited rather than `unlink`. Such an editor might rename `/dirA/name1` as `/dirA/name1.bak` before writing the new file. In this case, `/dirA/name1.bak` and `/dirB/name2` would have the same inode with two links as shown in Figure 3.7.

The behavior illustrated in Exercise 3.4 may be undesirable. Another type of link called a symbolic link behaves differently. A *symbolic link* is a file containing the name of another file or directory. A reference to the name of a symbolic link causes the operating system to locate the inode corresponding to that link. It assumes that the data blocks of the corresponding inode contain another filename. The operating system then looks up the new filename in a directory and continues to follow the chain until it finally encounters a hard link and a real file. POSIX.1 does not include symbolic links, but most implementations historically include them and Spec 1170 specifies them as well.

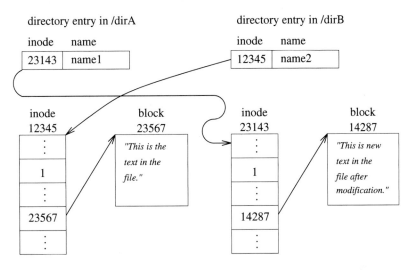

Figure 3.6: The situation editing a file. The original file had inode 12345 and two hard links prior to being edited.

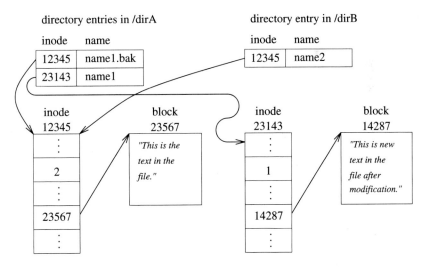

Figure 3.7: The situation after editing one file with an editor that makes a backup copy.

Create a symbolic link by using the `ln` command with the `-s` option or by invoking the `symlink` system call.

Example 3.8

Starting with the situation shown in Figure 3.4, the following command creates the symbolic link /dirB/name2 as shown in Figure 3.8.

```
ln -s /dirB/name2 /dirA/name1
```

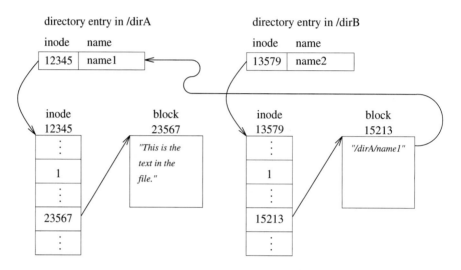

Figure 3.8: An ordinary file and a symbolic link to it.

Unlike Exercise 3.4, the `ln` command of Example 3.8 uses a new inode, 13579, for the symbolic link. Inodes contain information about the type of file they represent (i.e., ordinary, directory, special, or symbolic link), so inode 13579 contains information indicating that it is a symbolic link. The symbolic link requires at least one data block. In this case block 15213 is used. The data block contains the name of the file that /dirB/name2 is linked to, in this case /dirA/name1. The name may be fully qualified as in this example or it may be relative to its own directory.

Exercise 3.5

Suppose that /dirA/name1 is an ordinary file and /dirB/name2 is a symbolic link to /dirA/name1 as in Figure 3.8. How are the files /dirB/name2 and /dirA/name1 related after a user edits, changes, and saves /dirA/name1 as in Exercise 3.4?

Answer:

/dirA/name1 now refers to a different inode, but /dirB/name2 references
the name dirA/name1, so they still refer to the same file as shown in Figure 3.9. The link count in the inode counts only hard links, not symbolic links.
When the editor unlinks /dirA/name1, the operating system deletes the file
with inode 12345. If others try to edit /dirB/name2 in the interval during
which /dirA/name1 is unlinked but not yet created, they get an error.

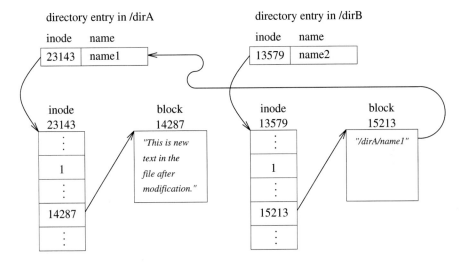

Figure 3.9: The situation after editing a file that has a symbolic link.

Exercise 3.6

Many programs assume that the header files for the X Window System are in
/usr/include/X11, but under Sun Solaris 2 these files are in the directory
/usr/openwin/share/include/X11. How can the system administrator
deal with the inconsistency?

Answer:

There are several ways to address this problem:

- Copy all of these files into /usr/include/X11.
- Move all of the files into /usr/include/X11.
- Have users modify all programs that contain lines in the form

      #include <X11/xyz.h>

  and replace these lines with

      #include "/usr/openwin/share/include/X11/xyz.h"

- Have users modify their makefiles so that compilers look for header files in

  /usr/openwin/share/include

  (See Section A.3 if unfamiliar with makefiles.)

- Create a symbolic link from /usr/include/X11 to the directory

  /usr/openwin/share/include/X11

All of the alternatives except the last have serious drawbacks. If the header files are copied to the directory /usr/include/X11, then two copies of these files exist. Aside from the additional disk space required, an update might cause these files to be inconsistent. Moving the files (copying them to the directory /usr/include/X11 and then deleting them from /usr/openwin/share/include/X11) may interfere with operating system upgrades. Having users modify all of their programs or even all makefiles is unreasonable. Another alternative not mentioned above is to use the appropriate environment variable to cause the compiler to search correctly for header files.

Exercise 3.7

Due to a large influx of user mail, the root partition of a server is becoming full. What can a system administrator do?

Answer:

Pending mail is usually kept in a directory with a name such as /var/mail or /var/spool/mail which may be part of the root partition. One possibility is to expand the size of the root partition. This expansion usually requires reinstallation of the operating system. Another possibility is to mount an unused partition on var. If a spare partition is not available, the /var/spool/mail directory can be a symbolic link to any directory in a partition that has sufficient space.

Exercise 3.8

Starting with Figure 3.8, execute the command rm /dirA/name1. What happens to /dirB/name2?

Answer:

This symbolic link still exists, but it is pointing to something that is no longer there. A reference to /dirB/name2 gives an error as if the symbolic link /dirB/name2 does not exist. However, if at a later time a new file named /dirA/name1 is created, the symbolic link then points to that file.

3.3 File Handle Representation

Files are designated within C programs either by file pointers or by file descriptors. The standard I/O library for ANSI C (`fopen`, `fscanf`, `fprintf`, `fread`, `fwrite`, `fclose`, and so on) uses file pointers, while the UNIX I/O library (`open`, `read`, `write`, `close`, and `ioctl`) uses file descriptors. File pointers and file descriptors provide logical names or *handles* for performing device-independent input and output. The file pointer handles for standard input, standard output, and standard error are `stdin`, `stdout`, and `stderr`, respectively, and are defined in `stdio.h`. The file descriptor handles for standard input, standard output, and standard error are `STDIN_FILENO`, `STDOUT_FILENO`, and `STDERR_FILENO`, respectively, and are defined in `unistd.h`.

An `fopen` or an `open` provides an association between a file or physical device and the logical handle used in the program. The file or physical device is specified by a character string (e.g., `/home/johns/my.dat` or `/dev/tty`). In the case of `open`, the handle is an index into a *file descriptor table*, while for an `fopen`, the handle is a pointer to a file structure.

3.3.1 File Descriptors

The `open` system call associates a file descriptor (the handle used in the program) with a file or physical device.

```
SYNOPSIS

   #include <sys/types.h>
   #include <sys/stat.h>
   #include <fcntl.h>

   int open(const char *path, int  oflag, ...);
                                              POSIX.1, Spec 1170
```

The POSIX.1 values for `oflag` include: `O_RDONLY`, `O_WRONLY`, `O_RDWR`, `O_APPEND`, `O_CREAT`, `O_EXCL`, `O_NOCTTY`, `O_NONBLOCK`, and `O_TRUNC`. Specify exactly one of the `O_RDONLY`, `O_WRONLY`, and `O_RDWR` flags designating read-only, write-only, or read-write access. Bitwise OR (`|`) several flags to get a combined effect.

Example 3.9

The following code segment opens the file `/home/ann/my.dat` *for reading.*

```
#include <sys/types.h>
#include <sys/stat.h>
#include <fcntl.h>

int myfd;
myfd = open("/home/ann/my.dat", O_RDONLY);
```

The open system call sets the file's status flags according to the value of the second parameter. O_RDONLY is defined in fcntl.h. If the oflag field has O_CREAT set, include a third parameter to open. This third parameter is of type mode_t and specifies the permissions for the file as a mode_t value.

Each file has three classes associated with it: a user (or owner), a group, and everybody else (others). The possible permissions or privileges are read(r), write(w), and execute(x). These privileges are specified separately for the user, the group, and others. Figure 3.10 shows a typical layout of the permissions mask. A 1 in the designated bit position in the mask indicates that the corresponding privilege is accorded to that class. POSIX.1 defines symbolic names for masks corresponding to these bits so that a user can specify modes in an implementation-independent manner. These names are defined in sys/stat.h. Table 3.1 lists the symbolic names and their meanings.

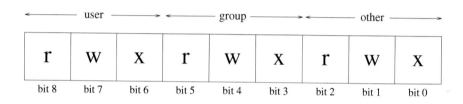

Figure 3.10: Typical layout of the permissions mask.

Example 3.10

The following code segment creates a file that can be read or written by the user and only read by everyone else.

```
#include <sys/types.h>
#include <sys/stat.h>
#include <fcntl.h>
#include <stdio.h>
int fd;
mode_t fd_mode = S_IRUSR | S_IWUSR | S_IRGRP | S_IROTH;

if ((fd = open("/home/ann/my.dat", O_RDWR | O_CREAT, fd_mode))
        == -1)
    perror("Could not open /home/ann/my.dat");
```

The O_CREAT flag specifies that if the file does not already exist, it should be created. If the value of the second parameter to the open in Example 3.10 were O_RDWR | O_CREAT | O_TRUNC and the file already existed, it would be truncated to zero length (i.e., its contents would be thrown away).

POSIX.1 File Modes

Symbol	Meaning
S_IRUSR	read permission bit for owner
S_IWUSR	write permission bit for owner
S_IXUSR	execute permission bit for owner
S_IRWXU	read, write, execute for owner
S_IRGRP	read permission bit for group
S_IWGRP	write permission bit for group
S_IXGRP	execute permission bit for group
S_IRWXG	read, write, execute for group
S_IROTH	read permission bit for others
S_IWOTH	write permission bit for others
S_IXOTH	execute permission bit for others
S_IRWXO	read, write, execute for others
S_ISUID	set user ID on execution
S_ISGID	set group ID on execution

Table 3.1: POSIX.1 symbolic names for file permission bits.

The file descriptor `myfd` of Example 3.10 is just an integer specifying the index into the file descriptor table as shown in Figure 3.11. The file descriptor table is specific to a process. It contains an entry for each open file in the process. The file descriptor table is in the process user area, but the program cannot access it except through system calls using the file descriptor.

Figure 3.11 shows an entry in the file descriptor table pointing to an entry in the system file table. The *system file table* contains an entry for each active `open` and is shared by all of the processes in the system. It contains information about whether the file is open for read or write, protection (i.e., read, write, execute for user, group, others), and lock information. The system file table entry also contains the file offset, indicating where the next data is read from or written to in the file.

Several entries in the system file table may correspond to the same physical file. Each of these entries points to the same entry in the *in-memory inode table*. The inode table contains an entry for each active file in the system. When a particular physical file is opened and no other process has it open, an entry in this inode table is created for that file. Figure 3.11 shows that the file `/home/ann/my.dat` had already been opened because there are two entries in the system file table with pointers to its entry in the inode table. (An earlier pointer is designated by B in the figure.)

The operating system keeps copies of the inodes for active files in memory for efficiency. Otherwise, according to the time scale of one processor cycle per second of

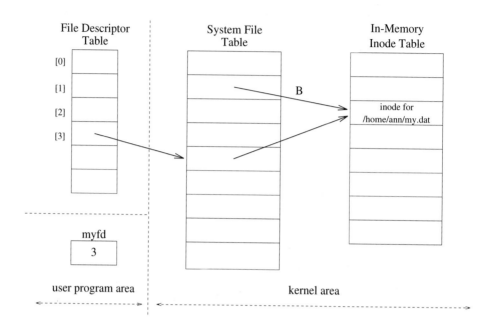

File Descriptor
Table

[0]

[1]

[2]

[3]

myfd

3

user program area

System File
Table

B

In-Memory
Inode Table

inode for
/home/ann/my.dat

kernel area

Figure 3.11: Relationship between the file descriptor table, the system file table, and the in-memory inode table.

Table 1.1, it would take eleven days to access the inode and at least another eleven days to access the data block itself.

Exercise 3.9

What happens when the process of Example 3.10 executes the `close(myfd)` system call?

Answer:

The operating system deletes the fourth entry in the file descriptor table and the corresponding entry in the system file table. (See Section 3.3.3 for a more complete discussion.) If the operating system also deleted the inode table entry, it would leave pointer B hanging in the system file table. Therefore, the inode table entry must have a count of the number of entries in the system file table that are pointing to it. When a process executes the `close` system call, the operating system decrements the count in the inode entry and if it is 0, deletes the inode entry from memory. (The operating system might not delete it right away on the off chance that it will be accessed again in the immediate future.)

Exercise 3.10

The system file table entry contains an offset which gives the current position in the file. If two processes have each opened a file for read, they each have their own offset into the file. Each process reads independently of the other, so each process reads the entire file. What happens with writes? What would happen if the file offset were stored in the inode table instead of the system file table?

Answer:

The writes are independent of each other. Each user can write over what the other user has written. On the other hand, if the offsets were stored in the inode table, the writes from different opens would be consecutive. In this case the processes would only read parts of the file because the file offset they were using could be updated by other processes.

Exercise 3.11

Suppose a process opens a file for reading and then forks. Both the parent and child can read from the file. How are reads by these two processes related? What about writes?

Answer:

The processes share a system file table entry and therefore also share the file offset. The two processes read different parts of the file. If no other processes have the file open, writes append to the end of the file and no data is lost on writes. Section 3.3.3 covers this situation in more detail.

3.3.2 File Pointers and Buffering

The ANSI C standard I/O library uses file pointers rather than file descriptors for I/O. A *file pointer* is a pointer to a data structure called a file structure in the user area of the process. This data structure contains a buffer and a file descriptor. (In System V this maps onto a stream interface but do not worry about that for the time being.)

Example 3.11

The following code segment opens the file /home/ann/my.dat *for output and then writes a string to the file.*

```
#include <stdio.h>
FILE *myfp;

if ((myfp = fopen("/home/ann/my.dat", "w")) == NULL)
    fprintf(stderr,"Could not fopen file\n");
else
    fprintf(myfp, "This is a test");
```

Figure 3.12 shows the file structure allocated by the fopen of Example 3.11. The file structure contains a buffer and a file descriptor value. The file descriptor value is the index to the entry in the file descriptor table that later fprintf's actually use to write the file to disk. In some sense the file pointer is a handle to a handle.

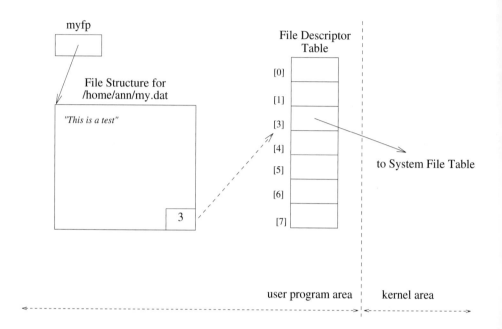

Figure 3.12: Schematic use of file pointer after `fopen`.

What happens when the program calls `fprintf`? The result depends on the type of file that was opened. Disk files are usually fully-buffered, meaning that the `fprintf` does not actually write the `This is a test` to disk but instead writes the string to a buffer in the file structure. When the buffer is full, the `fprintf` calls `write` with the file descriptor as in the previous section. The delay between when a program executes the `fprintf` and when the writing actually occurs may have interesting consequences, especially if the program crashes. Buffered data is sometimes lost on crashes, so it is possible for a program to complete normally, but its disk output be incomplete.

How can a program avoid the effects of buffering? A `fflush` call forces whatever has been buffered in the file structure to be written out. A program can call `setvbuf` to disable buffering.

Terminal I/O works a little differently. Files associated with terminals are line-buffered rather than fully-buffered (except for standard error which is not buffered). On output, line buffering means that the line is not written out until the buffer is full or until a newline symbol is encountered.

Example 3.12

   The `'a'` and `'b'` appear on the screen after the two standard error messages because standard output is line-buffered while standard error is not buffered.

```
#include <stdio.h>

fprintf(stdout, "a");
fprintf(stderr, "a has been written\n");
fprintf(stdout, "b");
fprintf(stderr, "b has been written\n");
fprintf(stdout, "\n");
```

Example 3.13

In the following code segment, the scanf flushes the buffer for stdout so the 'a' is displayed before the number is read in.

```
#include <stdio.h>
int i;

fprintf(stdout, "a");
scanf("%d", &i);
fprintf(stderr, "a has been written\n");
fprintf(stdout, "b");
fprintf(stderr, "b has been written\n");
fprintf(stdout, "\n");
```

The issue of buffering is more subtle than the previous discussion might lead one to believe. If a program that uses file pointers for a buffered device crashes, the last partial buffer created from the fprintf's may never be written out. When the buffer is full, a write is performed. Completion of a write does not mean that the data actually made it to disk. In fact the operating system copies the data to a system *buffer cache*. Periodically, the operating system writes these *dirty blocks* to disk. If the entire system crashes before the operating system writes the block to disk, the program still loses the data. Presumably a system crash is less likely to happen than an individual program crash.

3.3.3 Inheritance of File Descriptors

When fork creates a child, the child inherits a copy of most of the parent's environment and context including the signal state, the scheduling parameters, and the file descriptor table. The implications of inheritance are not always obvious. Because children inherit their parent's file descriptor table, the parent and children share the same file offset for files that are opened by the parent prior to the fork.

Example 3.14

In the following code segment the child inherits the file descriptor to my.dat.

```
#include <sys/types.h>
#include <sys/stat.h>
#include <fcntl.h>
```

```
#include <unistd.h>
#include <stdio.h>
int myfd;
pid_t childpid;

if ((myfd = open("my.dat", O_RDONLY)) == -1)
   perror("Could not open file");
else if ((childpid = fork()) == -1)
   perror("Could not fork");
else if (childpid == 0)
   /* child code is here */
else
   /* parent code is here */
```

Figure 3.13 shows the parent and child file descriptor tables for Example 3.14. The file descriptor table entries of the two processes point to the same entry in the system file table. The parent and child therefore share the file offset which is stored in the system file table.

When a program closes a file, the entry in the file descriptor table is freed. What about the corresponding entry in the system file table? It can only be freed if there are no more file descriptor table entries pointing to it. For this reason each system file table entry contains a count of the number of file descriptor table entries that are pointing to it. When a file is closed, the operating system decrements the count and only deletes the entry when the count becomes 0. In a similar way, the operating system decrements the link count in an inode after a hard link is removed as discussed in Section 3.2.2.

Example 3.15

In the following code segment, the parent and child have both opened my.dat *for reading.*

```
#include <sys/types.h>
#include <sys/stat.h>
#include <fcntl.h>
#include <unistd.h>
#include <stdio.h>
int myfd;
pid_t childpid;

if ((childpid = fork()) == -1)
   perror("Could not fork");
else if ((myfd = open("my.dat", O_RDONLY)) == -1)
   perror("Could not open file");
else if (childpid == 0)
      /* child code is here */
else
      /* parent code is here */
```

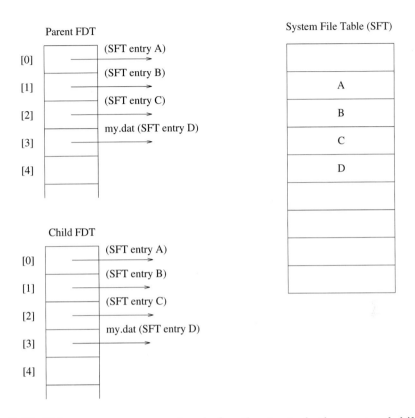

Figure 3.13: If the parent opens `my.dat` before the `fork,` both parent and child share the system file table entry.

Figure 3.14 shows the file descriptor tables for Example 3.15. The file descriptor table entries point to different system file table entries. Consequently the parent and child do not share the file offset. The child does not inherit the file descriptor because each process opened the file after the `fork,` so separate entries in the system file table are created. The parent and child still share system file table entries for standard input, standard output, and standard error.

3.4 Filters and Redirection

UNIX provides a large number of utilities that are written as filters. A *filter* reads from standard input, performs a transformation, and outputs the result to standard output. Filters write their error messages to standard error. All of the parameters of a filter are communicated as command-line arguments. The filter input data should have no headers or

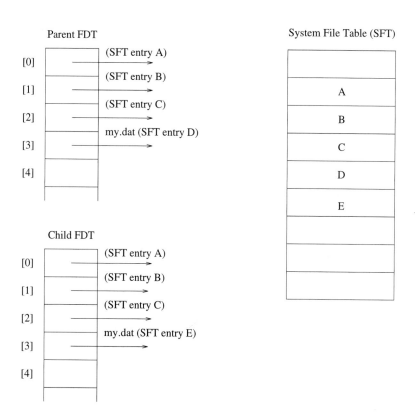

Figure 3.14: If the parent and child open my.dat after the fork, their file descriptor table entries point to different system file table entries.

trailers, and a filter should not require any interaction with the user.

Examples of useful UNIX filters include head, tail, more, sort, grep, and awk. The cat command takes a list of filenames as command-line arguments, reads each of the files in succession, and echoes the contents of each file to standard output. However, if no input file is specified, cat takes its input from standard input and sends its output to standard output. In this case cat behaves like a filter.

Recall that a file descriptor is an index into the process file descriptor table. Each entry in the file descriptor table points to an entry in the system file table which is created when the file is opened. A program can modify the file descriptor table entry so that it points to a different entry in the system file table. This action is known as *redirection*. Most shells interpret the greater than character (>) on the command line as redirection of standard output and the less than character (<) as redirection of standard input. (Associate > with output by picturing it as an arrow pointing in the direction of the output file.)

Example 3.16

The cat *command with no command-line arguments reads from standard input and echoes to standard output. The following command redirects standard output to* my.file *with the* >.

```
cat > my.file
```

The cat command of Example 3.16 gathers what is typed from the keyboard into the file my.file. Figure 3.15 depicts the file descriptor table for Example 3.16. Before redirection, entry [1] of the file descriptor table points to a system file table entry corresponding to the usual standard output device. After the redirection, entry [1] points to a system file table entry for my.file.

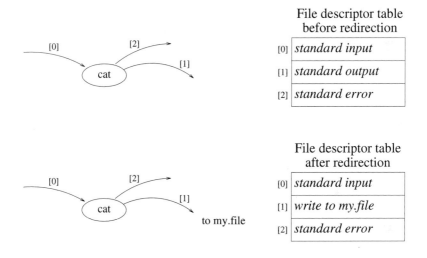

Figure 3.15: The status of the file descriptor table before and after redirection for the process that is executing cat > my.file.

The redirection of standard output in cat > my.file occurs because the shell changes the standard output entry of the file descriptor table (a pointer to the system file table) to point to a system file table entry associated with my.file. To accomplish this redirection in a C program, first open my.file to establish an appropriate entry in the system file table. After the open, copy the pointer to my.file into the entry for standard output by executing the dup2 system call. The dup2 takes two parameters, fildes and fildes2. It closes entry fildes2 of the file descriptor table and then copies the pointer of entry fildes into entry fildes2.

> *SYNOPSIS*
>
> ```
> #include <unistd.h>
>
> int dup2(int fildes, int fildes2);
> ```
>
> *POSIX.1, Spec 1170*

Example 3.17

The following code segment redirects standard output to the file `my.file`.

```
#include <stdio.h>
#include <sys/types.h>
#include <sys/stat.h>
#include <fcntl.h>
#include <unistd.h>
int fd;
mode_t fd_mode = S_IRUSR | S_IWUSR | S_IRGRP | S_IROTH;

if ((fd = open("my.file", O_WRONLY | O_CREAT, fd_mode)) == -1)
   perror("Could not open my.file");
else {
   if (dup2(fd, STDOUT_FILENO) == -1)
        perror("Could not redirect standard output");
   close(fd);
}
```

Figure 3.16 shows the effect of the redirection on the file descriptor table of Example 3.17. The `open` causes the operating system to create a new entry in the system file table and to set entry `[3]` of the file descriptor table to point to this entry.

The `dup2` closes the descriptor corresponding to the second parameter (standard output, `STDOUT_FILENO`) and then copies the entry corresponding to the first parameter (`fd`) into the entry corresponding to the second parameter (`STDOUT_FILENO`). From that point on in the program, a write to standard output goes to `my.file`.

3.5 Pipes

A programmer can build complicated transformations from simple filters by feeding the standard output of one filter into the standard input of the next.

Example 3.18

The following commands use the `sort` *filter in conjunction with* `ls` *to produce a directory listing sorted by size.*

```
ls -l > my.file
sort -n +4 < my.file
```

File descriptor table after open		File descriptor table after dup2		File descriptor table after close	
[0]	*standard input*	[0]	*standard input*	[0]	*standard input*
[1]	*standard output*	[1]	*write to my.file*	[1]	*write to my.file*
[2]	*standard error*	[2]	*standard error*	[2]	*standard error*
[3]	*write to my.file*	[3]	*write to my.file*		

Figure 3.16: The status of the file descriptor table during the execution of Example 3.17.

The first option to `sort` in Example 3.18 gives the type of sort (n means numeric). The second option indicates that the sort key should be found by skipping four fields. (The number of fields to skip depends on the version of UNIX.) The `ls` writes its output to an intermediate file (`my.file`) which `sort` then uses for input.

Example 3.19
The following alternative to the implementation in Example 3.18 produces a sorted directory listing without creating the intermediate file `my.file`.

```
ls -l | sort -n +4
```

The connection between `ls` and `sort` in Example 3.19 is different from redirection because `ls` and `sort` do not share a common file descriptor table. The standard output of `ls` is "connected" to the standard input of `sort` through a communication buffer called a *pipe*. Figure 3.17 shows a schematic of the connection and the corresponding file descriptor tables after the connection is established. The `ls` redirects its standard output to write to the pipe, and the `sort` redirects its standard input to read from the pipe. The `sort` reads the data that `ls` writes on a first-in-first-out basis. The `sort` does not have to consume data at the same rate as the `ls` writes it to the pipe.

```
SYNOPSIS

    #include <unistd.h>

    int pipe(int fildes[2]);
                                                     POSIX.1, Spec 1170
```

The `pipe` call creates a communication buffer which the caller can access through file descriptors `fildes[0]` and `fildes[1]`. The data written to `fildes[1]` is read from `fildes[0]` on a first-in-first-out basis. A pipe has no external or permanent

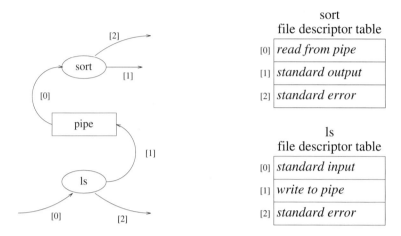

Figure 3.17: The status of the file descriptor table during the execution of Example 3.19.

name—so a program can only access it only through the two file descriptors. For this reason a pipe can be used only by the process that created it and by descendents that inherit the descriptors on `fork`.

Note: The `pipe` call described here creates a traditional unidirectional communication buffer. System V Release 4 implements pipes using a bidirectional communication mechanism called STREAMS. *STREAMS pipes* allow data written to `fildes[0]` to be read from `fildes[1]` as well as in the other direction. The POSIX.1 standard does not prohibit this extension. Chapter 12 discusses STREAMS.

Example 3.20

The following program implements the redirection of Example 3.19. For simplicity most of the error checking has been omitted in this code.

```
#include <stdio.h>
#include <stdlib.h>
#include <unistd.h>
#include <fcntl.h>

void main(void)
{
    int fd[2];
    pid_t childpid;

    pipe(fd);
    if ((childpid = fork()) == 0) {   /* ls is the child */
        dup2(fd[1], STDOUT_FILENO);
```

```
        close(fd[0]);
        close(fd[1]);
        execl("/usr/bin/ls", "ls", "-l", NULL);
        perror("The exec of ls failed");
    } else {                          /* sort is the parent */
        dup2(fd[0], STDIN_FILENO);
        close(fd[0]);
        close(fd[1]);
        execl("/usr/bin/sort", "sort", "-n", "+4", NULL);
        perror("The exec of sort failed");
    }
    exit(0);
}
```

Figures 3.18 to 3.20 depict the state of the file descriptor table for Example 3.20. In Figure 3.18 the child process inherits a copy of the file descriptor table of the parent. Figure 3.19 shows the file descriptor table after the child redirects its standard output and the parent redirects its standard input, but before either process closes unneeded file descriptors. Figure 3.20 shows the final configuration.

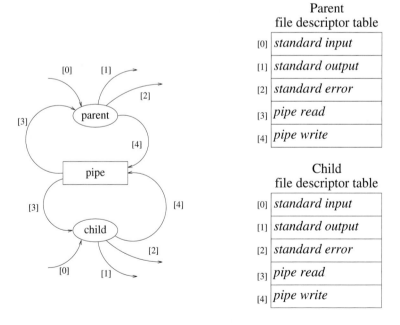

Figure 3.18: The status of the file descriptor table after the `fork` has been executed in Example 3.20.

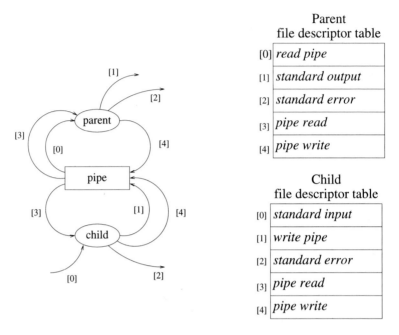

Figure 3.19: The status of the file descriptor table after the `dup2`'s have been executed in both processes of Example 3.20.

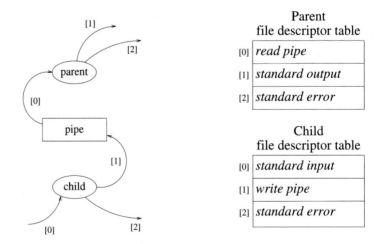

Figure 3.20: The status of the file descriptor table right before the `execl`'s have been executed in both processes of Example 3.20.

3.6 Reading to and Writing from Files

UNIX provides sequential access to files through the `read` and `write` system calls. These calls read or write a block of data starting from the current file offset. They update the offset so that the next operation occurs where the last one left off.

```
SYNOPSIS

   #include <unistd.h>

   ssize_t read(int fildes, void *buf, size_t nbyte);
                                              POSIX.1, Spec 1170
```

The `read` requests that `nbyte` bytes be read from the file with descriptor `fildes` and placed in `buf`. The caller must actually provide a buffer that is large enough to hold `nbyte` bytes of data. (A common mistake is to provide an uninitialized pointer to `char` rather than an actual buffer.) On success, `read` returns the number of bytes actually read. Error conditions for `read` are discussed on page 115.

```
SYNOPSIS

   #include <unistd.h>

   ssize_t write(int fildes, const void *buf, size_t nbyte);
                                              POSIX.1, Spec 1170
```

The `write` attempts to output `nbyte` bytes from `buf` to the file with descriptor `fildes`. On success `write` returns the number of bytes actually written.

Example 3.21

   The following code segment reads from `from_fd` *and writes to* `to_fd`.

```c
#include <sys/types.h>
#include <sys/uio.h>
#include <unistd.h>
#define BLKSIZE 1024

int from_fd, to_fd;
char buf[BLKSIZE];
int bytesread;

while ((bytesread = read(from_fd, buf, BLKSIZE)) > 0)
    if (write(to_fd, buf, bytesread) <= 0)
        break;
```

Notice that the `write` of Example 3.21 tries to write `bytesread` bytes rather than BLKSIZE bytes, thus taking into account that read may not actually read the full number of bytes requested. There is no guarantee, however, that the write outputs all of the bytes requested. Furthermore either read or write can be interrupted by a signal. In this case the call returns a −1 with errno set to EINTR.

Program 3.2 copies a file. The names of the source and destination files are passed as command-line arguments. Because the open for the destination file has O_CREAT | O_EXCL, the file copy fails if that file already exists. The loop for doing the copy handles partial writes and continues the copying even if there is an interruption by a signal. Chapter 5 discusses signals and interrupted system calls.

Program 3.2: A program to copy a file.

```
#include <sys/types.h>
#include <sys/uio.h>
#include <stdio.h>
#include <unistd.h>
#include <string.h>
#include <errno.h>
#include <sys/types.h>
#include <sys/stat.h>
#include <fcntl.h>
#define BLKSIZE 1024

void main(int argc, char *argv[])
{
    int from_fd, to_fd;
    int bytesread, byteswritten;
    char buf[BLKSIZE];
    char *bp;

    if (argc != 3) {
        fprintf(stderr, "Usage: %s from_file to_file\n", argv[0]);
        exit(1);
    }

    if ((from_fd = open(argv[1], O_RDONLY)) == -1) {
        fprintf(stderr, "Could not open %s: %s\n",
                argv[1], strerror(errno));
        exit(1);
    }

    if ((to_fd = open(argv[2], O_WRONLY | O_CREAT | O_EXCL,
                S_IRUSR | S_IWUSR)) == -1) {
        fprintf(stderr, "Could not create %s: %s\n",
                argv[2], strerror(errno));
        exit(1);
```

```
   }

   while (bytesread = read(from_fd, buf, BLKSIZE)) {
      if ((bytesread == -1) && (errno != EINTR))
         break;                   /* real error occurred on the descriptor */

      else if (bytesread > 0) {
         bp = buf;
         while(byteswritten = write(to_fd, bp, bytesread)) {
            if ((byteswritten == -1) && (errno != EINTR))
               break;
            else if (byteswritten == bytesread)
               break;
            else if (byteswritten > 0) {
               bp += byteswritten;
               bytesread -= byteswritten;
            }
         }
         if (byteswritten == -1)
            break;
      }
   }
   close(from_fd);
   close(to_fd);
   exit(0);
}
```

_____ **Program 3.2** _____

A read from an ordinary file returns with fewer bytes than requested if the read
has read up to the end of the file or if it is interrupted by a signal. When a read requests a
certain number of bytes from a pipe, the read returns as soon as the pipe is not empty.
The number of bytes read is less than or equal to the number of bytes requested. The
read returns the number of bytes actually read. If the read is interrupted by a signal
and no data has been transferred, it returns −1 and sets errno to EINTR.

The read system call returns 0 if a program tries to start reading past the current
end of an ordinary file. Once the end-of-file condition occurs, the program cannot read
beyond that point if the file is extended later. End-of-file detection for special files such
as pipes is more complicated. A pipe may be empty because the process writing to the
pipe has fallen behind. The end-of-file condition for pipes occurs only when the pipe is
empty and there are no more processes with write descriptors open to the pipe. *Close all
unused descriptors or the program will not be able to detect end-of-file.* Certain other
problems can occur with errant open file descriptors.

3.7 Nonblocking I/O

Communication buffers such as pipes can be empty if all of the information previously written to them has been read. The empty buffer is not an end-of-file indication. Rather it reflects the asynchronous nature of communication between processes. Normally when a process attempts to read such a buffer, it blocks (waits in the `read`) until input is available.

Blocking I/O presents a problem for a process that is monitoring more than one input communication buffer. The process has no way of knowing which input will arrive first—if it guesses wrong, the process might hang indefinitely.

One way to handle this problem is to use nonblocking I/O. By setting the appropriate control flags, a program can cause reads to return immediately if no input is available. The process then continuously attempts to read the input file descriptors, each in turn. This method, called polling, uses the CPU inefficiently.

A program does nonblocking I/O by setting the O_NONBLOCK flag associated with the file descriptor. The `fcntl` system call modifies the flags and status associated with an object that has a file descriptor.

```
SYNOPSIS

    #include <sys/types.h>
    #include <unistd.h>
    #include <fcntl.h>

    int fcntl(int fildes, int cmd, /* arg */ ...);
                                                       POSIX.1, Spec 1170
```

Example 3.22

The following code segment sets an already opened file descriptor `fd` *for non-blocking I/O.*

```c
#include <fcntl.h>
#include <stdio.h>
int fd_flags;

if ((fd_flags = fcntl(fd, F_GETFL, 0)) == -1)
    perror("Could not get flags for fd");
else {
    fd_flags |= O_NONBLOCK;
    if (fcntl(fd, F_SETFL, fd_flags) == -1)
        perror("Could not set flags for fd");
}
```

The code segment of Example 3.22 reads the current value of the flags associated with `fd`, performs a bitwise OR with `O_NONBLOCK`, and installs the modified flags. After this segment executes, `read` system calls associated with `fd` return immediately if there is no input available.

Example 3.23

The following code changes the I/O mode associated with file descriptor `fd` *to blocking by clearing the* O_NONBLOCK *file flag.*

```
#include <fcntl.h>
#include <stdio.h>
int fd_flags;

if ((fd_flags = fcntl(fd, F_GETFL, 0)) == -1)
    perror("Could not get flags for fd");
else {
    fd_flags &= ~O_NONBLOCK;
    if (fcntl(fd, F_SETFL, fd_flags) == -1)
        perror("Could not set flags for fd");
}
```

3.8 The `select` call

An alternative to polling is for the process to block until I/O is available from any of a set of file descriptors. Blocking until at least one member of a set of conditions becomes true is called *OR synchronization*. The condition for the case described is "input available" on a descriptor.

The `select` call provides a method of monitoring file descriptors for one of three possible conditions—a read can be done without blocking, a write can be done without blocking, or an exceptional condition is pending. (The latter does not mean an error occurred. Rather it indicates the presence of out-of-band data during network communication.)

```
SYNOPSIS
    #include <sys/time.h>
    #include <sys/types.h>

    int select(int nfds, fd_set *readfds, fd_set *writefds,
               fd_set *exceptfds, struct timeval *timeout);
                                                    Spec 1170
```

The first parameter of `select` is the number of bits to be checked in the file descriptor sets. This value must be at least one greater than the largest file descriptor to be checked. The `readfd` parameter specifies the set of descriptors to be monitored for reading.

Similarly `writefds` specifies the set of descriptors to be monitored for writing, and `exceptfds` specifies file descriptors to be monitored for exceptional conditions. The descriptor sets are of type `fd_set`.

On return, `select` clears all of the descriptors in each of `readfds`, `writefds`, and `exceptfds` except those descriptors that are ready. The return value for `select` is the number of file descriptors that are ready or −1 if there was an error. The last parameter is a timeout value used to force a return from the `select` after a certain period of time has elapsed even if no descriptors are ready. When `timeout` is `NULL`, the `select` may block indefinitely. If `select` is interrupted by a signal, it returns −1 and sets `errno` to `EINTR`.

Historically the descriptor set was implemented as an integer bit mask, but that implementation did not work for more than 32 file descriptors. The descriptor sets are now usually represented by bit fields in arrays of integers, and the macros `FD_SET`, `FD_CLR`, `FD_ISSET`, and `FD_ZERO` are provided for manipulating the descriptor sets in an implementation-independent way.

SYNOPSIS

```
#include <sys/time.h>
#include <sys/types.h>

void FD_SET(int fd, fd_set *fdset);
void FD_CLR(int fd, fd_set *fdset);
int FD_ISSET(int fd, fd_set *fdset);
void FD_ZERO(fd_set *fdset);
```
                                                                          Spec 1170

The `FD_SET` macro sets the bit in `fdset` corresponding to the `fd` file descriptor, while the `FD_CLR` macro clears the corresponding bit. The `FD_ZERO` macro clears all of the bits in `fdset`. Use these three macros to set up descriptor masks prior to calling `select`. Use the `FD_ISSET` macro after `select` to test whether the bit corresponding to the file descriptor `fd` is set in the mask `fdset`.

Example 3.24

The following code segment continuously monitors two file descriptors `pipe1` *and* `pipe2` *for input.*

```
#include <stdio.h>
#include <string.h>
#include <sys/time.h>
#include <sys/types.h>
#include <errno.h>

fd_set readset;
int maxfd;
int  pipe1;
```

```
int  pipe2;

    /* setup for pipe1 and pipe2 goes here */
maxfd = pipe1;                    /* find the biggest fd for select */
if (pipe2 > maxfd)
   maxfd = pipe2;

for( ; ; ) {
   FD_ZERO(&readset);
   FD_SET(pipe1, &readset);
   FD_SET(pipe2, &readset);
   if ( (select(maxfd+1, &readset, NULL, NULL, NULL) == -1) &&
      (errno != EINTR) )
      perror("Select failed");
   else {
      if (FD_ISSET(pipe1, &readset)) {
         /*  read and process pipe1 input */
      }
      if (FD_ISSET(pipe2, &readset)) {
         /*  read and process pipe2 input */
      }
   }
}
```

The `select` of Example 3.24 blocks until there is something to read on `pipe1` or on `pipe2`, so unlike polling, this method does not waste CPU cycles. The `select` call is not part of POSIX.1. A major shortcoming of POSIX is that there is no direct way to monitor two file descriptors without busy waiting. Although `select` is from 4.3 BSD UNIX, not System V, it is provided as part of Spec 1170. Section 9.1 gives additional examples of `select` and discusses `poll`, the System V counterpart of `select`.

3.9 FIFOs

Pipes are temporary in the sense that they disappear when no process has them open. *FIFOs*, also called *named pipes*, are represented by special files and persist even after all processes have closed them. Any process with the appropriate permissions can access a FIFO. FIFOs can be created with the `mkfifo` command from the shell or with the `mkfifo` system call from a program.

SYNOPSIS

```
#include <sys/types.h>
#include <sys/stat.h>

int mkfifo(const char *path, mode_t mode);
```
POSIX.1, Spec 1170

Example 3.25

The following code segment creates a named pipe called myfifo *that can be read by everybody but is only writable by the owner.*

```
#include <sys/stat.h>
#include <sys/types.h>

mode_t fifo_perms = S_IRUSR | S_IWUSR | S_IRGRP| S_IROTH;

if (mkfifo("myfifo", fifo_perms) == -1)
    perror("Could not create myfifo");
```

Program 3.3 creates a named pipe from a path specified on the command line. It then forks a child. The child process writes to the named pipe, and the parent reads what the child has written.

Program 3.3: The parent reads what its child has written to a named pipe.

```
#include <stdio.h>
#include <stdlib.h>
#include <unistd.h>
#include <string.h>
#include <sys/types.h>
#include <sys/wait.h>
#include <sys/stat.h>
#include <fcntl.h>
#include <errno.h>
#define BUFSIZE 256
void main (int argc, char *argv[])
{
    mode_t fifo_mode = S_IRUSR | S_IWUSR;
    int fd;
    int status;
    char buf[BUFSIZE];
    unsigned strsize;
    int mychild;

    if (argc != 2) {
        fprintf(stderr, "Usage: %s pipename\n", argv[0]);
        exit(1);
    }
                            /* create a named pipe with r/w for user */
    if ((mkfifo(argv[1], fifo_mode) == -1) && (errno != EEXIST)) {
        fprintf(stderr, "Could not create a named pipe: %s\n", argv[1]);
        exit(1);
    }

    if ((mychild = fork()) == -1){
```

```
        perror("Could not fork");
        exit(1);
    } else if (mychild == 0) {                    /* The child writes */
        fprintf(stderr, "Child[%ld] about to open FIFO %s\n",
                        (long)getpid(), argv[1]);
        if ((fd = open(argv[1], O_WRONLY))== -1) {
            perror("Child cannot open FIFO");
            exit(1);
        }
        sprintf(buf,
            "This was written by the child[%ld]\n", (long)getpid());
        strsize = strlen(buf) + 1;
        if (write(fd, buf, strsize) != strsize) {
            fprintf(stderr, "Child write to FIFO failed\n");
            exit(1);
        }
        fprintf(stderr, "Child[%ld] is done\n", (long)getpid());
    } else {                                      /* The parent does a read */
        fprintf(stderr, "Parent[%ld] about to open FIFO %s\n",
                        (long)getpid(), argv[1]);
        if ((fd = open(argv[1], O_RDONLY | O_NONBLOCK)) == -1) {
            perror("Parent cannot open FIFO");
            exit(1);
        }
        fprintf(stderr,"Parent[%ld] about to read\n", (long)getpid());
        while ((wait(&status)== -1) && (errno == EINTR))
            ;
        if (read(fd, buf, BUFSIZE) <= 0) {
            perror("Parent read from FIFO failed\n");
            exit(1);
        }
        fprintf(stderr, "Parent[%ld] got: %s\n", (long)getpid(), buf);
    }
    exit(0);
}
```

_____ **Program 3.3** _____

Exercise 3.12

Read the man page for open(2) and try to determine why the parent used O_NONBLOCK but the child did not. Why does the parent have to wait for the child process? Does it matter where the parent does the wait?

Answer:

If the child tries to do an open with O_NONBLOCK, it returns an error if the parent has not yet opened the pipe for reading. If neither uses O_NONBLOCK, then both block until the other succeeds causing a deadlock. If the parent tries to read before the child has written, the read returns an error since the parent opened with O_NONBLOCK. If the parent waits until the child completes before opening the pipe, the child blocks on its open.

The complication discussed in Exercise 3.12 can be avoided by having parent and child processes open the FIFO for both reading and writing. The open could be done before the fork, but it would then no longer illustrate the difference between FIFOs and pipes. The important difference is that for FIFOs the communicating processes do not need to be related; they only need to know the name of the FIFO and share a filesystem.

3.10 Special Files—The Audio Device

Most users want to know as little as necessary about the details of peripherals, and UNIX provides a device-independent interface by representing devices as *special files* which can be opened, read, or written as any other files. FIFOs are special files. Another example is the audio device available on many workstations (speaker and microphone). The device designation for this device on Sun workstations is /dev/audio. Note: If logged in on an ASCII terminal or on an X-terminal, a user cannot use the audio device even if the system has one.

Example 3.26
The following command plays the audio file sample.au *on the speaker of a Sun workstation.*

```
cat sample.au > /dev/audio
```

Program 3.4 contains a library of functions for reading and writing from the audio device. None of these library functions pass the file descriptor corresponding to the audio device. Rather, the audio library is treated as an object that calling programs access through the provided interface (open_audio, close_audio, read_audio, and write_audio).

The open_audio opens /dev/audio for read/write access using blocking I/O. If the audio device has already been opened, the open call hangs until the device is closed. If the audio device had been opened with the O_NONBLOCK flag, the open would have returned with an error if the device were busy.

The open_audio function attempts to open both the microphone and the speaker. A process that only wants to record can call open with O_RDONLY, while a process that only wants to play can call open with O_WRONLY. If it is interrupted by a signal, open_audio restarts the open.

Program 3.4: The audio device object and its basic operations.

```c
#include <unistd.h>
#include <stdio.h>
#include <fcntl.h>
#include <stropts.h>
#include <errno.h>
#define AUDIO_DEVICE "/dev/audio"

static int audio_fd = -1;   /* audio device file descriptor */

/* Open audio device.  Return 0 if successful or -1 if unsuccessful.*/
int open_audio(void)
{
   while (((audio_fd = open(AUDIO_DEVICE, O_RDWR)) == -1) &&
           (errno == EINTR))
       ;
   if (audio_fd <= 0)
      return -1;
   return 0;
}

/* Close the audio device. */
void close_audio(void)
{
   close(audio_fd);
   audio_fd = -1;
}

/* Read up to maxcnt bytes from audio.
 * Return bytes read or -1 if there was an error.
 */
int read_audio(char *buffer, int maxcnt)
{
   ssize_t bytes;

   while (((bytes = read(audio_fd, buffer, (size_t)maxcnt)) == -1) &&
           (errno == EINTR))
       ;
   return (int)bytes;
}

/* Write length bytes of buffer to audio.
 * Return number bytes written or -1 if there was an error.
 */
int write_audio(char *buffer, int length)
{
   ssize_t byteswritten;
```

```
   size_t bytestried;
   char *buffp;

   buffp = buffer;
   bytestried = length;
   while (bytestried != 0) {
      if ((byteswritten = write(audio_fd, buffp, bytestried)) >= 0) {
         bytestried -= byteswritten;
         buffp += byteswritten;
      } else if (errno != EINTR)
         break;
   }
   if (byteswritten == -1)
      return (int)byteswritten;
   else
      return length;
}
```

_____ **Program 3.4** _____

The speaker can handle data only at a predetermined rate, so the `write_audio` may not send the entire buffer to the speaker in one `write` system call. Similarly the `read_audio` reads only the data currently available from the microphone and returns the number of bytes actually read. Section 3.13 explores I/O to the audio device.

Program 3.5 reads from the microphone and writes to the speaker. Terminate the program by entering `ctrl-c` from the keyboard. It is best to use headphones when trying this program to avoid feedback caused by a microphone and speaker in close proximity. The `audio.h` header file contains the following audio function prototypes:

```
   int open_audio(void);
   void close_audio(void);
   int read_audio(char *buffer, int maxcnt);
   int write_audio(char *buffer, int length);
```

_____

Program 3.5: A simple program that reads from the microphone.

```
#include <stdio.h>
#include <stdlib.h>
#include "audio.h"

#define BUFSIZE 1024
void main (void)
{
   char buffer[BUFSIZE];
   int bytesread;
```

```
   if (open_audio() == -1) {
      perror("Could not open audio:");
      exit(1);
   }
   for( ; ; ) {
      if ((bytesread = read_audio(buffer, BUFSIZE)) == -1) {
         perror("Could not read microphone");
         break;
      } else if (write_audio(buffer, bytesread) == -1) {
         perror("Could not write to speaker");
         break;
      }
   }
   close_audio();
   exit(0);
}
```

_____ **Program 3.5** _____

If BUFSIZE is not commensurate with the size of the blocks transferred by the audio
device driver, the speech may sound discontinuous. Find out the appropriate buffer size
and other device-specific information by calling ioctl. The ioctl system call is not
part of POSIX.1 because the standards committee could not resolve some of the specification conflicts between various historical implementations of UNIX. Spec 1170 does
specify the ioctl system call for performing control on *STREAMS* devices. (Chapter 12 discusses STREAMS.)

```
┌─────────────────────────────────────────────────────────────────────────┐
│ SYNOPSIS                                                                  │
│                                                                           │
│    #include <stropts.h>                                                   │
│                                                                           │
│    int ioctl(int fildes, int request, .... /* arg */);                    │
│                                                              Spec 1170    │
└─────────────────────────────────────────────────────────────────────────┘
```

The ioctl system call provides a means of obtaining device status information
or setting device control options. Sun Solaris 2 uses the AUDIO_GETINFO request of
ioctl to provide information about the audio device. The audio_info_t type defined in audioio.h holds configuration information about the audio device:

```
   typedef struct audio_info {
      audio_prinfo_t   play;          /* output status information */
      audio_prinfo_t   record;        /* input status information */
      uint_t           monitor_gain;  /* input to output mix */
      uchar_t          output_muted;  /* nonzero if output muted */
      uchar_t _xxx[3];                /* Reserved for future use */
      uint_t _yyy[3];                 /* Reserved for future use */
   } audio_info_t;
```

where `audio_prinfo_t` is defined as

```
struct audio_prinfo {
    /* The following values describe the audio data encoding */
    uint_t    sample_rate;  /* samples per second */
    uint_t    channels;     /* number of interleaved channels */
    uint_t    precision;    /* number of bits per sample */
    uint_t    encoding;     /* data encoding method */

    /* The following values control audio device configuration */
    uint_t    gain;         /* volume level */
    uint_t    port;         /* selected I/O port */
    uint_t    avail_ports;  /* available I/O ports */
    uint_t    _xxx[2];      /* Reserved for future use */
    uint_t    buffer_size;  /* I/O buffer size */

    /* The following values describe the current device state */
    uint_t    samples;      /* number of samples converted */
    uint_t    eof;          /* End Of File counter (play only) */
    uchar_t   pause;        /* nonzero if paused, zero to resume */
    uchar_t   error;        /* nonzero if overflow/underflow */
    uchar_t   waiting;      /* nonzero if a process wants access */
    uchar_t   balance;      /* stereo channel balance */
    ushort_t minordev;

    /* The following values are read-only device state flags */
    uchar_t   open;         /* nonzero if open access granted */
    uchar_t   active;       /* nonzero if I/O active */
} audio_prinfo_t;
```

The `buffer_size` member of the `audio_prinfo_t` structure indicates how large a chunk of audio data the device driver accumulates before passing the data to a read request. The `buffer_size` for play indicates how large a chunk the device driver accumulates before sending the data to the speaker. Audio tends to sound better if the program sends and receives chunks that match the corresponding `buffer_size` settings. Use `ioctl` to determine these sizes in an audio application program.

Example 3.27

> *The* `get_record_buffer_size` *function returns the appropriate block size to use when reading from the microphone or* −1 *if an error occurs. This function can be added to the audio library of Program 3.4.*

```
#include <unistd.h>
#include <sys/audioio.h>

int get_record_buffer_size(void)
{
    audio_info_t myaudio;
```

```
    if (ioctl(audio_fd, AUDIO_GETINFO, &myaudio) == -1)
        return -1;
    else
        return myaudio.record.buffer_size;
}
```

The implementation of Program 3.4 opens the audio device for blocking I/O. Non-blocking reads are complicated by the fact that `read` can return −1 either if there is an error or if the audio device is not ready with the data. The latter case has an `errno` value of `EAGAIN` and should not be treated as an error. The primary reason for opening the audio device in nonblocking mode is so that the `open` does not hang when the device is already open. An alternative is to open the audio device in nonblocking mode and then to use `fcntl` to change the mode to blocking.

Example 3.28

The following code segment opens the audio device for nonblocking I/O. It then reads `BLKSIZE` *bytes from the audio device into a buffer.*

```c
#include <stdio.h>
#include <stdlib.h>
#include <unistd.h>
#include <fcntl.h>
#include <errno.h>
#define AUDIO_DEVICE "/dev/audio"

char buffer[BLKSIZE];
char *bp;
int bytes_read;
unsigned bytes_needed;
int audio_fd;

if ( (audio_fd = open(AUDIO_DEVICE, O_NONBLOCK | O_RDWR)) == -1) {
    perror("Could not open audio device");
    exit(1);
}

bp = buffer;
bytes_needed = BLKSIZE;
while(bytes_needed != 0) {
    bytes_read = read(audio_fd, bp, bytes_needed);
    if ((bytes_read == -1) && (errno != EAGAIN))
        break;
    if (bytes_read > 0) {
        bp += bytes_read;
        bytes_needed -= bytes_read;
    }
}
```

In testing audio programs, keep in mind that the audio device is closed when the program exits. If there is still data in the audio buffer that has not yet reached the speakers, it may be lost. The draining of a device after a `close` is system-dependent, so read the man page before deciding how to handle the situation.

3.11 Exercise: Traversing Directories

The exercises in this section develop programs to traverse directory trees in depth-first and breadth-first orders. Depth-first searches explore each branch of a tree to its leaves before looking at other branches. Breadth-first searches explore all of the nodes at a given level before descending lower in the tree.

Example 3.29

For the directory tree in Figure 3.1, depth-first ordering visits the nodes in the following order.

```
/
   dirC
      my3.dat
   dirA
      dirB
         my1.dat
      my1.dat
      my2.dat
```

The indentation of the filenames in Example 3.29 shows the level in the directory tree.

Exercise 3.13

The UNIX `du` command displays the sizes of the directories in a directory tree. Try to determine the search order that it uses.

Depth-first search is naturally recursive as indicated by the following pseudocode:

```
depth_first_search_tree(root) {
      for each node at or below root
            visit node;
            if node is a directory
                depth_first_search_tree(node);
      }
```

Example 3.30

For the directory tree in Figure 3.1, breadth-first order visits the nodes in the following order.

```
/
/dirC
/dirA
/dirC/my3.dat
/dirA/dirB
/dirA/my1.dat
/dirA/my2.dat
/dirA/dirB/my1.dat
```

Breath-first search can be implemented using a queue similar to the history queue of Program 2.3. As the program encounters each directory node at a particular level, it enqueues the complete pathname for later examination. The following pseudocode assumes the existence of a queue. The enqueue operation puts a node at the end of the queue, while the dequeue operation removes a node from the front of the queue.

```
breath_first_tree_search(root){
    enqueue(root);
    while (queue is not empty) {
        dequeue(&next);
        for each node directly below next:
            visit the node
            if node is a directory
                enqueue(node)
    }
}
```

- Write a function called isadirectory which has prototype

    ```
    int isadirectory(char *pathname);
    ```

    The isadirectory function uses stat to determine whether the file specified by pathname is a directory. It returns 1 if pathname is a directory and 0 if pathname is not a directory.

- Write a function called depth_first_apply which has prototype

    ```
    int depth_first_apply(char *pathname,
                          int pathfun(char *pathname1));
    ```

    The depth_first_apply function traverses the directory tree starting at pathname. It applies the pathfun function to each file that it encounters in the traverse. The depth_first_apply returns the sum of the return values of pathfun or −1 if it failed to traverse any subdirectories of the directory. An example of a possible pathfun is a function which prints the pathname with other stat information in a particular order. The pathfun returns the size of the file.

- Write a function called `sizepathfun` which has prototype

   ```
   int sizepathfun(char *pathname1);
   ```

   The   `sizepathfun`   returns the size in blocks of the file given by
   `pathname1` or −1 if `pathname1` does not correspond to an ordinary
   file.

- Use `depth_first_apply` with the `pathfun` given by `sizepathfun`
   to implement the command

   ```
   showtreesize pathname
   ```

   The `showtreesize` command writes `pathname` followed by its total size
   to standard output. If `pathname` is a directory, the total size corresponds
   to the size of the entire subtree rooted at `pathname`. If `pathname` is a
   special file, print an informative message, but no size.

- Write a command called `mydu` which is called with a command-line argument `rootpath`:

   ```
   mydu rootpath
   ```

   The `mydu` program calls a modified `depth_first_apply` with the function `sizepathfun`. It outputs the size of each directory followed by its
   pathname. The size of the directory does not count the size of subtrees of
   that directory. The program outputs the total size of the tree at the end and
   exits.

- Write `breadth_first_apply` which is similar to `depth_first_apply`
   but uses a breadth-first search strategy.

3.12 Exercise: `proc` Filesystem

Some implementations of UNIX such as Sun Solaris 2 provide a `proc` filesystem which
maps the image of each process in the system to a file in the `/proc` directory. Each
process has a corresponding file named by its process ID. The exercises in this section
assume a system with a `proc` filesystem similar to the one supported by Sun Solaris.

Example 3.31

The following partial output of the command `ls -l /proc` *shows processes
with their owners, size, time of creation, and process ID.*

```
total 396776
-rw-------   1 root      root            0 Jan 24 12:39 00000
-rw-------   1 root      root       724992 Jan 24 12:40 00001
-rw-------   1 root      root            0 Jan 24 12:40 00002
```

```
-rw-------   1 root      root             0 Jan 24 12:40 00003
-rw-------   1 root      root       1736704 Jan 24 12:40 00297
-rw-------   1 root      root       1236992 Jan 24 12:40 00299
-rw-------   1 root      root       1351680 Jan 24 12:40 00305
-rw-------   1 root      root       1454080 Jan 24 12:40 00314
-rw-------   1 root      root       1294336 Jan 24 12:50 00575
-rw-------   1 robbins   staff       675840 Feb  8 08:07 10522
-rw-------   1 robbins   staff      1449984 Feb  8 08:07 10526
```

The output of Example 3.31 indicates that the init process with process ID equal to 1 was started on January 24 at 12:40. The user robbins has two processes that were initiated on February 8 at 8:07.

On systems that support a proc filesystem, a program can use the standard system call interface: open, close, read, write, and ioctl to inspect or modify a process image. The program can also perform various control functions by calling ioctl. The specific headers required for the Sun Solaris proc filesystem are

```
#include <sys/types.h>
#include <sys/signal.h>
#include <sys/fault.h>
#include <sys/syscall.h>
#include <sys/procfs.h>
```

Sun Solaris uses the pr_status_t structure shown in Figure 3.21 to hold information about a process represented under the proc filesystem. The prstatus_t of Figure 3.21 provides detailed information about the process image. Most of the fields are self-explanatory. Possible values of the pr_flags, pr_why, and pr_what fields are related to the process state and are explained in the man pages.

Example 3.32

In the code segment below, the PIOCSTATUS *request of* ioctl *fills in a structure of type* prstatus_t *for the process corresponding to the specified* fd.

```
#include <sys/types.h>
#include <sys/signal.h>
#include <sys/fault.h>
#include <sys/syscall.h>
#include <sys/procfs.h>
#include <fcntl.h>
#include <stdio.h>
#include <stdlib.h>
#include <unistd.h>
#define NAMESIZE 25

prstatus_t my_status;
```

```
typedef struct prstatus {
    long            pr_flags;       /* Flags */
    short           pr_why;         /* Reason for stop (if stopped) */
    short           pr_what;        /* More detailed reason */
    id_t            pr_who;         /* Specific lwp identifier */
    u_short         pr_nlwp;        /* Number of lwps in the process */
    short           pr_cursig;      /* Current signal */
    sigset_t        pr_sigpend;     /* Set of process pending signals */
    sigset_t        pr_lwppend;     /* Set of lwp pending signals */
    sigset_t        pr_sighold;     /* Set of lwp held signals */
    struct siginfo  pr_info;        /* Info associated with signal or fault */
    struct sigaltstack  pr_altstack;/* Alternate signal stack info */
    struct sigaction  pr_action;    /* Signal action for current signal */
    struct ucontext *pr_oldcontext; /* Address of previous ucontext */
    caddr_t         pr_brkbase;     /* Address of the process heap */
    u_long          pr_brksize;     /* Size of the process heap, in bytes */
    caddr_t         pr_stkbase;     /* Address of the process stack */
    u_long          pr_stksize;     /* Size of the process stack, in bytes */
    short           pr_syscall;     /* System call number (if in syscall) */
    short           pr_nsysarg;     /* Number of arguments to this syscall */
    long            pr_sysarg[PRSYSARGS];   /* Arguments to this syscall */
    caddr_t         pr_brkbase;     /* Address of the process heap */
    u_long          pr_brksize;     /* Size of the process heap, in bytes */
    caddr_t         pr_stkbase;     /* Address of the process stack */
    u_long          pr_stksize;     /* Size of the process stack, in bytes */
    short           pr_syscall;     /* System call number (if in syscall) */
    short           pr_nsysarg;     /* Number of arguments to this syscall */
    long            pr_sysarg[PRSYSARGS];   /* Arguments to this syscall */
    pid_t           pr_pid;         /* Process id */
    pid_t           pr_ppid;        /* Parent process id */
    pid_t           pr_pgrp;        /* Process group id */
    pid_t           pr_sid;         /* Session id */
    timestruc_t     pr_utime;       /* Process user cpu time */
    timestruc_t     pr_stime;       /* Process system cpu time */
    timestruc_t     pr_cutime;      /* Sum of children's user times */
    timestruc_t     pr_cstime;      /* Sum of children's system times */
    char            pr_clname[PRCLSZ];   /* Scheduling class name */
    long            pr_instr;       /* Current instruction */
    prgregset_t     pr_reg;         /* General registers */
} prstatus_t;
```

Figure 3.21: The information held in `prstatus_t` under Sun Solaris 2.

```
char procname[NAMESIZE];
int fd;

sprintf(procname,"/proc/%05ld", (long)getpid());
if ((fd = open(procname, O_RDONLY)) == -1)
    perror("Could not open my process image");
else if (ioctl(fd, PIOCSTATUS, &my_status) == -1)
    perror("Could not get my process status");
```

Do the following exercises to become familiar with the `proc` filesystem.

- Look at the man page on `proc`. It has all of the details.
- Write the function `get_prstatus` which has the prototype

```
int get_prstatus (int pid, prstatus_t *sp)
```

The `get_prstatus` sets the `prstatus_t` structure pointed to by `sp` for the process with process ID `pid`. The function returns 0 on success and −1 otherwise. The outline of the `get_prstatus` procedure is
  * Open `/proc/pid` for read only.
  * Execute the system call `ioctl(fildes, code, s)` with code equal to `PIOCSTATUS` and `s` being a pointer to a `prstatus_t` structure.
  * Close the file.

Check for errors on each of the system calls in `get_prstatus`. Do not exit from the function on error—return an error code. Be sure to close open files—even if returning an error.

- Write the function `output_prstatus` with prototype

```
int output_prstatus(FILE *fp, prstatus_t s);
```

The `output_prstatus` function writes the contents of `s` in an easily readable format to the file `fp`. Do not worry about the members of type `sigset_t`. Section 5.11 discusses these members in an extension to this exercise.

3.13 Exercise: Audio

The exercises in this section expand and improve the audio library of Program 3.4.

- Add the following access functions to the audio object of Program 3.4:
  - The `play_file` function plays an audio file. It has prototype

    ```
    int play_file(char *filename);
    ```

    The `play_file` outputs the audio file specified by `filename` to the audio device, assuming that the speaker has already been opened. The function returns the total number of bytes output if successful or −1 if an error occurs.

  - The `record_file` function saves incoming audio to a disk file. It has prototype

    ```
    int record_file(char *filename, int seconds);
    ```

The `record_file` function saves audio information for a time interval of `seconds` in the file given by `filename` assuming that the microphone has already been opened. The function returns the number of bytes recorded if successful or −1 if unsuccessful.

➤ The `get_record_sample_rate` function determines the sampling rate for recording. It has prototype

```
int get_record_sample_rate(void);
```

The `get_record_sample_rate` returns the sampling rate used for recording or −1 if an error occurs.

➤ The `get_play_sample_rate` function determines the sampling rate for playing. It has prototype

```
int get_play_sample_rate(void);
```

The `get_play_sample_rate` returns the sampling rate used for playing audio files on the speaker or −1 if an error occurs. 8000 samples/second is considered voice quality.

- Use the `record_file` function to create eight audio files that are each of ten seconds in duration: `pid1.au`, `pid2.au`, and so on. In the file `pid1.au` record following the message (in your voice): "I am process 1 sending to standard error." Record similar messages in the remaining files. Play the files back using the `play_file` function.

- Be sure to create a header file (say `audio.h`) with the prototypes of the functions in the audio library. Include this header file in any program that calls functions from this library.

- Redesign the audio object representation and access functions so that processes have the option of opening for read and for write separately. Replace `audio_fd` with the descriptors `play_fd` and `record_fd`. Change the `open_audio` so that it sets both `play_fd` and `record_fd` to the file descriptor value returned by the `open`. Add the following access functions to the audio object of Program 3.4.

    ➤ The `open_audio_for_record` opens the audio device for read (O_RDONLY). It has prototype

    ```
    int open_audio_for_record(void);
    ```

    The function returns 0 if successful or −1 if an error occurs.

    ➤ The `open_audio_for_play` opens the audio device for write (O_WRONLY). It has prototype

    ```
    int open_audio_for_play(void);
    ```

The `open_audio_for_play` returns 0 if successful or −1 if an error occurs.

- Record your speaking of the individual numerical digits (from 0 to 9) in ten different files. Write a function called `speak_number` which takes a string representing an integer and speaks the number corresponding to the string by calling `play_file` to play the files for the individual digits. (How does the program sound compared to the computer-generated messages of the phone company?)

- Replace the `fprintf` statement that outputs the various IDs in Program 2.12 with a call to `play_file`. For the process with `i` having value 1, play the file `pid1.au` and so on. Listen to the results for different numbers of processes when the speaker is opened before the `fork` loop. What happens when the speaker is opened after the `fork`? Be sure to use `sprintf` to construct the filenames from the `i` value. Do not hardcode in the filenames.

- Make a recording of the following statement in file `pid.au`: "My process ID is." Instead of having each process in the previous part play a `pidi.au` file corresponding to its `i` number, use `speak_number` to speak the process ID. Handle the parent and child IDs in a similar manner.

- Add the following functions to the audio library:
  - ➤ The `set_play_volume` function changes the volume at which sound plays on the speaker. It has prototype

    ```
    int set_play_volume(double volume);
    ```

    The `set_play_volume` sets the gain on the speaker. The `volume` must be between 0.0 and 1.0. The function returns 0 if successful and −1 if an error occurs.

  - ➤ The `set_record_volume` function changes the volume of incoming sound from the microphone. It has prototype

    ```
    int set_record_volume(double volume);
    ```

    The `set_record_volume` sets the gain on the microphone. The `volume` must be between 0.0 and 1.0. The function returns 0 if successful and −1 if an error occurs.

3.14 Exercise: Terminal Control

If you do not have access to an audio device, you can still experiment with device control. POSIX.1 does not include `ioctl`. Since terminal control was thought to be essential, the POSIX.1 standards committee decided to include the following library functions for manipulating the characteristics of terminals and asynchronous communication ports.

```
#include <termios.h>
int tcgetattr(int fildes, struct termios *termios_p);
int tcsetattr(int fildes, int optional_actions,
        const struct termios *termios_p);
int tcsendbreak(int fildes, int duration);
int tcdrain(int fildes);
int tcflush(int fildes, int queue_selector);
int tcflow(int fildes, int action);
speed_t cfgetospeed(const struct termios *termios_p);
int cfsetospeed(struct termios *termios_p, speed_t speed);
speed_t cfgetispeed(const struct termios *termios_p);
int cfsetispeed(struct termios *termios_p, speed_t speed);
```

The `struct termios` structure includes the following members:

```
tcflag_t    c_iflag;        /* input modes */
tcflag_t    c_oflag;        /* output modes */
tcflag_t    c_cflag;        /* control modes */
tcflag_t    c_lflag;        /* local modes */
cc_t        c_cc[NCCS];     /* control chars */
```

Additional functions manipulate the process group and session ID for a terminal. These calls are used for job control.

```
SYNOPSIS

    #include <sys/types.h>
    #include <unistd.h>

    pid_t tcgetpgrp(int fildes);
    int tcsetpgrp(int fildes, pid_t pgid);
                                                POSIX.1, Spec 1170
```

```
SYNOPSIS

    #include <termios.h>

    pid_t tcgetsid(int fildes);
                                                        Spec 1170
```

Do the following to become more familiar with terminal control.

- Read the man page on `termio`.
- Execute `stty -a` and try to understand the different fields.
- Compare the facilities provided by the specific terminal calls to those provided using `ioctl`. Read the `termio` information in Section 7 of the man pages for additional information.

3.15 Additional Reading

The *USENIX Conference Proceedings* are a good source of current information on tools and approaches evolving under UNIX. *Operating Systems Review* is an informal publication of SIGOPS, the Association for Computing Machinery Special Interest Group on Operating Systems. *Operating Systems Review* sometimes has articles on recent developments in the area of file systems and device management.

Advanced Programming in the UNIX Environment by Stevens [86] has some nice case studies on user-level device control including a program to control a postscript printer, a modem dialer, and a pseudo terminal management program. *Data Communications Networking Devices* by Held [38] is a general reference on network device management. Finally, *SunOS 5.3 Writing Device Drivers* is a very technical guide to implementing drivers for block and character-oriented devices under Solaris [83].

Chapter 4

Project: *The Token Ring*

> This project explores pipes, forks, and redirection in the context of
> a ring of processes. Such a ring allows simple and interesting simu-
> lations of ring network topologies. The chapter also introduces fun-
> damental ideas of distributed algorithms including processor mod-
> els, pipelining, and parallel computation.

The ring topology is one of the simplest and least expensive configurations for connecting communicating entities. Figure 4.1 illustrates a unidirectional ring structure.
Each entity has one connection for input and one connection for output. Information
circulates around the ring in a clockwise direction. Rings are attractive because interconnection costs on the ring scale linearly—in fact only one additional connection is
needed for each additional node. The latency increases as the number of nodes increases,
because the time it takes for a message to circulate is longer. In most cases the rate at
which nodes can read information from the ring or write information to the ring does not
change with increasing ring size, so the bandwidth is independent of the size of the ring.
Several network standards, including *token ring* (IEEE 802.5), *token bus* (IEEE 802.4),
and *FDDI*, are based on ring connectivity.

This chapter develops an implementation of a ring of processes that communicate via
pipes. The processes represent nodes on the ring. Each process reads from standard input
and writes to standard output. Process $n - 1$ redirects its standard output to the standard
input of process n through a pipe. Once the ring structure is set up, the project can be
extended to simulate network standards or implement algorithms for mutual exclusion
and leader election based on the ring architecture.

Section 4.1 presents a step-by-step development of a simple ring of processes connected by pipes. Section 4.2 tests the ring connectivity and operation by having the

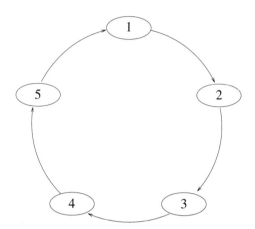

Figure 4.1: A unidirectional ring with five nodes.

ring generate a Fibonnaci sequence. Section 4.3 and Section 4.4 present two alternative approaches for protecting critical sections on the ring. The remaining sections of the chapter describe extensions exploring different aspects of network communication, distributed processing, and parallel algorithms. The extensions in a particular section are independent of those described in other sections.

4.1 Forming a Ring

This section develops a ring of processes starting with a ring containing a single process. The figures use [0] to designate standard input and [1] to designate standard output. Be sure to follow the POSIX standard and use STDIN_FILENO and STDOUT_FILENO when referring to these file descriptors in program code.

Example 4.1

The following code segment connects the standard output of a process to its standard input through a pipe. Error checking is omitted for simplicity.

```
#include <unistd.h>
int fd[2];

pipe(fd);
dup2(fd[0], STDIN_FILENO);
dup2(fd[1], STDOUT_FILENO);
close(fd[0]);
close(fd[1]);
```

Figures 4.2–4.4 illustrate the status of the process of Example 4.1 The numeric values in square brackets (e.g., [0]) are indices of the process file descriptor table. The entries in the file descriptor table are pointers to entries in the system file table. For example, *pipe a write* in entry [4] means "a pointer to the write entry in the system file table for *pipe a*," and *standard input* in entry [0] means "a pointer to the entry in the system file table corresponding to the default device for standard input"—usually the keyboard.

Figure 4.2 depicts the file descriptor table after *pipe a* has been created. File descriptor entries [3] and [4] point to system file table entries that were created by the pipe call. A program can write to the pipe at this point by using a file descriptor value of 4 in a write.

Figure 4.3 shows the status of the file descriptor table after the dup2's. At this point the program can write to the pipe using either 1 or 4 as the file descriptor value. Figure 4.4 shows the configuration after descriptors 3 and 4 are closed.

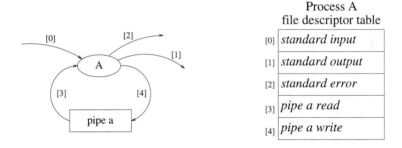

Figure 4.2: The status of the process of Example 4.1 after the pipe(fd) has been executed.

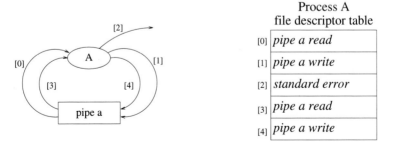

Figure 4.3: The status of the process of Example 4.1 after both dup2's have been executed.

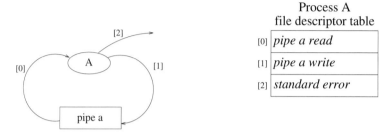

Figure 4.4: The status of the process of Example 4.1 after the `close(fd[0])` and `close(fd[1])` have been executed.

Exercise 4.1

What happens if, after connecting standard output to standard input via a pipe, the process of Example 4.1 executes the following code segment?

```
#include <unistd.h>
#include <stdio.h>
int i;
int myint;

for (i = 0; i < 10; i++) {
    write(STDOUT_FILENO, &i, sizeof(i));
    read(STDIN_FILENO, &myint, sizeof(myint));
    fprintf(stderr, "%d\n", myint);
}
```

Answer:

The code segment outputs the integers from 0 to 9 to the screen (assuming that standard error is displayed on the screen).

Exercise 4.2

What happens if the code in Exercise 4.1 is replaced by the following code?

```
#include <unistd.h>
#include <stdio.h>
int i;
int myint;

for (i = 0; i < 10; i++) {
    read(STDIN_FILENO, &myint, sizeof(myint));
    write(STDOUT_FILENO, &i, sizeof(i));
    fprintf(stderr, "%d\n", myint);
}
```

Answer:

The program hangs on the first `read` because nothing had been written to the pipe yet.

Exercise 4.3

What happens if the code in Exercise 4.1 is replaced by the following?

```
#include <unistd.h>
#include <stdio.h>
int i;
int myint;

for (i = 0; i < 10; i++) {
    printf("%d ", i);
    scanf("%d", &myint);
    fprintf(stderr, "%d\n", myint);
}
```

Answer:

The program hangs on the `scanf` because the pipe reading and writing are fully buffered. The `printf` does not write anything to the pipe until the buffer is full. Put a `fflush(stdout)` after the `printf` to get output.

Example 4.2

The following code segment creates a ring of two processes.

```
#include <unistd.h>
int fd[2];
pid_t haschild;

pipe(fd);
dup2(fd[0], STDIN_FILENO);
dup2(fd[1], STDOUT_FILENO);
close(fd[0]);
close(fd[1]);
pipe(fd);
if (haschild = fork())
    dup2(fd[1], STDOUT_FILENO); /* parent redirects std output */
else
    dup2(fd[0], STDIN_FILENO);  /* child redirects std input */
close(fd[0]);
close(fd[1]);
```

The parent process Example 4.2 redirects standard input through the first pipe to the standard output of the child and redirects standard output through the second pipe to standard input of the child. Figures 4.5–4.8 illustrate the connection mechanism. Figure 4.5 shows the file descriptor table after the parent process A has created a second pipe. Figure 4.6 shows the situation after child B has been forked. At this point neither

of the dup2's after the second pipe have been executed. Figure 4.7 shows the situation
after the parent and child have each executed their last dup2. Process A has redirected
its standard output to write to pipe b, while process B has redirected its standard input
to read from pipe b. Finally, Figure 4.8 shows the status of the file descriptors after all
unneeded descriptors have been closed and a ring of two processes has been formed.

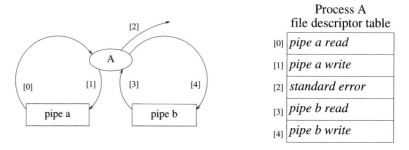

Process A
file descriptor table

[0]	*pipe a read*
[1]	*pipe a write*
[2]	*standard error*
[3]	*pipe b read*
[4]	*pipe b write*

Figure 4.5: The connections to the parent process of Example 4.2 after the second
pipe(fd) has been executed.

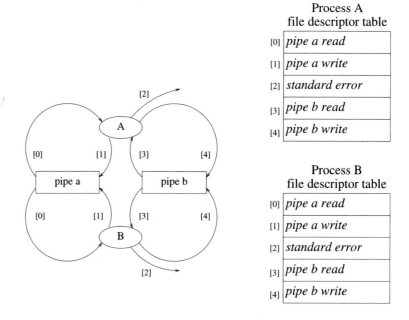

Process A
file descriptor table

[0]	*pipe a read*
[1]	*pipe a write*
[2]	*standard error*
[3]	*pipe b read*
[4]	*pipe b write*

Process B
file descriptor table

[0]	*pipe a read*
[1]	*pipe a write*
[2]	*standard error*
[3]	*pipe b read*
[4]	*pipe b write*

Figure 4.6: The connections of the processes of Example 4.2 after the fork but before
the rest of the if statement. Process A is the parent and process B is the child.

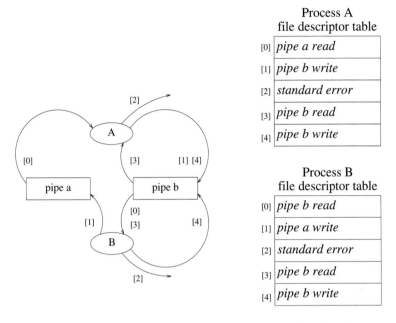

Figure 4.7: The connections of the processes of Example 4.2 after the `if` statement has been executed. Process A is the parent and process B is the child.

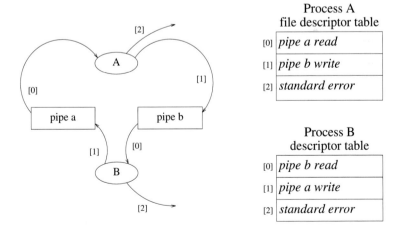

Figure 4.8: The connections of the processes of Example 4.2 after the code segment has been executed. Process A is the parent and process B is the child.

The code of Example 4.2 for forming a ring of two processes can be easily extended to rings of arbitrary size. Program 4.1 sets up a ring of n processes where n is passed on the command line (and converted to the variable nprocs). A total of n pipes are needed. Notice, however, that the program only needs an array of size 2 rather than $2n$ to hold the file descriptors. (Try to write your own code before looking at the ring program.)

Program 4.1: A program to create a ring of processes.

```c
#include <stdio.h>
#include <stdlib.h>
#include <unistd.h>
#include <string.h>
#include <errno.h>
/*
 * Sample C program for generating a unidirectional ring of processes.
 * Invoke this program with a command-line argument indicating the
 * number of processes on the ring.  Communication is done via pipes
 * that connect the standard output of a process to the standard input
 * of its successor on the ring.  After the ring is created, each
 * process identifies itself with its process ID and the process ID
 * of its parent.  Each process then exits.
 */

void main(int argc,  char *argv[ ])
{
    int    i;              /* number of this process (starting with 1)    */
    int    childpid;       /* indicates process should spawn another      */
    int    nprocs;         /* total number of processes in ring           */
    int    fd[2];          /* file descriptors returned by pipe           */
    int    error;          /* return value from dup2 call                 */

    /* check command line for a valid number of processes to generate */
    if ( (argc != 2) || ((nprocs = atoi (argv[1])) <= 0) ) {
        fprintf (stderr, "Usage: %s nprocs\n", argv[0]);
        exit(1);
    }
                           /* connect std input to std output via a pipe */
    if (pipe (fd) == -1) {
        perror("Could not create pipe");
        exit(1);
    }
    if ((dup2(fd[0], STDIN_FILENO) == -1) ||
        (dup2(fd[1], STDOUT_FILENO) == -1)) {
        perror("Could not dup pipes");
        exit(1);
    }
    if ((close(fd[0]) == -1) || (close(fd[1]) == -1)) {
```

```
      perror("Could not close extra descriptors");
      exit(1);
  }
       /* create the remaining processes with their connecting pipes */
  for (i = 1; i < nprocs;  i++) {
     if (pipe (fd) == -1) {
        fprintf(stderr,"Could not create pipe %d: %s\n",
            i, strerror(errno));
        exit(1);
     }
     if ((childpid = fork()) == -1) {
        fprintf(stderr, "Could not create child %d: %s\n",
            i, strerror(errno));
        exit(1);
     }
     if (childpid > 0)          /* for parent process, reassign stdout */
         error = dup2(fd[1], STDOUT_FILENO);
     else
         error = dup2(fd[0], STDIN_FILENO);
     if (error == -1) {
        fprintf(stderr, "Could not dup pipes for iteration %d: %s\n",
               i, strerror(errno));
        exit(1);
     }
     if ((close(fd[0]) == -1) || (close(fd[1]) == -1)) {
        fprintf(stderr, "Could not close extra descriptors %d: %s\n",
               i, strerror(errno));
        exit(1);
     }
     if (childpid)
        break;
  }
                             /* say hello to the world */
  fprintf(stderr,"This is process %d with ID %d and parent id %d\n",
      i, (int)getpid(), (int)getppid());
  exit (0);
}     /* end of main program here */
```

_____ **Program 4.1** _____

The following exercises test and modify Program 4.1. For each modification, make a new copy of the program. Suggested names for the executables are shown in parentheses.

- Run the program shown in Program 4.1 (ring).

- Create a makefile with descriptions for compiling and linting the program. Use make to compile the program. Add targets for additional parts of this project. (Refer to Section A.3 if unfamiliar with the make utility.)

- Make any corrections required to eliminate all lint errors and warning messages. (Refer to Section A.6 if unfamiliar with the `lint` utility.)

- Run `ring` for several values of the command-line argument and observe what happens as the number of processes in the ring varies from 1 to 20.

- Modify the original program by putting in a `wait` system call before the final `fprintf` statement (`ring1`). How does this affect the output of the program?

- Modify the original program by putting in a `wait` system call after the final `fprintf` statement (`ring2`). How does this affect the output of the program?

- Replace the `fprintf` statement in the original program, `ring`, with calls to `sprintf` and `prtastr` (`ring3`). Write the function

  ```
  void prtastr(const char *s, int fd, int n);
  ```

  which prints the `s` string one character at a time to the file specified by descriptor `fd` using `write`. After each character is output, `prtastr` executes the following loop:

  ```
  for (i = 0; i < n; i++);
  ```

  This loop just wastes some CPU time. Use `prtastr` to output the string to standard error. The value of `n` used by `prtastr` is passed as an optional command-line argument to `ring3`. The default value for this parameter is 1. (The single character at a time gives the ring processes more opportunity to interleave their output.) Run the program with a value of `n` that causes a small, but barely noticeable, delay between the output of characters.

- Compare the results of running the modified program `ring3` if
  * A `wait` is inserted before the call to `prtastr` (`ring4`).

  * A `wait` is inserted after the call to `prtastr` (`ring5`).

- Modify `ring1` as follows:
  * Before the `wait`, each process allocates an ID array of `nprocs` elements to hold the IDs of all the processes on the ring. The process puts its own process ID in element zero of the array and sets its variable `next_ID` to its process ID.

  * Do the following for `k` going from 1 to `nproc - 1`:
    ▪ Write `next_ID` to standard output.

    ▪ Read `next_ID` from standard input.

    ▪ Insert `next_ID` into position `k` of the ID array.

* Replace the `fprintf` after the `wait` with a loop that outputs the contents of the ID array to standard error in a readable format. This output tests the ring connectivity, since the ID array contains the processes in the order that they appear upstream from a given process.

- Modify `ring1` to be a bidirectional ring (information can flow in either direction between neighbors on the ring). Test the connections by accumulating ID arrays for each direction.

- Modify `ring1` to create a bidirectional torus of processes. Accumulate ID arrays to test connectivity. A torus has a two-dimensional structure. It is like a mesh except that the processes at the ends are connected together. The n^2 processes are arranged in n rings in each dimension. Each process has four connections (North, South, East, and West).

4.2 Simple Communication

Section 4.1 developed the connections for a ring of processes. This section develops a simple application in which processes generate a sequence of Fibonacci numbers on the ring. A sequence of Fibonacci numbers is generated by summing the last two numbers in the sequence to produce the next number.

In this project, the processes pass information in character string format. The original parent sends the string `"1 1"` representing the first two Fibonacci numbers. The other processes decode this string, calculate the next Fibonacci number and send a string representing the last two Fibonacci numbers calculated to the next process, display the result on standard error, and exit. The original parent exits after receiving a string and displaying the numbers received.

The following challenge makes the problem more interesting. Write the program in such a way that it handles the largest number of processes and still calculates all Fibonacci numbers exactly until an overflow occurs. If an overflow occurs, the process should detect the overflow, display a message on standard error, and send `"0 0"` to the next process. Attempt to calculate the largest Fibonacci number possible.

Start with the original `ring` of Program 4.1 and replace the `fprintf` with code to read two integers from standard input in the string format described below, calculate the next integer in a Fibonacci sequence, and write the result to standard output.

- Each string is the ASCII representation of two integers separated by a single space.

- The original parent writes out the string "`1 1`", representing two ones and then reads a string.

- All other processes first read a string and then write a string.

- Fibonacci numbers satisfy the formula $x_{n+1} = x_n + x_{n-1}$. Each process receives two numbers (e.g., a followed by b) calculates c = a + b, and writes b followed by c as a null-terminated string.
- After sending the string to standard output, the process writes a single-line message to standard error in the form

  ```
  Process i with PID x and parent PID y received a b and sent b c.
  ```
- After sending the message to standard error, the process exits.

Try to write the program in such a way that it handles the largest possible number of processes and still calculates the Fibonacci numbers correctly. The execution either runs out of processes or some process generates a numeric overflow when calculating the next number. Attempt to detect this overflow and send the string "0 0" if an overflow occurs.

Notes: The program should be able to calculate Fib(46) = 1, 836, 311, 903 using 45 processes or Fib(47) = 2, 971, 215, 073 using 46 processes. It may even be able to calculate Fib(78) = 8, 944, 394, 323, 791, 464 using 77 processes. With a little extra work, the program can compute higher values. A possible approach for detecting overflow is to halve the result and compare that value to one obtained when the values to be added are first halved and then summed.

This program puts a heavy load on the CPU of a machine. Don't try this project with more than a few processes unless running on a dedicated computer. Also, on some systems, a limit on the number of processes for a user may interfere with running the program for a large number of processes.

4.3 Mutual Exclusion with Tokens

All of the processes on the ring share the standard error device, and the call to `ptrastr` described in Section 4.1 is a critical section for these processes. A simple strategy for granting exclusive access to a shared device is based on tokens. The token can be a single character which is passed around the ring. When a given process acquires the token (reads the character from standard input), it has exclusive access to the shared device. When that process completes its use of the shared device, it writes the character to standard output so that the next process in the ring can acquire the token. The token algorithm for mutual exclusion is similar to the speaking stick (or a conch [35]) used in some cultures to enforce order at meetings. Only the person who holds the stick can speak.

The acquisition of mutual exclusion starts when the first process writes a token (just a single character) to its standard output. From then on the processes use the following strategy:

- Read the token from standard input.

- Access the shared device.
- Write the token to standard output.

If a process does not wish to access the shared device, it merely passes the token on.

What happens to the above algorithm at the end? After a process has completed writing its messages to standard error, it must continue passing the token until all of the other processes on the ring are done. One strategy for detecting termination is to replace the character token by an integer. The initial token has a zero value. If a process finishes an access but still wishes to access the shared device at a later time, it just passes the token unchanged. When a process no longer wishes to access the shared device, it performs the following shutdown procedure:

- Read the token.
- Increment the token.
- Write the token.
- Repeat until the token has value equal to the number of processes in the ring:
  - ∗ Read the token.
  - ∗ Write the token.
- Exit.

The repeat section of the shutdown procedure has the effect of forcing the process to wait until everyone is finished. This strategy requires that the number of processes on the ring be known.

Implement and test mutual exclusion with tokens as follows:

- Start with version `ring3` of the ring program from Section 4.1
- Implement mutual exclusion for standard error using the integer token method just described but without the shutdown procedure. The critical section should include the call to `prtastr`.
- Test the program with different values of the command-line arguments. In what order do the messages come out and why?
- Incorporate variation into the tests by having each process repeat the critical section a random number of times between 0 and r. Pass r as a command-line argument. Before each call to `prtastr`, read the token. After calling `prtastr`, write the token. When done with all output, execute a loop that just passes the token. (Hint: Read the man page on `drand48` and its related functions. The `drand48` function generates a pseudorandom double in the range $[0, 1)$. If `drand48` generates a value of x, then $y = $ `(int)(x*n)` is an integer satisfying $0 \leq y < n$.) Use the process ID for a seed so that the processes use independent pseudorandom numbers.
- The messages that each process writes to standard error should include the process ID and the time the operation began. Use `time` function to obtain a time in seconds. (See page 206 in Chapter 6 for a description of `time`.)

4.4 Mutual Exclusion by Voting

One problem with the token method is that it generates continuous traffic (a form of busy waiting) even when no process wants to enter its critical section. If all the processes want to enter their critical sections, access is granted by relative position as the token travels around the ring. An alternative approach uses an algorithm of Chang and Roberts for extrema finding [19]. Processes that want to enter their critical sections conduct a vote to see which process obtains access. This method only generates traffic when a process wants exclusive access and can be modified to accommodate a variety of priority schemes in the determination of which process goes next.

Each process that is contending for mutual exclusion generates a voting message with a unique two-part ID. The first part of the ID is called the sequence number, and it is based on a priority. The second part of the ID, the process ID, is used to break ties if two processes have the same priority. Examples of priority include sequence numbers based on the current clock time or on the number of times that the process has acquired mutual exclusion in the past. In each of these strategies the lower value corresponds to a higher priority. Use the latter strategy.

To vote, the process writes its ID message on the ring. Each process that is not participating in the vote merely passes the incoming ID messages to the next process on the ring. When a process that is voting receives an ID message, it bases its actions on the following:

- If the incoming message has a higher ID (lower priority) than its own vote, it throws away the incoming message.

- If the incoming message has a lower ID (higher priority) than its own vote, it forwards the message.

- If the incoming message is its own message, the process has acquired mutual exclusion and can begin the critical section. (Convince yourself that the winner is the process whose ID message is the lowest for that ballot.)

A process relinquishes mutual exclusion by sending a release message around the ring. Once a process detects that the vote has started either because it initiated the request or because it received a message, it cannot initiate another vote until it detects a release message. Thus, of the processes that decided earliest to participate, the process that received access the fewest times in the past wins the election.

Implement the voting algorithm for exclusive access to standard error. Incorporate random values of the delay value which is the last argument in `prtastr` function defined in Section 4.1. Devise a strategy for graceful exit after all of the processes have completed their output.

4.5 Leader Election on an Anonymous Ring

Specifications of distributed algorithms refer to the entities that execute the algorithm as *processes* or *processors*. Such algorithms often specify an underlying processor model in terms of a finite-state machine. The processor models are classified by how the state transitions are driven (synchrony) and whether the processors are labeled.

In the *synchronous processor model* the processors proceed in lock step and state transitions are clock-driven. In the *asynchronous processor model* state transitions are message-driven. The receipt of a message on a communication link triggers a change in processor state. The processor may send messages to its neighbors, perform some computation, or halt as a result of the incoming message. On any given link between processors, the messages arrive in the order they were sent. The messages incur a finite, but unpredictable, transmission delay.

A system of communicating UNIX processes connected by pipes, such as the ring of Program 4.1, is an example of an asynchronous system. A massively parallel SIMD (single instruction multiple data) machine such as the CM-2 is an example of a synchronous system.

A processor model must also specify whether the individual processors are labeled or whether they are indistinguishable. In an *anonymous system* the processors have no distinguishing characteristic. In general, algorithms involving systems of anonymous processors or processes are more complex than the corresponding algorithms for systems of labeled ones.

The UNIX `fork` creates a copy of the calling process. If the parent and child were completely identical, the `fork` would not accomplish anything beyond what would be accomplished by a single process. In fact, UNIX distinguishes the parent and child by their process IDs, and the `fork` returns different values to the parent and child so that each is aware of the other's identity. In other words, the `fork` breaks the symmetry between parent and child by assigning different process IDs. Systems of UNIX processors are not anonymous because the processes can be labeled by their process IDs.

Symmetry-breaking is a general problem in distributed computing in which identical processes (or processors) must be distinguished in order to accomplish useful work. Assignment of exclusive access is an example of symmetry-breaking. One possible way of assigning mutual exclusion is to give preference to the process with the largest process ID. Usually a more equitable method would be better. The voting algorithm of Section 4.4 assigns mutual exclusion to the process that has acquired it the fewest number of times in the past. The algorithm uses the process ID only in the case of ties.

Leader election is another example of a symmetry-breaking algorithm. Leader election algorithms are used in some networks to designate a particular processor to partition the network, regenerate tokens, or perform other operations. For example, what happens in a token-ring network if the processor holding the token crashes? When the crashed processor comes back up, it does not have a token and activity on the network comes to a standstill. One of the nonfaulty processors must take the initiative to generate another token. Who should decide which processor is in charge?

There are no deterministic algorithms for electing a leader on an anonymous ring. This section discusses the implementation of a probabilistic leader-election algorithm for an anonymous ring. The algorithm is an asynchronous version of the synchronous algorithm proposed in [42].

Itai and Roteh [42] proposed a probabilistic algorithm for leader election on an anonymous synchronous ring of size n. The synchronous version of the algorithm proceeds in phases.

- Phase zero:
    * Set local variable `m` to n.
    * Set `active` to `TRUE`.
- Phase k:
    * If `active` is `TRUE`:
        ▪ Choose a random number, `x`, between between 1 and `m`.
        ▪ If the number chosen was 1, send a one-bit message around the ring.
    * Count the number of one-bit messages received in the next $n-1$ clock pulses:
        ▪ If only one active process chose 1, the election is completed.
        ▪ If no active processes chose 1, go to the next phase with no change.
        ▪ If p processes chose 1, set `m` to p. If the process is active and it did not choose 1, set its local `active` to `FALSE`.

In summary, on each phase the active processes pick a random number between 1 and the number of active processes. Any process that picks a 1 is active on the next round. If no one picks a 1 on a given round, the active processes try again. The probability of a particular process picking a 1 increases as the number of active processes decreases. On the average, the algorithm eliminates processes from contention at a rapid rate. Itai and Roteh showed that the expected number of phases needed to choose a leader on a ring of size n is less than $e \approx 2.718$ independent of n.

Implement a simulation of this leader-election algorithm to measure the probability distribution $J(n, k)$ which is the probability that it takes k phases to elect a leader on a ring of size n.

The implementation has to address two problems. The first problem is that the algorithm is phrased for a synchronous ring, but the implementation is on an asynchronous ring. Asynchronous rings clock on the messages received (i.e., each time a process reads a message, it updates its clock). The processes must read messages at the correct point in the algorithm or they lose synchronization. Inactive processes must still write clock messages.

A second difficulty arises because the theoretical convergence of the algorithm relies on the processes having independent streams of random numbers. In practice the processes use a pseudorandom-number generator with an appropriate seed. The processes are supposedly identical, but if they start with the same seed, the algorithm will not work. The implementation can cheat by using the process ID to generate a seed, but ultimately it should include a method of generating numbers based on the system clock or other system hardware. (The first few sections of Chapter 6 discuss system calls for accessing the system clock and timers.)

4.6 Token Ring for Communication

This section develops a simulation of communication on a token-ring network. Each process on the ring now represents an IMP (Interface Message Processor) of a node on the network. The IMP handles message passing and network control for the host of the node. Each IMP process creates a pair of pipes to communicate with its host process as shown in Figure 4.9. The host is represented by a child process forked from the IMP.

Each IMP waits for messages from its host and from the ring. For simplicity, a message consists of five integers—a message type, the ID of the source IMP, the ID of the destination IMP, a status, and a message number. The possible message types are defined by the enumeration type `msg_t`:

```
typedef enum msg_const{TOKEN, HOST2HOST,
            IMP2HOST, HOST2IMP, IMP2IMP} msg_t;
```

The IMP must read a `TOKEN` message from the ring before it writes any message it originates to the ring. When it receives an acknowledgment of its message, it writes a new `TOKEN` message on the ring. The acknowledgments are indicated in the status member which is of type `msg_status_t` defined by

```
typedef enum msg_const_source{NONE, NEW, ACK} msg_status_t;
```

The IMP waits for a message from either its host or from the ring. When an IMP detects that the host wants to send a message, it reads the message into a temporary buffer and sets the `got_msg` flag. Once the `got_msg` flag is set, the IMP cannot read any additional messages from the host until the `got_msg` flag is clear.

When the IMP detects a message from the network, its actions depend on the type of message. If the IMP reads a `TOKEN` message and it has a host message to forward (`got_msg` is set), the IMP writes the host message to the network. If the IMP has no

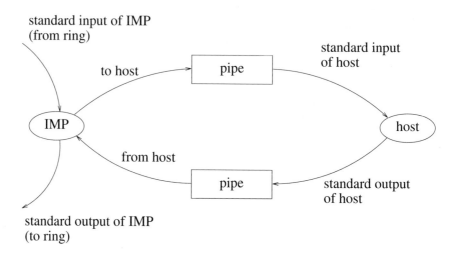

Figure 4.9: The IMP-host structure.

message to send (`got_msg` is clear), it writes the TOKEN message on the network.

If the IMP reads a message other than a TOKEN message from the ring, its actions depend on the source and destination IDs in the message.

- If the source ID of the message matches the IMP's ID, the message was its own. The IMP prints a message to standard error indicating whether the message was received by the destination. In any case the IMP writes a TOKEN message to the ring and clears `got_msg`.

- If the destination ID of the message matches the IMP's ID, the message is for the IMP or the IMP's host. The IMP prints a status message to standard error indicating the type of message. The IMP changes the status of the message to ACK and writes the message to the ring.

- Otherwise, the IMP writes the message to the ring unchanged.

The actual IEEE 802.5 token-ring protocol is more complicated than this. Instead of fixed-length messages, the IMPs use a token-holding timer set to a prespecified value when transmission starts. An IMP can transmit until the timer expires, so messages can be quite long. There can also be a priority scheme [84]. In the actual token-ring protocol, one IMP is designated as the active monitor for the ring. It periodically issues control frames to tell the other stations that the active monitor is present. The active monitor detects whether a token has been lost and is responsible for regenerating tokens. All of the stations periodically send `standby-monitor-present` control frames downstream to detect breaks in the ring.

For the first part of this project, start with Program 4.1. Modify it so that after the ring is created, each IMP process creates two pipes and a child host process as shown in Figure 4.9. Redirect standard output and standard input of the child host as shown in the figure. Write and test a separate program called `hostgen` which has two command-line arguments: an integer process number `n` and an integer sleep time `s`. The `hostgen` program does the following in a loop:

- Sleeps a random number of seconds between 0 and s.
- Writes a random integer between 0 and n to standard output.

For the second part of this project, again start with Program 4.1. Change the program so that the child host `exec`'s the program `hostgen` with the appropriate command-line arguments. The IMP enters an infinite loop to monitor its possible inputs using `select`. When input is available, the IMP performs the simple token-ring protocol described above.

4.7 A Pipelined Preprocessor

The C preprocessor, `cpp`, preprocesses C source code so that the C compiler itself does not have to worry about certain things. For example, if a C program has a line such as

```
#define BUFSIZE 250
```

`cpp` replaces all instances of the token `BUFSIZE` by `250`. The C preprocessor deals with tokens, so it does not replace an occurrence of `BUFSIZE1` with `2501`. This behavior is clearly needed for C source code. It is possible to get `cpp` into a loop with something like

```
#define BUFSIZE BUFSIZE + 1
```

Different versions of `cpp` handle this differently.

In other situations the program may not be dealing with tokens and might replace any occurrence of a string, even if that string is part of a token or consists of several tokens. One method of handling the loops that may be generated by recursion is not to perform any additional test on a string that has already been replaced. This method fails on something as simple as

```
#define BUFSIZE 250
#define BIGGERBUFSIZE BUFSIZE + 1
```

One inefficient way to handle this is to make several passes through the input file, one for each `#define` and make the replacements sequentially. The processing can be done more efficiently (and possibly in parallel) with a pipeline. Figure 4.10 shows a four-stage pipeline. Each stage in the pipeline applies a transformation to its input and then outputs the result for input to the next stage. A pipeline resembles an assembly line in manufacturing.

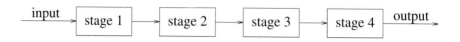

Figure 4.10: A four-stage pipeline.

This section develops a pipeline of preprocessors based on the ring of Program 4.1. To simplify the programming, the preprocessors just convert single characters to strings of characters.

- Write a function `pre_process_char` which has the following prototype:

  ```
  int pre_process_char(int fdin, int fdout, char inchar,
                       char *outstr);
  ```

  The `pre_process_char` function reads from file descriptor `fdin` until an end-of-file and writes to file descriptor `fdout`, translating any occurrence of the character `inchar` into the string `outstr`. It returns 0 if successful and −1 if not. Write a driver to test this program before using it with the ring.

- Modify Program 4.1 so that it now takes four command-line arguments (`ringpp`). Run the program as follows:

  ```
  ringpp n conf.in file.in file.out
  ```

  The value of the command-line argument `n` specifies the number of stages in the pipeline. It corresponds to `nprocs - 2` in Program 4.1. The original parent is responsible for generating pipeline input by reading `file.in` and the last child is responsible for removing output from the pipeline and writing it to `file.out`. Before `ringpp` creates the ring, the original parent opens the file `conf.in`, reads in `n` lines each containing a character and a string, and stores this information in an array.

  Assume that `n` is always less than or equal to `MAXPROCS` and each translation string contains at most `MAXSTR` characters including the string terminator. The `ringpp` program reads the `conf.in` file before forking any children so that the information in the array is available to all of the children.

- The original parent is responsible for copying the contents of the `file.in` input file to its standard output. When it encounters end-of-file on `file.in`, the process exits. The original parent generates the input for the pipeline and does not perform any pipeline processing.

- The last child is responsible for removing output from the pipeline. The process copies data from its standard input to `file.out`, but it does not perform any pipeline processing. The process exits when it encounters an end-of-file on its standard input.
- For `i` between 2 and `n + 1`, child process `i` uses the information in line `(i-1)` of the translation array to translate a character to a string. Each child process acts like a filter, reading the input from standard input, making the substitution, and writing the result to standard output. Call the function `pre_process_char` to process the input. When it receives an end-of-file on input, each process closes its standard output file and exits.
- After making sure that the program is working correctly, try it with a big file (many megabytes) and a moderate number (10 to 20) of processes.
- If possible, try the program on a multiprocessor machine to measure the speedup. (See Section 4.8 for a definition of speedup.)

Each stage of the pipeline reads from its standard input and writes to its standard output. The problem can be generalized by having each stage `execvp` an arbitrary process instead of calling the same function. The `conf.in` file could contain the command lines to `execvp` instead of the table of string replacements specific to this problem.

It is also possible to have the original parent handle both generation of pipeline input and removal of its output. In this case the parent opens `file.in` and `file.out` after forking its child. The process must now handle input from two sources: `file.in` and its standard input. It is possible to use `select` to handle this, but the problem is more complicated than might first appear. The process must also monitor its standard output with `select` because a pipe can fill up and block additional writes. If the process blocks while writing to standard output, it is not able to remove output from the final stage of the pipeline. The pipeline might deadlock in this case. The original parent is a perfect candidate for threading as discussed in Chapters 9 and 10.

4.8 Parallel Ring Algorithms

Parallel processing refers to the partitioning of a problem so pieces of the problem can be solved in parallel, thereby reducing the overall execution time. One measure of the effectiveness of the partitioning is the speedup, $S(n)$, which is defined as

$$S(n) = \frac{\text{execution time with one processor}}{\text{execution time with } n \text{ processors}}$$

Ideally the execution is inversely proportional to the number of processors, or the speedup $S(n)$ is just n. Unfortunately, linear speedup is a rare achievement in practical settings for a number of reasons. There is always a portion of the work that cannot be done in parallel, and the parallel version of the algorithm incurs overhead when the processors synchronize or communicate to exchange information.

The types of problems that are most amenable to parallelization have a regular structure and involve exchange of information following well-defined patterns. This section looks at two parallel algorithms for the ring: image filtering and matrix multiplication. The image filtering belongs to a class of problems in which each processor performs its calculation independently or by exchanging information with its two neighbors. In matrix multiplication, a processor must obtain information from all of the other processors in order to complete the calculation. However, the information can be propagated by a simple shift. Other parallel algorithms can also be adapted for efficient execution on the ring, but the communication patterns are more complicated than those of the examples done here.

4.8.1 Image Filtering

A filter is a transformation applied to an image. Filtering may remove noise, enhance detail, or blur image features depending on the type of transformation. This discussion considers a greyscale digital image represented by an $n \times n$ array of bytes. Common *spatial filters* replace each pixel value in such an image by a function of the original pixel and its neighbors. The filter algorithm specifies the neighborhood that contributes to the calculation by a mask. Figure 4.11 shows a 3×3 mask of nearest neighbors. This particular mask represents a *linear filter* because the function is a weighted average of the pixels in the mask. (In contrast a nonlinear filter cannot be written as a linear combination of pixels under the mask. Taking the median of the neighboring pixels is an example of a nonlinear filter.)

$$\frac{1}{9} \times \begin{array}{|c|c|c|} \hline 1 & 1 & 1 \\ \hline 1 & 1 & 1 \\ \hline 1 & 1 & 1 \\ \hline \end{array}$$

Figure 4.11: A mask for applying a smoothing filter to an image.

The values in the mask are the weights applied to each pixel in the average when the mask is centered on the pixel being transformed. In Figure 4.11 all of the weights are $1/9$. If $a_{i,j}$ is the pixel at position (i, j) of the original image and $b_{i,j}$ is the pixel at the corresponding position in the filtered image, the mask in Figure 4.11 represents the pixel transformation

$$b_{i,j} = \frac{1}{9}[a_{i-1,j-1} + a_{i,j-1} + a_{i+1,j-1} + a_{i-1,j} + a_{i,j} + a_{i+1,j} + a_{i-1,j+1} + a_{i,j+1} + a_{i+1,j+1}]$$

This transformation blurs sharp edges and eliminates contrast in an image. In filtering terminology, the mask represents a low-pass filter because it keeps slowly varying or low-frequency components and eliminates high-frequency components. The mask in Figure 4.12 is a high-pass filter which enhances edges and darkens backgrounds.

$$\frac{1}{9} \times \begin{array}{|c|c|c|} \hline -1 & -1 & -1 \\ \hline -1 & 8 & -1 \\ \hline -1 & -1 & -1 \\ \hline \end{array}$$

Figure 4.12: A mask for applying a difference filter to an image.

The ring of processes is a natural architecture for parallelizing the types of filters described by masks such as those of Figures 4.11 and 4.12. Suppose a ring of n processes is to filter an $n \times n$ image. Each process can be responsible for computing the filter for one row or one column of the image. Since C stores arrays in row-major format (i.e., the elements of a two-dimensional array are stored linearly in memory by first storing all elements of row zero followed by all elements of row one, and so on), it is more convenient to have each process handle one row.

To perform the filtering operation in process p, do the following:

- Obtain rows $p - 1$, p, and $p + 1$ of the original image. Represent the pixel values of three rows of the original image by an array

    ```
    unsigned char a[n+2][3];
    ```

    Put the image pixels of row $p - 1$ in `a[1][0]...a[n][0]`. Set `a[0][0]` and `a[n+1][0]` to 0 in order to compute the result for border pixels without worrying about array bounds. Handle rows p and $p+1$ similarly. If p is 1, set `a[0][0]...a[n+1][0]` to 0 corresponding to the row above the image. If p is n, set `a[0][2]...a[n+1][2]` to 0 corresponding to the row of pixels below the bottom of the image.

- Compute the new values for the pixels in row p and store the new values in an array:

    ```
    unsigned char b[n+2];
    ```

To compute the value of `b[i]`, use the formula

```
int sum;
int i;
int j;
int m;

sum = 0;
for (j = 0; j < 3; j++)
    for (m = i - 1; m < i + 2; m++)
        sum += a[m][j];
b[i] = (unsigned char) (sum/9);
```

The value of `b[i]` is the pixel value $b_{p,i}$ in the new image.
- Insert `b` in row p of the new image.

The above description is purposely vague about where the original image comes from and where it goes. This I/O is the heart of the problem. The simplest approach is to have each process read the part of the input image it needs from a file and write the resulting row to another file. In this approach the processes are completely independent of each other. Assume that the original image is stored as a binary file of bytes in row-major order. Use the system call `lseek` to position the file offset to the appropriate place in the file and use `read` to input the three needed rows. After computing the new image, use `lseek` and `write` to write the row in the appropriate place in the image. Be sure to open the input and output image files after the `fork` so that each process on the ring has its own file offsets.

A Bidirectional Ring

An alternative approach uses nearest-neighbor communication. Process p on the ring only reads in the pth row. It then writes the pth row to its neighbors on either side and reads rows $p - 1$ and $p + 1$ from its neighbors. This exchange of information requires the ring to be bidirectional, that is, a process node can read or write from the links in each direction. (Alternatively, replace each link in the ring by two unidirectional links, one in each direction.) It is probably overkill to implement the linear filter using nearest-neighbor communication, but several related problems require it. For example, the explicit method of solving the heat equation on an $n \times n$ grid uses a nearest-neighbor update of the form

$$b_{i,j} = a_{i,j} + D\left[a_{i-1,j} + a_{i+1,j} + a_{i,j-1} + a_{i,j+1}\right]$$

The constant D is related to the rate that heat diffuses on the grid. The array $b_{i,j}$ is the new heat distribution on the grid after one unit of time has lapsed. It becomes the initial array $a_{i,j}$ for the next time step. Clearly the program should not write the grid out to disk between each time step and here a nearest-neighbor exchange is needed.

Block Computation

Another important issue in parallel processing is the granularity of the problem and how it maps into the number of processors. The ring is typically under 100 processors while the images of interest may be 1024×1024 pixels. In this case each processor computes the filter for a block of rows.

Suppose the ring has m processes and the image has $n \times n$ pixels where $n = qm + r$. The first r processes are responsible for $q + 1$ rows and the remaining processes are responsible for q rows. Each processor computes the range of rows that it is responsible for from q and r. Pass m and n as command-line arguments to the original process in the ring.

4.8.2 Matrix Multiplication

Another problem that lends itself to parallel execution on a ring is matrix multiplication. To multiply two $n \times n$ matrices, A and B, form a third matrix C which has an entry in position (i, j) given by

$$c_{i,j} = \sum_{k=1}^{n} a_{i,k} b_{k,j}$$

In other words element (i, j) of the result is the product of row i of the first matrix with column j of the second matrix. Start by assuming that there are n processors on the ring. Each input array is stored as a binary file in row-major form. The elements of the array are of type `int`.

One approach to matrix multiplication is for process p to read row p of input file A and column p of input file B. Processor p accumulates row p of the output matrix C. It multiplies row p of A by column p of B and sets $c_{p,p}$ to the resulting value. It then writes column p of matrix B to the ring and reads column $p - 1$ from its neighbor. Process p then computes element $c_{p,p-1}$, and so on.

The row-column is very efficient once the processors have read the columns of B, but since B is stored in row-major form, the file accesses are inefficient if the process is accessing a column of B, since the read must seek for each element. In addition it is likely that matrix multiplication is an intermediate step in a larger calculation that might have the arrays A and B distributed to processes in row-major form. The following algorithm performs matrix multiplication when process p starts with row p of matrix A and row p of matrix B.

Process p is going to compute row p of the result. On each iteration, a row of B contributes one term to the sum needed to calculate each element of row p of the product matrix. Each process eventually needs all of the entries of the B matrix, and it receives the rows of B one at a time from its neighbors.

Use the following arrays:

```
int a[n+1];       /* holds the pth row of A */
int b[n+1];       /* starts with the pth row of B */
int c[n+1];       /* holds the pth row of C */
```

Initialize the elements of `a[]` and `b[]` from their respective files. Initialize `c[]` using

```
for (k = 1; k < n+1; k++)
    c[k] = a[p] * b[k];
```

In process p this accounts for row p of matrix B's contribution to row p of the output matrix C. In the matrix notation $c_{p,k} = a_{p,p}b_{p,k}$. Process p does the following:

```
m = p;
write(STDOUT_FILENO, &b[1], n*sizeof(int));
read(STDIN_FILENO, &b[1], n*sizeof(int));
for (k = 1; k < n+1; k++) {
    if ((m -= 1) == 0)
        m = n;
    c[k] += a[m]*b[k];
}
```

The `read` fills the `b[]` array with the values of the row of B held initially by the processor immediately before it on the ring. One execution of the `for` loop adds the contribution of row $p-1$ of B to row p of the result corresponding to $c_{p,k} = c_{p,k} + a_{p,p-1}b_{p-1,k}$. Execute this code $n-1$ times to multiply the entire array. Write the resulting array c as the pth row of the output file representing C.

4.9 The Flexible Ring

The flexible ring is a ring in which nodes can be added and deleted. The flexibility is useful for fault recovery and for network maintenance.

- Modify the `ring` of Program 4.1 to use named pipes or FIFOs instead of unnamed pipes. Devise an appropriate naming scheme for the pipes.
- Devise and implement a scheme for adding a node after node i in the ring. Pass i on the command line.
- Devise and implement a scheme for deleting a node i in the ring. Pass i on the command line.

After testing the strategies for inserting and deleting nodes, convert the token-ring implementation of Section 4.6 to one using named pipes. Develop a protocol so that any node can initiate a request to add or delete a node. Implement the protocol.

This project leaves most of the specification open. Figure out what it means to insert or delete a node.

4.10 Additional Reading

Early versions of the ring project described in this chapter can be found in [72]. *Local and Metropolitan Area Networks*, 4th ed. by Stallings [84] has a good discussion of the token ring, token bus, and FDDI network standards. Each of these networks is based on a ring architecture. Stallings also discusses the election methods used by these architectures for token regeneration and reconfiguration. The paper "A resilient mutual exclusion algorithm for computer networks" by Nishio et al. [51] analyzes the general problem of regenerating lost tokens in computer networks.

The theoretical literature on distributed algorithms for rings is large. The algorithms of Section 4.4 are based on a paper by Chang and Roberts [19], while the algorithms of Section 4.5 are discussed in Itai and Roteh [42]. A nice theoretical article on anonymous rings is "Computing on an anonymous ring" by Attiya et al. [5]. The book *Introduction to Parallel Computing: Design and Analysis of Algorithms* by Kumar et al. [45] presents a good overview of parallel algorithms and how to map these algorithms onto particular machine architectures.

Part II

Asynchronous Events

Chapter 5

Signals

Few people appreciate the insidious nature of asynchronous events
until they encounter an irreproducible problem. This chapter discusses signals and their effect on processes. The chapter also covers the new POSIX.1b signal handling and asynchronous I/O facilities. The new signal handling is particularly useful, allowing
queueing of signals and the transmittal of additional information
to the signal handler.

A *signal* is a software notification to a process of an event. A signal is *generated*
when the event that causes the signal occurs. A signal is *delivered* when the process takes
action based on that signal. The *lifetime* of a signal is the interval between its generation
and its delivery. A signal that has been generated but not yet delivered is *pending*. There
may be considerable time between signal generation and signal delivery. The process
must be running on a processor at the time action is taken.

A process *catches* a signal if it executes a *signal handler* when the signal is delivered.
A program installs a *signal handler* by calling `sigaction` with the name of a user-
written function or `SIG_DFL` or `SIG_IGN`. The `SIG_DFL` means take the default
action, while `SIG_IGN` means ignore the signal. If the process is set to *ignore* a signal,
the signal is thrown away when it is delivered and it has no effect on the process.

The action taken when a signal is generated depends on the current signal handler for
that signal and on the process *signal mask*. The signal mask contains a list of currently
blocked signals. It is easy to confuse blocking a signal with ignoring a signal. Blocked
signals are not thrown away as ignored signals are. If a pending signal is blocked, it is
delivered when the process unblocks that signal. A program blocks a signal by changing
the process signal mask using `sigprocmask`. A program ignores a signal by setting

the signal handler to `SIG_IGN` using `sigaction`.

This chapter discusses all aspects of POSIX signals. Section 5.1 introduces signals and presents examples of how to generate them. Section 5.2 discusses the signal mask and the blocking of signals, while Section 5.3 covers the catching and ignoring of signals. Section 5.4 shows how a process should block while waiting for the delivery of a signal, and Section 5.5 illustrates basic signal handling through a simple `biff` program. The remaining sections of the chapter cover more advanced signal handling topics. Section 5.6 discusses interactions between system calls and signal handling, Section 5.7 covers `siglongjmp`, Section 5.8 covers the POSIX.1b extension of realtime signals, and Section 5.9 introduces POSIX.1b asynchronous I/O.

5.1 Sending Signals

Every signal has a symbolic name starting with `SIG`. The signal names are defined in the file `signal.h` which any C program using signals must include. The names of the signals represent small integers greater than 0. Table 5.1 lists the required POSIX.1 signals. The default action associated with all of the required signals is to terminate the process abnormally.

Symbol	Meaning
SIGABRT	abnormal termination as initiated by `abort`
SIGALRM	timeout signal as initiated by `alarm`
SIGFPE	error in arithmetic operation as in division by zero
SIGHUP	hang up (death) on controlling terminal (process)
SIGILL	invalid hardware instruction
SIGINT	interactive attention signal
SIGKILL	terminate (cannot be caught or ignored)
SIGPIPE	write on a pipe with no readers
SIGQUIT	interactive termination
SIGSEGV	invalid memory reference
SIGTERM	termination
SIGUSR1	user-defined signal 1
SIGUSR2	user-defined signal 2

Table 5.1: The POSIX.1 required signals.

POSIX.1 also defines an optional group of signals for job control. Shells use these signals to control the interaction of background and foreground processes. If an implementation supports job control (_POSIX_JOB_CONTROL is defined), it must support the signals shown in Table 5.2. The default action for SIGCHLD is ignore. The SIGCONT always continues a stopped process immediately when it is generated (even if SIGCONT is blocked or ignored). The default action for the other job control signals is to stop the process.

POSIX.1 Job Control Signals

Symbol	Meaning
SIGCHLD	indicates child process terminated or stopped
SIGCONT	continue if stopped (done when generated)
SIGSTOP	stop signal (cannot be caught or ignored)
SIGTSTP	interactive stop signal
SIGTTIN	background process attempts to read from controlling terminal
SIGTTOU	background process attempts to write to controlling terminal

Table 5.2: The job control signals control foreground and background processes.

Some signals such as SIGFPE or SIGSEGV are generated when certain errors occur. Other signals are generated by specific calls. A user may send a signal only to processes that he or she owns. Specifically, the real or effective user IDs of the sending and receiving processes must match.

Generate signals from the shell with the kill command. While kill might seem like a bizarre name for a command to send signals, it is not as unreasonable as it seems because many of the signals have a default action of terminating the process.

```
SYNOPSIS

    kill -s signal pid...
    kill -l [exit_status]
    kill [-signal] pid...
                                              POSIX.2, Spec 1170
```

The traditional kill command is listed last in the synopsis. This form takes two command-line arguments, a signal number preceded by a minus sign and a process ID. The form is listed as obsolete in both the POSIX.2 and Spec 1170 standards because it does not follow the guidelines for arguments discussed in Section A.1.2. Use a symbolic name for the signal parameter in these commands by omitting the leading SIG from the corresponding POSIX signal name. Two signals, SIGUSR1 and SIGUSR2, are available for users and do not have a preassigned use.

Example 5.1

> *The following command sends the* `SIGUSR1` *signal to process* 3423.

```
kill -USR1 3423
```

Example 5.2

> *The* `kill -l` *command gives a list of symbolic signal names for the system.*
> *A system running Sun Solaris 2 produced the following sample output.*

```
% kill -l
HUP INT QUIT ILL TRAP ABRT EMT FPE
KILL BUS SEGV SYS PIPE ALRM TERM USR1
USR2 CLD PWR WINCH URG POLL STOP TSTP
CONT TTIN TTOU VTALRM PROF XCPU XFSZ WAITING
LWP FREEZE THAW RTMIN RTMIN+1 RTMIN+2 RTMIN+3 RTMAX-3
RTMAX-2 RTMAX-1 RTMAX
```

Use the `kill` system call from within a C program to send a signal to a process.
This call takes a process ID and a signal number as parameters.

SYNOPSIS

```
#include <sys/types.h>
#include <signal.h>

int kill(pid_t pid, int sig);
```

POSIX.1, Spec 1170

If the `pid` parameter is positive, `kill` sends the specified signal to the process with
that process ID. If the `pid` parameter is negative, `kill` sends the signal to the process
group with group ID equal to |pid|. If `pid` is 0, `kill` sends the signal to members
of the caller's process group. (Chapter 7 discusses process groups.) The `kill` call
returns 0 on success. The `kill` can fail if the caller does not have permission to send
the signal to any of the processes specified by `pid`. In this case, `kill` returns −1
and sets `errno`. For most signals, `kill` determines permissions by comparing the
user IDs of caller and receiver. `SIGCONT` is an exception. For `SIGCONT`, user IDs are
not checked if the `kill` is sent to a process which is in the same session. (Section 7.5
discusses sessions.)

Example 5.3

> *The following code segment sends* `SIGUSR1` *to process* 3423 *.*

```
#include <stdio.h>
#include <sys/types.h>
#include <signal.h>

if (kill(3423, SIGUSR1) == -1)
   perror("Could not send signal");
```

Normally a program would not use a specific process ID such as `3423` of Example 5.3. The usual way to find out relevant process IDs is with `getpid`, `getppid`, `getgpid`, or by saving the return value from `fork`.

Example 5.4

This scenario sounds grim, but a child process can kill its parent by executing the following code segment.

```
#include <stdio.h>
#include <unistd.h>
#include <signal.h>

if (kill(getppid(), SIGTERM) == -1)
    perror ("Error in kill");
```

A process can send a signal to itself with the `raise` function. The `raise` function takes just one parameter, a signal number.

SYNOPSIS

```
#include <signal.h>

int raise(int sig);
```

ISO C, Spec 1170

Example 5.5

The following C statement causes a process to send the `SIGUSR1` *signal to itself.*

```
#include <signal.h>

raise(SIGUSR1);
```

A key press causes a hardware interrupt which is handled by the device driver for the keyboard. This device driver and its associated modules may perform buffering and editing on the keyboard input. Two special characters, the `INTR` and `QUIT` characters, cause the device driver to send a signal to foreground processes. A user can send the `SIGINT` signal to a foreground process by entering the `INTR` character. This user-settable character is often `ctrl-c`. Similarly the user-settable `QUIT` character, which is is often `ctrl-|`, sends the `SIGQUIT` signal.

Example 5.6

The `stty -a` *command reports on the characteristics of the device associated with standard input including the settings of the signal-generating characters. A system running Sun Solaris 2 produced the following output.*

```
% stty -a
speed 9600 baud;
rows = 57; columns = 103; ypixels = 0; xpixels = 0;
eucw 1:0:0:0, scrw 1:0:0:0
intr = ^c; quit = ^|; erase = ^?; kill = ^u;
eof = ^d; eol = <undef>; eol2 = <undef>; swtch = <undef>;
start = ^q; stop = ^s; susp = ^z; dsusp = ^y;
rprnt = ^r; flush = ^o; werase = ^w; lnext = ^v;
-parenb -parodd cs8 -cstopb hupcl cread -clocal -loblk -crtscts
-parext -ignbrk brkint ignpar -parmrk -inpck -istrip -inlcr -igncr
icrnl -iuclc ixon -ixany -ixoff imaxbel
isig icanon -xcase echo echoe echok -echonl -noflsh
-tostop echoctl -echoprt echoke -defecho -flusho -pendin iexten
opost -olcuc onlcr -ocrnl -onocr -onlret -ofill -ofdel
```

The terminal in Example 5.6 interprets ctrl-c as the INTR character. Entering ctrl-c generates the SIGINT signal for the foreground processes. The QUIT character (ctrl-|) generates a SIGQUIT. The SUSP character (ctrl-z above) generates a SIGSTOP, and the DSUSP character (ctrl-y above) generates a SIGCONT.

The alarm function causes a SIGALRM signal to be sent to the calling process after a specified number of real seconds have elapsed.

SYNOPSIS

```
#include <unistd.h>

unsigned int alarm(unsigned int seconds);
```
                                                                POSIX.1, Spec 1170

Requests to alarm are not stacked, so if the program calls alarm before the previous one expires, the alarm is reset to the new value. The alarm function returns the number of seconds remaining on the alarm before the call reset the value. Call alarm with a zero value for seconds to cancel a previous alarm request.

Example 5.7

Since the default action for SIGALRM is to terminate the process, the following program runs for approximately ten seconds of wall-clock time.

```
#include <unistd.h>

void main(void)
{
    alarm(10);
    for ( ; ; ) {
    }
}
```

5.2 The Signal Mask and Signal Sets

A process can temporarily prevent a signal from being delivered by blocking it. Blocked signals do not affect the behavior of the process until they are delivered. The process *signal mask* gives the set of signals that are currently blocked. The signal mask is of type `sigset_t`.

Blocking a signal is different from ignoring a signal. When a process blocks a signal, an occurrence of the signal is held until the process unblocks the signal. A process blocks a signal by modifying its signal mask with `sigprocmask`. When a process ignores a signal, the signal is delivered and the process handles it by throwing it away. The process sets a signal to be ignored by calling `sigaction` with a handler of `SIG_IGN` as described in Section 5.3.

Specify operations (such as blocking or unblocking) on groups of signals using signal sets of type `sigset_t` with the following signal set functions.

```
SYNOPSIS

   #include <signal.h>

   int sigemptyset(sigset_t *set);
   int sigfillset(sigset_t *set);
   int sigaddset(sigset_t *set, int signo);
   int sigdelset(sigset_t *set, int signo);
   int sigismember(const sigset_t *set, int signo);
                                              POSIX.1, Spec 1170
```

The `sigemptyset` function initializes a signal set to contain no signals, while the `sigfillset` initializes a signal set to contain all of the signals. Initialize a signal set by calling either `sigemptyset` or `sigfillset` before using it.

The `sigaddset` puts a specified signal into the set. The `sigdelset` removes a specified signal from the set. The `sigismember` returns 1 if the specified signal is a member of a set and 0 otherwise. The other signal set functions return 0 if successful and −1 on error. Always access signal sets through the signal set functions so that the code is implementation-independent.

Example 5.8

The following code segment initializes signal set `twosigs` *to contain exactly the two signals,* `SIGINT` *and* `SIGQUIT`.

```
#include <signal.h>
sigset_t twosigs;

sigemptyset(&twosigs);
sigaddset(&twosigs, SIGINT);
sigaddset(&twosigs, SIGQUIT);
```

A process can examine or modify its process signal mask with the `sigprocmask` function.

SYNOPSIS

```
#include <signal.h>

int sigprocmask(int how, const sigset_t *set, sigset_t *oset);
```
                                                                                    POSIX.1, Spec 1170

The `how` parameter is an integer indicating the manner in which the signal mask is to be modified. The three possibilities for this parameter of `sigprocmask` are

> `SIG_BLOCK:`   add a collection of signals to those currently blocked.
>
> `SIG_UNBLOCK:`   delete a collection of signals from those currently blocked.
>
> `SIG_SETMASK:`   set the collection of signals being blocked to the collection given.

The `set` parameter of `sigprocmask` points to the set of signals to be used for the modification, and the `oset` parameter is the address of a `sigset_t` variable for holding the set of signals that were blocked before the call to `sigprocmask`. The second or third parameters may be NULL. If the second parameter is NULL, the third parameter provides the current signal mask without modification. If the third parameter is NULL, `sigprocmask` does not return the old value of the process signal mask in `*oset`. If an error occurs, `sigprocmask` returns −1 and sets `errno`. The `sigprocmask` returns 0 if the call was successful.

Example 5.9

The following code segment adds SIGINT *to the set of signals that the process has blocked.*

```
#include <stdio.h>
#include <signal.h>
sigset_t  newsigset;

sigemptyset(&newsigset);              /* start with a fresh set */
sigaddset(&newsigset, SIGINT);        /* add SIGINT to the set */
if (sigprocmask(SIG_BLOCK, &newsigset, NULL) < 0)
   perror("Could not block the signal");
```

If SIGINT is already blocked, the `sigprocmask` of Example 5.9 has no effect.

Example 5.10

The following program displays a message, blocks the SIGINT *signal while doing some useless work, unblocks the signal, and does more useless work. The program repeats this sequence continually in a loop.*

```
#include <stdio.h>
#include <stdlib.h>
#include <unistd.h>
#include <math.h>
#include <signal.h>

void main(int argc,  char * argv[])
{
   double y;
   sigset_t intmask;
   int i, repeat_factor;

   if (argc != 2) {
      fprintf(stderr,"Usage: %s repeat_factor\n", argv[0]);
      exit(1);
   }
   repeat_factor = atoi(argv[1]);
   sigemptyset(&intmask);
   sigaddset(&intmask, SIGINT);
   for( ; ; ) {
      sigprocmask(SIG_BLOCK, &intmask, NULL);
      fprintf(stderr, "SIGINT signal blocked\n");
      for (i = 0; i < repeat_factor; i++) y = sin((double)i);
      fprintf(stderr, "Blocked calculation is finished\n");
      sigprocmask(SIG_UNBLOCK, &intmask, NULL);
      fprintf(stderr, "SIGINT signal unblocked\n");
      for (i = 0; i < repeat_factor; i++) y = sin((double)i);
      fprintf(stderr, "Unblocked calculation is finished\n");
   }
}
```

If a user enters `ctrl-c` while the `SIGINT` is blocked, the program of Example 5.10 finishes the calculation before terminating. If a user types `ctrl-c` while `SIGINT` is unblocked, the program terminates immediately.

Example 5.11

The function `makepair` *takes two pathnames as parameters and creates two named pipes with these names. It returns 0 if successful and −1 if there is an error.*

```
#include <unistd.h>
#include <sys/stat.h>
#include <signal.h>
#include <errno.h>
#define R_MODE S_IRUSR | S_IRGRP | S_IROTH
#define W_MODE S_IWUSR | S_IWGRP | S_IWOTH
#define RW_MODE R_MODE | W_MODE
```

```
int makepair(char *pipe1, char *pipe2)
{
    sigset_t oldmask;
    sigset_t blockmask;
    int returncode = 0;

    sigfillset(&blockmask);
    sigprocmask(SIG_SETMASK, &blockmask, &oldmask);
    if ( ((mkfifo(pipe1, RW_MODE) == -1)
                && (errno != EEXIST)) ||
        ((mkfifo(pipe2, RW_MODE) == -1)
                && (errno != EEXIST)) ) {
        unlink(pipe1);
        unlink(pipe2);
        returncode = -1;
    }
    sigprocmask(SIG_SETMASK, &oldmask, NULL);
    return returncode;
}
```

If there is an error in making either pipe, `makepair` of Example 5.11 unlinks both pipes and returns an error. The function blocks all signals during the creation of the named pipes to be sure that it can deallocate both pipes if there is an error. The function restores the original signal mask before the return. The `if` statement relies on the conditional left-to-right evaluation of `&&` and `||`.

Exercise 5.1
What is wrong with the `makepair` function in Example 5.11?
Answer:
If one of the files already exists, `mkfifo` returns −1 and sets `errno` to `EEXIST`. This function does not determine whether that file was a FIFO or an ordinary file. It is possible for `makepair` to indicate success even if that previously existing file is not a FIFO.

Example 5.12
The following code segment blocks signals during creation of a child. Both the parent and child restore the signal mask to its original value after the `fork`.

```
#include <sys/types.h>
#include <unistd.h>
#include <stdio.h>
#include <stdlib.h>
#include <signal.h>

sigset_t oldmask, blockmask;
pid_t mychild;
```

```
sigfillset(&blockmask);
if (sigprocmask(SIG_SETMASK, &blockmask, &oldmask) == -1) {
   perror("Could not block all signals");
   exit(1);
}
if ((mychild = fork()) == -1) {
   perror("Could not fork child");
   exit(1);
} else if (mychild == 0) {   /* child code here */
      if (sigprocmask(SIG_SETMASK, &oldmask, NULL) == -1){
         perror("Child could not restore signal mask");
         exit(1);
      }
      /* .....rest of child code ..... */
} else {                        /* parent code here */
      if (sigprocmask(SIG_SETMASK, &oldmask, NULL) == -1){
         perror("Parent could not restore signal mask");
         exit(1);
      }
      /* .....rest of parent code ..... */
}
```

Processes inherit the signal mask after both `fork` and `exec`. The child created by the `fork` of Example 5.12 has a copy of the original signal mask saved in `oldmask`. An `exec` overwrites all program variables, so an `exec`'d process cannot restore the original mask once the `exec` takes place.

5.3 Catching and Ignoring Signals—`sigaction`

The `sigaction` function installs signal handlers for a process. A data structure of type `struct sigaction` holds the handler information. The `sigaction` system call has three parameters: the signal number, a pointer to the new handler structure (of type `struct sigaction`), and a pointer to the old structure (also of type `struct sigaction`).

When using `sigaction`, fill `*act` with handler information. The `sigaction` function fills in the `*oact` structure with values corresponding to the old status of the signal. If the first `sigaction` parameter is a `NULL` pointer, nothing is changed. If the program does not need the value of the previous signal handler, pass a `NULL` pointer for `oact`. The `sigaction` system call may seem confusing because it has the same name as the structure used to pass its handler information. When referring to the structure, always use the `struct` keyword.

```
SYNOPSIS

  #include <signal.h>

  int sigaction(int signo, const struct sigaction *act,
                           struct sigaction *oact);

  struct sigaction {
     void (*sa_handler)();  /* SIG_DFL, SIG_IGN, or
                               pointer to function */
     sigset_t sa_mask;      /* additional signals to be blocked
                               during execution of handler */
     int sa_flags;          /* special flags and options */
  };
                                                      POSIX.1, Spec 1170
```

The above `struct sigaction` structure shows three members. POSIX.1b specifies an additional member for realtime signals (Section 5.8). Do not define this structure in a program but instead use the definition given in `signal.h`.

Example 5.13

The following code segment sets the signal handler for SIGINT *to* mysighand.

```
#include <signal.h>
#include <stdio.h>
struct  sigaction  newact;

newact.sa_handler = mysighand;   /* set the new handler */
sigemptyset(&newact.sa_mask);    /* no other signals blocked */
newact.sa_flags = 0;             /* no special options */
if (sigaction(SIGINT, &newact, NULL) == -1)
   perror("Could not install SIGINT signal handler");
```

A signal handler is an ordinary function that returns `void` and has one integer parameter. When the operating system delivers the signal, it sets this parameter to the number of the signal that was delivered. Most signal handlers ignore this value, but it is possible to have a single signal handler for many signals. The usefulness of signal handlers is limited by the inability to pass values to them. This capability has been added to the realtime signals discussed in Section 5.8.

Two special values of the `sa_handler` member of `struct sigaction` are `SIG_DFL` and `SIG_IGN`. The `SIG_DFL` value specifies that `sigaction` should install the default handler for the signal. The `SIG_IGN` values specifies that the process should handle the signal by ignoring it.

Example 5.14

The following code segment causes the process to ignore SIGINT *if it is using the default handler for this signal.*

```
#include <signal.h>
#include <stdio.h>
struct  sigaction  act;
                                           /* Find old signal handler */
if (sigaction(SIGINT, NULL, &act) == -1)
   perror("Could not get old handler for SIGINT");
else if (act.sa_handler == SIG_DFL) {            /* ignore SIGINT */
   act.sa_handler = SIG_IGN;      /* set the new handler to ignore */
   if (sigaction(SIGINT, &act, NULL) == -1)
      perror("Could not ignore SIGINT");
}
```

Example 5.15

The following code segment sets up a signal handler that catches the SIGINT
signal generated by `ctrl-c`.

```
#include <sys/types.h>
#include <unistd.h>
#include <signal.h>
#include <string.h>

char handmsg[] = "I found ^c\n";
void catch_ctrl_c(int signo)
{
    write(STDERR_FILENO, handmsg, strlen(handmsg));
}
...
struct sigaction act;
...
act.sa_handler = catch_ctrl_c;
sigemptyset(&act.sa_mask);
act.sa_flags = 0;
if (sigaction(SIGINT, &act, NULL) < 0)
   /* handle error here */
...
```

POSIX.1 guarantees that `write` is async-signal safe, meaning that it can be called safely from inside a signal handler. There are no similar guarantees for `fprintf`, but `fprintf` may be async-signal safe in some implementations. Table 5.3 on page 191 lists the POSIX and Spec 1170 async-signal safe functions.

Example 5.16

The following code segment sets the action of SIGINT *to the default.*

```
#include <stdio.h>
#include <signal.h>
struct sigaction  newact;
```

```
newact.sa_handler = SIG_DFL;    /* new handler set to default */
sigemptyset(&newact.sa_mask);   /* no other signals blocked */
newact.sa_flags = 0;            /* no special options */
if (sigaction(SIGINT, &newact, NULL) == -1)
   perror("Could not set SIGINT handler to default action");
```

Example 5.17

The following function takes a signal number parameter and returns 1 if that signal is ignored and 0 otherwise.

```
#include <signal.h>

int test_signal_ignored(int signo)
{
   int returnvalue = 0;
   struct sigaction act;
   if (sigaction(signo, NULL, &act) == -1)
      returnvalue = 0;
   else if (act.sa_handler == SIG_IGN)
      returnvalue = 1;
   return returnvalue;
}
```

5.4 Waiting for Signals—`pause` and `sigsuspend`

One reason for using signals is to avoid busy waiting. Busy waiting means continually using CPU cycles to wait for an event. Typically a program does this by checking the value of a variable in a loop. A more efficient approach is to suspend the process until the waited-for event occurs, so that other processes can use the CPU productively. UNIX provides two functions that allow a process to suspend itself until a signal occurs: `pause` and `sigsuspend`.

The `pause` call suspends the calling process until a signal that is not being ignored is delivered to the process. If a signal is caught by the process, the `pause` returns after the signal handler returns.

SYNOPSIS

```
#include <unistd.h>

int pause(void);
```

POSIX.1, Spec 1170

The `pause` function always returns −1, so the return value is not significant.

To wait for a particular signal using `pause`, check which signal caused the `pause` to return. This information is not directly available, so the signal handler must set a flag for the program to check after `pause` returns.

Example 5.18

The following code segment causes a process to wait for a particular signal with `pause` *by having the signal handler set the* `signal_received` *variable to* 1. *Initially the* `signal_received` *variable is* 0.

```
#include <unistd.h>
int signal_received = 0;        /* external static variable */


...
while(signal_received == 0)
   pause();
```

Example 5.18 requires a loop because the `pause` returns when any signal is delivered to the process. If the signal was not the right one, `signal_received` is still 0 and the loop calls `pause` again. The implementation in Example 5.18 assumes that the signal does not occur between the test in the `while` loop and the `pause`.

Exercise 5.2

What happens if the signal in Example 5.18 is delivered between the test of `signal_received` and `pause`?

Answer:

The `pause` does not return until some other signal or another occurrence of the same signal is delivered to the process. A workable solution must test the value of `signal_received` while the signal is blocked.

Example 5.19

The following is an incorrect attempt to prevent a signal from being delivered between the test of `signal_received` *and the execution of the* `pause` *in Example 5.18.*

```
#include <unistd.h>
#include <signal.h>
int signal_received = 0;        /* external static variable */


...
sigset_t sigset;
int signum;

sigemptyset(&sigset);
sigaddset(&sigset, signum);
sigprocmask(SIG_BLOCK, &sigset, NULL);
while(signal_received == 0)
   pause();
```

Unfortunately, the program of Example 5.19 executes `pause` while the signal is blocked. As a result the program never receives the signal and `pause` never returns.

If the program unblocks the signal before executing the `pause,` it might receive the signal between the unblocking and the execution of the `pause.` This event is actually more likely than it seems. If a signal is generated while the process has it blocked, the process receives the signal right after unblocking it.

The delivery of a signal before `pause` was one of the major problems with the original UNIX signals, and there was no simple reliable way to get around the problem. The program must do two operations "at once": unblock the signal and start the `pause.` Another way of saying this is that the two operations together should be atomic (i.e., the program cannot be logically interrupted between execution of the two operations). The `sigsuspend` provides a method of doing this.

SYNOPSIS

```
#include <signal.h>

int sigsuspend(const sigset_t *sigmask);
```

POSIX.1, Spec 1170

The `sigsuspend` sets the signal mask to the one pointed to by `sigmask` and suspends the process until a signal is delivered to the process. The `sigmask` can be used to unblock the signal the program is looking for. When `sigsuspend` returns, the signal mask is reset to the value it had before the `sigsuspend.` The `sigsuspend` always returns -1, so the return value is not significant.

Example 5.20

The following code segment suspends a process until the signal given by the value of `signum` *occurs. It then restores the signal mask to its original value.*

```
#include <signal.h>
int signal_received = 0;        /* external static variable */
...
sigset_t sigset;
sigset_t sigoldmask;
int signum;

sigprocmask(SIG_SETMASK, NULL, &sigoldmask);
sigprocmask(SIG_SETMASK, NULL, &sigset);
sigaddset(&sigset, signum);
sigprocmask(SIG_BLOCK, &sigset, NULL);
sigdelset(&sigset, signum);
while(signal_received == 0)
    sigsuspend(&sigset);
sigprocmask(SIG_SETMASK, &sigoldmask, NULL);
```

The code segment in Example 5.20 assumes that `signal_received` is initially

0 and that the handler for `signum` sets `signal_received` to 1. It is important that the signal be blocked when the `while` is doing its test of `signal_received`. Otherwise, the signal can be delivered between the test of `signal_received` and the call to `sigsuspend`. In this case the process blocks until another signal causes the `sigsuspend` to return.

Exercise 5.3

Suppose the `sigsuspend` in Example 5.20 returns because of a different signal. Is the `signum` signal blocked when the `while` tests `signal_received` again?

Answer:

Yes, because after `sigsuspend` returns, the signal mask is restored to the state it had before the `sigsuspend`. The call to `sigprocmask` before the `while` guarantees that this signal is blocked.

5.5 An Example—biff

Section 2.8 presented a simple program to notify a user when mail is present. Program 5.1 shows a more sophisticated version of this program. It uses `stat` to determine the size of the mail file and notifies the user when the file size increases, indicating that new mail has arrived. This program also has a mechanism for turning notification on or off without killing the process. It can therefore be used as a true daemon that runs all the time but is active only when the user wants it to be.

The program uses the two user signals, `SIGUSR1` and `SIGUSR2`, to turn notification on or off. The program illustrates several important aspects of using signals. The two signal handlers change the global variable `notifyflag`. It is important that neither signal handler be interrupted by the other signal. During execution of a signal handler, the signal that caused that handler to execute is blocked by default. The `sigaction` allows the program to block other signals as well. In this program both signals are blocked when either signal handler is entered. The `sa_mask` member of the `sigaction` structure specifies which signals should be blocked during handler execution.

The program also illustrates the correct way to wait for a global variable to change its value. It is necessary to block the user signals before testing `notifyflag`.

Exercise 5.4

What is wrong with the following code to wait for `notifyflag` to be set?

```
#include <unistd.h>
int notifyflag = 0;    /* external static variable */
...
while (notifyflag == 0)
   pause();
```

Answer:

Suppose that `notifyflag` is 0 and the `SIGUSR1` signal is delivered to the process after it checked `notifyflag` but before it executed `pause()`. The `pause()` blocks until the *next* signal is delivered.

Exercise 5.5

Since `sigsuspend` unblocks the signals, what is the purpose of the second `sigprocmask` in Program 5.1?

Answer:

The `sigsuspend` is not called if `notifyflag` is 1. Also, when `sigsuspend` returns, it restores the signal mask to the value it had before the call.

Program 5.1: A biff program that uses signals.

```
#include <sys/types.h>
#include <sys/stat.h>
#include <fcntl.h>
#include <unistd.h>
#include <string.h>
#include <stdio.h>
#include <stdlib.h>
#include <errno.h>
#include <signal.h>
#include <pwd.h>
#define MAILDIR "/var/mail/"
#define SLEEPTIME 10
int notifyflag = 1;

 /* Return the size of file if no error.   Otherwise if
  * file does not exist return 0 otherwise return -1.
  */
int get_file_size(const char *filename)
{
   struct stat buf;

   if (stat(filename, &buf) == -1) {
      if (errno == ENOENT) return 0;
      else return -1;
   }
   return (long)buf.st_size;
}

/* Notify the user that mail has arrived */
void send_mail_notification()
{
   fprintf(stderr, "Mail has arrived\007\n");
}
```

```
/* Turn on mail notification */
void turn_notify_on(int s)
{
   notifyflag = 1;
}

/* Turn off mail notification */
void turn_notify_off(int s)
{
   notifyflag = 0;
}

/* Continuously check for mail and notify user of new mail */
int notify_of_mail(const char *filename)
{
   long old_mail_size;
   long new_mail_size;
   sigset_t blockset;
   sigset_t emptyset;

   sigemptyset(&emptyset);
   sigemptyset(&blockset);
   sigaddset(&blockset, SIGUSR1);
   sigaddset(&blockset, SIGUSR2);
   old_mail_size = get_file_size(filename);
   if (old_mail_size < 0) return 1;
   if (old_mail_size > 0) send_mail_notification();
   sleep(SLEEPTIME);
   for( ; ; ) {
      if (sigprocmask(SIG_BLOCK, &blockset, NULL) < 0)
         return 1;
      while (notifyflag == 0)
         sigsuspend(&emptyset);
      if (sigprocmask(SIG_SETMASK, &emptyset, NULL) < 0)
         return 1;
      new_mail_size = get_file_size(filename);
      if (new_mail_size > old_mail_size)
         send_mail_notification();
      old_mail_size = new_mail_size;
      sleep(SLEEPTIME);
   }
}

void main(void)
{
   char mailfile[80];
   struct sigaction newact;
   struct passwd *pw;
```

```
    if ((pw = getpwuid(getuid())) == NULL) {
        perror("Could not determine login name");
        exit(1);
    }
    strcpy(mailfile, MAILDIR);
    strcat(mailfile, pw->pw_name);
    newact.sa_handler = turn_notify_on;
    newact.sa_flags = 0;
    sigemptyset(&newact.sa_mask);
    sigaddset(&newact.sa_mask, SIGUSR1);
    sigaddset(&newact.sa_mask, SIGUSR2);
    if (sigaction(SIGUSR1, &newact, NULL) < 0)
        perror("Could not set signal to turn on notification");
    newact.sa_handler = turn_notify_off;
    if (sigaction(SIGUSR2, &newact, NULL) < 0)
        perror("Could not set signal to turn off notification");
    notify_of_mail(mailfile);
    fprintf(stderr, "Fatal error, terminating program\n");
    exit(1);
}
```

_____ **Program 5.1** _____

Exercise 5.6

Under what circumstances does Program 5.1 fail to notify of incoming mail?
Answer:

If a short message comes in right after the user has read a longer message, `biff` might not detect it.

5.6 System Calls and Signals

Be aware of two difficulties that can occur when signals interact with system calls. The first concerns whether system calls that are interrupted by signals should be restarted. The other problem occurs with nonreentrant system calls in signal handlers.

What happens when a process catches a signal while it is executing a system call? The answer depends on the type of system call. Some system calls, like those that do terminal I/O, can block the process for an undetermined length of time. There is no limit on how long it takes to get a key value from a keyboard or to read from a pipe. These are called "slow" system calls. Other system calls, like a disk I/O, can block for short periods of time. Still others, like `getpid()`, do not block at all. Neither of these latter types are considered to be "slow." The capability of interrupting slow system calls is needed so that the operating system can deliver signals to programs during indefinitely long waits for I/O.

In POSIX.1 slow system calls that are interrupted return -1 with `errno` set to `EINTR`. The program must handle this error explicitly and restart the system call if desired. Since I/O can be redirected, the compiler might not be able to resolve at compile time whether a particular I/O call is in the slow category. It is better to be on the safe side and insert the code to restart whenever relevant.

Example 5.21

The following code segment restarts the `read` *system call if it is interrupted by a signal.*

```
#include <sys/types.h>
#include <sys/uio.h>
#include <unistd.h>
#include <errno.h>
int fd;
int retval;
int  size;
char *buf;

while (retval = read(fd, buf, size),
                 retval == -1 && errno == EINTR)
    ;
if (retval == -1)
    /* handle errors here */
```

Notice the use of the comma operator in Example 5.21 and the semicolon after the `while`. The `read` sets the `retval` on return. The `while` continues as long as the second parameter of the comma operator is true, that is, as long as the `read` fails because it was interrupted by a signal. In this case the `while` restarts the `read`.

Under Spec 1170 the program can specify in the `sigaction` call that slow system calls should be restarted. The automatic restart is not part of POSIX.1, although the standard does not prohibit this extension. The restart specification is accomplished by using the `SA_RESTART` option in the `sa_flags` member of the `struct sigaction` structure for the handler. If writing library functions, try not to rely on the calling program setting up handlers to restart system calls. Sometimes the interruption of a system call by a signal is desirable. The next example uses a signal to prevent a system call from blocking indefinitely.

Example 5.22

The following code handles reading from a pipe on file descriptor `fd` *with a timeout of ten seconds.*

```
#include <unistd.h>
#include <sys/types.h>
#include <unistd.h>
```

```
#include <errno.h>
int fd;
int size;
char *buf;

alarm(10);
if (read(fd, buf, size) < 0) {
    if (errno == EINTR)
        /* handle timeout here */
    else
        /* handle other errors here */
}
alarm(0);
```

The `alarm` system call instructs the alarm clock of the calling process to send the SIGALRM signal to the process after a specified number of seconds. The default action of SIGALRM is to terminate a process. Example 5.22 assumes that the program has installed a signal handler to catch this signal without automatic restart of system calls. The final `alarm(0)` turns off the alarm timer. An alternative approach is to use `select` with a timeout to wait for I/O.

Recall that a function is *async-signal safe* if it can be safely called from within a signal handler. Many UNIX system calls and library functions are not async-signal safe because they use static data structures, call `malloc` or `free`, or use global data structures in a nonreentrant way. Consequently, a single process cannot correctly execute two occurrences of these calls concurrently.

Normally this is not a problem, but signals add concurrency to a program. Since signals occur asynchronously, a process may catch a signal while it is executing a system call or a library function. (For example, what happens if the program interrupts a `strtok` with another `strtok` and then tries to resume the first call?) Care must therefore be taken when executing system calls from inside signal handlers. Each UNIX standard has a list of system calls that may safely be used from inside signal handlers. Table 5.3 lists the functions that POSIX.1 and Spec 1170 guarantee a program can call safely from a signal handler. In addition, Spec 1170 requires that `fpathconf`, `raise`, and `signal` are async-signal safe.

Signal handling is complicated, but here are a few useful rules.

- When in doubt explicitly restart system calls within a program.

- Check each system call or library function used in a signal handler to make sure that it is on the list of *async-signal safe* calls.

- Carefully analyze the potential interactions between a signal handler that changes an external variable and other program code that accesses that variable. Block signals to prevent unwanted interactions.

_exit()	fstat()	read()	sysconf()
access()	getegid()	rename()	tcdrain()
alarm()	geteuid()	rmdir()	tcflow()
cfgetispeed()	getgid()	setgid()	tcflush()
cfgetospeed()	getgroups()	setpgid()	tcgetattr()
cfsetispeed()	getpgrp()	setsid()	tcgetpgrp()
cfsetospeed()	getpid()	setuid()	tcsendbreak()
chdir()	getppid()	sigaction()	tcsetattr()
chmod()	getuid()	sigaddset()	tcsetpgrp()
chown()	kill()	sigdelset()	time()
close()	link()	sigemptyset()	times()
creat()	lseek()	sigfillset()	umask()
dup2()	mkdir()	sigismember()	uname()
dup()	mkfifo()	sigpending()	unlink()
execle()	open()	sigprocmask()	utime()
execve()	pathconf()	sigsuspend()	wait()
fcntl()	pause()	sleep()	waitpid()
fork()	pipe()	stat()	write()

Table 5.3: Functions that POSIX.1 and Spec 1170 specify as async-signal safe.

5.7 siglongjmp and sigsetjmp

Programs sometimes use signals to handle errors that are not fatal but can occur in many places in a program. For example, a user might want to abort a long calculation or an I/O operation that has blocked for a long time without terminating the program. The program's response to ctrl-c should be to start over at the beginning (or at some other specified location). The program can use signals indirectly or directly to handle this situation.

In the indirect approach, the signal handler for SIGINT sets a flag. The program tests the flag in strategic places and returns to the main loop if the flag is set. The indirect approach is complicated since the program might have to return through several layers of functions. At each return layer, the program tests the return value for this special case.

In the direct approach, the signal handler jumps directly back to the main program. The jump requires unraveling the program stack. A pair of functions, sigsetjmp and siglongjmp, provide this capability. The sigsetjmp is analogous to a statement label and siglongjmp is analogous to a goto. The main difference is that the sigsetjmp and siglongjmp pair provide a mechanism for cleaning up the stack and signal states as well as doing the jump.

SYNOPSIS

```
#include <setjmp.h>

int sigsetjmp(sigjmp_buf env, int savemask);
void siglongjmp(sigjmp_buf env, int val);
```
POSIX.1, Spec 1170

Call the `sigsetjmp` at the point the program is to return to. The `sigsetjmp` provides a marker in the program similar to a statement label. The caller must provide a buffer of type `sigjmp_buf` which `sigsetjmp` initializes to the collection of information needed when jumping back to that marker. If `savemask` is nonzero, the current state of the signal mask is saved in the `env` buffer. When the program calls `sigsetjmp` directly, it returns 0. To jump back to the `sigsetjmp` point from a signal handler, execute `siglongjmp` with the same `sigjmp_buf` variable. The call makes it appear that the program is returning from `sigsetjmp` with a return value of `val`.

The C standard library provides functions `setjmp` and `longjmp` for the types of jumps referred to above. The reason for using `sigsetjmp` and `siglongjmp` rather than `setjmp` and `longjmp` is that the action of the latter pair on the signal mask is system-dependent. The `sigsetjmp` allows the program to specify whether the signal mask should be reset when jumping out of the signal handler.

Program 5.2 shows how to set up a SIGINT handler that causes the program to return to the main loop when `ctrl-c` is typed. It is important to execute `sigsetjmp` before calling `siglongjmp` in order to establish a point of return. The call to `sigaction` should appear before the `sigsetjmp` so that it is called only once. To prevent the signal handler from calling `siglongjmp` before the program executes `sigsetjmp`, Program 5.2 uses the flag `jumpok`. The signal handler tests this flag before calling `siglongjmp`. The `volatile` qualifier prevents this variable from being allocated to a register, and the type `sig_atomic_t` indicates that a write to it cannot be interrupted by a signal.

Program 5.2: Code to set up a signal handler that returns to the main loop when `ctrl-c` is typed.

```
#include <signal.h>
#include <stdio.h>
#include <setjmp.h>

static volatile sig_atomic_t jumpok = 0;
static sigjmp_buf jmpbuf;
...
void int_handler(int errno)
{
```

```
      if (jumpok == 0) return;
      siglongjmp(jmpbuf, 1);
}
...
void main(void)
{
      struct sigaction act;
            ...
      act.sa_handler = int_handler;
      sigemptyset(&act.sa_mask);
      act.sa_flags = 0;
      if (sigaction(SIGINT, &act, NULL) < 0) {
         perror("Error setting up SIGINT handler");
         exit(1);
      }
         ...
      if (sigsetjmp(jmpbuf, 1))
         fprintf(stderr, "Returned to main loop due to ^c\n");
      jumpok = 1;
            ...    /*  start of main loop */
}
```
_____ **Program 5.2** _____

5.8 Realtime Signals

A POSIX.1 signal handler is a function with a single parameter representing the signal number of the generating signal. POSIX.1b introduces several enhancements to POSIX.1 signal handling capabilities, including the queueing of signals and the passing of information to signal handlers. The standard expands the sigaction structure to allow for additional parameters to the signal handler. An implementation supports these expanded capabilities, known as the Realtime Signal Extension, if _POSIX_REALTIME_SIGNALS is defined.

```
SYNOPSIS

   #include <signal.h>

   struct sigaction {
       void (*sa_handler)(); /* SIG_DFL, SIG_IGN, or
                                 pointer to function */
       void (*sa_sigaction)(int, siginfo_t *, void *);
       sigset_t sa_mask;     /* additional signals to be blocked
                                 during execution of handler */
       int sa_flags;         /* special flags and options */
   };
```
                                                     POSIX.1b, Spec 1170

The new `sa_sigaction` member specifies an alternative type of signal handler. The new type of handler is used if `sa_flags && SA_SIGINFO` is true. The form of the new handler is

```
void func(int signo, siginfo_t *info, void *context);
```

The `signo` parameter is the same as before and is set to the number of the caught signal. The `context` is not currently defined by the POSIX standard. The `*info` structure contains at least the following members:

```
int si_signo;              /* signal number */
int si_code;               /* cause of the signal */
union sigval si_value;     /* signal value */
```

The `si_signo` contains the signal number. This value is the same as the value stored in `signo` . The `si_code` indicates the cause of the signal. The possible values are `SI_USER`, `SI_QUEUE`, `SI_TIMER`, `SI_ASYNCHIO`, and `SI_MESGQ`. A `SI_USER` value indicates that the signal was generated by `kill`, `raise`, or `abort`. In these situations there is no way of generating a `si_value` so it is not defined. `SI_QUEUE` indicates that the `sigqueue` function generated the signal. `SI_TIMER` value indicates that a timer generated the signal. Sections 6.2 and 6.9 discuss these timers. A `SI_ASYNCIO` value indicates the completion of asynchronous I/O (Section 5.9) and a `SI_MESGQ` value indicates the arrival of a message on an empty message queue.

The `sigval` union must have at least the following members:

```
int sival_int;
void *sival_ptr;
```

to allow either an integer or a pointer to be transmitted to the signal handler.

As mentioned earlier, the POSIX.1 standard does not specify what happens when multiple instances of a signal are pending. POSIX guarantees that at least one instance is delivered when the signal is unblocked, but additional instances may be lost. The `sigqueue` function is an extension to `kill` which permits signals to be queued.

SYNOPSIS

```
#include <signal.h>

int sigqueue(pid_t pid, int signo, const union sigval value);
```
POSIX.1b

The additional parameter specifies the value to be received by the signal handler in the `si_value` member of its `info` parameter.

To guarantee that multiple instances of a particular signal are queued, a program must use the `SA_SIGINFO` flag in the `sa_flags` when setting up the handler with sigaction. Multiple signals of the same signal number generated by sigqueue are queued up to a maximum of SIGQUEUE_MAX, which typically has a value of 32.

Whether signals are guaranteed to be queued is determined by the method used to generate the signals, not by how the signal handler is set up. Multiple instances of a signal generated with kill may not be queued even if instances of the same signal generated by sigqueue are.

Program 5.3 shows a program that sends queued signals to a process. The program behaves like the kill command but uses sigqueue instead of the kill system call. It allows the sending of queued signals and an integer value for each. Program 5.4 shows a program that prints its process ID, sets up a signal handler for SIGUSR1, blocks the signal, and waits for input before exiting. The signal handler just displays the values it receives from its parameters.

Program 5.3: A program that sends a queued signal to a process.

```
#include <stdio.h>
#include <stdlib.h>
#include <unistd.h>
#include <signal.h>

void main(int argc, char *argv[])
{
    union sigval qval;
    int val;
    int pid;
    int signo;

    if (argc != 4) {
        fprintf(stderr, "Usage: %s pid signal value\n", argv[0]);
        exit(1);
    }

    pid = atoi(argv[1]);
    signo = atoi(argv[2]);
    val = atoi(argv[3]);

    fprintf(stderr, "Sending signal %d with value %d to process %d\n",
        signo, val, pid);
    qval.sival_int = val;
    sigqueue(pid, signo, qval);
}
```

_____ **Program 5.3** _____

Program 5.4: A program that receives SIGUSR1 signals.

```
#include <stdio.h>
#include <stdlib.h>
#include <unistd.h>
#include <signal.h>

void my_handler(int signo, siginfo_t* info, void *context)
{
    fprintf(stderr, "Signal handler entered for signal number %d\n",
        signo);
    fprintf(stderr, "   si_signo = %3d\n", info->si_signo);
    fprintf(stderr, "   si_code  = ");

    if (info->si_code == SI_USER) fprintf(stderr, "USER\n");
    else if (info->si_code == SI_QUEUE) fprintf(stderr, "QUEUE\n");
    else if (info->si_code == SI_TIMER) fprintf(stderr, "TIMER\n");
    else if (info->si_code == SI_ASYNCIO) fprintf(stderr, "ASYNCIO\n");
    else if (info->si_code == SI_MESGQ) fprintf(stderr, "MESGQ\n");
    else fprintf(stderr, "%d\n", info->si_code);
    fprintf(stderr," si_value = %3d\n", info->si_value.sival_int);
}

void main(void)
{
    struct sigaction act;
    sigset_t sigset;

    fprintf(stderr, "Process ID is %ld\n", (long)getpid());

    sigemptyset(&sigset);
    sigaddset(&sigset, SIGALRM);
    sigprocmask(SIG_BLOCK, &sigset, NULL);
    sigemptyset(&act.sa_mask);
    act.sa_flags = SA_SIGINFO;
    act.sa_sigaction = my_handler;
    if (sigaction(SIGUSR1, &act, NULL) < 0) {
        perror("Sigaction failed");
        exit(1);
    }
    fprintf(stderr, "Signal SIGUSR1 = %d ready\n", SIGUSR1);

    for( ; ; )
        pause();
}
```

———————————————————— **Program 5.4** ————————————————————

5.9 Asynchronous I/O

Normally, when a process performs a read or write, the process blocks until the I/O completes. Sometimes a process would rather initiate the request and continue executing without waiting for the I/O to complete. The first type of request is called a *blocking* request, and the second type of request is called *nonblocking*.

Example 5.23

The following code segment opens the existing FIFO myfifo *for nonblocking reading.*

```
#include <stdio.h>
#include <fcntl.h>
int fd;

if ((fd = open("myfifo", O_RDONLY | O_NONBLOCK)) == -1)
    perror("Could not open myfifo");
```

If no data is available in the FIFO of Example 5.23, a read from fd returns −1 with errno set to EAGAIN.

In asynchronous I/O, the process issues a nonblocking I/O operation, and the operating system notifies it when the I/O completes. Spec 1170 uses SIGPOLL for asynchronous I/O notification, while the older BSD 4.3 uses SIGIO. Asynchronous I/O is not part of the original POSIX.1 standard, but POSIX.1b has an asynchronous I/O extension described below.

Example 5.24

The following code segment shows how to set up a file descriptor for asynchronous I/O as described by Spec 1170.

```
#include <unistd.h>
#include <stropts.h>
#include <fcntl.h>

if ((fd = open(pathname, O_RDONLY | O_NONBLOCK)) == -1)
    /* handle errors here */
if (ioctl(fd, I_SETSIG, S_RDNORM) == -1)
    /* could not set file descriptor for asynchronous read */
```

The S_RDNORM parameter Example 5.24 specifies that SIGPOLL should be generated when an ordinary message arrives on fd. The fd must be a stream as in Section 12.6. Files, pipes, FIFOs and network I/O fall into this category. Once the file descriptor is set for asynchronous I/O, the device driver generates a SIGPOLL signal if I/O (in Example 5.24 an ordinary message) becomes available on that file descriptor.

Of course, be sure to set up a handler for SIGPOLL before setting a file descriptor to use asynchronous I/O. The default action of SIGPOLL is to terminate the process. Section 9.1.2 provides a complete example of asynchronous I/O using SIGPOLL.

The POSIX.1b Realtime Extension defines asynchronous I/O based on aio_read and aio_write. The aio_read allows a process to queue a request for reading on an open file descriptor. The aio_write is similar. The aio_return returns the status of the asynchronous I/O operation, and the aio_error returns the error status of the asynchronous I/O operation.

```
SYNOPSIS

    #include <aio.h>

    int aio_read(struct aiocb *aiocbp);
    int aio_write(struct aiocb *aiocbp);
    ssize_t aio_return(struct aiocb *aiocbp);
    int aio_error(const struct aiocb *aiocbp);
```
                                                                                    POSIX.1b

The struct aiobc has at least the following members:

```
int              aio_fildes;    /* file descriptor */
volatile void    *aio_buf;      /* buffer location */
size_t           aio_nbytes;    /* length of transfer */
off_t            aio_offset;    /* file offset */
int              aio_reqprio;   /* request priority offset */
struct sigevent  aio_sigevent;  /* signal number and offset */
int              aio_lio_opcode; /* listio operation */
```

The first three members of this structure are similar to the parameters in an ordinary read or write. The aio_offset specifies the starting position for the I/O. If the implementation supports user scheduling (_POSIX_PRIORITIZED_IO and _POSIX_PRIORITY_SCHEDULING are defined), aio_reqprio lowers the priority of the request. The aio_sigevent specifies how the calling process is notified of the completion. If aio_sigevent.sigev_notify has the value SIGEV_NONE, the operating system does not post a signal when the I/O completes. If aio_sigevent.sigev_notify is SIGEV_SIGNAL, the operating system generates the signal specified in aio_sigevent.sigev_signo. The aio_lio_opcode is used by the lio_listio function to submit multiple I/O requests.

Program 5.5 illustrates the use of POSIX asynchronous I/O. The program monitors two slow input devices whose names are passed as command-line arguments one and two. Program 5.5 opens the two descriptors for input. The program queues a read request from fd_1 by calling aio_read. The operating system delivers a SIGRTMAX signal when the operation is complete. Similarly the program queues a first read request for fd_2 specifying notification by the SIGRTMAX-1 signal. The handler for each of these signals is `my_aio_handler`. The handler uses its second parameter to determine which signal was delivered. It writes the inputted information to standard error and initiates another asynchronous read on that descriptor. POSIX.1b asynchronous I/O was not supported at publication time on any systems that the authors have access to, so be warned that the code in Program 5.5 was not tested.

Program 5.5: A program to monitor two file descriptors using asynchronous I/O.

```
#include <aio.h>
#include <stdio.h>
#include <sys/types.h>
#include <sys/stat.h>
#include <stropts.h>
#include <fcntl.h>
#include <signal.h>
#include <unistd.h>
#include <string.h>
#include <errno.h>

#define BLKSIZE 1024

volatile char buf2[BLKSIZE];
volatile char buf1[BLKSIZE];
int fd_1 = 0;
int fd_2 = 0;
int fd1_error = 0;
int fd2_error = 0;
struct aiocb my_aiocb1;
struct aiocb my_aiocb2;

void my_aio_handler(int signo, siginfo_t *info, void *context)
{
    int   my_errno;
    int   my_status;
    struct aiocb *my_aiocbp;
    int *errorp;

    my_aiocbp = info->si_value.sival_ptr;
    if (signo == SIGRTMAX)
        errorp = &fd1_error;
    else
        errorp = &fd2_error;
    if ((my_errno = aio_error(my_aiocbp)) != EINPROGRESS) {
        my_status = aio_return(my_aiocbp);
        if (my_status >= 0) {
            write(STDERR_FILENO, (char *)my_aiocbp->aio_buf, my_status);
            *errorp = aio_read(my_aiocbp);
```

```
        }
        else
            *errorp = 1;
    }
}

void main(int argc, char *argv[])
{
    sigset_t oldmask;
    struct sigaction newact;
                                    /* open the file descriptors for I/O */
    if (argc != 3) {
        fprintf(stderr, "Usage: %s filename1 filename2\n", argv[0]);
        exit(1);
    }
    if ((fd_1 = open(argv[1], O_RDONLY)) == -1) {
        fprintf(stderr,"Could not open %s: %s\n",
            argv[1], strerror(errno));
        exit(1);
    }
    if ((fd_2 = open(argv[2], O_RDONLY)) == -1) {
        fprintf(stderr,"Could not open %s: %s\n",
            argv[2], strerror(errno));
        exit(1);
    }
                            /* Set up handlers for SIGRTMAX and SIGRTMAX-1 */
    sigemptyset(&newact.sa_mask);
    sigaddset(&newact.sa_mask, SIGRTMAX);
    sigaddset(&newact.sa_mask, SIGRTMAX-1);
    if (sigprocmask(SIG_BLOCK, &newact.sa_mask, &oldmask) == -1) {
        perror("Could not block SIGRTMAX or SIGRTMAX-1");
        exit(1);
    }
    newact.sa_sigaction = my_aio_handler;
    newact.sa_flags = SA_SIGINFO;
    if (sigaction(SIGRTMAX, &newact, NULL) == -1) {
        perror("Could not set SIGRTMAX handler");
        exit(1);
    }
    if (sigaction(SIGRTMAX-1, &newact, NULL) == -1) {
        perror("Could not set SIGRTMAX-1 handler");
        exit(1);
    }
                                            /* Unblock the signals */
    if (sigprocmask(SIG_UNBLOCK, &newact.sa_mask, NULL) == -1) {
        perror("Could not unblock SIGRTMAX or SIGRTMAX-1");
        exit(1);
    }
                                    /* Start first I/O operation on fd_1 */
```

```
    my_aiocb1.aio_fildes = fd_1;
    my_aiocb1.aio_offset = 0;
    my_aiocb1.aio_buf = (void *)buf1;
    my_aiocb1.aio_nbytes = BLKSIZE;
    my_aiocb1.aio_sigevent.sigev_notify = SIGEV_SIGNAL;
    my_aiocb1.aio_sigevent.sigev_signo = SIGRTMAX;
    my_aiocb1.aio_sigevent.sigev_value.sival_ptr = &my_aiocb1;
    fd1_error = aio_read(&my_aiocb1);
    if (fd1_error == -1) {
        if (errno == ENOSYS)
            fprintf(stderr,"                    !!!!! Not supported yet\n");
        else
            perror("The aio_read failed");
        exit(1);
    }

                            /* Start first I/O operation on fd_2 */
    my_aiocb2.aio_fildes = fd_2;
    my_aiocb2.aio_offset = 0;
    my_aiocb2.aio_buf = (void *)buf2;
    my_aiocb2.aio_nbytes = BLKSIZE;
    my_aiocb2.aio_sigevent.sigev_notify = SIGEV_SIGNAL;
    my_aiocb2.aio_sigevent.sigev_signo = SIGRTMAX-1;
    my_aiocb2.aio_sigevent.sigev_value.sival_ptr = &my_aiocb2;
    fd2_error = aio_read(&my_aiocb2);
    if (fd1_error == -1) {
        perror("The aio_read failed");
        exit(1);
    }

                            /* proceed with overlapping computations */
    while(!fd1_error || !fd2_error)
        /* do whatever */  ;
    exit(0);
}
```

_____ **Program 5.5** _____

5.10 Exercise: Dumping Statistics

The `atexit` function `show_times` of Program 2.11 also works as a signal handler to report the amount of CPU time used. Implement a signal handler for `SIGUSR1` that outputs this information to standard error. Read the man pages carefully to find out whether all of the calls are async-signal safe. Convert the handler to one that uses only safe calls. (Note: `fprintf` is not guaranteed to be async-signal safe in POSIX.1 or Spec 1170.)

5.11 Exercise: `proc` Filesystem II

This exercise builds on the exercises in Section 3.12. Write a program called `examps` that has a man page shown in Figure 5.1. Implement `examps` as follows:

- Write a first version of `examps` that parses the command line. If the `-s` option is given, `examps` sends a `SIGSTOP` to the process, prints a message to standard output, and then sends a `SIGCONT`. If `-s` is not given, `examps` just prints a message to standard output with the process ID.

- Implement the `get_prstatus` function of Section 3.12.

- Implement the full `examps` program described in the man page of Figure 5.1.

5.12 Exercise: Spooling a Slow Device

This exercise uses asynchronous I/O to overlap the handling of I/O from a slow device with other program calculations. Examples include printing or performing a file transfer over a slow modem. Another example is a program that plays an audio file in the background while doing something else. In both examples, a program reads from a disk file and writes to a slow device.

Write a program that uses asynchronous I/O to write to a slow device. The source of information is a disk file. Use the POSIX.1b signals with `aio_write` if they are available; otherwise use the Spec 1170 version with `SIGPOLL`. Pass the name of the input file and the output device as command-line arguments. Test this phase with the input file being a disk file and the output file being standard error. If a workstation with a supported audio device is available, use an audio file on disk as input and `"/dev/audio"` as the output device.

The signal handler should read another block of data from the input file and perform an asynchronous `write` to the output file. It should set an external flag if it encounters an I/O error.

The main program opens the input and output descriptors and sets up the appropriate signal handler. If using Spec 1170 system, use `ioctl` with the `I_SETSIG` command to set the write descriptor for asynchronous I/O. The main program performs a `read` of the input descriptor, followed by writing to the output descriptor. The main program then loops until the signal handler sets an external flag indicating that there was an error. Have the main program perform a calculation in the loop. This program is particularly interesting when the output goes to the audio device. It is possible to hear background talking or music overlapped with the computation. Estimate the percentage of time spent handling I/O as compared with calculation time.

```
NAME
     examps - examine a process

SYNOPSIS
     examps [-s] pid


DESCRIPTION

The examps utility examines the /proc/pid file and outputs
the following information to standard output:
     process ID,
     parent process ID,
     process group ID,
     session ID,
     process user CPU time,
     process system CPU time,
     scheduling class name,
     current instruction,
     names of the pending signals,
     current signal,
     start of the heap
     size of the process heap in bytes,
     start of stack,
     size of process stack in bytes,
     system call number (if in syscall),
     number of parameters to system call.

The process must be owned by the user executing the examps. If
the -s option is given, the process is stopped and restarted.
If the -s option is not given the process is not stopped and
the values may be modified while the read is taking place.

OPTIONS
     -s    Send the SIGSTOP signal to the process before obtaining the
           trace information.  Send SIGCONT when tracing information has
           been obtained.

EXAMPLES
     The following examines the status of process 3421:
           examps 3421
     Process 3421 is not stopped by examps.  It may have been stopped
     by another source.

FILES
     /proc

SEE ALSO
     proc(4)
```

Figure 5.1: The man page for examps.

5.13 Additional Reading

Advanced Programming in the UNIX Environment by Stevens [86] has a good historical overview of signals. See *POSIX.4: Programming for the Real World* by Gallmeister [31] for a thorough presentation of the new POSIX.1b Realtime Extension.

Chapter 6

Project: *Timers*

> Operating systems use timers for purposes such as process scheduling, timeouts for network protocols, and periodic updates of system statistics. This chapter discusses timers in detail but also emphasizes testing and the importance of careful signal handling. The chapter covers both Spec 1170 timers and the POSIX.1b realtime clocks and timers, providing a side-by-side comparison of their features.

A *timer* keeps track of the passage of time. The simplest timers measure *elapsed time* and give this information when queried. *Interval timers* generate an interrupt after a specific time interval. Operating systems use interval timers in many ways. An interval timer can cause a periodic interrupt, during which the operating system increments a counter. This counter can keep the time since the operating system was booted. UNIX systems traditionally keep the time of day as the number of seconds since January 1, 1970. If an underlying interval timer generates an interrupt after 100 microseconds and is restarted each time it expires, the timer interrupt service routine can keep a local counter to measure the number of seconds since January 1, 1970 by incrementing this local counter after each 10, 000 expirations of the interval timer.

Time-sharing operating systems also use interval timers for process scheduling. When the operating system schedules a process, it starts an interval timer for a time interval called the *scheduling quantum*. If this timer expires and the process is still executing, the scheduler moves the process to a ready queue so that another process can execute. Multiprocessor systems need one of these interval timers for each processor.

Most scheduling algorithms have a mechanism for raising the priority of processes that have been waiting for a long time to execute. The scheduler might use an interval timer for priority management. Every time the timer expires, the scheduler raises the priority of the processes that have not executed.

The standard C library contains a function called `sleep`.

SYNOPSIS

```
#include <unistd.h>

unsigned sleep(unsigned seconds);
```
                                                                                    POSIX.1, Spec 1170

When a process executes `sleep`, it blocks for the number of seconds specified. An implementation of `sleep` could use an interval timer for each process.

A computer system typically has a small number of hardware interval timers, and the operating system implements multiple software timers using these hardware timers. Section 6.1 discusses representations of times in UNIX, and Section 6.2 looks at various types of interval timers including the new timer facilities which are part of the POSIX.1b Realtime Extension. The next sections develop the central project of the chapter—an implementation of multiple interval timers using a single programmable interval timer. Finally Section 6.9 explores more advanced issues such as timer drift.

6.1 Times in UNIX

System time is kept as seconds since the Epoch which is defined as 00:00 (midnight) January 1, 1970, Coordinated Universal Time (also called UTC, Greenwich Mean Time or GMT). A program can access the system time by calling the `time` function.

SYNOPSIS

```
#include <time.h>

time_t time(time_t *tloc);
```
                                                                                    POSIX.1, Spec 1170

The `time` function returns the time in seconds since the Epoch. If `tloc` is not `NULL`, the `time` function also stores the time in `*tloc`. If an error occurs, `time` returns -1 and sets `errno`.

Exercise 6.1

The `time_t` type is usually implemented as a `long`. If a `long` is 32 bits, at approximately what date would a `time_t` overflow? Remember that one bit is used for the sign. What date would cause overflow if an `unsigned long` were used? What date would cause overflow if a `long` were 64 bits?

Answer:

It would take about 68 years from January 1, 1970 for time to overflow with a 32-bit `long`, so UNIX is safe until the year 2038. For a `time_t` value that is `unsigned long`, the overflow would occur in the year 2106. For a 64-bit `long`, UNIX would be safe until about the year 292 billion, long after the sun has died (:-().

The `time_t` type is convenient for calculations requiring the difference between times, but it is cumbersome for printing dates. The C library function `ctime` converts a time to an ASCII string suitable for printing.

SYNOPSIS

```
#include <time.h>

char *ctime(const time_t *clock);
```
                                                    ISO C, POSIX.1, Spec 1170

The `ctime` function takes one parameter which is a pointer to a variable of type `time_t` and returns a pointer to a twenty-six-character string. The `ctime` function takes into account both the time zone and daylight saving time. Each of the fields in the string has a constant width. The string might look like this:

```
Sun Oct 06 02:21:35 1986\n\0
```

The `time` function measures *real time* or wall-clock time. In a multiprogramming environment many processes share the CPU, so real time is not an accurate measure of execution time. The *virtual time* for a process is the amount of time that the process spends in the running state. Execution times are expressed in virtual time. The `times` function returns information about the execution times of a process and its children.

SYNOPSIS

```
#include <sys/times.h>

clock_t times(struct tms *buffer);
```
                                                    POSIX.1, Spec 1170

The `clock_t` type holds a number of clock ticks. The `struct tms` structure contains at least the following members:

```
clock_t    tms_utime;  /* user CPU time */
clock_t    tms_stime;  /* system CPU time */
clock_t    tms_cutime  /* user CPU time of terminated children */
clock_t    tms_cstime; /* system CPU time of terminated children */
```

The `times` function returns the amount of elapsed time in clock ticks since an arbitrary point in the past. The `times` function returns -1 and sets `errno` if unsuccessful. (Program 2.11 shows how to use `sysconf` to determine the number of clock ticks per second on a system.)

Example 6.1

The following code segment calculates the fraction of time that a process is running on a processor while performing a computation.

```c
#include <sys/times.h>
#include <limits.h>
#include <stdio.h>

clock_t real_start;
clock_t real_end;
clock_t ticks_used;
struct tms process_start;
struct tms process_end;

if ((real_start = times(&process_start)) == -1)
   perror("Could not get starting times");
else {
   /* perform calculation to be timed */
   if ((real_end = times(&process_end)) == -1)
      perror("Could not get ending times");
   else {
      ticks_used = process_end.tms_utime + process_end.tms_cstime -
         process_start.tms_utime - process_start.tms_cstime;
      printf("Fraction of time running = %f\n",
         (double)(ticks_used)/(real_end - real_start));
   }
}
```

A time scale of seconds is too coarse for timing programs or controlling program events. Traditional UNIX systems and Spec 1170 use the `struct timeval` structure to express time on a finer scale. The `struct timeval` structure includes the following members:

```c
long    tv_sec;    /* seconds since Jan. 1, 1970 */
long    tv_usec;   /* and microseconds */
```

The POSIX.1b Realtime Extension defines a fine-grained timer facility based on the structure `struct timespec` which has a least the following members:

```c
time_t  tv_sec;   /* seconds */
long    tv_nsec;  /* nanoseconds */
```

The `tv_nsec` member is only valid if it is greater than or equal to 0 and less than 10^9. The `struct timespec` structure specifies time for both POSIX.1b clocks and timers. An implementation supports these clocks and timers if `_POSIX_TIMERS` is defined. POSIX.1b timers are not implemented in many systems as of this writing, so this chapter discusses both Spec 1170 and POSIX timers.

A program can use the Spec 1170 facility to time code by retrieving the time before and after with the `gettimeofday`.

SYNOPSIS

```
#include <sys/time.h>

int gettimeofday(struct timeval *tp, void *tzp);
```
Spec 1170

The `gettimeofday` function fills in the `struct timeval` structure pointed to by `tp` with the time. It returns 0 on success. It returns −1 and sets `errno` on failure. The `tzp` pointer must be `NULL`. This second parameter is included for historical reasons.

The `gettimeofday` is not part of POSIX, and there are many versions of it in use, some of which take only a single parameter. Check your man page before using `gettimeofday`. The POSIX committee could not decide on which `gettimeofday` to adopt, so POSIX does not define a function for returning the current time to an accuracy greater than one second. The `time` function can be used if this accuracy is sufficient.

Example 6.2

The following code segment uses `gettimeofday` *to measure the running time of the function* `function_to_time`.

```
#include <stdio.h>
#include <sys/time.h>
#define MILLION 1000000

struct timeval tpstart;
struct timeval tpend;
long timedif;

gettimeofday(&tpstart,NULL);
function_to_time();             /* timed code goes here */
gettimeofday(&tpend,NULL);
timedif = MILLION*(tpend.tv_sec - tpstart.tv_sec) +
                tpend.tv_usec - tpstart.tv_usec;
fprintf(stderr, "It took %ld microseconds\n", timedif);
```

The POSIX.1b Realtime Extension also contains clocks. A *clock* is a counter that increments at fixed intervals called the *clock resolution*. POSIX.1b provides functions to set the time (`clock_settime`), retrieve the time (`clock_gettime`), and determine the clock resolution (`clock_getres`).

```
SYNOPSIS

    #include <time.h>

    int clock_settime(clockid_t clock_id,
                      const struct timespec *tp);
    int clock_gettime(clockid_t clock_id, struct timespec *tp);
    int clock_getres(clockid_t clock_id, struct timespec *res);
                                                              POSIX.1b
```

These functions return 0 on success. On failure they return −1 and set errno. POSIX.1b clocks may be systemwide or only visible within a process. All implementations must support a systemwide clock of CLOCK_REALTIME which corresponds to the system realtime clock. Only privileged users may set this clock, but any user can read it.

Example 6.3

The following code segment measures the running time of `function_to_time` *by using the POSIX.1b clocks.*

```
#include <stdio.h>
#include <time.h>
#define MILLION 1000000

struct timespec tpstart;
struct timespec tpend;
long timedif;

clock_gettime(CLOCK_REALTIME, &tpstart);
function_to_time();                    /* timed code goes here */
clock_gettime(CLOCK_REALTIME, &tpend);
timedif = MILLION*(tpend.tv_sec - tpstart.tv_sec) +
             (tpend.tv_nsec - tpstart.tv_nsec)/1000;
fprintf(stderr,"It took %ld microseconds\n", timedif);
```

6.2 Interval Timers

The interval timers available in Spec 1170 and POSIX.1b are similar, but they differ in certain significant ways. Spec 1170 timers are based on the traditional UNIX timers and are available on most systems. POSIX.1b interval timers provide the capability of increased accuracy and flexibility.

6.2.1 Interval Timers in Spec 1170

Many operating systems allocate several user timers to each process. A conforming Spec 1170 implementation must provide each process with the following three interval timers:

ITIMER_REAL: decrements in real time and generates a SIGALRM signal when it expires.

ITIMER_VIRTUAL: decrements in virtual time (time used by the process) and generates a SIGVTALRM signal when it expires.

ITIMER_PROF: decrements in virtual time and system time for the process and generates a SIGPROF signal when it expires.

The Spec 1170 interval timers use a struct itimerval structure that contains the following members:

```
struct timeval it_value;    /* time until next expiration */
struct timeval it_interval; /* value to reload into the timer */
```

Here it_value holds the time remaining before the timer expires, and it_interval holds the time interval to be used for resetting the timer after it expires.

Spec 1170 provides the setitimer function for starting and stopping the user interval timers.

SYNOPSIS

```
#include <sys/time.h>

int setitimer (int which, const struct itimerval *value,
                   struct itimerval *ovalue);
```

Spec 1170

The setitimer function returns 0 on success. It returns −1 and sets errno on failure. The which parameter specifies the timer (i.e., ITIMER_REAL, ITIMER_VIRTUAL, or ITMER_PROF). The caller specifies the time interval for setting the timer in *value. Although the caller passes a pointer to this struct itimerval structure, it must supply values for the structure's members. The setitimer function does not change *value. If the it_interval member of *value is not 0, the timer restarts with this value when it expires. If the it_interval of *value is 0, the timer does not restart after it expires. If the it_value of *value is 0, setitimer stops the timer if it is running.

The setitimer function fills the members of the structure pointed to by ovalue with the current timer values. If the timer was running, the it_value member of *ovalue is nonzero and contains the time remaining before the timer would have expired. The ovalue pointer may be NULL , in which case no information is returned.

The `setup_interval_timer` function in Program 6.1 causes the process to print out an asterisk for each two seconds of CPU time used. The `ITIMER_PROF` timer generates a `SIGPROF` signal after every two seconds of CPU time used by the process. The process catches the `SIGPROF` signal and handles it with `myhandler`.

Program 6.1: A program that prints an asterisk for each two seconds of CPU time used.

```c
#include <stdio.h>
#include <stdlib.h>
#include <signal.h>
#include <sys/time.h>

char astbuf[] = "*";
static void myhandler(int s)
{
   write(STDERR_FILENO, astbuf, sizeof(char));
}

/* set up the myhandler handler for signal SIGPROF */
void init_timer_interrupt(void)
{
   struct sigaction newact;
   newact.sa_handler = myhandler;
   newact.sa_flags = SA_RESTART;
   sigemptyset(&newact.sa_mask);
   sigaction(SIGPROF, &newact, NULL);
}

/* set the ITIMER_PROF interval timer for 2-second intervals */
void setup_interval_timer(void)
{
   struct itimerval value;
   value.it_interval.tv_sec = 2;
   value.it_interval.tv_usec = 0;
   value.it_value = value.it_interval;
   setitimer(ITIMER_PROF, &value, NULL);
}

void main(int argc, char *argv[])
{
   init_timer_interrupt();
   setup_interval_timer();
   /* execute rest of main program here */
   exit(0);
}
```

─────────────────────── **Program 6.1** ───────────────────────

Exercise 6.2

Write a program that sets the `ITIMER_REAL` to expire in two seconds and then sleeps for ten seconds. How long does it take for the program to terminate? Why?

Answer:

The program terminates in two seconds because the default action of the `SIGALRM` signal terminates the process.

Exercise 6.3

Modify the program of Exercise 6.2 to catch `SIGALRM` before it sets the timer. The signal handler should print a message to standard error and return. Now how long does it take the program to terminate? Replace the `sleep` by an infinite loop. What happens?

Answer:

If the program uses `sleep`, it prints the message and terminates two seconds after it was started because the `sleep` terminates prematurely when the process receives the `SIGALARM` signal. If the program uses an infinite loop, it never terminates.

Use `getitimer` to determine the amount of time remaining on a Spec 1170 timer.

```
SYNOPSIS

   #include <sys/time.h>

   int getitimer (int which, struct itimerval *value);
                                                         Spec 1170
```

The `getitimer` sets the `*value` structure with the time remaining until the `which` timer expires. The `getitimer` returns 0 on success. It returns −1 and sets the `errno` on failure.

Exercise 6.4

What is wrong with the following code, which should print out the number of seconds remaining on the `ITIMER_VIRTUAL` interval timer?

```
#include <sys/time.h>
#include <stdio.h>
struct itimerval *value;

getitimer(ITIMER_VIRTUAL, value);
fprintf(stderr, "Time left is %ld seconds\n",
   value->it_value.tv_sec);
```

Answer:

The variable `value` is not initialized. It is declared as a pointer to a `struct itimerval`, but it does not point to anything. That is, there is no declaration of an actual `struct itimerval` structure that `value` can point to.

Program 6.2 uses the interval timer `ITIMER_VIRTUAL` to measure the execution time of the `function_to_time` function. This example, unlike Example 6.2, uses virtual time. Remember that the value returned by `getitimer` is the time remaining, and so the quantity is decreasing.

Program 6.2: A program segment that uses a Spec 1170 interval timer to measure the execution time of a function.

```
#include <stdio.h>
#include <sys/time.h>
#define MILLION 1000000

    struct itimerval value;
    struct itimerval ovalue;
    long timedif;

    value.it_interval.tv_sec = 0;
    value.it_interval.tv_usec = 0;
    value.it_value.tv_sec = MILLION;      /* a large number */
    value.it_value.tv_usec = 0;
    setitimer(ITIMER_VIRTUAL, &value, NULL);
    getitimer(ITIMER_VIRTUAL, &ovalue);
    function_to_time();                    /* timed code goes here */
    getitimer(ITIMER_VIRTUAL, &value);
    timedif = MILLION*(ovalue.it_value.tv_sec - value.it_value.tv_sec) +
              ovalue.it_value.tv_usec - value.it_value.tv_usec;
    printf("It took %ld microseconds\n", timedif);
```

———————————————— **Program 6.2** ————————————————

6.2.2 Interval Timers in POSIX

In Spec 1170 each process has a small fixed number of timers, one of each type: `ITIMER_REAL`, `ITIMER_VIRTUAL`, `ITIMER_PROF`, and so on. In POSIX.1b there are a small number of clocks such as `CLOCK_REALTIME`, and a process can create many independent timers for each clock.

POSIX.1b timers are based on the `struct itimerspec` structure which has the following members:

```
struct timespec  it_interval;  /* timer period */
struct timespec  it_value;     /* timer expiration */
```

As with Spec 1170 timers, the `it_interval` is the time used for resetting the timer after it expires. The `it_value` member holds the time remaining before expiration.

A process can create specific timers by calling `timer_create`. The timers are per-process timers that are not inherited on `fork`.

SYNOPSIS

```
#include <signal.h>
#include <time.h>

int timer_create(clockid_t clock_id, struct sigevent *evp,
    timer_t *timerid);

struct sigevent {
    int          sigev_notify   /* notification type */
    int          sigev_signo;   /* signal number */
    union sigval sigev_value;   /* signal value */
};

union sigval {
    int          sival_int;     /* integer value */
    void         *sival_ptr;    /* pointer value */
};
```

POSIX.1b

The `clock_id` specifies which clock the timer is based on, and `*timerid` holds the ID of the created timer. The `timer_create` returns 0 on success. It returns −1 and sets `errno` on failure.

The members of the `sigevent` structure and the `sigval` union shown in the synopsis are required by the POSIX.1b standard. The standard does not prohibit an implementation from including additional members.

The `*evp` parameter of `timer_create` specifies which signal should be sent to the process when the timer expires. If `evp` is `NULL`, the timer generates the default signal when it expires. For `CLOCK_REALTIME`, the default signal is `SIGALRM`. In order for the timer expiration to generate a signal other than the default signal, the program must set `evp->sigev_signo` to the desired signal number. The `evp->sigev_notify` member of `struct sigevent` indicates the action to be taken when the timer expires. Normally this member is `SIGEV_SIGNAL`, which indicates that the timer expiration generates a signal. The program can prevent the timer expiration from generating a signal by setting the `evp->sigev_notify` member to `SIGEV_NONE`.

If several timers generate the same signal, the handler can use `evp->sigev_value` to distinguish which timer generated the signal. In order to do this, the program must use the `SA_SIGINFO` flag in the `sa_flags` member of `struct sigaction` when it installs the handler for the signal. (See Program 6.7 on page 243 for an example of how to do this.)

The following three functions manipulate the per-process POSIX.1b timers.

```
SYNOPSIS

    #include <time.h>

    int timer_settime(timer_t timerid, int flags,
        const struct itimerspec *value,
        struct itimerspec *ovalue);
    int timer_gettime(timer_t timerid, struct itimerspec *value);
    int timer_getoverrun(timer_t timerid);

                                                                    POSIX.1b
```

The `timer_settime` function starts or stops a timer that was created by calling `timer_create`. The `flags` parameter indicates whether the timer uses relative or absolute time. Relative time is similar to the Spec 1170 timers, while absolute time allows for greater accuracy and control of timer drift. This is further discussed in Section 6.9. The last two parameters have the same meaning as for `setitimer`. The `timer_settime` and `timer_gettime` functions return 0 on success, while `timer_getoverrun` returns the number of timer overruns. On failure these functions return −1 and set `errno`.

Use `timer_gettime` like `getitimer` to get the time remaining on an active timer. It is possible for a timer to expire while a signal is still pending from a previous expiration of the same timer. In this case one of the signals generated may be lost. This is called timer overrun. A program can determine the number of such overruns for a particular timer by calling `timer_getoverrun`. Timer overruns occur only for signals generated by the same timer. Signals generated by multiple timers, even timers using the same clock and signal, are queued and not lost.

Program 6.3 creates a POSIX.1b timer to measure the running time of the function `function_to_time`. It is very similar to Program 6.2, but it uses real time rather than virtual time.

Program 6.3: A program segment that uses a POSIX.1b interval timer to measure the running time of a function.

```
#include <stdio.h>
#include <signal.h>
#include <time.h>
#include <unistd.h>
#define MILLION 1000000
#define THOUSAND 1000
```

```
timer_t time_ID;
struct itimerspec value;
struct itimerspec ovalue;
long timedif;

if (timer_create(CLOCK_REALTIME, NULL, &time_ID) < 0) {
    perror("Could not create a timer based on CLOCK_REALTIME");
    exit(1);
}
value.it_interval.tv_sec = 0;
value.it_interval.tv_nsec = 0;
value.it_value.tv_sec = MILLION;      /* a large number */
value.it_value.tv_nsec = 0;
timer_settime(time_ID, 0, &value, NULL);
timer_gettime(time_ID, &ovalue);
function_to_time();                   /* timed code goes here */
timer_gettime(time_ID, &value);
timedif = MILLION*(ovalue.it_value.tv_sec - value.it_value.tv_sec) +
    (ovalue.it_value.tv_nsec - value.it_value.tv_nsec)/THOUSAND;
printf("It took %ld microseconds\n", timedif);
```
_____ **Program 6.3** _____

Section 6.9 contains additional information about POSIX.1b timers. The timing project is described in terms of Spec 1170 timers, because POSIX.1b timers are not yet available in many implementations.

6.3 Project Overview

This chapter's project develops an implementation of multiple timers in terms of a single operating-system timer. The project consists of five semi-independent modules. Three of these are created as objects; the other two are main programs.

Figure 6.1 shows the five modules and their relationships. The dashed line shows communication through a pipe. Standard output of the `testtime` program is fed into standard input of the `timermain` program. The solid lines represent the calling of functions in the objects. The `timermain` program calls only functions in the `mytimers` object. The `mytimers` object calls functions in the `hardware_timer` and `showall` objects. The `hardware_timer` object calls functions in the `showall` object. The `showall` object, which is only for debugging, calls functions in both the `mytimers` and `hardware_timer` objects.

At the lowest level is the `hardware_timer` object. This object consists of a single operating-system timer that generates a signal when it expires. The un-

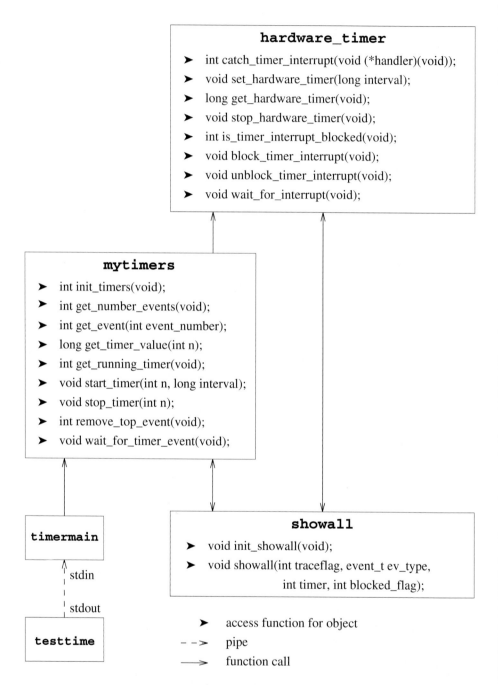

Figure 6.1: The five timers modules to be created in this project.

derlying timer object can be either a Spec 1170 or a POSIX.1b timer. While not truly a hardware timer, it is treated as such. The object provides interface functions which hide the underlying timer from outside users and in this sense behaves like a hardware timer. In theory, if the program has access to a real hardware timer, the underlying object can be this timer and the interface remains the same. The interface functions manipulate a single timer that generates a signal when it expires.

At the next level is the multiple timers object, `mytimers`. This object has interface functions which manipulate multiple timers by calling functions from the `hardware_timer` module.

A third object, the `showall` object, is for debugging and is called by functions in the other two objects to display a running log of the timer operations. It also calls functions from these other modules to obtain status information about the timers.

Each of the objects has a corresponding header file with the same name and a `.h` extension containing prototypes for the functions that are accessible from the outside. The object and any module that uses the object include this header file. Each object also has a local header file containing definitions and prototypes for items that are used internally to the object but hidden from the outside.

Two main programs are used for testing the timer objects. The first one, `timermain`, receives input from standard input to call functions in the `mytimers` object. It might, for example, start a timer to expire after a given interval. The timer is started when `timermain` receives this input.

It is critical to the debugging process that experiments producing incorrect results be precisely repeatable. Then, when a bug is detected, the programmer can fix the code and repeat the same experiment with the modified code. If the experiments rely on the timing of keyboard input, they are almost impossible to repeat. To solve this problem, the `testtime` program pipes data into `timermain` at precise intervals. The `testtime` program reads lines from standard input and interprets the first integer on the line as a delay time. After waiting for this amount of time, it sends the rest of the input line to standard output. The `testtime` program then reads its next input line and continues. This setup allows `testtime` to read input from a file and to simulate precisely-timed keyboard input for `timermain`.

The project is implemented in stages. Section 6.4 introduces the data structures and gives examples of setting a single timer. Section 6.5 introduces the three objects and specifies how to handle the setting of a single timer. Section 6.6 handles multiple active timers, Section 6.7 discusses some of the race conditions that can occur with multiple timers and how to avoid them, and Section 6.8 introduces a simple timer application. Section 6.9 discusses advanced timer issues in terms of POSIX timers and how POSIX timers can implement a timer facility.

6.4 Simple Timers

Operating systems often implement multiple software timers based on a single hardware timer. A software timer can be represented by a timer number and an indication of when the timer expires. The implementation depends on the type of hardware timer available.

Suppose the hardware timer generates interrupts at regular short intervals. The time interval is usually referred to as the clock tick time. The timer interrupt service routine keeps track of the time remaining on each timer (in terms of clock ticks) and decrements this time for each tick of the clock. When it decrements the timer to 0, the program takes the appropriate action. This approach is inefficient if the number of timers is large or if the clock tick time is short.

Alternatively a program can keep the timer information in a list sorted by expiration time. Each entry contains a timer number and an expiration time. The first entry in the list contains the first timer to expire and the time until expiration (in clock ticks). The second entry contains the next timer to expire and the expiration time relative to the time the first timer expired, and so on. With this representation, the interrupt service routine only decrements one counter on the each clock tick, but there is additional overhead involved when the program starts a timer. It must insert the new timer in a sorted timer list and update the time of the timer that expires immediately after the new one.

Exercise 6.5

For each of the two cases described above, what is the time complexity of the interrupt handler and the start timer function in terms of the number of timers?

Answer:

Suppose there are n timers. For the first method, the interrupt handler is $O(n)$ since all timer values must be decremented. The start timer function is $O(1)$ since a timer can be started independently of the other timers. For the second method, the interrupt handler is usually $O(1)$ since only the first timer value must be decremented. However, when this causes the timer to expire, the next entry has to be examined to make sure it did not expire at the same time. This can degenerate to $O(n)$ in the worst case, but in practice the worst case is unlikely. The start timer function is $O(n)$ to insert the timer in the sorted list or less if using a more complex data structure such as a heap.

If the system has a hardware interval timer instead of a simple clock, a program can set the interval timer to expire at a time corresponding to the software timer with the earliest expiration. There is no overhead unless a timer expires, one is started, or one is stopped. Interval timers are efficient when the timer intervals are long.

Exercise 6.6

Analyze the interrupt handler and the start timer function for an interval timer.

Answer:

The complexity depends on whether the timers are kept in a sorted list. The interrupt handler is the same order as the clock tick timer above. The start timer function is $O(n)$ if the timer is kept in a sorted list because all entries in the timer structure might have to be accessed.

The project uses an interval timer to implement multiple timers, replacing the hardware timer by the ITIMER_REAL. When the ITIMER_REAL expires, it generates a SIGALRM signal and the SIGALRM signal handler puts an entry in an event list.

Figure 6.2 shows a simple implementation of five software timers. The individual timers (designated by 0 through 4) are represented by long's in the array active. An array entry of −1 is used for a timer that is not active. The event array keeps a list of timers that have expired, and num_events holds the number of unhandled events.

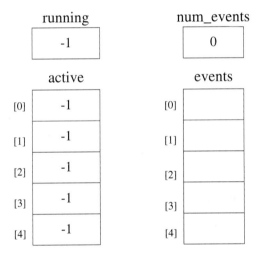

Figure 6.2: The timers data structure with no timers active.

Start a timer by specifying a timer number and an interval in microseconds. Figure 6.3 shows the data structures after timer 2 is started for five seconds (5, 000, 000 microseconds). No timers have expired so the event list is still empty.

Just writing the information into the active array in Figure 6.2 is not enough to implement a timer. The program must set the ITIMER_REAL timer for 5, 000, 000 microseconds. When SIGALRM is delivered, the program must clear the active array entry and mark an entry in the event array. Figure 6.4 shows the timer data structure after ITIMER_REAL expires.

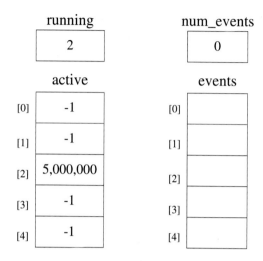

Figure 6.3: The `timers` data structure after timer 2 has been set for five seconds.

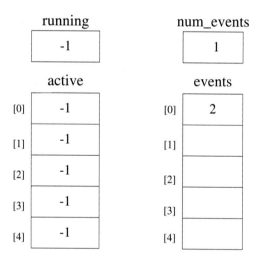

Figure 6.4: The `timers` data structure after timer 2 has expired.

6.5 Setting One of Five Single Timers

This section describes an implementation for setting one of five possible software timers using the underlying process interval timer ITIMER_REAL. The main program takes the timer number and the timer interval (in microseconds) as command-line arguments and calls the start_timer function. The main program then waits for the timer to expire, prints out a message that the timer has expired, and exits.

6.5.1 The mytimers Object

Implement the software timers in an object called mytimers. Use a static variable called timers of type timer_data_t to hold the internal timer data for the object. The timer_data_t data structure is

```
#define MAXTIMERS 5
typedef struct timer_data_t {
    int running;
    long active[MAXTIMERS];
    int num_events;
    int events[MAXTIMERS];
} timer_data_t;
```

The members of timer_data_t structure have the following meanings:

running   is the number of the timer that is running or -1 if none are active. The running timer is the one that is next to expire. It is the one whose expiration time causes the one real timer (set with set_hardware_timer specified on page 226) to generate a signal.

active   has an entry for each timer giving the expiration time (in μsec) relative to the starting time of the running timer. A negative value indicates the timer is not active. (In this part only one timer is ever active.)

num_events   is the number of entries in the events array.

events   is a list of timers that have expired in the order in which they have expired. (There is at most one timer on the list for the program of this section.)

The integer representation of the time intervals simplifies the code but limits the length of the intervals to about 2000 seconds (a little more than half an hour) for 32-bit integers. This should be more than enough for testing the algorithms.

Place the timers data structure in mytimers.c along with the following functions which are callable from outside the object:

➤ `init_timers` initializes the `timers` data structure as shown in Figure 6.2.
The function also calls initialization functions for the `hardware_timer`
object and the `showall` object. The `init_timers` function returns 0 on
success and −1 on failure. Its prototype is

```
int init_timers(void);
```

➤ `get_number_events` returns the value of `num_events`. Its prototype is

```
int get_number_events(void);
```

➤ `get_event` returns the timer number associated with a particular entry in
the `events` array. Its prototype is

```
int get_event(int event_number);
```

The `event_number` parameter specifies the position in the `events` array, which is indexed from 0. The `get_event` functions returns −1 if
`event_number` is negative or greater than or equal to `num_events`.

➤ `get_timer_value` returns the current value of a specified timer from the
`active` array or −1 if the timer is not active or the timer number is invalid.
Its prototype is

```
long get_timer_value(int n);
```

The parameter `n` is the number of the timer.

➤ `get_running_timer` returns the timer number of the running timer or −1
if there is no running timer. Its prototype is

```
int get_running_timer(void);
```

➤ `start_timer` starts a timer with the time interval given in microseconds.
For this part assume that no other timers are or were ever running. Its prototype is

```
void start_timer(int n, long interval);
```

The parameter `n` specifies the timer to be started, and `interval` is the
number of microseconds in the future after which the timer should expire.
To start timer `n`

* Remove timer `n` from the event list if it is there.
* Set `running` to timer `n`.
* Set `active[n]` to the appropriate time value.
* Start the interval timer by calling the `set_hardware_timer` func-
tion in the `hardware_timer` object.

➤ `stop_timer` stops a timer if it is running and removes the timer from the
event list if it is there. Its prototype is

```
void stop_timer(int n);
```

This function is needed later when multiple timers are handled.

➤ `remove_top_event` removes the top event from the event list and returns the timer number or -1 if the event list is empty. Its prototype is

```
int remove_top_event(void);
```

This function is needed later when multiple timers are handled.

➤ `wait_for_timer_event` waits until there is an event on the event list and then returns without changing the event list. Its prototype is

```
void wait_for_timer_event(void);
```

The `mytimers` object also contains the following functions which are not directly accessible from the outside. These include

- `myhandler` handles the timer signal. This function is called by the actual signal handler to maintain the `timers` structure when the real hardware timer expires. It must do the following:
  * Add the running timer to the end of the event list.

  * Make the running timer inactive.

  * Update the `timers` data structure.

  * Reset the interval timer if there is an active timer. (There will not be one in the single timer case.)

  Its prototype is

  ```
  static void myhandler(void);
  ```

- `put_on_event_list_and_deactivate` sets a timer to be inactive, removes it from the event list if it was there, and puts it at the end of the event list. Its prototype is

  ```
  static void put_on_event_list_and_deactivate(int n);
  ```

  The parameter n is the number of the timer to be deactivated. The function `put_on_event_list_and_deactivate` takes no action if n is negative or greater than or equal to `MAXTIMERS`.

Since the `hardware_timer` object handles the signals, it must contain the actual signal handler. The prototype of the signal handler may depend on the implementation and should not be part of the `mytimers` object. Since the timers must be manipulated when the signal is caught, this work should be done in the `mytimers` object. The real signal handler calls `myhandler` to do this. Since `myhandler` is declared to have internal linkage, it is passed to the `catch_timer_interrupt` in the `hardware_timer` object.

6.5.2 The `hardware_timer` Object

The `hardware_timer` object contains the code to handle a single "hardware" timer. The functions that are accessible from outside the object are

> ➤ `catch_timer_interrupt` uses `sigaction` to set up a signal handler to catch the `SIGALRM` signal. The function returns 0 if successful or −1 if there was an error. Its prototype is

```
int catch_timer_interrupt(void (*handler)(void));
```

> The `handler` parameter is the name of the function that does the work of handling the signal. The actual signal handler in `hardware_timer` just calls the `handler` function. The `mytimers` object calls the function `catch_timer_interrupt` to set up signal handling.

> ➤ `set_hardware_timer` starts the `ITIMER_REAL` timer running with the given interval in microseconds. Call `set_hardware_timer` only when the timer interrupt is blocked or the interval timer is stopped. Its prototype is

```
void set_hardware_timer(long interval);
```

> The `interval` parameter specifies the interval for setting the timer in microseconds. Use `setitimer` to implement this function.

> ➤ `get_hardware_timer` returns the time remaining on the hardware timer if it is running or 0 if it is not running. Use `getitimer` to implement this function. Its prototype is

```
long get_hardware_timer(void);
```

> ➤ `stop_hardware_timer` stops the hardware timer if it is running. Its prototype is

```
void stop_hardware_timer(void);
```

> ➤ `is_timer_interrupt_blocked` returns 1 if the `SIGALRM` is blocked and 0 otherwise. Its prototype is

```
int is_timer_interrupt_blocked(void);
```

> ➤ `block_timer_interrupt` blocks the `SIGALRM` signal. Its prototype is

```
void block_timer_interrupt(void);
```

> ➤ `unblock_timer_interrupt` unblocks the `SIGALRM` signal. Its prototype is

```
void unblock_timer_interrupt(void);
```

> ➤ `wait_for_interrupt` calls `sigsuspend` to wait until a signal is caught. It does not guarantee that the signal was from a timer expiration. This func-

tion is normally entered with the timer signal blocked. The signal set used by `sigsuspend` must not unblock any signals that were already blocked other than the one being used for the timers. If the main program has blocked `SIGINT`, the program should not terminate if a `ctrl-c` is pushed. The prototype of `wait_for_interrupt` is

```
void wait_for_interrupt(void);
```

Some of these functions are not needed until a later part of this project. The interface to the hardware timer is isolated in this file, so using POSIX.1b timers or a different underlying timer than `ITIMER_REAL` only requires changing these functions. Define a header file called `hardware_timer.h` that has the prototypes of the functions in the `hardware_timers` object.

6.5.3 Main Program Implementation

Write a main program that does the following:

- Initializes everything by calling `init_timers`.
- Calls `start_timer` with the values passed on the command line.
- Detects when the timer has expired by calling `remove_top_event()` in a loop until an event is removed. This form of busy waiting is called *polling* and is quite inefficient.
- Outputs an informative message to standard output.
- Exits.

Once the program is working, call `wait_for_timer_event` instead of looping.

6.5.4 Instrumenting the Timer Code, the `showall` Object

Code with signal handlers and timers is hard to test because of the unpredictable nature of the events that drive the program. A particular timing of events that causes an error might occur rarely and not be easily reproducible. Furthermore, the behavior of the program depends not only on the input values but also on the rate at which input data is generated.

This section describes how to instrument the code with calls to a `showall` function as a preliminary step in testing. This instrumentation is critical for debugging the later parts of the project. The code for the `showall` function is provided. This subsection explains what `showall` does and how to use it in the program.

The prototype for `showall` is

```
void showall(int traceflag, event_t ev_type, int timer,
             int blocked_flag);
```

If `traceflag` is 1, the `showall` function displays a message corresponding to the value of `ev_type` and displays the `timers` data structure in a single line format. It also displays the value of the `timer` parameter if it makes sense to do so for the event. Program 6.4 shows the `showall.h` file to be included by programs that call `showall`.

Program 6.4: The `showall.h` header file.

```
typedef enum ev_t {TIMER_INITIALIZE,
       TIMER_INTERRUPT_ENTER, TIMER_INTERRUPT_EXIT,
       TIMER_START_ENTER, TIMER_START_EXIT,
       TIMER_STOP_ENTER, TIMER_STOP_EXIT,
       TIMER_REMOVE_EVENT_ENTER, TIMER_REMOVE_EVENT_EXIT,
       TIMER_REMOVE_EVENT_NONE, TIMER_REMOVE_EVENT_OK,
       TIMER_START_NONE_RUNNING, TIMER_START_THIS_NOT_RUNNING,
       TIMER_START_THIS_RUNNING, TIMER_STOP_RUNNING,
       TIMER_STOP_EXIT_NOT_ACTIVE, TIMER_STOP_EXIT_NOT_RUNNING,
       TIMER_WAIT_INPUT, TIMER_GOT_INPUT} event_t;

void init_showall(void);
void showall(int traceflag, event_t ev_type, int timer,
             int blocked_flag);
```

_____ **Program 6.4** _____

Example 6.4

The following statement shows how `showall` *is called. Place this call early in the* `myhandler` *function of the* `mytimers` *object.*

```
showall(traceflag, TIMER_INTERRUPT_ENTER, this_timer, 1);
```

The `showall` call of Example 6.4 appears at the beginning of `myhandler`. The `myhandler` gets the value of `this_timer` from `timers.running`. The last parameter indicates that `showall` can assume that the timer signal is blocked. If `traceflag` is 1, then each time the interrupt handler is entered, `showall` causes a line similar to the following to be displayed:

```
****   6.39043: Timer Interrupt Enter 1 B(1,1.00) A:(1,1:00) (0E)
```

The interpretation of the `showall` output is

- The leading four asterisks (****) identify the message as output from `showall`.

- The first numeric field is the current time in seconds since the start of the program.

- Next comes a string indicating the event that caused this message to appear. In Example 6.4 showall was called with the TIMER_INTERRUPT_ENTER event type.
- Next comes the number of the timer that was running when the signal was caught.
- The letter B indicates that the timer interrupt was blocked when showall was entered. This information is obtained from the last parameter to showall. Three more asterisks follow if the parameter does not agree with the actual blocked status of the timer signal as reported by is_timer_interrupt_blocked, indicating a bug in one of the functions.
- The next values in parentheses are the running timer and the time active[running] displayed in seconds.
- The next field starts with an A: and contains a list of all active timers with their active entries. In the above case only timer 1 is active.
- Lastly, (0E) indicates that there are no events on the event list. If there are events, the number of events is displayed followed by E followed by the events.

Program 6.4 shows the possible values of event_t. Here are the event_t values relevant to the start_timer function. In each case the timer parameter is the number of the timer being started.

TIMER_START_ENTER:	first statement of start_timer
TIMER_START_EXIT:	before each return statement.
TIMER_START_THIS_NOT_RUNNING:	when start_timer determines that no timers are active.
TIMER_START_ONE_RUNNING:	when start_timer determines that at least one timer is active.
TIMER_START_THIS_RUNNING:	when start_timer determines that the timer to be started is already running.

The single timer implementation needs only the first two of these. Program 6.5 has the source code for showall and the other files that are needed. The showall function uses printf even though it is not on the list of POSIX async-signal safe functions. Sun Solaris has an async-signal safe printf function, and it was easier to succumb to nonportability than to use write.

The showall function and its supporting functions should be in a separate file. The showall function does most of its work with the timer signal blocked so that the timer structure does not change during its calculation. It blocks the signal if it is not already blocked. Before returning, showall unblocks the signal only if it was unblocked at the time `showall` was called. The last parameter to `showall` indicates whether the signal is already blocked. The calling function should have this information. As a debugging aid, `showall` checks to see if the `blocked_flag` correctly has this information.

Program 6.5: The `showall` function

```
#include <stdio.h>
#include <stdlib.h>
#include <signal.h>
#include <sys/time.h>
#include "mytimers.h"
#include "hardware_timer.h"
#include "showall.h"
extern int gettimeofday(struct timeval *tp, void *tzp);

static double initial_tod = 0.0;

/* get_time returns seconds since January 1, 1970 as a double */
static double get_time(void)
{
    struct timeval tval;
    double thistime = 0.0;

    if (gettimeofday(&tval,NULL) == -1)
        perror("Warning, cannot get time of day");
    else
        thistime = tval.tv_sec + (double)tval.tv_usec/MILLION;
    return thistime;
}

/* get_relative_time returns seconds since init_showall was called */
static double get_relative_time(void)
{
    return get_time() - initial_tod;
}

/* init_showall sets global initial_tod to seconds since Jan 1, 1970 */
void init_showall(void)
{
    initial_tod = get_time();
}

/* time_to_double converts microseconds to seconds in double format */
static double time_to_double(long interval)
{
    return (double)interval/MILLION;
}
```

```
/* show_timer_data displays the timers data structure. */
static void show_timer_data(void)
{
   int i;

   printf("(%d,%.2f) A:", get_running_timer(),
      time_to_double(get_timer_value(get_running_timer())));
   for (i = 0; i < MAXTIMERS; i++)
      if (get_timer_value(i) >= 0)
         printf("(%d,%.2f) ", i, time_to_double(get_timer_value(i)));
   printf(" (%dE", get_number_events());
   for (i = 0; i < get_number_events(); i++)
      printf(" %d", get_event(i));
   printf(")\n");
}

/* showall displays timers with  message corresponding to ev_type */
void showall(int traceflag, event_t ev_type, int timer,
            int blocked_flag)
{
   int actual_blocked_flag;

   if (!traceflag)
      return;
   actual_blocked_flag = is_timer_interrupt_blocked();
   if (!blocked_flag)
      block_timer_interrupt();
   printf("**** %8.4f: ", get_relative_time());
   switch(ev_type) {
      case TIMER_INITIALIZE:
         printf("Timer Initialize ");
         break;
      case TIMER_INTERRUPT_ENTER:
         printf("Timer Interrupt Enter %d ", timer);
         break;
      case TIMER_INTERRUPT_EXIT:
         printf("Timer Interrupt Exit  %d ", timer);
         break;
      case TIMER_START_ENTER:
         printf("Timer Start Enter %d ", timer);
         break;
      case TIMER_START_EXIT:
         printf("Timer Start Exit  %d ", timer);
         break;
      case TIMER_STOP_ENTER:
         printf("Timer Stop Enter %d ", timer);
         break;
      case TIMER_STOP_EXIT:
```

```
        printf("Timer Stop Exit   %d ", timer);
        break;
    case TIMER_REMOVE_EVENT_ENTER:
        printf("Timer Remove Event Enter ");
        break;
    case TIMER_REMOVE_EVENT_EXIT:
        printf("Timer Remove Event Exit  ");
        break;
    case TIMER_REMOVE_EVENT_NONE:
        printf("Timer Remove Event None  ");
        break;
    case TIMER_REMOVE_EVENT_OK:
        printf("Timer Remove Event OK    ");
        break;
    case TIMER_START_NONE_RUNNING:
        printf("Timer Start None Running ");
        break;
    case TIMER_START_THIS_NOT_RUNNING:
        printf("Timer Start This Not Running ");
        break;
    case TIMER_START_THIS_RUNNING:
        printf("Timer Start This Running ");
        break;
    case TIMER_STOP_RUNNING:
        printf("Timer Stop Running ");
        break;
    case TIMER_STOP_EXIT_NOT_ACTIVE:
        printf("Timer Stop Exit Not Active ");
        break;
    case TIMER_STOP_EXIT_NOT_RUNNING:
        printf("Timer Stop Exit Not Running ");
        break;
    case TIMER_WAIT_INPUT:
        printf("Timer Wait Input ");
        break;
    case TIMER_GOT_INPUT:
        printf("Timer Got Input ");
        break;
    default:
        printf("**** Unknown Event Type ");
        break;
    }
if (blocked_flag)
    printf("B");
else
    printf("U");
if (blocked_flag != actual_blocked_flag)
    printf("***");
show_timer_data();
```

```
    fflush(stdout);
    if (!blocked_flag)
        unblock_timer_interrupt();
}
```

_____ **Program 6.5** _____

Put the code of Program 6.5 in a separate file. Instrument the timer functions so that each time something of interest occurs, the program calls `showall` with the appropriate `event_t` value. For this part, just insert the following four lines:
Early in `myhandler`:

```
    showall(traceflag, TIMER_INTERRUPT_ENTER, this_timer, 1);
```

Before returning from `myhandler`:

```
    showall(traceflag, TIMER_INTERRUPT_EXIT, this_timer, 1);
```

First line of `start_timer`:

```
    showall(traceflag, START_TIMER_ENTER, timer, 0);
```

Before returning from `start_timer`:

```
    showall(traceflag, START_TIMER_EXIT, timer, 0);
```

Test the program with a variety of appropriate inputs and observe the output of `showall`.

After testing the instrumented code, modify the main program so that instead of setting a timer from command-line arguments, it reads the timer number and interval from standard input. Add an outer loop so that the main program repeats the following until it encounters an end-of-file on standard input:

- Read a timer number and an interval in microseconds from standard input.

- Call `start_timer` to set the timer.

- Wait for the timer to expire as before.

6.6 Multiple Timers

The potential interactions of multiple timers make their implementation more complex than single timers. All of the times in the `active` array are specified relative to the start of the underlying `ITIMER_REAL` interval timer. Suppose that a program wants to set timer 4 for seven seconds and that two seconds have elapsed since it set timer 2 for five seconds. The procedure to use is

- Find out how much time is left on the real timer by calling the function `get_hardware_timer`.
- Find the start of the real timer relative to the currently running timer by subtracting the time left on the real timer from the timer value of the `running` timer. (Use `get_running_timer`.)
- Calculate the time of the timer to be set relative to the start time by adding the relative start time from step 2 to the requested time.

Figure 6.3 shows the `timers` data structures after a program sets timer 2 for five seconds $(5,000,000$ microseconds). Suppose that two seconds later, the program sets timer 4 for seven seconds $(7,000,000$ microseconds). Figure 6.5 shows the `timers` data structure after timer 4 is set. The program calls `get_hardware_timer` to find that there are three seconds left $(3,000,000$ microseconds) on the interval timer, so two seconds $(5,000,000 - 3,000,000$ microseconds) have elapsed since it set timer 2. The program then computes the time for timer 4 relative to the start of the original setting of the real timer as nine seconds $(2,000,000 + 7,000,000$ microseconds).

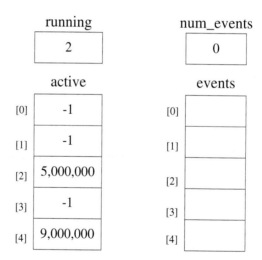

Figure 6.5: The `timers` data structure after timer 4 has been set.

The `running` timer is the same in Figure 6.3 and Figure 6.5 because timer 4 expires after timer 2. The program did not change the `running` timer designation or reset the timer in this case. Continuing the situation of Figure 6.5, suppose that a program wants to set timer 3 for one second and a call to `get_hardware_timer` shows that the real timer has two seconds left. Timer 3 should expire before the real timer is scheduled to expire so the program must reset the real timer. Figure 6.6 shows the situation after the program sets timer 3. The program resets the real timer to expire in one second and adjusts all of the other times in `active`. The new times are relative to the start time of timer 3 rather than to that of timer 2 (three seconds ago), so the program subtracted three seconds from each of the active times.

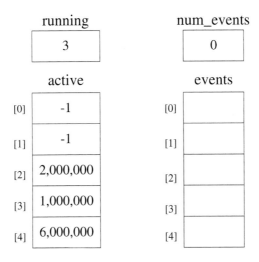

Figure 6.6: The `timers` data structure after timer 3 has been set.

Figure 6.7 shows the situation a little over a second after timer 3 was set. Timer 3 expires and timer 2 becomes the running timer. All of the times are readjusted to expire relative to timer 2.

Figure 6.8 shows the situation two seconds later. Timer 2 expires and timer 4 becomes the running timer.

6.6.1 Setting Multiple Timers

This section discusses the handling of simultaneous timers. Modify the `start_timer` function and add a `stop_timer` function to handle all of the cases of timers being set while other timers are running. At any moment, each timer is either active or inactive. An active timer cannot appear on the event list but is added to the event list when it expires. If any of the timers is active, exactly one of them is *running*. The running timer is the one that is next to expire. Its expiration time has been used in `set_hardware_timer` so that a signal is generated when its time expires.

The choice of how starting and stopping a timer affect the event list is arbitrary. This implementation removes an event corresponding to the timer to be started or stopped if

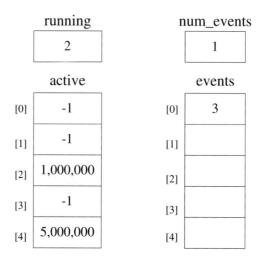

Figure 6.7: The `timers` data structure after timer 3 expires.

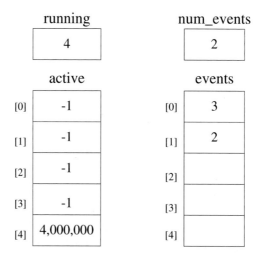

Figure 6.8: The `timers` data structure after timer 2 expires.

one is there. This choice ensures that no timer is represented by more than one event on the event list, so that the size of the event list cannot exceed the number of timers. The bound on the event list simplifies the implementation.

With multiple timers active, the signal handler must update the `timers` data structure by subtracting `active[running]` from all active times. If the time becomes 0, the corresponding timer has expired and that timer should be placed on the event list and made inactive. This method handles multiple timers expiring at the same time.

Section 6.5 handles the simplest case, that of starting a timer when no timer is running. The case in which the timer to be started is already running but all other timers are inactive is similar.

Suppose some other timer is running when a timer is started. If the timer to be started expires after the running timer, only one entry in the `timers` data structure needs to be modified. However, if starting this timer causes it to expire before the currently running timer, the interval timer must be reset. The entries in the `active` array also need to be adjusted so they are relative to the starting time of the new running timer. This can be done by decrementing the active times by the time that the currently running timer has been running (`runtime`).

Use `get_hardware_timer` to find the `remaining` time on the interval timer and calculate `runtime = active[running] - remaining`. Some of the things that have to be done in this case are

- Remove the timer from the event list.

- Adjust all active times by `runtime`.

- Set a new `running` timer.

- Start the interval timer by calling `set_hardware_timer`.

The case in which the timer to be started is the running timer can be treated either as a special case of the above or as a separate case.

A call to `stop_timer` for a timer that is not active just removes the timer from the event list. If the timer was active but not running, set it to be inactive. The interesting case is that of stopping the running timer. This case is similar to the case of starting a timer that becomes the running timer because the `timers` data structure needs to be updated using `runtime` and a new running timer has to be selected.

In this part, the program should handle all combinations of starting and stopping timers as well as removing events from the event list. Enhance the `start_timer` and `myhandler` functions appropriately and write the functions `remove_top_event` and `stop_timer` which were not needed before.

Modify the main program so that it interprets a negative interval as a command to stop the timer. Instrument the functions with `showall` for testing. The following summarizes where `showall` should be called.

In `myhandler` with `timer` equal to `timers.running`:

`TIMER_INTERRUPT_ENTER:`	early in the function
`TIMER_INTERRUPT_EXIT:`	last statement before return

In `remove_top_event` with `timer` equal to 0:

TIMER_REMOVE_EVENT_ENTER :	first statement
TIMER_REMOVE_EVENT_EXIT :	last statement before return
TIMER_REMOVE_EVENT_NONE :	if no events to remove
TIMER_REMOVE_EVENT_OK :	if there is an event to remove

In `start_timer` with `timer` set to the timer to be started:

TIMER_START_ENTER :	first statement
TIMER_START_EXIT :	last statement before return
TIMER_START_NONE_RUNNING :	if no timer is running
TIMER_START_THIS_NOT_RUNNING :	if the running timer is not this one
TIMER_START_THIS_RUNNING :	if this timer is running

In `stop_timer` with `timer` set to the timer to be stopped:

TIMER_STOP_ENTER :	first statement
TIMER_STOP_EXIT :	last statement before return
TIMER_STOP_EXIT_NOT_ACTIVE :	last statement before return if this timer was not active
TIMER_STOP_EXIT_NOT_RUNNING :	last statement before return if this timer was active but not running
TIMER_STOP_RUNNING :	if this timer was running

6.6.2 Testing with Multiple Timers

Even code instrumented by `showall` is difficult to test systematically, since the action of the program depends on the speed of the input typing. One approach to this problem is to use a driver, `testtime`, to generate the input for the program. Program 6.6 shows the `testtime` program. It must be linked to the `hardware_timer` object.

As with any filter, `testtime` takes input from standard input and sends output to standard output. The input consists of lines containing three integers, `n`, `m`, and `p`. The filter reads in these three integers, waits `n` microseconds and then outputs `m` and `p` on a single line. The `testtime` program ignores any characters on the line after the three integers so that a user can add comments to the end of each input line.

Example 6.5

When `testtime` *receives the following input*

```
1000000   2   5000000
2000000   4   7000000
1000000   3   1000000
```

`testtime` *waits one second* (1, 000, 000 *microseconds) and outputs the line*

```
2 5000000
```

The program then waits two more seconds and outputs the line

```
4 7000000
```

and then waits one second and outputs the line

```
3 1000000
```

Suppose the data is in the file `timer.input` and the timer program is called `timermain`. Use the filter as follows:

```
testtime < timer.input | timermain
```

This command causes timer 2 to start at time 1 second and to expire five seconds later (at time 6). Two seconds later (at time 3) timer 4 starts and expires in seven seconds (at time 10). One second later (at time 4) timer 3 is set to expire in one second (at time 5). This is exactly the situation illustrated in Figure 6.6 on page 235.

The main program reads input timer values from standard input as before. Pipe the output of `testtime` to standard input of the main program. Develop an extensive set of input data for testing the program.

Program 6.6: The program `testtime`.

```c
#include <stdio.h>
#include <stdlib.h>
#include <signal.h>
#include <sys/time.h>
#include "hardware.h"

static int timer_expired = 0;
static void myalarm(int s)
{
    timer_expired = 1;
}

void main(int argc, char *argv[])
{
    long interval;
    int n1;
    int n2;

    if (argc != 1) {
        fprintf(stderr, "Usage: %s\n", argv[0]);
        exit(1);
    }
    catch_timer_interrupt(myalarm);
    for( ; ; ){
```

```
      if (scanf("%ld%d%d%*[^\n]", &interval, &n1, &n2) == EOF)
         break;
      if (interval <= 0)
         break;
      block_timer_interrupt();
      set_hardware_timer(interval);
      while (!timer_expired)
         wait_for_interrupt();
      timer_expired = 0;
      printf("%d %d\n", n1, n2);
      fflush(stdout);
      fprintf(stderr,"%d %d\n", n1, n2);
   }
   exit(0);
}
```

_____ **Program 6.6** _____

6.7 A Robust Implementation of Multiple Timers

What happens if a SIGALRM signal is delivered during execution of the start_timer
function? Both the signal handler and the start_timer function modify the timers
data structure, a shared resource. This is the classical critical section problem for shared
variables, and care must be taken to ensure that the timers data structure is not cor-
rupted. It is very difficult to determine if such a problem exists in the code by testing
alone. The events that might cause corruption of the data structure are rare and usually
would not show up during testing. If such an event occurred, it would not be easily repeatable and so there might be little information about its cause.

   It is therefore important to analyze the problem to determine where the critical sections are. In this case, the analysis is simple since there is only one global variable, the
timers data structure. Any function that modifies this structure must do so at a time
when the SIGALRM signal handler may not be entered. The simplest approach is to
block the SIGALRM signal before modifying the timers data structure.

   Just blocking SIGALRM may not be sufficient. What happens if the interval timer
expires during the execution of the start_timer function and SIGALRM is blocked?
The start_timer function might make a new timer the running timer and reset the
interval timer. Before the start_timer function terminates, it unblocks SIGALRM.
At this point the signal is delivered and the handler assumes that the new timer had expired. While this sequence of events is extremely unlikely, Exercise 6.7 shows another
problem.

Exercise 6.7

Describe a sequence of events in which the stop_timer function could fail even if it blocked the signal on entry and unblocked it on exit.

Answer:

The stop_timer function blocks the SIGALRM signal. The timer to be stopped then expires (i.e., the interval timer generates a signal). This signal is not immediately delivered to the process since the signal is blocked. The stop_timer function then starts the interval timer corresponding to the next timer to expire. Before it returns, the stop_timer function unblocks the signal and the signal is delivered. The signal handler behaves as if the running timer just expired, when in fact a different timer had expired.

The simplest way to handle the problem described in Exercise 6.7 is to ignore the signal rather than block it. An ignored signal cannot be pending. After ignoring the signal and manipulating the data structure, it is necessary to catch the signal again. Care must be taken to not ignore the signal unless that signal corresponds to the timer's being stopped. The program does not work if stop_timer ignores the signal on entry and catches it again before returning. Suppose the stop_timer function were entered and the timer to be stopped was not the running timer. If the signal were ignored and the running timer expired before the signal was caught again, this timer would be lost.

Another possible approach that does not involve ignoring the signal is to have a global variable indicating to myhandler that the next signal should not be acted upon. In any case it will probably be necessary to add functions to the hardware_timer object to handle this problem.

Do a complete analysis of the start_timer and stop_timer functions and modify the implementation of Section 6.6 so that the timers are handled robustly. Devise a method of testing to verify that the program works correctly. (The test will involve simulating rare events.)

6.8 mycron, a Small Cron Facility

The cron facility in UNIX allows users to execute commands at specified dates and times. This facility is quite flexible and allows regularly scheduled commands. It is implemented with a cron daemon which analyzes a file containing timing and command information.

Implement a simplified personal cron facility called mycron. Write a program that takes one command-line argument. The argument represents a data file containing time intervals and commands. Each line of the data file specifies a command and how often that command is to be executed. The lines of the data file have the following format:

```
interval command
```

The `interval` specifies the number of seconds between execution of instances of the command. The `command` is the command to execute with its arguments.

- Implement the above cron facility assuming none of the intervals in the cron data file are longer than the maximum interval that the timers can handle (about thirty minutes). Call the executable `mycron`.
- Handle the case in which the intervals can be arbitrarily large. Assume that the number of seconds in the interval will fit in a `long`. Try to do this without modifying the timer functions.
- Find a way to adjust the starting times so that if two commands have commensurate intervals, they will not always be executing at the same time.

6.9 POSIX Timer Implementation

POSIX.1b timers have several advantages over Spec 1170 timers. Under POSIX a program can create several timers for a given clock such as `CLOCK_REALTIME`. The timers have a potentially greater resolution since values are given to the nearest nanosecond rather than the nearest microsecond. The program can specify which signal is delivered for each timer, and the signal handler can determine which timer generated the signal. Also, the signals generated by the timers are queued, and program can determine when signals have been lost due to overruns.

There are several possible implementations of multiple timers of Section 6.6 with POSIX timers. The simplest method is to use one timer and make minor changes in the data types to accommodate the higher resolution. Alternatively, a separate POSIX timer can implement each software timer. Starting and stopping a timer as well as handling the timer signal is independent of the other timers, so the only shared structure is the event queue. The `mytimers` and `hardware_timer` object might have to be reorganized. There may be a limit to the number of timers that are supported for each process given by the constant `TIMER_MAX`. If the number of timers needed is small, this method would be the easiest to implement. A third approach is to use a single POSIX timer but modify the method of implementation to make the timing more accurate. The remainder of this section develops a test program illustrating how to do this.

One of the problems with the original timer implementation of this chapter is that there can be a significant amount of timer drift if the time intervals are small. A *timer drift* occurs because signals are not delivered immediately when they are generated and signal handling takes a nonzero amount of time. There is always a delay between when an interval timer expires and when it is restarted. If the expiration time is short, the drift can be a significant portion of the time lapsed. For Spec 1170 timers there is no way to take into account the amount of time between when a timer expires and the next timer is started.

Suppose the multiple software timer program of Section 6.6 starts two timers—one timer expires at time 5 seconds and the other at time 5.1 seconds. When the signal handler catches the first signal, it restarts the timer for an additional .1 seconds. On a heavily loaded system, a signal generated at time 5 might not be caught until time 5.05, or later. If the handler catches the signal at 5.05, it still sets the next timer to expire .1 seconds later at time 5.15 instead of time 5.1. The delay (timer drift) affects all active timers.

The timer drift arises because the program uses relative expiration times and small errors in expiration time accumulate. This approach is mandated by the nature of the underlying interval timer. If the underlying timer can be set to expire at a particular time rather than a particular interval, the program can use actual or absolute time to eliminate the drift because delays in signal handling do not change the time of next expiration in this case.

POSIX timers support both relative times like the Spec 1170 timers and absolute times. To set a timer using absolute times, set the `flags` parameter of `timer_settime` to `TIMER_ABSTIME`. A program uses absolute times to solve the timer drift problem described above as follows.

- Before starting the first timer, determine the current time and add five seconds to compute the absolute expiration time.
- Call `timer_settime` using the absolute expiration time for the `value` parameter and `TIMER_ABSTIME` for the `flags` parameter.
- When the timer expires, have the interrupt handler add .1 second to the saved absolute time and start the timer using this value. As long as the second timer is started before it is to expire, there is no timer drift.

It is possible for the signal handler to set the timer to expire at a time that is earlier than the current time if the latency in handling the signal is high. The past expiration is not considered to be an error, and in this case the timer expires immediately.

Program 6.7, called `abstime`, allows user experimentation with absolute and relative POSIX.1b timers by making it easy to set a timer that expires at regular intervals. The `abstime` program also computes the timer drift to give the user a feeling for the size of the drift when the interval times are small. It includes a settable amount of busy-waiting in the signal handler to simulate varying system loads.

Program 6.7: The `abstime` program illustrates POSIX.1b timers with absolute time.

```c
#include <stdio.h>
#include <stdlib.h>
#include <unistd.h>
#include <signal.h>
#include <string.h>
#include <time.h>
```

```
#define BILLION  1000000000
#define D_BILLION 1000000000.0
#define INCTIME 0.01
#define NUMTIMES 1
#define SPINTIME 0.0

struct itimerspec interval;
int tflags;
int exitflag = 0;
double inctime = INCTIME;
int numtimes = NUMTIMES;
double spintime = SPINTIME;
int absflag = -1;

double time_to_double(struct timespec t)
{
    return t.tv_sec + t.tv_nsec/D_BILLION;
}

struct timespec double_to_time(double tm)
{
    struct timespec t;

    t.tv_sec = (long)tm;
    t.tv_nsec = (tm - t.tv_sec)*BILLION;
    return t;
}

struct timespec add_to_time(struct timespec t, double tm)
{
    struct timespec t1;

    t1 = double_to_time(tm);
    t1.tv_sec = t1.tv_sec + t.tv_sec;
    t1.tv_nsec = t1.tv_nsec + t.tv_nsec;
    while (t1.tv_nsec > BILLION) {
        t1.tv_nsec = t1.tv_nsec - BILLION;
        t1.tv_sec++;
    }
    return t1;
}

/*
 * spinit loops for stime seconds before returning.  It
 * returns 0 on success.  On failure it returns -1 and
 * sets errno.
 */
int spinit (double stime)
```

```
{
    struct timespec timecurrent;
    double timenow;
    double timeend;

    if (spintime == 0.0)
        return 0;
    if (clock_gettime(CLOCK_REALTIME, &timecurrent) < 0)
        return -1;
    timenow = time_to_double(timecurrent);
    timeend = timenow + stime;
    while (timenow < timeend) {
        if (clock_gettime(CLOCK_REALTIME, &timecurrent) < 0)
            return -1;
        timenow = time_to_double(timecurrent);
    }
    return 0;
}

void my_handler(int signo, siginfo_t* info, void *context)
{
    static int timesentered = 0;
    int timid;

    timesentered++;
    if (timesentered < numtimes) {
        if (inctime < 0.0)
            return;
        if (spinit(spintime) == -1) {
            perror("Spin failed in my_handler");
            exit(1);
        }
        if (absflag)
            interval.it_value = add_to_time(interval.it_value, inctime);
        timid = *(int *)(info->si_value.sival_ptr);
        if (timer_settime(timid, tflags, &interval, NULL) < 0){
            perror("Could not start timer in handler");
            exit(1);
        }
    }
    else
        exitflag = 1;
}

void main(int argc, char *argv[])
{
    struct sigaction act;
    struct sigevent evp;
    struct timespec currenttime;
```

```
struct timespec res;
sigset_t sigset;
timer_t timid;
double total_time;
double calctime;
double starttime;
double endtime;

if (argc > 1) {
    if (!strcmp(argv[1], "-r"))
        absflag = 0;
    else if (!strcmp(argv[1], "-a"))
        absflag = 1;
}
if ( (argc < 2) || (absflag < 0) ){
    fprintf(stderr,
        "Usage:  %s -r | -a [inctime [numtimes [spintime]]]\n",
        argv[0]);
    exit(1);
}

if (argc > 2)
    inctime = atof(argv[2]);
if (argc > 3)
    numtimes = atoi(argv[3]);
if (argc > 4)
    spintime = atof(argv[4]);
fprintf(stderr, "pid = %ld\n", (long)getpid());

sigemptyset(&act.sa_mask);
act.sa_flags = SA_SIGINFO;
act.sa_sigaction = my_handler;
if (sigaction(SIGALRM, &act, NULL) < 0) {
    perror("sigaction failed");
    exit(1);
}
evp.sigev_notify = SIGEV_SIGNAL;
evp.sigev_signo = SIGALRM;
evp.sigev_value.sival_ptr = &timid;
if (timer_create(CLOCK_REALTIME, &evp, &timid) < 0) {
    perror("Could not create a timer");
    exit(1);
}
if (clock_getres(CLOCK_REALTIME, &res) < 0)
    perror("Can not get clock resolution");
else
    fprintf(stderr, "Clock resolution is %0.3f microseconds\n",
        1000000.0*time_to_double(res));
interval.it_interval.tv_sec = 0;
```

```
    interval.it_interval.tv_nsec = 0;
    if (inctime < 0.0)
        sleep(100);
    if (clock_gettime(CLOCK_REALTIME, &currenttime) < 0) {
        perror("Cannot get current time");
        exit(1);
    }
    starttime = time_to_double(currenttime);
    if (absflag) {
        fprintf(stderr,
            "abs time: interrupts: %d at %.6f seconds, spinning %.6f\n",
            numtimes, inctime, spintime);
        tflags = TIMER_ABSTIME;
        interval.it_value = currenttime;
    }
    else {
        fprintf(stderr,
            "rel time: interrupts: %d at %.6f seconds, spinning %.6f\n",
            numtimes, inctime, spintime);
        tflags = 0;
        interval.it_value.tv_sec = 0;
        interval.it_value.tv_nsec = 0;
    }
    interval.it_value = add_to_time(interval.it_value, inctime);
    if (timer_settime(timid, tflags, &interval, NULL) < 0){
        perror("Could not start timer");
        exit(1);
    }
    sigemptyset(&sigset);
    for( ; ; ){
        sigsuspend(&sigset);
        if (exitflag) {
            if (clock_gettime(CLOCK_REALTIME, &currenttime) < 0) {
                perror("Can not get current time");
                exit(1);
            }
            endtime = time_to_double(currenttime);
            total_time=endtime - starttime;
            calctime = numtimes*inctime;
            fprintf(stderr,
                "Total time: %1.7f, calculated: %1.7f, error = %1.7f\n",
                total_time, calctime, total_time - calctime);
            exit(0);
        }
    }
}
```

_____ **Program 6.7** _____

Program 6.7 has one required command-line argument and three optional ones. The program synopsis is

```
abstime -a|-r  [inctime [numtimes [spintime]]]
```

The first command-line argument must be either -a or -r indicating absolute or relative time. The additional arguments are called inctime, numtimes, and spintime. The program generates numtimes SIGALARM signals which are inctime seconds apart. The signal handler wastes spintime seconds before handling the timer expiration. For absolute times, the abstime program initializes the it_value member to the current absolute time (time since January 1, 1970) plus the inctime value. If relative time is set, the program sets it_value to inctime. The inctime and spintime are double values.

Example 6.6

The following command simulates a signal handler that takes an appreciable time to execute.

```
abstime -a 0.02 1000 0.01
```

Exercise 6.8

The command of Example 6.6 uses absolute time. Are there differences in output when it is run with relative time instead?

Answer:

For an execution of

```
abstime -a 0.02 1000 0.01
```

the output might look something like

```
pid = 6766
Clock resolution is 1.000 microseconds
abs time: interrupts:1000 at 0.020000 seconds, spinning 0.010000
Total time: 20.1690290, calculated: 20.0000000, error = 0.1690290
```

While for an execution of

```
abstime -r 0.02 1000 0.01
```

the output might be

```
pid = 6767
Clock resolution is 1.000 microseconds
rel time: interrupts:1000 at 0.020000 seconds, spinning 0.010000
Total time: 30.1253541, calculated: 20.0000000, error = 10.1253541
```

When absolute timers are used, the error is less than one percent while relative timers show the expected drift corresponding to the amount of processing time.

The resolution of the clock is displayed using a call to `clock_getres`. A typical value for this might be anywhere from 1000 nanoseconds to 20 milliseconds. The 20 milliseconds (20, 000, 000 nanoseconds or 50 Hertz) is the lowest resolution allowed by POSIX.1b. One microsecond (1000 nanoseconds) is the time it takes to execute a few hundred instructions on most fast machines. Just because a system has a clock resolution of 1 microsecond does not imply that a program can use timers with anything near this resolution. A context switch is often needed before the signal handler can be entered and, as Table 1.1 indicates, a context switch takes considerably longer than this.

Example 6.7

The following command uses Program 6.7 to estimate the effective resolution of the hardware timer on a machine.

```
abstime -a 0
```

Example 6.8

The following command uses Program 6.7 to determine the maximum number of timer signals that can be handled per second.

```
abstime -a 0.0 1000 0.0
```

Exercise 6.9

Run Program 6.7 with a value of `inctime` that is negative:

```
abstime -a -1.0 1000 0.0
```

In this case the program displays its process ID and sleeps for a while. The signal handler does not restart the timer if `inctime` is negative. Program 6.8, called `multikill`, sends multiple signals to a process until that process dies. After starting Program 6.7 with a negative `inctime` use Program 6.8 to send SIGALRM signals to `abstime`. Since SIGALRM = 14, use

```
multikill pid 14
```

Program 6.7 prints its process ID before sleeping. Use this value for the `pid` above. How many signals can the process receive per second?

Answer:
Do not be surprised if the timer resolution is considerably worse than the signal handling capability of a machine. A fast Sun SPARCstation under Solaris 2.4 could handle only 100 timer-generated signals per second, while it could handle over 4000 signals generated externally by Program 6.8. A considerably slower machine running the same operating system could handle the same 100 timer-generated signals in a second but could handle only about 600 signals generated externally.

Program 6.8: The `multikill` program continually sends signals to another process until the process dies.

```
#include <stdio.h>
#include <stdlib.h>
#include <signal.h>

void main(int argc, char *argv[])
{
    int pid;
    int sig;
    if (argc != 3) {
        fprintf(stderr, "Usage: %s pid signal\n", argv[0]);
        exit(1);
    }
    pid = atoi(argv[1]);
    sig = atoi(argv[2]);
    while (kill(pid, sig) == 0) ;
}
```

_____ **Program 6.8** _____

Program 6.7 illustrates some other useful tips in using POSIX timers. Information about the timer that generated the signal is available in the signal handler, When a timer is created, an integer or a pointer can be stored in the `sigev_value` member of the `struct sigevent`. If the signal handler is to restart that timer or if multiple timers are to share a signal handler, the signal handler must have access to the timer ID of the timer that generated the signal. If the signal handler was set up using the `SA_SIGINFO` flag, it can access the value that `timer_create` stored in `sigev_value` through its second argument. The `timer_create` cannot directly store the timer ID in its `sigev_value` because the ID is not known until after the timer has been created. It therefore stores a pointer to the timer ID in the `sival_ptr` member of `union sigval`.

6.10 Additional Reading

An array representation for timers works well when the number of timers is small. Consider other possible implementations of the basic structures: a priority queue for timers and a linked list for events, for example. It might be worthwhile to look at the paper "Hashed and hierarchical timing wheels: Data structures for efficient implementation of a timer facility" by G. Varghese and T. Lauck [95]. The POSIX.1b Realtime Extension [53] provides an excellent discussion of the issues involved in implementing timers at the system level.

Realtime issues promise to become more important in the future. The book *POSIX.4: Programming for the Real World* by Gallmeister [31] provides a general introduction to realtime programming under the POSIX.1b standard. POSIX.4 was the name of the standard before it was approved. It is now an extension of the POSIX.1 standard referred to as POSIX.1b.

Chapter 7

Project: *Cracking Shells*

This chapter develops a shell from the bottom up and explores the intricacies of process creation, termination, identification, and the correct handling of signals. The chapter also looks at job control and terminal I/O. The closing project integrates these concepts by incorporating job control into a shell.

A *shell* is a process that does command-line interpretation. It reads from its standard input and executes the command corresponding to the input line. Execution of a command generally means the creation of a child process for the execution. In the simplest case the shell reads in a command and forks a child to execute the command. The parent then waits for the child to complete before reading in another command. A real shell handles process pipelines and redirection as well as foreground and background processes and signals.

This chapter starts with the simplest of shells and builds a working shell piece-by-piece. All of the sample shells in this chapter include the `ush.h` header file given in Program 7.1. The examples also use `makeargv` which is shown in Program 1.2 on page 22.

Program 7.1: The `ush.h` file is included by all programs in this chapter.

```
#include <string.h>
#include <sys/types.h>
#include <sys/stat.h>
#include <fcntl.h>
#include <unistd.h>
#include <stdlib.h>
```

```
#include <stdio.h>
#include <sys/wait.h>
#include <limits.h>

#define STDMODE 0600
#define DELIMITERSET " ><|&"

#ifndef MAX_CANON
#define MAX_CANON 256
#endif
#define TRUE 1
#define FALSE 0
#define BLANK_STRING  " "
#define PROMPT_STRING ">>"
#define QUIT_STRING "q"
#define BACK_STRING "&"
#define PIPE_STRING "|"
#define NEWLINE_STRING "\n"
#define IN_REDIRECT_SYMBOL '<'
#define OUT_REDIRECT_SYMBOL '>'
#define NULL_SYMBOL '\0'
#define PIPE_SYMBOL '|'
#define BACK_SYMBOL '&'
#define NEWLINE_SYMBOL '\n'

int makeargv(char *s, char *delimiters, char ***argvp);
int parsefile(char *inbuf, char delimiter, char **v);
int redirect(char *infilename, char *outfilename);
void executecmdline(char *cmd);
int connectpipeline(char *cmd, int frontfd[], int backfd[]);
```

———————————————————— **Program 7.1** ————————————————————

The initial parts of the shell project build a simple shell for user experimentation. Section 7.1 presents the most basic of command-line interpreters. Section 7.2 adds redirection, and Section 7.3 adds pipelines. Section 7.4 explains how a shell handles signals for a foreground process. The programs for each of these phases are given along with a series of exercises that point out the important issues. Work through these exercises before going on to the main part of the project.

The heart of this project is signal handling and job control. Section 7.5 introduces the machinery needed for job control. Write the showid program described in that section and experiment with it for different shells. Section 7.6 describes how background processes are handled without job control, and Section 7.7 introduces job control at the user level. Finally Section 7.8 specifies the implementation of a complete shell with job control.

7.1 A Simple Shell

Program 7.2 shows Version 1 of ush (ultra-simple shell). The shell process forks a child which builds an argv type array and execvp's commands entered from standard input.

Program 7.2: The code for Version 1 of the ush program.

```
#include "ush.h"
#define MAX_BUFFER 256

void main (void)
{
    char inbuf[MAX_BUFFER];
    char **chargv;

    for( ; ; ) {
       gets(inbuf);
       if (strcmp(inbuf, QUIT_STRING) == 0)
          break;
       else {
          if (fork() == 0) {
             if (makeargv(inbuf, BLANK_STRING, &chargv) > 0)
                execvp(chargv[0], chargv);
          }
          wait(NULL);
       }
    }
    exit(0);
}
```

——————————————— **Program 7.2** ———————————————

Exercise 7.1

Run Program 7.2 with a variety of commands such as ls, grep, and sort. Does it behave as expected?

Answer:

No. The ush of Program 7.2 does not display a prompt or expand filenames containing wildcards such as * and ?. This shell also does not handle some important commands that are available in all shells (e.g., cd).

The ush of Program 7.2 also does not handle quotes in the same way as the standard shells do. The standard shells allow quotes to guarantee that a particular argument is passed to the exec in its entirety and is not interpreted by the shell as something else.

Exercise 7.2

What happens if Program 7.2 doesn't call wait?

Answer:

If a user enters a command before the previous one completes, the commands execute concurrently. Both commands are still affected by keyboard input and `ctrl-c`.

Another problem is that Version 1 of `ush` does not trap errors on the `execvp`. This omission has some interesting consequences if the user enters an invalid command. When the `execvp` succeeds, control never comes back from the child. However, when it fails, the child falls through and tries to get a command line too!

Exercise 7.3

Run Program 7.2 with several invalid commands. Do a `ps` and observe the number of shells that are running. Try to quit. What happens?

Answer:

Each time an invalid command is entered, the new process acts like an additional shell. The user must enter `q` once for each shell.

Another minor problem with Program 7.2 is the use of MAX_BUFFER, a user-defined, nonportable constant. Version 1 of `ush` also uses `gets` rather than `fgets`, so there is a possibility that it can overflow the space allocated for input.

Program 7.3 shows an improved version of `ush` that has a prompt and handles an unsuccessful `execvp`. The system-defined constant MAX_CANON replaces the nonportable MAX_BUFFER. The `fgets` replaces `gets`.

Program 7.3: Version 2 of `ush`.

```c
#include "ush.h"

void main (void)
{
    char inbuf[MAX_CANON+1];
    pid_t child_pid;

    for( ; ; ) {
        fputs(PROMPT_STRING, stdout);
        if (fgets(inbuf, MAX_CANON, stdin) == NULL)
            break;
        if (*(inbuf + strlen(inbuf) - 1) == NEWLINE_SYMBOL)
            *(inbuf + strlen(inbuf) - 1) = 0;
        if (strcmp(inbuf, QUIT_STRING) == 0)
            break;
        else {
            if ((child_pid = fork()) == 0) {
```

```
            executecmdline(inbuf);
            exit(1);
        }
        else if (child_pid > 0)
            wait(NULL);
    }
}
exit(0);
}
```

_____ **Program 7.3** _____

The shell in Program 7.3 does not exit if there is an error on the `fork`. In general the shell should be impervious to errors—and bullet-proofing takes a lot of effort. The function `executecmdline` replaces the `makeargv` and `execvp` calls. Control should never return from this function.

Example 7.1

The following is a sample `executecmdline` *for Program 7.3.*

```
void executecmdline(char *incmd)
{
    char **chargv;
    if (makeargv(incmd, BLANK_STRING, &chargv) > 0) {
        if(execvp(chargv[0], chargv) == -1) {
            perror("Invalid command");
            exit(1);
        }
    }
    exit(1);
}
```

Exercise 7.4

Why is there not a `perror` before the last `exit(1)` in Example 7.1? Observe the effect when an empty command string is entered.

Answer:

For the empty command, `makeargv` returns 0, and `perror` prints out a message corresponding to the current value of `errno`. Since there was no system error, the message displayed by `perror` is not necessarily appropriate.

Exercise 7.5

Only the child parses the command line in Program 7.2 and Program 7.3. What happens if the parent parses the command line before the `fork`? What are the memory allocation and deallocation issues involved in moving the `makeargv` call prior to the `fork` in these programs.

Answer:

When the child exits, all memory allocated by the child is freed. If the parent called `makeargv` before the `fork`, the shell would have to worry about freeing the memory allocated by `makeargv`.

Exercise 7.6

Try the `cd` command as input to Program 7.3. What happens? Why? Hint: Read the man page on `cd` for an explanation.

Answer:

Since `cd` must change the user's environment, it cannot be external to the shell because external commands are executed by children of the shell and a process cannot change the environment of its parent. Most shells implement `cd` as an internal command.

Exercise 7.7

Try giving `ush` commands such as `ls -1` and `q` with leading and interspersed extra blanks. What happens?

Answer:

Program 7.3 correctly handles commands such as `ls -1` because `makeargv` handles leading and interspersed blanks. The `q` command does not work because this command is handled directly by `ush` which has no provision for handling interspersed blanks.

Exercise 7.8

Execute the command `stty -a` and record the current settings of the terminal control characters. The following is a possible example of what might appear:

```
intr = ^c; quit = ^|; erase = ^?; kill = ^u;
eof = ^d; eol = <undef>; eol2 = <undef>; swtch = <undef>;
start = ^q; stop = ^s; susp = ^z; dsusp = ^y;
rprnt = ^r; flush = ^o; werase = ^w; lnext = ^v;
```

Try each of the control characters under `ush` and under a regular shell and compare the results.

Exercise 7.9

Run the `cat` command under `ush` and enter a few lines from the terminal. Terminate with the `eof` character (usually `ctrl-d`). Follow this with another command such as `ls -1`. Does it work? On some systems, once the end-of-file is reached for a particular file descriptor, it must be explicitly reset with the `rewind` call. Where should the `rewind` be placed in Program 7.3?

Answer:

The `rewind` has to be executed directly after the `wait(NULL)`.

In Exercise 7.8 the `erase` and `werase` continue to work even though there is no explicit code to handle them in `ush`. The reason is that the shell program does not receive characters directly as they are entered from the keyboard. Instead, the terminal device driver processes input from the keyboard and passes the input through additional modules to the program. Terminals can operate in either canonical (line-buffered) or noncanonical mode. Canonical mode is the default.

In canonical mode, input is returned one line at a time. Thus, a program does not receive any input until the newline character is entered even if it just reads in a single character. The input is buffered by a terminal line driver until it encounters a newline symbol. The terminal line driver then makes the line available to the program upon request. Some processing of the line takes place while the line is being gathered. If the terminal line driver encounters the `erase` or `werase` characters, it adjusts the buffer appropriately.

Noncanonical mode allows flexibility in the handling of I/O. For example, an editing application might display the message `"entering cbreak mode"` to indicate that it is entering noncanonical mode with echo disabled and one-character-at-a-time input. In noncanonical mode, input is made available to the program after a user-specified number of characters have been entered or after a specified time has elapsed. The canonical mode editing features are not available. Programs such as editors usually operate with the terminal in noncanonical mode, while user programs generally operate with the terminal in canonical mode.

Examine and change the terminal modes by calling `tcgetattr` and `tcsetattr`, respectively. The driver and its associated modules also handle special editing characters. Call `tcsetattr` to change the individual editing actions of the driver and its modules. If it is defined, the constant `MAX_CANON` gives the maximum allowed input line length for processing in canonical mode.

7.2 Redirection

UNIX handles I/O in a device-independent way through file descriptors. A program must open a file or device such as a terminal (represented by a special file) before accessing it. The program then accesses the file or device using a handle returned by the `open`. Redirection allows a program to reassign a handle that has been opened for one file to designate another file. (See Section 3.4 for a review of redirection.)

Most shells in UNIX allow redirection of standard input, standard output, and possibly standard error from the command line. Filters are programs that read from standard input and write to standard output. Redirection on the command line allows filters to operate on other files without recompilation.

Example 7.2

The following `cat` command redirects its standard input to `my.input` and its
standard output to `my.output`.

```
cat < my.input > my.output
```

   Recall that open file descriptors are inherited on `exec` (unless specifically prevented). For shells this means that the child can first handle redirection before calling
`exec`. (After the `exec` the process won't be able to handle the redirection.)
   Program 7.4 shows a version of `executecmdline` that handles redirection of standard input and standard output designated by an input command line, `incmd`. The
`redirect` function shown in Program 7.5 performs the appropriate redirection. The
`parsefile` in Program 7.6 splits off the filenames for the redirection. It removes the
first occurrence of `search_symbol` and the token following it from `input_buffer`.
On return `*tokenp` points to the token. The `parsefile` function returns 0 if successful or −1 on failure.

Program 7.4: A version of `executecmdline` that handles redirection.

```c
/*
 * The executecmdline function parses incmd for possible redirection.
 * It calls redirect to perform the redirection and makeargv to create
 * the command  argument array. It then execvp's the command executable.
 * The function exits on error so it never returns to the caller.
 */
void executecmdline(char *incmd)
{
    char **chargv;
    char *infilename;
    char *outfilename;

    if (parsefile(incmd, IN_REDIRECT_SYMBOL , &infilename) == -1)
        fprintf(stderr, "Incorrect input redirection\n");
    else if (parsefile(incmd, OUT_REDIRECT_SYMBOL, &outfilename) == -1)
        fprintf(stderr, "Incorrect output redirection\n");
    else if (redirect(infilename, outfilename) == -1)
        fprintf(stderr, "Redirection failed\n");
    else if (makeargv(incmd, BLANK_STRING, &chargv) > 0) {
        if (execvp(chargv[0], chargv) == -1)
            perror("Invalid command");
    }
    exit(1);
}
```

--- **Program 7.4** ---

Program 7.5: A program that redirects standard input and standard output.

```
/*
 * The redirect function redirects standard  output to outfilename and
 * standard input to infilename. If either infilename or outfilename is
 * NULL, the corresponding redirection does not occur.
 * It returns 0 if successful and -1 if unsuccessful.
 */
int redirect(char *infilename, char *outfilename)
{
   int indes;
   int outdes;

   if (infilename != NULL) {   /* redirect standard in to infilename */
      if ((indes = open(infilename, O_RDONLY, STDMODE)) == -1)
         return -1;
      if (dup2(indes, STDIN_FILENO) == -1) {
         close(indes);
         return -1;
      }
      close(indes);
   }
   if (outfilename != NULL) {/* redirect standard out to outfilename */
      if ((outdes =
            open(outfilename, O_WRONLY|O_CREAT, STDMODE)) == -1)
         return -1;
      if (dup2(outdes, STDOUT_FILENO) == -1) {
         close(outdes);
         return -1;
      }
      close(outdes);
   }
   return 0;
}
```

_____ **Program 7.5** _____

Program 7.6: The `parsefile` function searches for tokens.

```
/*
 * parsefile removes the token following delimiter if present in s.
 * On return *v points to the token. The delimiter and token have been
 * been removed from s.  It returns 0 if parse was successful or -1
 * if there is an error.
 */
int  parsefile(char *s, char delimiter, char **v)
```

```
{
    char *p;
    char *q;
    int offset;
    int error = 0;

                        /* Find position of the delimiting character */
    *v = NULL;
    if ((p = strchr(s, delimiter)) != NULL)  {
                        /* Split off the token following delimiter */
        if ((q = (char *)malloc(strlen(p + 1) + 1)) == NULL)
            error = -1;
        else {
            strcpy(q, p + 1);
            if ((*v = strtok(q, DELIMITERSET)) == NULL)
                error = -1;
            offset = strlen(q);
            strcpy(p, p + offset + 1);
        }
    }
    return error;
}
```

———————————————————— **Program 7.6** ————————————————————

7.3 Pipelines

Pipelines are used to connect filters in an assembly line to perform more complicated functions.

Example 7.3

The following command redirects the output of ls -l *to the standard input of the* sort *and the standard output of the* sort *to the file* temp.

```
ls -l | sort -n +4 > temp
```

The ls and the sort are distinct processes connected together in a pipeline. The connection does not imply that the processes share file descriptors, but rather that the shell creates an intervening pipe to act as a buffer between them as shown in Figure 7.1. The shell creates the pipe before forking its children since both processes access it.

Program 7.7 shows a function that parses the command line and connects a process in a pipeline with pipe frontfd on the standard input side and backfd on the standard output side.

Figure 7.1: A pipe acts as a buffer between two processes in a pipeline.

Program 7.7: The `connectpipeline` function redirects standard input to front[0] and standard output to back[1].

```
/*
 * connectpipeline connects the process to a pipeline by redirecting
 * standard input to frontfd[0] and standard output to backfd[1].
 * If frontfd[0] = -1, the process is at the front of the pipeline and
 * standard input may be redirected to a file.  If backfd[1] = -1,
 * the process is at the back of the pipeline and standard output may
 * be redirected to a file.  Otherwise redirection to a file is
 * an error.  If explicit redirection occurs in cmd, it is removed
 * in processing.  A 0 is returned if connectpipeline is successful
 * and a -1 is returned otherwise.
 */
int connectpipeline(char *cmd, int frontfd[], int backfd[])
{
   int error = 0;
   char *infilename, *outfilename;

   if (parsefile(cmd, IN_REDIRECT_SYMBOL , &infilename) == -1)
      error = -1;
   else if (infilename != NULL && frontfd[0] != -1)
      error = -1;    /* no redirection allowed at front of pipeline */
   else if (parsefile(cmd, OUT_REDIRECT_SYMBOL, &outfilename) == -1)
      error = -1;
   else if (outfilename != NULL && backfd[1] != -1)
      error = -1;    /* no redirection allowed at back of pipeline */
   else if (redirect(infilename, outfilename) == -1)
      error = -1;
   else {                          /* now connect up appropriate pipes */
      if (frontfd[0] != -1) {
         if (dup2(frontfd[0], STDIN_FILENO) == -1)
            error = -1;
      }
      if (backfd[1] != -1) {
         if (dup2(backfd[1], STDOUT_FILENO) == -1)
            error = -1;
      }
   }
}
```

```
                                            /* close unneeded file descriptors */
    close (frontfd[0]);
    close (frontfd[1]);
    close (backfd[0]);
    close (backfd[1]);
    return error;
}
```

_____ **Program 7.7** _____

The last step in `connectpipeline` of Program 7.7 is to close the unneeded file descriptors so that processes can detect end-of-file for pipes. Because a pipe is a buffer, it behaves more like a terminal than an ordinary file in the sense that not all of the input is immediately available to a process reading from a pipe. The end-of-file condition is therefore only raised when the pipe is empty and there are no writers connected to it. If there are extra unused descriptors open on the pipe (particularly write descriptors), the process does not detect the end-of-file and hangs indefinitely.

The version of `executecmdline` given in Program 7.8 handles an arbitrary length pipeline. For each element in the pipeline, the calling program creates front and back pipes before forking the process to execute the element.

_____

Program 7.8: A version of `executecmdline` that handles pipes.

```
/*
 * executecmdline parses a command line into its individual pipeline
 * elements.  It creates a pipe to connect each intermediate member of
 * the pipeline to its successor and forks children to exec the
 * individual pipeline elements.   The executecmdline function should
 * never return.   It handles all errors by calling exit(1).
 */
void executecmdline(char *incmd)
{
    char **chargv;
    pid_t child_pid;
    char *cmd;
    char *nextcmd;
    int frontfd[2];
    int backfd[2];

    frontfd[0] = -1;
    frontfd[1] = -1;
    backfd[0] = -1;
    backfd[1] = -1;

    child_pid = 0;
```

```
    if ((nextcmd = incmd) == NULL)
        exit(1);

    for ( ; ; ) {
        cmd = nextcmd;
        if (cmd == NULL) break;
                        /* if last in pipeline, do not fork another */
        if ((nextcmd = strchr(nextcmd, PIPE_SYMBOL)) == NULL) {
            backfd[1] = -1;
            child_pid = 0;
        }
        else {
                        /* fork a child to execute next pipeline command */
            *nextcmd = NULL_SYMBOL;
            nextcmd++;
            if (pipe(backfd)== -1) {
                perror("Could not create back pipe");
                exit(1);
            } else if ((child_pid = fork()) == -1) {
                perror("Could not fork next child");
                exit(1);
            }
        }
        if (child_pid == 0) {
                                /* the child execs the command */
            if (connectpipeline(cmd, frontfd, backfd) == -1) {
                perror("Could not connect to pipeline");
                exit(1);
            } else if (makeargv(cmd, BLANK_STRING, &chargv) > 0) {
                if (execvp(chargv[0], chargv) == -1)
                    perror("Invalid command");
            }
            exit(1);
        }
            /* the parent closes front pipe and makes back pipe, front */
        close(frontfd[0]);
        close(frontfd[1]);
        frontfd[0] = backfd[0];
        frontfd[1] = backfd[1];
    }
    close(backfd[0]);
    close(backfd[1]);
    exit(1);
}
```

_____ **Program 7.8** _____

7.4 Signals

Signal handling is an integral part of user control for shells. A shell that supports job control allows users to terminate running processes, flush command lines in the middle of entry, and move processes between foreground and background. The ordinary user may not be explicitly aware that signals control these actions.

Suppose a user enters a ctrl-c to terminate a running process. The terminal device driver buffers and interprets characters as they are typed from the keyboard. If the driver encounters the intr character (usually ctrl-c), it sends a SIGINT signal to that process. In normal shell operation, the ctrl-c causes the executing command to be terminated but does not cause the shell to exit.

This section discusses shell signal handling for foreground processes and introduces the concept of a process group. Section 7.5 introduces process groups and controlling terminals, Section 7.6 develops a version of ush that correctly handles signals for background processes, and Section 7.7 addresses job control. These sections lead up to the main part of the chapter's project as specified in Section 7.8.

If a user enters ctrl-c with Version 2 of ush in Program 7.3, the shell takes the default action which is to terminate the program. Program 7.9 shows Version 3 of ush. This shell ignores SIGINT and SIGQUIT.

Program 7.9: Version 3 of ush ignores SIGINT and SIGQUIT.

```
#include "ush.h"
#include <signal.h>
void main (void)
{
    char inbuf[MAX_CANON];
    pid_t child_pid;
    struct sigaction ignorehd;
    struct sigaction defaulthd;
    sigset_t blockmask;

                        /* Set up the handlers for prompt and default */
    ignorehd.sa_handler = SIG_IGN;
    sigemptyset(&ignorehd.sa_mask);
    ignorehd.sa_flags = 0;
    defaulthd.sa_handler = SIG_DFL;
    sigemptyset(&defaulthd.sa_mask);
    defaulthd.sa_flags = 0;
    if ((sigaction(SIGINT, &ignorehd, NULL) < 0) ||
        (sigaction(SIGQUIT, &ignorehd, NULL) < 0))  {
      perror("Shell failed to install signal handlers");
      exit(1);
    }
```

```
                                /* Set up a mask to block SIGINT and SIGQUIT */
    sigemptyset(&blockmask);
    sigaddset(&blockmask, SIGINT);
    sigaddset(&blockmask, SIGQUIT);
    sigprocmask(SIG_BLOCK, &blockmask, NULL);

    for( ; ; ) {
       fputs(PROMPT_STRING, stdout);
       if (fgets(inbuf, MAX_CANON, stdin) == NULL)
          break;
       if (*(inbuf + strlen(inbuf) - 1) == NEWLINE_SYMBOL)
          *(inbuf + strlen(inbuf) - 1) = 0;
       if (strcmp(inbuf, QUIT_STRING) == 0)
          break;
       else {
          if ((child_pid = fork()) == 0) {
             if ((sigaction(SIGINT, &defaulthd, NULL) < 0) ||
                 (sigaction(SIGQUIT, &defaulthd, NULL) < 0)) {
                perror("Child could not restore default handlers");
                exit(1);
             }
             sigprocmask(SIG_UNBLOCK, &blockmask, NULL);
             executecmdline(inbuf);
             exit(1);
          }
          else if (child_pid > 0)
             wait(NULL);
       }
    }
    exit(0);
}
```

_____ **Program 7.9** _____

Exercise 7.10

If a user enters `ctrl-c` while Program 7.9 is executing the `fgets`, nothing appears until the return key is pressed. What happens if the user enters `ctrl-c` in the middle of a command line?

Answer:

When the user pushes `ctrl-c` in the middle of a command line, the symbols `^C` are displayed. All the characters on the line before the `ctrl-c` are ignored because the terminal driver empties the input buffer when `ctrl-c` is pushed (canonical input mode), but these characters still appear on the current input line because `ush` does not redisplay the prompt.

In order to handle `SIGINT` correctly, `ush` should catch the signal rather than ignore it. The `ush` must also block the signal at critical times so that unwanted signals are not delivered while the shell is setting up signal handlers or during other signal-sensitive operations. Remember that ignoring is different from blocking. Ignore a signal by setting the signal handler to be `SIG_IGN`, and block a signal by setting a flag in the signal mask. Blocked signals are not delivered to the process but are held for later delivery.

The parent shell and the child command must handle the `SIGINT` in different ways. The parent shell clears the input line and goes back to the prompt, which the shell accomplishes by calls to `sigsetjmp` and `siglongjmp`.

The strategy for the child is different. When the child forks, it inherits the signal mask and has the same signal handler as the parent. The child should not go to the prompt if a signal occurs. Instead, the child should take the default action which is to exit. In order to accomplish this, the parent blocks the signal before the `fork`. The child then installs the default handler before unblocking the signal. When the child `execvp`'s, the default handler is automatically installed, since the process was catching the signal before it was blocked. The program cannot afford to wait until then to install the default handler because the child needs to unblock the signal before it `execvp`'s and a signal may come in between unblocking the signal and the `execvp`.

The shell in Program 7.10 uses `sigsetjmp` to return to the prompt when it receives `ctrl-c`. The child installs the default handler before unblocking the signal after the fork.

Program 7.10: A shell that uses `siglongjmp` to handle `ctrl-c`.

```
#include "ush.h"
#include <signal.h>
#include <setjmp.h>
static void jumphand(int);
static sigjmp_buf jump_to_prompt;
static volatile sig_atomic_t okaytojump = 0;
void main (void)
{
    char inbuf[MAX_CANON];
    pid_t child_pid;
    struct sigaction jumphd;
    struct sigaction defaulthd;
    sigset_t blockmask;
                        /* Set up a mask to block SIGINT and SIGQUIT */
    sigemptyset(&blockmask);
    sigaddset(&blockmask, SIGINT);
    sigaddset(&blockmask, SIGQUIT);
                        /* Set up the handlers for prompt and default */
    jumphd.sa_handler = jumphand;
    jumphd.sa_mask=blockmask;
    jumphd.sa_flags = 0;
    defaulthd.sa_handler = SIG_DFL;
```

```
   sigemptyset(&defaulthd.sa_mask);
   defaulthd.sa_flags = 0;
                                    /* Set up to handle jump to prompt */
   if ((sigaction(SIGINT, &jumphd, NULL) < 0) ||
       (sigaction(SIGQUIT, &jumphd, NULL) < 0)) {
      perror("shell failed to install signal handlers");
      exit(1);
   }
   for( ; ; ) {
      if (sigsetjmp(jump_to_prompt, 1))
            /* Redisplay prompt on a new line if return from signal */
         fputs(NEWLINE_STRING, stdout);
      okaytojump = 1;
      fputs(PROMPT_STRING, stdout);
      if (fgets(inbuf, MAX_CANON, stdin) == NULL)
         break;
      if (*(inbuf + strlen(inbuf) - 1) == NEWLINE_SYMBOL)
         *(inbuf + strlen(inbuf) - 1) = 0;

      if (!strcmp(inbuf, QUIT_STRING))
         break;
      else {
         sigprocmask(SIG_BLOCK, &blockmask, NULL);
         if ((child_pid = fork()) == 0) {
            if ((sigaction(SIGINT, &defaulthd, NULL) < 0) ||
                (sigaction(SIGQUIT, &defaulthd, NULL) < 0)) {
               perror("Child could not restore default handlers");
               exit(1);
            }
            sigprocmask(SIG_UNBLOCK, &blockmask, NULL);
            executecmdline(inbuf);
            exit(1);
         }
         else if (child_pid > 0)
            wait(NULL);
         sigprocmask(SIG_UNBLOCK, &blockmask, NULL);
      }
   }
   exit(0);
}

static void jumphand(int signalnum)
{
   if (!okaytojump) return;
   okaytojump = 0;
   siglongjmp(jump_to_prompt, 1);
}
```

_____ **Program 7.10** _____

The sigsetjmp (Section 5.7) stores the signal mask and current environment in a designated jump buffer. When the signal handler calls siglongjmp with that jump buffer, the environment is restored and control is transferred to the point of the sigsetjmp call. Program 7.10 sets the jump_to_prompt point just above the shell prompt. When called directly, sigsetjmp returns 0, and when called through a siglongjmp, it returns a nonzero value. This distinction allows the shell to output a newline when a signal has occurred. The siglongjmp call pops the stack and restores the register values to those at the point that the sigsetjmp was originally called.

Sometimes compilers allocate local variables in registers for efficiency. It is important that variables that should not be changed when a siglongjmp is executed not be stored in registers. Use the volatile qualifier from ISO C to suppress this type of assignment.

Program 7.10 uses the same signal handler for both SIGINT and SIGQUIT. Therefore it sets the jumphd.sa_mask to block the delivery of both of these signals when jumphd is called.

7.5 Process Groups, Sessions, and Controlling Terminals

The previous section implemented signal handling for ush with simple commands. Signal handling for pipelines and background processes requires additional machinery. Pipelines need process groups; background processes need sessions and controlling terminals.

A *process group* is a collection of processes established for such purposes as signal delivery. Each process has a *process group ID* which identifies the process group to which it belongs. Both the kill command and the kill function treat a negative process ID value as a process group ID and send a signal to each member of the corresponding process group.

Example 7.4

The following command sends SIGINT *to the process group* 3245.

```
kill -INT -3245
```

In contrast, the following command sends SIGINT *just to the process* 3245.

```
kill -INT 3245
```

Example 7.5

If a user executes the following command and then pushes a ctrl-c, *all three processes (i.e.,* ls, sort, *and* more *) react to the* SIGINT *signal, but the shell does not.*

```
ls -l | sort -n +4 | more
```

One way to implement the signal-handling behavior of Example 7.5 is for the members of the pipeline to be in a single process group that is different from the shell. (See Exercise 7.11.)

The *process group leader* is a process whose process ID has the same value as the process group ID. A process group persists as long as any process is in the group. Thus, a process group may not have a leader if the leader dies or joins another group. A process can obtain its process group ID with the `getpgrp` and can change its process group with the `setpgid`.

SYNOPSIS

```
#include <sys/types.h>
#include <unistd.h>

pid_t getpgrp(void);
int setpgid(pid_t pid, pid_t pgid);
```
                                                                    POSIX.1, Spec 1170

The `setpgid` system call sets the process group ID of process `pid` to have process group ID `pgid`. It uses the process ID of the calling process if `pid` is 0 or if `pgid` is 0. In the latter case, the process starts a new group with itself as the leader.

When a child is created with `fork`, it gets a new process ID, but it inherits the process group ID of its parent. The parent can also use `setpgid` to change the group ID of a child as long as the child has not yet issued an `exec`. A child process can give itself a new process group ID by setting its process group ID equal to its process ID. The new process group ID is exactly what the child of the parent shell needs to ensure that signals are delivered correctly.

Processes that are running in the background or that may be put in the background in the future are more complicated than foreground processes. Background processes do not receive `ctrl-c`. If a background process is brought to the foreground, it again receives `ctrl-c`.

Example 7.6

If a user executes the following command and then pushes a `ctrl-c`, *none of the processes in the pipeline get the* `SIGINT` *signal since the pipeline is in the background.*

```
ls -l | sort -n +4 | more &
```

The background pipeline of Example 7.6 is not affected by `ctrl-c`. One way to implement similar behavior in `ush` is to have the processes ignore this signal. The shell can do this before the processes are `execvp`'d, but this approach does not work if any of `execvp`'d processes then catch the `SIGINT` signal. Also, if a user moves the pipeline back into the foreground, the `ctrl-c` should again be delivered to the processes in the pipeline, without these processes taking any action related to `SIGINT`.

In order to make the signal delivery transparent, POSIX uses sessions and controlling terminals. A *session* is a collection of process groups established for job control purposes. A session is identified by a session ID. A process can determine its session ID by calling `getsid`. Every process belongs to a session, but a process can change its session by calling `setsid`.

```
SYNOPSIS

    #include <unistd.h>
    #include <sys/types.h>

    pid_t getsid(pid_t pid);

                                                                    Spec 1170
```

```
SYNOPSIS

    #include <sys/types.h>
    #include <unistd.h>

    pid_t setsid(void);

                                                              POSIX.1, Spec 1170
```

The `setsid` sets both the process group ID and the session ID of the caller to its process ID. The shell becomes the session leader by creating a new session.

Figure 7.2 shows a shell with several process groups. Each solid rectangle represents a process. The process ID, process group ID, and the session ID are all shown for each process. All of the processes have session ID 1357 which is the process ID and session ID of the shell. Each of the four jobs is a process group. The process group ID is the same as the process ID of one of its members, the process group leader. Depending on the implementation of the shell, this could be either the first or the last process of the pipeline.

Example 7.7

The following sequence of commands might give rise to the process group structure of Figure 7.2.

```
ls -l | sort -n +4 | grep testfile > testfile.out&
grep process | sort  > process.out &
du . > du.out &
cat /etc/passwd | grep users | sort | head > users.out &
```

Exercise 7.11

Write a short program called `showid` that takes one command-line argument. It displays its argument along with its process ID, parent process ID, process group

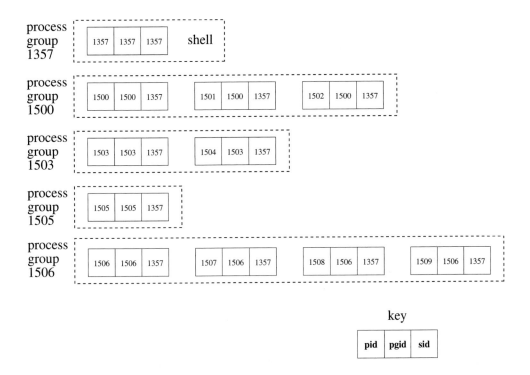

Figure 7.2: Five process groups for session 1357.

ID, and session ID, all on one line, and then starts an infinite loop. Execute the following commands to verify how your login shell handles process groups and sessions for pipelines.

```
showid 1 | showid 2 | showid 3
```

Which process in the pipeline is the process group leader? Is the shell in the same process group as the pipeline? Which processes in the pipeline are children of the shell and which are grandchildren? How does this change if the pipeline is started in the background?

Answer:

The results will vary based on the shell used. Some shells make all of the processes children of the shell. Others have only the first or last in the pipeline as a child of the shell and the rest are grandchildren. Either the first or the last may be the process group leader. If a shell does not support job control, it is possible for the shell to be the process group leader of the pipeline unless the pipeline is started in the background.

The session has a controlling terminal which is the controlling terminal of the shell. At most one process group in the session is the foreground process group at any one time. This process group gets the signals caused by keyboard input from the controlling terminal. All other process groups are background process groups. The background process groups are not affected by keyboard input from the controlling terminal of the session. If all of the process groups are in the background, the shell is the foreground process group of the controlling terminal and the others jobs are background process groups. If one of the jobs is brought into the foreground, it becomes the foreground process group and the shell becomes one of the background process groups. Keyboard input and `SIGINT` signals generated by pushing `ctrl-c` at the keyboard of the controlling terminal are sent only to the processes in the foreground process group.

A shell is said to have job control if it allows a user to move the foreground process group into the background and move a process group from the background to the foreground. Job control involves changing the foreground process group of a controlling terminal. The `tcgetpgrp` function returns the process group ID of the foreground process of a particular controlling terminal.

```
SYNOPSIS

    #include <sys/types.h>
    #include <termios.h>

    pid_t tcgetpgrp(int fildes);
    int tcsetpgrp(int fildes, pid_t pgid);
                                                  POSIX.1, Spec 1170
```

```
SYNOPSIS

    #include <sys/types.h>
    #include <termios.h>

    pid_t tcgetsid(int fildes);
                                                          Spec 1170
```

The `tcsetpgrp` changes the process group associated with a controlling terminal `fildes`. The `tcgetsid` returns the session ID of the terminal associated with `fildes`.

7.6 Handling Background Processes in `ush`

The main operational properties of a background process are that the shell does not wait for it to complete and that it is not terminated by a `SIGINT` sent from the keyboard. In fact, a background process appears to run independently of the terminal. This section explores how ush should handle signals for background processes. A correctly working shell must prevent terminal-generated signals and input from being delivered to a background process and must handle the problem of having a child divorced from its controlling terminal.

An ampersand (&) at the end of a command indicates to ush that it should run the command in the background. Assume that there is at most one & on the line, and that if present, it is at the end. The shell must determine whether the command is to be executed in the background before forking the child, since they both must know whether it is in the background. The examples in this section build on Version 2 of the ush shown in Program 7.3.

Program 7.11 shows a modification of ush that allows a command to be executed in the background. If the command is executed in the background, the child calls setpgid so that it no longer is the foreground process of its controlling terminal. In this case the parent shell does not wait for its child.

Program 7.11: A shell that attempts to handle background processes by changing their process groups.

```
#include "ush.h"
void main (void)
{
    char inbuf[MAX_CANON];
    pid_t child_pid;
    int inbackground;
    char *backp;

    for( ; ; ) {
        fputs(PROMPT_STRING, stdout);
        if (fgets(inbuf, MAX_CANON, stdin) == NULL)
            break;
        if (*(inbuf + strlen(inbuf) - 1) == NEWLINE_SYMBOL)
            *(inbuf + strlen(inbuf) - 1) = 0;
        if (strcmp(inbuf, QUIT_STRING) == 0)
            break;
        else {
            if ((backp = strchr(inbuf, BACK_SYMBOL)) == NULL)
                inbackground = FALSE;
            else {
                inbackground = TRUE;
                *(backp) = NULL_SYMBOL;
            }
            if ((child_pid = fork()) == 0) {
                if (inbackground)
                    if (setpgid(getpid(), getpid())== -1)
```

```
                exit(1);
            executecmdline(inbuf);
            exit(1);
        }
        else if (child_pid > 0 && !inbackground)
            waitpid(child_pid, NULL, 0);
    }
}
exit(0);
}
```

_____ **Program 7.11** _____

Exercise 7.12

Execute the command `ls &` several times under the shell in Program 7.11.
Then execute `ps -a` (still under this shell). Observe that the previous `ls`
processes still appear as `<defunct>`. Exit from the shell and execute `ps -a`
again. Explain the status of these processes before and after the shell exits.

Answer:

Since no process has waited for them, the background processes become zombie processes. They stay in this state until the shell exits. At that time `init`
becomes the parent of these processes, and since `init` periodically waits for
its children, they eventually die.

The shell in Program 7.12 fixes the problem of zombie or defunct processes. When
a command is to be run in the background, the shell does an extra `fork`. The first
child exits immediately, leaving the background process as an orphan which can then be
adopted by `init`. The shell now waits for all children even for background processes,
since the background children exit immediately and the grandchildren are adopted by
`init`.

_____

Program 7.12: A shell that handles zombie background processes.

```
#include "ush.h"
void main (void)
{
    char inbuf[MAX_CANON];
    pid_t child_pid;
    char *backp;

    for( ; ; ) {
        fputs(PROMPT_STRING, stdout);
        if (fgets(inbuf, MAX_CANON, stdin) == NULL)
            break;
        if (*(inbuf + strlen(inbuf) - 1) == NEWLINE_SYMBOL)
```

```
             *(inbuf + strlen(inbuf) - 1) = 0;
        if (strcmp(inbuf, QUIT_STRING) == 0)
             break;
        else if ((child_pid = fork()) == 0) {
             if ((backp = strchr(inbuf, BACK_SYMBOL)) != NULL) {
                 *(backp) = NULL_SYMBOL;    /* end command line before & */
                 if (fork() != 0) exit(0);
                 if (setpgid(getpid(), getpid())== -1)
                     exit(1);
             }
             executecmdline(inbuf);
             exit(1);
        } else if (child_pid > 0)
             waitpid(child_pid, NULL, 0);
    }
    exit(0);
}
```
_____ **Program 7.12** _____

Exercise 7.13

Execute a long-running background process such as rusers & under the shell given in Program 7.12. Do a ctrl-c. Observe that the background process is not interrupted even though the shell exits. (Remember that the version of the program in Program 7.12 does not trap SIGINT.)

Exercise 7.14

Use the showid function from Exercise 7.11 to determine which of the three processes in a pipeline becomes the process group leader and which are children of the shell for the version of ush in Program 7.12. Do this for pipelines started both in the foreground and background.

Answer:

If the pipeline is started in the foreground, all the processes have the same process group as the shell and the shell is the process group leader. The last process in the pipeline is a child of the shell and the others are grandchildren of it. If the pipeline is started in the background, the last process in the pipe is the process group leader and its parent is init. The other processes are children of the last process in the pipeline.

The zombie child problem is more complicated if the shell does job control. In this case, the shell must be able to detect whether the background process is stopped because of a signal (e.g., SIGSTOP). The waitpid has an option for detecting children stopped by signals, but not for detecting grandchildren. The background process of Program 7.12 is a grandchild because of the extra fork, so ush cannot detect it.

Program 7.13: A shell that handles zombie background processes by using `waitpid`.

```c
#include "ush.h"
void main (void)
{
    char inbuf[MAX_CANON];
    pid_t child_pid;
    pid_t wait_pid;
    char *backp;
    int inbackground;

    for( ; ; ) {
        fputs(PROMPT_STRING, stdout);
        if (fgets(inbuf, MAX_CANON, stdin) == NULL)
            break;
        if (*(inbuf + strlen(inbuf) - 1) == NEWLINE_SYMBOL)
            *(inbuf + strlen(inbuf) - 1) = 0;
        if (strcmp(inbuf, QUIT_STRING) == 0)
            break;
        else {
            if ((backp = strchr(inbuf, BACK_SYMBOL)) == NULL)
                inbackground = FALSE;
            else {
                inbackground = TRUE;
                *(backp) = NULL_SYMBOL;
            }
            if ((child_pid = fork()) == 0) {
                if (inbackground)
                    if (setpgid(getpid(), getpid()) == -1) exit(1);
                executecmdline(inbuf);
                exit(1);
            }
            else if (child_pid > 0) {
                if (!inbackground)
                    while((wait_pid = waitpid(-1, NULL, 0)) > 0)
                        if (wait_pid == child_pid) break;
                while (waitpid(-1, NULL, WNOHANG) > 0)
                    ;
            }
        }
    }
    exit(0);
}
```

_____ **Program 7.13** _____

Program 7.13 shows a direct approach for handling zombies using `waitpid`. In order to detect whether background processes are stopped for a signal, this version of ush uses waitpid with the WNOHANG for background processes rather than forking an extra child. The −1 for the first argument to waitpid means to wait for any process. If the command is not a background command, ush explicitly waits for the corresponding child to complete.

Exercise 7.15

Repeat Exercise 7.14 for Program 7.13

Answer:

The results are the same as for Exercise 7.14 except that the last process in the pipeline is a child of the shell.

7.7 Job Control

Job control allows users to selectively stop processes and resume their execution later. One purpose of job control is to allow users to run long programs in the background and periodically halt them to check their status or provide them with input. The C shell and the KornShell allow job control, but the Bourne shell does not. This section describes job control in the C shell. The KornShell is almost identical with respect to job control.

A job consists of the processes needed to run a single command line. When a shell starts a job in the background, it assigns a job number and displays the job number and process IDs of the processes in the job. If a pipeline is started in the background, all processes in the pipe have the same job number. The job number is typically a small integer. If there are no other jobs in the background, the shell assigns the command the job number one. In general the shell assigns a background job the number one greater than the current largest background job number.

The jobs command displays the jobs running under a shell.

Example 7.8

The following commands illustrate job control for the C shell. The shell displays the prompt ospmt%. *The commands appear after this prompt. The shell produces the other messages shown.*

```
ospmt% du .  | sort -n > duout &
[1] 23145 23146
ospmt% grep mybook *.tex > mybook.out &
[2] 23147
ospmt% rusers | grep myboss > myboss.out &
[3] 23148 23149
ospmt% jobs
[1]   + Running              du .  | sort -n > duout
[2]   - Running              grep mybook *.tex > mybook.out
[3]     Running              rusers | grep myboss > myboss.out
```

The jobs *command shows three running background jobs. The job number is at the start of the line in square brackets. If the second job finishes first, the shell displays the following line when the user presses the return.*

```
[2]     Done                    grep mybook *.tex > mybook.out
```

If at that time the user executes another jobs *command, the following output appears.*

```
[1]   + Running                du . | sort -n > duout
[3]   - Running                rusers | grep myboss > myboss.out
```

Example 7.8 shows that when a shell starts a job in the background, it displays the job number followed by the process IDs of the processes corresponding to that job. Refer to job n by %n.

Example 7.9

The following command kills job two without referring to process IDs.

```
kill -KILL %2
```

Example 7.8 shows job one preceded by a + meaning it is the *current job* and is the default if no number is used after %. The - represents the previous job. Note that the current job is the first one started, not the last.

A background job can be either running or stopped. To stop a running job, use the stop command. The stopped job becomes the current job and is suspended.

Example 7.10

The following command stops job two.

```
stop %2
```

To start a stopped job running in the background, use the bg command. In this case bg or bg % or bg %2 all work since job two is the current job.

Use the fg command to move a background job (either running or stopped) into the foreground, and the SIGSTOP character (typically ctrl-z) to move the foreground job into the background in the stopped state. The combination ctrl-z and bg makes the foreground job a running background job.

The fg, bg, and jobs commands usually do not have their own man pages, since these commands are built into the shell. To get information on these commands in the C shell, execute man csh.

Exercise 7.16

Experiment with job control (assuming that it is available). Move processes in and out of the foreground.

A shell that supports job control must keep track of all of the foreground and background process groups in its session. When the terminal generates a SIGSTOP interrupt (usually in response to ctrl-z), the foreground process group is placed in the stopped state. How should the shell get back in control? Fortunately, the waitpid blocks the parent shell until the state of one of its children changes. Thus, an appropriate call to waitpid by the parent shell allows the shell to get back in control after the foreground process group is suspended. The shell can start a suspended process group by sending it the SIGCONT signal. If the shell wants to restart that group in the foreground, it has to use tcsetpgrp to tell the controlling terminal what the foreground process group is. Since a given process or process group can run in the foreground or the background at different times during its execution, each child command must start a new process group regardless of whether it is started as a background process or a foreground process.

One job control problem not yet addressed in this discussion concerns how a process obtains input from standard input. If this process is in the foreground, there is no problem. If there is no job control and the process is started in the background, its standard input is redirected to /dev/null to prevent it from grabbing characters from the foreground process. This simple redirection does not work with job control. Once standard input is redirected, it would be difficult to get input from the original controlling terminal when the process is brought to the foreground. The solution specified by POSIX is for the kernel to generate a SIGTTIN signal when a background process attempts to read from the controlling terminal. The default handler for SIGTTIN stops the job. The shell detects a change in the status of the child when it does a waitpid and displays a message. The user can then choose to move the process to the foreground so it can receive input.

In POSIX.1, background jobs can write to standard error. If they attempt to write to standard output (and standard output is still the controlling terminal), the terminal device driver generates a SIGTTOU for the process if the c_lflag member of the struct termios for the terminal has the TOSTOP flag set. If so, a user then has the option of moving the job to the foreground so that it can send output to the controlling terminal. If the process has redirected standard input and standard output, it does I/O from the redirected sources.

Exercise 7.17

Write a simple program that writes to standard output. Start it in the background and see if it can write to standard output without generating a SIGTTOU signal.

7.8 Job Control for `ush`

This section describes an implementation of job control for ush. Start by combining the signal handling of Program 7.10 with the background processing handling of Program 7.13 to produce a shell that correctly handles the `SIGINT` and `SIGQUIT`. Test the program appropriately for the following cases:

- Simple commands.
- Incorrect commands.
- Commands with standard input and output redirected.
- Pipelines.
- Background processes.
- All of the above interrupted by `ctrl-c`.

7.8.1 A Job List Object

In order to do job control, `ush` must keep track of its children. Use a list object similar to the one used in Program 2.4 to keep a program history. The nodes in the list should have the following structure:

```
typedef enum jstatus
        {FOREGROUND, BACKGROUND, STOPPED, DONE, TERMINATED}
    job_status_t;

typedef struct job_struct {
    char *cmdstring;
    pid_t pgid;
    int job;
    job_status_t jobstat;
    struct job_struct *next_job;
} joblist_t;

static joblist_t *job_head = NULL;
static joblist_t *job_tail = NULL;
```

Place the list structure in a separate file along with the following functions to manipulate the job list:

➤ The `add_list` function adds the specified job to the list. The prototype for `add_list` is

```
int add_list(pid_t pgid, char *cmd, job_status_t status);
```

The `pgid` is the process group ID, and `cmd` is the command string for the job. The `status` value can be either `FOREGROUND` or `BACKGROUND`. The `add_list` function returns the job number if successful or -1 on failure.

➤ The `delete_list` function removes the node corresponding to the specified job from the list. The prototype for `delete_list` is

```
int delete_list(int job);
```

> The `delete_list` returns the job number if the node is successfully deleted or −1 on failure. Be sure to free all space associated with the deleted node.

➤ The `show_jobs` function outputs a list of jobs and each one's status. Use a format similar to

```
[job]     status          pgid           cmd
```

➤ The `set_status` function sets the status value of the node of the corresponding job to either `FOREGROUND` or `BACKGROUND`. Its prototype is

```
int set_status(int job, job_status_t status);
```

The `set_status` function returns 0 on success and −1 on failure.

➤ The `get_status` function returns the status value associated with the specified job. Its prototype is

```
int get_status(int job, job_status_t *pstatus);
```

The `get_status` function returns 0 on success and −1 on failure.

➤ The `get_process` function returns the process group ID of the specified job. The prototype for `get_process` is

```
pid_t get_process(int job);
```

If `job` doesn't exist, `get_process` returns 0.

➤ The `get_largest_job_number` scans the job list for the largest job number currently in the list. The prototype for `get_largest_job_number` is

```
int get_largest_job_number(void);
```

The `get_largest_job_number` returns the largest job number if there are any nodes on the list or 0 if the list is empty.

Write a driver program to test thoroughly the list functions independently of `ush`.

7.8.2 The Job List in `ush`

After the job list functions are working, add the job list object to `ush` as follows:

- Each time `ush` forks a child to run a background process, it adds a node to the job list. It sets the `pgid` member of the `joblist_t` node to the value returned from the `fork`. The process status is `BACKGROUND`. It calls `get_largest_job_number` to determine the largest job number of current background processes and assigns the new background process a job number which is one greater.

- If the command is executed in the background, `ush` outputs a message of the form

```
[job]     pid1  pid2   ....
```

where `job` is the job number and `pid1`, `pid2`, and so on are the process IDs of the children in the process group for the command. The parent `ush` knows only the process ID of the initial child, so the child that does the `executecmdline` must produce this message.

- The `ush` calls the `show_jobs` function when a user enters the `jobs` command.

- Replace the `waitpid` call in `ush` with a more sophisticated approach by using `waitpid` in a loop with the WUNTRACED option. The WUNTRACED option specifies that `waitpid` should report the status of any stopped child whose status has not yet been reported. This report is necessary for implementing job control in the next stage.

SYNOPSIS

```
#include <sys/types.h>
#include <sys/wait.h>

pid_t waitpid(pid_t pid, int *stat_loc, int options);
```
POSIX.1, Spec 1170

Use -1 for the `pid` parameter. If the command is running in the foreground, loop until the foreground child completes. If the command is running in the background, use the WNOHANG option in addition to WUNTRACED. When the shell successfully waits for some child, it should use the following macros to determine that child's status:

```
WIFSTOPPED(status)   /* nonzero if child is stopped */

WIFSIGNALED(status)  /* signal number if child terminated
                             by a signal that  was not caught */
WIFEXITED(status)    /* nonzero if child terminated normally */
```

The `status` is the integer value pointed to by `stat_loc` in the `waitpid`.

- When a child terminates normally (WIFEXITED returns a nonzero value) or terminates because of a signal (WIFSIGNALED returns a nonzero value), the `ush` removes the corresponding node from its job list.

Test `ush` with the job list. Do not add job control in this step. Execute the `jobs` command frequently to see the status of the background processes. Carefully experiment with an existing shell that has job control (e.g., C shell or KornShell). Make sure that `ush` handles background and foreground processes similarly.

7.8.3 Job Control in `ush`

Incorporate job control into `ush` by adding the following commands to `ush` in addition to the `jobs` command of the previous section:

`stop`	stops the current job
`bg`	starts the current job running in the background
`bg %n`	starts job `n` running in the background
`fg %n`	starts job `n` running in the foreground
`mykill -SIGNUM %n`	sends the signal `SIGNUM` to job `n`

Some of these commands refer to the current job. When there are a number of jobs, one is *the current job*. The current job starts out as the first background job to be started. A user can make another job the current job by bringing it to the foreground with `fg`.

The `ush` now must handle `SIGCONT`, `SIGTSTP`, `SIGTTIN`, and `SIGTTOU` in addition to `SIGINT` and `SIGQUIT`. When `ush` detects that a child has stopped because of a `SIGTTIN` or a `SIGTTOU`, it writes an informatory message to standard error indicating that the child is waiting for input or output, respectively. The user can move that job to the foreground so that it can read to or write from the controlling terminal.

Test the program thoroughly. Pay particular attention to how the C Shell does job control and adjust `ush` to look as similar as possible.

7.9 Additional Reading

An elementary book on C shell programming is *UNIX Shell Programming* by Arthur [4]. The book *Learning the Korn Shell* by Rosenblatt [74] is a clear reference on the Korn-Shell. Another book on the KornShell is *The New KornShell Command and Programming Language*, 2nd ed. by Bolsky and Korn [12]. The upcoming book *Using* `csh` *and* `tsch` by DuBois [28] promises to be a good technical reference.

Part III

Concurrency

Chapter 8

Critical Sections and Semaphores

Programs that manage shared resources must execute portions of code called *critical sections* in a mutually exclusive manner. This chapter discusses the protection of critical sections using semaphores. In addition to presenting an overview of the semaphore abstraction, the chapter covers both POSIX.1b semaphores and System V semaphores.

Imagine a computer system in which all users share a single printer and can simultaneously print. How would the output appear? If lines of users' jobs were interspersed, the system would be unusable. Shared devices, such as printers, are called *exclusive resources* because they must be accessed by one process at a time. Processes that share access to these resources must execute in a *mutually exclusive* manner.

A *critical section* is a code segment that must be executed in a mutually exclusive manner. Code that modifies a shared variable usually has the following parts:

Entry Section:	The code that requests permission to modify the shared variable.
Critical Section:	The code that modifies the shared variable.
Exit Section:	The code that releases access.
Remainder Section:	The remaining code.

The *critical-section problem* refers to the problem of executing critical sections in a fair, symmetric manner. Solutions to the critical-section problem must satisfy each of the following:

Mutual Exclusion:	At most one process is in its critical section at any time.
Progress:	If no process is executing its critical section, a process that wishes to enter can get in. Only those processes

that are not in their remainder section can participate in the decision to determine which process enters its critical section next.

Bounded Waiting:　No process is postponed indefinitely. In addition, there must be a bound on the number of times that other processes are allowed to enter their critical sections after a process has made a request to enter its critical section.

Program 8.1 contains a modification of Program 2.12. The program generates a process chain. After falling out of the forking loop, each process outputs an informative message to standard error one character at a time. Since standard error is shared by all processes in the chain, that part of the code is a critical section and should be executed in a mutually exclusive manner. The critical section of Program 8.1 is not protected, so output from the different processes is interleaved in a random manner, different for each run.

Program 8.1: A program to generate a chain of processes.

```
#include <stdio.h>
#include <stdlib.h>
#include <limits.h>
#include <unistd.h>

void main   (int argc, char *argv[])
{
    char buffer[MAX_CANON];
    char *c;
    int i;
    int n;
    pid_t childpid;

    if ( (argc != 2) || ((n = atoi(argv[1])) <= 0) ) {
       fprintf (stderr, "Usage: %s number_of_processes\n", argv[0]);
       exit(1);
    }

    for (i = 1; i < n;   ++i)
       if (childpid = fork())
          break;

    sprintf(buffer,
         "i:%d  process ID:%ld  parent ID:%ld  child ID:%ld\n",
         i, (long)getpid(), (long)getppid(), (long)childpid);
```

```
   c = buffer;
      /*****************start of critical section *******************/
   while (*c != '\0') {
      fputc(*c, stderr);
      c++;
   }
   fputc('\n', stderr);
      /******************end of critical section *******************/

   exit(0);
}
```

_____ **Program 8.1** _____

Each process in Program 8.1 executes the statements in sequential order, but the statements (and hence the output) from the different processes can be arbitrarily interleaved. An analogy to this arbitrary interleaving comes from a deck of cards. Cut a deck of cards. Think of each section of the cut as representing one process. The individual cards in each section represent the statements in the order that the corresponding process is executing them. Now shuffle the two sections by interleaving. There are many possibilities for a final ordering depending on the shuffling mechanics. Similarly, there are many possible interleavings of the statements of two processes because the exact timing of processes relative to each other depends on outside factors (e.g., how many other processes are competing for the CPU or how much time each process spent in previous blocked states waiting for I/O). The challenge for programmers is to develop programs that work for all realizable interleavings of program statements.

8.1 Atomic Operations

An *atomic operation* is an operation that, once started, completes in a logically indivisible way (i.e., without any other related instructions interleaved). Most solutions of the critical-section problem rely on the existence of certain atomic operations.

On many machines that have a single processor, individual machine instructions are not interruptible and hence are atomic. However, look carefully at the hardware reference manual for a given machine before concluding that a given machine instruction is an atomic operation. Since RISC machines provide very limited types of operations on memory, even a simple C assignment statement may not compile into an atomic machine instruction. As examples, memory-to-memory transfers and operations in which arithmetic is done on a value in a memory location are usually not atomic. On machines in which several CPUs share a memory, effective implementation of atomic operations is more complicated.

Example 8.1

The following code segment is a typical implementation of the C statement
counter++.

```
a:|    R1 <-- counter
b:|    R1 <-- R1 + 1
c:|    counter <-- R1
```

R1 in Example 8.1 represents a machine register. While each of the individual statements a, b, and c is indivisible, other instructions can be executed between a and b if a signal occurs or if the process loses the CPU at the wrong instant. If those other instructions modify counter, the program can produce inconsistent results.

Let a_1 denote process one executing statement a. An interleaving of statements for processes can be represented by a sequence of such values. Thus a_1, b_1, a_2 means that process one executed statements a and b, and then process two executed statement a. The code is in error if any possible interleaving fails.

Example 8.2

The following are two possible interleavings of the pseudocode of Example 8.1.

$$a_1, b_1, c_1, a_2, b_2, c_2$$
$$a_1, b_1, a_2, b_2, c_2, c_1$$

Suppose counter of Example 8.1 has an initial value of 1. After the first sequence in Example 8.2, counter has a final value of 3, while after the second sequence counter has a final value of 2. Thus, execution of three statements in Example 8.1 does not produce consistent results. The failure in Example 8.1 has nothing to do with the fact that the two processes were using the same registers. When the context switch occurs, the registers are saved. The same problem occurs if a local variable replaces R1.

One method for implementing mutual exclusion is to have a simple, shared variable indicating whether it is safe to enter the critical section. The variable represents a *lock* and a variable value of 1 indicates that some process is currently executing code in its critical section. A zero value indicates that it is safe to enter the critical section.

Example 8.3

The following pseudocode illustrates an incorrect method of implementing mutual exclusion. The strategy uses the shared variable lock *which is initially set to 0.*

```
a:|    while (lock)
b:|        ;
c:|    lock = 1;
d:|        <critical section>
e:|    lock = 0;
```

A process executes the `while` loop of Example 8.3 as long as `lock` is 1. When `lock` becomes 0, the process sets `lock` to 1 to prevent other processes from entering the critical section and clears `lock` when it completes the critical section. The locking method of Example 8.3 fails if two processes are in their `while` loops when `lock` becomes 0 and one process loses the CPU between leaving the `while` loop and setting `lock`.

Example 8.4

The following interleaving of the statements of Example 8.3 allows both processes one and two to execute their critical sections at the same time.

$$a_1, b_1, a_2, b_2, c_2, d_2, c_1, d_1, e_1, e_2$$

Implementing and debugging critical sections is difficult because interleavings that fail may not occur very often and are not directly repeatable. So, exercise care when using shared variables. Even with no explicitly shared variables, a program can have critical section difficulties. A frequent and insidious interleaving problem is the use of external variables in signal handlers. Nonreentrant system calls and library functions also interact badly with signal handlers.

Exercise 8.1

Example 8.3 does not satisfy mutual exclusion. What other requirements of the critical-section problem are not satisfied by this example?

Answer:

This example does not satisfy bounded waiting.

Example 8.3 fails to execute consistently because the test of `lock` and the setting of `lock` are not atomic. For a one-CPU system, the problem with Example 8.3's not satisfying mutual exclusion can be corrected by preventing the process from losing the CPU between testing the lock variable and setting it. For multiple CPUs, disabling all interrupts is not sufficient, because a process executing on another CPU can modify a shared variable at any time.

Many systems provide an atomic `TestAndSet` instruction or an atomic `Swap` instruction to handle the problem. `TestAndSet` sets a variable to 1 and returns the old value of the variable. `Swap` is more general than `TestAndSet`. It has two arguments and swaps the values of its arguments atomically.

Example 8.5

The following C function implements a `TestAndSet`-like operation.

```
int TestAndSet(int *target)
{
    int returnval;
```

```
                returnval = *target;
                *target = 1;
                return returnvalue;
         }
```

The important point here is that the `TestAndSet` function must be executed atomically, even on a multiprocessor system. If `TestAndSet` instructions are attempted simultaneously (by different CPUs on the same machine), they are executed sequentially. If they are executed concurrently (two processes in a multitasking environment), neither one is interrupted by the other.

Exercise 8.2

What is the effect of the following statement if the `lock` variable is 0 before the statement executes?

```
mytemp = TestAndSet(&lock);
```

Answer:

After execution `mytemp` is 0 and `lock` is 1.

Exercise 8.3

What is the effect of the following statement if the `lock` variable is 1 before the statement executes?

```
while (TestAndSet(&lock))
    ;
```

Answer:

If the value of `lock` is never changed elsewhere, the process loops forever.

Example 8.6

The following pseudocode uses `TestAndSet` *to protect a critical section. The* `lock` *variable is initialized to 0 before any process executes the segment.*

```
a:|    while(TestAndSet(&lock))
b:|        ;
c:|    <critical section>
d:|    lock = 0;
e:|    <remainder section>
```

The first process to execute the `TestAndSet` in Example 8.6 causes `lock` to be set to 1. The `TestAndSet` returns the old value of `lock` (which is 0) to terminate the `while` loop, and the first process goes on to execute its critical section. If another process executes the `while` loop while `lock` is 1, it continues to loop because `TestAndSet` returns 1. Eventually the first process finishes and sets `lock` back to 0.

The next process to execute the `TestAndSet` then gets a zero return value and drops out of the `while` loop. Example 8.6 assumes that statement d is atomic.

Exercise 8.4

Suppose processes one and two are executing their critical sections as specified in Example 8.6. Is the following a possible interleaving of instructions for these processes?

$$a_1, a_2, c_2, c_1, d_1, e_1, d_2, e_2$$

Answer:

The interleaving is not possible. After a_1, the value of `lock` is 1. Therefore the `TestAndSet` in a_2 must return 1, and process two cannot leave its `while` loop.

Exercise 8.5

Does the `TestAndSet` solution of Example 8.6 solve the critical-section problem?

Answer:

No, the code provides mutual exclusion, but it does not satisfy bounded waiting.

Exercise 8.6

Suppose that `key` has value 1 and `lock` has value 1. What is the effect of the following code? What if `lock` is initialized to 0 instead of 1?

```
while(key == 1)
    Swap(&lock, &key);
```

Answer:

If `lock` is initially 1, the process is stuck in the `while` loop. If `lock` is initially 0, the process drops out of the loop after the first iteration.

Example 8.7

The following pseudocode uses `Swap` *to protect a critical section. The shared variable* `lock` *is initially* 0.

```
key = 1;
while(key == 1)
    Swap(&lock, &key);
<critical section>
lock = 0;
<remainder section>
```

The first process to execute the `while` loop in Example 8.7 drops through after the first iteration because `lock` is 0. Subsequent processes are stuck in the `while` loop until the first process completes its critical section and resets `lock` to 0. One of the processes then executes the `Swap` when `lock` is 0 and falls through the `while` loop.

Remember, the `Swap` is atomic so only one process at a time sees the zero value of `lock` and gets through.

The `TestAndSet` implementation of Example 8.6 and the `Swap` implementation of Example 8.7 use *busy waiting*, meaning that a process continually performs an operation to determine whether it can proceed. This continual testing consumes machine cycles without accomplishing useful work. The preferred approach is to block a process until it can proceed.

`TestAndSet` is not a user-level solution to the critical-section problem because it uses busy waiting and is machine-dependent. The operating system uses instructions like `TestAndSet` to provide atomicity for higher-level synchronization primitives such as *semaphores*, *event counters*, or *condition variables*. The remainder of the chapter concentrates on semaphores. Section 8.2 introduces the semaphore abstraction, Section 8.3 covers the new POSIX.1b semaphores, and Section 8.4 discusses the older System V semaphores. Chapter 10 explores additional synchronization mechanisms such as condition variables which are part of the POSIX.1c threads specification.

8.2 Semaphores

In 1965, E.W. Dijkstra [25] proposed the semaphore abstraction for high-level management of mutual exclusion and synchronization. A semaphore is an integer variable with two atomic operations: `wait` and `signal`. Other names for `wait` are `down`, `P`, and `lock`. Other names for `signal` are `up`, `V`, `unlock`, and `post`.

A process that executes a `wait` on a semaphore variable `s` cannot proceed until the value of `s` is positive. It then decrements the value of `s`. The `signal` operation increments the value of the semaphore variable. In the POSIX.1b terminology [53] these operations are called *semaphore lock* and *semaphore unlock*.

This section assumes that semaphore variables are of type `semaphore_t`. The `semaphore_t` type always contains an integer variable that a process can test, increment, or decrement through the associated semaphore operations. Sometimes the semaphore is just an integer variable, and sometimes there is more structure depending on the underlying implementation. For now, think of `semaphore_t` as an `int`.

Example 8.8
The following pseudocode implements the semaphore operations.

```
void wait(semaphore_t *sp)
{
    while(*sp <= 0)
        ;
    (*sp)--;
}
```

```
void signal(semaphore_t *sp)
{
    (*sp)++;
}
```

The `wait` and `signal` operations of Example 8.8 must be atomic. In this context being atomic means that if the caller reaches the decrement statement in the `wait`, no other process attempts to change the semaphore variable between the final test in the `while` and the completion of the decrement. Naturally the C code for `wait` given above does not work correctly because it is not atomic as presented.

Example 8.9

The following pseudocode protects a critical section if the semaphore variable `S` *is initially* 1.

```
wait(&S);
<critical section>
signal(&S);
<remainder section>
```

Processes using semaphores must cooperate to assure mutual exclusion. The code of Example 8.9 protects a critical section as long as all processes execute the `wait(&S)` before entering their critical sections and the `signal(&S)` when they leave. If any process fails to execute the `wait(&S)` due to a mistake or oversight, the processes may not execute mutually exclusively. If a process fails to execute `signal(&S)` when it finishes its critical section, other cooperative processes are blocked from entering their critical sections.

Exercise 8.7

What happens if `S` is initially 0 in the previous example? What happens if `S` is initially 8.

Answer:

If `S` is initially 0, every `wait(&S)` blocks and a deadlock results unless some other process sets `S` to 1. If `S` is initially 8, at most eight processes execute concurrently in their critical sections.

Example 8.10

Suppose process one must execute statement a_1 before process two executes statement b_2. The semaphore `sync` *enforces the ordering in the following pseudocode, provided* `sync` *is initially* 0.

```
Process 1 executes:              Process 2 executes:
    a;                               wait(&sync);
    signal(&sync);                   b;
```

Because `sync` of Example 8.10 is initially 0, process two blocks on its `wait` until process one executes the `signal`.

Exercise 8.8

What happens in the following pseudocode if the semaphores `S` and `Q` are both initially 1?

```
Process 1 executes:                 Process 2 executes:
    for( ; ; ) {                        for( ; ; ) {
        wait(&S);                           wait(&Q);
        a;                                  b;
        signal(&Q);                         signal(&S);
    }                                   }
```

Answer:

Either process might execute its `wait` statement first. The semaphores ensure that a given process is no more than one iteration ahead of the other. If one semaphore is initially 1 and the other 0, the processes proceed in strict alternation. If both semaphores are initially 0, a deadlock occurs.

Exercise 8.9

What happens when `S` is initially 8 and `Q` is initially 0 in Exercise 8.8? Hint: Think of `S` as representing buffer slots and `Q` as representing items in a buffer.

Answer:

Process one is always between zero and eight iterations ahead of process two. If the value of `S` represents empty slots and the value of `Q` represents items in the slots, process one acquires slots and produces items, while process two acquires items and produces empty slots. This generalization synchronizes access to a buffer with room for no more than eight items.

Exercise 8.10

What happens in the following pseudocode if semaphores `S` and `Q` are both initially 1?

```
Process 1 executes:                 Process 2 executes:
    for( ; ; ) {                        for( ; ; ) {
        wait(&Q);                           wait(&S);
        wait(&S);                           wait(&Q);
        a;                                  b;
        signal(&S);                         signal(&Q);
        signal(&Q);                         signal(&S);
    }                                   }
```

Answer:

The result depends on the order in which the processes get the CPU. It should work most of the time, but if process one loses the CPU after executing `wait(&Q)` and process two gets in, both processes block on their second `wait` and a deadlock occurs.

8.2.1 Implementing Semaphores with `TestAndSet`

Operating systems use hardware `TestAndSet` or its equivalent to enforce atomicity of high-level synchronization constructs (at least on single-CPU systems). However, semaphores and other high-level synchronization mechanisms are more convenient. Semaphores are architecture-independent, so the programmer need not be aware of the architectural details of the target machine. In addition, a user process cannot block a process directly but must invoke a system call to request the service from the kernel. Thus, a program cannot directly call a `TestAndSet` and then block itself (at least not by putting itself directly in the appropriate kernel-level list). Since the program must invoke a system call for blocking anyway, the `TestAndSet` might as well be in the system call too. In other words, the use of `TestAndSet` to enforce mutual exclusion without kernel intervention implies a busy waiting implementation.

The remainder of this section looks at a busy waiting implementation of semaphores using `TestAndSet`. The main point of the discussion is that the `TestAndSet` should be used to lock for only short periods of time.

Exercise 8.11

What is wrong with the following implementation of `wait` and `signal`? Assume that `lock` is initially 0, and `*sp` is initially 1.

```
         void wait(semaphore_t *sp)
         {
a: |          while(TestAndSet(&lock))
b: |              ;
c: |          while((*sp) <= 0)
d: |              ;
e: |          (*sp)--;
f: |          lock = 0;
         }

         void signal(semaphore_t *sp)
         {
g: |          while(TestAndSet(&lock))
h: |              ;
i: |          (*sp)++;
k: |          lock = 0;
         }
```

Answer:

Suppose process two calls `wait`, finds `*sp` equals 1, decrements it to 0, and returns from `wait` to execute its critical section. The value of `lock` was briefly 1, but now it is 0 again. Now suppose process one executes `wait`. Process one is now looping indefinitely at statements c and d with `lock` having the value 1. When process two calls `signal`, it hangs on statements g and h because `lock` is held by process one. A deadlock results. An example interleaving sequence in which process one executes a `wait` and process two blocks on a `signal` is

$$a_1, b_1, c_1, d_1, c_1, d_1, g_2, h_2, g_2, h_2$$

The implementation in Exercise 8.11 fails because the `wait` holds `lock` too long (not just long enough to do an assignment but all of the time it is waiting on the semaphore variable). The `signal` implementation is fine because it holds `lock` only long enough to increment the semaphore variable. A correct implementation carefully holds `lock` just long enough to assure atomicity.

Example 8.11

The following implementation of a semaphore in terms of `TestAndSet` *does not cause a deadlock.*

```
        void wait(semaphore_t *sp)
        {
a:  |       for( ; ; ) {
b:  |           while(TestAndSet(&lock))
c:  |               ;
c:  |           if (*sp > 0) {
d:  |               (*sp)--;
e:  |               break;    /* exits the loop */
f:  |           }
g:  |           lock = 0;
h:  |       }
i:  |       lock = 0;
        }


        void signal(semaphore_t *sp)
        {
j:  |       while(TestAndSet(&lock))
k:  |           ;
l:  |       (*sp)++;
m:  |       lock = 0;
        }
```

The `wait` of Example 8.11 sets `lock` to 1, performs a single test to see if the semaphore is positive, and sets `lock` to 0. The semaphore variable can be a simple `int` for this implementation. Of course, this implementation uses busy waiting.

8.2.2 Semaphores without Busy Waiting

An implementation of semaphores that relies on busy waiting is inefficient and does not guarantee bounded waiting. A better implementation blocks the process when it has to wait. When a process begins waiting, the operating system puts it on a special queue of processes waiting for a semaphore, similar to a queue of processes waiting for I/O. The operating system manages this queue (say as a FIFO queue) and removes a process when a semaphore `signal` occurs. One possible implementation represents the `semaphore_t` type as a structure, `s`, consisting of an integer member (denoted by `s.value`) and a linked list (denoted by `s.list`) of waiting processes. The integer member represents the number of available resources.

Example 8.12

The following pseudocode shows a blocking implementation of semaphores.

```
void wait(semaphore_t *sp)
{
    if (sp->value > 0)
        sp->value--;
    else {
        <Add this process to sp->list>
        <block>
    }
}
void signal(semaphore_t *sp)
{
    if (sp->list != NULL)
        <remove a process from sp->list and put in ready state>
    else
        sp->value++;
}
```

Remember that the `wait` and `signal` must be atomic, and Example 8.12 does not show the extra code needed to assure atomicity. The type of ordering used for the semaphore list determines which process is serviced next. A FIFO queue guarantees bounded waiting. Other queuing techniques may result in a process being completely overlooked. This problem is called *starvation*.

8.2.3 *AND* Synchronization

The semaphore synchronizes processes by requiring that the value of the semaphore variable be greater than 0. There are more general forms of synchronization than those discussed so far (e.g., condition variables allow synchronization on arbitrary conditions), and there are also mechanisms for combining synchronization conditions. *OR synchronization* refers to waiting until any condition in a specified set is satisfied. The use of `select` or `poll` to monitor multiple file descriptors for input is a form of OR synchronization. *NOT synchronization* refers to waiting until some condition in a set is not true. NOT synchronization can be used to enforce priority ordering [64].

AND synchronization refers to waiting until all of the conditions in a specified set of conditions are satisfied. AND synchronization can be used for simultaneous control of multiple resources. This subsection explores the use and implementation of simultaneous semaphores which are a form of AND synchronization. UNIX System V semaphores sets, discussed in Section 8.4, use a form of AND synchronization.

Example 8.13

Consider a system that has two tape drives labeled A and B. Process one periodically dumps to tape using drive A. Process two copies from drive A to drive B. Process three periodically dumps to tape using drive B. The following pseudocode correctly synchronizes the interactions of the three processes using simple semaphores, A *and* B, *initialized to* 1.

```
Process 1:          Process 2:                Process 3:
   wait(&A);           wait(&A);                 wait(&B);
   <use tape A>        wait(&B);                 <use tape B>
   signal(&A);         <use tapes A and B>       signal(&B);
                       signal(&B);
                       signal(&A);
```

Unfortunately process two of Example 8.13 can hold tape A while waiting for tape B to become available. Thus, tape A can sit idle if process three is active and process two is blocked. A better solution to Example 8.13 has process two waiting for both tape drives before acquiring either one. The notation wait(&A, &B) denotes a *simultaneous wait* on two semaphores A and B. The process blocks if it would block on either semaphore individually, that is, it does not decrement the semaphore variables unless it can decrement both semaphore variables without blocking.

Example 8.14

The following pseudocode illustrates the use of simultaneous wait for the tape drive problem of Example 8.13.

```
Process 1:          Process 2:                Process 3:
   wait(&A);           wait(&A, &B);             wait(&B);
   <use tape A>        <use tapes A and B>       <use tape B>
   signal(&A);         signal(&A, &B);           signal(&B);
```

When a process executes a simultaneous wait, it atomically tests all of the semaphores in the set to see if any would cause the process to block. If none would cause blocking, the process atomically decrements all of the semaphores variables and proceeds. If any of the decrement operations would cause blocking, the process blocks without modifying the semaphore values.

When a process executes a simultaneous semaphore signal, all of the processes blocked on the semaphores are awakened. The newly unblocked processes then attempt to perform their decrements again. In this way the unblocked processes compete to pass through the simultaneous wait. Example 8.15 shows pseudocode for a two-variable simultaneous `wait`. Compare the two-variable implementation to the one-variable implementation of Section 8.2.2.

Example 8.15

In the following pseudocode implementation of a two-variable simultaneous `wait`, *a process appears in at most one list. The* `wait` *must be executed atomically.*

```
void wait(semaphore_t *ap, semaphore_t *bp)
{
    if ((ap->value > 0) && (bp->value > 0)){
        (ap->value)--;
        (bp->value)--;
    }
    else {
        if (ap->value <= 0)
            <Add this process to ap->list>
        else
            <Add this process to bp->list>
        <reset program counter to beginning of wait>
        <block>
    }
}
```

The simultaneous two-variable semaphore `signal` awakens all processes waiting on either semaphore. Since each process tries to reacquire its needed semaphores when it is awakened, only one process whose semaphores are available proceeds and the other processes block again.

Example 8.16

The following pseudocode implements a simultaneous semaphore signal.

```
void signal(semaphore_t *ap, semaphore_t *bp)
{
    ap->value++;
    <move all processes on ap->list to the ready queue>
    bp->value++;
    <move all processes on bp->list to the ready queue>
}
```

The simultaneous semaphore signal of Example 8.16 awakens all waiting processes when the semaphores are incremented. This approach appears to be inefficient, but alternative implementations are very complicated.

Suppose instead, the simultaneous wait puts the process on all queues and the simultaneous signal only wakes the first waiting process on each queue. These processes could be waiting for other semaphores and there is no guarantee that the right process is selected. Example 8.12 illustrates the problems with the alternative implementation.

Exercise 8.12

The semaphores A, B, and C are all initially 0. How can the following pseudocode fail if the simultaneous signal implementation only awakens the first process in each semaphore queue?

```
Process 1                        Process 2
a:|  wait(&A, &B);               a:|    wait(&B, &C);
b:|  <critical section>          b:|    <critical section>
c:|  signal(&A, &B);             c:|    signal(&B, &C);

Process 3
a:|  signal(&B, &C);
```

Answer:

If the execution order is a_1 followed by a_2, the semaphore queues are

```
A:   1
B:   1, 2
C:   2
```

If the simultaneous semaphore signal wakes only the first process in each queue, statement a_3 removes process one from queue B and process two from queue C.

```
A:   1
B:   2
C:
```

Process one holds semaphore B while blocking on A. Process two is now blocked until process one gets semaphore A violating the purpose of simultaneous acquisition.

Both simultaneous `wait` and `signal` generalize to any number of semaphores. A program does not have to call the `signal` with the same number of semaphores as the `wait`. A `signal` awakens all processes waiting on the corresponding semaphores. Since the awakened processes recompete for semaphore resources in an uncontrolled fashion, it is possible that an unlucky process never acquires its semaphore resources.

8.3 Semaphores in POSIX

Semaphores are part of the POSIX.1b standard adopted in 1993 [53]. Since this is a fairly new addition, POSIX semaphores may not be available in all operating systems that claim to be POSIX.1 compliant. An implementation supports POSIX semaphores if it defines _POSIX_SEMAPHORES in unistd.h.

A POSIX.1b semaphore is a variable of type sem_t with associated atomic operations for initializing, incrementing, and decrementing its value. The POSIX.1b standard defines two types of semaphores: named and unnamed. A POSIX.1b *unnamed semaphore* can be used by a single process or by children of the process that created it. A POSIX.1b *named semaphore* can be used by any process. The difference between unnamed and named semaphores is analogous to the difference between ordinary pipes and named pipes (FIFOs).

Example 8.17

The following code segment declares a semaphore variable called sem.

```
#include <semaphore.h>
sem_t sem;
```

The POSIX.1b standard does not specify the underlying type of sem_t. One possibility is that this acts like a file descriptor and is an offset into a local table. The table entries point to entries in a system file table. A particular implementation may not use the model of a file descriptor table or a system file table, so information about the semaphore may be stored with the sem variable, and the semaphore functions all take a pointer to the semaphore variable as a parameter.

All of the POSIX.1b semaphore functions return -1 and set errno to indicate an error. One of the possible errno values for sem_init is ENOSYS indicating that sem_init is not supported by an implementation. (_POSIX_SEMAPHORES may be defined, but the system does not yet support using the POSIX.1b semaphores.) The number of semaphores that the system can support may be limited, and if this limit is exceeded, the value of errno is ENOSPC. POSIX does not indicate what the semaphore operations must return on success, but the standard states that a later amendment might require them to return 0.

8.3.1 Initialization of Unnamed Semaphores

POSIX.1b semaphores are counting semaphores that have nonnegative values and must be initialized before they are used. Section 8.3.3 discusses initialization techniques for named semaphores. The sem_init function initializes an unnamed semaphore.

```
SYNOPSIS

   #include <semaphore.h>

   int sem_init(sem_t *sem, int pshared, unsigned int value);
                                                        POSIX.1b
```

The `sem_init` function initializes the semaphore to have the value `value`. The `value` parameter cannot be negative. If the value of `pshared` is not 0, the semaphore can be used between processes (i.e., by the process that initializes it and by children of that process). Otherwise it can be used only by threads within the process that initializes it.

Think of `sem` as referring to the semaphore, rather than as the semaphore itself. In fact, the `sem_init` function creates the semaphore and sets `sem` to refer to it. As a result, if `pshared` is not 0, children inherit semaphores in the same way they inherit open file descriptors.

8.3.2 POSIX Semaphore Operations

The following functions manipulate unnamed or named semaphores after initialization.

```
SYNOPSIS

    #include <semaphore.h>

    int sem_destroy(sem_t *sem);
    int sem_wait(sem_t *sem);
    int sem_trywait(sem_t *sem);
    int sem_post(sem_t *sem);
    int sem_getvalue(sem_t *sem, int *sval);
```
                                                                        POSIX.1b

The `sem_destroy` function destroys a previously initialized semaphore. If a process attempts to destroy a semaphore that has another process waiting for it, `sem_destroy` may return an error with `errno` set to `EBUSY`. Unfortunately the POSIX.1b specification does not require that the system detect this.

The `sem_wait` is a standard semaphore wait operation. If the semaphore value is 0, the `sem_wait` blocks until it can successfully decrement the semaphore value or until it is interrupted by a signal such as `SIGINT`. Section 8.5 discusses this further. The `sem_trywait` function is similar to `sem_wait` except that instead of blocking when attempting to decrement a zero-valued semaphore, it returns -1 and sets `errno` to `EAGAIN`.

The `sem_post` increments the semaphore value and is the classical semaphore signal operation. The POSIX.1b standard requires that `sem_post` be reentrant with respect to signals, that is, it is async-signal safe and may be invoked from a signal-handler.

The `sem_getvalue` function allows a user to examine the value of either a named or unnamed semaphore. This function sets the integer referenced by `sval` to the value of the semaphore. If there are processes waiting for the semaphore, the POSIX.1b standard allows this function to set `sval` either to 0 or to a negative number whose absolute value represents the number of processes waiting for the semaphore at some unspecified time during the call to sem_getvalue. The ambiguity makes this feature unusable. A positive value of sval represents the value of the semaphore during some unspecified time of execution of sem_getvalue, not necessarily the time at which sem_getvalue returns. The function returns 0 on success. On error sem_getvalue returns −1 and sets errno.

Program 8.2 shows a modification of Program 8.1 that protects the critical section by a POSIX.1b semaphore, my_lock. The code initializes my_lock to 1 to provide mutual exclusion.

Program 8.2: A program with a critical section protected by a POSIX.1b semaphore.

```c
#include <stdio.h>
#include <stdlib.h>
#include <limits.h>
#include <unistd.h>
#include <semaphore.h>

void main  (int argc, char *argv[])
{
    char buffer[MAX_CANON];
    char *c;
    int i;
    int n;
    pid_t childpid;
    sem_t my_lock;

    if ( (argc != 2) || ((n = atoi(argv[1])) <= 0) ) {
        fprintf (stderr, "Usage: %s number_of_processes\n", argv[0]);
        exit(1);
    }
    if (sem_init(&my_lock, 1, 1) == -1) {
        perror("Could not initialize mylock semaphore");
        exit(1);
    }
    for (i = 1; i < n;   ++i)
        if (childpid = fork())
            break;

    sprintf(buffer,
        "i:%d  process ID:%ld  parent ID:%ld  child ID:%ld\n",
        i, (long)getpid(), (long)getppid(), (long)childpid);

    c = buffer;
        /************************entry section ************************/
```

```
      if (sem_wait(&my_lock) == -1)   {
         perror("Semaphore invalid");
         exit(1);
      }
      /***************start of critical section ********************/
      while (*c != '\0') {
         fputc(*c, stderr);
         c++;
      }
      fputc('\n', stderr);
      /*****************end of critical section ********************/

      /********************* exit section ************************/
      if (sem_post(&my_lock) == -1) {
         perror("Semaphore done");
         exit(1);
      }
      /****************** remainder section ********************/
      exit(0);
}
```

_____ **Program 8.2** _____

8.3.3 Named Semaphores

POSIX.1b named semaphores can synchronize processes that do not have a common
ancestor. Named semaphores have a name, a user ID, a group ID, and permissions just
as files do. A semaphore name is a character string that conforms to the construction
rules for a pathname. POSIX.1b does not require that the name appear in the filesystem
nor does POSIX.1b specify the consequences of having two processes refer to the same
name unless the name begins with the slash character. If the name begins with a slash
(/), then two processes (or threads) that open the semaphore with that name refer to
the same semaphore. Consequently, always use names beginning with a / for named
POSIX semaphores.

The sem_open function establishes the connection between a named semaphore
and a sem_t value. There are two forms of sem_open.

SYNOPSIS

```
   #include <semaphore.h>

   sem_t *sem_open(const char *name, int oflag);
   sem_t *sem_open(const char *name, int oflag, mode_t mode,
                   unsigned int value);
```
POSIX.1b

If the call is successful, `sem_open` returns a pointer identifying the semaphore in future calls to `sem_wait`, `sem_trywait`, `sem_post`, `sem_destroy`, and `sem_getvalue`. Notice the analogy between semaphore names and `sem_t` values with filenames and file descriptors. Remember, however, that semaphore functions use pointers to `sem_t` values.

The `oflag` value determines whether `sem_open` accesses a previously-created semaphore or creates a new one. An `oflag` of 0 specifies the first form, and `sem_open` returns a handle to a previously opened semaphore of the same name. If no such semaphore has been previously opened, `sem_open` returns −1 and sets `errno` to `ENOENT`.

An `oflag` value of `O_CREAT` or `O_CREAT | O_EXCL` requires the second form of `sem_open` with two additional parameters. The third parameter specifies the permissions of the semaphore if it is being created, as with the `open` system call. The fourth parameter specifies the initial value of the semaphore if it is being created.

If `oflag` is `O_CREAT`, `sem_open` creates a semaphore if one does not already exist. If a semaphore of the same name already exists, the `sem_open` accesses the previously created semaphore. In the latter case, the `sem_open` ignores the third and fourth arguments.

If `oflag` is `O_CREAT | O_EXCL`, `sem_open` creates a semaphore if one does not already exist. If a semaphore with the same name already exists, `sem_open` returns −1 and sets `errno` to `EEXIST`. POSIX.1b only defines `oflag` values of 0, `O_CREAT`, and `O_CREAT | O_EXCL`. Other values are system-dependent.

Two additional functions are available for use with named semaphores, the `sem_close` and the `sem_unlink`.

```
SYNOPSIS

   #include <semaphore.h>

   int sem_close(sem_t *sem);
   int sem_unlink(const char *name);
                                                     POSIX.1b
```

Both `sem_close` and `sem_unlink` return 0 on success. On error, these functions return −1 and set `errno`. Although POSIX.1b does not require that named semaphores correspond to entries in a filesystem, it is convenient to think of this representation and to compare `sem_close` and `sem_unlink` to the `close` and `unlink` system calls.

When a process is finished with a named semaphore, it calls `sem_close` to deallocate any system resources allocated to the caller for this semaphore. The `sem_close` function does not necessarily remove the named semaphore, but it makes the semaphore inaccessible to the process. The `_exit` or `exec` system calls also deallocate process semaphore resources.

The `sem_unlink` function removes a named semaphore from the system. If other processes still reference the semaphore, `sem_unlink` postpones the destruction until all other references are closed by `sem_close`, `_exit`, or `exec`. Calls to `sem_open` with the same name refer to a new semaphore after the `sem_unlink`, even if other processes still have the old semaphore open. The `sem_unlink` always returns immediately, even if other processes have the semaphore open.

POSIX.1b does not specify where the resources for POSIX semaphores are allocated. System V semaphores, discussed in the next section, are an example of kernel-level semaphores because their resources reside in the kernel.

8.4 Semaphores in System V (Spec 1170)

The System V semaphores are part of a general System V interprocess communication facility (IPC) which also includes shared memory (Section 8.9) and message queues (Section 8.10). A process creates a System V semaphore by executing a `semget` system call. The call creates a semaphore data structure in the kernel and returns an integer handle to the semaphore. Processes cannot access the semaphore data structures directly, only through system calls. The semaphore IDs or handles are analogous to file descriptors.

The System V semaphores, shared memory, and message queues are not part of POSIX.1 but are included in the Spec 1170 specification. Their data structures are created and kept in the kernel and referenced through integer handles. In contrast, a program declares a variable of type `sem_t` and passes a pointer to that variable when invoking the POSIX semaphore functions.

8.4.1 Semaphore Sets

A UNIX System V semaphore is actually a *semaphore set* consisting of an array of *semaphore elements*. The semaphore elements correspond to the classical integer semaphores proposed by Dijsktra. A process can perform operations on the entire set in a single system call.

The internal representation of the semaphore sets and the individual semaphore elements is not directly accessible, but each semaphore element includes at least the following:

- A nonnegative integer representing the value of the semaphore element.
- The process ID of the last process to manipulate the semaphore element.
- The number of processes waiting for the semaphore element value to increase.
- The number of processes waiting for the semaphore element value to equal 0.

Semaphore operations allow a process to block until a semaphore element value is 0 or until it becomes positive. Each element has two queues associated with it—a queue of processes waiting for the semaphore element value to increase and a queue of processes waiting for the value to equal 0.

8.4.2 Semaphore Creation

The `semget` creates a semaphore set and initializes each element to 0.

```
SYNOPSIS

    #include <sys/types.h>
    #include <sys/ipc.h>
    #include <sys/sem.h>

    int semget(key_t key, int nsems, int semflg);
                                                         Spec 1170
```

The `semget` takes three arguments: a key identifying the semaphore set, the size of the semaphore set, and flags. The `semget` returns an integer handle for subsequent calls to `semop` and `semctl`. The `semget` returns a −1 and sets `errno` if the call fails. A failure can occur if the arguments are invalid or if there are not enough system resources to allocate the semaphore.

The `key` parameter indicates the particular semaphore set to be created or accessed. A program specifies a key in one of these three ways: use `IPC_PRIVATE` and have the system come up with a key, pick a random key number, or use `ftok` to generate a key from a pathname.

The `nsems` parameter specifies the number of semaphore elements in the set. The individual semaphore elements within a semaphore set are referenced by the integers 0 through `nsems` - 1. Semaphores have permissions specified by the `semflg` argument of `semget`. Set permission values in the same way as described in Section 3.3.1 for files, and change the permissions by calling `semctl`. If a process attempts to create a semaphore that already exists, it receives a handle to the existing semaphore unless it specifies a `semflg` value including both `IPC_CREAT` and `IPC_EXCL`. In the latter case, `semget` fails and sets `errno` equal to `EEXIST`.

Example 8.18

The following code segment creates a private semaphore set containing three semaphore elements.

```
#include <stdio.h>
#include <sys/stat.h>
#include <sys/types.h>
#include <sys/ipc.h>
#include <sys/sem.h>
```

```
#define PERMS S_IRUSR|S_IWUSR
#define SET_SIZE 3

int semid;

if ((semid = semget(IPC_PRIVATE, SET_SIZE, PERMS)) < 0)
    perror("Could not create new private semaphore");
```

The `PERMS` value in Example 8.18 specifies that the semaphore can be read or written only by the owner. The `IPC_PRIVATE` key guarantees that `semget` creates a
new semaphore. To get a new semaphore set from a made-up key or a key derived from
a pathname, the process must specify that it is creating a new semaphore by using the
`IPC_CREAT` flag.

Example 8.19
*The following code segment creates a semaphore set with a single element iden-
tified by the key value* 99887.

```
#include <stdio.h>
#include <sys/stat.h>
#include <sys/ipc.h>
#include <sys/sem.h>
#include <string.h>
#include <errno.h>

#define PERMS S_IRUSR|S_IWUSR|S_IRGRP|S_IWGRP|S_IROTH|S_IWOTH
#define SET_SIZE 1
#define KEY ((key_t)99887)

int semid;
if ((semid = semget(KEY, SET_SIZE, PERMS | IPC_CREAT)) < 0)
    fprintf(stderr, "Error creating semaphore with key %d: %s\n",
        (int)KEY, strerror(errno));
```

Giving a specific key value allows cooperating processes to agree on a common semaphore set. The permissions in Example 8.19 allow all user processes to
access the semaphore. If the semaphore already exists, the `semget` returns a handle to the existing semaphore. Replace the `semflg` argument of `semget` with
`PERMS | ICP_CREAT | IPC_EXCL`, and `semget` returns an error when the semaphore already exists.

The third way to identify a semaphore set is to derive a key from a pathname by
calling `ftok`. The file must exist and be accessible to the processes that want to access
the semaphore. The combination of pathname `path` and integer `id` uniquely identifies
the semaphore. The `id` parameter allows several semaphore sets keyed from a single
pathname.

SYNOPSIS

```
#include <sys/types.h>
#include <sys/ipc.h>

key_t ftok(const char *path, int id);
```

Spec 1170

Program 8.3 creates a semaphore set with two elements from a derived key. The `path` and `id` parameters are command-line arguments.

Program 8.3: A program that creates a semaphore from a pathname key.

```c
#include <stdio.h>
#include <stdlib.h>
#include <sys/stat.h>
#include <sys/ipc.h>
#include <sys/sem.h>
#include <string.h>
#include <errno.h>

#define PERMS S_IRUSR|S_IWUSR|S_IRGRP|S_IWGRP|S_IROTH|S_IWOTH
#define SET_SIZE 2

void main(int argc, char *argv[])
{
   int semid;
   key_t mykey;

   if (argc != 3) {
      fprintf(stderr, "Usage: %s filename id\n", argv[0]);
      exit(1);
   }
   if ((mykey = ftok(argv[1], atoi(argv[2]))) == (key_t) -1) {
      fprintf(stderr, "Could not derive key from filename %s: %s\n",
              argv[1], strerror(errno));
      exit(1);
   }
   else if ((semid = semget(mykey, SET_SIZE, PERMS | IPC_CREAT)) < 0) {
      fprintf(stderr, "Error creating semaphore with key %d: %s\n",
              (int)mykey, strerror(errno));
      exit(1);
   }
   printf("semid = %d\n", semid);
   exit(0);
}
```

_____ **Program 8.3** _____

8.4.3 System V Semaphore Operations

A process can increment, decrement, or test individual semaphore elements for a zero value by using the `semop` system call.

```
SYNOPSIS

    #include <sys/types.h>
    #include <sys/ipc.h>
    #include <sys/sem.h>

    int semop(int semid, struct sembuf *sops, int nsops);
                                                            Spec 1170
```

The `semid` parameter is the handle returned by `semget`, and the `sops` parameter points to an array of element operations. The `nsops` parameter specifies the number of element operations in the `sops` array. If `semop` is interrupted by a signal, it returns -1 with `errno` set to `EINTR`. A careful implementation of mutual exclusion with System V semaphores restarts the `semop` if interrupted by a signal.

All of the operations specified in `struct sembuf` are performed atomically on a single semaphore set. If any of the individual element operations would cause the process to block, the process blocks and none of the operations are performed.

The `struct sembuf` structure, which specifies a semaphore element operation, includes the following members:

`short sem_num:`	The number of the semaphore element.
`short sem_op:`	The particular operation to be performed on the semaphore element.
`short sem_flg:`	The flags to specify options for the operation.

The `sem_op` element operations are values indicating the amount by which the semaphore value is changed:

- If `sem_op` is a positive number, `semop` adds the value to the corresponding semaphore element value and awakens all processes that are waiting for the element to increase.

- If `sem_op` is 0 and the semaphore element value is not 0, `semop` blocks the calling process (waiting for 0) and increments the count of processes waiting for a zero value of that element.

- If `sem_op` is a negative number, `semop` adds the value to the corresponding semaphore element value provided the result would not be negative. On the other hand, if the operation would make the element value negative, `semop` blocks the process on the event that the semaphore element value increases. If the resulting value is 0, `semop` wakes the processes waiting for 0.

The description of `semop` assumes that `sem_flg` is 0. If `sem_flg & IPC_NOWAIT` is true, the call never blocks, but instead, returns a -1 with `errno` set to `EAGAIN`. If `sem_flg & SEM_UNDO` is true, the function also modifies the semaphore adjustment value for the process. This adjustment value allows the process to *undo* its effect on the semaphore when it exits.

Example 8.20

An undesirable practice is to initialize a `struct sembuf` *in a declaration. The following C code declares the* `struct sembuf` *structure* `myopbuf` *and initializes it so that* `sem_num` *is 1,* `sem_op` *is 1, and* `sem_flg` *is 0.*

```
struct sembuf myopbuf = {1, -1, 0};
```

Do not use the initialization method of Example 8.20 because it is not implementation-independent. The `struct sembuf` structure, which specifies the operations for `semop` structure, is guaranteed to have the members `sem_num`, `sem_op`, and `sem_flg`. The Spec 1170 standard does not specify the order these members appear in the definition, nor does the standard restrict `struct sembuf` to contain only these members.

Example 8.21

The function `set_sembuf_struct` *initializes the* `struct sembuf` *structure members* `sem_num`, `sem_op`, *and* `sem_flg` *in an implementation-independent manner.*

```
#include <sys/types.h>
#include <sys/ipc.h>
#include <sys/sem.h>

void set_sembuf_struct(struct sembuf *s, int num, int op, int flg)
{
   s->sem_num = (short) num;
   s->sem_op = op;
   s->sem_flg = flg;
   return;
}
```

Example 8.22

The following code segment atomically increments the elements of the semaphore set defined in Program 8.3.

```
#include <stdio.h>
#include <sys/types.h>
#include <sys/ipc.h>
#include <sys/sem.h>
#include <string.h>
```

```
#include <errno.h>
struct sembuf myop[2];

set_sembuf_struct(&(myop[0]), 0, 1, 0);
set_sembuf_struct(&(myop[1]), 1, 2, 0);
if (semop(semid, myop, 2) == -1)
   perror("Semaphore operation failed");
```

Element zero in Example 8.22 is incremented by one and element one is incremented by two. The code uses `set_sembuf_struct` from Example 8.21 to initialize the operations.

Example 8.23

Suppose a two-element UNIX System V semaphore set, `S`, represents the tape drive system in Example 8.13. `S[0]` represents tape A and `S[1]` represents tape B. Both elements of `S` are initialized to 1. The following pseudocode segment defines semaphore operations to access one or both tape drives.

```
#include <sys/types.h>
#include <sys/ipc.h>
#include <sys/sem.h>
struct sembuf GET_TAPES[2];
struct sembuf RELEASE_TAPES[2];

set_sembuf_struct(&(GET_TAPES[0]), 0, -1, 0);
set_sembuf_struct(&(GET_TAPES[1]), 1, -1, 0);
set_sembuf_struct(&(RELEASE_TAPES[0]), 0, 1, 0);
set_sembuf_struct(&(RELEASE_TAPES[1]), 1, 1, 0);

Process 1:        semop(S, GET_TAPES, 1);
                  <use tape A>
                  semop(S, RELEASE_TAPES, 1);

Process 2:        semop(S, GET_TAPES, 2);
                  <use tapes A and B>
                  semop(S, RELEASE_TAPES, 2);

Process 3:        semop(S, GET_TAPES + 1, 1);
                  <use tape A>
                  semop(S, RELEASE_TAPES + 1, 1);
```

Program 8.4 is a modification of Program 8.1 that uses System V semaphores to protect the critical section. The program calls `set_sembuf_struct` defined in Example 8.21 and `remove_semaphore` defined in Example 8.26. It restarts `semop` operations if interrupted by a signal.

Program 8.4: A modification of Program 8.1 that uses System V semaphores to protect the critical section.

```
#include <stdlib.h>
#include <unistd.h>
#include <stdio.h>
#include <limits.h>
#include <errno.h>
#include <string.h>
#include <sys/stat.h>
#include <sys/wait.h>
#include <sys/ipc.h>
#include <sys/sem.h>
#define PERMS S_IRUSR | S_IWUSR
#define SET_SIZE 2

void set_sembuf_struct(struct sembuf *s, int semnum,
                                         int semop, int semflg);
int remove_semaphore(int semid);

void main (int argc, char *argv[])
{
    char buffer[MAX_CANON];
    char *c;
    int i;
    int n;
    pid_t childpid;
    int semid;
    int semop_ret;
    struct sembuf semwait[1];
    struct sembuf semsignal[1];
    int status;

    if ( (argc != 2) || ((n = atoi (argv[1])) <= 0) ) {
        fprintf (stderr, "Usage: %s number_of_processes\n", argv[0]);
        exit(1);
    }
            /* Create a semaphore containing a single element */
    if ((semid = semget(IPC_PRIVATE, SET_SIZE, PERMS)) == -1) {
        fprintf(stderr, "[%ld]: Could not access semaphore: %s\n",
            (long)getpid(), strerror(errno));
        exit(1);
    }
                        /* Initialize the semaphore element to 1 */
    set_sembuf_struct(semwait, 0, -1, 0);
    set_sembuf_struct(semsignal, 0, 1, 0);

    if (semop(semid, semsignal, 1) == -1) {
```

```
        fprintf(stderr, "[%ld]: semaphore increment failed - %s\n",
            (long)getpid(), strerror(errno));
        if (remove_semaphore(semid) == -1)
            fprintf(stderr, "[%ld], could not delete semaphore - %s\n",
                (long)getpid(), strerror(errno));
        exit(1);
    }

    for (i = 1; i < n;  ++i)
        if (childpid = fork())
            break;
    sprintf(buffer,
        "i:%d  process ID:%ld  parent ID:%ld  child ID:%ld\n",
        i, (long)getpid(), (long)getppid(), (long)childpid);

    c = buffer;
        /**********************entry section **********************/
    while(( (semop_ret = semop(semid, semwait, 1)) == -1) &&
            (errno == EINTR))
        ;
    if (semop_ret == -1)
        fprintf(stderr, "[%ld]: semaphore decrement failed - %s\n",
            (long)getpid(), strerror(errno));
    else {
        /***************start of critical section ******************/
        while (*c != '\0') {
            fputc(*c, stderr);
            c++;
        }
        fputc('\n', stderr);
        /****************end of critical section ******************/
        /********************* exit section ***********************/
        while(((semop_ret = semop(semid, semsignal, 1)) == -1) &&
                (errno == EINTR))
            ;
        if (semop_ret == -1)
            fprintf(stderr, "[%ld]: semaphore increment failed - %s\n",
                (long)getpid(), strerror(errno));
    }
        /***************** remainder section **********************/
    while((wait(&status) == -1) && (errno == EINTR))
        ;
    if (i == 1)   /* the original process removes the semaphore */
        if (remove_semaphore(semid) == -1)
            fprintf(stderr, "[%ld], could not delete semaphore - %s\n",
                (long)getpid(), strerror(errno));
    exit(0);
}
```

_____ **Program 8.4** _____

System V semaphores do creation and initialization in separate system calls. If one process creates a semaphore and another process tries a `semop` before the original process has a chance to initialize the semaphore, the results of the execution are unpredictable. This unpredictability is an example of a *race condition* because the occurrence of the error depends on the precise timing between instructions in different processes. Program 8.4 does not have the problem because the original parent creates and initializes the semaphore before doing a `fork`. Since the semaphore is private, only the original process can access it at the time of creation.

One approach to solving the initialization problem when the semaphores are not private is to wait for 0 rather than to wait for a positive value [85]. The traditional signal operation then becomes a decrement to 0, and the traditional wait operation becomes an increment to 1.

Example 8.24

The following code segment implements a semaphore wait as an increment rather than as a decrement.

```
#include <stdio.h>
#include <sys/types.h>
#include <sys/ipc.h>
#include <sys/sem.h>
#include <string.h>
#include <errno.h>
#define SET_SIZE 2
struct sembuf myop[SET_SIZE];

set_sembuf_struct(&(myop[0]), 0, 0, 0);
set_sembuf_struct(&(myop[1]), 0, 1, 0);
if (semop(semid, myop, 2) == -1)
   perror("Semaphore operation failed");
```

Notice that both operations in `myop` of Example 8.24 refer to element number zero. If element zero does not currently have the value 0, the process blocks until it is 0. When the element is 0, it is incremented to 1 in an atomic operation. Since `semget` initializes the semaphore elements to 0, the semaphore is ready to use right after the `semget` without an intervening initialization.

The approach of Example 8.24 assumes that the semaphore operations are attempted in order [85]. Spec 1170 does not explicitly mandate this implementation, so it is unwise to rely on it. The `create_and_initialize` function of Program 8.5 illustrates an alternative approach to initializing a semaphore element to a particular value.

The semaphore element to be initialized in Program 8.5 has an associated lock element. The semaphore is element one and the lock is element zero. The function returns a handle to the semaphore on success or −1 on failure. If the semaphore already exists, the caller waits until the lock element is set to 1 before proceeding. The error checking for `semop` is not shown for clarity, but in fact, the call to `semop` should be replaced by a call to `semop_restart` of Example 8.29 to restart the call after interruption by signals. Program 8.5 should deallocate the semaphore before returning if a real `semop` error occurs.

Program 8.5: A function that atomically creates and initializes a System V semaphore.

```c
#include <sys/stat.h>
#include <sys/ipc.h>
#include <sys/sem.h>
#include <stdio.h>
#include <errno.h>
#define PERMS S_IRUSR|S_IWUSR
#define SET_SIZE 2

int create_and_initialize(key_t mykey, int value)
{
    int semid;
    struct sembuf getlock, setlock, setinit;

    semid = semget(mykey, SET_SIZE, PERMS|IPC_CREAT|IPC_EXCL);
    if ((semid < 0) && (errno != EEXIST)) {
        perror("Semaphore create failed");
        return -1;
    } else if (semid > 0) {
        /* initialize the semaphore and open the lock */
        set_sembuf_struct(&setinit, 1, value, 0);
        semop(semid, &setinit, 1);
        set_sembuf_struct(&setlock, 0, 1, 0);
        semop(semid, &setlock, 1);
    } else {
        /* semaphore already exists -- wait for initialization */
        if ((semid = semget(mykey, SET_SIZE, PERMS)) < 0) {
            perror("Could not access existing semaphore");
            return -1;
        }
        set_sembuf_struct(&getlock, 0, -1, 0);
        semop(semid, &getlock, 1);
        set_sembuf_struct(&setlock, 0, 1, 0);
        semop(semid, &setlock, 1);
    }
    return 0;
}
```

---------------------------------- **Program 8.5** ----------------------------------

8.4.4 Semaphore Control

The `semctl` function queries or sets the values of individual semaphore elements. It also performs other control functions including semaphore destruction.

```
SYNOPSIS

   #include <sys/types.h>
   #include <sys/ipc.h>
   #include <sys/sem.h>

   int semctl(int semid, int semnum, int cmd,
                        /* union semun arg */ ...);
                                                     Spec 1170
```

Here `semid` identifies the semaphore set, and `semnum` indicates the semaphore element within the set if `cmd` refers to individual elements. The `cmd` argument specifies which command is to be executed, and `arg` is used differently for the various `cmd` values. The following are the most important commands to be used with `semctl`:

GETVAL:	Return the value of a specific semaphore element.
GETPID:	Return process ID of last process to manipulate element.
GETNCNT:	Return number of processes waiting for element to increment.
GETZCNT:	Return number of processes waiting for element to become 0.
SETVAL:	Set the value of a specific semaphore element to `arg.val`
IPC_RMID:	Remove the semaphore identified by `semid`.
IPC_SET:	Set the permissions of the semaphore.

The `union semun` definition may need to be included directly in programs, since some systems do not define it in the header files for semaphores. Its definition is

```
union semun {
   int val;
   struct semid_ds *buf;
   ushort *array;
};
```

The `semctl` returns -1 and sets `errno` if an error occurs. The return value when there is no error depends on `cmd`. The GETVAL, GETPID, GETNCNT, and GETZCNT values of `cmd` cause `semctl` to return the value associated with `cmd`. All other values of `cmd` cause `semctl` to return 0.

Example 8.25

The `initialize_sem_element` *function sets the value of the specified semaphore element to* `semvalue`.

```
#include <sys/types.h>
#include <sys/ipc.h>
```

```
#include <sys/sem.h>

int initialize_sem_element(int semid, int semnum, int semvalue)
{
    union semun arg;
    arg.val = semvalue;
    return semctl(semid, semnum, SETVAL, arg);
}
```

The `semid` and `semnum` parameters of `initialize_sem_element` in Example 8.25 identify the semaphore set and the element within the set whose value is to be set to `semvalue`. The `initialize_sem_element` function returns 0 on success. On failure it returns −1 with `errno` set (since `semctl` sets the `errno`).

Example 8.26

   The `remove_semaphore` *function deletes the semaphore specified by* `semid`.

```
#include <sys/types.h>
#include <sys/ipc.h>
#include <sys/sem.h>

int remove_semaphore(int semid)
{
    return semctl(semid, 0, IPC_RMID);
}
```

The `remove_semaphore` function of Example 8.26 returns 0 on success. On failure it returns −1 with `errno` set (since `semctl` sets the `errno`).

8.4.5 Semaphore Status

Typically System V semaphore implementations keep a single table of the semaphore sets in the kernel. Investigate the status of these semaphore sets from the shell with the `ipcs` command. Remove personally-owned semaphore sets with the `ipcrm` command.

Example 8.27

   The following command lists all semaphores.

```
ipcs -s
```

The `ipcs` command of Example 8.27 may produce a message indicating that the semaphore facility is not in the system. Under Sun Solaris 2, the semaphore facility is loaded only after some program performs a semaphore operation, usually the creation of a semaphore. The facility then stays loaded until the system is rebooted or until it is specifically unloaded.

Example 8.28

> *The following command deletes the semaphore with ID* 12345.
>
> ```
> ipcrm -s 12345
> ```

8.5 Semaphores and Signals

In the context of semaphores, the word *signal* has two meanings: incrementing a semaphore and generating a notification of a UNIX event. This section uses signal to mean a UNIX signal not a semaphore signal operation.

During execution of slow system calls (those that can block forever), the action of a signal depends on how the signal has been caught. Under System V and Spec 1170, sigaction provides the option of restarting the system call after the signal handler exits (SA_RESTART). That option is not part of POSIX and when writing library functions used by others, the developer may not have control over how signals are set up. If slow system calls are not automatically restarted by the signal handlers, a semaphore operation such as a semaphore wait (decrement a semaphore) may return without the semaphore having been decremented. If semop is interrupted by a signal, it returns −1 and sets errno to EINTR.

Example 8.29

> *Inserting restart code for each* semop *is tedious. The* semop_restart *is like* semop *but restarts the call if it is interrupted by a signal.*
>
> ```
> #include <sys/types.h>
> #include <sys/ipc.h>
> #include <sys/sem.h>
> #include <errno.h>
>
> int semop_restart(int semid, struct sembuf *sops, int nsops)
> {
>     int retval;
>     while ( ((retval = semop(semid, sops, nsops)) == -1) &&
>             (errno == EINTR) )
>         ;
>     return retval;
> }
> ```

Example 8.30

> *The POSIX.1b* sem_wait *also returns if it is interrupted by a signal. The* sem_wait_restart *function restarts the call if it is interrupted by a signal.*
>
> ```
> #include <semaphore.h>
> #include <errno.h>
> ```

```
int sem_wait_restart(sem_t *sem)
{
    int retval;
    while ( ((retval = sem_wait(sem)) == -1) &&
            (errno == EINTR) )
        ;
    return retval;
}
```

8.6 Exercise: POSIX Unnamed Semaphores

This exercise describes an implementation of POSIX-like unnamed semaphores in terms
of System V semaphores. The prototypes for the semaphore functions are

```
#include "mysem.h"
int mysem_init(mysem_t *sem, int pshared, unsigned int value);
int mysem_destroy(mysem_t *sem);
int mysem_wait(mysem_t *sem);
int mysem_post(mysem_t *sem);
```

All of these functions return 0 if successful. On error, they return -1 and set `errno`
appropriately. Actually the last point is a little subtle. It will probably turn out that the
only statements that can cause an error are the System V semaphore calls and they set
the `errno`. If that is the case, the functions return the correct `errno` value as long
as there are no intervening system or library calls. Remember that POSIX.1c permits
`errno` to be a macro, so avoid explicitly setting this variable.

Define a type called `mysem_t` for the semaphores. For this exercise, `mysem_t` is
simply an `int`. Put the declarations and any needed type definitions in a header file
called `mysem.h` so that users can include the header file in programs that call the functions. Since a process that is going to share an unnamed semaphore with its children must
call `mysem_init` before it forks, there is no need to worry about race conditions when
implementing the initialization in terms of System V semaphores. The `mysem_t` value
is the semaphore ID of a System V semaphore. Ignore the value of `pshared`, since
System V semaphores are sharable between processes. Use a key of `IPC_PRIVATE`.

Implement the `mysem_wait` and `mysem_post` directly with calls to `semop`.
The details will depend on how `sem_init` initializes the semaphore. Implement
`mysem_destroy` with a call to `semctl`.

Write a test driver based on Program 8.2 and test the library to see that it enforces
mutual exclusion. The test program must create and delete all semaphores that it uses.

Before logging out, use `ipcs -s` from the command line. If semaphores still exist
(because of a program bug), delete each of them using

```
ipcrm -s n
```

This command deletes the semaphore with ID n. The semaphore should be created only once by the test program. It should also be deleted only once, not by all of the children in the process chain.

8.7 Exercise: POSIX Named Semaphores

This exercise describes an implementation of POSIX-like named semaphores in terms of System V semaphores. The prototypes for the semaphore functions are

```
#include "mysem.h"
mysem_t *mysem_open(const char *name, int oflag, mode_t mode,
                    unsigned int value);
int mysem_close(mysem_t *sem);
int mysem_unlink(const char *name);
int mysem_wait(mysem_t *sem);
int mysem_post(mysem_t *sem);
```

All of these functions return −1 and set errno when there is an error. To simplify the interface, always call mysem_open with four parameters.

Use an ordinary file to represent the semaphore. This file contains the semaphore ID of the System V semaphore used to implement the POSIX semaphore. The mysem_open function creates the file, allocates a System V semaphore, and stores its ID in the file. The mysem_open function returns a pointer to a file descriptor representing the file. It must allocate space for this file descriptor. The mysem_unlink, mysem_wait, and mysem_post functions use a pointer to this descriptor as their parameter. The mysem_close function makes the semaphore inaccessible to the caller. The mysem_unlink function deletes the semaphore, its corresponding file, and the integer containing the file descriptor. The mysem_wait function decrements the semaphore, and the mysem_post function increments the semaphore.

Put all of the semaphore functions in a separate library and treat this as an object in which the only items with external linkage are the five functions listed above. Do not worry about race conditions in using mysem_open to create the file until a rudimentary version of the test program is working. Devise a mechanism for freeing the System V semaphore after the last sem_unlink only after the last process has closed this semaphore. The mysem_unlink cannot directly do the freeing, because other processes may still have the POSIX semaphore open. One possibility is to have mysem_close check the link count in the inode and free the System V semaphore if the link count becomes 0.

When everything else is working, try to handle the various race conditions by using an additional System V semaphore to protect the critical sections for semaphore initialization. Use the same semaphore for all copies of the POSIX semaphore library to protect against interaction between unrelated processes. Refer to this semaphore by a filename which can be converted to a key using `ftok`.

8.8 Exercise: License Manager

The exercises in this section are along the lines of the `runsim` program developed in the exercises of Section 2.13. In those exercises `runsim` reads commands from standard input and forks a child to `execvp` each command. That `runsim` program takes a single command-line argument specifying the number of child processes allowed to execute simultaneously. It also keeps a count of the children and uses `wait` to block when it reaches the limit.

In these exercises, `runsim` again reads commands from standard input and forks a child. The child in turn forks a grandchild to do the `execvp`. The first child waits for the grandchild to complete and then exits. Figure 8.1 shows the structure of `runsim` while three such pairs are executing. This program uses semaphores to control the number of simultaneous executions.

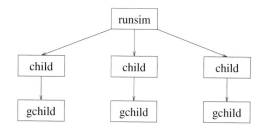

Figure 8.1: The structure of `runsim` when the `execvp`'s are performed by grandchildren rather than children.

Write a `runsim` program that runs up to n processes at a time. Start the `runsim` program by typing the command

    runsim n

Prior to starting the `runsim` program, create the following file if it does not already exist:

    /tmp/license.uid

The `uid` should be the numerical value of the process user ID. Be sure to remove this file before logging out.

Implement `runsim` as follows:

- Check for the correct number of command-line arguments and output a usage message if incorrect.
- Generate a semaphore key by calling the function `ftok` with the pathname `/tmp/license.uid`, where `uid` is the process user ID. Also use the user ID for the `id` parameter of `ftok`.
- Create a semaphore set using the key generated from the previous step. The semaphore set has one element in it which is initialized to `n`. Use the variable `license` to hold the semaphore ID returned from `semget`.
- Perform the following in a loop until end-of-file on standard input:
  - * Read a command from standard input of up to MAX_CANON characters.
  - * Perform a semaphore wait operation on the `license` semaphore.
  - * Fork a child that calls `perform_command` and then exits. Pass the input string to `perform_command`.
  - * Check to see if any of the children have finished (`waitpid` with the WNOHANG option).
- Wait for all children to finish and then remove the `license` semaphore. If the program crashes during debugging, be sure to remove the semaphore using the `ipcrm` command prior to starting `runsim` again.

The `perform_command` function has the following prototype:

```
void perform_command(char *cline);
```

Implement `perform_command` as follows:

- Fork a child (a grandchild of the original). This grandchild calls `makeargv` on `cline` and `execvp`'s the command.
- Wait for this child and then do a semaphore signal on the `license` semaphore.
- Exit.

Test the program as in Section 2.13. Improve the error messages to make them more readable. Write a test program that takes two command-line arguments: the sleep time and the repeat factor. The test program simply repeats a loop the specified number of times. In the loop it sleeps and then outputs a message with its process ID to standard error. It then exits. Use `runsim` to run multiple copies of the test program.

Now modify `runsim` so that if the `license` semaphore already exists, the program accesses this semaphore without changing its value. The `runsim` program still waits for its children but does not remove the sempahores. Try executing several copies of `runsim` concurrently. Since they all use the same semaphore, the number of grandchildren processes should still be bounded by `n`. When done, be sure to use `ipcrm` to remove the semaphore.

8.9 Exercise: System V Shared Memory

The System V Interprocess Communication facility provides three types of objects: semaphores, shared memory, and message queues. This section describes an implementation of a simple software pipe using semaphores and shared memory. Section 8.10 introduces a similar implementation for message queues.

8.9.1 An Overview of System V Shared Memory

The rules for creating and accessing System V shared memory are very similar to those for semaphores.

```
SYNOPSIS

    #include <sys/types.h>
    #include <sys/ipc.h>
    #include <sys/shm.h>

    int shmget(key_t key, int size, int shmflg);
    void *shmat(int shmid, void *shmaddr, int shmflg);
    int shmdt(void *shmaddr);
    int shmctl(int shmid, int cmd, struct shmid_ds *buf);
                                                        Spec 1170
```

The `shmget` creates a shared memory segment using a specified key. The `size` is the number of bytes in the memory segment, and `shmflg` gives the access permissions for the segment. Programs using the shared memory facility call `shmat` or `shmdt` to attach or detach shared memory segments from their user space. The `shmat` function returns a `void *` pointer, so a program may use the return value like an ordinary memory pointer obtained from `malloc`. Use a `shmaddr` of `NULL`. On some systems it may be necessary to set `shmflg` so that the memory segment is properly aligned. When finished with a shared memory segment, a program should detach it with a call to `shmdt`. The last process to detach the segment should deallocate the shared memory segment by calling `shmctl`.

8.9.2 Specification of Software Pipe Implementation

This section develops a specification for a software pipe consisting of a semaphore set to protect access to the pipe and a shared memory segment to hold the pipe data and state information. The pipe state information includes the number of bytes of data in the pipe, the position of next byte to be read, and status information. The pipe can hold at most one message of maximum size `_POSIX_PIPE_BUF`. Represent the pipe by the following `pipe_t` structure allocated in shared memory:

```
typedef struct pipe {
    int semid;                        /* ID of protecting semaphore set */
    int shmid;                        /* ID of the shared memory segment */
    char data[_POSIX_PIPE_BUF];        /* buffer for the pipe data */
    int data_size;                    /* bytes currently in the pipe */
    void *current_start;          /* pointer to current start of data */
    int end_of_file;            /* true after pipe closed for writing */
} pipe_t;
```

A program creates and references the pipe using a pointer to `pipe_t` as a handle. For simplicity, assume that only one process can read from the pipe and one process can write to the pipe. It is the responsibility of the reader to clean up the pipe when it closes the pipe. When the writer closes the pipe, it sets the `end_of_file` member of `pipe_t` so that the reader can detect end-of-file.

The semaphore set protects the `pipe_t` data structure during shared access by the reader and the writer. Element zero of the semaphore set controls exclusive access to `data`. It is initially 1. Readers and writers acquire access to the pipe by decrementing this semaphore element and release access by incrementing it. Element one of the semaphore set controls synchronization of writes so that the `data` buffer contains only one message, that is, the output of a single `write` operation. When this semaphore element is 1, the pipe is empty. When it is 0, the pipe has data or an end-of-file has been encountered. Initially, element one is 1. The writer decrements element one before writing any data. The reader waits until element one is 0 before reading. When it has read all of the data from the pipe, the reader increments element one to indicate that the pipe is now available for writing. Write the following functions:

- The `pipe_open` function creates a software pipe and returns a pointer of type `pipe_t *` to be used as a handle in the other calls. The prototype for `pipe_open` is

      ```
      pipe_t *pipe_open(void);
      ```

  The algorithm for `pipe_open` is
    * Create a shared memory segment to hold a `pipe_t` data structure by calling `shmget`. Use a key of `IPC_PRIVATE` and owner read/write permissions.
    * Attach the segment by calling `shmat`. Cast the return value of `shmat` to a `pipe_t *` and assign it to a local variable `p`.
    * Set `p->shmid` to the ID of the shared memory segment returned by the `shmget`.
    * Set `p->data_size` and `p->end_of_file` to 0.
    * Create a semaphore set containing two elements by calling `semget` with `IPC_PRIVATE` key and owner read, write, execute permissions.

* Initialize both semaphore elements to 1, and put the resulting semaphore ID value in `p->semid`.
* If all of the calls were successful, return `p` .
* If an error occurs, deallocate all resources and return a `NULL` pointer.

- The `pipe_read` has prototype

      int pipe_read(pipe_t *p, char *buf, int bytes);

  The `pipe_read` function behaves like an ordinary blocking `read` system call. The algorithm for `pipe_read` is

  * Perform a `semop` on `p->semid` to atomically decrement semaphore element zero and test semaphore element one for 0. Element zero provides mutual exclusion. Element one is only 0 if there is something in the buffer.
  * If `p->data_size` is greater than 0, copy at most `bytes` bytes of information starting at position `p->current_start` of the software pipe into `buf`. Take into account that the pipe data buffer is only of total size `_POSIX_PIPE_BUF`.
  * Update the `p->current_start` and `p->data_size` members of the pipe data structure.
  * Set the return value to the number of bytes actually read or to -1 if there was an error. If `p->data_size` is 0 and `p->end_of_file` is true, set the return value to 0 to indicate an end-of-file.
  * Perform another `semop` operation to release access to the pipe. Increment element zero. If there is no more data in the pipe, also increment element one unless `p->end_of_file` is true. Perform these operations atomically by a single `semop` call.

- The `pipe_write` has prototype

      int pipe_write(pipe_t *p, char *buf, int bytes);

  The `pipe_write` function behaves like an ordinary blocking `write` system call. The algorithm for `pipe_write` is

  * Perform a `semop` on `p->semid` to decrement atomically both semaphore elements zero and one.
  * Copy at most `_POSIX_BUF_MAX` bytes from `buf` into the pipe buffer.
  * Set `p->data_size` to the number of bytes actually copied and `p->current_start` to 0.
  * Perform another `semop` call to increment atomically semaphore element zero of the semaphore set.

* Return the number of bytes copied or −1 if either call to semop failed.

- The pipe_close has prototype

    ```
    int pipe_close(pipe_t *p, int how);
    ```

    The how parameter determines whether the pipe is closed for reading or writing. Its possible values are O_RDONLY and O_WRONLY. The algorithm for pipe_close is
    * Use the semop function to decrement atomically element zero of p->semid. If the semop fails, return −1.
    * If how & O_WRONLY is true,
        - Set p->end_of_file to true.
        - Perform a semctl to set element one of p->semid to 0.
        - Copy p->semid into a local variable, semid_temp.
        - Perform a shmdt to detach p.
        - Perform a semop to increment atomically element zero of semid_temp.

        If any of the semop, semctl, or shmdt calls fail, return −1 immediately.
    * If how & O_RDONLY is true,
        - Perform a semctl to remove the semaphore p->semid. (If the writer is waiting on the semaphore set, its semop returns an error when this happens.)
        - Copy p->shmid into a local variable, shmid_temp.
        - Call shmdt to detach p.
        - Call shmctl to deallocate the shared memory segment identified by shmid_temp.

        If any of the semctl, shmdt, or shmctl calls fails, return −1 immediately.

Test the software pipe by writing a main program that is similar to Program 3.3. The program creates a software pipe and then forks a child. The child reads from standard input and writes to the pipe. The parent reads what the child has written to the pipe and outputs it to standard output. When the child detects end-of-file on standard input, it closes the pipe for writing. The parent then detects end-of-file on the pipe, closes the pipe for reading (which destroys the pipe), and exits. Check to see that everything was properly destroyed by executing the ipcs command.

The above specification describes blocking versions of the functions pipe_read and pipe_write. Modify and test a nonblocking version also.

8.10 Exercise: System V Message Queues

The message queue facility of System V IPC allows a program to enqueue or dequeue messages of different types. After creating a queue with `msgget`, a program inserts messages into the queue with `msgsnd`, removes messages with `msgrcv`, and deallocates a message queue or changes permissions with `msgctl`.

```
SYNOPSIS

    #include <sys/types.h>
    #include <sys/ipc.h>
    #include <sys/msg.h>

    int msgget(key_t key, int msgflg);
    int msgsnd(int msqid, const void *msgp, size_t msgsz,
               int msgflg);
    int msgrcv(int msqid, void *msgp, size_t msgsz, long msgtyp,
               int msgflg);
    int msgctl(int msqid, int cmd, struct msqid_ds *buf);
                                                    Spec 1170
```

Formulate a specification of a software pipe implementation in terms of message queues. Implement the following functions:

```
pipe_t *pipe_open(void);
int pipe_read(pipe_t *p, char *buf, int chars);
int pipe_write(pipe_t *p, char *buf, int chars);
int pipe_close(pipe_t *p);
```

Design a `pipe_t` structure to fit the implementation. Test the implementation as in Section 8.9.

8.11 Additional Reading

Most books on operating systems [80, 92] discuss the classical semaphore abstraction. *UNIX Network Programming* by Stevens [85] has an extensive discussion on System V Interprocess Communication including semaphores, shared memory, and message queues. The book *UNIX Systems for Modern Architectures: Symmetric Multiprocessing and Caching for Kernel Programmers* by Schimmel [77] presents an advanced look at how these issues apply to design of multiprocessor kernels.

Chapter 9

POSIX Threads

One method of achieving parallelism is for multiple processes to cooperate and synchronize through shared memory. An alternative is to use multiple threads of execution in a single address space. This chapter motivates threads by comparing approaches to the problem of monitoring multiple file descriptors for input. The chapter then presents an overview of basic thread management under the POSIX.1c standard. The chapter discusses different thread models and how these models are accommodated under the standard.

When a program executes, the CPU uses the process program counter value to determine which instruction to execute next. The resulting stream of instructions is called the program's *thread of execution*. It is the flow of control for the process represented by the sequence of instruction addresses taken on by the program counter during the execution of the program's code.

Example 9.1

Process one executes the statements 245, 246, and 247 in a loop. Its thread of execution can be represented as: 245_1, 246_1, 247_1, 245_1, 246_1, 247_1, 245_1, 246_1, 247_1.... The subscripts identify the thread of execution. In this case there is a single thread of execution.

The sequence of instructions in a thread of execution appears to the program as an uninterrupted stream of addresses as shown in Example 9.1. From the point of view of the processor, however, the threads of execution from different processes are intermixed, and the point at which execution switches from one process to another is called a *context switch*.

Example 9.2

Process one executes its statements 245, 246, and 247 in a loop as in Example 9.1, and process two executes its statements 10, 11, 12.... The CPU executes instructions in the order 245_1, 246_1, 247_1, 245_1, 246_1, 10_2, 11_2, 12_2, 13_2, 247_1, 245_1, 246_1, 247_1.... Context switches occur between 246_1 and 10_2 and between 13_2 and 247_1. The processor sees the threads of execution interleaved, while the individual processes see continuous sequences.

A natural extension of the process model is to allow multiple threads to execute within the same process. This extension provides an efficient way to manage threads of execution that share both code and data by avoiding context switches. The approach also has great potential for performance gains because machines with multiple processors are capable of simultaneously executing multiple threads. Programs with natural parallelism in the form of independent tasks operating on shared data can take advantage of added execution power on these multiple-processor machines. Operating systems, in particular, fall into the category of having significant natural parallelism and can experience substantial performance enhancements by having multiple, simultaneous threads of execution. Vendors advertise *symmetric multiprocessing* support meaning that the operating system and applications can have multiple undistinguished threads of execution and can take advantage of parallel hardware.

Each thread of execution is associated with a *thread*, an abstract data type representing flow of control within a process. A thread has its own execution stack, program counter value, register set, and state. By declaring many threads within the confines of a single process, a programmer can achieve parallelism at low overhead. While threads provide low-overhead parallelism, they add certain complications in requirements for synchronization.

This chapter addresses basic implementation issues—how threads are created and managed. Section 9.1 provides a motivation for threads by looking at a simple problem with natural parallelism—the monitoring of multiple input descriptors. Five approaches to solving this problem are discussed. The complexity of an efficient nonthreaded implementation should be convincing evidence of the usefulness of threads for such problems. The remainder of this chapter discusses basic thread structure and management as specified by the POSIX.1c standard. Chapter 10 covers thread synchronization, signal handling, and cancellation under POSIX.1c.

One of the difficulties with using multiple threads of execution is that until recently there has not been a standard. The POSIX.1c extension was approved in June 1995. With the adoption of a POSIX standard for threads, threaded commercial applications should become more common.

9.1 A Motivating Problem: Monitoring File Descriptors

As a motivating example, this section looks at the difficulties presented when an un-threaded program must monitor multiple file descriptors. (If already convinced of the utility of threading, skip ahead to Section 9.1.5.)

When a process performs a blocking I/O operation such as a read, it blocks until input becomes available. Blocking can create problems when a process expects input from more than one source since the process has no way of knowing which file descriptor will produce the next input. The six general approaches to monitoring multiple file descriptors for input under UNIX are

- Use nonblocking I/O with polling.
- Use asynchronous I/O with the `SIGPOLL` signal.
- Use POSIX.1b asynchronous I/O (covered in Example 5.5).
- Use `select` to block until input is available.
- Use `poll` to block until input is available.
- Create a separate thread to monitor each file descriptor.

In this section five of the approaches are implemented for the problem of reading and processing input from two file descriptors. (Example 5.5 uses POSIX.1b asynchronous I/O for a similar problem, so a program using POSIX asynchronous I/O is not imple-mented here.) Compare the different approaches in order to understand the advantages of multiple threads.

9.1.1 Simple Polling

A nonblocking I/O operation returns a -1 immediately with `errno` set to `EAGAIN` if it would encounter a delay. The calling process can then try the operation later. (Sec-tion 3.7 introduces the syntax for nonblocking I/O.) The repeated query of descriptors to see if input is available is called *polling*. This form of busy waiting wastes CPU cycles and should not be used unless the file descriptors need only occasional querying.

The `poll_and_process` function of Program 9.1 reads from the open file descrip-tor `fd`. The `fd` file descriptor has been opened for nonblocking read. The function reads up to `BLKSIZE` bytes and returns -1 if there is an error or end-of-file. It returns 0 if there was no error.

Program 9.1: The `poll_and_process` function reads from an open file descriptor.

```
#include <sys/types.h>
#include <unistd.h>
#include <errno.h>
#define BLKSIZE 1024
```

```
void process_command(char *, int);

int poll_and_process(int fd)
{
    int nbytes;
    char buf[BLKSIZE];

    nbytes = read(fd, buf, BLKSIZE);
    if ( ((nbytes < 0) && (errno != EAGAIN) && (errno != EINTR))
          || !nbytes)
        return -1;
    else if (nbytes > 0)
        process_command(buf, nbytes);
    return 0;
}
```

_____ **Program 9.1** _____

Nonblocking I/O complicates the handling of error codes. A `read` return value of
-1 may indicate a real error. However, a nonblocking `read` also returns a -1 if no input was available or if it was interrupted by a signal. Neither of these conditions should
cause the polling to stop even though there is nothing available to be processed. The
`poll_and_process` function of Program 9.1 determines whether either of these conditions have occurred by testing `errno` for values `EAGAIN` and `EINTR`, respectively.
The function calls `process_command` only if input was actually available.

Program 9.2 opens two files for nonblocking read. The filenames are passed on the
command line. The program then monitors the file descriptors by alternately polling
them until all of the input is exhausted. The program calls the `poll_and_process`
function from Program 9.1 to perform the polling and to process the information.

_____

Program 9.2: A program that polls on nonblocking file descriptors.

```
#include <stdio.h>
#include <sys/types.h>
#include <sys/stat.h>
#include <stropts.h>
#include <fcntl.h>
#include <string.h>
#include <errno.h>
#include <unistd.h>

#define FALSE 0

int poll_and_process(int fd);
void do_some_other_stuff(void);
```

```
void main (int argc, char *argv[])
{
   int fd_1;
   int fd_2;
   int fd_1_done = FALSE;
   int fd_2_done = FALSE;

   if (argc != 3) {
      fprintf(stderr, "Usage: %s filename1 filename2\n", argv[0]);
      exit(1);
   }

   if ((fd_1 = open(argv[1], O_RDONLY | O_NONBLOCK)) == -1) {
      fprintf(stderr, "Could not open %s: %s\n",
         argv[1], strerror(errno));
      exit(1);
   }
   if ((fd_2 = open(argv[2], O_RDONLY | O_NONBLOCK)) == -1) {
      fprintf(stderr, "Could not open %s: %s\n",
         argv[2], strerror(errno));
      exit(1);
   }

   while(!fd_1_done || !fd_2_done) {
      if (!fd_1_done)
         fd_1_done = poll_and_process(fd_1);
      if (!fd_2_done)
         fd_2_done = poll_and_process(fd_2);
      do_some_other_stuff();
   }
   exit(0);
}
```

_____ **Program 9.2** _____

9.1.2 Asynchronous I/O to Eliminate Busy Waiting

Program 9.2 uses polling to monitor two input file descriptors that have been opened for nonblocking I/O. A more efficient method uses asynchronous I/O. In this strategy, the program does not perform an I/O operation until the operating system indicates that something is available by sending the SIGPOLL signal. The SIGPOLL is a System V signal that is only supported for STREAMS devices, but almost all I/O in System V is implemented in terms of STREAMS. (See Section 12.6.) Asynchronous I/O with SIGPOLL is part of Spec 1170 but not of POSIX. (BSD UNIX uses the SIGIO signal for asynchronous I/O.)

The general strategy for asynchronous I/O is

- Open the file descriptors for nonblocking I/O.
- Block the SIGPOLL signal.
- Install a signal handler to catch the SIGPOLL signal. The signal handler just sets a global variable indicating that a SIGPOLL signal has arrived.
- Enable the SIGPOLL signal by calling ioctl with the I_SETSIG flag for each file descriptor to be monitored.
- Perform the polling and sigsuspend in a loop.

Program 9.3 shows how to monitor asynchronous I/O on two file descriptors. The program calls poll_and_process of Program 9.1 to perform the actual polling of the device. The program blocks the SIGPOLL signal before setting the file descriptors to generate this signal. After attempting to read from the file descriptors, the program goes into a loop and blocks until it catches the SIGPOLL signal. The SIGPOLL signal is blocked during the entire execution except when sigsuspend is active. The program returns from sigsuspend with its signal mask automatically reset to the previous state with SIGPOLL blocked.

Program 9.3: A program to monitor two file descriptors using asynchronous I/O.

```
#include <stdio.h>
#include <sys/types.h>
#include <sys/stat.h>
#include <stropts.h>
#include <fcntl.h>
#include <signal.h>
#include <unistd.h>
#include <string.h>
#include <errno.h>

int poll_and_process(int fd);

int sigpoll_received = 0;

static void mypoll_handler(int signo)
{
    sigpoll_received = 1;
}

void main(int argc, char *argv[])
{
    int fd_1;
    int fd_2;
    int fd_1_done = 0;
    int fd_2_done = 0;
    sigset_t oldmask;
```

```
sigset_t newmask;
sigset_t zeromask;
struct sigaction newact;

                    /* open the file descriptors for nonblocking I/O */
if (argc != 3) {
   fprintf(stderr, "Usage: %s filename1 filename2\n", argv[0]);
   exit(1);
}
if ((fd_1 = open(argv[1], O_RDONLY | O_NONBLOCK)) == -1) {
   fprintf(stderr,"Could not open %s: %s\n",
       argv[1], strerror(errno));
   exit(1);
}
if ((fd_2 = open(argv[2], O_RDONLY | O_NONBLOCK)) == -1) {
   fprintf(stderr,"Could not open %s: %s\n",
       argv[2], strerror(errno));
   exit(1);
}

                    /* block the SIGPOLL signal and set up handler */
sigemptyset(&newmask);
sigaddset(&newmask, SIGPOLL);
if (sigprocmask(SIG_BLOCK, &newmask, &oldmask) == -1) {
   perror("Could not block SIGPOLL");
   exit(1);
}
newact.sa_handler = mypoll_handler;
sigemptyset(&newact.sa_mask);
newact.sa_flags = 0;
if (sigaction(SIGPOLL, &newact, NULL) == -1) {
   perror("Could not set SIGPOLL handler");
   exit(1);
}
           /* tell driver to generate SIGPOLL if message comes in */
if ((ioctl(fd_1, I_SETSIG, S_INPUT | S_HANGUP) == -1) ||
    (ioctl(fd_2, I_SETSIG, S_INPUT | S_HANGUP) == -1)) {
   perror("Could not set descriptors for SIGPOLL");
   exit(1);
}
             /*  now monitor by suspending until SIGPOLL arrives */
sigemptyset(&zeromask);
while(!fd_1_done || !fd_2_done) {
   if (!fd_1_done)
      fd_1_done = poll_and_process(fd_1);
   if (!fd_2_done)
      fd_2_done = poll_and_process(fd_2);
   while (!sigpoll_received && (!fd_1_done || !fd_2_done) )
      sigsuspend(&zeromask);
```

```
        sigpoll_received = 0;
   }
   exit(0);
}
```

_____ **Program 9.3** _____

9.1.3 Using `select` to Eliminate Busy Waiting

An alternative to asynchronous I/O is to use `select`. Section 3.8 introduced `select`, a BSD construct for monitoring file descriptors. The `select` call is available on most UNIX systems and is part of Spec 1170 but not of POSIX. It uses separate masks for read, write, and exceptional conditions. The masks indicate which descriptors are to be monitored. The `select` causes the thread of execution to block until input arrives.

The `monitor_fd` function in Program 9.4 monitors an array of open file descriptors `fd`. When input is available on file descriptor `fd[i]`, the program reads in a command and calls `process_command`. The `monitor_fd` function has three parameters: an array of open file descriptors, the number of file descriptors in the array, and an integer that is at least one more than the largest file descriptor to be monitored.

_____

Program 9.4: A function to monitor file descriptors using `select`.

```
#include <sys/time.h>
#include <sys/types.h>
#include <unistd.h>

void process_command(char *, int);

/* monitor an array fd[] of open file descriptors using select */
void monitor_fd(int fd[], int num_fds, int max_fd)
{
   fd_set readset;
   int i;
   int num_ready;
   int num_now;
   int bytes_read;
   char buf[BUFSIZE];

   num_now = num_fds;
   while (num_now > 0) {
      FD_ZERO(&readset);    /* set up the file descriptor mask */
      for (i = 0; i < num_fds; i++)
         if (fd[i] >= 0)
            FD_SET(fd[i], &readset);
```

```
    num_ready = select(max_fd, &readset, NULL, NULL, NULL);
    for (i = 0; i < num_fds && num_ready > 0; i++)
        if ( (fd[i] >= 0) && FD_ISSET(fd[i], &readset)) {
            bytes_read = read(fd[i], buf, BUFSIZE);
            num_ready--;
            if (bytes_read > 0)
                process_command(buf, bytes_read);
            else {
                fd[i] = -1;
                num_now--;
            }
        }
    }
  }
}
```

_____ **Program 9.4** _____

The control in Program 9.4 is relatively simple because input from the two file de-scriptors is processed independently. If process_command blocks for some reason, the processing of the other file descriptors waits until process_command completes. To overlap reading of another descriptor during the process_command, the program would require some fairly complex logic.

9.1.4 Using `poll` to Eliminate Busy Waiting

The poll function is part of System V Release 4 and Spec 1170 but not of POSIX. It is similar to the select, but it organizes the information by descriptor rather than by type of condition. In contrast, select has separate descriptor masks for read, write, and exceptional conditions.

```
SYNOPSIS

   #include <stropts.h>
   #include <poll.h>

   int poll(struct pollfd *fds, size_t nfds, int timeout);
                                                           Spec 1170
```

Each element of the fds array represents the monitoring information for one file de-scriptor. The nfds parameter gives the number of descriptors to be monitored. The struct pollfd includes the following members:

```
    int fd;            /* file descriptor */
    short events;      /* requested events */
    short revents;     /* returned events */
```

The fd is the file descriptor number, and the events and revents are constructed by taking the logical OR of flags representing various conditions. Set `events` to contain the events to monitor, and `poll` fills in the `revents` with the events that have occurred. The man page for `poll` describes the flags associated with descriptor events. Only normal read of data from descriptors is considered here. The `timeout` value is in milliseconds. The special value `INFTIM` is used when the `poll` should never time out. The `select` call modifies the file descriptor sets that are passed to it, and the program must reset these descriptor sets each time it calls the `select`. The `poll` uses separate variables for input and return values, so it is not necessary to reset the list of monitored descriptors after each call to `poll`. The `poll` function returns the number of file descriptors that are ready or −1 if an error occurs.

Program 9.5 implements `monitor_fd` in terms of `poll`. The `poll` has a number of advantages. The masks do not need to be reset after each call. Unlike the `select`, the `poll` treats errors as events that cause the `poll` to return, and `poll` does not need a `max_fd` argument.

Program 9.5: A function to monitor an array of file descriptors using `poll`.

```c
#include <stdlib.h>
#include <stdio.h>
#include <sys/types.h>
#include <unistd.h>
#include <stropts.h>
#include <poll.h>
#include <errno.h>

void process_command(char *, int);

void monitor_fd(int fd[], int num_fds)
{
    int i;
    int num_ready;
    int num_now;
    int bytes_read;
    char buf[BUFSIZE];
    struct pollfd *myfd;
    short errormask;

    errormask = POLLERR|POLLHUP;

                                    /* initialize the polling structure */
    if ((myfd = (void *)calloc(num_fds, sizeof(struct pollfd))) == NULL)
        return;
    for (i = 0; i < num_fds; i++) {
        (myfd + i)->fd = *(fd + i);
        (myfd + i)->events = POLLRDNORM;
```

```
            (myfd + i)->revents = 0;
        }

    num_now = num_fds;

            /* Continue monitoring until all I/O on all descriptors done */
        while (num_now > 0) {
            if ( ((num_ready = poll(myfd, num_fds, INFTIM)) == -1) &&
                 (errno != EINTR) )
               break;

            for (i = 0; i < num_fds && num_ready > 0; i++)   {
                if ( (myfd + i)->events && (myfd + i)->revents ) {
                        /* if an error occurred, do not monitor fd anymore */
                    if ((myfd + i)->revents & errormask) {
                        num_now--;
                        (myfd + i)->events = 0;
                    }
                                /* if a normal data arrival, read the data */
                    else if ((myfd + i)->revents & POLLRDNORM) {
                        bytes_read = read(fd[i], buf, BUFSIZE);
                        num_ready--;
                        if (bytes_read > 0)
                            process_command(buf, bytes_read);
                        else {
                            num_now--;
                            (myfd + i)->events = 0;
                        }
                    }
                }
            }
            if (!num_now) break;
        }
}
```

_____ **Program 9.5** _____

9.1.5 Multiple Threads

Multiple threads can simplify the programming of problems such as the monitoring and processing inputs from multiple file descriptors because dedicated threads can monitor each descriptor. Threads also provide capability for overlap of I/O and processing not available in the other approaches.

The process_fd function of Program 9.6 monitors a file descriptor using blocking I/O. It returns upon encountering an end-of-file or upon detecting an error that occurs on the descriptor. The file descriptor is passed by a pointer to void so that process_fd can be called either as an ordinary function or as a thread.

Program 9.6: The `process_fd` function monitors a file descriptor for input.

```
#include <sys/types.h>
#include <unistd.h>
#include <errno.h>
void process_command(char *, int);

void *process_fd(void *arg)
{
    int fd;
    int nbytes;
    char buf[BUFSIZE];

    fd = *((int *)(arg));
    for ( ; ; )   {
        if (((nbytes = read(fd, buf, BUFSIZE)) == -1) &&
               (errno != EINTR))
            break;
        if (!nbytes)
            break;
        process_command(buf, nbytes);
    }
    return NULL;
}
```

—————————————————————— **Program 9.6** ——————————————————————

Example 9.3

The following code segment calls `process_fd` *as an ordinary function.*

```
#include <stdio.h>
#include <sys/types.h>
#include <sys/stat.h>
#include <fcntl.h>
#include <string.h>
#include <errno.h>
void *process_fd(void *);
int fd_1;

if ((fd_1 = open("my.dat", O_RDONLY)) == -1)
    perror("Could not open my.dat");
else process_fd(&fd_1);
```

Figure 9.1 shows the thread of execution when Program 9.6 is called as an ordinary function. The thread of execution for the calling program traverses the statements in the function and then resumes execution at the statement after the call. Since `process_fd` uses blocking I/O, the thread of execution blocks on the `read` until input becomes avail-

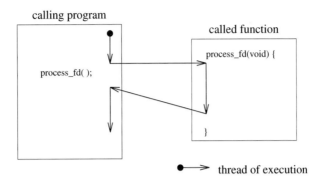

Figure 9.1: The thread of execution for an ordinary call to `process_fd`.

able on the file descriptor. Remember that the thread of execution is represented by the sequence of statements that the thread executes. There is no timing information in this sequence. The fact that execution blocks on a `read` is transparent.

A program can also create a separate thread to execute `process_fd` as shown in Figure 9.2. The thread splits off and executes an independent stream of instructions, never returning to the point of call. The calling program continues to execute concurrently. In contrast, when `process_fd` is called as an ordinary function, the caller's thread of execution moves through the function code and returns to the point of call.

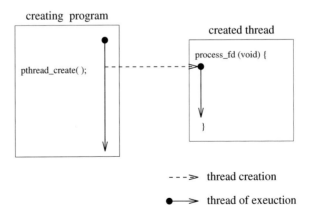

Figure 9.2: A new thread executes `process_fd`.

Example 9.4

The following code segment creates a new thread to run `process_fd`.

```
#include <stdio.h>
#include <sys/types.h>
#include <sys/stat.h>
#include <fcntl.h>
#include <pthread.h>
#include <string.h>
#include <errno.h>

pthread_t tid;
int fd;
void *process_fd(void *arg);

if ((fd = open("my.dat", O_RDONLY)) == -1)
   perror("Could not open my.dat");
else if (pthread_create(&tid, NULL, process_fd, (void *)&fd))
   perror("Could not create thread");
else
   pthread_join(tid, NULL);
```

The beauty of threads is that a program can create a lot of them without much work. The remainder of the chapter discusses the mechanics of creating threads, so do not be overly concerned with the syntax at this point. The function `monitor_fd` of Program 9.7 uses threads to monitor an array of file descriptors. Compare this implementation with those of Program 9.4 and Program 9.5. The threaded version takes advantage of parallelism without any user intervention. If `process_command` causes the calling thread to block for some reason, the thread runtime system schedules another ready thread. In this way processing and reading are overlapped in a natural way. In contrast, with a single thread of execution, blocking in `process_command` causes the entire process to block.

Program 9.7: A function to monitor an array of file descriptors using threads.

```
#include <stdlib.h>
#include <stdio.h>
#include <sys/types.h>
#include <unistd.h>
#include <fcntl.h>
#include <pthread.h>
#include <string.h>
#include <errno.h>

void process_fd(void *arg);
```

```
void monitor_fd(int fd[], int num_fds)
{
    int i;
    pthread_t *tid;

    if ((tid = (pthread_t *)calloc(num_fds, sizeof(pthread_t))) == NULL)
        return;
                        /* create a thread for each file descriptor */
    for (i = 0; i < num_fds; i++) {
        if (pthread_create((tid + i), NULL, process_fd, (void *)(fd + i)))
            fprintf(stderr, "Could not create thread %i: %s\n", i,
                    strerror(errno));
    }
    for (i = 0; i < num_fds; i++)
        pthread_join(*(tid + i), NULL);
}
```

_____ **Program 9.7** _____

9.2 POSIX Threads

A typical thread package contains a runtime system to manage threads in a transparent way (i.e., the user is not aware of the runtime system). A thread package usually includes calls for thread creation and destruction, mutual exclusion, and condition variables. Both Sun Solaris 2 and POSIX.1c standard thread libraries have such calls. These packages provide for the dynamic creation and destruction of threads, so the number of threads does not have to be known until runtime. Table 9.1 summarizes the common thread functions in POSIX and in Sun Solaris 2.

Most of the thread functions return 0 if successful and a nonzero error code if unsuccessful. The pthread_create (thr_create) creates a thread to execute a specified function. The pthread_exit (thr_exit) causes the calling thread to terminate without causing the entire process to exit. The pthread_kill (thr_kill) sends a signal to a specified thread. The pthread_join (thr_join) causes the calling thread to wait for the specified thread to exit. This call is similar to waitpid at the process level. Finally, pthread_self (thr_self) returns the caller's identity. The remaining calls in the table refer to synchronization mechanisms discussed in the next chapter.

POSIX.1c threads and Sun Solaris threads are quite similar. One major difference is the manner in which properties are associated with the threads. POSIX threads use attribute objects to represent properties of threads. Properties such as stack size or scheduling policy are set for a thread attribute object. Several threads can be associated with the same thread attribute object. If a property of the object changes, the change is reflected

Description	POSIX	Solaris 2
Thread management	pthread_create	thr_create
	pthread_exit	thr_exit
	pthread_kill	thr_kill
	pthread_join	thr_join
	pthread_self	thr_self
Mutual exclusion	pthread_mutex_init	mutex_init
	pthread_mutex_destroy	mutex_destroy
	pthread_mutex_lock	mutex_lock
	pthread_mutex_trylock	mutex_trylock
	pthread_mutex_unlock	mutex_unlock
Condition variables	pthread_cond_init	cond_init
	pthread_cond_destroy	cond_destroy
	pthread_cond_wait	cond_wait
	pthread_cond_timedwait	cond_timedwait
	pthread_cond_signal	cond_signal
	pthread_cond_broadcast	cond_broadcast

Table 9.1: A comparison of calls for POSIX.1c threads and Sun Solaris 2 threads.

in all of the threads associated with that object. Solaris threads explicitly set properties of threads and other primitives, so some calls have long lists of parameters for setting these properties. Solaris threads offer more control over how threads are mapped to processor resources, while POSIX threads offer a more robust method of cancellation and thread termination. This book concentrates on POSIX threads.

9.3 Basic Thread Management

A thread has an ID, a stack, an execution priority, and starting address for execution. POSIX threads are referenced by an ID of type `pthread_t`. A thread can find out its ID by calling `pthread_self`. The thread's internal data structure might also contain scheduling and usage information. The threads for a process share the entire address space of that process. They can modify global variables, access open file descriptors, or interfere with each other in other ways.

Threads are called *dynamic* if they can be created at any time during the execution of a process and if the number of threads does not need to be specified in advance. In POSIX, threads are created dynamically with the `pthread_create` function. The `pthread_create` creates a thread and puts it in a ready queue.

SYNOPSIS

```
#include <pthread.h>

int pthread_create(pthread_t *tid, const pthread_attr_t *attr,
               void *(*start_routine)(void *), void *arg);
void pthread_exit(void *value_ptr);
int pthread_join(pthread_t thread, void **value_ptr);
```

POSIX.1c

The `tid` parameter of `pthread_create` points to the ID of the thread that is created. The attributes of the thread are encapsulated by the attribute object pointed to by `attr`. If `attr` is `NULL`, the new thread has the default attributes. The third parameter, `start_routine`, is the name of a function that the thread calls when it begins execution. The `start_routine` takes a single parameter specified by `arg`, a pointer to void. The `start_routine` returns a pointer to `void` which is treated as an exit status by `pthread_join`. Do not let the prototype of `pthread_create` be intimidating—threads are easy to create and use.

The `pthread_exit` function terminates the calling thread. The `value_ptr` parameter value is available to a successful `pthread_join`. However, the `value_ptr` in `pthread_exit` must point to data that exists after the thread exits, so it cannot be allocated as automatic local data for the thread that is exiting.

Example 9.5

The following segment code creates a thread with the default attributes.

```
#include <stdio.h>
#include <sys/types.h>
#include <sys/stat.h>
#include <fcntl.h>
#include <pthread.h>
pthread_t copy_tid;
int myarg[2];
void *copy_file(void *arg);

if ((myarg[0] = open("my.in", O_RDONLY)) == -1)
   perror("Could not open my.in");
else if ((myarg[1] = open("my.out",
      O_WRONLY | O_CREAT, S_IRUSR | S_IWUSR)) == -1)
   perror("Could not open my.out");
else if (pthread_create(&copy_tid, NULL, copy_file, (void *)myarg))
   perror("Thread creation was not successful");
```

In Example 9.5, `copy_tid` holds the ID of the created thread, and `copy_file` is the name of the function that the thread is to execute. The `myarg` is a pointer to the parameter value to be passed to the thread function. In this case the `myarg` array contains open file descriptors to the files `my.in` and `my.out`.

Program 9.8 shows an implementation of a `copy_file` function that reads from one file and outputs to another file. The `arg` parameter has a pointer to a pair of open descriptors representing the source and destination files. The variables `infile`, `outfile`, `bytes_read`, `bytes_written`, `bytes_copied_p`, `buffer`, and `bufp` are allocated on `copy_file`'s local stack and are not directly accessible to other threads. The thread also `malloc`'s space for returning the total number of bytes copied. The implementation assumes that `malloc` is thread-safe, otherwise a `malloc_r` version should be used. The `copy_file` function could return the `bytes_copied` pointer rather than calling `pthread_exit`. The `pthread_exit` function calls thread exit handlers while `return` does not.

Program 9.8: The `copy_file` function copies the contents of `infile` to `outfile`.

```
#include <sys/types.h>
#include <stdlib.h>
#include <unistd.h>
#include <pthread.h>
#include <errno.h>

#define BUFFERSIZE 100

void *copy_file(void *arg)
{
    int infile;
    int outfile;
    int bytes_read = 0;
    int bytes_written = 0;
    int *bytes_copied_p;
    char buffer[BUFFERSIZE];
    char *bufp;
            /* open file descriptors for source and destination files */
    infile = *((int *)(arg));
    outfile = *((int *)(arg) + 1);
    if ((bytes_copied_p = (int *)malloc(sizeof(int))) == NULL)
        pthread_exit(NULL);
    *bytes_copied_p = 0;

    for ( ; ; ) {
        bytes_read = read(infile, buffer, BUFFERSIZE);
        if ((bytes_read == 0) || ((bytes_read < 0) && (errno != EINTR)))
            break;
        else if ((bytes_read < 0) && (errno == EINTR))
            continue;
        bufp = buffer;
        while (bytes_read > 0) {
            bytes_written = write(outfile, bufp, bytes_read);
```

```
                if ((bytes_written < 0) && (errno != EINTR))
                    break;
                else if (bytes_written < 0)
                    continue;
                *bytes_copied_p += bytes_written;
                bytes_read -= bytes_written;
                bufp += bytes_written;
            }
        if (bytes_written == -1)
            break;
    }
    close(infile);
    close(outfile);
    pthread_exit(bytes_copied_p);
}
```

——————————————————————— **Program 9.8** ———————————————————————

Program 9.9 shows a main program with three command-line arguments: an input file basename, an output file basename, and the number of copier files. The program creates `numcopiers` number of threads. Thread `i` copies `infile_name.i` to `outfile_name.i`.

Program 9.9: A program that creates threads to copy multiple file descriptors.

```
#include <stdio.h>
#include <stdlib.h>
#include <sys/types.h>
#include <sys/stat.h>
#include <string.h>
#include <errno.h>
#include <fcntl.h>
#include <pthread.h>

#define MAXNUMCOPIERS 10
#define MAXNAMESIZE 80

void *copy_file(void *arg);

void main(int argc, char *argv[])
{
    pthread_t copiertid[MAXNUMCOPIERS];
    int fd[MAXNUMCOPIERS][2];
    char filename[MAXNAMESIZE];
    int numcopiers;
    int total_bytes_copied=0;
    int *bytes_copied_p;
```

```
    int i;

    if (argc != 4) {
       fprintf(stderr, "Usage: %s infile_name outfile_name copiers\n",
           argv[0]);
       exit(1);
    }
    numcopiers = atoi(argv[3]);
    if (numcopiers < 1 || numcopiers > MAXNUMCOPIERS) {
       fprintf(stderr, "%d invalid number of copiers\n", numcopiers);
       exit(1);
    }
                                         /* create the copier threads */
    for (i = 0; i < numcopiers; i++) {
       sprintf(filename, "%s.%d", argv[1], i);
       if ((fd[i][0] = open(filename, O_RDONLY)) < 0) {
          fprintf(stderr, "Unable to open copy source file %s: %s\n",
                          filename, strerror(errno));
          continue;
       }
       sprintf(filename, "%s.%d", argv[2], i);
       if ((fd[i][1]=
          open(filename, O_WRONLY | O_CREAT, S_IRUSR | S_IWUSR)) < 0) {
          fprintf(stderr,
             "Unable to create copy destination file %s: %s\n",
             filename, strerror(errno));
          continue;
       }
       if (pthread_create(&copiertid[i], NULL, copy_file,
             (void *)fd[i]) != 0)
          fprintf(stderr, "Could not create thread %i: %s\n",
             i, strerror(errno));
    }
                                         /* wait for copy to complete */
    for (i = 0; i < numcopiers; i++) {
       if (pthread_join(copiertid[i], (void **)&(bytes_copied_p)) != 0)
          fprintf(stderr, "No thread %d to join: %s\n",
             i, strerror(errno));
       else {
          printf("Thread %d copied %d bytes from %s.%d to %s.%d\n",
             i, *bytes_copied_p, argv[1], i, argv[2], i);
          total_bytes_copied += *bytes_copied_p;
       }
    }
    printf("Total bytes copied = %d\n", total_bytes_copied);
    exit(0);
}
```

———————————————————————— **Program 9.9** ————————————————————————

When a `copy_file` thread completes its work, it exits by calling `pthread_exit`. The exit status of a thread that calls `pthread_exit` is maintained until another thread joins with it or until it is the last thread in the process. The `pthread_join` is similar to `waitpid` for child processes in that the calling thread blocks until the indicated thread terminates. The calling thread retrieves the number of bytes copied by the thread through the return `status_value` on the `pthread_join`. The thread dynamically allocates space for `status_value` so that the variable persists after the thread exits. Finally the main thread exits.

Threads have a `detachstate` attribute of `PTHREAD_CREATE_JOINABLE` by default. The other possible value of `detachstate` is `PTHREAD_CREATE_DETACHED`. Detached threads must call `pthread_detach` rather than `pthread_exit` to free their resources.

Exercise 9.1

What happens in Program 9.9 if the `malloc` of `copy_file` fails?

Answer:

In the main program after `pthread_join` returns, `bytes_copied_p` is NULL and the program crashes when it tries to dereference this pointer. The problem can be fixed by having the main program check for this NULL pointer.

In traditional UNIX implementations, `errno` is a global external variable that is set when system functions produce an error. This implementation does not work for multithreading (see Section 1.5), and in most thread implementations `errno` is a macro that returns thread-specific information. In essence, each thread has a private copy of `errno`. The main program does not have direct access to the `errno` of a joined thread, so if needed, this information must be returned through the last parameter of `pthread_join`.

Exercise 9.2

What happens in Program 9.9 if the `write` in `copy_file` fails?

Answer:

The `copy_file` returns the number of bytes successfully copied, and the main program does not detect an error. The problem can be fixed by having `copy_file` return a pointer to a structure containing both the number of bytes copied and an error value.

One tricky aspect is the passing of the parameters when there are multiple threads. In Program 9.9 several threads are created, but each thread has its file descriptors passed in different entries of the `fd` array so that the threads do not interfere. Be careful about reusing variables that are passed by reference to threads on creation. The created thread may not be scheduled in time to use the values before they are overwritten.

Program 9.10 shows a modification of Program 9.9 that uses a single pair of locations for the file descriptors. This program fails if the file descriptor for thread i is overwritten by the next for loop iteration before thread i has a chance to copy the descriptor to its local storage.

Program 9.10: A program that incorrectly passes multiple file descriptors to threads.

```c
#include <stdio.h>
#include <stdlib.h>
#include <sys/types.h>
#include <sys/stat.h>
#include <string.h>
#include <errno.h>
#include <fcntl.h>
#include <pthread.h>

void *copy_file(void *arg);
#define MAXNUMCOPIERS 10
#define MAXNAMESIZE 80

void main(int argc, char *argv[])
{
    pthread_t copiertid[MAXNUMCOPIERS];
    int fd[2];
    char filename[MAXNAMESIZE];
    int numcopiers;
    int total_bytes_copied=0;
    int *bytes_copied_p;
    int i;

    if (argc != 4) {
        fprintf(stderr, "Usage: %s infile_name outfile_name copiers\n",
            argv[0]);
        exit(1);
    }
    numcopiers = atoi(argv[3]);
    if (numcopiers < 1 || numcopiers > MAXNUMCOPIERS) {
        fprintf(stderr, "%d invalid number of copiers\n", numcopiers);
        exit(1);
    }

                            /* create the copier threads */
    for (i = 0; i < numcopiers; i++) {
        sprintf(filename, "%s.%d", argv[1], i);
        if ((fd[0] = open(filename, O_RDONLY)) < 0) {
            fprintf(stderr, "Unable to open copy source file %s: %s\n",
                            filename, strerror(errno));
```

```
            continue;
      }
      sprintf(filename, "%s.%d", argv[2], i);
      if ((fd[1] =
          open(filename, O_WRONLY | O_CREAT, S_IRUSR | S_IWUSR)) < 0) {
          fprintf(stderr,
              "Unable to create copy destination file %s: %s\n",
              filename, strerror(errno));
          continue;
      }
      if (pthread_create(&copiertid[i], NULL, copy_file,
              (void *)fd) != 0)
          fprintf(stderr, "Could not create thread %i: %s\n",
              i, strerror(errno));
   }
                                  /* wait for copy to complete */
   for (i = 0; i < numcopiers; i++) {
      if (pthread_join(copiertid[i], (void **)&(bytes_copied_p)) != 0)
          fprintf(stderr, "No thread %d to join: %s\n",
              i, strerror(errno));
      else {
          printf("Thread %d copied %d bytes from %s.%d to %s.%d\n",
              i, *bytes_copied_p, argv[1], i, argv[2], i);
          total_bytes_copied += *bytes_copied_p;
      }
   }
   printf("Total bytes copied = %d\n", total_bytes_copied);
   exit(0);
}
```

_____ **Program 9.10** _____

Exercise 9.3

Try the code from Program 9.10. Print out each file descriptor when it is opened and at the beginning of the thread to which it was passed as a parameter. Are the two values of the descriptor the same? What happens if a sleep(5) is inserted inside the for loop after the pthread_create?

Answer:

A different pair of file descriptors is opened for each thread, but the fd array is reused for each thread. All of the threads are created at the same priority as the main thread and go into the ready queue. If the next iteration of the loop starts before the thread created by the previous iteration is scheduled, the file descriptors are overwritten and the thread copies the wrong files. If a sleep is placed after the pthread_create, the thread will probably have a chance to execute before this happens and the program should work correctly.

The individual copier threads in Program 9.9 are working on independent problems and do not interact with each other. In more complicated applications, a thread may not exit after completing its assigned task. Instead, a worker thread may request additional tasks or share information. Chapter 10 explains how this type of interaction can be controlled by synchronization primitives such as mutex locks and condition variables.

A hidden problem with threads is that they may call library functions or system calls that are not thread-safe, possibly producing spurious results. Even functions such as `sprintf` and `fprintf` may not be thread-safe, so beware. POSIX.1c specifies that all of the required functions, including the standard C library, be implemented in a thread-safe manner. Those functions whose traditional interfaces preclude making them thread-safe must have an alternative thread-safe version designated with a `_r` suffix. Sun Solaris 2 man pages usually indicate whether a function is thread-safe under the heading `MT_LEVEL`.

9.4 User versus Kernel Threads

Recall that a processor runs by executing its instruction cycle and that the program counter value determines which process is executing. The operating system has opportunities to regain control by changing the program counter value when interrupts occur and when programs request services through system calls. With threads, similar control issues arise at the process level. The two traditional models of thread control are *user-level threads* and *kernel-level threads*.

User-level threads packages usually run on top of an existing operating system. The threads within the process are invisible to the kernel. These threads compete among themselves for the resources allocated to a process, as shown in Figure 9.3. The threads are scheduled by a thread runtime system which is part of the process code. Programs using a user-level threads package usually link to a special library in which each library function and system call is enclosed by a jacket. The jacket code calls the runtime system to do thread management.

System calls such as `read` or `sleep` could be a problem for user-level threads because they can cause the process to block. In order to avoid the problem of a blocking call causing the entire process to block, each potentially blocking call is replaced in the jacket by a nonblocking version. The thread runtime system tests to see if the call would cause the thread to block. If the call would not block, the runtime system does the call right away. If the call would block, however, the runtime system blocks the thread, adds the call to a list of things to try later, and picks another thread to run. All of this control is invisible to the user and to the operating system.

User-level threads have extremely low overhead, but they have some disadvantages. The model relies on having threads that allow the thread runtime system to regain con-

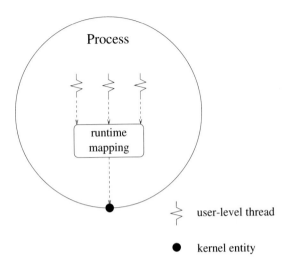

Figure 9.3: User-level threads are not visible outside of the process.

trol. A *CPU-bound thread* rarely performs system calls or library calls and thus prevents the thread runtime system from regaining control to schedule other threads. The programmer has to avoid the lockout situation by explicitly forcing CPU-bound threads to yield control at appropriate points. A second, more serious problem with user-level threads is that the threads can share only processor resources allocated to their encapsulating process. This restriction limits the amount of parallelism because the threads can run on only one processor at a time. Since one of the prime motivations for using threads is to take advantage of the parallelism provided by multiprocessor workstations, user-level threads alone are not an acceptable approach.

With kernel-level threads, the kernel is aware of each thread as a schedulable entity. Threads compete for processor resources on a systemwide basis as shown in Figure 9.4. The scheduling of kernel-level threads can be almost as expensive as scheduling processes themselves, but kernel-level threads can take advantage of multiple processors. The synchronization and sharing of data that kernel-level threads provide is less expensive than for full processes, but kernel-level threads are considerably more expensive than user-level threads.

Hybrid thread models have advantages of both user-level and kernel-level models by providing two levels of control. Figure 9.5 illustrates a typical hybrid approach. The user writes the program in terms of user-level threads and then specifies how many kernel-schedulable entities are associated with the process. The user-level threads are mapped into the kernel-schedulable entities as the process is running to achieve parallelism. The

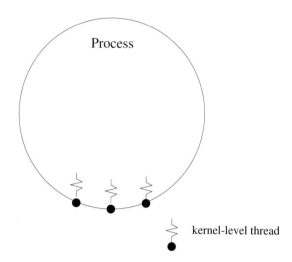

Figure 9.4: Kernel-level threads are scheduled just like individual processes.

level of control a user has over the mapping depends on the implementation. In the Sun Solaris thread implementation, for example, the user-level threads are called threads and the kernel-schedulable entities are called *lightweight processes*. The user can specify that a particular thread have a dedicated lightweight process or that a particular group of threads be run by a pool of lightweight processes.

The POSIX.1c thread scheduling model is a hybrid model which is flexible enough to support both user-level and kernel-level threads in particular implementations of the standard. The model consists of two levels of scheduling—threads and kernel entities. The threads are analogous to user-level threads. The kernel entities are scheduled by the kernel. The thread library decides how many kernel entities it needs and how they will be mapped.

POSIX.1c introduces the idea of a *thread scheduling contention scope*, which gives the programmer some control over how kernel entities are mapped to threads. A thread can have a `contentionscope` attribute of either `PTHREAD_SCOPE_PROCESS` or `PTHREAD_SCOPE_SYSTEM`. Threads that are `PTHREAD_SCOPE_PROCESS` contend for processor resources with the other threads in their process. POSIX does not specify how such a thread contends with threads outside its own process, so `PTHREAD_SCOPE_PROCESS` threads can be strictly user-level threads or they can be mapped to a pool of kernel entities in some more complicated way.

Threads that are `PTHREAD_SCOPE_SYSTEM` contend for processor resources on a systemwide basis much like kernel-level threads. POSIX leaves the mapping be-

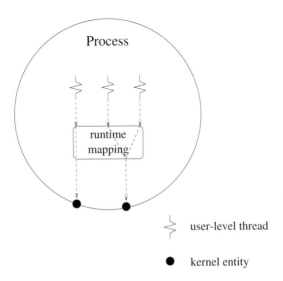

Figure 9.5: The hybrid model has two levels of scheduling with user-level threads mapped into kernel entities.

tween `PTHREAD_SCOPE_SYSTEM` threads and kernel entities up to the implementation, but the obvious mapping is to bind such a thread directly to a kernel entity. A POSIX thread implementation can support either `PTHREAD_SCOPE_PROCESS` or `PTHREAD_SCOPE_SYSTEM` or both.

Table 9.2 shows the relative cost of user-level versus kernel-level threads as presented in the *Sun Solaris 2.3 Software Developer Answerbook*. Solaris 2 uses a two-level thread model that is similar to the POSIX specification. In the Sun Microsystems terminology, an *unbound thread* is a user-level thread, and a *bound thread* is a kernel-level thread because it is bound to a lightweight process. The `fork` is the cost of the creation of an entire process. The synchronization refers to two threads synchronizing with semaphores as in the producer-consumer problem. A kernel-level thread is between six and seven times more costly to create and to synchronize than a user-level thread. It costs about thirty times more to create a full process with a `fork` than to create a user-level thread.

9.5 Thread Attributes

POSIX.1c takes an object-oriented approach to representation and assignment of properties. Each POSIX.1c thread has an associated attribute object that represents its properties. A thread attribute object can be associated with multiple threads, and POSIX.1c

Operation	Microseconds
Unbound thread create	52
Bound thread create	350
`fork()`	1700
Unbound thread synchronize	66
Bound thread synchronize	390
Between process synchronize	200

Table 9.2: Times for thread services under Solaris 2.3 on a SPARCstation 2.

has functions to create, configure, and destroy attribute objects. The object-oriented approach allows a program to group entities such as threads and associate the same attribute object with all members of the group. When a property of the attribute object changes, all of the entities in the group have the new property. The thread attribute objects are of type `pthread_attr_t`. Table 9.3 shows the settable properties of thread attributes and the functions associated with the properties. Other entities, such as condition variables or mutex locks, have their own attribute object types and functions as discussed in Chapter 10.

Property	Function
Initialization	`pthread_attr_init`
	`pthread_attr_destroy`
Stack Size	`pthread_attr_setstacksize`
	`pthread_attr_getstacksize`
Stack Address	`pthread_attr_setstackaddr`
	`pthread_attr_getstackaddr`
Detach State	`pthread_attr_setdetachstate`
	`pthread_attr_getdetachstate`
Scope	`pthread_attr_setscope`
	`pthread_attr_getscope`
Inheritance	`pthread_setinheritsched`
	`pthread_getinheritsched`
Schedule Policy	`pthread_attr_setschedpolicy`
	`pthread_attr_getschedpolicy`
Schedule Parameters	`pthread_attr_setschedparam`
	`pthread_attr_getschedparam`

Table 9.3: Summary of settable properties for POSIX.1c thread attribute objects.

The `pthread_attr_init` initializes a thread attribute object with the default values. The `pthread_attr_destroy` sets the value of the attribute object to be invalid. POSIX does not specify the behavior of the object after it has been destroyed. Both `pthread_attr_init` and `pthread_attr_destroy` take a single argument that is a pointer to a thread attribute object.

All of the get/set thread attribute functions have two parameters—the first is a pointer to a thread attribute object. The second parameter is the value of the attribute or a pointer to a value. For example, the synopsis for the functions to manipulate the scheduling policy is

```
SYNOPSIS

   #include <pthread.h>
   #include <sched.h>

   int pthread_attr_setschedparam(pthread_attr_t *attr,
                           const struct sched_param *param);
   int pthread_attr_getschedparam(pthread_attr_t *attr,
                           struct sched_param *param);
                                                        POSIX.1c
```

A thread has a stack whose location and size can be examined or set by the calls `pthread_attr_getstackaddr` , `pthread_attr_setstackaddr` , `pthread_attr_getstacksize` , and `pthread_attr_setstacksize` , respectively. A thread that is detached cannot be waited for with a `pthread_join`. The functions `pthread_attr_getdetachstate` and `pthread_attr_setdetachstate` can examine and set the `detachstate` of a thread. The possible values of `detachstate` are `PTHREAD_CREATE_JOINABLE` or `PTHREAD_CREATE_DETACHED`. By default, threads are joinable. Detached threads call `pthread_detach` when they complete to release their resources.

The `pthread_attr_getscope` and `pthread_attr_setscope` examine and set the `contentionscope` attribute which controls whether the thread competes within the process or at the system level for resources. The possible values of `contentionscope` are `PTHREAD_SCOPE_PROCESS` and `PTHREAD_SCOPE_SYSTEM`.

The `pthread_attr_getinheritsched` examines the `inheritsched` attribute which controls whether the scheduling parameters are inherited from the creating thread or explicitly specified. The `pthread_attr_setinheritsched` function sets this attribute. The possible values of `inheritsched` are `PTHREAD_INHERIT_SCHED` and `PTHREAD_EXPLICIT_SCHED`.

A thread's schedule policy is stored in a structure of type `struct sched_param`. The `sched_policy` submember of `struct sched_param` holds the scheduling policy. The possible scheduling policies are first-in-first-out (`SCHED_FIFO`), round robin (`SCHED_RR`), or implementation-defined (`SCHED_OTHER`). Preemptive priority policy is the most common implementation of SCHED_OTHER. A POSIX-compliant implementation can support any of these scheduling policies. The actual behavior of the policy in the implementation depends on the scheduling scope and other factors.

The property most likely to change is the priority of a thread, which is part of the schedule policy. The sched_priority submember of struct sched_param holds an int priority value. Larger priority values correspond to higher priorities.

Example 9.6

The following code segment creates a do_it *thread with the default attributes and then changes the priority to* HIGHPRIORITY.

```
#include <stdio.h>
#include <errno.h>
#include <string.h>
#include <sys/types.h>
#include <sys/stat.h>
#include <fcntl.h>
#include <pthread.h>
#include <sched.h>

#define HIGHPRIORITY 10

pthread_attr_t my_tattr;
pthread_t my_tid;
struct sched_param param;
int fd;

if (pthread_attr_init(&my_tattr))
   perror("Could not initialize thread attribute object");
else if (pthread_create(&my_tid, &my_tattr, do_it, (void *)&fd))
   perror("Could not create copier thread");
else if (pthread_attr_getschedparam(&my_tattr, &param))
   perror("Could not get scheduling parameters");
else {
   param.sched_priority = HIGHPRIORITY;
   if (pthread_attr_setschedparam(&my_tattr, &param))
      perror("Could not set priority");
}
```

The pthread_create of Example 9.6 associates the my_tattr thread attribute object with the my_tid thread at creation so that this thread's associated attributes can later be changed. Notice that the priority of thread my_tid is changed by modifying a property of the thread attribute object my_tattr which has been associated with the thread.

9.6 Exercise: Parallel File Copy

This section develops a parallel file copy as an extension of the copier application of Program 9.9. Be sure to use thread-safe calls in the implementation. The main program takes two command-line arguments that are directory names and copies everything from the first directory into the second directory. The copy program preserves subdirectory structure. The same filenames are used for source and destination. Implement the parallel file copy as follows:

- Write a function called `copy_directory` that has the prototype

  ```
  void *copy_directory(void *arg)
  ```

  The `copy_directory` function copies all of the files from one directory to another directory. The directory names are passed in `arg` as two consecutive strings (separated by a `NULL`). Assume that both source and destination directories exist when `copy_directory` is called. In this version, only ordinary files are copied and subdirectories are ignored. For each file to be copied, create a thread to run the `copy_file` function of Program 9.8. Wait for the thread to complete execution before copying the next file.

- Write a main program that takes two command-line arguments for the source and destination directories. The main program creates a thread to run `copy_directory` and then does does a `pthread_join` to wait for the `copy_directory` thread to complete. Use the main program to test the first version of `copy_directory`.

- Modify the `copy_directory` function so that if the destination directory does not exist, it creates the directory. Test the new version.

- Modify the `copy_directory` so that after it creates a thread to copy a file, it continues on to create threads to copy the other files. Keep the thread ID and open file descriptors for each `copy_file` thread in a linked list with a node structure similar to

  ```
  typedef struct copy_struct {
      char *namestring;
      int source_fd;
      int destination_fd;
      pthread_t tid;
      struct copy_struct *next_thread;
  } copyinfo_t;
  copyinfo_t *copy_head = NULL;
  copyinfo_t *copy_tail = NULL;
  ```

  Implement the list as an object by putting its declaration in a separate file along with access functions to insert, retrieve, and delete nodes. After the `copy_directory` function creates threads to copy all of the files in the directory, it does a `pthread_join` on each thread in its list and frees the `copyinfo_t` structure.

- Modify the `copy_file` function of Program 9.8 so that its argument is a pointer to a `copyinfo_t` structure. Test the new version of `copy_file` and `copy_directory`.

- Modify `copy_directory` so that if a file is a directory instead of an ordinary file, the `copy_directory` creates a thread to run a `copy_directory` instead of `copy_file`. Test the new function.

- Devise a method for performing timings to compare an ordinary copy with the threaded copy.

- If run on a large directory, the program may attempt to open more file descriptors than are allowed for a process. Devise a method for handling this situation. With some shells this maximum can be changed by the user.

- See if there is a difference in running time if the threads have scope `PTHREAD_SCOPE_SYSTEM` instead of `PTHREAD_SCOPE_PROCESS`.

9.7 Additional Reading

The book *Distributed Operating Systems* by Tanenbaum [93] presents an understandable general discussion of threads. Different approaches to thread scheduling are discussed in the papers [3, 10, 27, 48]. The upcoming book entitled *Programming with Threads* by Kleiman, et al. [44] covers advanced programming techniques with threads. Finally, the POSIX.1c standard itself [54] is a surprisingly readable account of the conflicting issues and choices involved in implementing a usable threads package.

Chapter 10

Thread Synchronization

POSIX.1c supports a synchronization mechanism called a mutex for short-term locking, and it supports condition variables for waiting on events of unbounded duration. Multithreaded programs can also use POSIX.1b semaphores for synchronization. Signal handling in threaded programs presents additional complications which can be reduced if signal handlers are replaced with dedicated threads. This chapter illustrates these thread synchronization concepts through variations on the producer-consumer problem.

Threads are created within the address space of a process and share resources such as static variables and open file descriptors. When threads use such shared resources, they must synchronize their interaction in order to get consistent results. There are two distinct types of synchronization—locking and waiting. *Locking* refers to typically short-duration holding of resources. *Waiting*, which can be of unbounded duration, refers to blocking until some event occurs. POSIX.1c provides mutexes and condition variables to support these two types of synchronization in multithreaded programs. POSIX.1c also allows the use of semaphores in multithreaded programs.

This chapter develops the concepts of thread synchronization in terms of the producer-consumer problem. Producer threads or processes manufacture data (such as messages) and deposit these items in a FIFO queue. Consumer threads remove data items from the queue. When the queue is of specified size, the producer-consumer problem is called the *bounded-buffer problem*. An example of a producer-consumer application is a network printer manager where the producers are users generating print requests, and the consumers are the printers. Other examples include scheduling queues in a multiprocessor system or the network message buffers used in routing messages through intermediate nodes on a wide-area network.

Figure 10.1 shows a schematic of the producer-consumer problem. Producer and consumer threads share the queue and must lock this resource when inserting or removing items. Producers acquire the lock only when they have an item to insert and hold the lock only during the period in which they are actually doing the insertion. Similarly, consumers lock the queue only while they are removing the items and release the lock prior to processing the items they have removed. When the queue is empty, consumer threads should block until there are items to remove. In addition, if the queue is limited in size, producers must wait for room to become available before producing more data. Locking is typically short duration while waiting can be long duration. Here are some problems to avoid in programming the producer-consumer:

- A consumer removes an item while a producer is in the process of putting it in the buffer *(locking)*.

- A consumer removes items that are not there at all *(waiting)*.

- A consumer removes items that have already been removed *(locking)*.

- A producer puts something in the buffer when there is no free slot *(waiting)*.

- A producer overwrites an item that has not been removed *(locking)*.

More complicated producer-consumer flow control might include *high-water* and *low-water marks*. When a queue reaches a certain size (the high-water mark), producers block until the queue empties to the low-water mark. Mutexes, condition variables, and semaphores can be used to control various aspects of the problem. The next three sections illustrate the use of these primitives to control and synchronize producers and consumers. Section 10.1 introduces POSIX.1c mutex locks and uses them to implement exclusive access to the producer-consumer queue. Section 10.2 uses POSIX.1b semaphores to synchronize the producer and consumer threads when the number of items is known. Section 10.3 introduces POSIX.1c condition variables and uses them to implement the producer-consumer synchronization with more complex termination requirements. Section 10.4 covers signal handling with threads. Section 10.5 presents an application of a threaded print server.

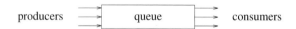

Figure 10.1: A schematic of the producer-consumer problem.

10.1 Mutexes

The *mutex* or *mutex lock* is the simplest and most efficient thread synchronization mechanism. Programs use mutexes to preserve critical sections and to obtain exclusive access to resources.

```
SYNOPSIS

  #include <pthread.h>

  int pthread_mutex_init(pthread_mutex_t *mutex,
                         const pthread_mutexattr_t *attr);
  int pthread_mutex_destroy(pthread_mutex_t *mutex);
  int pthread_mutex_lock(pthread_mutex_t *mutex);
  int pthread_mutex_trylock(pthread_mutex_t *mutex);
  int pthread_mutex_unlock(pthread_mutex_t *mutex);
                                                        POSIX.1c
```

To use these function, a program must declare a variable of type `pthread_mutex_t` and initialize it prior to using it for synchronization. Typically mutex variables are static variables that are accessible to all of the threads in the process. A program can initialize a mutex either by calling `pthread_mutex_init` or by using the static initializer `PTHREAD_MUTEX_INITIALIZER`.

Example 10.1

The following code segment initializes the mutex `my_lock` *with the default attributes. The* `my_lock` *variable must be accessible to all of the threads that use it.*

```
#include <stdio.h>
#include <pthread.h>
#include <string.h>
#include <errno.h>
pthread_mutex_t my_lock;

if (!pthread_mutex_init(&my_lock, NULL))
   perror("Could not initialize my_lock");
```

The static initializer method has two advantages over the `pthread_mutex_init` for initializing mutex locks—it is usually more efficient, and it is guaranteed to be performed exactly once before any threads begin execution.

Example 10.2

The following code segment initializes the mutex `my_lock` *to the default attributes using the static initializer.*

```
#include <pthread.h>
pthread_mutex_t my_lock = PTHREAD_MUTEX_INITIALIZER;
```

A thread can use a `pthread_mutex_lock` to protect its critical sections. In order to preserve the critical section semantics, the mutex must be released by the same thread that acquired it. That is, do not have one thread acquire a lock (`pthread_mutex_lock`) and a different thread release it (`pthread_mutex_unlock`). Once a thread acquires a mutex, it should hold that mutex only for a short period of time. Threads waiting for events of unpredictable duration should use other synchronization mechanisms such as semaphores or condition variables.

Example 10.3

The following code segment uses a mutex to protect a critical section.

```
#include <pthread.h>
pthread_mutex_t my_lock = PTHREAD_MUTEX_INITIALIZER;

pthread_mutex_lock(&my_lock);
    /*   critical section */
pthread_mutex_unlock(&my_lock);
```

Locking and unlocking are voluntary in the sense that mutual exclusion is achieved only when all threads correctly lock the mutex before entering their critical sections. There is nothing to prevent an uncooperative thread from entering its critical section without acquiring a lock. One way to ensure exclusive access to objects is to permit access only through well-defined functions and to put the locking calls in these functions. The locking mechanism is then transparent to the calling threads.

Figure 10.2 shows an implementation of a queue as a circular buffer with eight slots and three data items. The `bufout` value indicates the slot number of the next data item to be removed, and the `bufin` value indicates the next slot to be filled. If producer and consumer threads do not update `bufout` and `bufin` in a mutually exclusive manner, a producer may overwrite an item that has not been removed or a consumer may remove an item that has already been used.

Program 10.1 shows code for implementing a circular buffer as a shared object. The data structures for the buffer are declared to have internal linkage class using the `static` qualifier to limit their scope. (See Section 2.1 for a discussion of the two meanings of the `static` qualifier in C.) The code is in a separate file so that the program can access `buffer` only through `get_item` and `put_item`.

Program 10.1: A circular buffer protected by mutex locks.

```
#include <pthread.h>
#define BUFSIZE 8
static int buffer[BUFSIZE];
static int bufin = 0;
static int bufout = 0;
```

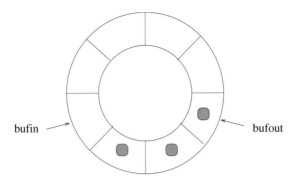

Figure 10.2: A circular-buffer implementation of a bounded queue for the producer-consumer problem.

```
static pthread_mutex_t  buffer_lock = PTHREAD_MUTEX_INITIALIZER;

/* Get the next item from buffer and put it in *itemp. */
void get_item(int *itemp)
{
   pthread_mutex_lock(&buffer_lock);
   *itemp = buffer[bufout];
   bufout = (bufout + 1) % BUFSIZE;
   pthread_mutex_unlock(&buffer_lock);
   return;
}

/* Put item into  buffer at position bufin and update bufin. */
void put_item(int item)
{
   pthread_mutex_lock(&buffer_lock);
   buffer[bufin] = item;
   bufin = (bufin + 1) % BUFSIZE;
   pthread_mutex_unlock(&buffer_lock);
   return;
}
```

_____ **Program 10.1** _____

Program 10.2 shows a simple example where a producer thread writes the squares of the integers from 1 to 100 into the circular buffer and a consumer thread removes the values and sums them. Although the buffer is protected with mutex locks, the producer-consumer synchronization is not correct. The consumer may remove items from empty slots or the producer may overwrite full slots.

Program 10.2: An incorrect implementation of the producer-consumer problem. The producer and consumer threads are not synchronized.

```c
#include <pthread.h>
#include <stdio.h>
#include <stdlib.h>
#include <string.h>
#include <errno.h>
#define SUMSIZE 100
int sum = 0;

void put_item(int);
void get_item(int *);

void *producer(void * arg1)
{
    int i;
    for (i = 1; i <= SUMSIZE; i++)
        put_item(i*i);
    return NULL;
}

void *consumer(void *arg2)
{
    int  i, myitem;
    for (i = 1; i <= SUMSIZE; i++) {
        get_item(&myitem);
        sum += myitem;
    }
    return NULL;
}

void main(void)
{
    pthread_t prodtid;
    pthread_t constid;
    int i, total;
                                                    /* check value */
    total = 0;
    for (i = 1; i <= SUMSIZE; i++)
        total += i*i;
    printf("The actual sum should be %d\n", total);

                                                    /*  create threads */
    if (pthread_create(&constid, NULL, consumer, NULL))
        perror("Could not create consumer");
    else if (pthread_create(&prodtid, NULL, producer, NULL))
        perror("Could not create producer");
```

```
                              /* wait for the threads to finish */
    pthread_join(prodtid, NULL);
    pthread_join(constid, NULL);
    printf("The threads produced the sum %d\n", sum);
    exit(0);
}
```

_____ **Program 10.2** _____

Exercise 10.1

Provide a scenario in which Program 10.2 produces an incorrect answer. Assume that only one thread can run at a time and that preemptive priority scheduling is used.

Answer:

Suppose that only one thread is allowed to run at a time. The consumer and producer are created at the same priority so there is no preemption for these compute-bound threads. The consumer thread starts first and runs to completion, consuming zeroes from the buffer since the producer has not produced anything. Afterwards the producer gets in and produces the values, but to no avail.

Exercise 10.2

As an attempt to fix the problem with the code in Program 10.2, interchange the creation of the consumer and the producer so that the producer starts first. What happens?

Answer:

This time the producer runs to completion. Since the buffer has only eight slots, the values from 93 to 100 are in the buffer when the consumer starts.

A running thread or process that executes `sched_yield` yields until it again becomes the head of its scheduling list. For threads scheduled by preemptive priority, a calling thread yields to all higher priority threads and until all threads of its priority have run and either yielded or blocked.

```
SYNOPSIS

    #include <sched.h>

    int sched_yield(void);
                                                            POSIX.1b
```

The `sched_yield` function returns 0 on success. On failure it returns −1 and sets `errno`.

The difficulties with Program 10.2 can be partially addressed by forcing the producer and consumer threads to yield.

Example 10.4

The following modification of Program 10.2 forces the producer and consumer threads to yield on each iteration of their respective loops.

```c
#include <pthread.h>
#include <sched.h>
#define SUMSIZE 100
int sum = 0;

void put_item(int);
void get_item(int *);

void *producer(void *arg1)
{
    int i;
    for (i = 1; i <= SUMSIZE; i++)
        put_item(i*i);
        sched_yield();
    return NULL;
}

void *consumer(void *arg2)
{
    int  i, myitem;
    for (i = 1; i <= SUMSIZE; i++) {
        get_item(&myitem);
        sum += myitem;
        sched_yield();
    }
    return NULL;
}
```

With the `sched_yield` in place in Example 10.4, the producer and consumer operate in strict alternation provided that only one thread executes at a time. In order for the program to work exactly right, it has to start the producer thread first and the consumer thread must be active by the time the producer first yields. The strict alternation does not solve the problem for arbitrary numbers of producers and consumers. The `sched_yield` is part of POSIX.1b, while the threads are part of POSIX.1c. It may be necessary to search for the library containing `sched_yield`. In Sun Solaris 2, this library is called `libposix4`. The man page should indicate the library.

The behavior of the examples in this section depends on exactly how many threads are allowed to run concurrently and in what order they begin execution. A multithreaded program should perform correctly regardless of execution order and level of parallelism. The items and slots in the producer-consumer problem must be synchronized so that the program is independent of thread execution order. The next section discusses a traditional method of synchronization using POSIX.1b semaphores.

10.2 Semaphores

The traditional semaphore solution to the producer-consumer problem uses counting semaphores to represent resources (e.g., POSIX.1b semaphores of Section 8.3). In the producer-consumer problem the resources are items in the queue and free slots (in the bounded-buffer case). Each of these resource types is represented by a semaphore. When a thread needs a resource of a particular type, it decrements the corresponding semaphore (sem_wait). When the thread releases a resource, it increments the appropriate semaphore (sem_post). Since the semaphore variable never falls below zero, threads cannot use resources that are not there. Always initialize a counting semaphore to the number of resources initially available.

Program 10.3 shows a correctly synchronized version of the bounded producer-consumer problem using POSIX unnamed semaphores. The slots semaphore, which is initialized to BUFSIZE, represents the number of free slots available. It is decremented by the producer and incremented by the consumer. The items semaphore, which is initialized to 0, represents the number of items in the buffer. It is decremented by the consumer and incremented by the producer.

Program 10.3: A producer-consumer program for threads synchronized by semaphores.

```
#include <stdio.h>
#include <string.h>
#include <errno.h>
#include <pthread.h>
#include <semaphore.h>

#define SUMSIZE 100
#define BUFSIZE 8

int sum = 0;
sem_t items;
sem_t slots;

void put_item(int);
void get_item(int *);

static void *producer(void *arg1)
{
    int i;

    for (i = 1; i <= SUMSIZE; i++) {
        sem_wait(&slots);
        put_item(i*i);
        sem_post(&items);
```

```
    }
    return NULL;
}

static void *consumer(void *arg2)
{
    int i, myitem;

    for (i = 1; i <= SUMSIZE; i++) {
        sem_wait(&items);
        get_item(&myitem);
        sem_post(&slots);
        sum += myitem;
    }
    return NULL;
}

void main(void)
{
    pthread_t prodtid;
    pthread_t constid;
    int i, total;
                                        /* check value */
    total = 0;
    for (i = 1; i <= SUMSIZE; i++)
        total += i*i;
    printf("The checksum is %d\n", total);

                            /* initialize the semaphores */
    sem_init(&items, 0, 0);
    sem_init(&slots, 0, BUFSIZE);

                                    /* create threads */
    pthread_create(&prodtid, NULL, producer, NULL);
    pthread_create(&constid, NULL, consumer, NULL);

                        /* wait for the threads to finish */
    pthread_join(prodtid, NULL);
    pthread_join(constid, NULL);
    printf("The threads produced the sum %d\n", sum);
}
```

_____ **Program 10.3** _____

Exercise 10.3

What happens when Program 10.3 runs on a machine with a single processor, the BUFSIZE is 8, and the producer starts first? In what order are the items processed under preemptive priority scheduling?

Answer:

The answer depends on the level of concurrency allowed. Suppose that only one thread can execute at a time. The producer produces eight items and then blocks, thereby allowing the consumer to get in for the first time. The consumer then gets the first eight items. The producer then produces the next eight items, and so on. This alternation of blocks is a consequence of the preemptive priority scheduling. A thread does not give up control unless it must. If two threads are allowed to execute at a time, the order of execution depends on the underlying kernel scheduling mechanism.

Exercise 10.4

Would Program 10.3 work correctly if two consumer threads were created?

Answer:

No. If there is more than one consumer thread, the modification of the `sum` is a critical section which must be protected. Also, both consumers try to process `SUMSIZE` items and eventually block since the producer exits after producing a total of `SUMSIZE` items.

Semaphores solve the producer-consumer problem when producers and consumers loop indefinitely or loop for a specified number of times. Things are not so simple when the producers or consumers are controlled by more complicated exit conditions. In a *producer-driven* variation on the producer-consumer problem, there is one producer and an arbitrary number of consumer threads. The producer puts a certain number of items in the queue and then exits. The consumers continue until all items have been consumed and the producer has exited. A possible approach is for the producer to set a flag indicating that it has completed its operation. Program 10.4 illustrates some of the difficulties in using semaphores to handle this situation.

Program 10.4 shows an incorrect solution to producer-driven exit conditions in the producer-consumer problem. The producer inserts `SUMSIZE` items in the queue, but the consumers do not exit until the producer does. Suppose the buffer is empty and consumers are waiting on the `items` semaphore. If the producer then decides it is done and sets the `producer_done` flag, the consumers hang indefinitely waiting for a final item to be produced.

Program 10.4: An incorrect solution to the producer-driven producer-consumer problem

```
#include <stdio.h>
#include <string.h>
#include <errno.h>
#include <pthread.h>
#include <semaphore.h>
```

```c
#define BUFSIZE 8
#define SUMSIZE 100

int producer_done = 0;
int sum = 0;
sem_t items;
sem_t slots;
pthread_mutex_t my_lock = PTHREAD_MUTEX_INITIALIZER;

void put_item(int);
void get_item(int *);

void *producer(void *arg1)
{
   int i;

   for (i = 1; i <= SUMSIZE; i++) {
      sem_wait(&slots);
      put_item(i*i);
      sem_post(&items);
   }
   pthread_mutex_lock(&my_lock);
      producer_done = 1;
   pthread_mutex_unlock(&my_lock);
   return NULL;
}

void *consumer(void *arg2)
{
   int myitem;

   for ( ; ; ) {
      pthread_mutex_lock(&my_lock);
      if (producer_done) {
         pthread_mutex_unlock(&my_lock);
         if (sem_trywait(&items)) break;
      } else {
         pthread_mutex_unlock(&my_lock);
         sem_wait(&items);
      }
      get_item(&myitem);
      sem_post(&slots);
      sum += myitem;
   }
   return NULL;
}
```

_____ **Program 10.4** _____

A difficulty with the semaphore implementation is that once a consumer is waiting on a semaphore, there is no way to unblock that consumer except by incrementing the semaphore with a `sem_post`. A producer who is finished cannot `sem_post` without making the consumer think that an item is available. The producer might try a `sem_destroy`, but unfortunately, POSIX does not guarantee that threads waiting for a semaphore unblock when it is destroyed.

Exercise 10.5

Program 10.5 shows an attempt to fix the problem described above. What is wrong with this solution?

Answer:

If the producer sets `producer_done` before the consumer has used all remaining items, the consumer breaks from the loop without consuming the last items.

Program 10.5: A second incorrect solution to the producer-driven producer-consumer problem.

```
#include <stdio.h>
#include <string.h>
#include <errno.h>
#include <pthread.h>
#include "psemaphore.h"

#define BUFSIZE 8
#define MAXCONSUMERS 1
#define SUMSIZE 100
int producer_done = 0;
int sum = 0;
sem_t items;
sem_t slots;
pthread_mutex_t my_lock = PTHREAD_MUTEX_INITIALIZER;

void put_item(int);
void get_item(int *);

void *producer(void *arg1)
{
    int i;

    for (i = 1; i <= SUMSIZE; i++) {
        sem_wait(&slots);
        put_item(i*i);
        sem_post(&items);
    }
    pthread_mutex_lock(&my_lock);
    producer_done = 1;
```

```
        for (i = 0; i < MAXCONSUMERS; i++)
            sem_post(&items);
        pthread_mutex_unlock(&my_lock);
        return NULL;
}

void *consumer(void *arg2)
{
    int myitem;

    for ( ; ; ) {
        sem_wait(&items);
        pthread_mutex_lock(&my_lock);
        if (!producer_done) {
            pthread_mutex_unlock(&my_lock);
            get_item(&myitem);
            sem_post(&slots);
            sum += myitem;
        } else {
            pthread_mutex_unlock(&my_lock);
            break;
        }
    }
    return NULL;
}
```

———————————————————————— **Program 10.5** ————————————————————————

Note: At the time this book was printed, no POSIX.1b semaphore implementation was available. The examples in this section were tested with an implementation of the functions specified in Sections 8.6 and 8.7 The next section presents a solution to the problem of shutdown in terms of condition variables.

10.3 Condition Variables

The sem_wait on a semaphore variable, s, waits atomically on the predicate $s > 0$. A condition variable waits atomically on arbitrary predicates and is a convenient mechanism for blocking until a combination of events occurs.

Condition variables have atomic operations for waiting and signaling (cond_wait and cond_signal) which are analogous, but not identical, to the semaphore operations sem_wait and sem_post. For semaphores, the test of the predicate $s > 0$ is part of the sem_wait, and the thread blocks only if the predicate is false. The key point is that the testing and the blocking are done atomically.

Read the next two paragraphs slowly and carefully. Condition variables are hard to understand the first time through. The information in these two paragraphs is repeated several times in this section. Once understood, condition variables are not hard to use.

Suppose a thread needs to wait on some predicate involving a set of shared variables, say that a particular pair of them are equal. These shared variables will be protected by a mutex lock since any code that uses these variables is part of a critical section. An additional condition variable provides a mechanism for threads to wait on predicates involving these variables. Whenever a thread changes one of these shared variables, it signals on the condition variable that a change has taken place. This signal wakes up a waiting thread, which then checks to see if its predicate is now satisfied.

When a waiting thread is signaled, it must lock the mutex before testing its predicate. If the predicate is false, the thread should release the lock and block again. The mutex must be released before the thread blocks so that another thread can gain access to the mutex and change the protected variables. The release of the mutex and the blocking must be atomic so that another thread does not change the variables between these two operations. Since the signal only means that the variables may have changed and not that the predicate is now true, the blocked thread must retest the predicate each time it is signaled.

Follow these steps when using a condition variable to synchronize on an arbitrary predicate:

a) Acquire the mutex.

b) Test the predicate.

c) If the predicate is true, do some work and release the mutex.

d) If the predicate is false, call `cond_wait` and go to b) when it returns.

The `cond_wait` atomically blocks the calling thread and releases the mutex. Thus, the mutex is released explicitly if the predicate is true and released implicitly if the predicate is false. When a thread waiting on a condition variable is unblocked, it reacquires the mutex automatically as part of the unblocking process. If necessary, it changes from waiting on the condition variable to waiting on the mutex. Always use the same mutex with a particular condition variable.

Example 10.5

The following pseudocode illustrates the use of a condition variable, v, and its associated mutex lock, m, to force a thread to wait until the variables x and y have the same value.

```
a: | lock_mutex(&m);
b: |    while (x != y)
c: |        cond_wait(&v, &m);
d: |    /* do stuff related to x and y */
e: | unlock_mutex(&m);
```

In Example 10.5 the predicate or condition which must be true for the thread to proceed is $x == y$. (Notice this is negation of the actual test that appears in the `while` loop.) The thread locks the mutex, m, before testing $x != y$. The thread executing this code segment does not execute statement d until x is equal to y. The test is performed in a `while` loop rather than with a single `if` statement to be sure that the desired predicate is actually true.

When a thread waiting on a simple semaphore s awakens, it is guaranteed that $s > 0$ unless the wait was interrupted by a signal. Condition variables are not associated with particular predicates, so a program does not know if the predicate is true, but only that some thread signaled on that condition variable.

Example 10.6

The following pseudocode illustrates the signaling related to condition variables.

```
f:|   lock_mutex(&m);
g:|       x++;
h:|       cond_signal(&v);
i:|   unlock_mutex(&m);
```

The thread of Example 10.6 changes the value of x and then signals on v so that a waiting thread can check the predicate. The indentation in the pseudocode segments of Examples 10.5 and 10.6 shows which statements are executed while the mutex lock is held. The actual mechanism for blocking is a bit complicated. If the thread continues to hold the lock when it blocks on the `cond_wait` of statement c, another process cannot acquire the mutex lock in statement f in order to signal on the condition variable and unblock the thread. A deadlock would occur. To solve this problem, the implementation guarantees that if the thread blocks on a condition variable, the `cond_wait` atomically releases the mutex and blocks. Since these operations are atomic, another thread cannot modify a shared variable and signal before this thread blocks. When the thread is unblocked, it reacquires the mutex lock before executing anything else. The second argument of the `cond_wait` tells the thread which mutex lock is the one to acquire before going on.

Exercise 10.6

Suppose that thread one executes the code of Example 10.5 and thread two executes the code of Example 10.6. The initial values of x and y are 0 and 2, respectively. What happens when the statements from the execution of the two threads are interleaved as follows: $a_1, b_1, c_1, f_2, g_2, h_2, i_2$. What statement does thread one execute next?

Answer:

In this interleaving, thread one acquires mutex lock m and tests x != y. Since x is 0 and y is 2, the test succeeds and thread one blocks on condition variable v and releases the lock m. Thread two then acquires the lock, increments the variable x, signals the condition variable v, and releases the mutex m. The signal unblocks thread one, and it reacquires the mutex lock which is freed in statement i_2. Thread one then retests the predicate. Since x != y is still true, thread one executes the `cond_wait` and blocks again. The next statements executed by thread one are b_1 and c_1. These statements may be interleaved with statements from other threads.

Exercise 10.7

Are the following interleavings of the pseudocode from Examples 10.5 and 10.6 possible?

$$a_1, b_1, c_1, f_2, g_2, h_2, b_1, c_1, i_2$$
$$a_1, b_1, f_2, g_2, c_1, h_2$$

Answer:

Neither interleaving is possible. In the first interleaving, thread one awakens from a `cond_wait` and must reacquire the mutex lock before proceeding. Thread two has the lock when it signals. Therefore i_2 must come before the second b_1 in the interleaving. The second interleaving is not possible because thread one does not release the mutex until the `cond_wait` in statement c_1. Therefore thread two cannot acquire the lock in statement f_2 before it is released in c_1.

The `cond_signal` does not guarantee that the predicate has become true. It merely is a way of telling the blocked process that the variables involved in the predicate may have changed and that the thread should retest the predicate. The `while` loop in statement b of Example 10.5 is necessary to ensure that the predicate is actually true. If the `while` loop test succeeds (the predicate is false), the thread blocks itself again doing a `cond_wait`. When another thread modifies the variables in the predicate, it can awaken the blocked thread by calling `cond_signal` again.

10.3.1 Condition Variables for POSIX.1c Threads

POSIX.1c threads provide condition variable synchronization in a manner similar to the description at the beginning of this section. Initialize a condition variable either by using a static initializer or with a call to `pthread_cond_init`. If `attr` is NULL, `pthread_cond_init` uses the default condition variable attributes.

SYNOPSIS

```
#include <pthread.h>

int pthread_cond_init(pthread_cond_t *cond,
                      const pthread_condattr_t *attr);
int pthread_cond_destroy(pthread_cond_t *cond);
int pthread_cond_wait(pthread_cond_t *cond,
                      pthread_mutex_t *mutex);
int pthread_cond_timedwait(pthread_cond_t *cond,
                      pthread_mutex_t *mutex,
                      const struct timespec *abstime);
int pthread_cond_signal(pthread_cond_t *cond);
int pthread_cond_broadcast(pthread_cond_t *cond);
```

POSIX.1c

Condition variables derive their name from the fact that they are always used with a condition, that is, a predicate. A thread tests a predicate and calls `pthread_cond_wait` if the predicate is false. When another thread changes variables that might make the predicate true, it awakens the blocked thread by executing `pthread_cond_signal`. Other actions such as the delivery of a UNIX signal can also cause the blocked thread to return from `pthread_cond_wait`. The previously blocked thread normally retests the predicate and calls `pthread_cond_wait` again if the predicate is still false.

To guarantee that the test of the predicate and the wait are atomic, the calling thread must obtain a mutex before it tests the predicate. The implementation guarantees that if the thread blocks on a condition variable, the `pthread_cond_wait` atomically releases the mutex and blocks. Another thread cannot signal before this thread blocks.

Example 10.7

Let v *be a condition variable and* m *be a mutex lock. The following is a proper use of the condition variable to access a resource if the predicate defined by* `test_condition()` *is true.*

```
#include <pthread.h>
pthread_mutex_t m = PTHREAD_MUTEX_INITIALIZER;
pthread_cond_t v = PTHREAD_COND_INITIALIZER;

pthread_mutex_lock(&m);
while (!test_condition())
    pthread_cond_wait(&v, &m);
        /* get resource (make test_condition return false) */
pthread_mutex_unlock(&m);
        /*  do stuff */
pthread_mutex_lock(&m);
        /* release resource (make test_condition return true) */
pthread_cond_signal(&v);
pthread_mutex_unlock(&m);
```

In Example 10.7, the thread must lock the mutex `m` specified in the function `pthread_cond_wait` before `pthread_cond_wait` is called. If `test_condition` returns false, the thread executes `pthread_cond_wait`, releases the mutex `m`, and blocks on the condition variable `v`.

When a thread executes the `pthread_cond_wait` in Example 10.7, it is holding the mutex `m`. It blocks atomically and releases the mutex, permitting another thread to acquire the mutex and modify the variables in the predicate. When a thread returns successfully from a `pthread_cond_wait`, it has acquired the mutex and can retest the predicate without explicitly reacquiring the mutex. Even if the program signals on a particular condition variable only when a certain predicate is true, waiting threads must still retest the predicate.

The `pthread_cond_wait` awakens one thread waiting on a condition variable. If more threads are waiting, one is selected in a manner consistent with the scheduling algorithm. The `pthread_cond_broadcast` wakes up all threads waiting on a condition variable. These awakened threads contend for the mutex lock before returning from `pthread_cond_wait`.

Here are some rules for using condition variables:

- Acquire the mutex before testing the predicate.
- Retest the predicate after returning from a `pthread_cond_wait`, since the return might have been caused by some unrelated event or by a `pthread_cond_signal` that did not signify that the predicate had become true.
- Acquire the mutex before changing any of the variables appearing in the predicate.
- Acquire the mutex before calling the functions `pthread_cond_signal` or `pthread_cond_broadcast`.
- Hold the mutex only for a short period of time—usually while testing the predicate. Release the mutex as soon as possible either explicitly (with `pthread_mutex_unlock`) or implicitly (with `pthread_cond_wait`).

Program 10.6 shows a condition variable solution to the producer-driven bounded-buffer problem. The producer exits after producing a fixed number of items. The consumer continues until it processes all items and detects that the producer has exited.

Program 10.6: A condition variable solution to the producer-driven bounded-buffer problem.

```
#include <stdio.h>
#include <stdlib.h>
#include <pthread.h>
#define SUMSIZE 100
```

```
#define BUFSIZE 8

int sum = 0;
pthread_cond_t slots = PTHREAD_COND_INITIALIZER;
pthread_cond_t items = PTHREAD_COND_INITIALIZER;
pthread_mutex_t slot_lock = PTHREAD_MUTEX_INITIALIZER;
pthread_mutex_t item_lock = PTHREAD_MUTEX_INITIALIZER;
int nslots = BUFSIZE;
int producer_done = 0;
int nitems = 0;

void get_item(int *itemp);
void put_item(int item);

void *producer(void * arg1)
{
    int i;

    for (i = 1; i <= SUMSIZE; i++) {
        pthread_mutex_lock(&slot_lock);      /* acquire right to a slot */
            while (nslots <= 0)
                pthread_cond_wait (&slots, &slot_lock);
            nslots--;
        pthread_mutex_unlock(&slot_lock);

        put_item(i*i);
        pthread_mutex_lock(&item_lock);    /* release right to an item */
            nitems++;
            pthread_cond_signal(&items);
        pthread_mutex_unlock(&item_lock);
    }
    pthread_mutex_lock(&item_lock);
        producer_done = 1;
        pthread_cond_broadcast(&items);
    pthread_mutex_unlock(&item_lock);
    return NULL;
}

void *consumer(void *arg2)
{
    int myitem;

    for ( ; ; ) {
        pthread_mutex_lock(&item_lock);    /* acquire right to an item */
            while ((nitems <=0) && !producer_done)
                pthread_cond_wait(&items, &item_lock);
            if ((nitems <= 0) && producer_done) {
                pthread_mutex_unlock(&item_lock);
                break;
```

```
            }
         nitems--;
      pthread_mutex_unlock(&item_lock);
      get_item(&myitem);
      sum += myitem;
      pthread_mutex_lock(&slot_lock);    /* release right to a slot */
         nslots++;
         cond_signal(&slots);
      pthread_mutex_unlock(&slot_lock);
   }
   return NULL;
}

void main(void)
{
   pthread_t prodtid;
   pthread_t constid;
   int i, total;
                                              /* check value */
   total = 0;
   for (i = 1; i <= SUMSIZE; i++)
      total += i*i;
   printf("The checksum is %d\n", total);
                                         /* create threads */
   pthread_create(&prodtid, NULL, producer, NULL);
   pthread_create(&constid, NULL, consumer, NULL);
                          /* wait for the threads to finish */
   pthread_join(prodtid, NULL);
   pthread_join(constid, NULL);
   printf("The threads produced the sum %d\n", sum);
   exit(0);
}
```
_____ **Program 10.6** _____

The producer in Program 10.6 blocks until the predicate `nslots > 0` becomes true. Its test can be written as `while(!(nslots > 0))` or `while(nslots <= 0)`. The consumer blocks until the predicate `(nitems > 0) || producer_done` is true (i.e., the consumer must take action if either an item is available or the producer is done). Its test is therefore `while((nitems <= 0) && !producer_done)`. The consumer completes only if the producer is done and there are no items left.

10.4 Signal Handling and Threads

The interaction of threads with signals involves several complications. All of the threads share the process signal handlers, but each thread can have its own signal mask. In ad-

dition, different types of signals are handled in different ways. Table 10.1 summarizes
the types of signals and their methods of handling.

Type	Delivery Action
Asynchronous	Delivered to some thread that has it unblocked.
Synchronous	Delivered to the thread that caused it.
Directed	Delivered to the identified thread (`pthread_kill`).

Table 10.1: Signal delivery in threads.

Signals such as `SIGFPE` (floating point exception) are synchronous to the thread
that caused them (i.e., they are always generated at the same point in the thread's execution). Synchronous signals are sometimes called traps. Traps are handled by the thread
that caused them. Other signals are asynchronous in that they are not generated at a pre-
dictable time and they are not associated with a particular thread.   If several threads
have an asynchronous signal unblocked, one of them is selected to handle the signal.
Signals can also be directed to a particular thread with the `pthread_kill`. A thread
can examine or set its signal mask with the `pthread_sigmask` function.

```
SYNOPSIS

    #include <signal.h>
    #include <pthread.h>

    int pthread_kill(pthread_t thread, int sig);
                                                                    POSIX.1c
```

```
SYNOPSIS

    #include <pthread.h>
    #include <signal.h>

    int pthread_sigmask(int how, const sigset_t *set,
                        sigset_t *oset);
                                                                    POSIX.1c
```

The `pthread_sigmask` call is similar to `sigprocmask`. The `how` parameter can be
one of `SIG_BLOCK`, `SIG_UNBLOCK`, or `SIG_SETMASK`. Signal handlers are processwide and are installed with calls to `sigaction` as in single-threaded processes. The
distinction between signal handlers which are processwide and signal masks which are
thread-specific is important.

Recall from the discussion of signals that when the signal handler is entered, the
signal that caused the event is automatically blocked. With a multithreaded application,

there is nothing to prevent another signal of the same type from being delivered to another thread that has the signal unblocked. It is possible to have multiple threads executing within the same signal handler. It is absolutely critical that the call to `sigaction` explicitly block the signal being handled. Installing the signal handler to block the signal causes all threads to have the signal blocked when the signal handler is active.

An alternative strategy for dealing with signals in multithreaded processes is to dedicate particular threads to signal handling. The main thread blocks all of signals before creating the threads. The signal mask is inherited from the creating thread so all threads have the signal blocked. The thread dedicated to handling the signal then executes a `sigwait` on that signal. (See page 391.)

To illustrate the two approaches (signal handler versus dedicated thread), consider a variation of the bounded-buffer problem in which the producer inserts items in the buffer until the program receives a `SIGUSR1` signal. At that point the producer finishes its current item and exits. The program cannot just kill the producer thread, because it might be holding a mutex lock which would leave that mutex in an undetermined state.

Program 10.7 illustrates the signal handler approach to the signal-driven bounded-buffer problem. The signal handler sets the `producer_shutdown` variable to indicate that the producer thread should exit. Because the `producer_shutdown` variable in Program 10.7 is shared by the handler and the producer thread, it must be protected in the handler by the same mutex as in the producer thread. If a `SIGUSR1` signal came in while the producer was holding this lock, the signal handler deadlocks. In order to avoid this, the producer blocks the signal when it is holding the mutex. The solution assumes that all other threads have also blocked `SIGUSR1`. Because the producer blocks the signal while it is doing the condition wait, it does not detect that it should shut down until a slot becomes available and it produces the next item.

The functions in Program 10.7 have been instrumented so that they can be tested. The main program displays its process ID and then sleeps for five seconds before creating the threads. This allows the user to move to another window and prepare to execute a command to send the `SIGUSR1` signal to the process. The thread IDs of the producer and consumer threads are displayed to indicate when the threads have started. On most machines the calculation of the sum of squares in this simple program will overflow a 32-bit integer rather quickly (after 1861 items), so a small delay has been added in various places to slow it down. The amount of delay is controlled by the `SPIN` constant and has to be modified for different machines. A warning is displayed when the program terminates if an overflow is detected. The consumer in Program 10.7 is almost identical to the one in Program 10.6 except for the delay. The main program blocks the `SIGUSR1` signal before creating the threads so the threads inherit a signal mask with that signal blocked. The producer needs to have the signal blocked while holding the `slot_lock` mutex. The producer thread uses `pthread_sigmask` to unblock this signal so that it is unblocked only for that thread.

Program 10.7: Signal-handler approach in the signal-driven bounded-buffer problem.

```
#include <stdio.h>
#include <stdlib.h>
#include <unistd.h>
#include <signal.h>
#include <pthread.h>

#define SUMSIZE 1861
#define BUFSIZE 8
#define SPIN 10000

int sum = 0;
pthread_cond_t slots = PTHREAD_COND_INITIALIZER;
pthread_cond_t items = PTHREAD_COND_INITIALIZER;
pthread_mutex_t slot_lock = PTHREAD_MUTEX_INITIALIZER;
pthread_mutex_t item_lock = PTHREAD_MUTEX_INITIALIZER;
int nslots = BUFSIZE;
int producer_done = 0;
int nitems = 0;
int totalproduced = 0;
int producer_shutdown = 0;

void get_item(int *itemp);
void put_item(int item);

/* spinit loops to waste time */
void spinit(void)
{
    int i;
    for (i = 0; i < SPIN; i++) ;
}

/* signal handler for shutdown */
void catch_sigusr1(int signo)
{
    pthread_mutex_lock(&slot_lock);
        producer_shutdown = 1;
    pthread_mutex_unlock(&slot_lock);
}

void *producer(void * arg1)
{
    int i;
    sigset_t intmask;

    sigemptyset(&intmask);
    sigaddset(&intmask, SIGUSR1);
```

```
    for (i = 1;  ; i++){
        spinit();
        pthread_sigmask(SIG_BLOCK, &intmask, NULL);
        pthread_mutex_lock(&slot_lock);     /* acquire right to a slot */
        spinit();
        while ((nslots <= 0) && (!producer_shutdown))
            pthread_cond_wait (&slots, &slot_lock);
        if (producer_shutdown) {
            pthread_mutex_unlock(&slot_lock);
            break;
        }
        nslots--;
        pthread_mutex_unlock(&slot_lock);
        pthread_sigmask(SIG_UNBLOCK, &intmask, NULL);

        spinit();
        put_item(i*i);
        pthread_mutex_lock(&item_lock);    /* release right to an item */
            nitems++;
            totalproduced++;
            pthread_cond_signal(&items);
        pthread_mutex_unlock(&item_lock);
        spinit();
    }
    pthread_mutex_lock(&item_lock);
        producer_done = 1;
        pthread_cond_broadcast(&items);
    pthread_mutex_unlock(&item_lock);
    return NULL;
}

void *consumer(void *arg2)
{
    int myitem;

    for ( ; ; ) {
        pthread_mutex_lock(&item_lock);     /* acquire right to an item */
            while ((nitems <= 0) && !producer_done)
                cond_wait(&items, &item_lock);
            if ((nitems <= 0) && producer_done) {
                pthread_mutex_unlock(&item_lock);
                break;
            }
            nitems--;
        pthread_mutex_unlock(&item_lock);
        spinit();
        get_item(&myitem);
        spinit();
        sum += myitem;
```

```
        pthread_mutex_lock(&slot_lock);    /* release right to a slot */
            nslots++;
            cond_signal(&slots);
        pthread_mutex_unlock(&slot_lock);
    }
    return NULL;
}

void main(void)
{
    pthread_t prodtid;
    pthread_t constid;
    double total;
    double tp;
    struct sigaction act;
    sigset_t set;

    fprintf(stderr, "Process ID is %ld\n", (long)getpid());
    sleep(5);
                                        /* setup signal handler and block */
    act.sa_handler = catch_sigusr1;
    sigemptyset(&act.sa_mask);
    act.sa_flags = 0;
    sigaction(SIGUSR1, &act, NULL);
    sigemptyset(&set);
    sigaddset(&set,SIGUSR1);
    sigprocmask(SIG_BLOCK, &set, NULL);
                                                    /* create threads */
    pthread_create(&prodtid, NULL, producer, NULL);
    pthread_create(&constid, NULL, consumer, NULL);
    fprintf(stderr,"Producer ID = %d, Consumer ID = %d\n",
        (int)prodtid, (int)constid);
                                        /* wait for the threads to finish */
    pthread_join(prodtid, NULL);
    pthread_join(constid, NULL);
    printf("The threads produced the sum   %d\n", sum);
                                                /* show correct value */
    total = 0.0;
    tp = (double) totalproduced;
    total = tp*(tp+1)*(2*tp+1)/6.0;
    if (tp > SUMSIZE)
        fprintf(stderr,"*** Overflow occurs for more than %d items\n",
            SUMSIZE);
    printf("The checksum for %4d items is %1.0f\n",
        totalproduced, total);
    exit(0);
}
```

_____ **Program 10.7** _____

The `pthread_mutex_lock` and `pthread_mutex_unlock` are *async-signal safe*, meaning they can be called from a signal handler. However, all of the threads must block the signal before acquiring such a mutex lock or the program may deadlock.

An alternative approach is to use a dedicated thread for signal handling. All threads except the dedicated thread block the signal in question. The dedicated thread does a `sigwait` on the specified signal.

SYNOPSIS

```
#include <signal.h>

int sigwait(sigset_t *sigmask, int *signo);
```
                                                                    POSIX.1c

---

The `sigwait` function blocks until the thread receives any of the signals specified by `*sigmask`. The `*signo` value is the number of the signal that caused the return from `sigwait`. The `sigwait` function returns 0 if the call was successful and −1 otherwise. It sets the `errno` in case of an error.

Note the differences between `sigwait` and `sigsuspend`. Both functions have a first parameter that is a pointer to a signal set (`sigset_t *`). For `sigsuspend`, this set holds the new signal mask and so the signals that are *not in* the set are the ones that can cause `sigsuspend` to return. For `sigwait`, this parameter holds the set of signals to be waited for, so the signals *in* the set are the ones that can cause the `sigwait` to return. In both cases, the program blocks the signals of interest before the call. With `sigsuspend`, the signal is delivered to the process and `sigsuspend` returns only after a normal return from the signal handler. With `sigwait`, the pending signal is removed without its being delivered, so no signal handler is necessary.

Program 10.8 shows a solution to the signal-driven bounded-buffer problem that uses a separate thread to wait for the `SIGUSR1` signal. The dedicated thread approach is simpler than the signal-handler approach in several respects. The threads are not restricted to calling async-signal safe functions, and the producer thread can be informed that it should exit while it is waiting for a slot to free up.

The main program in Program 10.8 blocks the `SIGUSR1` signal before creating any threads. Since the created threads inherit the signal mask, all of the threads have `SIGUSR1` blocked. The main program creates a dedicated thread to handle the signal. Program 10.8 was tested on a system that supported only preemptive priority scheduling. The thread that waits for the signal, `sigusr1_thread`, has a higher priority than the default to guarantee that `sigusr1_thread` gets in to catch the signal. When Program 10.8 executes on the same system without first increasing `sigusr1_thread`'s priority, the program still works correctly, but sometimes several seconds elapse between when the signal is generated and when it is caught. The priority is set by initializing a thread attribute to the default using `pthread_attr_init`, putting its priority in a variable, increasing the priority in that variable, resetting the priority of the attribute, and then creating the thread with this new attribute. If a round-robin scheduling policy were available, all of the threads could have the same priority.

The dedicated signal-handling thread, `sigusr1_thread`, displays its priority to confirm that the priority is set correctly and then calls `sigwait` on the `SIGUSR1` signal. No signal handler is needed since `sigwait` removes the signal from those pending. The signal is always blocked, so the default `SIGUSR1` handler (which would terminate the process) is never entered.

Program 10.8 is set up to be tested by sending the `SIGUSR1` to the process using the `kill` command from another window. The program starts by displaying its process ID and then starts the calculation as in Program 10.7. If left to its own, the program would overflow the integer used to store the sum after 1861 items in a fraction of a second on a fast machine. The function `spinit` slows down the program in various places. The parameter `SPIN` determines how long it spins and must be adjusted for the speed of the target machine. A sleep-type function would have made the program more portable, but it was not used since it could affect the scheduling of the threads.

Program 10.8: A solution to the signal-driven bounded-buffer problem using a dedicated thread.

```
#include <stdio.h>
#include <stdlib.h>
#include <unistd.h>
#include <signal.h>
#include <pthread.h>
#include <sched.h>
#define SUMSIZE 1861
#define BUFSIZE 8
#define SPIN 1000000

int sum = 0;
pthread_cond_t slots = PTHREAD_COND_INITIALIZER;
pthread_cond_t items = PTHREAD_COND_INITIALIZER;
pthread_mutex_t slot_lock = PTHREAD_MUTEX_INITIALIZER;
pthread_mutex_t item_lock = PTHREAD_MUTEX_INITIALIZER;
int nslots = BUFSIZE;
int producer_done = 0;
int nitems = 0;
int totalproduced = 0;
int producer_shutdown = 0;

void get_item(int *itemp);
void put_item(int item);
```

```
void spinit(void)
{
   int i;
   for (i = 0; i < SPIN; i++) ;
}

void *sigusr1_thread(void *arg)
{
   sigset_t intmask;
   struct sched_param param;
   int policy;

   sigemptyset(&intmask);
   sigaddset(&intmask, SIGUSR1);

   pthread_getschedparam(pthread_self(), &policy, &param);
   fprintf(stderr,
       "sigusr1_thread entered with policy %d and priority %d\n",
       policy, param.sched_priority);

   sigwait(&intmask);
   fprintf(stderr, "sigusr1_thread returned from sigwait\n");
   pthread_mutex_lock(&slot_lock);
      producer_shutdown = 1;
      pthread_cond_broadcast(&slots);
   pthread_mutex_unlock(&slot_lock);
   return NULL;
}

void *producer(void *arg1)
{
   int i;

   for (i = 1;   ; i++) {
       spinit();
       pthread_mutex_lock(&slot_lock);     /* acquire right to a slot */
          while ((nslots <= 0) && (!producer_shutdown))
             pthread_cond_wait (&slots, &slot_lock);
          if (producer_shutdown) {
             pthread_mutex_unlock(&slot_lock);
             break;
          }
          nslots--;
       pthread_mutex_unlock(&slot_lock);
       spinit();

       put_item(i*i);
       pthread_mutex_lock(&item_lock);    /* release right to an item */
          nitems++;
```

```
            pthread_cond_signal(&items);
        pthread_mutex_unlock(&item_lock);
        spinit();
        totalproduced = i;
    }
    pthread_mutex_lock(&item_lock);
        producer_done = 1;
        pthread_cond_broadcast(&items);
    pthread_mutex_unlock(&item_lock);
    return NULL;
}

void *consumer(void *arg2)
{
    int myitem;

    for ( ; ; ) {
        pthread_mutex_lock(&item_lock);    /* acquire right to an item */
            while ((nitems <=0) && !producer_done)
                cond_wait(&items, &item_lock);
            if ((nitems <= 0) && producer_done) {
                pthread_mutex_unlock(&item_lock);
                break;
            }
            nitems--;
        pthread_mutex_unlock(&item_lock);
        get_item(&myitem);
        sum += myitem;
        pthread_mutex_lock(&slot_lock);    /* release right to a slot */
            nslots++;
            cond_signal(&slots);
        pthread_mutex_unlock(&slot_lock);
    }
    return NULL;
}

void main(void)
{
    pthread_t prodtid;
    pthread_t constid;
    pthread_t sighandid;
    double total;
    double tp;
    sigset_t set;
    pthread_attr_t high_prio_attr;
    struct sched_param param;
    fprintf(stderr, "Process ID is %ld\n", (long)getpid());
                                            /* block the signal */
    sigemptyset(&set);
```

```
    sigaddset(&set, SIGUSR1);
    sigprocmask(SIG_BLOCK, &set, NULL);
    fprintf(stderr, "Signal blocked\n");
                                                    /* create threads */
    pthread_attr_init(&high_prio_attr);
    pthread_attr_getschedparam(&high_prio_attr, &param);
    param.sched_priority++;
    pthread_attr_setschedparam(&high_prio_attr, &param);
    pthread_create(&sighandid, &high_prio_attr, sigusr1_thread, NULL);
    pthread_create(&prodtid, NULL, producer, NULL);
    pthread_create(&constid, NULL, consumer, NULL);
                                        /* wait for the threads to finish */
    pthread_join(prodtid, NULL);
    pthread_join(constid, NULL);
    printf("The threads produced the sum   %d\n", sum);
                                                /* show correct value */
    tp = (double) totalproduced;
    total = tp*(tp + 1)*(2*tp + 1)/6.0;
    if (tp > SUMSIZE)
        fprintf(stderr, "*** Overflow occurs for more than %d items\n",
            SUMSIZE);
    printf("The checksum for %4d items is %1.0f\n",
        totalproduced, total);
    exit(0);
}
```

_____ **Program 10.8** _____

10.5 Exercise: Threaded Print Server

The `lp` command on most systems does not send a file directly to the specified printer. Instead `lp` sends the request to a process called a *print server* or a *printer daemon*. The print server places the request in a queue and makes available an identification number in case the user decides to cancel the print job. When a printer becomes free, the print server begins copying the file to the printer device. The file to be printed may not be copied to a temporary spool device unless the user explicitly specifies that it should be. Many implementations of `lp` try to create a hard link to the file while it is waiting to be printed so that the file cannot be removed completely. It is not always possible for `lp` to link to the file, and the man page warns the user not to change the file until after it is printed.

Example 10.8

> *The following UNIX* `lp` *command outputs the file* `myfile.ps` *to the printer designated as* `ps`.

```
lp -dps myfile.ps
```

The `lp` *command might respond with a request number similar to the follow-ing.*

```
Request ps-358 queued
```

Use the `ps-358` *in a* `cancel` *command to delete the job.*

Printers are slow devices relative to process execution times, and one print server process can handle many printers. Like the problem of handling input from multiple descriptors, print serving is a natural for multithreading. Figure 10.3 shows a schematic organization of a threaded print server. The server uses a dedicated thread to read user requests from an input source. The request thread allocates space for the request and adds it to the request queue.

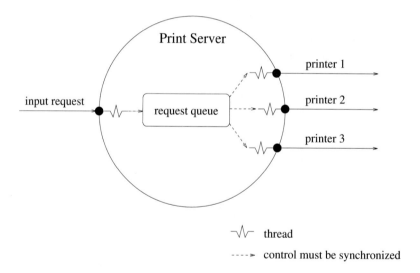

Figure 10.3: A schematic of a threaded print server.

The print server of Figure 10.3 also has dedicated threads for handling its printers. Each printer thread removes a request from the request queue and copies the file specified in the request to the printer. When the copying is complete, the printer thread frees the request and handles another request.

The threads within the print server require producer-consumer synchronization with a single producer (the request thread) and multiple consumers (the printer threads). The queue itself must be protected with mutexes so that items are removed and added in a consistent manner. The consumers must synchronize on the requests available in the queue, so that they do not attempt to remove nonexistent requests. The request queue is not bounded, because the request thread dynamically allocates space for requests as they come in. The request thread could also use a *high-water mark* to limit the number of requests that it queues before blocking. In this more complicated situation, the request thread synchronizes on a predicate involving the size of the queue.

Several aspects of the print server are simplified for this exercise. In a real server, input is redirected from a certain network port or the requests are done by remote procedure calls. There is no requirement for printers to be identical, and realistic print requests allow a variety of options for users to specify how the printing is to be done. The system administrator can install default filters that act on files of particular types. The print server can analyze request types and direct requests to the best printer for the job. Printer requests may be allowed to have priorities or other characteristics that affect the way in which they are printed. The individual printer threads should respond to error conditions and status reports from the printer device drivers.

This exercise describes the print server represented schematically in Figure 10.3. Keep pending requests in a request queue. Synchronize the number of pending requests with a condition variable called `items` in a manner similar to the standard producer-consumer problem. This exercise does not require a condition variable for `slots` since the request queue can grow arbitrarily large.

- Represent print requests by an integer user ID followed by a string specifying the full pathname of the file to be printed.

- Represent the request queue by a linked list of nodes of type `prcmd_t`. A sample definition is

```
typedef struct pr_struct {
    int owner;
    char filename[PATH_MAX];
    struct pr_struct *next_prcmd;
} prcmd_t;
static prcmd_t *pr_head = NULL;
static prcmd_t *pr_tail = NULL;
static int pending_requests = 0;
static pthread_mutex_t prmutex = PTHREAD_MUTEX_INITIALIZER;
```

Put the request queue data structures in a separate file and access them only through the following functions.

> The `add_queue` function adds a node to the request queue. It has prototype

```
int add_queue(prcmd_t *node);
```

The `add_queue` increments `pending_requests` and inserts the node at the end of the request queue. It returns 0 on success and -1

on failure.

➤ The `remove_queue` function removes a node from the request queue. It has prototype

```
int remove_queue(prcmd_t **node);
```

If the queue is not empty, the `remove_queue` function decrements `pending_requests` and removes the first node from the request queue. It sets `*node` to point to the removed node. The `remove_queue` returns 0 if it successfully removed a node or −1 if the queue is empty.

➤ The `get_number_requests` returns the size of the request queue, which is the value of `pending_requests`. It has prototype

```
int get_number_requests(void);
```

• Define a condition variable called `items` and an associated mutex lock called `items_lock`.

• Write the following function that is called as a thread to enqueue input requests:

```
void *get_requests(void *arg);
```

The `get_requests` function adds incoming requests to the printer request queue. The parameter `arg` points to an open file descriptor from where the requests are read. The `get_requests` reads the user ID and the pathname of the file to be printed, creates a `prcmd_t` node to hold the information, and calls `add_queue` to add the request to the printer request list. The `get_request` function then signals on the condition variable `items` to inform waiting printer threads that requests are available. If `get_request` fails to allocate space for `prcmd_t` or if it detects an end-of-file, it returns. Otherwise, it continues to monitor the open file descriptor for the next request.

• Write a main program to test `get_requests`. The main program creates the `get_requests` thread with `STDIN_FILENO` as the input file. It then goes into a loop in which it waits for `pending_requests` to become nonzero. Use the condition variable `items` and its associated mutex lock to synchronize with the `get_requests` thread. The main thread removes the next request from the queue and outputs the user ID and the filename to standard output. Run the program with input requests typed from the keyboard. Also test the program with standard input redirected from a file.

• Write a function called `printer` which removes a request from the printer request queue and "prints" it. The prototype for `printer` is

```
void *printer(void *arg);
```

The parameter `arg` points to an open file descriptor to which `printer` outputs the file to be printed. The `printer` function waits for the counter `pending_requests` to become nonzero in a manner similar to the loop of the main program in the previous step. Use the condition variable `items` and its associated mutex to access `pending_requests` properly. When a request is available, remove the request from the queue, open the file specified by the `filename` field for reading, and copy the contents of the file to the output file. Then close the input file, free the space occupied by the request node, and resume waiting for more requests. If an error is encountered in reading the input file, output an appropriate error message, close the input file, and resume waiting for more requests. Since the output file plays the role of the printer in this exercise, an output error corresponds to a printer failure. If `printer` encounters an error on output, close the output file, output an appropriate error message, and return.

- Write a new main program to implement the print server. The server supports a maximum of `MAX_PRINT` printers. (Five should suffice for testing.) The main program takes two command-line arguments: the output file basename and the number of printers. The input requests are taken from standard input which may be redirected to take requests from a file. The output for each printer goes to a separate file whose filename starts with the output file basename. For example if the basename is `printer.out`, the output files are `printer.out.1`, `printer.out.2`, and so on. The main program creates a thread to run `get_requests` and a `printer` thread for each printer to be supported. It then waits for all of the threads to exit before exiting itself. Thoroughly test the print server.

- Add facilities so that each `printer` thread keeps track of statistics such as total number of files output and total number of bytes output. When the server receives a `SIGUSR1` signal, it outputs the statistics for all of the printers to standard error. Handle the `SIGUSR1` signal by adding a thread that does a `sigwait` on `SIGUSR1`, acquires the appropriate locks, and outputs the statistics. All other threads including the main thread should block `SIGUSR1`.

- Add facilities so that the input now includes a command as well as a user ID and filename. The commands are

`lp:`	Add the request to the queue and output a request ID to standard output.
`cancel:`	Remove the request from the queue if it is there
`lpstat:`	Output a summary of all of the pending requests and of the requests currently being printed on each printer.

Add appropriate functions to the queue file as needed. The `lp` command writes a request number to standard output which can be used by later `cancel` commands.

- Add synchronization so that `get_request` uses a `high_water_mark` and `low_water_mark` to control the size of the request queue. Once the number of requests reaches the `high_water_mark` value, the `get_request` blocks until the size of the request queue is less than `low_water_mark`.

10.6 Additional Reading

Most classical books on operating systems discuss some variation of the producer-consumer problem. See, for example, [80, 92]. Unfortunately in most classic treatments, producers and consumers loop forever, uninterrupted by signals or other complications that arise from a finite universe. The upcoming book *Programming with Threads* [44] has a comprehensive section on signal handling with threads. The *Solaris Multithreaded Programming Guide* [100], while dealing primarily with Solaris threads, contains some interesting examples of synchronization.

Chapter 11

Project: *The Not Too Parallel Virtual Machine*

Grace Murray Hopper, a vocal early advocate of parallel computing, was fond of reminding her audiences that the way to pull a heavier load was not to grow a bigger ox. The prospect of harnessing cheap workstations to solve large problems has become increasingly appealing, but the difficulties in providing software to coordinate the activity of these machines continue to prevent widespread use. PVM (Parallel Virtual Machine) provides a high-level, but not transparent, system for a user to coordinate tasks spread across workstations on a network. This project compares two approaches for implementing the Not Too Parallel Virtual Machine (NTPVM) dispatcher which is a simplified PVM system. The single-threaded approach uses `select` or `poll` to manage file descriptors, while the multithreaded approach allocates a dedicated thread for each input descriptor. The latter approach simplifies the logic and enhances parallelism.

Programming systems such as PVM (Parallel Virtual Machine) [87] and Linda [18] use groups of heterogeneous, interconnected machines to provide a transparent parallel-computing environment. These systems allow users to solve large problems on networks of workstations by providing the illusion of a single parallel machine. Linda is based on a tuple-space programming model and provides a distributed shared-memory abstraction, while PVM operates at the task level and provides a message-passing abstraction. In either case, the user perceives a single, unified system and the details of the network and

401

individual machines that make up the *virtual machine* are not directly visible. This chapter concentrates on a PVM-like implementation, while Chapter 15 explores the Linda paradigm.

The basic unit of computation in PVM is called a *task* and is analogous to a UNIX process. A PVM program calls PVM library functions to create and coordinate tasks. The tasks can communicate by passing messages to other tasks through calls to PVM library functions. Tasks that cooperate either through communication or synchronization are organized into groups called *computations*. PVM supports direct communication, broadcast, and barriers within a computation.

Figure 11.1 shows a logical view of a typical PVM application. A PVM application generally starts with an input and partitioning task which controls how the problem is going to be solved. The user specifies in this task how other tasks cooperate to solve a problem. The input and partitioning task creates several computations. Tasks within each computation share data and communicate with each other. The PVM application also has a dedicated task to handle output and user display. The other tasks in the PVM application forward their output to this task for display on the application's console.

To run a PVM application, a user first designates the pool of machines or *hosts* that make up the *virtual machine* and then starts the PVM control daemon, pvmd, on each of these hosts. The control daemon communicates with the user's console and handles communication and control of tasks on its machine. To send input to a particular task, PVM sends the data to the pvmd daemon on the destination host which then forwards it

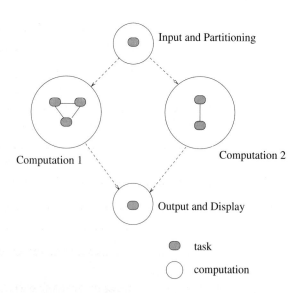

Figure 11.1: A logical view of an application running on a PVM virtual machine.

to the appropriate task. Similarly, a task outputs by sending a message to its pvmd which in turn forwards it to the console's pvmd which in turn forwards it to the application's output task. The underlying message passing is transparent, so the user sees only that a particular task has sent a message to the console. Figure 11.2 shows how an application is mapped onto the virtual machine. The tasks that make up a logical computation are not necessarily mapped to the same host but might be spread across all of the hosts on the virtual machine.

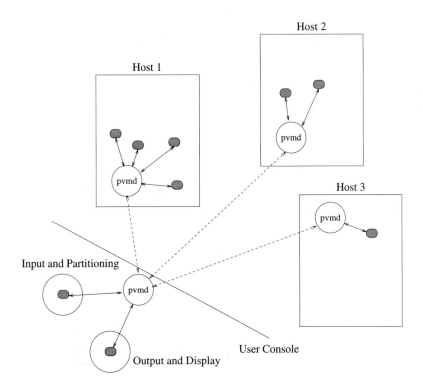

Figure 11.2: A schematic of a PVM virtual machine.

11.1 The Not Too Parallel Virtual Machine

The Not Too Parallel Virtual Machine (NTPVM) is a dispatcher which shares many characteristics of a PVM control daemon, pvmd. The NTPVM dispatcher is responsible for creating and managing tasks as shown schematically in Figure 11.3. The dispatcher receives requests through its standard input and responds through its standard output. (Later standard input and standard output can be redirected to network communication ports.) The dispatcher might receive a request to create a task or to forward data to a task under its control.

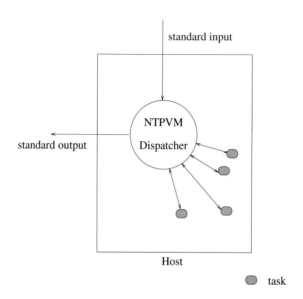

Figure 11.3: A schematic of the NTPVM dispatcher.

A task is just a process which executes a specified program. Each task is identified by a computation ID and a task ID. When the dispatcher receives a request to create a task with a particular computation ID and task ID, it creates a pair of pipes and forks a child to execute the task. Figure 11.4 shows the communication layout between a task and its dispatcher. The pipe that carries communication from the dispatcher to the child task is labeled `writefd` on the dispatcher end. The child redirects its standard input to this pipe. Similarly the pipe that carries communication from the child to the dispatcher is labeled `readfd` on the dispatcher end. The child redirects its standard output to this pipe.

The dispatcher supports the delivery of data to the tasks, delivery of output from the tasks, broadcast to tasks that have the same computation ID, numbered barriers for tasks with the same computation ID, and cancellation. NTPVM is simpler than the real PVM in several respects. PVM has in-order message delivery and allows any task to communicate with other tasks in its computation. It has a buffering mechanism for holding messages. PVM also provides sophisticated computation monitoring tools. NTPVM delivers messages whenever it gets them, does not support point-to-point task communication, and has primitive monitoring capabilities.

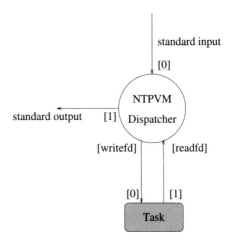

Figure 11.4: The NTPVM dispatcher communicates with its children via pipes.

11.2 NTPVM Project Overview

This chapter specifies two implementations of the Not Too Parallel Virtual Machine. One version, designated A, has a single thread of execution and uses `select` or `poll` to manage multiple file descriptors. The other version, designated B, is multithreaded. Try to do the first few parts of both versions, and then choose additional parts to implement from either the A series or the B series.

The tasks in NTPVM are independent processes grouped into units called computations. The dispatcher is responsible for creating and managing tasks. In general, the tasks of a computation do not have to reside on the same machine, and the specification of the project is designed with this extension in mind. However, a single dispatcher controls all of the computations for the project described in this chapter.

The dispatcher communicates with the outside world by reading packets from its standard input and writing packets to its standard output. The dispatcher might receive a packet indicating that it should create a new task, or it might receive a data packet intended for a task under its control. The dispatcher forwards output generated by the tasks under its control to its own standard output in the form of packets. For the first parts of the project, the tasks send ASCII data and the dispatcher wraps the data in a packet. Later, the tasks generate the packets themselves.

Program 11.1 shows the `ntpvm.h` header file which contains the relevant type definitions for the dispatcher. Include this file in all of the programs in this project.

Program 11.1: The `ntpvm.h` header file.

```
typedef enum ptype {START_TASK, DATA, BROADCAST, DONE,
                    TERMINATE, BARRIER} packet_t;

typedef struct {
      int comp_id;
      int task_id;
      packet_t type;
      int length;
} task_packet_t;

typedef struct {
      int comp_id;                    /* computation ID for task */
      int task_id;                      /* task ID for the task */
      int writefd;               /* holds dispatcher->child fd */
      int readfd;                /* holds child->dispatcher fd */
      int total_packs_sent;
      int total_bytes_sent;
      int total_packs_recv;
      int total_bytes_recv;
      pid_t task_pid;           /* process ID of the forked task */
      int barrier; /* -1 if not at barrier, else barrier number */
      int end_of_input;        /* true if no more input for task */
} task_t;

#define MAX_PACK_SIZE 1024
#define MAX_TASKS 10
```

_____ **Program 11.1** _____

The dispatcher packets have the following format:

- A computation ID.
- A task ID.
- A packet type.
- The length of the packet information.
- The packet information.

The first four items in a packet make up a fixed-length *packet header* which is stored in a structure of type `task_packet_t`. Assume that the information portion of the packet contains no more than `MAX_PACK_SIZE` bytes.

The dispatcher keeps information about each active task in a global `tasks` array of type `task_t`. Do not allow the dispatcher to execute more than `MAX_TASKS` simultaneous tasks. The `tasks` array is declared by

```
task_t tasks[MAX_TASKS];
```

Initially set the `comp_id` member of each element of the `tasks` array to -1 indicating that the slot is empty. When the dispatcher creates a task, it finds an empty slot in the `tasks` array to hold the relevant information about the new task.

There are six types of dispatcher packets in all: `START_TASK`, `DATA`, `BROADCAST`, `DONE`, `TERMINATE`, and `BARRIER`. The dispatcher interprets these packet types as follows:

- When the dispatcher receives a `START_TASK` on standard input, it initiates a new task. The information portion of this packet gives the command line to be `execvp`'d by the forked child task. The dispatcher creates two pipes (the `readfd` and `writefd` of Figure 11.4) and forks a child to `execvp` the specified command.

- `DATA` packets passed to the dispatcher from standard input are treated as input data for the task identified by the computation ID and task ID members of the packet header. For the first few parts of the project, the dispatcher strips off the packet header and writes the actual packet data to `writefd` of the appropriate task.

- When a task writes data to its standard output, the dispatcher forwards the data to standard output. The first parts of this project run standard UNIX utilities as the tasks. Since these commands produce just ASCII text as output, the dispatcher packages the data into `DATA` packets before sending it to standard output.

- When the dispatcher receives a `DONE` packet on standard input, it closes the `writefd` file descriptor for the task identified by the computation ID and task ID members of the packet header. The corresponding task then detects end-of-file on its standard input.

- When the dispatcher detects an end-of-file on the `readfd` of a task, it performs the appropriate cleanup and sends a `DONE` packet on standard output indicating that the task has completed.

- The dispatcher forwards any `BROADCAST` packets from standard input to all tasks in the specified computation.

- If a task sends a `BROADCAST` packet to the dispatcher, the dispatcher forwards the request to all tasks in the same computation and also forwards the request on its standard output. In this way, all of the tasks within a computation receive the message.

- If the dispatcher receives a `TERMINATE` packet on its standard input, it kills the task identified by the packet computation ID and task ID.

- The `BARRIER` packets synchronize tasks of a computation at a particular point in their execution.

The NTPVM project has the following parts:

Part I: Setup of I/O and testing [Section 11.3].

Part II: Single task with no input (handle START_TASK and outgoing data) [Section 11.4].

Part III: One task at a time (handle START_TASK, DATA, and DONE packets) [Section 11.5].

Part IV: Multiple tasks and computations (handle START_TASK, DATA, and DONE packets) [Section 11.6].

Part V: Handling BROADCAST and BARRIER packets [Section 11.7].

Part VI: Handling TERMINATION packets and signals [Section 11.8].

In the first parts of the project, the child tasks do not communicate using packets, and the dispatcher strips off the packet headers before writing to writefd. This format allows the dispatcher to run ordinary UNIX utilities such as cat or ls as tasks. In Part V the tasks communicate with the dispatcher using packets. At that point the project requires specific task programs for NTPVM testing. The remainder of this section gives examples of different types of packets and how the dispatcher should handle them.

11.2.1 START_TASK Packets

The NTPVM dispatcher receives commands from its standard input (denoted by [0]) and reports results via its standard output (denoted by [1]). The dispatcher waits for a START_TASK packet from standard input. Such a packet includes a computation ID, a task ID, and a command-line string.

Example 11.1

The following START_TASK *packet requests that task two in computation three be created to execute* ls -l.

Computation ID:	3
Task ID:	2
Packet Type:	START_TASK
Packet Data Length:	5
Packet Information:	ls -l

The data contained in the packet of Example 11.1 is not a null-terminated string. The dispatcher must convert the data to such a string before handing it to makeargv or execvp.

The dispatcher selects a free entry in the tasks array to store the information about the new task and initializes the total_packs_sent, total_bytes_sent, total_packs_recv, total_bytes_recv, and end_of_input members of the `tasks` array entry to 0. It also initializes the `barrier` member to −1 to indicate that the task is not waiting at a barrier.

The dispatcher then creates two pipes for two-way communication with a task child. The dispatcher uses two of the four resulting pipe file descriptors for communication with the child task. These descriptors are stored in the `readfd` and `writefd` members of the `tasks` array entry. The dispatcher forks a child and stores the child process ID in the `task_pid` member of the `tasks` entry. It closes unused pipe file descriptors. The dispatcher then waits for I/O either from its standard input or from the `readfd` descriptors of its tasks.

When the child is forked, it redirects its standard input and output to the pipes and closes the unused file descriptors. The child then `execvp`'s the command to perform the task. Use the `makeargv` function of Program 1.2 to create an argument array for input to `execvp`.

11.2.2 DATA Packets

When a `DATA` packet arrives on standard input, the dispatcher checks to see if it has a task with matching task ID and computation ID. If there is no match, the packet is discarded. If there is a match, the dispatcher updates the `total_packs_recv` and `total_bytes_recv` members of the task's entry in the `tasks` array. For the first parts of the project, the tasks are standard UNIX utilities that accept ASCII input. The dispatcher forwards the information portion of the packet to the task on the task's `writefd` descriptor. In Parts V and VI, the tasks receive the full data packets directly.

Example 11.2

After receiving the following `DATA` *packet, the dispatcher sends the words* `This is my data` *to task two in computation three.*

Computation ID:	3
Task ID:	2
Packet Type:	DATA
Packet Data Length:	15
Packet Data:	This is my data

The dispatcher also forwards data received from individual tasks to its standard output in the form of `DATA` packets. For the first few parts of the project, the dispatcher interprets input from `readfd` as raw input from the task. It creates a `DATA` packet with the task's computation ID and task ID and uses the information read from `readfd` as the information portion of the packet. The dispatcher then writes the `DATA` packet to standard output. Starting with Section 11.7, each task reads and writes its data in packet format.

11.2.3 DONE Packets

When the dispatcher receives a DONE packet on standard input, it sets the corresponding task's end_of_input member in the tasks array and closes the writefd descriptor for the task. The dispatcher discards any additional DONE or DATA packets that arrive for the task.

Example 11.3

The following DONE packet indicates that there is no more input data for task two in computation three.

Computation ID:	3
Task ID:	2
Packet Type:	DONE
Packet Data Length:	0
Packet Data:	NULL

When the dispatcher receives an end-of-file indication on readfd, it closes that descriptor and forwards a DONE packet on standard output. If the writefd descriptor for the task is still open, the dispatcher closes it. The dispatcher must eventually perform a wait on the child task process and set the comp_id member of the tasks array entry to −1 so that the array entry can be reused.

If the dispatcher receives an end-of-file indication on its standard input, it closes the writefd descriptors of all active tasks and sets the end_of_input member of each active task to 1. When it has received an end-of-file indication on the readfd descriptors for all active tasks, the dispatcher waits for each task and exits.

11.3 I/O and Testing of Dispatcher

This section develops dispatcher I/O functions and debugging layout. The dispatcher receives input data from standard input by calling get_packet and sends output data on standard output by calling put_packet as shown in Figure 11.5. The data is always transferred in two parts. First, the dispatcher reads or writes a header of type task_packet_t. Second, it uses the length member in the header to determine how many bytes of packet information to read or to write. Finally, it reads or writes the data portion of the packet. Assume that the packet information field contains no more than MAX_PACK_SIZE bytes so that the dispatcher can use a fixed-length buffer of MAX_PACK_SIZE bytes to hold the packet information during input and output.

The get_packet function has the following prototype:

```
int get_packet(int fd, int *comp_idp, int *task_idp,
               packet_t *typep, int *lenp, unsigned char *buf);
```

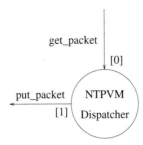

Figure 11.5: Basic dispatcher I/O.

The `get_packet` function reads a `task_packet_t` header from `fd` and then reads the number of bytes specified by the `length` member into `buf`. The `get_packet` returns 0 if successful or -1 if there is an error. The `get_packet` function sets `*comp_idp`, `*task_idp`, `*typep`, and `*lenp` from the `comp_id`, `task_id`, `type`, and `length` members of the packet header, respectively.

The `put_packet` function has the following prototype:

```
int put_packet(int fd, int comp_id, int task_id,
               packet_t type, int len, unsigned char *buf);
```

The `put_packet` function assembles a `task_packet_t` header from `comp_id`, `task_id`, `type`, and `len`. It then writes the packet header to `fd` followed by `len` bytes from `buf`. The `put_packet` returns 0 if successful or -1 if there is an error.

Example 11.4

The following program uses `get_packet` *and* `put_packet` *to copy packets from standard input to standard output.*

```
#include <stdio.h>
#include <unistd.h>
#include "ntpvm.h"

int get_packet(int, int *, int *, packet_t *, int *, unsigned char *);
int put_packet(int, int, int, packet_t, int, unsigned char *);

void main(void)
{
    int in, out;
    int comp_id;
    int task_id;
    packet_t type;
    int len;
    unsigned char buf[MAX_PACK_SIZE];
```

```
    in = STDIN_FILENO;
    out = STDOUT_FILENO;
    while (get_packet(in, &comp_id, &task_id, &type, &len, buf) != -1) {
        if (put_packet(out, comp_id, task_id, type, len, buf) == -1)
            break;
    }
}
```

The specification for Part I of the project is

- Convert the code segment of Example 11.4 into a main program.
- Write the `get_packet` and `put_packet` functions.
- Compile and lint the program to make sure that there are no syntax errors.
- Test the program using named pipes as described below.
- Add debugging messages to the loop of the main program to indicate what values are being read and written. All debugging messages should go to standard error.

The hardest part of the NTPVM project is the testing of the dispatcher. The dispatcher communicates with standard input and standard output using packets that have non-ASCII components. During debugging, the dispatcher should produce messages on standard error indicating its progress. A small amount of work is needed to isolate the dispatcher output and input from the informatory messages by directing the three types of I/O to appear in ASCII format on different screens.

Start with the two simple filters, `a2ts` and `ts2a`, shown in Program 11.2 and Program 11.3, respectively. The `a2ts` filter reads ASCII characters from standard input, constructs a task packet, and writes it to standard output. For interactive use, `a2ts` prompts for the required information sending the prompts to standard error. The `ts2a` filter reads a task packet from standard input and writes the contents of the packet to standard output in ASCII format. For this project, assume that the information portion of a task packet always contains ASCII information.

Program 11.2: The filter `a2ts` prompts for information and sends a packet to standard output.

```
/*
 * This filter converts ASCII text to task packets.
 * It takes prompts for three integers using standard error:
 *     comp_id, task_id, type,
 * The three integers are in free format.
 *
 * The ASCII text must be a collection of lines
 * terminated by a line containing only 5 !'s.
 * The ASCII text must consist of full lines.
```

```
 *
 * This function is meant to be used by someone knowledgeable,
 *  so error checking is minimal.
 */
#include <stdio.h>
#include <stdlib.h>
#include <unistd.h>
#include <string.h>
#include "ntpvm.h"
#define MAX_LINE_SIZE 100
#define TERMINATE_STRING "!!!!!"

void main(void)
{
    task_packet_t pack;
    int type_int;
    int wsize;
    int line_len;
    char buf[MAX_PACK_SIZE + MAX_LINE_SIZE];
    char *bufptr;


    wsize = sizeof(task_packet_t);
    fprintf(stderr, "Ready for first packet\n");
    for( ; ; ) {
        fprintf(stderr, "Enter comp_id:");
        if (scanf("%d", &pack.comp_id) == EOF) {
            fprintf(stderr, "Exiting ...\n");
            break;
        }
        fprintf(stderr, "Enter task_id:");
        scanf("%d", &pack.task_id);
        fprintf(stderr, "Enter task type:\n");
        fprintf(stderr, "   0 = START_TASK\n");
        fprintf(stderr, "   1 = DATA\n");
        fprintf(stderr, "   2 = BROADCAST\n");
        fprintf(stderr, "   3 = DONE\n");
        fprintf(stderr, "   4 = TERMINATE\n");
        fprintf(stderr, "   5 = BARRIER\n");
        scanf("%d", &type_int);
        pack.type = type_int;
        gets(buf);                          /* Skip new line after 3rd int */
        pack.length = 0;
        bufptr = buf;
        *bufptr = 0;
        fprintf(stderr, "Enter first line of data (%s to end):\n",
            TERMINATE_STRING);

        while (fgets(bufptr, MAX_LINE_SIZE+ 1, stdin) != NULL) {
```

```
           line_len = (int)strlen(bufptr);
           if (line_len == 0)
              continue;
           if (*(bufptr + line_len - 1) != '\n') {
              *(bufptr + line_len - 1) = '\n';
              *(bufptr + line_len) = 0;
              line_len++;
           }
           if ( (line_len == (strlen(TERMINATE_STRING) + 1)) &&
                !strncmp(bufptr,TERMINATE_STRING,line_len - 1) )
              break;
           bufptr = bufptr + line_len;
           pack.length = pack.length + line_len;
           if (pack.length >= MAX_PACK_SIZE) {
              fprintf(stderr, "**** Maximum packet size exceeded\n");
              exit(1);
           }
           fprintf(stderr,

              "Length %d received, total=%d, Enter line (%s to end):\n",
               line_len, pack.length, TERMINATE_STRING);
        }
        fprintf(stderr, "Writing packet header: %d %d %d %d\n",
            pack.comp_id, pack.task_id, (int)pack.type, pack.length);
        if (write(STDOUT_FILENO, &pack, wsize) != wsize) {
           fprintf(stderr, "Error writing packet\n");
           exit(1);
        }
        fprintf(stderr, "Writing %d bytes\n", pack.length);
        if (write(STDOUT_FILENO, buf, pack.length) != pack.length) {
           fprintf(stderr,"Error writing packet\n");
           exit(1);
        }
        fprintf(stderr, "Ready for next packet\n");
     }
     exit(0);
}
```

——————————————— **Program 11.2** ———————————————

Program 11.3: The `ts2a` filter reads a packet from standard input and displays the header and data on standard output in ASCII format.

```
/*
 * This filter reads task packets from standard input
 * and displays them in ASCII format at standard output.
 * Waiting messages appear on standard error.
```

```
*/
#include <stdio.h>
#include <stdlib.h>
#include <unistd.h>
#include "ntpvm.h"
#define MAX_LINE_SIZE 100

char *get_type_string(packet_t ptype)
{
    switch (ptype) {
        case START_TASK:
            return "Start Task";
        case DATA:
            return "Data";
        case BROADCAST:
            return "Broadcast";
        case DONE:
            return "Done";
        case TERMINATE:
            return "Terminate";
        case BARRIER:
            return "Barrier";
        default:
            return "Unknown";
    }
}

void main(void)
{
    task_packet_t pack;
    int wsize;
    char buf[MAX_PACK_SIZE + MAX_LINE_SIZE];
    char *type_string;
    int bytes_read;

    wsize = sizeof(task_packet_t);
    fprintf(stderr, "***** Waiting for first packet\n");
    for( ; ; ) {
        bytes_read =  read(STDIN_FILENO, &pack, wsize);
        if (bytes_read == 0) {
            fprintf(stderr, "End of File received\n");
            exit(0);
        }
        if (bytes_read != wsize) {
            fprintf(stderr, "Error reading packet header\n");
            exit(1);
        }
        type_string = get_type_string(pack.type);
        printf("Received packet header of type %s\n", type_string);
```

```
        printf("   comp_id = %d, task_id = %d, length = %d\n",
               pack.comp_id, pack.task_id, pack.length);
        fflush(stdout);
        if (pack.length > MAX_PACK_SIZE) {
            fprintf(stderr, "Task data is too long\n");
            exit(1);
        }
        if (read(STDIN_FILENO, buf, pack.length) != pack.length) {
            fprintf(stderr, "Error reading packet data\n");
            exit(1);
        }
        write(STDOUT_FILENO, buf, pack.length);
        fprintf(stderr, "***** Waiting for next packet\n");
    }
}
```

────────────────── **Program 11.3** ──────────────────

Example 11.5

The following command prompts for the fields of a packet. It then echoes the packet to standard output in ASCII format.

```
a2ts | ts2a
```

In Example 11.5 the `a2ts` program interactively prompts for packet information and outputs it to its standard output in binary format. The standard output of `a2ts` is piped into standard input of `ts2a`. The `ts2a` program reads binary packets from its standard input and outputs them in ASCII format to its standard output.

Example 11.6

The following command shows a possible method of testing the dispatcher interactively.

```
a2ts| dispatcher | ts2a
```

Example 11.6 pipes standard output of `a2ts` into standard input of the dispatcher and standard output of the dispatcher into `ts2a`. While the command of Example 11.6 allows a user to enter ASCII data and displays the task packet output in ASCII, it is not as useful as it can be because there is too much data coming to the screen from many different sources. It is difficult to distinguish what information is coming from which program. A better solution is to use a windowing system with three windows allocated to testing the dispatcher as shown in Figure 11.6. Use the *input window* to enter packets in ASCII format and to send them to the standard input of the dispatcher. Use the *output window* to display the packets coming from standard output of the dispatcher. The *dispatcher window* shows the standard-error output of the dispatcher indicating what the dispatcher is doing.

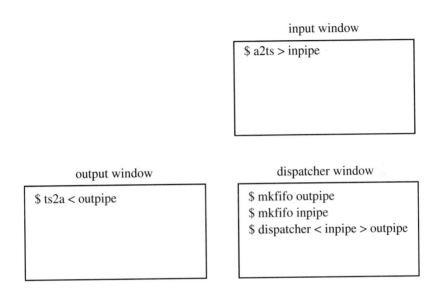

Figure 11.6: Use three windows to debug the NTPVM dispatcher.

Figure 11.6 shows the setup for the three windows. Be sure to use the same working directory in all three windows. The procedure for running the dispatcher is as follows:

- Create two named pipes in the dispatcher window by executing the following commands:

```
mkfifo outpipe
mkfifo inpipe
```

- Start the dispatcher in the dispatcher window by executing the following command:

```
dispatcher < inpipe > outpipe
```

This window displays only the messages that the dispatcher sends to standard error, since both standard input and standard output are redirected.

- In the output window, execute the following command:

```
ts2a < outpipe
```

This window displays the packets coming from the standard output of the dispatcher.

- In the input window, execute the following command:

    ```
    a2ts > inpipe
    ```

    This window displays the prompts for the user to enter packets. The `a2ts` program converts the entered information from ASCII to packet format and writes it to the standard input of the dispatcher.

Figure 11.7 shows the layout of the windows for the debugging. If a workstation that supports multiple windows is not available, try to persuade your system administrator to install a program such as `screen` which supports multiple screens on an ASCII terminal.

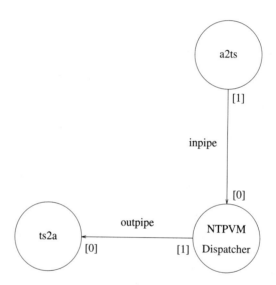

Figure 11.7: Logical process layout for debugging the dispatcher.

11.4 Single Task with No Input

This part of the project uses a single task that has no input to allow testing of the code to create the task and the pipes for communication without the added complication of monitoring multiple file descriptors for input.

The dispatcher reads a single `START_TASK` packet from standard input, creates the appropriate pipes, and forks the child task. The dispatcher then monitors the `readfd` pipe file descriptor for output from the task and forwards what it reads as `DATA` packets on standard output. When the dispatcher encounters an end-of-file on `readfd`, it waits for the child task to exit and then exits. The dispatcher has the following structure:

```
get_packet(STDIN_FILENO, &comp_id, &task_id, &type, &len, buf);
if (type != START_TASK)
    /* handle expecting a START_TASK error */
else {
    /* create the pipes ... */
    /* fork the child for the task ... */
    /* close the unneeded descriptors ... */
    while ((nbytes = read(readfd, buf, MAX_PACK_SIZE)) > 0) {
        if (put_packet(STDOUT_FILENO, comp_id, task_id,
                    DATA, nbytes, buf) == -1)
            break;
    }
}
```

Implement the NTPVM dispatcher as described above. The dispatcher has the following specification:

- Read a packet from standard input using `get_packet`. If the packet is not a `START_TASK` packet, then exit after outputting an error message.
- Create the appropriate pipes for communication with a child task.
- Fork a child to `execvp` the command given in the `START_TASK` packet of step 1. Use the `makeargv` function of Program 1.2 to construct the argument array in the child.
- Close all unneeded pipe descriptors so that the parent can detect end-of-file on `readfd`.
- Wait for output from the child on `readfd`. For testing, assume that the child outputs only text. The dispatcher reads the child task's output from `readfd`, wraps this output in a `DATA` packet, and sends the packet to standard output by calling `put_packet`.
- If an end-of-file on `readfd` occurs, close the `readfd` and `writefd` descriptors for the task. Send a `DONE` packet to standard output identifying the task.

The child task redirects its standard input and output to the appropriate pipes before it `execvp`'s the requested command. Be sure to close all unnecessary file descriptors before doing the `execvp`.

The dispatcher should use standard error liberally to display informatory messages about what it is doing. For example, when it receives something from a `readfd`, the dispatcher should display information about the task it was from, the number of bytes read, and the message read. It is worthwhile to invest time in designing a readable layout for the informative messages, so that all of the relevant information is available at a glance. Test the program by using `ls -l` as the command to be `execvp`'d.

11.5 Sequential Tasks

This section describes the behavior of the dispatcher when the child task has both input
and output. Although the dispatcher handles only one task at a time, it must monitor two
input file descriptors. Complete Section 11.4 before starting this part.

    The dispatcher keeps information about the child task in the `tasks` array. For sim-
plicity, the discussion refers to members of the `task_t` array such as `readfd` without
their qualifying structure. Implement the `tasks` array as an object with appropriate
access functions. The `tasks` array and its access functions should be in a file separate
from the dispatcher main program. The array and its access functions are referred to as
the `tasks` object, and an individual element of the `tasks` array is referred to as an
entry in the `tasks` object.

11.5.1 Version A: Implementation of a Nonthreaded Dispatcher

Implement the single-task-at-a-time NTPVM dispatcher by executing the following algorithm in a loop:

- Monitor input file descriptors to data. To start, the dispatcher has its standard
  input as its only input file descriptor. Once a child task starts, the dispatcher
  also must monitor the child's output. Use `select` or `poll` to monitor the
  `STDIN_FILENO` and `readfd` file descriptors efficiently.
- If input is available on standard input, read a packet by calling the
  `get_packet` function. Handle the packets as follows:
    * If the packet is a `START_TASK` packet and the dispatcher is already
      executing a task, discard the packet and output an error message. If the
      dispatcher doesn't currently have a task, create the appropriate pipes,
      update the `tasks` object, and fork a child to `execvp` the command
      given in the packet. Use the `makeargv` function of Program 1.2 to
      construct the argument array.
    * If the packet is a `DATA` packet:
        ▪ If the packet's IDs don't match those of the executing task or if
          the task's `end_of_input` is true, output an error message and
          discard the packet.
        ▪ Otherwise, copy the data portion to `writefd`.
        ▪ Update the `total_packs_recv` and `total_bytes_recv`
          members of the appropriate entry in the `tasks` object.
    * If the packet is a `DONE` packet:
        ▪ If the packet's task ID and computation ID do not match those
          of the executing task, output an error message and discard the
          packet.

  ▪ Otherwise, close the `writefd` descriptor if it is still open.

  ▪ Set the `end_of_input` member for this task.

  * If the packet is of type `BROADCAST`, `BARRIER`, or `TERMINATE`, output an error message and discard the packet.

- If input is available from the child task on `readfd`:
  * Read the information and call `put_packet` to send a `DATA` packet on standard output.

  * Update the `total_packs_sent` and `total_bytes_sent`.

For testing, assume that the child outputs only text so that the child can `execvp` standard commands such as `ls` or `cat`.

- If an end-of-file occurs on the dispatcher's standard input and there is an active task, close the `writefd` descriptor, wait for the task to exit, and then exit the dispatcher.

- If an end-of-file occurs on `readfd`:
  * Close the `readfd` and `writefd` descriptors for the task.

  * Wait for the task to complete.

  * Send a `DONE` packet identifying the task to standard output.

  * Output the following information about the finished task to standard error:
    ▪ The computation ID.

    ▪ The task ID.

    ▪ The total bytes sent by the task.

    ▪ The total packets sent by the task.

    ▪ The total bytes received by the task.

    ▪ The total packets received by the task.

  * If an end-of-file has already been received on standard input, wait for the task to exit, and then exit the dispatcher.

  * If an end-of-file has not been received on the dispatcher's standard input, clear the `tasks` entry for this task by setting the `comp_id` member to -1 and go back and look for a `START_TASK` packet.

Test the program by starting tasks to execute various `cat` and `ls -l` commands. Try other filters such as `sort` to test the command-line parsing.

11.5.2 Version B: Implementation of a Threaded Dispatcher

Version A of this part of the project uses `select` or `poll` to block the dispatcher until input arrives from standard input or from the task via `readfd`. Version B uses threads.

One obvious question is how the `fork` system call interacts with threads. Recall that a `fork` results in a creation of a copy of the process. Which thread starts executing in the child of a multithreaded process? POSIX.1c specifies that the child has only one thread of execution—the thread that did the `fork`. (Sun Solaris threads use `fork1` to designate a `fork` that results in a single-threaded child process.)

Figure 11.8 shows the structure of the threaded version. The thread design suggested here has an *input thread* that monitors standard input and writes to the appropriate `writefd` descriptor. An *output thread* monitors the `readfd` descriptor for input from the child task and outputs to standard output.

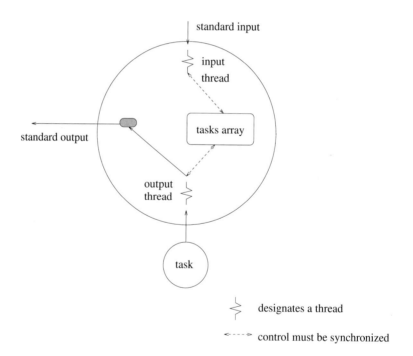

Figure 11.8: A schematic of a threaded NTPVM dispatcher.

The input and output threads share the `tasks` object and must synchronize their access to this structure. One possible mechanism for synchronizing threads is for a mutex lock to protect the entire `tasks` object. This choice cuts down on the potential parallelism, because only one thread at a time can access the `tasks` object. Since mutex locks are low cost, add a mutex lock member to the `task_t` definition. Each entry in the `tasks` object then has a member containing a mutex lock and a member containing the thread ID of the output thread for that task. The new `task_t` is now

```
typedef struct {
    int comp_id;                    /* computation ID for task */
    int task_id;                      /* task ID for the task */
    int writefd;                 /* holds dispatcher->child fd */
    int readfd;                  /* holds child->dispatcher fd */
    int total_packs_sent;
    int total_bytes_sent;
    int total_packs_recv;
    int total_bytes_recv;
    pid_t task_pid;             /* process ID of the forked task */
    pthread_t task_tid;      /* thread ID of task output thread */
    int barrier; /* -1 if not at barrier, else barrier number */
    int end_of_input;         /* true if no more input for task */
    pthread_mutex_t mlock;            /* mutex lock for element */
} task_t;
```

The `input_thread` monitors standard input and takes action according to the input it receives. The prototype for `input_thread` is

```
void *input_thread(void *arg);
```

The `arg` parameter is not used. Write an `input_thread` which executes the following steps in a loop until it encounters an end-of-file on standard input.

- Read a packet from standard input using `get_packet`.

- If the packet is a `START_TASK` and no task is already active:
    * Initialize the `tasks` object entry.

    * Create the appropriate pipes.

    * Update the `tasks` object entry.

    * Fork a child to `execvp` the command given in the packet. Use the `makeargv` function of Program 1.2 to construct the argument array.

    * Create `output_thread` thread by calling `pthread_create`. Pass the element number of the `tasks` object entry as an argument to the `output_thread`.

    * Update all appropriate fields in `tasks`.

- If the packet is a `START_TASK` and another task is already active, output an error message and discard the packet.

- If the packet is a DATA packet and the computation ID and task ID match the corresponding IDs of the currently active task, then send the information portion of the packet to the task by copying it to writefd. Update the total_packs_recv and total_bytes_recv entries of the tasks object.

- If the packet is a DONE packet and the computation ID and task ID match the corresponding IDs of the currently active task, close the writefd descriptor if it is still open and set the end_of_input member for this task.

- If any other type of packet is encountered, output an error message and discard the packet.

After falling through the loop, close the writefd and call pthread_exit.

The output_thread handles input from the readfd of a particular task. Its prototype is

```
void *output_thread(void *arg);
```

The arg parameter is a pointer to the entry in tasks for the particular task. Write an output_thread function that executes the following steps in a loop until it encounters an end-of-file on readfd.

- Read data from the readfd. The input_thread passes the entry number of the tasks object for which this thread is responsible to the thread as a parameter when it creates the thread. The thread finds out the readfd by looking it up in the tasks object entry.

- Call put_packet to construct a DATA packet and send it to standard output.

- Update the total_packs_sent and total_bytes_sent members of the appropriate entry in the tasks object.

After falling through the loop because of an end-of-file or an error on readfd, the output thread does the following.

- Close the readfd and writefd descriptors for the task.

- Perform a wait on the child task.

- Write a DONE packet with the appropriate computation ID and task ID to standard output.

- Deactivate the tasks entry by setting the computation ID to -1. (When the input_thread reuses the entry, it waits for this output_thread.)

- Call pthread_exit.

The resources in the `tasks` object are shared between the `input_thread` and the `output_thread`, so each thread must do a `pthread_mutex_lock` on the entry in the `tasks` object before accessing the resources. Write a main program that initializes the `tasks` object with the corresponding mutex locks and creates the `input_thread`.

The resources of a thread that has exited are not released until another thread joins with it or the process exits. The input thread joins with the output thread before reusing a `tasks` entry to limit the number of "zombie" threads during execution of the dispatcher.

11.6 Concurrent Tasks

Modify the program to allow multiple computations and tasks. Use a `MAX_TASKS` value of 10 for this part. A new `START_TASK` packet may come in before the data from previous tasks has been completely transmitted, so the dispatcher may be monitoring several file descriptors.

When a new `START_TASK` packet comes in, find an available entry in the `tasks` object, create a new set of pipes, and fork a new child to `execvp` the command. Assume that there are no duplicate computation or task IDs in header packets.

11.6.1 Version A: Implementation with `select` or `poll`

In order to service multiple tasks, Version A requires that the dispatcher add new file descriptors to the input file descriptor set when new tasks are created. Modify the Version A implementation from Section 11.5 to allow the dispatcher to handle up to `MAX_TASKS` tasks simultaneously. Consider carefully when the dispatcher should wait for child tasks to finish and at what point it is valid to free an entry of the `tasks` object.

11.6.2 Version B: Implementation with Threads

Figure 11.9 shows a schematic of a threaded NTPVM dispatcher. When another calculation request comes in, the input thread creates a new output thread. Since multiple output threads write to standard output, define an additional mutex lock to synchronize output on the dispatcher's standard output. Another issue to be addressed in the concurrent implementation is the cleanup process. The dispatcher eventually must wait for child tasks or the program accumulates defunct processes. Similarly, it must join with each `output_thread` before freeing the corresponding entry in the `tasks` object.

11.7 Broadcast and Barriers

Once the dispatcher handles multiple simultaneous tasks, implement the handling of the `BROADCAST` and `BARRIER` packets. The child tasks now have to communicate with the

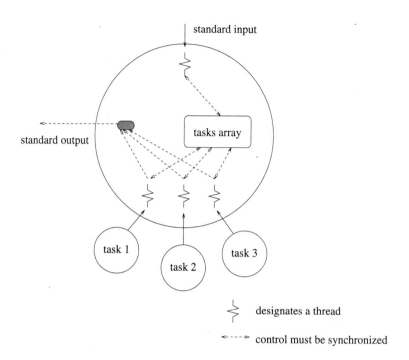

standard input

tasks array

standard output

task 1

task 2

task 3

designates a thread

control must be synchronized

Figure 11.9: A schematic of a threaded NTPVM dispatcher.

dispatcher in packet format so that the dispatcher and its tasks can distinguish control information (broadcast or barrier) from data information.

When the dispatcher receives a BROADCAST request from standard input, it forwards the packet on the writefd descriptors for each task whose computation ID matches that in the BROADCAST packet. If the dispatcher receives a BROADCAST request from one of the readfd descriptors, it forwards the packet on the writefd descriptors for each task whose computation ID matches that in the BROADCAST packet. Since in a future extension tasks from the computation may reside on other hosts, the dispatcher also forwards the packet on its standard output.

When the dispatcher receives a BARRIER packet from a task, it sets the barrier member for that task to the barrier number indicated by the packet data. When all of the tasks in a computation have indicated that they are waiting for the barrier, the dispatcher sends a BARRIER message on standard output.

When the dispatcher reads a BARRIER message for that barrier number from standard input, it resets the barrier member to -1 and sends a SIGUSR1 signal to all of the tasks in the computation. The BARRIER packet from standard input indicates that all tasks in the computation are waiting at the designated barrier and that they can be released. Assume that the dispatcher never receives a `BARRIER` message from standard input before it has forwarded a corresponding `BARRIER` packet on standard output.

Implement the barrier on the task side by blocking the `SIGUSR1` signal, writing a `BARRIER` packet to standard output, and then executing `sigsuspend` in a loop until the `SIGUSR1` signal arrives. Example 5.20 shows how this is done.

Write a dummy task program to generate appropriate broadcast and barrier messages.

11.8 Termination and Signals

Implement signal handling so that the dispatcher shuts down gracefully when it receives a `ctrl-c`. Also add code to kill a task when the dispatcher receives a `TERMINATE` packet for a particular task.

11.9 Additional Reading

The PVM system was developed by Oak Ridge National Laboratory and Emory University. The paper "PVM: A framework for parallel distributed computing" by V. S. Sunderam [87] provides an overview of the development and implementation of the PVM system. Other articles of interest include "Visualization and debugging in a heterogeneous environment" by Beguelin et al. [7] and "Experiences with network-based concurrent computing on the PVM system" by Geist and Sunderam [29]. The PVM distribution is available electronically from `netlib@ornl.gov`.

Part IV

Communication

Chapter 12

Client-Server Communication

In the client-server model, processes called servers provide services to clients on a network. Most local-area networks have file servers which manage common disk space, making it easier to share files and perform backups. Standard UNIX network services such as mail and file transfer also use the client-server paradigm. This chapter develops a special library called the Universal Internet Communication Interface (UICI) for simplifying client-server programming and shows how to program different client-server strategies in terms of UICI. The chapter then develops implementations of UICI in terms of three different UNIX communication mechanisms—sockets, TLI, and STREAMS. A side-by-side comparison of the implementations clarifies some of the differences between the mechanisms. POSIX does not yet standardize network communication, and this chapter follows the Spec 1170 version of sockets and TLI.

Many network applications and services such as mail, file transfer (`ftp`), authentication (Kerberos), remote login (`telnet`), and access to remote filesystems (NFS) are based on the client-server model. In that computational model, a client makes a request for a service to a server, and the server provides the service to clients. The server can be on the same machine or on a different machine, in which case communication takes place over a network.

Two classes of low-level communication protocols supporting the client-server paradigm are connection-oriented protocols and connectionless protocols. In the connection-oriented communication model, a server waits for a connection request from a client. Once a connection is established, communication takes place using handles (file descriptors), and the server address is not included in the user message. Connection-oriented protocols have setup overhead. An alternative approach is to use a connectionless protocol. The client sends a single message to a server. The server performs the service and returns a reply. This chapter emphasizes low-level connection-oriented client-server communication.

Both connectionless and connection-oriented protocols are considered to be low-level in that the request for service involves visible communication. The programmer is explicitly aware of the server and its location and must explicitly name the particular server to be accessed.

The naming of servers in a network environment is a difficult problem. The obvious method is to designate a server by its process ID and host ID. However, since the process ID is assigned chronologically at the time that the process starts running, it is difficult to know in advance the process ID of a particular process on a host. The most common naming convention is for servers to be named by small integers called ports. A server "listens" at a well-known port that has been designated in advance for a particular service. The client explicitly specifies a host address and a port number on the host when setting up the connection.

Chapter 14 discusses the intermediate-level naming services provided by remote procedure calls (RPCs). While still requiring explicit specification of the host, RPCs allow a user to request a particular service on the host by name rather than by port number. One of the goals of a distributed operating systems is to provide a unified user interface to system services across the network. Ideally, more than one server on the network could perform a particular service. It would be convenient to request the service by name and have the system designate the server. Unfortunately, that type of high-level interface is not yet part of UNIX.

12.1 Client-Server Strategies

The simplest client-server communication takes place over a single communication port such as shown in Figure 12.1. If the client and server share a filesystem and are executing on the same machine, the single port can be a FIFO. On a network, that port can be a socket or TLI connection.

When the server starts up, it opens its well-known FIFO (or socket connection to a well-known port) and waits for client requests. When a client needs a service, it opens the FIFO (or a socket connection to the server's well-known port) and writes its request. The server then performs the service. This approach works fine as long as there is only one client and the client does not require a reply. If there is more than one client, a convention for sending the client's process ID must be established so that the requests from different clients can be distinguished. (Of course it would be convenient if the identification mechanism prevented clients from forging another user's ID and claiming to be someone else.)

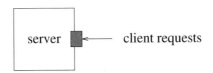

Figure 12.1: A server receives client requests from a single, well-known port.

A single port will not do in the case where the client requires a response from the server, because there is no mechanism for the client to obtain the correct response. Suppose the server uses a single FIFO for responses. Since items are removed from the FIFO when they are read and there is nothing to prevent a client from taking someone else's request, each client needs its own channel for responses to the server as shown in Figure 12.2.

In the FIFO implementation the server can open a client-specific FIFO by incorporating the client process ID into the name of the response FIFO. The client makes a request that includes its (unforgable) ID and opens an agreed upon FIFO for reading the server's response. The server must be sure to create such a response FIFO with the appropriate permissions so that an unfriendly client cannot steal responses meant for someone else.

The socket implementation has a `recvfrom` call which allows the server to listen at a well-known socket port for requests. Each request identifies the sender. The server simply uses the identification in a `sendto` response to the client. The `recvfrom` and `sendto` form the basis of the socket *connectionless* protocol.

If the client and server require additional interaction during the processing of the request, it is useful to have a two-way communication channel that is private but does not require an exchange of process ID information with each message. Figure 12.3 illustrates a hand-off mechanism in which the initial client request serves merely to establish the two-way communication channel that is private and not client-specific. The channel is private because it is not accessible to other processes. It is not client-specific because it is not identified by the client process ID. Connection-oriented protocols use the hand-off mechanism to establish a communication channel between client and server. The remainder of the chapter uses connection-oriented protocols.

Once a server receives a request and establishes a channel of communication, it can use a number of different strategies for handling the request. One possibility is that when a server receives a request, it completely devotes itself to handling that request before taking any additional requests. Figure 12.3 depicts the *serial-server* strategy.

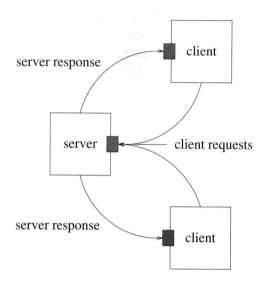

Figure 12.2: In a connectionless protocol, the server has a well-known port for client requests, but client-specific ports for responses.

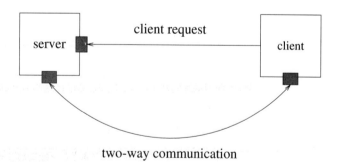

Figure 12.3: The client requests a service from a server by accessing a well-known port. The server responds by providing a private, two-way communication channel.

Example 12.1

The following pseudocode illustrates the serial-server strategy.

```
for ( ; ; ) {
    listen for client request
    create private two-way communication channel
    while(no error on communication channel)
        read client request
        handle request and respond to client
    close communication channel
}
```

A busy server handling long-lived requests such as file transfers cannot use the serial-server strategy because it allows only one request to be serviced at a time. In the *parent-server* strategy, the server forks a child to handle the actual service to the client while the server resumes listening for additional requests. Figure 12.4 depicts the parent-server strategy. The strategy is ideal for services such as file transfers, which take a relatively long period of time and involve a lot of blocking.

Example 12.2

The following pseudocode illustrates the parent-server strategy.

```
for( ; ; ) {
    listen for client request
    create a private two-way communication channel
    fork a child to handle the request
    close the communication channel
    clean up zombies
}
```

Since the server child handles the actual service in the parent-server strategy, the server can accept multiple clients requests in rapid succession. The strategy is analogous to the old-fashioned switchboard at some hotels. A client calls the main number at the hotel (the connection request). The switchboard operator (server) answers the call, patches the connection to the appropriate room (the server-child), steps out of the conversation, and resumes listening for additional calls.

The *threaded-server* strategy depicted in Figure 12.5 is a low-overhead alternative to the parent-server strategy. Instead of forking a child to handle the request, the server creates a thread in its own process space. Threads have considerably less overhead and the approach can be very efficient, particularly if the request is small or I/O intensive. A drawback of the threaded-server strategy is possible interference among multiple requests due to the shared address space. For computationally intensive services, the additional threads may reduce the efficiency of or block the main server thread. The server-design must have sufficient kernel-level parallelism in order to perform well.

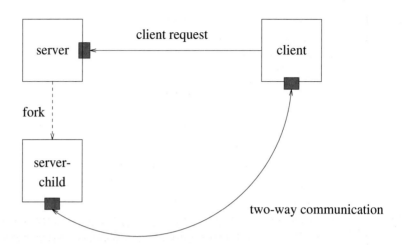

Figure 12.4: The parent-server strategy for client-server implementation.

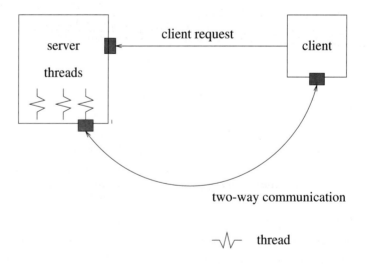

Figure 12.5: The threaded-server strategy for client-server implementation.

12.2 The Universal Internet Communication Interface (UICI)

It is possible to implement the connection-oriented client-server communication paradigm using sockets, TLI, or STREAMS. All three implementations share common elements. The server listens for a connection request at a well-known port. Usually the server translates the port into an appropriate handle (e.g., file descriptor) before listening. When the server detects a request, it generates a new handle for the communication. At this point, client and server can communicate using the handle. On the client side, the client makes a connection request to the well-known port of the server. The connection request returns a handle for the communication.

This section develops a Universal Internet Communication Interface (UICI) library which is summarized in Table 12.1. The UICI library provides a simplified, transport-independent interface to connection-oriented communication in UNIX. UICI is not part of any UNIX standard, and this chapter introduces the library to clarify client-server communication. Appendix B provides complete UICI implementations in terms of sockets, TLI, and STREAMS, respectively. This section presents a client-server example in terms of UICI. The following sections discuss the underlying implementation using each of the three UNIX communication mechanisms.

UICI Prototype	Description
`int u_open(u_port_t port)`	Opens file descriptor bound to `port`. Returns listening file descriptor.
`int u_listen(int fd, char *hostn)`	Listens for connection request on `fd`. Returns communication file descriptor.
`int u_connect(u_port_t port,` `char *the_host)`	Initiates connection to server on port `port` and host `the_host`. Returns communication file descriptor.
`int u_close(fd)`	Closes file descriptor `fd`.
`ssize_t u_read(int fd, char *buf,` `size_t nbyte)`	Reads up to `nbyte` bytes from `fd` into `buf`. Returns number of bytes actually read.
`ssize_t u_write(int fd, char *buf,` `size_t nbyte)`	Writes `nbyte` bytes from `buf` to `fd`. Returns number of bytes actually written.
`void u_error(char *errmsg)`	Outputs `errmsg` followed by a UICI error message.
`int u_sync(int fd)`	Updates relevant kernel information after calls to `exec` .

Table 12.1: Summary of UICI calls.

The `u_error` function returns `void`, while the remaining UICI functions return −1 on error. Use `u_error` to display the error message associated with a UICI error on standard error in a manner similar to `perror` for system calls. The server listens for a connection (`u_open`, `u_listen`). The client requests the connection (`u_connect`). Once client and server have established a connection, they communicate over the network using `u_read` and `u_write` in a manner similar to the ordinary `read` and `write` system calls.

The `copy_from_network_to_file` function of Program 12.1 copies data from a network communication file descriptor to a file. It returns the total number of bytes copied. The `copy_from_network_to_file` function assumes that a network connection with handle `communfd` has been established and that `filefd` is open. It calls `u_error` if `u_read` returns an error and `perror` if `write` returns an error.

Program 12.1: The `copy_from_network_to_file` function.

```
#include <stdio.h>
#include <unistd.h>
#include <errno.h>
#include "uici.h"
#define BLKSIZE 1024
int copy_from_network_to_file(int communfd, int filefd)
{
    int bytes_read;
    int bytes_written;
    int bytes_to_write;
    int total_bytes = 0;
    char buf[BLKSIZE];
    char *bufp;

    for ( ; ; ) {
        if ((bytes_read = u_read(communfd, buf, BLKSIZE)) < 0) {
            u_error("Server read error");
            break;
        } else if (bytes_read == 0) {
            fprintf(stderr, "Network end-of-file\n");
            break;
        } else {     /* allow for interruption of write by signal */
            for (bufp = buf, bytes_to_write = bytes_read;
                 bytes_to_write > 0;
                 bufp += bytes_written, bytes_to_write -= bytes_written) {
                bytes_written = write(filefd, bufp, bytes_to_write);
                if ((bytes_written) == -1 && (errno != EINTR)) {
                    perror("Server write error");
                    break;
                } else if (bytes_written == -1)
                    bytes_written = 0;
                total_bytes += bytes_written;
            }
        }
```

```
            if (bytes_written == -1)
                break;
        }
    }
    return total_bytes;
}
```

_____ **Program 12.1** _____

12.2.1 UICI Servers

UICI servers are organized as follows:

- Open a well-known listening port (u_open). The u_open returns a _listening file descriptor_.
- Listen for a connection request on the listening file descriptor (u_listen). The u_listen blocks until a client requests a connection and then returns a _communication file descriptor_ to use as a handle for the private, two-way client-server communication.
- Communicate directly or through a surrogate (child or thread) with the client using the communication file descriptor (u_read and u_write).
- Close the communication file descriptor (u_close).

Program 12.2 shows a serial-server program for copying files from a client using the UICI library. The "uici.h" file defines the needed UICI prototypes. The server takes a single command-line argument specifying the port number on which the server listens. The server obtains a listening file descriptor for the port with u_open. It then listens for a client request by calling u_listen. The u_listen function returns a communication file descriptor. The server then calls copy_from_network_to_file of Program 12.1 to perform the actual copying. Once the copying is complete, the server outputs the number of bytes copied and resumes listening.

Program 12.2: A serial server implemented using UICI.

```
#include <stdio.h>
#include <stdlib.h>
#include <unistd.h>
#include <limits.h>
#include "uici.h"
int copy_from_network_to_file(int communfd, int filefd);

/*
 *
 *                         UICI Server
 *    Open a UICI port specified as a command-line argument
 *    and listen for a request.  When a request
```

```
 *    arrives, use the provided communication file descriptor to
 *    read from the UICI connection and echo to standard output
 *    until the connection is terminated.  Then the server resumes
 *    listening for additional requests.
 */
void main(int argc, char *argv[])
{
    u_port_t portnumber;
    int listenfd;
    int communfd;
    char client[MAX_CANON];
    int bytes_copied;

    if (argc != 2) {
        fprintf(stderr, "Usage: %s port\n", argv[0]);
        exit(1);
    }
    portnumber = (u_port_t) atoi(argv[1]);
    if ((listenfd = u_open(portnumber)) == -1) {
        u_error("Unable to establish a port connection");
        exit(1);
    }
    while ((communfd = u_listen(listenfd, client)) != -1) {
        fprintf(stderr, "A connection has been made to %s\n",client);
        bytes_copied = copy_from_network_to_file(communfd, STDOUT_FILENO);
        fprintf(stderr, "Bytes transferred = %d\n", bytes_copied);
        close(communfd);
    }
    exit(0);
}
```

_____ **Program 12.2** _____

In the serial-server strategy of Program 12.2 the server copies the complete file before accepting another client request. That strategy can result in long delays for other clients, suggesting that the parent-server strategy is more appropriate. In the parent-server strategy additional client requests are delayed only while the server forks a child to process the request. Program 12.3 implements the parent-server strategy. If the parent does not close communfd, the child cannot detect end-of-file on its network connection.

Program 12.3: A server program that forks a child to handle communication.

```
#include <stdio.h>
#include <stdlib.h>
#include <unistd.h>
#include <limits.h>
```

```c
#include <sys/wait.h>
#include "uici.h"

int copy_from_network_to_file(int communfd, int filefd);

/*
 *                        UICI Server
 *  Open a UICI port specified as a command-line arugment
 *  and listen for requests.  When a request
 *  arrives, fork a child to handle the communication and
 *  listen again.
 */
void main(int argc, char *argv[])
{
   u_port_t portnumber;
   int listenfd;
   int communfd;
   char client[MAX_CANON];
   int bytes_copied;
   int child;

   if (argc != 2) {
      fprintf(stderr, "Usage: %s port\n", argv[0]);
      exit(1);
   }

   portnumber = (u_port_t) atoi(argv[1]);
   if ((listenfd = u_open(portnumber)) == -1) {
      u_error("Unable to establish a port connection");
      exit(1);
   }

   while ((communfd = u_listen(listenfd, client)) != -1) {
      fprintf(stderr, "[%ld]: A connection has been made to %s\n",
               (long) getpid(), client);
      if ((child = fork()) == -1) {
         fprintf(stderr, "Could not fork a child\n");
         break;
      }

      if (child == 0) {                             /* child code */
         close(listenfd);
         fprintf(stderr, "[%ld]: A connection has been made to %s\n",
                    (long) getpid(), client);
         bytes_copied =
              copy_from_network_to_file(communfd, STDOUT_FILENO);
         close(communfd);
         fprintf(stderr, "[%ld]:Bytes transferred = %d\n",
                    (long) getpid(), bytes_copied);
```

```
            exit(0);

        } else {                                    /* parent code */
            close(communfd);
            while (waitpid(-1, NULL, WNOHANG) > 0)
                ;
        }
    }
    exit(0);
}
```

_____ **Program 12.3** _____

12.2.2 UICI Clients

UICI clients are organized as follows:

- Connect to a specified host and port (u_connect). The connection request
  returns the communication file descriptor.
- Communicate with the server (u_read and u_write) using the communication file descriptor.
- Close the communication file descriptor (u_close).

Program 12.4 shows the client side of the file copy. The client makes a connection to
a specified port on a specified host by calling u_connect. The u_connect function
returns the communication file descriptor. The client reads the file from standard input,
transfers the file, and exits.

_____

Program 12.4: A client implemented with UICI.

```
#include <stdio.h>
#include <stdlib.h>
#include <unistd.h>
#include <string.h>
#include <errno.h>
#include "uici.h"

#define BLKSIZE 1024

/*
 *                      UICI Client
 *  Make a UICI connection request to the host and port specified
 *  as command-line arguments.  Read from standard input and
 *  write to the UICI communication file descriptor until
 *  end-of-file.
 */
```

```c
void main(int argc, char *argv[])
{
    u_port_t portnumber;
    int communfd;
    ssize_t bytesread;
    char buf[BLKSIZE];

    if (argc != 3) {
        fprintf(stderr, "Usage: %s host port\n", argv[0]);
        exit(1);
    }
    portnumber = (u_port_t)atoi(argv[2]);
    if ((communfd = u_connect(portnumber, argv[1])) < 0) {
        u_error("Unable to establish an Internet connection");
        exit(1);
    }
    fprintf(stderr, "A connection has been made to %s\n",argv[1]);
    for ( ; ; ) {
        if ((bytesread = read(STDIN_FILENO, buf, BLKSIZE)) < 0) {
            perror("Client read error");
            break;
        } else if (bytesread == 0) {
            fprintf(stderr, "Client detected end-of-file on input\n");
            break;
        } else if (bytesread !=
                    u_write(communfd, buf, (size_t)bytesread)) {
            u_error("Client write_error");
            break;
        }
    }
    u_close(communfd);
    exit(0);
}
```

_____ **Program 12.4** _____

Example 12.3

If the executable for the server given in Program 12.2 is called `uici_server,` *the following command causes the server to listen on port* `8652` *for a client connection request.*

```
uici_server 8652
```

Example 12.4

If the executable for the client of Program 12.4 is called `uici_client` *and the server is on a host called* `vip,` *the following command causes the client to make the connection request.*

```
uici_client vip 8652
```

UICI	Sockets	TLI	STREAMS
u_open	socket bind listen	t_open t_bind	create pipe push connld fattach
u_listen	accept	t_alloc t_listen t_bind t_accept	ioctl of I_RECVFD
u_connect	socket connect	t_open t_bind t_alloc t_connect	open
u_read	read	t_rcv	read
u_write	write	t_snd	write
u_sync		t_sync	

Table 12.2: A summary of the UICI connection protocol and its underlying implementations.

Exercise 12.1

Start the server and client in different windows on different machines using the commands of Example 12.3 and Example 12.4. Once the connection is established, enter text for the client and see the server output it.

12.2.3 UICI Implementation

Table 12.2 shows the steps needed to implement each UICI function in terms of three different communication paradigms—sockets, TLI, or STREAMS. The sockets and TLI implementations allow for network communication. The STREAMS implementation works only when the client and server are on the same machine.

All of the underlying mechanisms (sockets, TLI, and STREAMS) allow for the possibility of nonblocking I/O, but the UICI interface provides only blocking I/O. That is, a u_read or u_write call causes the caller to block. A u_read blocks until the information is available from the network connection.

What blocking means for u_write is less obvious. In the present context it means that u_write returns when the output has been transferred to a buffer used by the transport mechanism. It does not mean that the message has actually been delivered to the destination. Writes can also block if, because of message delivery problems in the lower protocol layers, all of the buffers for the network protocols are full. Fortunately, the issues of blocking and buffering are transparent for most applications.

The next section gives a brief overview of network layers and communication on the Internet. The remaining sections of the chapter give an overview of each underlying mechanism and develop implementations of the `u_open`, `u_listen`, and `u_connect` in terms of these mechanisms. Section 12.4 introduces the socket calls and discusses an implementation of UICI using sockets. Section 12.5 presents some of the technical details of TLI and discusses an implementation of UICI using TLI. Section 12.6 introduces STREAMS, and Section 12.7 gives a STREAMS implementation of UICI. Appendix B presents complete implementations of UICI for sockets, TLI, and STREAMS. The UICI interface has been designed to look like a simplified version of TLI or sockets. Because of the problems in detecting errors, it is difficult to make that interface safe to use with threads. Section 12.8 discusses a thread-safe version of the UICI interface.

12.3 Network Communication

The International Standards Organization (ISO) has a standard for network design called the Open Systems Interconnection (OSI) reference model. Figure 12.6 shows the seven protocol layers in the OSI model. Each layer consists of a set of functions to handle a particular aspect of the network communication. Functions in a layer communicate only with the layers directly above and below. The lowest layers in the OSI model deal with issues that are closely related to hardware, and the highest layers deal with the user interface.

In peer-to-peer communication with layered protocols, each layer on one host appears to be communicating with the same layer on the other host. Such a logical view of the communication simplifies and isolates the implementation of a layer's functions. For example, the logical view of communication at the transport layer in Figure 12.6 might be an error-free stream of bytes. The actual mechanism is that the transport layer passes its data to the layer below. That layer performs its function and passes the information on. Eventually the information flows on the physical network to the other host and is passed up through successive layers to the transport layer on the other host.

The *physical layer* and the *data link layer* are concerned with point-to-point transmission of data. Ethernet is a common low-cost implementation of these layers. Each host on the network has a hardware Ethernet adapter that is connected to a communication link consisting of coaxial cable or twisted pair wire. The host is identified by a unique 6-byte Ethernet address that is hard-wired into the adapter hardware. Other commonly used possibilities for these two layers include token ring, token bus, ISDN, ATM, and FDDI.

The *network layer* handles network addressing and routing through bridges and routers interconnecting networks. The most common network layer protocol used by

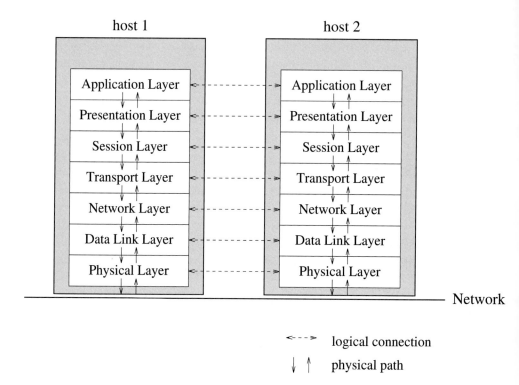

Figure 12.6: Peer-to-peer communication in the OSI model.

UNIX systems is called IP, the Internet Protocol. Every host has one or more IP addresses each consisting of 4 bytes. It is conventional to refer to the 4 bytes of the IP address by representing them in decimal with decimal points between the bytes (e.g., `198.86.40.81`).

Although the IP software only deals with IP address numbers, users typically refer to a machine by name (e.g., `sunsite.unc.edu`). Convert from name to address using `gethostbyname` and from address to name using `gethostbyaddr`. There is usually a correspondence between the first part of the IP address (1, 2, or 3 bytes) called the Internet domain with the last part of the machine name, but the exact details of the correspondence are complicated and are not relevant here.

The *transport layer* handles end-to-end communication between hosts. The two main protocols used at this layer are TCP (Transmission Control Protocol) and UDP (User Datagram Protocol). UNIX networks use both TCP and UDP. UDP is a connec-

tionless protocol without any guarantee of delivery. The `tftp` (trivial file transfer protocol) program is usually implemented using UDP. TCP is a reliable, connection-oriented
protocol. The `ftp` (file transfer protocol) program is typically implemented using TCP.

More than one user at a time may be using TCP or UDP between a given pair of
machines. To distinguish between the various processes that might be communicating,
TCP and UDP use 16-bit integers called ports. Some of these port numbers have been
permanently assigned to specific applications and are called *well-known addresses*. For
example, `ftp` always uses port 21, `telnet` uses 23, `tftp` uses 69, and `finger`
uses 79. User processes should choose port numbers above $7,000$ so as not to interfere
with system services and X.

The *session layer* contains interfaces to the transport layer. This chapter discusses
two standard interfaces called sockets and TLI (transport layer interface). The *presentation layer*, and the *application layer* consist of general utilities and application programs.
The presentation layer may handle compression or encryption.

One drawback of using the OSI model is that many networks were already established by the time the OSI reference model was accepted; thus the organization of many
networks does not exactly fit the model. Still, it is a valuable conceptual framework for
comparing protocols.

12.4 Socket Implementation of UICI

The first socket interface originated with 4.1cBSD UNIX in the early 1980s. Spec 1170
incorporates the 4.3BSD version, and POSIX will probably standardize sockets in the not
too distant future. Sockets are now often implemented on top of STREAMS in System
V systems.

To use the socket calls, compile programs with the library options `-lsocket` and
`-lnsl`. All of the socket system calls return -1 in case of failure and set the external
variable `errno`.

Table 12.2 on page 444 summarizes the socket calls needed to establish communication. The server creates a handle (`socket`), associates it with a physical location on
the network (`bind`), and sets up the queue size for pending requests (`listen`). The
server then listens for client requests (`accept`).

The client also creates a handle (`socket`) and then associates this handle with the
network location of the server (`connect`). The server and client handles, sometimes
called *transmission endpoints*, are file descriptors. Once the client and server have established a connection, they can communicate using ordinary `read` and `write` calls.

The `socket` call creates an endpoint for communication and returns a file descriptor.

SYNOPSIS

```
#include <sys/types.h>
#include <sys/socket.h>

int socket(int domain, int type, int protocol);
```
                                                                    Spec 1170

The `domain` selects the protocol family to be used. Spec 1170 requires that the domains `AF_UNIX` and `AF_INET` be supported. The `AF_UNIX` can be used only between processes on a single UNIX system, while `AF_INET` is for the Internet and allows communication between remote hosts.

A `type` value of `SOCK_STREAM` provides sequenced, reliable, two-way, connection-oriented byte streams and is typically implemented with TCP. A `type` value of `SOCK_DGRAM` provides connectionless communication using unreliable messages of a fixed length and is typically implemented with UDP.

The `protocol` specifies a particular protocol to be used. However, there is usually only one protocol available for each value of `type` (e.g., TCP with `SOCK_STREAM` and UDP with `SOCK_DGRAM`). The `protocol` is therefore usually given as 0.

Example 12.5

The following code segment sets up a socket transmission endpoint for Internet communication using a connection-oriented protocol.

```
#include <sys/types.h>
#include <sys/socket.h>
#include <stdio.h>
int sock;

if ((sock = socket(AF_INET, SOCK_STREAM, 0)) == -1)
    perror("Could not create socket");
```

The `bind` call associates a socket transmission endpoint or handle with a specific physical network connection. Internet domain protocols specify the physical connection by a port number, while UNIX domain protocols specify the connection by a pathname.

SYNOPSIS

```
#include <sys/types.h>
#include <sys/socket.h>

int bind(int s, const struct sockaddr *address,
         size_t address_len);
```
                                                                    Spec 1170

The `s` is the file descriptor returned by the `socket` call, and `address_len` is the number of bytes in the `*address` structure. The `*address` structure contains a family name and protocol-specific information. The Internet domain uses `struct sockaddr_in` for `struct sockaddr`. The `struct sockaddr_in` is defined by

```
struct sockaddr_in {
        short   sin_family;
        u_short sin_port;
        struct  in_addr sin_addr;
        char    sin_zero[8];
};
```

The `sin_family` is `AF_INET`, and the `sin_port` is the port number. The `sin_addr` can be set to `INADDR_ANY` to allow communication from any host. The `sin_zero` array fills out the structure so that it has the same size as `struct sockaddr`.

A server may process multiple simultaneous communication requests for a given well-known port number by forking a child or starting a new thread to handle each communication. While the server is processing a communication request for a client, it cannot respond to additional client requests. The `listen` call specifies how many pending client requests can be backlogged before the server refuses a connection. The client receives an `ECONNREFUSED` error if the server refuses its connection request.

SYNOPSIS

```
#include <sys/types.h>
#include <sys/socket.h>

int listen(int s, int backlog);
```
Spec 1170

The `s` value is the descriptor returned by `socket`, and `backlog` is the number of pending client requests allowed.

The combination of `open`, `bind`, and `listen` establishes a handle for the server to monitor communication requests from a well-known port. Program 12.5 gives an implementation of `u_open` in terms of the socket calls.

If an attempt is made to write to a pipe or socket that no process has open for reading, the `write` generates a `SIGPIPE` signal in addition to returning an error and setting `errno` to `EPIPE`. Since the default action of `SIGPIPE` is to terminate the process, that signal prevents a graceful shutdown when the remote host closes the connection (unless a user-defined handler is used). For this reason, the socket implementation of UICI ignores the signal if the default handler is active.

The `sin_port` member of the second argument to `bind` represents the port number using the network byte ordering. Machines that use a different byte ordering must do a conversion. The macro `htons`, host to network short, can be used to do the conversion for port numbers. It should be used even when not necessary to maintain portability.

Program 12.5: A socket implementation of the UICI `u_open`.

```
int u_open(u_port_t port)
{
   int sock;
   struct sockaddr_in server;

   if ( (u_ignore_sigpipe() != 0) ||
        ((sock = socket(AF_INET, SOCK_STREAM, 0)) < 0) )
      return -1;

   server.sin_family = AF_INET;
   server.sin_addr.s_addr = INADDR_ANY;
   server.sin_port = htons((short)port);

   if ( (bind(sock, (struct sockaddr *)&server, sizeof(server)) < 0) ||
        (listen(sock, MAXBACKLOG) < 0) )
      return -1;
   return sock;
}
```

_____ **Program 12.5** _____

Once it associates a handle with the physical connection, the server waits for a client to initiate a connection with the `accept` call.

```
SYNOPSIS

   #include <sys/types.h>
   #include <sys/socket.h>

   int accept(int s, struct sockaddr *address, int *address_len);
                                                             Spec 1170
```

The parameters are similar to those of `bind`, except that `accept` fills `*address` with information about the client making the connection. In particular, the `sin_addr` member of the `struct sockaddr_in` structure contains a member, `s_addr`, to hold the Internet address of the client.

The value of the `*address_len` parameter of `accept` specifies the size of the buffer pointed to by `address`. Before the call, fill this with the size of the `address` structure. After the call, `*address_len` contains the number of bytes of the buffer actually filled in by the `accept` call. The `accept` returns a file descriptor for communicating with the client. The server can then fork a child to handle the communication and resume monitoring the original file descriptor.

Convert this address to a name by calling `gethostbyaddr`.

SYNOPSIS

```
#include <netdb.h>

struct hostent *gethostbyaddr(const void *addr, size_t len,
        int type);
```
Spec 1170

The `struct hostent` structure includes a member, `h_name` which is a pointer to the official name of the host. On error, `gethostbyaddr` returns `NULL` and sets the external integer `h_errno`. The `gethostbyaddr` function is not thread-safe and the use of `gethostbyaddr_r` is preferred. (See Section 12.8.)

Program 12.6 shows the implementation of `u_listen`. The socket `accept` call waits for a connection request and returns a communication file descriptor. If the `accept` is interrupted by a signal, it returns a −1 with `errno` set to `EINTR`. The `u_listen` reinitiates an `accept` in this case.

Program 12.6: A socket implementation of the UICI `u_listen`.

```
int u_listen(int fd, char *hostn)
{
    struct sockaddr_in net_client;
    int len = sizeof(struct sockaddr);
    int retval;
    struct hostent *hostptr;

    while ( ((retval =
            accept(fd, (struct sockaddr *)(&net_client), &len)) == -1) &&
            (errno == EINTR) )
       ;
    if (retval == -1)
       return retval;
    hostptr =
       gethostbyaddr((char *)&(net_client.sin_addr.s_addr), 4, AF_INET);
    if (hostptr == NULL)
       strcpy(hostn, "unknown");
    else
       strcpy(hostn, (*hostptr).h_name);
    return retval;
}
```
_____ **Program 12.6** _____

The client code for establishing a socket connection is simpler. The client calls `socket` to set up a transmission endpoint and then uses `connect` to establish a link to the well-known port of the remote server.

SYNOPSIS

```
#include <sys/types.h>
#include <sys/socket.h>

int connect(int s, struct sockaddr *address,
            size_t address_len);
```

Spec 1170

Fill in the `struct sockaddr_in` structure as with `bind`.

Program 12.7 shows the socket implementation of `u_connect`. Because a connection request is possibly for a different host, the specification of the address is slightly complicated. Convert the host name string to an appropriate Internet address by calling gethostbyname.

SYNOPSIS

```
#include <netdb.h>

struct hostent *gethostbyname(const char *name);
```

Spec 1170

The `struct hostent` structure includes two members of interest that are filled in by `gethostbyname`. The `h_addr_list` is an array of pointers to network addresses used by this host. Use the first one, `h_addr_list[0]`. The integer member, `h_length` is filled with the number of bytes in the address. On error, `gethostbyname` returns `NULL` and sets the external integer `h_error`. Macros exist to determine the error. `gethostbyname` is not thread-safe and `gethostbyname_r` should be used in threaded applications. (See Section 12.8.)

The client creates a socket and makes the connection request. The `connect` call can be interrupted by a signal, and the loop reinitiates the call in this case. The program does not use `strncpy` to copy the server's address into `server.sin_addr`, since the source may have an embedded zero byte.

Program 12.7: A socket implementation of the UICI `u_connect`.

```
int u_connect(u_port_t port, char *hostn)
{
    struct sockaddr_in server;
    struct hostent *hp;
    int sock;
    int retval;

    if ( (u_ignore_sigpipe() != 0) ||
         !(hp = gethostbyname(hostn)) ||
         ((sock = socket(AF_INET, SOCK_STREAM, 0)) < 0) )
```

```
        return -1;

    memcpy((char *)&server.sin_addr, hp->h_addr_list[0], hp->h_length);

    server.sin_port = htons((short)port);
    server.sin_family = AF_INET;

    while ( ((retval =
            connect(sock, (struct sockaddr *)&server, sizeof(server))) == -1)
            && (errno == EINTR) )
        ;
    if (retval == -1) {
            close(sock);
            return -1;
    }
    return sock;
}
```

_____ **Program 12.7** _____

Once the client and server establish a connection, they can exchange information using u_read and u_write with their communication file descriptors. Sockets also support connectionless communication, passing of file descriptors, and out-of-band data, but these features are not part of UICI. Appendix B gives a complete socket implementation of UICI.

12.5 Transport Layer Interface (TLI)

TLI is an alternative to sockets for doing client-server network communication. TLI, which stands for *Transport Layer Interface*, was introduced in System V Release 3 in 1986. In System V, TLI is implemented on top of STREAMS. Compile the programs with -lnsl in order to access the TLI library.

TLI programs are more complicated than those using sockets because these programs must explicitly allocate space for the communication data structures by calling the general purpose t_alloc. In order to avoid memory leaks in long running programs, be sure to free these structures using t_free. Another complication with TLI is that the TLI data structures are in the user area and are not accessible after an exec. Use the t_sync function to copy the required information from the user area.

Error handling is also more complicated in TLI. TLI does not directly set the external variable errno when it encounters an error. Instead TLI provides its own external variable t_errno for specifying errors and a function t_look for examining the status of the communication channel. If a problem was the result of a system error, TLI sets t_errno to TSYSERR. In that case errno contains relevant information.

The function `t_open` is the first step in establishing communication by either the server or the client. It establishes a handle or transmission endpoint for the communication.

SYNOPSIS

```
#include <xti.h>
#include <fcntl.h>

int t_open(const char *path, int oflag, struct t_info *info);
```
                                                                        Spec 1170

The `path` parameter indicates the underlying communication protocol, for example `/dev/tcp` (connection-oriented) or `/dev/udp` (connectionless). The `oflag` is similar to the flag used for the usual `open` system call and is typically `O_RDWR`. Upon successful completion, the `*info` parameter contains information about the underlying protocol. If this parameter is the `NULL` pointer, `t_open` does not return any information about the underlying protocol. If successful, `t_open` returns a communication file descriptor. Otherwise, it returns -1 and sets `t_errno`.

The `t_bind` function is similar to the `bind` function for sockets. It associates the file descriptor created by `t_open` with a physical connection.

SYNOPSIS

```
#include <xti.h>

int t_bind(int fildes, const struct t_bind *req,
           struct t_bind *ret);
```
                                                                        Spec 1170

The `fildes` parameter is the handle returned by `t_open`. Fill the `req` structure with information about the server network port prior to calling `t_bind`. If `ret` is not a `NULL` pointer, the `t_bind` fills `ret` with information about the port provided that `t_bind` is successful. The function `t_bind` returns 0 if successful. It returns -1 and sets `t_errno` if an error occurs.

The `struct t_bind` structure contains the following members:

```
struct netbuf addr;
unsigned qlen;
```

Here `addr` is of type `struct netbuf`, which for the Internet domain is the same as the `struct sockaddr_in` structure discussed for sockets in Section 12.4. The `qlen` member is an unsigned integer specifying the number of outstanding connections and is similar to the value set by `listen` for sockets. Handling the backlog of connection requests is complicated in TLI, and the UICI implementation does not allow a backlog.

Program 12.8 shows a TLI implementation of u_open in terms of t_open and t_bind. Most of the code in u_open involves setting up the appropriate address structures for the Internet connection. The t_open creates the file descriptor for the TLI connection. The t_bind associates that file descriptor with the appropriate network port for communication with the outside world.

Program 12.8: A TLI implementation of the UICI u_open.

```
int u_open(u_port_t port)
{
    int fd;
    struct t_info info;
    struct t_bind req;
    struct sockaddr_in server;

    /* Create a TLI endpoint */
    fd = t_open("/dev/tcp", O_RDWR, &info);
    if (fd < 0)
        return -1;

    /* Specify server information with wildcards */
    memset(&server, 0, (size_t)sizeof(server));
    server.sin_family = AF_INET;
    server.sin_addr.s_addr = INADDR_ANY;
    server.sin_port = htons((short)port);

    req.addr.maxlen = sizeof(server);
    req.addr.len = sizeof(server);
    req.addr.buf = (char *)&server;
    req.qlen = 1;

    /* bind the TLI endpoint to port */
    if (t_bind(fd, &req, NULL) < 0)
        return -1;
    return fd;
}
```

_____ **Program 12.8** _____

A TLI server calls t_listen to wait for a connection request from a client, which is more like the socket function accept than the socket function listen. Recall that for sockets, listen sets only the buffer size for pending connections. For TLI, t_bind uses the qlen member of req to set the buffer size.

SYNOPSIS

```
#include <xti.h>

int t_listen(int fildes, struct t_call *call);
```
                                                     Spec 1170

The `fildes` is just the handle returned by `t_open`. If successful, `t_listen` returns 0 and fills the `*call` structure with information about the connection. If not successful, `t_listen` returns -1 and sets `t_errno`.

Because of the intended generality of TLI, use of the `struct t_call` structure is complicated. TLI uses many types of data structures whose size depends on the transport protocol; therefore, it is not possible to use automatic variables for these. Instead, TLI provides a method of allocating these structures with the `t_alloc` function.

SYNOPSIS

```
#include <xti.h>

char *t_alloc(int fildes, int struct_type, int fields);
```
                                                     Spec 1170

The `t_alloc` uses the `fildes` returned by `t_open` to determine the transport protocol, and thus the size of the structure needed. To allocate a `struct t_call` structure for use by `t_listen`, use `t_alloc` with the `struct_type` equal to `T_CALL` and the `fields` equal to `T_ADDR`. It is unnecessary to initialize the `t_call` structure before executing `t_listen`.

Once `t_listen` returns, the server calls `t_accept` to accept the communication request. The server creates a new file descriptor for the actual communication so that the original file descriptor returned by `t_open` can be used to listen for another connection. For sockets, `accept` automatically returns a new communication file descriptor.

SYNOPSIS

```
#include <xti.h>

int t_accept(int fildes, int resfd, struct t_call *call);
```
                                                       Spec 1170

The `fildes` is the handle returned by the original `t_open` and `resfd` is the handle returned by the second `t_open`. The last parameter is the `struct t_call` structure returned by `t_listen`. It need not be modified before calling `t_accept`.

Program 12.9 shows the TLI implementation of the `u_listen` function. The `t_listen` causes the caller to block until a connection request arrives or until there is an error or an asynchronous event on the communication channel. In the case of an asynchronous event, the external variable `t_errno` is set to `TLOOK`. Call the `t_look` function to investigate further.

Program 12.9: A TLI implementation of the UICI `u_listen`.

```
int u_listen(int fd, char *hostn)
{
   struct t_call *callptr;
   struct sockaddr_in *client;
   struct hostent *hostptr;
   int newfd;
   int tret;

   if ( (callptr =
         (struct t_call *)t_alloc(fd, T_CALL, T_ADDR)) == NULL) {
      return -1;
   }

   while( ((tret = t_listen(fd, callptr)) < 0) &&
          (t_errno == TSYSERR) && (errno == EINTR) )
      ;                          /* t_listen interrupted and restarted */
   if ( (tret < 0) ||
        ((newfd = t_open("/dev/tcp", O_RDWR, NULL)) < 0 ) ||
        (t_bind(newfd, NULL, NULL) < 0 ) ||
        (t_accept(fd, newfd, callptr) < 0) ) {
      t_free((char *)callptr, T_CALL);
      return -1;
   }
   client = (struct sockaddr_in *)(callptr->addr).buf;
   hostptr =
      gethostbyaddr((char *)&(client->sin_addr.s_addr), 4, AF_INET);
   if (hostptr == NULL)
      strcpy(hostn, "unknown");
   else
      strcpy(hostn, hostptr->h_name);
   t_free((char *)callptr, T_CALL);
   return newfd;
}
```

_____ **Program 12.9** _____

If a TLI call fails because of interruption by a signal, the call returns −1, sets `t_errno` to `TSYSERR`, and sets `errno` to `EINTR`. The `u_listen` call automatically restarts `t_listen` when it detects that the call was interrupted by a signal.

If an error occurs, the memory allocated by `t_alloc` should be freed. While that may not be necessary for programs that terminate when an error occurs, a server may listen again after a failed request. Long-running programs can develop serious memory leaks if care is not taken to free all allocated memory.

The TLI client calls t_open, t_bind, and t_connect.

```
SYNOPSIS

    #include <xti.h>

    int t_connect(int fildes, const struct t_call *sndcall,
                  struct t_call *rcvcall);
                                                            Spec 1170
```

The client allocates *sndcall with t_alloc as before and fills it in with information about the server. If the connection is successful, the t_connect function fills the *rcvcall structure with information about the connection. If the information is not needed, the caller can pass a NULL pointer for rcvcall.

Program 12.10 shows the u_connect function for making a TLI connection. The communication channel is created (t_open and t_bind). Considerable setup is required to address the remote host and to the allocate the user data structures.

Program 12.10: A TLI implementation of the UICI u_connect.

```
int u_connect(u_port_t port, char *inetp)
{
    struct t_info info;
    struct t_call  *callptr;
    struct sockaddr_in server;
    struct hostent *hp;
    int fd;
    int trynum;
    unsigned int slptime;

    fd = t_open("/dev/tcp", O_RDWR, &info);
    if (fd < 0)
        return -1;

    /* Create TCP addresses for communication with port */
    memset(&server, 0, (size_t)sizeof(server));
    server.sin_family = AF_INET;              /* Internet address family    */
    hp = gethostbyname(inetp);        /* convert name to Internet address */
                                      /* copy Internet address to buffer   */
    if (hp == NULL) {
        fprintf(stderr, "gethostbyname returned NULL\n");
        return -1;
    }
    memcpy(&(server.sin_addr.s_addr), hp->h_addr_list[0],
```

```
                 (size_t)hp->h_length);
    server.sin_port = htons((short)port);

                                /* set buffer with destination info */
    if (t_bind(fd, NULL, NULL) < 0)
        return -1;

                                /* allocate structure for connect    */
    if ( (callptr =
            (struct t_call *)t_alloc(fd, T_CALL, T_ADDR)) == NULL)
        return -1;

    callptr -> addr.maxlen = sizeof(server);
    callptr -> addr.len = sizeof(server);
    callptr -> addr.buf = (char *)&server;
    callptr -> opt.len = 0;
    callptr -> udata.len = 0;

                                /* Keep trying until the server is ready */
    for (trynum = 0, slptime = 1;
        (trynum < RETRIES) && (t_connect(fd, callptr, NULL) < 0);
        trynum++, slptime = 2*slptime) {
        t_rcvdis(fd, NULL);
        sleep(slptime);
    }
    callptr -> addr.buf = NULL;
    t_free((char *)callptr, T_CALL);
    if (trynum >= RETRIES)
        return -1;
    return fd;
}
```

_____ **Program 12.10** _____

The way the TLI server handles queued requests produces a complication. If the queue of pending requests has length 1, then connection requests are denied while a previous request is being serviced. This problem also occurs with sockets, but for sockets, the problem can be avoided by using a larger queue length. Unfortunately, when the TLI queue length is greater than 1, the server becomes very complicated. A t_accept fails if another connection request is in the queue, so a server must listen for all pending connections and queue them before the t_accept succeeds.

To avoid the pending queue complication, the TLI version of UICI uses a queue length of 1. That means a connection request can fail simply because the server has not yet accepted a previous request. Program 12.10 shows an implementation of u_connect. The u_connect retries a connection when the connection fails. After a failed connection attempt, the u_connect calls t_rcvdis to receive notification of the rejection. This call to `t_rcvdis` is required before the next connection attempt, even though `u_connect` does not use the information returned by `t_rcvdis`. There are several strategies on how long to wait between requests and how many times to attempt a connection before giving up. In the implementation given, the client doubles the time it waits after each unsuccessful try until a maximum number of tries.

As with the server, the client uses `t_free` to free dynamically allocated memory if an error occurs. The `t_free` attempts to free all memory referenced by the structure passed to it. It not only frees the `callptr`, but also the memory pointed to by `callptr->addr.buf`. Since that buffer is part of an automatic variable, an error would result. The `u_connect` implementation solves the problem by setting `callptr->addr.buf` to `NULL` before calling `t_free`.

The TLI version of UICI uses `t_rcv` and `t_snd` to implement `u_read` and `u_write`, respectively.

SYNOPSIS

```
#include <xti.h>

int t_rcv(int fildes, char *buf, unsigned nbytes, int *flags);
int t_snd(int fildes, char *buf, unsigned nbytes, int flags);
```
Spec 1170

These functions are like `read(2)` and `write(2)` except for the extra parameter `flags` that distinguishes high priority communication.

Note: Spec 1170 specifies the header file `xti.h` should be included in programs referencing the TLI functions. Since that header file does not appear to be available on many systems, the examples use the older `tiuser.h` header file.

12.6 STREAMS

STREAMS is a general, standardized interface in System V between the user and character-oriented device drivers. Chances are if a program is communicating with a character-oriented device in System V, it is doing so through a *stream*. (Find out by calling `isastream` for the file descriptor in question.) STREAMS supports a variety of services ranging from network protocol suites to device drivers for modems and printers. The STREAMS interface promotes modular, portable design.

Dennis Ritchie of AT&T developed the original streams mechanism in 1982. The first commercial versions of the STREAMS interface appeared in System V Release 3.0 in 1986 and its name was capitalized to distinguish it from the precommercial version. Most users find STREAMS somewhat incomprehensible, but STREAMS are unavoidable for programs that interact with device drivers in any significant way. System V socket and TLI interfaces are, in fact, usually implemented as STREAMS modules.

Figure 12.7 shows a schematic representation of a stream. The entry point into the kernel is called the *stream head*. The entry point is a full-duplex communication channel accessed by a file descriptor through the system calls `open`, `close`, `read`, `write`, `ioctl`, `putmsg`, and `getmsg`. When a program reads from a stream, information travels *upstream*. When a program writes to a stream, information travels *downstream*.

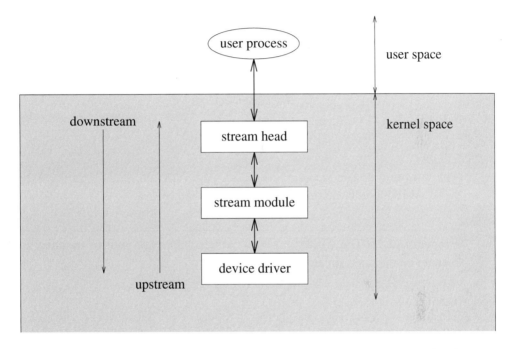

Figure 12.7: A stream is a System V interface between a user process and a character-oriented device driver.

Information in the form of messages is passed from the stream head through an arbitrary number of processing modules to the device driver. The device driver has an entry point that appears in the `/dev` directory. Some of the device drivers correspond to real physical devices such as the speaker and microphone on a workstation. Other device drivers correspond to *simulated* or *pseudodevices*. The latter device drivers are called *pseudodevice drivers*.

Common STREAMS processing modules are found in `/kernel/strmod` and include `bufmod`, `connld`, `ldterm`, `pipemod`, `ptem`, `rpcmod`, `sockmod`, `timod`, `tirdwr`, and `ttcompat`. In theory, programmers can develop their own STREAMS modules, but since the modules reside in the kernel after being pushed on the stream, superuser privileges are needed to install the modules in the system device directories.

The I_LIST option of ioctl lists the modules on a stream. The synopsis for this variation of ioctl is

```
#include <unistd.h>
int ioctl(int fd, I_LIST, struct str_list *mlist)
```

The fd parameter is an open file descriptor for the stream in question. The *mlist contains the module names in a structure of type struct str_list which is defined as

```
struct str_mlist {
        char l_name[FMNAMESZ+1];
};

struct str_list {
        int sl_nmods;
        struct str_mlist *sl_modlist;
};
```

The function list_stream_modules of Program 12.11 outputs a list of the STREAMS modules on the open stream specified by fd.

Program 12.11: The list_stream_modules function lists the modules and drivers that are on the open stream fd.

```
#include <stdio.h>
#include <stdlib.h>
#include <unistd.h>
#include <sys/conf.h>
#include <sys/types.h>
#include <fcntl.h>
#include <stropts.h>

/* Outputs the names of the modules on the stream fd to stdout.
 * Returns -1 if error or 0 if successful.
 */
int list_stream_modules(int fd)
{
    struct str_list mlist;
    int num_mods, i;

    if (!isastream(fd)) {
        printf("The descriptor %d is not a stream\n", fd);
        return -1;
    }
    if ((num_mods = ioctl(fd, I_LIST, NULL)) == -1)
        return -1;
```

```
    mlist.sl_nmods = num_mods;
    mlist.sl_modlist =
        (void *) calloc(num_mods, sizeof(struct str_mlist));
    if (mlist.sl_modlist == NULL)
        return -1;
    if (ioctl(fd, I_LIST, &mlist) == -1)
        return -1;

    printf("Module(s) on the stream:\n");
    for (i = 0; i < num_mods; i++) {
        printf("%s\n", mlist.sl_modlist->l_name);
        mlist.sl_modlist++;
    }
    return 0;
}
```

_____ **Program 12.11** _____

Example 12.6

The following execution of who _shows that the user_ robbins _is logged in to the machine twice through two pseudoterminal device drivers_ pts/1 _and_ pts/2 _from remote machine_ vip.

```
% who
robbins         pts/1         Oct  9 09:26          (vip)
robbins         pts/2         Oct  9 09:26          (vip)
```

The following code segment calls list_stream_modules _to produce a list of stream modules on_ /dev/pts/2 _for user_ robbins.

```
#include <sys/types.h>
#include <sys/stat.h>
#include <fcntl.h>
#include <stdio.h>

if ((fd = open("/dev/pts/2", O_RDONLY)) == -1)
    perror("Could not open /dev/pts/2");
else if (list_stream_modules(fd) == -1)
    fprintf(stderr, "Could not list command modules\n");
}
```

A typical pseudoterminal might have the following modules on its stream.

```
Module(s) on the stream:
    ttcompat
    ldterm
    ptem
    pts
```

The top two modules on the pseudoterminal stream of Example 12.6, `ttcompat` and `ldterm`, provide the terminal line discipline. That is, these modules make the stream appear to be coming from a terminal. The `ldterm` module handles the delete character, line buffering, and other features. The `ttcompat` allows older versions of `ioctl`'s to work. The `ptem` module provides terminal-like control such as keeping track of the window size and ignoring changes to the baud rate or parity. The underlying pseudoterminal device driver is `pts`.

System V implements pipes by connecting two stream heads as shown in Figure 12.8. Here `fd[0]` and `fd[1]` are distinct streams, and the read end of `fd[0]` is connected to the write end of `fd[1]` and vice versa.

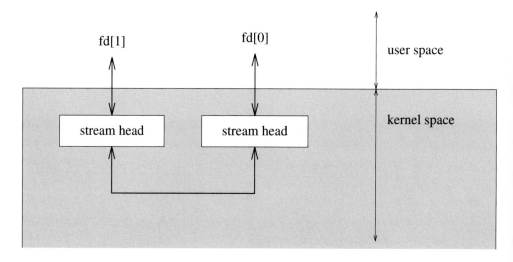

Figure 12.8: System V implements pipes by connecting two stream heads.

Exercise 12.2

What output should the following code segment produce?

```
#include <stdio.h>
#include <unistd.h>
int fd[2];

if (pipe(fd) == -1)
    perror("Bad pipe");
else if (list_stream_modules(fd[1]) == -1)
    fprintf(stderr, "Could not list modules\n");
```

Answer:

It should indicate that there are no modules or device drivers on the stream.

The STREAMS interface is appealing because a programmer can push processing modules onto the stream and change the fundamental appearance of the device without having to modify any kernel code.

Example 12.7

The following code segment makes a pipe appear to be a terminal by pushing the appropriate modules on the stream.

```
#include <unistd.h>
#include <stropts.h>
int fd[2];

if (pipe(fd) == -1)
    return -1;
if (ioctl(fd[0], I_PUSH, "ldterm") == -1)
    return -1;
if (ioctl(fd[0], I_PUSH, "ttcompat") == -1)
    return -1;
```

The `fd[0]` end of the pipe in Example 12.7 should handle the delete character and be line-buffered.

Streams modules pass information upstream and downstream in the form of messages of type `struct strbuf` defined by

```
struct strbuf {
    int     maxlen;     /* no. of bytes in buffer */
    int     len;        /* no. of bytes returned */
    char    *buf;       /* pointer to data */
};
```

Each STREAMS module consists of a read queue, a write queue, and processing entry points as shown in Figure 12.9. The read queue holds messages that are moving upstream, and the write queue holds messages that are moving downstream. The `open` performs initialization, and the `close` performs shutdown activities prior to the module's removal from the stream. A module transfers a message to another module's queue by calling the other module's `put` procedure. The `put` procedure can either process the message immediately or place the message on the queue for later processing by `service`. The `service` entry point handles deferred processing of messages.

12.7 STREAMS Implementation of UICI

STREAMS uses `connld` to do connection-oriented communication. A server pushes `connld` on the end of a pipe and attaches a name to the pipe. A client can then open that pipe by name and receive a unique connection to the server.

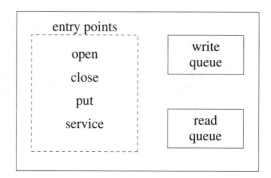

Figure 12.9: A STREAMS module consists of a pair of queues and entry points.

Example 12.8

The following code segment uses the `ioctl` *system call with the* `I_PUSH` *function to push the* `connld` *processing module on one end of a STREAMS pipe as shown in Figure 12.10.*

```
#include <unistd.h>
#include <stropts.h>
int fd[2];
if (pipe(fd) == -1)
   perror("Bad pipe");
else if (ioctl(fd[1], I_PUSH, "connld") == -1)
   perror("Could not push connld");
```

After pushing the `connld` processing module on the stream, attach a name to the `fd[1]` pipe with `fattach`.

```
SYNOPSIS

   #include <stropts.h>

   int fattach(int fildes, const char *path);
                                                          Spec 1170
```

The `fattach` attaches a STREAMS file descriptor to a pathname. The pathname corresponds to an existing file with privileges set so that both the client and server can access it. The pathname serves as the well-known port referenced by the client. When the server does an `I_RECVFD ioctl` on the original file descriptor, it blocks until another process does an `open` on the corresponding filename. The `open` returns a file descriptor that the client can use for communication. The `I_RECVFD ioctl` returns to the server a new file descriptor that it can use to communicate with the client.

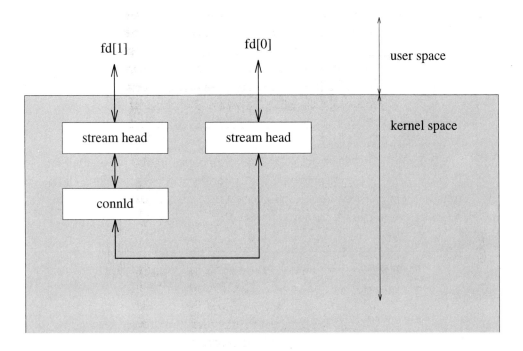

Figure 12.10: Connections after `connld` has been pushed on `fd[1]`.

Program 12.12 shows an implementation of the `u_open` function based on STREAMS pipes. The pathname used for the well-known port is just a file in the `/tmp` directory whose name is constructed by appending an agreed upon number to `streams_uici_`. If an error occurs in any of the intermediate calls, `u_open` returns −1. Use `u_error` to display a message.

Program 12.12: A STREAMS implementation of the UICI `u_open`.

```
int u_open(u_port_t port)
{
    char buffer[MAX_CANON];
    int mtpoint;
    int fd[2];

    sprintf(buffer, "/tmp/streams_uici_%d", (int)port);
    unlink(buffer);
    if ( ((mtpoint = creat(buffer, MTMODE)) != -1) &&
         (close(mtpoint) != -1) &&
         (pipe(fd) != -1) &&
```

```
            (ioctl(fd[1], I_PUSH, "connld") != -1) &&
            (fattach(fd[1], buffer) != -1) )
            return fd[0];
      close (fd[0]);
      close (fd[1]);
      return -1;
}
```

_____ **Program 12.12** _____

Program 12.13 shows the STREAMS implementation of u_listen. The server does an ioctl to request the file descriptor for the private stream. The ioctl blocks until a client calls u_connect. At that time, the ioctl creates a new stream and returns the new file descriptor to the server.

Program 12.13: A STREAMS implementation of the UICI u_listen.

```
int u_listen(int fd, char *hostn)
{
    mystrrecvfd conversation_info;
    int retval;

    while ( ((retval =
            ioctl(fd, I_RECVFD, &conversation_info)) == -1) &&
            (errno == EINTR) )
        ;
    if (retval == -1)
        return -1;
    *hostn = 0;
    return conversation_info.f.fd;
}
```

_____ **Program 12.13** _____

Program 12.14 shows the STREAMS implementation of the client call u_connect. The client opens the file that the server is waiting on. The open returns the communication file descriptor. Since the STREAMS implementation of UICI does not support network communication, u_listen sets the host name to the empty string and u_connect does not use its second parameter.

Program 12.14: A STREAMS implementation of the UICI u_connect.

```
int u_connect(u_port_t port, char *hostn)
{
    char buffer[MAX_CANON];
```

```
    sprintf(buffer, "/tmp/streams_uici_%d", (int)port);
    return open(buffer, O_RDWR);
}
```
_____ **Program 12.14** _____

12.8 Thread-Safe UICI

This section discusses the problems with implementing UICI in a thread-safe manner
and gives the details of an implementation that can be used with threads.

The UNIX `read` and `write` system calls are inherently unsafe for threads because
of the way they use `errno` to return error information. That problem has been solved
for multithreading by using thread-specific data for `errno`. Similarly, thread-safe TLI
uses thread-specific data for `t_errno`. The representation is necessary to preserve the
syntax for the standard UNIX system calls. User programs cannot easily use thread-
specific data, nor should they try to. The implementation of UICI in terms of sockets is
almost thread-safe because the underlying implementation of sockets is thread-safe.

The sockets and TLI implementations in Sections 12.4 and 12.5 ignore a few small
problems. The TLI implementation uses `t_errno` for saving error information. That
works as long as all errors produced are generated by the network calls. There are
cases in which that does not work. The `u_connect` calls `gethostbyname`, and
`u_listen` calls `gethostbyaddr`. These functions set `h_errno` rather than `errno`
or `t_errno`. This can cause `u_error` to produce a misleading message. These calls
also use static storage and are therefore not thread-safe. The returned `struct hostent`
structure contains pointers into this static storage. The thread-safe version of UICI uses
`gethostbyname_r` and `gethostbyaddr_r`.

```
┌──────────────────────────────────────────────────────────────────────┐
│ SYNOPSIS                                                              │
│                                                                      │
│   #include <netdb.h>                                                 │
│                                                                      │
│   struct hostent *gethostbyname_r(const char *name,                  │
│        struct hostent *result, char *buffer, int buflen,             │
│        int *h_errnop);                                               │
│   struct hostent *gethostbyaddr_r(const char *addr,                  │
│        int length, int type, struct hostent *result,                 │
│        char *buffer,  int buflen, int *h_errnop);                    │
│                                                                      │
└──────────────────────────────────────────────────────────────────────┘
```

These functions perform the same tasks as their unsafe counterparts but do not use
static storage. The `result` parameter is a pointer to a user-supplied `struct hostent`
structure that contains the result. Pointers in this structure point into the user-supplied

buffer `buffer` which has length `buflen` and must be large enough for the generated data. Error information is put in `*h_errorp` if the function returns `NULL`.

Even with these functions, the sockets and TLI implementations of UICI would still have a problem because `errno` and `t_error` would not be set and so `u_error` would not produce the correct message.

To keep the thread-safe version of the UICI functions similar to the original unsafe ones, the interpretation of the return values of these functions has not changed. Instead, they each take an additional parameter representing the error. All of these functions except for `u_error_r` pass a pointer to a `uerror_t` structure. If error information is not needed, a `NULL` pointer may be passed. The calling thread provides the storage for error information. New versions of all of the functions have an `_r` suffix indicating that they are thread-safe.

The `uerror_t` structure may be implementation-dependent. In the socket implementation, it contains a two integers. One contains the value of `errno` if this was set, and the other contains a value indicating an error from `gethostbyname_r` or `gethostbyaddr_r`. In the TLI implementation, three integers are needed, the extra one for `t_errno`. The TLI version of `uerror_t` is

```
typedef struct {
    int tli_error;
    int syserr;
    int hosterr;
} uerror_t;
```

The prototypes of the new UICI functions are

```
int u_open_r(unsigned short port, uerror_t *errorp);
int u_listen_r(int fd, char *hostn, uerror_t *errorp);
int u_connect_r(unsigned short port, char *inetp,
               uerror_t *errorp);
int u_close_r(int fd, uerror_t *errorp);
ssize_t u_read_r(int fd, void *buf, size_t nbyte,
               uerror_t *errorp);
ssize_t u_write_r(int fd, void *buf, size_t nbyte,
                uerror_t *errorp);
void u_error_r(char *s, uerror_t error);
int u_sync_r(int fd, uerror_t *errorp);
```

Program 12.15 shows the TLI implementation of `u_error_r` and Program 12.16 shows an implementation of `u_connect_r`. If the function `gethostbyname_r` returns an error, the `u_connect_r` sets the `hosterr` member of the `error` structure. All other errors set the `tli_error` member and possibly the `syserror` member of the `error` structure. The function does not set `t_errno` directly, since POSIX allows this to be a macro. The `u_set_error` function sets the error structure. A complete implementation of the thread-safe UICI is given in Appendix B.

_____

Program 12.15: TLI implementation of the thread-safe UICI `u_error_r`.

```
#define GETHOSTNOERROR      0
#define GETHOSTBYNAMEERROR 1
#define GETHOSTBYADDRERROR 2

void u_error_r(char *s, uerror_t error)
{
   if (error.hosterr == GETHOSTBYNAMEERROR)
      fprintf(stderr,"%s: error in getting name of remote host\n", s);
   else if (error.hosterr == GETHOSTBYADDRERROR)
      fprintf(stderr,"%s: error converting host name to address\n", s);
   else if (error.tli_error == TSYSERR)
      fprintf(stderr,"%s: %s\n", s, strerror(error.syserr));
   else
      fprintf(stderr,"%s: %s\n", s, t_errlist[error.tli_error]);
}
```
_____ **Program 12.15** _____

_____

Program 12.16: TLI implementation of the thread-safe UICI client call `u_connect_r`.

```
static void u_set_error(uerror_t *errorp)
{
   if (errorp == NULL)
      return;
   errorp -> hosterr = GETHOSTNOERROR;
   errorp -> tli_error = t_errno;
   if (t_errno == TSYSERR)
      errorp ->syserr = errno;
}

int u_connect_r(unsigned short port, char *inetp, uerror_t *errorp)
{
   struct t_info info;
   struct t_call *callptr;
   struct sockaddr_in server;
   struct hostent *hp;
   struct hostent hostresult;
   int fd;
   int trynum;
   unsigned int slptime;
   int herror;
   char hostbuf[HOSTBUFFERLENGTH];

   fd = t_open("/dev/tcp", O_RDWR, &info);
   if (fd < 0) {
```

```
    u_set_error(errorp);
    return -1;
}
                /* Create TCP addresses for communication with port */
memset(&server, 0, (size_t)sizeof(server));
server.sin_family = AF_INET;           /* Internet address family   */
                               /* convert name to internet address */
hp = gethostbyname_r(inetp, &hostresult, hostbuf, HOSTBUFFERLENGTH,
                &herror);
if (hp == NULL) {
    errorp -> hosterr = GETHOSTBYNAMEERROR;
    return -1;
}
                               /* copy Internet address to buffer   */
memcpy(&(server.sin_addr.s_addr), hostresult.h_addr_list[0],
    (size_t)hostresult.h_length);
server.sin_port = htons(port);
                               /* set buffer with destination info */
if ( (t_bind(fd, NULL, NULL) < 0) ||
    ((callptr =
        (struct t_call *)t_alloc(fd, T_CALL, T_ADDR)) == NULL) ) {
    u_set_error(errorp);
    return -1;
}

callptr -> addr.maxlen = sizeof(server);
callptr -> addr.len = sizeof(server);
callptr -> addr.buf = (char *)&server;
callptr -> opt.len = 0;
callptr -> udata.len = 0;
                                           /* Retry if this fails */
for (trynum = 0, slptime = 1;
    (trynum < RETRIES) &&
        (t_connect(fd, callptr, NULL) < 0);
    trynum++, slptime = 2*slptime) {
    t_rcvdis(fd, NULL);
    sleep(slptime);
}

callptr -> addr.buf = NULL;
t_free((char *)callptr, T_CALL);
if (trynum >= RETRIES) {
    u_set_error(errorp);
    return -1;
}
return fd;
}
```

_____ **Program 12.16** _____

A thread-safe version of UICI can also be produced using the `gethostbyname` and `gethostbyaddr` functions as long as these functions are protected by mutex locks.

12.9 Exercise: Transmission of Audio

This section extends the UICI server and client of Program 12.2 and Program 12.4 to send audio information from the client to the server. These programs can be used to implement a network intercom, network telephone service, or network radio broadcasts as described in Chapter 13. Start by incorporating audio into the UICI server and client:

- Implement file copying with the UICI server and client shown in Program 12.2 and Program 12.4.
- Test the program with the three different implementations of UICI. (Make sure to `diff` the input and output files to verify that each transfer completes correctly.)
- Modify the server and client to call the audio functions developed in Chapter 3 to transmit audio from the microphone of the client to the speaker of the server.
- Test the audio functions.

The program sends even if no one is talking, because once the program opens the audio device, the underlying device driver and interface card sample the audio input at a fixed rate until the program closes the file. The continuous sampling produces a prohibitive amount of data for transmission across the network. Use a filter to detect whether a packet contains voice and throw away audio packets that contain no voice. A simple method of filtering is to convert the u-law data to a linear scale and reject packets that fall below a threshold. Program 12.17 shows an implementation of this filter for Solaris 2. The `has_voice` function returns 1 if the packet contains voice and 0 if it should be thrown away. Incorporate `has_voice` or another filter so that the client does not transmit silence.

Program 12.17: Threshold function for filtering data with no voice.

```
#include <stdlib.h>
#include "/usr/demo/SOUND/include/multimedia/audio_encode.h"

    /* amplitude of ambient room noise, linear PCM */
#define THRESHOLD 20

/* Return 1 if anything in audio_buffer is above THRESHOLD. */
```

```
int has_voice(char *audio_buffer, int length)
{
    int i;

    for (i = 0; i < length; i++)
        if (abs(audio_u2c(audio_buffer[i])) > THRESHOLD)
            return 1;
    return 0;
}
```

—————————————————— **Program 12.17** ——————————————————

Write the following enhancements to the basic audio transmission service:

- Develop a calibration function that allows the threshold for voice detection to be adjusted based on the current value of the ambient room noise.
- Use filtering algorithms more sophisticated than simple thresholds.
- Keep track of total number of packets and the actual number that contain voice data. Display the information on standard error when the client receives a SIGUSR1 signal.
- Add volume control options on both client and server sides.
- Design an interface for accepting or rejecting connections based on sender information.
- Devise protocols analogous to caller ID and call-waiting.
- Add an option on the server side to record the incoming audio to a file for later playback. Recording is easy if the client is sending all packets. However, since the client is sending only packets with voice, straight recording will not sound right on playback because all silences are compressed. Keep timing information as well as the audio information in the recorded data.

12.10 Exercise: Ping Server

When a user pings a node on the network, ping responds with a message indicating that the host is up.

Example 12.9

The following command queries the vip *host.*

```
ping vip
```

The command might output the following message to indicate that vip *is responding to network communication.*

```
vip is alive
```

This section describes an exercise that uses `UICI` to implement a slightly fancier version of the `ping` service called `myping`. The `myping` function responds with

```
vip: 5:45am up 12:11, 2 users, load average: 0.14, 0.08, 0.07
```

Like `ping`, the `myping` program is a client-server application. A `myping` server running on the host listens at a well-known port for client requests. The server forks a child to respond to the request. The original server process continues listening. Assume that the `myping` well-known port number is defined by the constant `MYPINGPORT`.

- Write the code for the `myping` client. The client takes the host name as a command-line argument, makes a connection to the `MYPINGPORT`, reads what comes in on the connection and echoes it to standard output until end-of-file, closes the connection, and exits. Assume that if the connection attempt to the host fails, the client sleeps for `SLEEPTIME` seconds and then retries. After the number of connection attempts without success exceeds `RETRIES`, the client outputs the message that the host is not available and exits.

- Write code for the `myping` server. The server listens for connections on the `MYPINGPORT`. If a connection is made, the server forks a child to handle the request and the original process resumes listening at `MYPINGPORT`. The child closes the listening file descriptor, calls the `process_ping` function, closes the communication file descriptor, and exits. Write a `process_ping` that outputs just an error message for this step.

- Write a `process_ping` function with prototype

  ```
  int process_ping(int communfd);
  ```

  The `process_ping` function writes the response message to the communication file descriptor. An example message is

  ```
  vip: 5:45am up 12:11, 2 users, load average: 0.14, 0.08, 0.07
  ```

  The message consists of the hostname and the results of executing the `uptime` command. Use `uname` to get the hostname.

SYNOPSIS

```
#include <sys/utsname.h>

int uname(struct utsname *name);
```
POSIX.1, Spec 1170

One member of `struct utsname` is `char nodename[Sys_NMLN]` which specifies the name of the host. Use the `system` function to execute the `uptime` command. The `system` call forks a child to `execvp` the

command given by `string`. For the call, the `string` is `"uptime"`.
Since `uptime` outputs its result to standard output, redirect standard output
to the `communfd` before calling `system`.

SYNOPSIS

```
#include <stdlib.h>

int system(const char *string);
```
                                                                    Spec 1170

12.11 Additional Reading

Computer Networks, 2nd ed., by Tanenbaum [90] is a standard reference on computer
networks and the OSI model. *UNIX Network Programming* by Stevens [85] is a classic
in the area of network communication, but it is somewhat dated. *UNIX System V Network Programming* by Rago [71] is an excellent up-to-date reference book on network
programming under System V. Network services are not yet addressed in POSIX, but
Spec 1170 [99] standardizes both sockets and TLI.

Chapter 13

Project: *Internet Radio*

Broadcast, telephone, and network technologies are converging rapidly. Cable companies are offering telephone service and connections to the Internet. Telephone companies want to enter the entertainment business with video-on-demand and high-speed data services. Software for video conferencing and telephone conferencing on the Internet is widely available. The final outcome of the conflicts among these competing forces will probably be determined more by politics and regulatory decisions than by technical merit. Whatever the outcome, more computers will be handling voice and audio streams in addition to data. This chapter explores the interaction of threads with network communication through a producer-consumer application called a multiplex buffer. The project uses the buffer to synchronize a radio broadcast over a network, making delays in network transmission and synchronization audible.

Internet Talk Radio is an outgrowth of the rapid expansion of multimedia facilities on the Internet. Professionally produced audio broadcasts of interest to travelers on the *Information Highway* are encoded in Sun `.au` format and spooled to regional servers. Once a show has been distributed to regional spool sites, it is available for local broadcast using a multicast program called `radio` which is available by `ftp`.

Independently of Internet Talk Radio, a multicast backbone called MBone has been defined for the Internet [63]. The MBone is a combination of multicast and point-to-point links designed to facilitate the distribution of broadcast information on the Internet. The term *broadcast* means that a packet is distributed to every node on a network. The term *multicast* means that a packet is distributed to a subset of nodes on the network. A *point-to-point* connection implies a packet is sent by a specific source node to a specific destination.

Local networks are interconnected by *bridges* and *routers* [69] to form wide-area networks which in turn are interconnected to form the Internet. The network-layer protocol underlying the Internet (appropriately called IP for Internet Protocol) supports multicast communication for local-area networks. Bridges and routers generally do not forward broadcast and multicast packets in order to prevent an unruly node from flooding the Internet. However, there are situations when such multicast facilities are useful—such as in the distribution of a radio broadcast to receivers on the Internet. Rather than sending a distinct copy of the same packet to each receiver, a multicast distributes one copy of the packet along the network to all specified receivers.

In order to support efficient multicasting across bridges and routers, the MBone Project defines a virtual network consisting of subnetworks of the Internet connected by special routers that support multicasting. The special routers are called *mrouters*. Disconnected islands of the MBone are connected by point-to-point communication links. When a node with a point-to-point link detects a multicast packet, it encapsulates the multicast packet in IP packets and transmits the encapsulated packets on the link. The destination mrouter converts the packets back to multicast packets and transmits them on its local backbone.

13.1 Overview of the Multiplexer

This chapter develops a point-to-point system for distributing audio and data files to multiple destinations. The implementation is based on a multiplexer server shown in Figure 13.1 and does not take advantage of the IP multicast capabilities. Input received by the server is multiplexed or duplicated on all of the output lines. The output lines are network connections to clients. Imagine a generalization where the output lines are connected to multicast routers that are responsible for multicasting the information to their local networks. The project uses the multiplexer server to distribute an audio broadcast to a group of receiving workstations, hence the term Internet Radio in the chapter title.

This project is a variation of the producer-consumer problem. There is one producer (the broadcaster) and an arbitrary number of consumers (the receivers). The problem has some additional twists—in the ordinary producer-consumer problem, each packet is consumed by only one consumer. In the multiplexer each consumer must consume all of the packets, and consumers can join (tune in) or leave (tune out) the broadcast at any time.

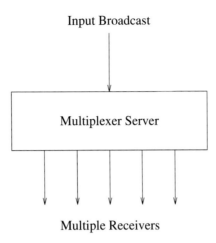

Figure 13.1: A multiplexer server buffers and copies its input to all output ports.

13.2 One-Way Communication

The first stage of the project establishes one-way communication over a network using the UICI communication interface described in Chapter 12. Use either the socket or TLI version of UICI. Communication follows a client-server model where a server program is running on the remote host and a client program on the local machine seeks to establish communication as shown in Figure 13.2.

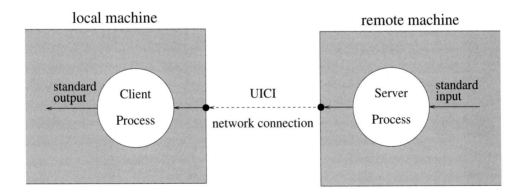

Figure 13.2: One-way communication on a network.

The following specification refers to the server program as do_broadcast and the client program as get_broadcast.

- Write a server program called do_broadcast to transmit from standard input over a network using one of the network versions of UICI discussed in Chapter 12. The do_broadcast listens at a well-known port for a client connection by calling u_listen. The u_listen function returns a *conversation file descriptor* which is actually used in the communication. Pass the well-known port number as a command-line argument to the server program.

- Once it has established a communication link, the do_broadcast program calls a writer function (described below) to transmit from standard input to the network. When the writer function returns, the server resumes listening at the well-known port for another do_broadcast client. Instrument the code so that do_broadcast writes informative messages to standard error.

- Write a writer function to handle the transmission of data from standard input to the network. The prototype for the writer function is

    ```
    void *writer(void *fdp);
    ```

    The writer function reads from standard input by calling read and outputs to the network by calling u_write on the open file descriptor specified by *fdp. Perform the operations in a loop until the end-of-file on standard input or until an error occurs. The writer's parameter and return value are pointers to void so that this function can be called as a thread without modification.

- Write a client program called get_broadcast that receives one-way communication over the network using UICI. The client connects to the well-known port on a remote machine by calling u_connect. Pass the hostname and the port number as command-line arguments to the get_broadcast client. After establishing network communication, the get_broadcast client calls a reader function (described below) to transmit from the network to standard output. When reader returns, the client exits.

- Write a reader function to handle the transmission of data from the network to standard output. The prototype for the reader function is

    ```
    void *reader(void *fdp);
    ```

    The reader function reads information from the network connection by calling u_read on the open file descriptor specified by *fdp and writes to standard output using write. Perform the operations in a loop until the end-of-file on *fdp or until an error occurs.

- Test the programs by running the `do_broadcast` server on one machine and the `get_broadcast` client on another machine. Run the client several times. Each time, halt the client with a `ctrl-c`. Make sure it is possible to start another client without restarting the server. Enter data at the keyboard for the standard input of `do_broadcast`.
- Test the program by transmitting a large file, say `my.file`. Suppose that the machine host name is `vip` and that it is using port `8623` for transmission. Execute the following commands on the `vip` host:

```
do_broadcast 8623 < my.file
get_broadcast vip 8623 > my.file.out
diff my.file.out my.file
```

If the transmission is working properly and the program is detecting end-of-file correctly, the files `my.file` and `my.file.out` should have no differences. Be sure to test an input file of significant size, say a megabyte or more. Use `diff` to compare the input and output files.

- Test the program with audio transmission. Suppose that the `do_broadcast` server executes on the `vip` host and the `get_broadcast` on another machine. The server machine must have a microphone, and the client machine must have a speaker. The test is

```
do_broadcast 8623 < "/dev/audio"
get_broadcast vip 8623 > "/dev/audio"
```

Speak into the microphone and listen for the transmission. Use `ctrl-c` to stop the programs. Remember data is transmitted even if no one is saying anything. (The `"/dev/audio"` is a Sun Microsystems device name for a workstation speaker and microphone. Substitute the appropriate device name as needed.)

13.3 Two-Way Communication

This section develops a client-server version of two-way communication [75]. After the client and server establish a UICI network connection, they communicate in a symmetric fashion. Each program monitors standard input and an input channel from its remote connection. A nonthreaded program might use `select` or `poll` to monitor the two file descriptors. (See Section 9.1.) This implementation uses the `reader` and `writer` functions of Section 13.2 as independent threads to do the two-way communication.

Recall that `writer` copies from standard input to a file descriptor, while `reader` copies from a file descriptor to standard output. Together they provide two-way communication. Figure 13.3 shows a schematic of the two-way communication. The `reader` and the `writer` threads are independent of each other and require no synchronization.

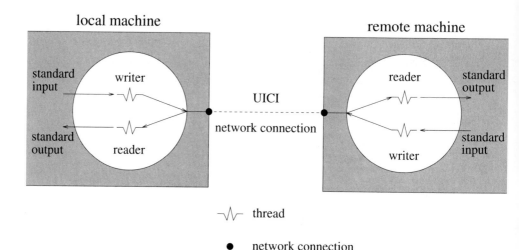

Figure 13.3: A schematic of the threaded implementation of two-way communication.

Modify the client and server programs of Section 13.2 as follows to convert one-way communication to two-way communication:

- Make a copy of the source for the `get_broadcast` and modify it as follows. Call the modified executable `call_up`. After making a network connection using `u_connect`, the `call_up` client creates two threads, one to execute `reader` and the other to execute `writer`. Pass a pointer to the network file descriptor returned by `u_connect` to both threads.

- Make a copy of the source for the `do_broadcast` and modify it as follows. Call the modified executable `answer_call`. After the `answer_call` server makes a network connection to the client through `u_listen`, it creates two threads, one to execute `reader` and the other to execute `writer`. Pass a pointer to the network file descriptor returned by `u_listen` to both threads for the network communication.

- Test the programs by transmitting a large file in each direction and using `diff` to verify that the transmission completes accurately.

- Test the programs as an audio intercom by redirecting both standard input and standard output to `"/dev/audio"`. To do that requires two machines equipped with microphones and speakers. Test the program by conscripting two users to talk at the same time.

13.4 The Transmit Buffer

The audio intercom of Section 13.3 supports two-way communication between processes over a network. In a radio application, one process (the broadcaster) sends to many processes (the receivers). This section introduces a transmit buffer between the broadcaster and the receiver in preparation for multiple receivers. Figure 13.4 represents the transmit buffer as a circular buffer with elements of type `buffer_t`.

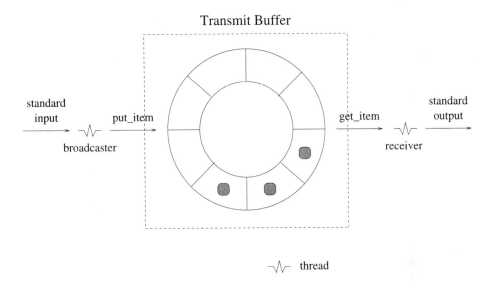

Figure 13.4: A schematic of the transmit buffer.

Define `transmit_buffer` by

```
#define MAXBUFSIZE 10
#define PACKETSIZE 1024
typedef struct buf {
    char buffer[PACKETSIZE];
    int packet_size;
    int number_unread;
    pthread_mutex_t element_lock;
} buffer_t

static int transmit_buffer_size;
static buffer_t transmit_buffer[MAXBUFSIZE];
static int current_start;
static int current_active_receivers;
```

Implement the `transmit_buffer` as an object with the access functions to insert and retrieve items from the buffer. A `broadcaster` thread transfers information from an input file to the buffer by calling `put_item`. A `receiver` thread transfers information from the buffer to an output file by calling `get_item`.

Modify the circular buffer object given in Program 10.1 so that instead of having a mutex lock protect the entire buffer, there is a mutex for each slot in the buffer. A thread only holds an element mutex while it is modifying the `number_unread` member of that element. As in Chapter 10, the access functions do not provide synchronization between broadcaster and receiver.

The implementation of the circular buffer of Program 10.1 included variables `bufin` and `bufout` for designating the slots to insert into and remove from. In the `transmit_buffer` implementation, each thread keeps its own pointers and passes them as part of the `get_item` and `put_item`. Another modification is that the `put_item` does not explicitly pass the data item to be inserted and `get_item` does not return the data item that was extracted. Instead, both functions pass open file descriptors. The `get_item` function copies the buffer value directly to the file represented by the `outfd` file descriptor. Similarly, `put_item` obtains the data to be inserted directly by reading `infd`. The modification eliminates a copying operation for each packet access.

This section specifies the implementation of the transmit buffer object and describes how to test the object. Implement the following access functions for the `transmit_buffer` object:

> ➤ Write an `initialize_transmit_buffer` function to initialize the transmit buffer. The prototype of `initialize_transmit_buffer` is
>
> ```
> int initialize_transmit_buffer(int buffer_size);
> ```
>
> The `initialize_transmit_buffer` initializes the `element_lock` and `number_unread` members of each element. It also sets the `transmit_buffer_size` to `buffer_size`. The `buffer_size` must be less than `MAXBUFSIZE`. On success, `initialize_transmit_buffer` returns 0, otherwise it returns −1.

> ➤ Write a `get_item` function that copies the item in slot `*outp` of the `transmit_buffer` to the file specified by `outfd`. The prototype for `get_item` is
>
> ```
> int get_item(int outfd, int *outp);
> ```
>
> The `get_item` increments `*outp` modulo `transmit_buffer_size` so that the variable always specifies the next location for the caller to read from. The `get_item` function also decrements the `number_unread` and returns the new value of `number_unread`.

➤ Write a `put_item` function that reads the next packet from the input file specified by the open file descriptor `infd` and puts it into the `transmit_buffer` slot number `*inp`. The prototype for `put_item` is

```
int put_item(int infd, int *inp);
```

The `put_item` function sets the `packet_size` of the corresponding slot to the size of the packet read, and it sets `number_unread` to the current number of active receiver threads which is specified by the global variable, `current_active_receivers`. The `put_item` function increments `*inp` modulo `transmit_buffer_size` so that the variable always specifies the next location for the calling thread to write to. The `put_item` function returns the number of bytes transferred to the buffer if successful or −1 otherwise.

➤ Write a `get_current_start` function that returns the current value of `current_start`. Its prototype is

```
int get_current_start(void);
```

The `transmit_buffer` object includes the static variables `current_start` and `current_active_receivers` which are initialized to 0 and 1, respectively. These static variables have values that are constant for this part of the project.

In order to test the `transmit_buffer` object, do the following:

- Copy Program 10.6 into a new directory. Rename the `producer` thread as `broadcaster` and the `consumer` thread as `receiver`. Call the executable `test_buffer`.
- Modify `broadcaster` so that instead of calculating a fixed number of items, the `broadcaster` continues until `put_item` returns a −1. The `broadcaster` keeps a local buffer position, `in`, which it initializes to `current_start`. The `broadcaster` passes `&in` as the second argument to `put_item` and `STDIN_FILENO` as the first argument.
- Modify `receiver` to keep a local buffer position, `out`, which it initializes by calling `get_current_start`. The `receiver` passes `&out` as the second argument to `get_item` and `STDOUT_FILENO` as the first argument.
- Modify the main program to take the size of the transmit buffer as a command-line argument. Make any other modifications necessary to test the transmit buffer library.
- Use `test_buffer` to transmit a large file. For example, to copy `my.file` through a transmit buffer of size 10 execute

```
test_buffer 10 < my.file > my.file.out
diff my.file my.file.out
```

13.5 Multiplexing the Transmit Buffer

This section develops the multiplexing synchronization for the transmit buffer shown in
Figure 13.5. Assume that a fixed number of receivers are active throughout the broadcast. The main program takes the size of the transmit buffer and the number of receivers
as command-line arguments.

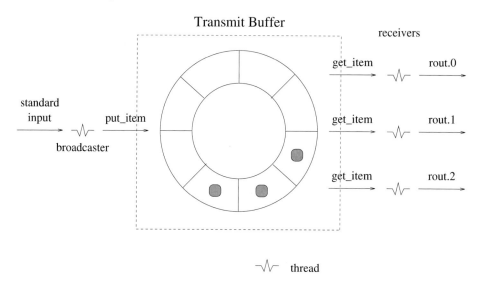

Figure 13.5: A schematic of the multiplexed transmit buffer.

- Rewrite the `receiver` function of Section 13.4 so that it no longer writes
  data to standard output. Rather, it takes an argument that is an open file descriptor of the file it should write to.
- Rewrite the `broadcaster` function of Section 13.4 so that it no longer
  reads data from standard input. Rather, it takes an argument that is an open
  file descriptor for the file it should read from.
- Modify the `test_buffer` program of Section 13.4 as described below:
  - * Pass the size of the transmit buffer and the number of active receivers
    on the command line.
  - * Call the function `initialize_transmit_buffer` to initialize
    `transmit_buffer`.
  - * Initialize all of the necessary synchronization variables.
  - * Open `current_active_receivers` files that are named `rout.n`
    where `n` is the number of the `receiver` thread to be created (starting
    with `0`). The resulting file descriptors are passed to the corresponding
    `receiver` threads that the main program creates.

> * Create `current_active_receivers` number of `receiver` threads and pass the corresponding `rout.n` file descriptor as a parameter to each thread through `pthread_create`.
>
> * Create a `broadcaster` thread as in Section 13.4 and pass the file descriptor `STDIN_FILENO` as the parameter to `broadcaster` through the `pthread_create`.
>
> * Wait to join with all of the other threads.
>
> Test the program with files of different lengths. Make sure that the files are transmitted correctly, (i.e, that all of the files `rout.n` have the same contents as the input file). Use `diff` to make sure that the files agree.

13.6 Network Receivers

This section develops the network version of the `receiver` threads. Create a new subdirectory and copy all of the code developed in Section 13.5 into the directory. Rename the main program `test_receivers`. The `test_receivers` program now takes three command-line arguments: the size of the transmit buffer, the number of receivers, and the well-known port that the receivers connect on. Figure 13.6 shows a schematic of the `test_receivers` program when the number of receiver threads is three.

Implement the `test_receivers` program as follows:

- Listen for the specified number of receiver requests on the well-known receiver port and create a `receiver` thread for each request. Pass the conversation descriptor returned by `u_listen` as the parameter for the thread in the `pthread_create`.

- Create the `broadcast` thread and pass `STDIN_FILENO` as the parameter for the thread in the `pthread_create`.

- Join with the `broadcaster` thread.

- Join with all `receiver` threads.

- Clean up.

Use the `get_broadcast` program of Section 13.2 for the receiver client. Test the program first by transmitting a large file and then by transmitting audio as in Section 13.2. When transmitting audio to more than one client, be sure to run the clients on different machines, each of which is equipped with a speaker. Experiment with the following:

- Different values for the `transmit_buffer_size`.

- Different priorities for `broadcaster` and `receiver` threads.

- The `broadcaster` and `receiver` threads having scope `SYSTEM`.

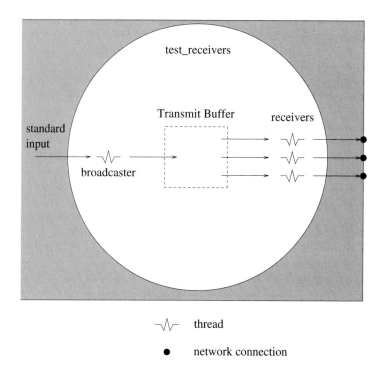

Figure 13.6: The `test_receivers` has remote receivers connecting to the transmit buffer through a well-known port.

13.7 Tuning In and Out

This section allows receivers to join the broadcast in progress and to leave the broadcast early.

- Make a new directory and copy the programs from Section 13.6 into it. Rename the main program `test_tuning`.
- The `test_tuning` program takes three command-line arguments: the transmit buffer size, the maximum number of receivers (`max_receivers`), and the well-known port that the external receiver clients connect on.
- The `test_tuning` program creates a `get_receivers` thread which listens for connection requests on the receiver well-known port.
- The main thread then calls `pthread_create` to create a `broadcaster` thread with `STDIN_FILENO` as the parameter.
- Write a `get_receivers` function that has the following prototype:

```
void *get_receivers(void *arg);
```

The `get_receivers` function should do the following in a loop:
* Listen for a connection request from the well-known receiver port by calling `u_listen`.
* When a request is received, create a new `receiver` thread and pass it the file descriptor returned by `u_listen`.

The `get_receivers` thread creates up to `max_receivers` threads before returning or being killed.

- The `current_active_receivers` and `current_start` are no longer constant. Define a mutex to protect these shared variables. Update their values in the appropriate places.
- If a remote receiver is killed, the corresponding `receiver` thread experiences an error in writing output. The `receiver` decrements the `current_active_receivers` and decrements the appropriate counts in the `transmit_buffer`.
- Devise a strategy for graceful exit.

13.8 Network Broadcaster

This section converts the Internet Radio program so that it takes input from the network instead of from standard input.

- Modify the `test_tuning` program so that the main thread creates the `get_receivers` thread and then does a `u_listen` on the input well-known port. Call the executable of the modified program `test_network`.
- When a broadcast source makes the connection, the main thread creates the `broadcaster` thread using the descriptor returned by `u_listen` as the argument for `pthread_create`. The `test_network` program now takes four command-line arguments: the transmit buffer size, the maximum number of receivers, the well-known port that the external receiver clients connect on, and the well-known port that the broadcaster listens on.
- Write a `broadcast_source` client program to provide the network source. Figure 13.7 shows a schematic of the connection.

13.9 Signal Handling

Incorporate signal handling into the `test_network` program of Section 13.8. If `test_network` receives the `SIGUSR1` signal, it should kill the `broadcaster` thread and allow the `receiver` threads to finish transmitting what is left in the `transmit_buffer`. Investigate the cancellation points mechanism provided by

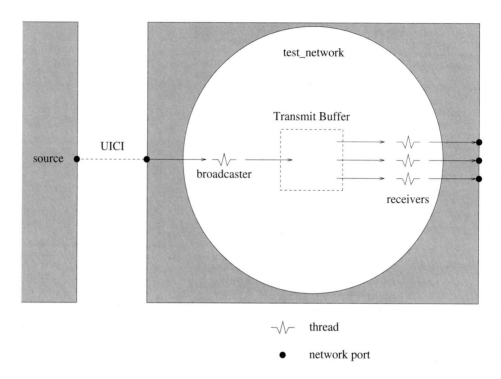

Figure 13.7: A network version of the broadcaster.

POSIX.1c threads. Use a dedicated thread with `sigwait` to handle the `SIGUSR1` signal.

13.10 Additional Reading

Many audio files are available on the Internet. To receive a FAQ, send a mail message to `inforadio.com` . For a list of sites archiving radio files, send mail to `sitesradio.com` . No subject or message body is necessary. The Web page of Internet Talk Radio is `http://town.hall.org/radio`. The article "MBone provides audio and video across the Internet" discusses MBone availability and provides pointers to a number of Internet sites [63]. "Handling audio and video streams in a distributed environment" discusses the general issues that arise in audio and video transmissions [43]. The May 1995 issue of *IEEE Computer* was devoted to multimedia systems [30, 34, 49, 73]. Some early experiments on audio that formed the basis of this project were reported in [75].

Chapter 14

Remote Procedure Calls

Opinion is divided on the remote procedure call (RPC): Is it the best or worst development to hit distributed computing? Unfortunately, the user-interface for RPCs is an emerging standard which is not as simple as it should be. In any case, this chapter discusses the basics of RPCs and allows the reader to form his or her own opinion about their future. The chapter illustrates, by example, the mechanics of converting a local function to a remote service. The discussion then turns to such critical issues as server state, idempotent calls, and semantics under failures. Sun NFS (Network File System) is an important commercial application whose protocols illustrate many of these ideas. The chapter closes with an explanation of how to develop a threaded server for RPCs.

In traditional structured programming and top-down design, programmers organize large programs into smaller functional units in order to produce modular designs in which the functions (or procedures) represent high-level operations. A program invokes these operations on different data by passing arguments to the functions through their parameters.

It seems natural to generalize the idea of a function call to a distributed setting by allowing a program to call a function that is not located in the process address space. If such a *remote function call* or *remote procedure call* were available, a programmer could distribute an ordinary program on networked hosts and take advantage of services not available locally, while still preserving a modular design. The Sun Open Network Computing (ONC) Transport Independent Remote Procedure Call (TI-RPC) is an emerging standard, and this chapter develops the remote procedure call under that system. The first section explains the philosophy of remote procedure calls. Later sections present examples that convert local calls to remote calls and explore general issues of binding, naming, and failures. Section 14.9 shows how to convert an ordinary RPC server to a threaded one.

14.1 Basic Operation

When a program calls a function, the return address and other state information are pushed on a run-time stack, and control is transferred to the start of the function. The storage allocated on the stack is called the *activation record* for the function. The activation record also holds initial values of parameters and locations for the automatic variables declared within the function. The call to a function is part of a single thread of execution as shown in Figure 14.1. The function call causes a change in the execution address representing the thread of execution.

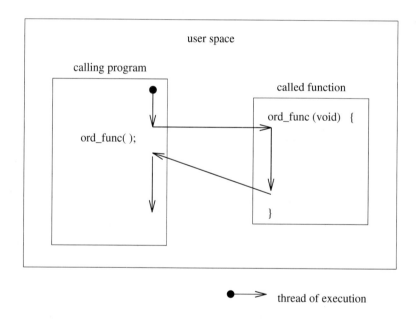

Figure 14.1: Thread of execution for an ordinary function call.

The function return pops the activation record and sets the program counter to the return address. (The return may also restore registers and do other cleanup.) The return causes the thread to resume execution of the calling program at the statement after the call.

Example 14.1
The following sequence represents a thread of execution for process one.

$$2998_1, 2999_1, 3000_1, 4000_1, 4001_1, 4002_1, 4003_1, 3001_1, 3002_1$$

The subscripts in Example 14.1 label the particular thread of execution. At statement 3000, thread one calls a function. The function statements are 4000, 4001, 4002, and 4003. The thread of execution then returns to statement 3001_1 of the calling program.

A program requests a system service by executing a *system call*, which appears to work like an ordinary function call except that the call refers to code in the operating system rather than in the program. From the viewpoint of the thread of execution, however, there are important differences between a system call and an ordinary function call. Figure 14.2 shows the thread of execution for a system call.

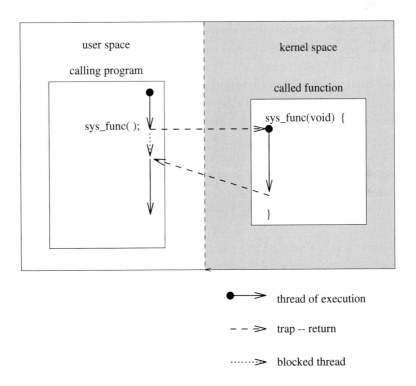

Figure 14.2: Thread of execution for a system call.

A system call is a trap to an entry point into the kernel which causes the thread of execution for the calling program to block. A separate thread of execution with a stack in the kernel executes the system call. When the trap returns, the original thread of execution unblocks. A program may invoke a system call directly or through C library functions. The library functions form *jackets* for the underlying services. A jacket might massage the parameters and do other bookkeeping before actually making the system call trap in order to provide a more transparent user service.

Figure 14.3 shows the underlying mechanism for system calls. The calling program executes an instruction that causes a software interrupt or trap. The kernel trap handler gains control, examines the request, executes the requested service, and returns the result. The system call is handled that way to prevent user code from directly accessing any data structures in the kernel and possibly doing damage.

The trap changes the hardware to a different mode of operation, sometimes called supervisor mode, in order to access system resources not available to the ordinary user. From the user's viewpoint, a system call is just an opaque function call. The program blocks until the call is executed and then resumes execution at the statement after the call.

The philosophy of system calls is to make them look as much like ordinary function calls as possible. While the two mechanisms appear the same to the calling program, there are essential differences. The system call is executed by a distinct thread operating from a different stack, while the function call is executed by the calling program thread and uses the calling program's stack. In other words the system call is *executed on behalf of* the calling program, while an ordinary function call is *executed by* the calling program.

Now suppose that instead of calling a function that is in the kernel, a program calls a function located in the address space of another process, possibly a process residing on another machine. Logically, the program should make the call and block until the function returns. Such an operation is referred to as a *remote procedure call (RPC)*. Figure 14.4 shows the threads of execution for an RPC. Like a system call, the remote call generates a new thread of execution (this time in the address space of a remote server), and the caller blocks until the new thread completes.

Figure 14.5 shows the basic setup for the remote procedure call. A client makes a function call just as it would make an ordinary call and waits for control to return (as indicated by *logical call* and *logical return* in the figure).

The actual call is more circuitous than would first appear. The client program is compiled with additional code called the *client stub* to form a single process. The client stub (which plays a role analogous to the system call jacket) is responsible for converting the arguments and assembling them into a message that is appropriate for network transmission. The conversion to a network message is known as *marshaling the arguments*. The program actually calls a function in the *client stub* that is essentially a jacket used to package up arguments for the underlying request. The client stub performs the marshaling by converting the arguments to a machine-independent format so that machines with different architectures can participate. The standard format for machine-

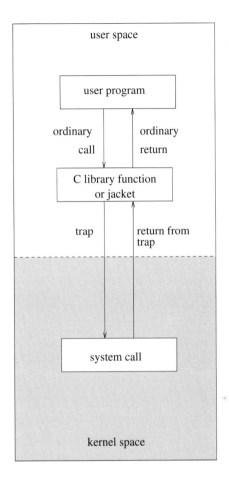

Figure 14.3: A system call generates a trap into the kernel. The kernel returns values to the calling program.

independent representation of data is called the XDR or *external data representation* format. The client stub then performs a trap to network functions in the kernel that are responsible for sending a message to the remote server. The client stub then waits for a reply message.

The functions that are to be called remotely are also compiled with additional code called the *server stub*. The server stub acts as a jacket for the server functions. When a client request arrives over the network, the kernel of the remote host passes it to the waiting server stub. The server stub unmarshals the arguments and calls the requested service as an ordinary function call.

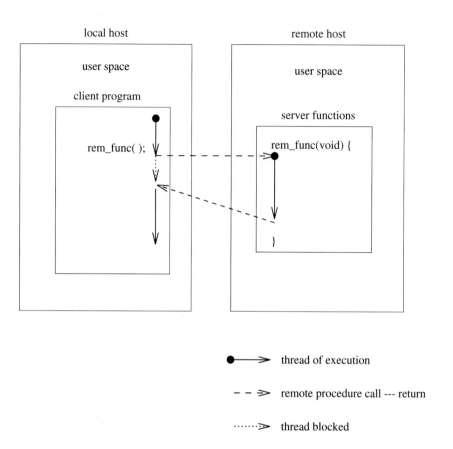

Figure 14.4: Thread of execution for a remote procedure call.

When the service function call returns, the server stub marshals the return values into an appropriate network message and performs a system call to the server kernel requesting transmission of the response over the network to the client's host. The kernel passes the message to the waiting client stub which unmarshals it and passes it to the client as an ordinary return value.

The RPC mechanism is transparent to the caller. All the client program sees is an ordinary function call to the client stub, and the underlying network communication is hidden from view. On the server side, the server functions are called as ordinary functions because the server stub is part of the server process. The underlying mechanism for transporting requests and return values over the network is called the *transport protocol*. Remote procedure calls are designed to be independent of the transport protocol that is used to provide the service.

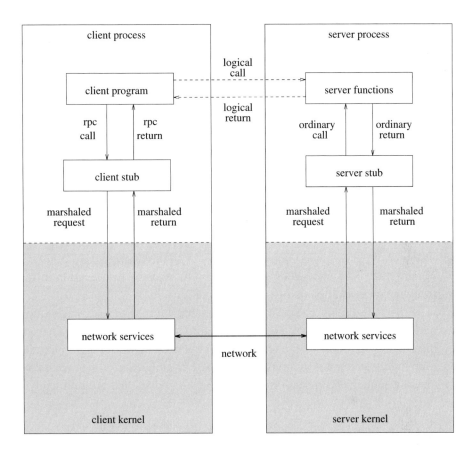

Figure 14.5: Protocol for remote procedure calls.

14.2 Converting a Simple Local Call to an RPC

The most natural approach for developing remote calls is to debug functions first as local functions and then to analyze how remote execution changes them. The two main issues involved in converting a local function to a remotely called one are establishing a handle to the remote function so that the correct service is called and passing parameters in a form that is recognizable by different kinds of server hosts.

In an ideal world, a programmer could create a program with local calls, indicate which calls should be remote, and have the system generate the client and server code. Unfortunately, high-level generation of client and server code is not yet available. Sun provides a command called rpcgen which generates the remote version from a specification file whose name ends in .x. The rpcgen program uses information in the function prototypes (return value type and parameter types) and makes skeleton functions into which the programmer inserts code. The skeletons indicate how to call the remote functions and how the remote functions return their values.

This section illustrates the process by converting a simple local service for generating pseudorandom numbers into a remote service. The service is based on the `drand48` family of pseudorandom-number generators from the UNIX standard library.

```
SYNOPSIS

  #include <stdlib.h>

  double drand48(void);
  double erand48(unsigned short xsubi[3]);
  void srand48(long seedval);
  unsigned short *seed48(unsigned short seed16v[3]);
```
Spec 1170

This section uses `srand48` and `drand48`, and the next section introduces a more robust implementation using `erand48` and `seed48`.

Prior to invoking `drand48` a program must initialize a starting value by calling the `srand48` function with a `long` parameter value called the *seed*. The seed determines the starting position in a predetermined sequence of pseudorandom numbers. After initializing the generator by invoking `srand48`, call `drand48` to return successive values in a sequence of pseudorandom `double` values that are uniformly distributed in the interval $[0, 1)$.

Example 14.2

The following code segment produces ten pseudorandom numbers. The generator seed is 3243.

```
#include <stdio.h>
#include <stdlib.h>
int myseed;
int iters;
int i;

myseed = 3243;
iters = 10;
srand48(myseed);
for (i = 0; i < iters; i++)
    printf("%d : %f\n", i, drand48());
```

The design of a local service is the first step in RPC development. Program 14.1 shows such a local service for generating pseudorandom numbers. The service has two functions—`initialize_random` and `get_next_random` which encapsulate the `srand48` and `drand48` functions, respectively.

Program 14.1: Local service for generating pseudorandom numbers.

```
#include "rand.h"
void initialize_random(long seed)
{
    srand48(seed);
}

double get_next_random(void)
{
    return drand48();
}
```
_____ **Program 14.1** _____

Program 14.2 calls the functions of Program 14.1. The seed value and the number of iterations are command-line arguments. The program calls the `initialize_random` service to initialize the underlying pseudorandom-number generator and then outputs a specified number of pseudorandom numbers by calling `get_next_random`.

Program 14.2: A program that calls a local service for generating pseudorandom numbers.

```
#include <unistd.h>
#include <stdio.h>
#include "rand.h"

void main(int argc, char *argv[])
{
    int iters;
    int i;
    long myseed;

    if (argc != 3) {
        fprintf(stderr, "Usage: %s seed iterations\n", argv[0]);
        exit(1);
    }
    myseed = (long)atoi(argv[1]);
    iters = atoi(argv[2]);
    initialize_random(myseed);
    for (i = 0; i < iters; i++)
        printf("%d : %f\n", i, get_next_random());
    exit(0);
}
```
_____ **Program 14.2** _____

Program 14.3 shows the `rand.h` header file for the service. The remainder of this section explains the steps in converting `initialize_random` and
`get_next_random` to remote functions. The first step in converting a local function to a remote one is to produce a specification file for the remote service. The
specification file has a `.x` extension and is written in the Sun RPC Language, a C-like
specification language. Fortunately a standard template is sufficient for simple services.

Program 14.3: The `rand.h` header file.

```
#include <stdlib.h>
void initialize_random(long seed);
double get_next_random(void);
```
—————————————————————— **Program 14.3** ————————————————————

A remote procedure call specification contains three unsigned numbers that identify
the program, the version, and the procedure or function within the program. (The RPC
terminology uses procedure instead of function, but the meaning is the same.) Program
numbers are administered by a central authority. Some program numbers, including
those used in the examples here, are available for experimentation (but see Section 14.6).
The version number may be any value, but it typically starts at `1`. Each time the service
is updated, choose a new version number so that old copies of the server may be active
while newer versions are in testing. The old versions of the clients continue to communicate with the old servers while the new clients use the new server. A server may
encapsulate several functions that can be called remotely. The correspondence between
functions and procedure numbers is part of the specification of the service.

Program 14.4 shows a sample `rand.x` specification file for the remote pseudorandom-number server `RAND_PROG` which is identified by the number `0x31111111`.
The version number of the server, referred to symbolically as `RAND_VERS`, is `1`. The
`RAND_PROG` server exports services `initialize_random` and `get_next_random`.

Program 14.4: The `rand.x` specification file.

```
/*       rand.x          */
program RAND_PROG {
    version RAND_VERS{
        void INITIALIZE_RANDOM(long) = 1;
        double GET_NEXT_RANDOM(void) = 2;
    } = 1;
} = 0x31111111;
```
—————————————————————— **Program 14.4** ————————————————————

The function names in Program 14.4 are the same as those of the local functions in Program 14.1 except that they are all in uppercase. The `rpcgen` utility converts these to lowercase when it forms the skeleton functions. The functions are numbered, so that the `initialize_random` function is service number `1` within the `RAND_PROG` server, and the `get_next_random` function is service number `2` within the server.

The `rpcgen` program generates the files needed to create the remote service.

```
SYNOPSIS

   rpcgen infile
   rpcgen [ -a ] [ -A ] [ -b ] [ -C ] [ -D name [ = value ] ]
          [ -i size ] [ -I [ -K seconds ] ] [ -L ]
          [ -M ] [ -N ] [ -T ] [ -Y pathname ] infile
   rpcgen [ -c | -h | -l | -m | -t | -Sc | -Ss | -Sm ]
          [ -o outfile ] [ infile ]
   rpcgen [ -s nettype ] [ -o outfile ] [ infile ]
   rpcgen [ -n netid ] [ -o outfile ] [ infile ]
```

The `-C` option indicates ANSI C is used, and the `-a` option tells `rpcgen` to generate all of the supporting files. The `infile` should have a `.x` extension to indicate that it is a specification file.

Example 14.3

Figure 14.6 shows the files generated when the following command is executed. The `proto.x` *is a user-constructed specification file.*

```
rpcgen -C -a proto.x
```

The `-a` option of `rpcgen` requests that all of the files shown in Figure 14.6 be generated. If the `-a` option is omitted, `rpcgen` only generates the files in the unshaded boxes. The `rpcgen` incorporates whatever name occurs before `.x` in the specification filename as the prefix or suffix in the filenames for the various files it generates. The files in Figure 14.6 contain the following information for the `proto.x` service:

`makefile.proto`	This file is the makefile for compiling all of the client and server code.
`proto_clnt.c`	This file contains the client stub, which is usually not modified.
`proto_svc.c`	This file contains the server stub, which is usually not modified.
`proto.h`	This header file contains all of the XDR types generated from the specification. Look here to see how `rpcgen` converted any types defined in the `.x` file.
`proto_client.c`	This file contains a skeleton client main program with

dummy calls to the remote service. Insert code to set up the argument values for the remote service before the dummy call in the client program.

`proto_server.c`   This file contains the stubs for the remote services. Insert the code for the local version of the services into these stubs. It may prove necessary to modify the way these functions use the parameters.

`proto_xdr.c`   If this file is generated, it contains XDR filters needed by the client and server stubs. This file is usually not modified.

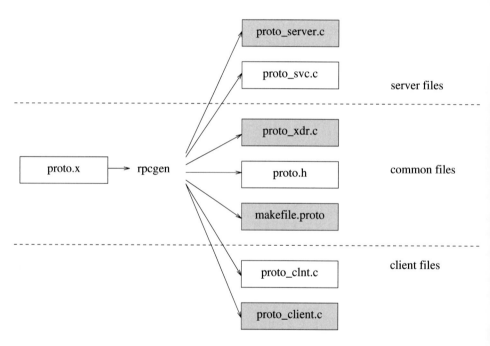

Figure 14.6: Files generated by `rpcgen` from the `proto.x` file. Shaded files are optionally generated by the `-a` option of `rpcgen`.

Example 14.4

The following command generates the client and server programs for the pseudorandom-number service from the `rand.x` *specification file of Program 14.4.*

```
rpcgen -C -a rand.x
```

To convert the local pseudorandom-number service to a remote service, follow these steps:

- Execute `rpcgen` to generate the needed files from the `rand.x` specification file.
- Modify the `rand_client.c` file to contain the client code.
- Modify the `rand_svc.c` file to contain the functions to be called remotely.

Program 14.5 shows the `rand_client.c` program generated by `rpcgen`. The dummy main program is just a vehicle for getting the host name from the command line. The host name is the Internet address in ASCII form (e.g., `vip.cs.utsa.edu`).

Program 14.5: The `rand_client.c` program generated by `rpcgen`.

```c
/*
 * This is sample code generated by rpcgen.
 * These are only templates and you can use them
 * as a guideline for developing your own functions.
 */

#include "rand.h"


void
rand_prog_1(char *host)
{
CLIENT *clnt;
void   *result_1;
long   initialize_random_1_arg;
double *result_2;
char * get_next_random_1_arg;

#ifndef DEBUG
clnt = clnt_create(host, RAND_PROG, RAND_VERS, "netpath");
if (clnt == (CLIENT *) NULL) {
clnt_pcreateerror(host);
exit(1);
}
#endif /* DEBUG */

result_1 = initialize_random_1(&initialize_random_1_arg, clnt);
if (result_1 == (void *) NULL) {
clnt_perror(clnt, "call failed");
}
result_2 = get_next_random_1((void *)&get_next_random_1_arg, clnt);
if (result_2 == (double *) NULL) {
clnt_perror(clnt, "call failed");
```

```
}
#ifndef DEBUG
clnt_destroy(clnt);
#endif /* DEBUG */
}


main(int argc, char *argv[])
{
char *host;

if (argc < 2) {
printf("usage:   %s server_host\n", argv[0]);
exit(1);
}
host = argv[1];
rand_prog_1(host);
}
```

_____ **Program 14.5** _____

Most of the interesting code in Program 14.5 is in the jacket function `rand_prog_1`. The `clnt_create` call generates a handle for the remote service. The `RAND_PROG` and `RAND_VERS` parameters are the program and version names specified in `rand.x`. The `"netpath"` parameter indicates that the program should look for an available network transport mechanism as specified by the `NETPATH` environment variable. (See Section 14.6 for a discussion.) If the `clnt_create` fails, it returns a `NULL` pointer.

The converted remote calls to `initialize_random` and `get_next_random` have the version number appended to the function names, so `initialize_random` is called as `initialize_random_1`. Another difference between the local calls and the remote calls is that the parameters and return values are designated by pointers. In fact these pointers refer to data structures defined in the client stub. The `clnt` pointer returned from `clnt_create` is the handle for the remote service. It is used as an additional parameter to each of the remote procedure calls. The `clnt` handle should be deallocated with a `clnt_destroy` when the program no longer needs to make remote calls.

Program 14.6 shows a revised `rand_client.c` program. It is a combination of the main program in Program 14.2 and Program 14.5. Start with the original program for local service of Program 14.2 and insert the call to `create_client` near the beginning of the program and the call to `clnt_destroy` at the end. The host name is now passed as the first command-line argument. The main program calls the remote functions directly, so there is no need for `rand_prog_1`.

The next change involves the conversion of the calls to `initialize_random` and

get_next_random from local calls to remote calls. The remote names have an appended _1 because the version number is 1. The remote functions pass their parameters by pointer and return a pointer to the return value. The clnt handle is passed as
an additional parameter in the calls. The client side conversion is now complete.

Program 14.6: The rand_client.c program.

```
#include <stdlib.h>
#include <stdio.h>
#include "rand.h"

void main(int argc, char *argv[])
{
    int iters, i;
    long myseed;
    CLIENT *clnt;
    void *result_1;
    double *result_2;
    char *arg;

    if (argc != 4) {
        fprintf(stderr, "Usage: %s host seed iterations\n", argv[0]);
        exit(1);
    }
    clnt = clnt_create(argv[1], RAND_PROG, RAND_VERS, "netpath");
    if (clnt == (CLIENT *) NULL) {
        clnt_pcreateerror(argv[1]);
        exit(1);
    }
    myseed = (long)atoi(argv[2]);
    iters = atoi(argv[3]);
    result_1 = initialize_random_1(&myseed, clnt);
    if (result_1 == (void *) NULL) {
        clnt_perror(clnt, "call failed");
    }
    for (i = 0; i < iters; i++) {
        result_2 = get_next_random_1((void *)&arg, clnt);
        if (result_2 == (double *) NULL) {
            clnt_perror(clnt, "call failed");
        }
        else
            printf("%d : %f\n", i, *result_2);
    }
    clnt_destroy(clnt);
    exit(0);
}
```

_____ **Program 14.6** _____

The code generated by `rpcgen` for `rand_server.c` is shown in Program 14.7. The server functions have the version number and `_svc` appended to their names. The return values are static because they are passed by pointer to the server stub. If these values were not static, the storage for them would be deallocated when the call returned and the server stub would not have an opportunity to marshal them.

Program 14.7: The skeleton `rand_server.c` code generated from the `rpcgen` of Example 14.4.

```
/*
 * This is sample code generated by rpcgen.
 * These are only templates and you can use them
 * as a guideline for developing your own functions.
 */

#include "rand.h"

void *
initialize_random_1_svc(long *argp, struct svc_req *rqstp)
{
static char * result;

/*
 * insert server code here
 */

return((void *) &result);
}

double *
get_next_random_1_svc(void *argp, struct svc_req *rqstp)
{
static double  result;

/*
 * insert server code here
 */

return (&result);
}
```
──────────────────────────── **Program 14.7** ────────────────────────────

Program 14.8 shows the final `rand_server.c` after the code for the function `initialize_random` and `get_next_random` of Program 14.1 is inserted into the dummy server stubs of `rand_server.c`. The `#include <stdlib.h>` provides the prototypes for `srand48` and for `drand48`.

Program 14.8: The final version of the server program for the pseudorandom-number service.

```
#include <stdlib.h>
#include "rand.h"

void *
initialize_random_1_svc(long *argp, struct svc_req *rqstp)
{
    static char *result;
    srand48(*argp);
    result = (void *)NULL;
    return (void *) &result;
}

double *
get_next_random_1_svc(void *argp, struct svc_req *rqstp)
{
    static double  result;
    result = drand48();
    return &result;
}
```

———————————————— **Program 14.8** ————————————————

Use the makefile generated by `rpcgen` to produce executables for the client and the server.

Example 14.5

The following command produces the two executables `rand_client` *and* `rand_server` *for the client and server, respectively.*

```
make -f makefile.rand
```

Example 14.6

The following command registers the pseudorandom-number server.

```
rand_server
```

After execution of the command of Example 14.6 `rand_server` service is registered on the current host and ready to receive remote requests. (See Section 14.6 for a discussion about removing the service.)

Example 14.7

Suppose the server of Example 14.6 was running on the host with Internet name `vip.cs.utsa.edu`. *The following command runs the client with initial seed* `4323` *and produces ten pseudorandom numbers by invoking the remote pseudorandom-number service.*

```
rand_client vip.cs.utsa.edu 4323 10
```

In summary, follow these steps in converting local calls to remote calls:

- Get the program to work using local functions.
- Restructure each function so it has only one parameter which is passed by value, and be sure that it works when called locally.
- Create a specification file having a `.x` extension.
- Call `rpcgen` with the `-a` and `-C` options to generate a complete set of files as shown in Figure 14.6.
- Before making any changes to the generated files, use the generated makefile to compile them. It is often possible to catch mistakes in the specification file type definitions at this stage.
- Insert the calling program into the `_client.c` file generated by `rpcgen`. (Here the specification filename appears before the `_client.c`.)
- Insert the local function code into the `_server.c` file generated by `rpcgen`.
- Try compiling the programs using the generated makefile.
- Fiddle with the `_server.c` and `_client.c` sources until they work. Fiddling should not be needed if only simple data types are used, but things are not always so simple.

Because the pseudorandom-number service contained functions that had at most one parameter and the parameter was not changed in the function, there was no need to restructure the functions to take a single parameter. The next section describes a more complicated version of the pseudorandom-number service.

14.3 An Improved Remote Pseudorandom-Number Service

One problem with the implementation in the previous section is that another client can request seed reinitialization at any time. One approach for preventing arbitrary reinitialization is to add a static flag to `initialize_random_1` indicating whether the generator has already been initialized. The `initialize_random_1` function then calls the `srand48` function only if the flag is clear. That approach prevents the seed function from being called more than once, but it still does not isolate individual clients or allow a client to restart with a different seed. All of the clients depend on the initial value chosen by the first caller of `initialize_random_1`. This section develops a more satisfactory approach—a version of the pseudorandom-number service that is capable of supplying independent streams of pseudorandom numbers. The calling parameters are more complicated, so there is additional conversion of the `rpcgen`-generated code.

The `drand48` and related functions generate pseudorandom numbers using the linear congruential algorithm and 48-bit integer arithmetic according to the formula $X_{n+1} = (aX_n + c) \bmod m$ where $n \geq 0$. The default values of the other parameters are $a = 0x5DEECE66D$, $c = 0xB$ and $m = 2^{48}$. An internal buffer keeps the current value of the 48-bit integer X_n, so that the next value of X_{n+1} can be directly computed from the previous one. The `drand48` function extracts the appropriate bits from X_{n+1} and returns a converted pseudorandom number. Normally the caller supplies a `long` seed value, and `srand48` produces the initial X_0. The man page indicates that the current method of doing that is to copy the seed value into the upper 32 bits of X_0 and to insert the arbitrary value $0x330E16$ in the low 16 bits to produce a 48-bit value.

In an alternative form of the pseudorandom-number generator, `erand48`, the caller supplies the X_n value in an array of three unsigned shorts. The `erand48` function fills the array with the new 48-bit X_n value and returns the pseudorandom number. Thus, `erand48` does not need to use static variables and can be used to generate multiple independent streams of pseudorandom numbers. In order to get an initial X_n value from the seed value, call `srand48` with the desired seed to set the internal static X_n value of the pseudorandom-number generator. The `seed48` function sets a seed from an X_n value and returns a pointer to the previous X_n value. Call `seed48` with any argument, but save the return value to find the X_n value associated with the first call to `srand48`.

Example 14.8

The following code segment shows how to generate the internal X_0 value without any knowledge of the exact mechanism used in the calculation.

```
#include <stdlib.h>

void initialize_random(long seed, unsigned short xsubi[3])
{
    unsigned short *xp;
    srand48(seed);
    xp = seed48(xsubi);
    xsubi[0] = *xp;
    xsubi[1] = *(xp + 1);
    xsubi[2] = *(xp + 2);
}

double get_next_random(unsigned short xsubi[3])
{
    return erand48(xsubi);
}
```

The internal X_n values are held in a three-element array of unsigned short values. The initial call to srand48 in Example 14.8 sets the values of the internal seed array. The call to seed48 resets the seed to some value, but returns the previously set seed array. The return value is the starting point for calls to erand48.

The version of get_next_random in Example 14.8 returns the pseudorandom number and sets the next value of X_n. The standard old-style Sun calling mechanism requires that each remote function have a single parameter and that the parameter not be used to return information to the calling program. (An option for passing multiple parameters has recently been added to rpcgen under Sun Solaris.) All information is returned through the return value, so this section illustrates restructuring of initialize_random and get_next_random to single-parameter format as an intermediate step. To make things easier, define a structure of type struct randpack to hold both the internal 48-bit integer and the double which is the pseudorandom value of interest. Program 14.9 shows a revised rand.h.

Program 14.9: The rand.h header file for local service.

```
#include <stdlib.h>
struct randpack {
    double pseudo;
    unsigned short xi[3];
};
struct randpack initialize_random(long seed);
struct randpack get_next_random(struct randpack p);
```

———————————————————— **Program 14.9** ————————————————————

Program 14.10 shows the local functions after conversion to single-parameter format. The revised initialize_random takes the original long seed as a parameter and returns a structure of type struct randpack containing the 48-bit value to be passed to erand48. The get_next_random takes a structure of type struct randpack holding the 48-bit value and returns the pseudorandom number and the new 48-bit value in a struct randpack.

Program 14.10: A local service for generating independent streams of pseudorandom numbers.

```
#include "rand.h"

struct randpack initialize_random(long seed)
{
```

```
        struct randpack result;
        unsigned short *xp;
        srand48(seed);
        xp = seed48(result.xi);
        result.xi[0] = *xp;
        result.xi[1] = *(xp + 1);
        result.xi[2] = *(xp + 2);
        return result;
}

struct randpack get_next_random(struct randpack p)
{
        struct randpack result;
        double rpseudo;
        rpseudo = erand48(p.xi);
        result = p;
        result.pseudo = rpseudo;
        return result;

}
```
_____ **Program 14.10** _____

Program 14.11 shows the main program for the local pseudorandom-number service. Each call to `get_next_random` resets the internal seed of the `drand48` generator, so the result does not depend on state information saved from previous calls.

Program 14.11: A main program illustrating the use of the new local pseudorandom-number service.

```
#include <stdio.h>
#include "rand.h"
void main(int argc, char *argv[])
{
        int iters, i;
        long myseed;
        unsigned short xi[3];
        struct randpack next_seed;

        if (argc != 3) {
            fprintf(stderr, "Usage: %s seed iterations\n", argv[0]);
            exit(1);
        }

        myseed = (long)atoi(argv[1]);
        iters = atoi(argv[2]);
        next_seed = initialize_random(myseed);
```

```
    for (i = 0; i < iters; i++)   {
       next_seed = get_next_random(next_seed);
       printf("%d : %f\n", i, next_seed.pseudo);
    }
    exit(0);
}
```

_____ **Program 14.11** _____

Example 14.9

The specification file in Program 14.12 describes a remote service for generating independent streams of pseudorandom numbers. The following command generates the skeleton files for the service.

```
rpcgen -C -a rand.x
```

Program 14.12: Specification file for an independent pseudorandom-number service.

```
/*       rand.x          */
struct randpack {
    double pseudo;
    unsigned short xi[3];
};

program RAND_PROG {
    version RAND_VERS{
        randpack INITIALIZE_RANDOM(long) = 1;
         randpack GET_NEXT_RANDOM(randpack) = 2;
    } = 2;
} = 0x31111111;
```

_____ **Program 14.12** _____

Example 14.10

The rpcgen *output for Example 14.9 contains the following translation for the* struct randpack *in the* rand.h *file.*

```
struct randpack {
        double pseudo;
        u_short xi[3];
};
typedef struct randpack randpack;
```

The rpcgen translation of struct randpack is typedef struct randpack randpack, so avoid using typedef's in the original definition in rand.x.

Program 14.13 shows the final version of rand_client.c. The main changes from the local call are the use of a client handle clnt and the use of pointers for parameters and return values. The version number is 2 so the client program calls the services as `initialize_random_2` and `get_next_random_2`, respectively.

Program 14.13: Final client for a remote service for independent streams of pseudorandom numbers.

```
#include <stdlib.h>
#include <stdio.h>
#include "rand.h"

void main(int argc, char *argv[])
{
    int iters, i;
    long myseed;
    CLIENT *clnt;
    randpack next_seed;
    randpack  *result;
    char *host;

    if (argc != 4) {
        fprintf(stderr, "Usage: %s host seed iterations\n", argv[0]);
        exit(1);
    }
    host = argv[1];
    clnt = clnt_create(host, RAND_PROG, RAND_VERS, "netpath");
    if (clnt == (CLIENT *) NULL) {
        clnt_pcreateerror(host);
        exit(1);
    }
    myseed = (long)atoi(argv[2]);
    iters = atoi(argv[3]);
    result = initialize_random_2(&myseed, clnt);
    if (result == (randpack *) NULL) {
        clnt_perror(clnt, "cannot initialize generator");
        exit(1);
    }
    next_seed = *result;
    for (i = 0; i < iters; i++) {
        result = get_next_random_2(&next_seed, clnt);
        if (result == (randpack *) NULL)
            clnt_perror(clnt, "call for next number failed");
        printf("%d : %f\n", i, result->pseudo);
        next_seed = *result;
    }
    exit(0);
}
```
_____ **Program 14.13** _____

Program 14.14 shows the remote server for the client of Program 14.13. Calls to `initialize_random_2_svc` and `get_next_random_2_svc` do not use any static information and are independent of each other.

Program 14.14: Final version of server functions for a remote service to generate independent streams of pseudorandom numbers.

```
#include <stdlib.h>
#include "rand.h"

randpack *
initialize_random_2_svc(long *argp, struct svc_req *rqstp)
{
    static randpack  result;
    unsigned short *xp;

    srand48(*argp);
    xp = seed48(result.xi);
    result.xi[0] = *xp;
    result.xi[1] = *(xp + 1);
    result.xi[2] = *(xp + 2);
    return &result;
}

randpack *
get_next_random_2_svc(randpack *argp, struct svc_req *rqstp)
{
    static randpack result;
    double rpseudo;

    rpseudo = erand48(argp->xi);
    result = *argp;
    result.pseudo = rpseudo;
    return &result;
}
```
_____ **Program 14.14** _____

Exercise 14.1

Experiment with the remote pseudorandom-number service. Take a look at the code in the `rand_clnt.c` and the `rand_svc.c` which are the stubs for the client and server, respectively. Try to understand the code generated by `rpcgen`. (Most of the complexity arises in the XDR conversion functions for the parameters.)

14.4 Server State and Idempotent Requests

Remote procedure calls are designed to look as much like local calls as possible, but there are some unavoidable complications with the execution of remote calls. The discussion in this section is based on the example of writing a certain number of bytes to a file. To simplify the discussion, assume that the local and remote calls look exactly the same and concentrate on the effect of a local call versus that of a remote call.

Example 14.11

The following `write_file` *function writes* `nbytes` *of* `buf` *to the file designated by* `fd`. *The function returns the number of bytes written if the operation succeeds or* −1 *if the operation fails.*

```
int write_file(int fd, char *buf, int nbytes)
{
    return put_block(fd, nbytes, buf);
}
```

The `put_block` of Example 14.11 is a remote version of an ordinary `write`; that is, `put_block(fd, nbytes, buf)` is the same as `write(fd, buf, nbytes)` except that it is executed on a remote host. The order of the parameters in `put_block` is different from those in `write_file` because the `write_file` is similar to an ordinary `write`, while `put_block` is analogous to the remote call in NFS (Network File System).

When a program executes an ordinary `write`, the file descriptor refers to an entry in the local file descriptor table of the process, and the `write` causes an update of the offset in the system file table on the host of the calling program.

When `write_file` calls `put_block`, the remote equivalent of `write`, the file descriptor refers to an entry in the server's file descriptor table. The corresponding remote file descriptor table entry points to an entry in the system file table of the remote host as shown in Figure 14.7. The `put_block` updates the file offset in the server host's system file table entry.

The remote service of Example 14.11 works fine when the network is reliable and none of the participants crash. Remote calls are complicated by the fact that a client or a server can fail separately. It is not always possible to know whether lack of response is due to network failure or a host crash. In contrast, local calls are delivered reliably. If the host operating system crashes, both the client and the server terminate.

Consider the situation in which a client issues a request but does not receive a response. After a certain period, the client retries the request. What happens? The answer depends on why the client did not receive a response. The possibilities include:

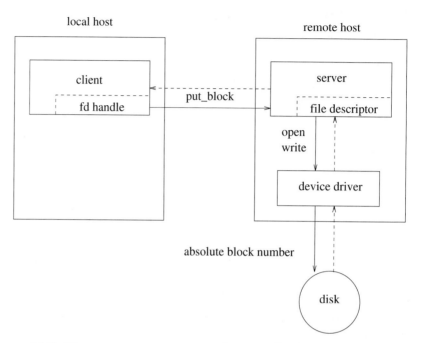

Figure 14.7: The remote `put_block` refers to a file descriptor on the server.

- The initial request is lost on the network.
- The server receives the request and services it, but the response is lost.
- The server is no longer active.

If the initial request is lost, the client can retry without adverse effects. On the other hand, if the server actually serviced the original request, but the response was lost, a retry produces an incorrect result because the server's file offset is updated each time `put_block` is called. A possible solution is to identify each request by a sequence number. The server keeps track of the sequence number of the last request serviced and the result of the last request. If a duplicate request comes in, the server resends the response rather than redoing the request. The sequence number solution does not solve the problem of server crashes because the sequence numbers are lost upon crash.

An approach to both the lost response and the server crash problems is to convert the problem to one in which the same request can be reexecuted without changing the results. Such a request is called *idempotent*. The `put_block` of Example 14.11 is not idempotent because writing updates the file offset in the remote system file table. If a client repeats the same request, the server uses the updated value of the file offset. The second call results in the writing of the same information directly after the end of the previously written block. One approach to solving this problem is to have the client keep track of its own file offset.

Example 14.12

The following idempotent version of `put_block` *adjusts the file offset to a specified position before writing the information.*

```
int put_block(int file, int offset, int count, char *data)
{
    int returncode = 0;
    if (lseek(file, offset, SEEK_SET) == -1)
        returncode = -1;
    else
        returncode = write(file, data, count);
    return returncode;
}
```

The `put_block` function of Example 14.12 is idempotent in the sense that a client can repeat the call and have it write the same data to the same place in the file. Of course, the repeated call changes the time of modification on the file, but ignore that complication for the time being.

In order to call the `put_block` of Example 14.12 as a remote call, a client keeps track of where in the file it wants to write. The client then updates the information when it receives confirmation that the `put_block` has succeeded.

Example 14.13

The `write_file` *is a jacket for a idempotent remote call* `put_block` *of Example 14.12.*

```
static int fd_offset = 0;
int write_file(int fd, char *buf, int nbytes)
{
    int bytes_written;
    if ((bytes_written =
            put_block(fd, fd_offset, nbytes, buf)) != -1)
        fd_offset += bytes_written;
    return bytes_written;
}
```

The client variable `fd_offset` in Example 14.13 keeps track of the file offset of the last successful request. Before calling `write_file` the program must remotely open the file to obtain a handle for subsequent requests. Example 14.13 uses the integer handle `fd`, but in an actual remote implementation the handle might be an opaque structure.

The remote open creates an entry in the system file table of the remote host. If the file was not opened by other processes, a new entry in the in-memory inode table is also created. The `lseek` and the `write` calls of `put_block` update the offset stored in the remote host system file table entry created by the remote open.

The `put_block` of Example 14.12 does not completely solve the problem of server crashes. Consider how `put_block` executes on a remote server. The file descriptor `file` refers to an entry in the server's file descriptor table, and the client must open the file and receive the handle back prior to making any remote requests. Each `put_block` call from the client updates the server's local file offset. The server retains the file descriptor and its corresponding entry in the system file table until it receives an explicit request from the client to close the file. If the server crashes and is restarted, it has no way of knowing what file to reopen when it gets the next `put_block` request from the client.

Crashes of the client are also a problem. The remote files are not automatically closed as part of the `exit` of the client. If the client forgets to close the remote file or crashes before closing it, the server is left with a hanging entry in its file descriptor table. During long periods of operation these hanging descriptors could cause the server to fail because there was no more room in its descriptor table. The problem arises in that situation because the client request causes the server to keep state information (an open file descriptor). Even if the requests are idempotent, a client crash may result in invalid or unneeded state information on the server.

Figure 14.8 illustrates an idempotent and stateless approach for the remote write. The `put_block` opens the file, seeks to the appropriate position, writes the block, and closes the file. The client keeps track of the file offset locally to determine the seek position of the calls.

Example 14.14

The following version of `put_block` *is completely self-contained. If it were called remotely, it would leave no state on the server.*

```
int put_block(char *fname, int offset, int count, char *data)
{
    int returncode = 0;
    int file;
    if ((file = open(fname, O_WRONLY|O_CREAT, 0600)) == -1)
        returncode = -1;
    else if (lseek(file, offset, SEEK_SET) == -1)
        returncode = -1;
    else
        returncode = write(file, data, count);
    close(file);
    return returncode;
}
```

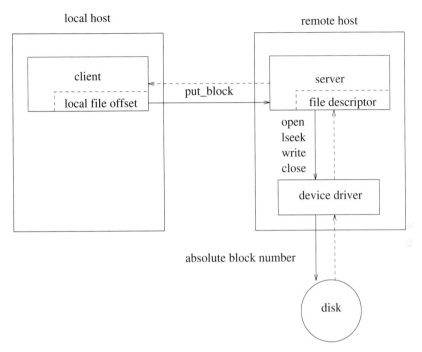

Figure 14.8: An idempotent and stateless version of `put_block`.

The client keeps a file offset locally and updates it when it receives an acknowledgment that the server completed the request. The server does not care if the client crashes, since it has retained no state information from client requests. The client cannot distinguish between slow response and a crashed server. Because the requests are idempotent, the client can continue to retry the request until it is successful. If the remote system reboots and the server is restarted, the retried client request goes to the new server.

A *stateless* server is one for which client requests are completely self-contained and leave no residual state information on the server. Stateless servers are robust under crashes. Not all problems can be cast in stateless form, but there are some well-known examples of stateless servers. The Sun NFS (Network File System) is implemented as an RPC-based stateless server as discussed in Section 14.8.

14.5 Remote Idempotent File Service

This section develops a remote version of the `put_block` of Example 14.14. It also illustrates some of the complications which can arise in the XDR conversion.

Program 14.15 shows the specification for a stateless version of the `put_block` remote service. Remember that specifications are not written in C, but in a special C-like specification language. The `string` of Program 14.15 is a type built into `rpcgen`. The `< >` instead of `[ ]` indicates strings or arrays of variable length.

Program 14.15: The specification of a stateless remote file service.

```
/*    rfile.x                  */
const MAX_BUF = 1024;
const MAX_STR = 256;

struct packet {
    string fname<MAX_STR>;
    int count;
    int offset;
    char  data<MAX_BUF>;
};

program RFILEPROG {
    version RFILEVERS {
        int PUT_BLOCK(packet) = 1;
    } = 1;
} = 0x31111112;
```

_____ **Program 14.15** _____

Example 14.15

 The following command creates the skeleton files.

```
rpcgen -C -a rfile.x
```

 The `rpcgen` _translates_ `struct packet` _into the following C code in the_ `rfile.h` _header file._

```
#define MAX_BUF 1024
#define MAX_STR 256

struct packet {
    char *fname;
    int offset;
    int count;
    struct {
        u_int data_len;
        char *data_val;
    } data;
};
typedef struct packet packet;
```

Notice that rpcgen translates a string, such as the fname member in Program 14.15, into a pointer instead of a fixed array. The data variable-length array becomes a structure which has a pointer to char and a length member. The example emphasizes the importance of looking at the header file generated by rpcgen before inserting code into the client and server skeleton files.

Program 14.16 shows the final version of rfile_server.c. Each call to the service is completely self-contained. Program 14.17 shows the corresponding client.

Program 14.16: Final version of rfile_server.c.

```c
#include <stdio.h>
#include <unistd.h>
#include <sys/stat.h>
#include "rfile.h"
#define PERMS S_IRUSR | S_IWUSR

int *
put_block_1_svc(packet *pack, struct svc_req *rqstp)
{
    static int   result;
    int file;
    result = 0;
    if ((file = open(pack->fname, O_WRONLY|O_CREAT, PERMS)) == -1)
        result = -1;
    else if (lseek(file, pack->offset, SEEK_SET) == -1)
        result = -1;
    else
        result = write(file, pack->data.data_val, pack->count);
    close(file);
    return &result;
}
```
_____ **Program 14.16** _____

Program 14.17: The client code for Program 14.16.

```c
#include <stdio.h>
#include <unistd.h>
#include <stdlib.h>
#include <string.h>
#include "rfile.h"
static int fd_offset = 0;

int write_file(CLIENT *clnt, char *filename, char *buf, int nbytes)
{
    int   bytes_written;
```

```
    struct packet pack;
    int *result;
    pack.count = nbytes;
    pack.offset = fd_offset;
    pack.fname = filename;
    pack.data.data_val = buf;
    pack.data.data_len = nbytes;
    result = put_block_1(&pack, clnt);
    if (result == (void *)NULL)
        bytes_written = -1;
    else{
        bytes_written = *result;
        fd_offset += bytes_written;
    }
    return bytes_written;
}

void main(int argc, char *argv[])
{
    int i, blocks, block_size;
    char stuff[256];
    CLIENT *clnt;
    char *host;

    if (argc != 4) {
        fprintf(stderr,"Usage: %s host filename blocks\n", argv[0]);
        exit(1);
    }

    host = argv[1];
    clnt = clnt_create(host, RFILEPROG, RFILEVERS, "netpath");
    if (clnt == (CLIENT *) NULL) {
        clnt_pcreateerror(host);
        exit(1);
    }

    blocks = atoi(argv[3]);
    sprintf(stuff, "This is a test\n");
    block_size = strlen(stuff);
    for (i = 0; i < blocks; i++) {
        if (write_file(clnt, argv[2], stuff, block_size) <= 0) {
            fprintf(stderr, "Error in writing file\n");
            break;
        }
    }
    clnt_destroy(clnt);
    exit(0);
}
```

_____ **Program 14.17** _____

14.6 Binding and Naming of Services

Each RPC message has three unsigned numbers which identify the program, the version, and the procedure number within the program. The Sun Microsystems convention for program numbers is

00000000 - 1fffffff	Defined by and administered by Sun
20000000 - 3fffffff	Defined by user (for debugging services)
40000000 - 5fffffff	Transient (applications which dynamically generate numbers)
60000000 - ffffffff	Reserved for future use

Multiple versions of the same service are allowed so that services can be upgraded and clients using older versions continue to work. The servers which are listening on ports as RPC services must register with rpcbind. The registration code is automatically included in the _svc.c server stub generated by rpcgen. Use rpcinfo to find out what RPC services are available on a given host.

```
SYNOPSIS

  rpcinfo [ -m ] [ -s ] [ host ]
  rpcinfo -p [ host ]
  rpcinfo -T transport host prognum [ versnum ]
  rpcinfo -l [ -T transport ] host prognum [ versnum ]
  rpcinfo [ -n portnum ] -u host prognum [ versnum ]
  rpcinfo [ -n portnum ] -t host prognum [ versnum ]
  rpcinfo -a serv_address -T transport prognum [ versnum ]
  rpcinfo -b [ -T transport ] prognum versnum
  rpcinfo -d [ -T transport ] prognum versnum
```

Example 14.16

The command

```
rpcinfo -s
```

produced the following partial output on a particular machine.

```
program version(s)       netid(s)                        service  owner
100000  2,3,4  udp,tcp,ticlts,ticotsord,ticos  rpcbind  superuser
100029  2,1    ticots,ticotsord,ticlts         keyserv  superuser
100078  4      ticots,ticotsord,ticlts         kerbd    superuser
100087  10     udp                             admind   superuser
100011  1      ticlts,udp                      rquotad  superuser
100002  3,2    ticlts,udp                      rusersd  superuser
100099  1      ticots,ticotsord,ticlts         -        superuser
100012  1      ticlts,udp                      sprayd   superuser
100008  1      ticlts,udp                      walld    superuser
```

```
100001   4,3,2  ticlts,udp                           rstatd    superuser
100024   1      ticots,ticotsord,ticlts,tcp,udp status    superuser
100021   2,3,1  ticots,ticotsord,ticlts,tcp,udp nlockmgr superuser
100068   4,3,2  udp                                  -         superuser
100020   2      ticots,ticotsord,ticlts,tcp,udp llockmgr superuser
100083   1         tcp,udp                           -         superuser
1342177279  1,2     tcp                                 -            5001
```

Each RPC service has an identifying program number and version number. The `netid` field of the `rpcinfo` output gives the underlying transport providers. The two commonly supported transport mechanisms are UDP and TCP. UDP is a connection-less protocol which does not guarantee error-free delivery. TCP is a connection-oriented protocol which provides error-free, in-order delivery. The `TICOTS`, `TICOTSORD`, and `TICLTS` are protocols for use on the same machine. They are called *loopback transport providers*. The TICLTS is analogous to UDP, while `TICOTS` is a connection-oriented transport provider analogous to TCP. The `TICOTSORD` is a connection-oriented provider which has an orderly release mechanism.

Example 14.17

The following command deletes version 1 *of service* 1342177279 *belonging to user* 5001 *as listed in Example 14.16.*

```
rpcinfo -d 1342177279 1
```

The new TI-RPC mechanism promotes the development of code that is transport in-dependent. A given service may have several different transports available. In transport-independent remote procedure calls, the client does not explicitly say which transport to use. The `clnt_create` tries the transports in the order specified by the `NETPATH` environment variable.

The `rpcbind` facility provides a registry of the remote services provided by a par-ticular host. Clients call `clnt_create` to contact the `rpcbind` service at runtime in order to obtain the address of the service. Each supported transport must have a specified notion of a *well-known address* which is represented in a *Universal Address* format. The *Universal Address* for a given transport is a string in a predefined format. An inquiry to `rcpbind` returns the address in the Universal Address format. The client and server stubs have functions to translate the Universal Address string into a local TLI transport-specific address structure. Thus, a supported transport must have a TLI interface on the local host in order to be used. (Chapter 12 describes the addressing mechanism for TLI.)

The `rpcbind` allows the client to access a service by 32-bit program number, and it returns the local port information. In contrast, an ordinary TLI client must know the server's 16-bit well-known port. Because the port number can be any number that is agreed upon by `rpcbind` and the server, the potential for port conflicts is considerably less than with an implementation requiring direct specification of well-known ports. In addition to having more bits, these RPC service numbers are administered by a central authority, unlike port numbers for sockets or TLI.

Example 14.18

The following value of NETPATH *says that the client should first try UDP, then TCP and then TP4.*

```
udp:tcp:tp4
```

If NETPATH is not set, the application defaults to the visible transports specified in the system netconfig file. While the selection of transport may not appear to be critical, it does affect the way failures are handled as discussed in the next section.

14.7 Failures

Failures present a sticky problem for remote procedure call designers. Unlike the local calls, failure of a client and failure of a server do not always happen together. If a client program attempts a remote procedure call and does not receive a response, a number of scenarios are possible:

- The network was slow and the client did not wait long enough.
- The initial message was lost.
- The server received the message, performed the request, and then crashed.
- The server performed the service, but the acknowledgment was lost.

Because of the possibility of a remote crash, most implementations of remote procedure calls have an associated timeout value. If an answer is not received within the timeout period, the remote procedure call returns a failure to the calling program. Because of the predominance of network transmission media that do not have an upper bound on the time for delivery of messages (e.g., Ethernet), the calling program cannot distinguish between a network failure and a server failure. In order to decide what to do, the calling program has to know how the underlying call was performed, that is, the *calling semantics under failure*. There are several common choices for calling semantics:

- In *exactly once semantics* the call is guaranteed to have been performed exactly once. Exactly once semantics is impossible to guarantee if a remote server can crash.
- In *maybe semantics* no guarantees are made. The call is made once and if no reply is received in a certain period of time, the call returns with an error. If the call returns with an error, the client has no idea whether the request was performed and the acknowledgment was lost or whether the initial request was lost.

- In *at most once semantics* the calling mechanism tries to make the call. If it does not receive a reply, it retries. The server filters duplicate requests and sends replies without reexecuting the request. As long as the server does not crash, at most once semantics guarantees that the request is executed exactly once. If the server crashes, the request could have been executed once or not at all depending on the timing of the crash. The server must save these request numbers in permanent storage in order to restart after a crash.

- In *at least once semantics*, the underlying calling mechanism continues to retry the call until it gets a response.

Recall from Chapter 12 that UDP is a connectionless protocol which provides no error checking. A single packet is sent and no follow-up occurs verifying that it arrived. The UDP transport mechanism for the ONC TI-RPC remote procedure calls provides maybe semantics because there is no guarantee that a packet arrives. Use UDP for applications that implement error-checking at the user-level anyway. The Sun NFS file server software uses ONC TI-RPC with a UDP transport.

The TCP transport provides connection-oriented, error-free transmission of data. As long as the server does not crash, the request arrives at the server and the client receives the reply. The TCP protocol achieves fault tolerance by acknowledging each packet and retransmitting packets for which it receives a negative acknowledgment. The TCP transport provides at most once semantics for ONC TI-RPC.

14.8 NFS—Network File System

Sun NFS (Network File System) is a widely-ported system for performing network file access. NFS, which was first released in 1985, strives to provide efficient and transparent access to remote file systems on a heterogeneous network. Version 3 became available in 1994. NFS is implemented as a stateless server over RPC in much the same way as the stateless `put_block` of Example 14.16.

Most of the standard UNIX file and directory calls have NFS counterparts for remote access. Program 14.18 shows the RPC specification of the remote services for NFS Version 3. Most of the services are self-explanatory and are analogous to corresponding UNIX system calls for local files. There are remote procedures for getting or setting attributes, reading, writing, creating or removing directories or symbolic links, and obtaining status information. Each remote service in NFS has a distinct type for its parameters and a type for its return value.

The NFS function for writing to a file, `NFSPROC3_WRITE,` has a parameter and return values specified by `WRITE3args` and `WRITE3res`, respectively. Program 14.19 shows the specifications for these types. Remember the specification is in an RPC specification language, not in C.

Program 14.18: NFS Version 3 remote procedure specification.

```
program NFS_PROGRAM {
   version NFS_V3  {
      void NFSPROC3_NULL(void)                                      = 0;
      GETATTR3res NFSPROC3_GETATTR(GETATTR3args)                    = 1;
      SETATTR3res NFSPROC3_SETATTR(SETATTR3args)                    = 2;
      LOOKUP3res NFSPROC3_LOOKUP(LOOKUP3args)                       = 3;
      ACCESS3res NFSPROC3_ACCESS(ACCESS3args)                       = 4;
      READLINK3res NFSPROC3_READLINK(READLINK3args)                 = 5;
      READ3res NFSPROC3_READ(READ3args)                             = 6;
      WRITE3res NFSPROC3_WRITE(WRITE3args)                          = 7;
      CREATE3res NFSPROC3_CREATE(CREATE3args)                       = 8;
      MKDIR3res NFSPROC3_MKDIR(MKDIR3args)                          = 9;
      SYMLINK3res NFSPROC3_SYMLINK(SYMLINK3args)                    = 10;
      MKNOD3res NFSPROC3_MKNOD(MKNOD3args)                          = 11;
      REMOVE3res NFSPROC3_REMOVE(REMOVE3args)                       = 12;
      RMDIR3res NFSPROC3_RMDIR(RMDIR3args)                          = 13;
      RENAME3res NFSPROC3_RENAME(RENAME3args)                       = 14;
      LINK3res NFSPROC3_LINK(LINK3args)                             = 15;
      READDIR3res NFSPROC3_READDIR(READDIR3args)                    = 16;
      READDIRPLUS3res NFSPROC3_READDIRPLUS(READDIRPLUS3args)        = 17;
      FSSTAT3res NFSPROC3_FSSTAT(FSSTAT3args)                       = 18;
      FSINFO3res NFSPROC3_FSINFO(FSINFO3args)                       = 19;
      PATHCONF3res NFSPROC3_PATHCONF(PATHCONF3args)                 = 20;
      COMMIT3res NFSPROC3_COMMIT(COMMIT3args)                       = 21;
   } = 3;
} = 100003;
```

_____ **Program 14.18** _____

Program 14.19: Specification of parameter and return types for `NSFPROC3_WRITE`.

```
enum stable_how {
   UNSTABLE = 0,
   DATA_SYNC = 1,
   FILE_SYNC = 2
};

struct WRITE3args {
   nfs_fh3       file;
   offset3       offset;
   count3        count;
   stable_how    stable;
   opaque        data<>;
}
```

```
struct WRITE3resok {
   wcc_data      file_wcc;
   count3        count;
   stable_how  committed;
   writeverf3  verf;
};

struct WRITE3resfail {
   wcc_data      file_wcc;
};

union WRITE3res switch (nfsstat3 status) {
   case NFS3_OK;
      WRITE3resok   resok;
   default;
      WRITE3resfail resfail;
};
```

_____ **Program 14.19** _____

All of the parameter and return specifications for NFS functions follow the format
of Program 14.19. The `file` is the NFS file handle for the file to be written. It is an
opaque identifier which is provided by the server when the file is initially located. The
`offset`, `count`, and `data` members have the same meanings as the members of
`struct packet` of the `put_block` specification of Program 14.15.

The usual value of `stable` is `FILE_SYNC` which indicates that the server should
actually complete its write to disk before returning from the remote call. The other possibilities are discussed later in this section.

The NFS services return different structures on success and failure. Return values
are handled by the switched union `union WRITE3res`. If the RPC call is successful,
it returns a `struct WRITE3resok`. Included in that structure is a count of the number
of bytes actually written and an indication of whether the data was written to permanent storage or to a memory cache. On failure `NFSPROC3_WRITE` returns a `struct`
`WRITE3resfail`.

The user-level implementation of `put_block` in Example 14.16 requires an explicit `open` on each block that is written because it has to access the disk through the
file system calls. The NFS server implementation of `NFSPROC3_WRITE` is part of the
kernel. It can bypass the user-level file system calls and fetch blocks directly without doing an explicit `open`. The direct fetch has considerably less overhead than the `open`,
`lseek`, `write`, and `close` sequence.

Since NFS servers are essentially stateless, they do not keep information about open files. The client kernel keeps information about the files that have been opened by its users. In the `put_block` of Program 14.15, the file is identified by the complete path-name and the server traverses its directory tree to locate the file. In NFS, the client tra-verses the server directory tree by doing a series of lookup calls. Each lookup produces a NFS file handle for that node in the directory tree and allows the client to read the direc-tory in order to obtain the file handle of the next node down in the tree. The file handles are opaque to the client, so servers that use different file formats can be accessed by the same client. A consequence of client traversal of the directory tree is that each filesys-tem accessed remotely through NFS must be mounted somewhere in the client's root filesystem. The mount procedure is separate from the NFS protocol.

14.8.1 Caching and Consistency

The philosophy of the NFS is to make the server as simple as possible and off-load most of the work to the client. Keep in mind that the program that does the RPC calls is not a user program, but rather it is part of the NSF client's operating system. Figure 14.9 shows a schematic of the operation. A user program running on an NFS client performs ordinary file operations such as a `read`. If the `read` refers to a remote file, the client kernel initiates a remote NFS request on behalf of the user. In the standard NFS protocol, the client kernel blocks until the remote server responds with the block. Needless to say that is quite slow.

Although it is not part of the NFS specification, practical implementations of NFS use caching on both the client and server to improve performance. *Caching* refers to the retention of data in memory so that it can be reused without being refetched. Caching does not affect the way client and server exchange information, but it does cut down considerably on the traffic between client and server.

The conventional UNIX kernel uses caching in several ways to make file access more efficient. It keeps a copy of the inodes of all open files in memory. The kernel may also cache inodes of recently accessed files and recently accessed directory nodes. It may keep tables of pathname and inode numbers to speed traversal of directory trees. The kernel also keeps a large cache of recently accessed data blocks. When a process requests a block of data from a file, the kernel first checks to see whether it is available in memory. Most implementations use read-ahead to prefetch additional file blocks when a particular block is accessed in order to anticipate future requests. When a process does a write, the block is written to the memory buffer rather than directly to disk. The operating system periodically writes modified data blocks to disk. This periodic write-out is called a `sync` operation and typically happens every 30 seconds. If the system crashes between `sync` operations, the copy on disk may not reflect the latest changes, but other than that everything is consistent because reads and writes on the system go through the same

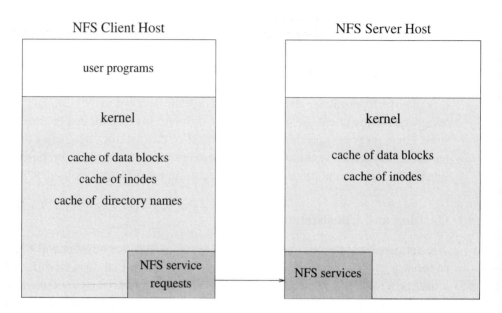

Figure 14.9: A schematic diagram of the relationship between NFS client and server.

system cache.

Caching on both NFS clients and servers can considerably improve performance in remote file service, but caching also causes serious consistency problems. Most implementations do caching and provide additional mechanisms for improving, but not guaranteeing, consistency.

Client-side caching looks like conventional file caching in many respects. User programs read and write blocks to the data block cache. The kernel prefetches blocks and periodically writes modified blocks. The prefetches and the modified writes are calls to the NFS server rather than to local disk device drivers. When an NFS request is made, the client blocks until the call returns.

The NFS server keeps a large cache of recently requested blocks. It also uses read-ahead to anticipate future client read requests. Writes are more complicated. In the NFS Version 2 protocol, the server had to complete the write to stable storage before responding to the client. When the NFSPROC3_WRITE request has a stable member value of FILE_SYNC, the server writes to stable storage before returning to the client. When the stable member is UNSTABLE, the server is required only to write the block to its own cache. It may later write it to disk as part of its normal sync operation or in response to a client NFSPROC3_COMMIT request. When stable is DATA_SYNC, the server must write the data to stable storage but does not have to commit the metadata. *System metadata* refers to state and attribute information that is usually stored in the file's inode.

One big problem with caching is that clients and servers do not share a single cache. Copies of a data block can become inconsistent if a user on one client writes a block to its local cache and a user on another client accesses a local copy of the same block before it has received the update. NFS does not specify a mechanism for assuring that cached copies of data blocks are consistent. Each implementation is free to use its own method of determining consistency. A typical approach is for the client to inquire periodically about the last modification time for a given block by calling NFSPROC3_GETATTR. If the client detects that the copy on the server has been modified since the client retrieved it, it can invalidate its own copy. The technique provides "pretty good" (*weak cache consistency*), but not absolute, consistency. It is based on the assumption that only about 5 percent of the remote accesses are writes and that writes are usually made to files that are not shared. A separate locking service is often provided for applications that write to shared blocks.

One difficulty with using timestamps to approximate cache consistency is that client and server are not exactly synchronized. The lack of synchronization between client and server clocks is called *time skew*. Client and server may need to exchange information periodically to keep track of how far their clocks are out-of-sync.

Another difficulty with time concerns side effects on otherwise idempotent operations. Suppose a client does an NFSPROC3_WRITE request and fails to receive a reply from the server. In the usual implementation, the client backs off for a certain amount of time and then retries the request. Suppose the server performed the first request, but the reply was lost. Since writes have the side effect of changing the time of modification, the second write changes the state of the file. In order to cut down on side effects and to improve efficiency, the NFS Version 3 protocol specification recommends that servers keep a cache of recent requests called the *duplicate request cache*. The cache retains the completion status of recent requests. If the server receives a request that is a duplicate of one held in the duplicate request cache, it merely returns the original return status and does not attempt the operation again.

14.9 Threads and Remote Procedure Calls

Normal RPC operations are synchronous and serial meaning that a client blocks on an RPC call until it receives a response. A client can therefore issue only one request at a time. On the server side, the server processes only one request at a time. The traditional approach for increasing parallelism on the server side is to install multiple servers (such as NSF server daemons) on a host.

Threads provide new opportunities for parallelism for both the clients and servers. An RPC client side can dedicate a thread to issuing RPC calls and waiting for responses while the rest of the program does something else. Multiple client threads can make simultaneous RPC calls provided that each thread creates its own handle with `clnt_create`. If the client threads share a single RPC handle, the calls are processed sequentially rather than in parallel.

Threading of RPC servers is more complicated because each remote service can be called as an independent thread. Obviously the program must protect shared variables and use appropriate mechanisms to synchronize interaction of the services. A good approach is to develop a threaded local version with a main program that creates a new thread to call the service and wait for the result. The main program can launch many simultaneous threads and test the interactions among services.

The parameters and return values present a subtle problem that arises because of the traditional structure of RPC stubs. A single-threaded server stub uses static variables to unmarshal information and pass parameters to the services. The remote function communicates its return value by returning a pointer to a static variable. The stub then uses the static variable to marshal a return value. A threaded server must allocate space for the parameters and return value before creating the service thread. When the thread completes, the server stub must free the space that is allocated. These changes require modification of the server stub.

Fortunately `rpcgen` now provides a `-A` option for automatically generating a multithreaded server. The resulting server runs in *automatic MT mode*. The `-A` option causes `rpcgen` to generate remote services whose parameters and return values are dynamically allocated rather than assigned to static variables. The `_server.c` template file also includes functions that the server stub calls to free dynamically allocated storage after the service returns.

Example 14.19
Program 14.20 shows the `rfile_server.c` *template file for a threaded server produced by the following command.*

```
rpcgen -a -A -C rfile.x
```

The `*result` in the `put_block_1_svc` of Program 14.20 is the return value for the `put_block` service specified in `rfile.x`. The actual return value for `put_block_1_svc` is just a boolean flag indicating that the function executed. Simply set `retval` to 1 to indicate to the client that the call executed.

Program 14.20: Template for threaded version of `put_block` server.

```
#include "rfile.h"

bool_t
put_block_1_svc(packet *argp, int *result, struct svc_req *rqstp)
{
    bool_t retval;
    /*  insert server code here */
    return (retval);
}

int
rfileprog_1_freeresult(SVCXPRT *transp, xdrproc_t xdr_result,
                       caddr_t result)
{
    (void) xdr_free(xdr_result, result);
    /* Insert additional freeing code here, if needed */
}
```

_____ **Program 14.20** _____

Example 14.20

    Program 14.21 shows a `rfile_server.c` _template file for a nonthreaded server produced by the following_ `rpcgen` _command. The function returns_ `result` _to the server stub by a pointer to a static variable._

    `rpcgen -a -C rfile.x`

Program 14.21: The `rfile_server.c` template file for a nonthreaded server.

```
#include "rfile.h"

int *
put_block_1_svc(packet *argp, struct svc_req *rqstp)
{
    static int  result;
    /*  insert server code here */
    return (&result);
}
```

_____ **Program 14.21** _____

Program 14.22 shows a threaded version of the `rfile_server.c` file after the code has been inserted into the template. Since the `put_block_1_svc` does not refer to any static variables, simultaneous invocations of the function do not interfere with each other.

Program 14.22: The `put_block` service in a threaded server.

```
#include "rfile.h"

bool_t
put_block_1_svc(packet *pack, int *result, struct svc_req *rqstp)
{
    bool_t retval;
    int fd;

    *result = 0;
    if ((fd = open(pack->fname, O_WRONLY|O_CREAT, 0600)) == -1)
        *result = -1;
    else if (lseek(fd, pack->offset, SEEK_SET) == -1)
        *result = -1;
    else
        *result = write(fd, pack->data.data_val, pack->count);
    close(fd);
    retval = 1;
    return retval;
}

int
rfileprog_1_freeresult(SVCXPRT *transp, xdrproc_t xdr_result,
    caddr_t result)
{
    (void) xdr_free(xdr_result, result);
    return 0;
}
```

—————————————— **Program 14.22** ——————————————

In calls to a nonthreaded server, the client detects an RPC failure when the remote call returns a NULL pointer to the return value. In calls to threaded servers, the remote call returns an error code specifying whether the call succeeded. The error code is RPC_SUCCESS when the function succeeds. The constant RPC_SUCCESS has a numerical value of 0, which is confusing since a 0 return value for the service on the server side specifies a failure. Notice that the `put_block_1_svc` function of Program 14.22 returns 1 to indicate success.

The actual result of a call to a threaded service is returned as a parameter, so a client call to a threaded server has an extra parameter containing a pointer to the return value.

Program 14.23 shows the client-side call to the remote service on the threaded server. The call returns an error code rather than a pointer to a result.

Program 14.23: The client `write_file` function calls a service in a threaded RPC server.

```
#include "rfile.h"

int write_file(CLIENT *clnt, char *filename, char *buffer, int nbytes)
{
    int  bytes_written;
    enum clnt_stat retval_1;
    int result_1;
    packet  pack;

    pack.count = nbytes;
    pack.offset = fd_offset;
    pack.fname = filename;
    pack.data.data_val = buffer;
    pack.data.data_len = nbytes;
    retval_1 = put_block_1(&pack, &result_1, clnt);
    if (retval_1 != RPC_SUCCESS)
        bytes_written = -1;
    else {
        bytes_written = result_1;
        fd_offset += bytes_written;
    }
    return bytes_written;
}
```

_____ **Program 14.23** _____

In a single-threaded server created by `rpcgen`, the stub sets up communication using a transport mechanism such as `TCP` with sockets. It then calls a `svc_run` function to monitor the communication descriptors using `select` or `poll`. When a request comes in, the server unmarshals it, calls the service as an ordinary function, marshals the results, and replies on the communication descriptor. The server then resumes monitoring the descriptors for additional requests. The `-A` option of `rpcgen` not only handles the problem of parameter passing, but it automatically generates a `svc_run` that creates a new thread for each service request. Sun Solaris 2.4 uses 16 as the default maximum number of simultaneous threads, but the server stub may change the value by calling `rpc_control`.

The `rpcgen` uses Solaris threads rather than POSIX threads. The Solaris documentation indicates that a program can mix POSIX synchronization mechanisms and Solaris synchronization mechanisms in the same program. Be sure to add `-lpthreads` to the `LDLIB` in the `makefile` and the appropriate `pthreads.h` header files in the source.

The threaded RPC calls appear to be in a state of flux and there are no standards, as yet, about their format. Read current documentation before developing threaded servers on a particular system. Here are some guidelines to follow when developing a threaded server:

- Develop the remote services as simple local calls.
- Convert the local calls to threaded local calls.
- For testing, use a program that creates multiple threads to call the local functions. Each thread calls the local function as an ordinary call, waits for a return value, and exits. Synchronization problems are more easily detected in a local environment than in a remote one. Do not go on to the next step until the local threaded version works.
- Create a `.x` specification file (e.g., `rfile.x` or `rand.x`). (The specification files for threaded and the nonthreaded versions are the same.)
- Run `rpcgen` with the command

      rpcgen -a -A -C rfile.x

  (Substitute the name of the specification file for `rfile.x`.) The `-A` option designates *automatic MT mode*. With that option, `rpcgen` generates a server stub that automatically creates threads to service each request.
- If using POSIX threads rather than Solaris threads, be sure to add `-lpthreads` to the makefile and include the `pthreads.h` header file in the source.

14.10 Exercise: Stateless File Server

This exercise explores various aspects of the ONC TI-RPC remote procedure call facility.

- Make a new directory and copy the `rfile.x` specification for the remote version of `put_block` into the directory.
- Run `rpcgen -C -a rfile.x` to generate the needed files.
- Use the resulting files to implement a remote client similar to the one given in Program 14.17.
- Modify the `rfile_server.c` file to implement a remote server similar to the one given in Program 14.16.
- Make the files using the `makefile.rfile` makefile.
- Execute `rfile_server` to register the service with `rpcbind`.

- On the same machine, execute `rfile_client` with the appropriate command-line arguments. Verify correct transmission of a file.
- Execute `rfile_server` on a different machine than `rfile_client` to verify that it correctly transmits files.
- Experiment with different values of NETPATH. In particular try transmitting a large file with UDP and then with TCP. See if the UDP version was correct. Compare the transmission times for the two transports. Try the same experiment when several simultaneous `ftp` transfers of large files going on at the same time. Are there differences between UDP and TCP in performance and accuracy under these circumstances?
- Add `get_block` and `read_file` functions to the local version of the program. These functions are analogous to `put_block` and `write_file`. Their prototypes are

  ```
  int get_block(char *fname, int offset, int count,
                char *data);
  int write_file(int fd, char *buf, int nbytes);
  ```

  Debug the local version and then add the function `get_block` as a remote service to the file server.
- Add a `myrddir` function to the local version of the program. `myrddir` is similar to the C `readdir` library function. Its prototype is

  ```
  struct dirent myrddir(char *pathname, int cookie);
  ```

  The function returns an entry in the directory `pathname` as specified by `cookie`. A `cookie` value of 0 indicates the first entry, a `cookie` value of 1 indicates a second filename, and so on. Write the function as an idempotent function. After debugging the local version, add `myrddir` as a remote service to the file server.
- Add a `mystat` function to the local version of the program. The `mystat` function is similar to `stat`. Its prototype is

  ```
  struct stat mystat(char *pathname)
  ```

  The function returns a `struct stat` structure for the file indicated by `pathname`. Write the function as an idempotent function. After debugging the local version, add `mystat` as a remote service to the file server.
- Write a `showdir` function that lists the contents of a remote directory. Its prototype is

  ```
  int showdir(int fd, char *pathname);
  ```

  The function lists the entries of directory `pathname` one per line to the file `fd`. The function calls the `myrddir` to read the directory. The `showdir` function is part of the client program and does not have to be idempotent.

- Write a `showall` function that lists a directory entry followed by its inode information (e.g., owner, time of creation, and so on). The function has a prototype

    ```
    int showall(int fd, char *pathname);
    ```

    The function lists the directory entry followed by its inode information. Use `myrddir` and `mystat` to implement the function. The `showall` function is part of the client program and does not have to be idempotent.

14.11 Additional Reading

The remote procedure call was initially proposed by Birrell and Nelson [8] in a classic paper entitled "Implementing remote procedure calls." The book *UNIX System V Network Programming* by Stephen Rago has a discussion of XDR and low-level RPC programming [71]. The most extensive discussion of RPCs can be found in *Power Programming with RPC* by John Bloomer [11]. Russel Sandberg gives an overview of the original implementation of NFS in a Sun White Paper [76] entitled "The Sun Network File System: Design, implementation, and experience." The complete specification of NFS Version 3 is available via Internet at the anonymous ftp site `ftp.uu.net`.

Chapter 15

Project: *Tuple Space*

Linda is an elegant programming language designed to support parallel processing on networks of computers. The language is built on simple primitives and a tuple-space model that uses shared data for communication and synchronization, in contrast to traditional message-passing or shared-memory approaches. David Gelernter, Linda's originator, says in expressing the philosophy of Linda, "Elegance in writing software is achieving maximum functionality from minimal complexity,... It's the same as good prose—getting the most value from each word you write." This chapter develops a specification of a simplified tuple-space model and illustrates its use by building a distributed cooperative search application. The project integrates most concepts covered in previous chapters, culminating with a threaded remote-procedure-call server for a Linda subset. The machinery developed in this chapter is amazingly powerful, building the foundation for a truly distributed operating system.

A *tuple space* contains objects called *tuples*, which are ordered collections of data items. When a process needs to communicate, it generates a tuple and inserts it in tuple space. Other processes can then retrieve tuples from tuple space. Senders and receivers are uncoupled in this programming model and do not know each other's identity. They only communicate through shared information. A surprising number of parallel-programming problems fit well into this programming paradigm, and every parallel primitive can be simulated using it [33].

The tuple space appears as a shared associative memory which holds tuples and supports four operations: `out`, `in`, `rd`, and `eval`. The `out` operation places a tuple in tuple space. The `in` operation finds an appropriate tuple in tuple space, removes it, and returns its value. The `rd` operation is similar to `in`, but `rd` does not remove the tuple before returning its value. Finally, `eval` creates an active tuple (a process).

The tuple-space model forms the foundation of the Linda parallel communication system developed at Yale University [17] and now marketed by Scientific Computing Associates. Linda has two types of tuples—ordinary and active. Ordinary tuples contain data while active tuples represent processes. In addition to the four standard tuple-space operations (`out`, `in`, `rd`, and `eval`), the commercial version of Linda has nonblocking versions of `in` and `rd` which it designates as `inp` and `rdp`, respectively.

One goal of parallel computing is to make the development of parallel and distributed applications completely transparent to the programmer. Parallelizing compilers are one approach to this; the tuple-space abstraction is another. The average programmer is not going to be happy writing an application in PVM (see Chapter 11). The development of Linda is an important contribution to the field of parallel computing because of Linda's simplicity and expressive power. It allows users to develop distributed applications at a very high level compared with other distributed coordination systems such as PVM. The user writes programs using the tuple abstraction and has no knowledge of or control over the underlying distribution of the problem on the network.

The abstraction of Linda is a two-edged sword in practice—if the Linda implementation is efficient, all is well, but if the implementation performs poorly, the result is an elegant but impractical or useless system. The commercial versions of Linda claim to be efficient, but they do not provide convincing evidence that this is the case. Still, most distributed systems have a lot of overhead anyway when compared to single-processor operating systems, and starting with an abstract model offers the hope of improved performance as the underlying implementation becomes more sophisticated.

This chapter's project is ambitious—implementation of a fully working tuple-space system called Richard. (The name Richard follows the tradition of selecting famous Lovelaces for the namesakes of programming languages: Richard Lovelace was a seventeenth-century British poet who romanticized his life in prison and died penniless.) The next section briefly describes Linda, and the following section introduces Richard. Section 15.3 specifies an implementation of a Richard tuple space accessed by remote procedure calls. It makes no claims of efficiency. Section 15.4 discusses cooperative optimization as an application of tuple spaces and develops a greedy backtracking algorithm for the *n*-queens problem as an example. Section 15.5 extends Richard to include active tuples, while Section 15.6 extends Richard to include tuples that are themselves tuple spaces. Section 15.7 describes how to thread the Richard tuple space server. These three extensions to the basic Richard system are independent of each other, but together they provide the foundation for building a distributed computing system.

15.1 Linda

The Linda programming model is based on four operations on tuples—out, in, rd, and eval which augment a standard programming language such as FORTRAN or C. Special Linda preprocessors and optimizing compilers translate programs for the underlying target architecture and try to minimize the amount of runtime expense.

Example 15.1

A tuple is an ordered collection of data items. The following out *operation inserts a tuple with three elements into tuple space.*

```
out("element", 5, 3.0);
```

The ordering of the values in a Linda tuple is important, so a tuple ("element", 3.0, 5) is not the same as the tuple in Example 15.1. Identical copies of elements can reside in tuple space, so two out operations of the same tuple insert two copies into tuple space. The out operation never blocks.

There are two types of tuples in Linda, ordinary and active. Active tuples are created by eval and correspond to execution of a function. When the function completes execution, the active tuple becomes an ordinary one. The in and rd operations retrieve ordinary tuples from tuple space. The main difference between the two operations is that in removes the tuple while rd just returns a copy. These operations block if an appropriate tuple is not in tuple space and return later when such a tuple appears, either because of an out or because an eval completes execution.

The question of what constitutes an appropriate tuple is complicated. The in or rd contains a template which specifies what an appropriate tuple is. Linda selects at random among tuples matching the template. The template can take the wildcard ? indicating that a particular element can be matched to anything of a given type. Templates and tuples match when they have the same length and each field has the same type.

Example 15.2

Each of the following statements presents a template containing five elements.

```
rd("x", ?b, 3.0, "this", ?c);
rd(?y, "uuu", 3.0, ?z, 5.0);
```

Both requests in Example 15.2 match the tuple ("x", "uuu", 3.0, "this", 5.0) provided that y, b, and z are char * and c is a double. The notation ?b specifies a Linda *formal*. It says that the rd operation should replace the variable b with the corresponding value in the tuple returned by the rd. The calling program does not actually get the returned tuple; rather the variables that appear as formals are filled with values from the tuple. If rd were an ordinary C function, an &b parameter would designate a pointer to the variable b for the function to fill in. It would be hard to write a general rd function because the function has no way of knowing which of its parameters are formals and which contain values to be matched. The ?b notation allows a preprocessor to replace the b with the appropriate assignment statement without any work from the user. Without compiler support this would be tough for an ordinary programmer to deal with.

Linda's elegance arises from its expressive power—the common synchronization mechanisms are easy to program with Linda. Mutex locks and atomic updates of shared variables are naturally expressed by *in-out* pairs.

Example 15.3

> *The following Linda statements atomically increment a shared variable* x.

```
in(x, ?i);
out(x, i+1);
```

The x in Example 15.3 is a tag that labels the shared variable. The i is a local program variable of the same type as the shared variable (e.g., int). The in operation searches for a tuple that contains two elements, the first of which is x. The second value can be any int. The in removes the tuple. The out operation writes a new tuple whose first value is x and whose second element has a value that is one more than the corresponding element in the original tuple. The in-out pair is atomic if there is only one tuple with first value x, because other processes block when they attempt to perform an in operation on a tuple that is not there.

Linda supports message passing with in-order delivery by a sequence of tuples of the form

```
(comun_id, sequence_number, message)
```

The commun_id identifies the communication session and is analogous to well-known ports for sockets. The sequence_number identifies the position of the message in the sequence, and message is one of the individual messages within the sequence.

Example 15.4

> *The sender executes the following code segment to send* n *integers of an array* A, *each as an individual message.*

```
int A[MAX_SIZE];
int s_seq;
int n;

for (s_seq = 0; s_seq < n; s_seq++)
      out("ID1", s_seq, A[i]);
```

Similarly, the receiver executes the following.

```
int B[MAX_SIZE];
int r_seq;
int n;

for (r_seq = 0; r_seq < n; r_seq++)
     in("ID1", r_seq,  ?B[r_seq]);
```

Example 15.4 guarantees error-free in-order communication between sender and receiver as long as no one else refers to a tuple with leading tag value of `"ID1"`. The sender and receiver must agree in advance to identify their communication by the tag `"ID1"`. The `?B[r_seq]` is a just a variable to be filled with the corresponding `int` tuple value. The blocking `in` controls the flow of control between sender and receiver. If the receiver attempts to read a message that has not been sent, it blocks until the sender inserts the needed tuple.

In the bounded-buffer problem, the sender can block if there is no room in the buffer to hold the next message. Here, the sender inserts tuples as long as there is room in the tuple space. An `out` can fail if there is no room in the tuple space, but that possibility is unlikely for correctly working programs. In effect, all of the Linda processes are sharing a global buffer, providing considerably more flexibility than if a process allocates a fixed set of buffers for each communication session.

The Linda `eval` operation creates a new process to evaluate each of its parameters. The `eval` operation is usually used when one or more of the parameters is a function call. The `eval` operation never blocks. Linda inserts an active tuple into tuple space and creates a new process to evaluate each function in the tuple. When a process completes, it deposits the function return value into the corresponding entry of the tuple. When all of the return values arrive, the tuple becomes an ordinary tuple.

Example 15.5

The following Linda statement creates a process to run the function `myfun`.

```
eval("MY", i, j, myfun(i, j));
```

The `eval` statement of Example 15.5 inserts an active tuple into tuple space and creates a process to evaluate `myfun`. When the process completes, it replaces the active tuple with an ordinary tuple of the form `("MY", i, j, result)`, where `result` contains the value returned by `myfun`. The `in` and `read` operations never match active tuples. A blocked `in` or `read` can unblock if an active tuple changes to an ordinary one.

A distributed hash table is a natural setting for current Linda implementations, though eventually more advanced techniques such as large-scale associative memories or multilevel caching may come into play. Because tuples are typed, current implementations use hash tables that are partitioned by the number of components in the tuples and the types of their values.

15.2 Richard, a Simplified Linda

Linda implementations require extensive preprocessor, compiler, and runtime support. This chapter develops a specification for a tuple-space server called Richard with simplified semantics and no extra compiler support. The Richard specification restricts the allowable tuples and templates to make implementation easier.

In contrast to Linda tuples which can be of arbitrary length, a Richard tuple contains exactly two items: an integer tuple ID and a value. For the initial implementation the value can only be an integer or a character array. Section 15.5 describes an extension in which tuple values can be functions, and Section 15.6 describes an extension in which tuple values can themselves be tuple spaces. These extensions provide functionality for Richard that is similar to that of Kernel Linda [46], the basis of the QIX operating system.

Richard also differs from Linda in its search semantics. Linda permits arbitrary search operations and returns a random tuple matching the search template. Richard allows only two types of searches—searching for a tuple with a certain ID value and searching for any tuple that contains a certain type of value field. On searches for a tuple with a specific tuple ID, Richard returns the matching tuples in the order in which they were inserted in the tuple space. The Richard semantics implies that `out` operations queue tuples having the same tuple ID.

Since it is implemented without compiler support and its operations must be sandwiched into RPC format, Richard dispenses with the `?i` formal notation and replaces `?` with ugly `union` and `struct` specifications. (See Section 15.3 for the grim details.) The examples in this section use a Richard pseudocode similar to Linda syntax. Section 15.3 introduces Richard syntax.

Example 15.6

The following Richard pseudocode removes the first tuple that was inserted that has x *as its first value. (Never mind what a Richard tuple looks like for now.)*

```
in(x, ?i);
```

In contrast to Example 15.6, the equivalent Linda `in` statement removes a random tuple matching the template. Another important difference is that Linda matches the types of the formals, so if `i` is an integer, the tuples matching the `in` of Example 15.6 must have an integer second value. Richard allows any supported-type to match the formal. This flexibility is required unless extensive preprocessor or compiler support is available. It will also be used later to allow the implementation of active tuples.

Example 15.7

The following Richard pseudocode implements error-free in-order message passing for a communication session identified by x. *The sender writes tuples containing consecutive elements of the array* A *as follows.*

```
int A[MAX_SIZE];
int i;
int n;

for (i = 0; i < n; i++)
   out(x, A[i]);
```

After the sender completes, the receiver removes the tuples as follows.

```
int B[MAX_SIZE];
int i;
int n;

for (i = 0; i < n; i++)
   in(x, ?B[i]);
```

The code given in Example 15.7 is Richard pseudocode. The receiver receives the messages in the order the sender wrote them because Richard queues tuples with duplicate tuple IDs. In Example 15.4, each Linda tuple needed an additional sequence number to ensure in-order delivery of messages. Since Richard is implemented on top of C without additional compiler support, the ?B[i] syntax cannot be used. Section 15.3 describes the details of the actual Richard syntax.

In Example 15.7 the sender must insert all of its messages before the receiver starts, since Richard and Linda have different blocking semantics. Linda in and rd operations block indefinitely if no tuple in the space matches the request template. Some important algorithms rely on this blocking mechanism. The Richard implementation of this chapter has nonblocking semantics (i.e., an in or rd returns an error if there is no match) because blocking operations are hard to implement correctly using remote procedure calls. If the tuple server is not threaded, a blocking call can cause a deadlock. Furthermore, remote procedure calls time out if the server does not respond in a preset amount of time.

Blocking remote procedure calls may be implemented with *client callbacks*. The idea of a client callback is that the server immediately returns a null response when it starts to process the call. Later, when the server is ready with the actual result, it does a remote procedure call to the client. The parameters of this server call to the client are the return values for the original call. The client has to register its own server when it starts execution. Unfortunately, using callbacks requires adding server event-loop processing on both the client and server sides, and the interaction of callbacks with threaded servers and clients is very complicated.

Example 15.8

Example 15.7 does not work under Richard unless the sender inserts messages before the receiver attempts to remove them. The following Richard pseudocode implements message passing without this restriction but in an inefficient manner. The sender writes tuples containing consecutive elements of the array A *as follows.*

```
int A[MAX_SIZE], i, n;

for (i = 0; i < n;  i++)
    out(x, A[i]);
```

The receiver removes the tuples as follows.

```
int B[MAX_SIZE], i, n;

for (i = 0; i < n; i++)
    while (!in(x, ?B[i]))
        ;
```

The in *returns a 0 error code if the operation fails. The receiver retries until it successfully fetches the value.*

A *barrier* is a point in program execution where a group of processes synchronize by waiting until all members of the group reach that point. A tuple-space application can implement barrier synchronization for n processes by inserting a barrier tuple that contains the integer value n as part of its initialization. When a process in the application reaches the barrier, it decrements the barrier tuple value (in, decrement, out) and then waits for the barrier tuple value to reach 0 (rd). The continual examination of the barrier tuple until it reaches 0 is an example of *spinning*, a form of busy waiting.

Example 15.9

The following Richard pseudocode implements a barrier assuming that a tuple with ID barrier_ID *and value* n *is in the tuple space.*

```
while(!in(barrier_ID, ?i))
    ;
i--;
out(barrier_ID, i);
while (!rd(barrier_ID, ?i) || (i != 0))
    ;
```

Example 15.10

> *The following Linda pseudocode implements the barrier of Example 15.9 without spinning.*

```
in(barrier_ID, ?i);
i--;
out(barrier_ID, i);
if (i > 0)
   rd(barrier_ID, 0);
```

Each process in Example 15.9 does both an `in` and an `out` operation to decrement the barrier count. An alternative implementation initializes the barrier by inserting n identical tuples. Each process removes a tuple when it reaches the barrier and then spins until all barrier tuples are gone.

Example 15.11

> *The following Richard pseudocode implements a barrier assuming that exactly n copies of a tuple with ID* `barrier_ID` *are in the tuple space.*

```
in(barrier_ID, ?i);
while(rd(barrier_ID, ?i))
   ;
```

Although Example 15.11 requires the same number of `out` operations as Example 15.9, it may need fewer tuple-space accesses after the barrier is reached and allows greater parallelism because the `in` operations do not have to wait on the completion of decrements by other processes.

15.3 A Simple Richard Tuple Space

This section specifies a Richard server with `out`, `in`, and `rd` operations. The specification first develops a completely local version of Richard and then describes how to convert the system so that the tuple space has a remote server.

15.3.1 Tuple Data Structures

A Richard tuple consists of an integer tuple ID and a value. Represent tuples in a structure of type `struct tuple_t` defined by the declarations of Program 15.1. The `tuple_val_u` union holds the value of the tuple. The `tuple_type` member designates the type of value. These definitions do not contain `typedef`'s in order to please `rpcgen` later. To keep the memory management from being too complex and to allow implementation in terms of RPCs, arrays are assumed to have a maximum size of `MAX_BUF`.

Program 15.1: The tuple declarations for Richard.

```
#define MAX_BUF 1024
enum tuple_value_type {
    INTEGER = 0,
    ARRAY = 1
};

struct array_t {
    unsigned int array_len;
    char *array_val;
};

struct tuple_val_t {
    enum tuple_value_type  tuple_type;
    union {
        int     ival;
        struct array_t array;
    } tuple_val_u;
};

struct tuple_t {
    unsigned int tuple_ID;
    struct tuple_val_t tuple_val;
};
```

———————————————————— **Program 15.1** ————————————————————

Richard has two types of tuple values—integer and array of characters. The value of the integer is in the tuple, but array-valued tuples only contain pointers. The program must allocate additional space to hold the actual array and set a pointer to it.

Example 15.12

The following C code segment creates a tuple with tuple ID 45 to hold the string "This is a test".

```
char *p = "This is a test";
struct tuple_t *t;

t = (struct tuple_t *)malloc(sizeof(struct tuple_t) +
                            strlen(p) + 1);
t->tuple_ID = 45;
t->tuple_val.tuple_type = ARRAY;
t->tuple_val.tuple_val_u.array.array_len = strlen(p) + 1;
t->tuple_val.tuple_val_u.array.array_val =
                            (char *)t + sizeof(struct tuple_t);
memcpy(t + sizeof(struct tuple_t), p, strlen(p) + 1);
```

The `malloc` in Example 15.12 allocates space for both `struct tuple_t` and the array data. Later a single `free` can deallocate both items. Use this block allocation technique to allocate space for the nodes that hold tuples in the hash table described below.

15.3.2 Tuple Space Representation

Represent the Richard tuple space by a hash table such as the one shown in Figure 15.1. Keep the tuples whose tuple IDs hash to the same value in a linked list pointed to by the corresponding entry in the hash table. Queue tuples with identical tuple ID values within the linked list so that `in` and `rd` can retrieve them on a first-in-first-out basis. Keep a counter with the largest tuple ID used so far (`largest_ID`) in order to assign an unused tuple ID to a tuple, if necessary.

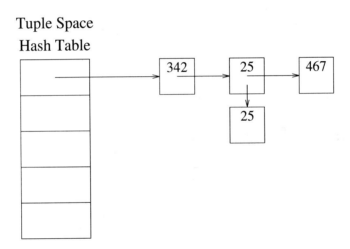

Figure 15.1: A hash-table representation for the Richard tuple space.

Example 15.13

In the hash table of Figure 15.1, tuples with key values 342, 25, *and* 467 *hash to the same location. The two tuples with ID* 25 *are queued.*

Choose a hash-table representation that is efficient for Richard searches (i.e., search-by-tuple-ID and search-by-tuple-type). To perform a search-by-tuple-ID, calculate the hash-table entry based on the tuple ID and then scan for nodes containing the tuple ID.

For randomized search applications such as the backtracking problem of Section 15.4, the randomness (or lack of it) of the search-by-tuple-type can affect the outcome of the solution. Keeping counts of the number of each type of tuple hashed to that value may improve the performance of random search-by-tuple-type. The program can approximate random search by first selecting a random hash-table entry. If the entry contains any tuples of the specified type, use the counts in the hash-table entry to select a random tuple of the given type.

The specification assumes that new tuple IDs are unique over the lifetime of the system. That is, if an `out` operation uses a 0 `tuple_ID` value, the tuple will be assigned an ID that has not been used. A 32-bit `tuple_ID` is sufficient for testing but not for a real system. A more realistic representation number might include an incarnation number. Each time the tuple IDs wrap around, increment the incarnation number. This representation is equivalent to keeping a 64-bit tuple ID.

15.3.3 Tuple-Space Operations

Implement the Richard tuple-space operations `out`, `in`, and `rd` as described below. Place the hash-table data structures with the three Richard functions in a separate file. Write a main test program that performs various combinations of `out`, `in`, and `rd` function calls to establish that the local implementation works correctly.

- The `out` function inserts the specified tuple into tuple space. The `out` function has the prototype

  ```
  unsigned int out(struct tuple_t val);
  ```

  On success, `out` returns the tuple ID of the inserted tuple. On failure `out` returns 0. If the `val.tuple_ID` value is positive, queue the tuple behind all other existing tuples with the same tuple ID value. If the ID is greater than `largest_ID`, update `largest_ID` to this value. If `val.tuple_ID` is 0, assign the tuple a new ID value that is one greater than `largest_ID` and increment `largest_ID`.

- The `in` function removes a tuple that matches the specified template and returns the tuple value. The `in` function has the prototype

  ```
  struct tuple_t in(struct tuple_t val);
  ```

  The template is based on the value of the `val.tuple_ID`. If the `val.tuple_ID` is positive, search for the first tuple with matching tuple ID. If the `val.tuple_ID` is 0, search for a random tuple of type `val.tuple_val.tuple_type` (ideally, a uniformly distributed random tuple). If no tuple matches the template, the `tuple_ID` member of the returned tuple is 0.

- The `rd` function behaves like `in` except that it does not remove the tuple from tuple space. The `rd` function has the prototype

  ```
  struct tuple_t rd(struct tuple_t val);
  ```

At first glance these specifications seem deceptively simple—so much so that the temptation may arise to change the return values of `in` and `rd` to pointers to `struct tuple_t` rather than the structures themselves. Resist the temptation. (Also refer to the improved pseudorandom-number service specified in Example 14.9.) The remote version cannot return a pointer to the client, so it is better to address the difficulty in the local version right away.

The problem arises because the `struct tuple_t` definition has a pointer to an array rather than the actual array. Pass the `val` parameter by value in the calling program, and the called program can locate the string if necessary. When a string tuple is returned by an `in` or `rd`, where should the string be located?

Example 15.14

The following code segment calls the `out` *function to insert an array containing* `"this is a test"` *into tuple space.*

```
struct tuple_t myval;
char myarray[MAX_BUF];

strcpy(myarray, "this is a test");
myval.tuple_ID = 0;
myval.tuple_val.tuple_type = ARRAY;
myval.tuple_val.tuple_val_u.array.array_len = strlen(myarray) + 1;
myval.tuple_val.tuple_val_u.array.array_val = myarray;
if (!out(myval))
    fprintf(stderr, "Out failed\n");
```

Since the tuple in Example 15.14 is an `ARRAY` type, the `out` function performs a single block allocate of a `struct hash_node` with enough space to hold the array values. The `out` then copies the `struct tuple_t` values, explicitly sets its `array_val` pointer to refer to the extra space allocated with its node, and performs a `memcpy` of the array pointed to in the parameter into its own space similar to the allocation of Example 15.12. After the conversion to a remote call, the `struct tuple_t` parameter of `out` refers to a static variable in the server stub.

The `in` operation finds a node in the tuple space that matches the search template. It then copies the `struct tuple_t` portion of the node into a special static return value, and frees the node. The calling program must be sure to copy the array value into its own space before calling another `in`, since `in` reuses the static array on the next call of that type. The problem is similar to those arising from library functions that use static storage as discussed in Section 1.5.

Example 15.15

The following code segment within in *handles the return values for the local version.*

```
static struct tuple_t return_tuple;
static char return_array[MAX_BUF];

/* within in function */
struct hash_node *p;

if ((p = find_and_remove(val)) == NULL) {
    return_tuple.tuple_ID = 0;
    return return_tuple;
}
return_tuple = p->tuple;
if (return_tuple.tuple_val.tuple_type == ARRAY) {
    return_tuple.tuple_val.tuple_val_u.array.array_val = return_array;
    memcpy(return_array,
            p->tuple.tuple_val.tuple_val_u.array.array_val,
            p->tuple.tuple_val.tuple_val_u.array.array_len);
}
free(p);
return return_tuple;
```

15.3.4 Conversion to a Remote Server

Once the local implementation works, convert the tuple space implementation to a server accessed by remote procedure calls. The local out, in, and rd functions now contain remote calls to the tuple server. Test the server to make sure it is working. Design appropriate formats for passing tuples as discussed in Chapter 14.

One problem area is the tuple_val_u union in the struct tuple_val_t because the RPC specification language uses a switched union instead of a union. Replace the struct tuple_t definition by something equivalent to

```
/* Sun RPC Specification Language.  This is not C */
const MAX_BUF = 1024;

enum tuple_value_type {
    INTEGER = 0,
    ARRAY = 1
};

union tuple_val_t switch(enum tuple_value_type tuple_type) {
    case INTEGER:
        int ival;
    case ARRAY:
        char array<MAX_BUF>;
};
```

```
struct tuple_t {
    unsigned int tuple_ID;
    struct tuple_val tuple_val;
};
```

The `rpcgen` uses the switched union information to generate an ordinary structure. An explicit upper bound on the size of the character array (`MAX_BUF`) must be given. The switched union syntax and variable-sized arrays are not part of C but rather are part of the Sun RPC specification language. This syntax appears in the `.x` files, and `rpcgen` generates C code from the specification. Program 15.2 shows a specification file for the Richard server. The `struct array_t` is now a variable-length character array.

Program 15.2: The `richard.x` specification file for a remote Richard server.

```
/*  richard.x: Sun RPC Specification Language.  This is not C. */

const MAX_BUF = 1024;

enum tuple_value_type {
    INTEGER = 0,
    ARRAY = 1
};

union tuple_val_t switch(enum tuple_value_type tuple_type) {
    case INTEGER:
        int ival;
    case ARRAY:
        char array<MAX_BUF>;
};

struct tuple_t {
    unsigned int tuple_ID;
    struct tuple_val tuple_val;
};

program RICHPROG {
    version RICHVERS {
        int OUT(tuple_t) = 1;
        tuple_t IN(tuple_t) = 2;
        tuple_t RD(tuple_t) = 3;
    } = 1;
} = 0x31234566;
```
_____ **Program 15.2** _____

Example 15.16

The command

```
rpcgen -a -C richard.x
```

creates several skeleton files and a `richard.h` *header file that includes the following type definitions.*

```
#define MAX_BUF 1024

enum tuple_value_type {
        INTEGER = 0,
        ARRAY = 1
};
typedef enum tuple_value_type tuple_value_type;

struct tuple_val_t {
        tuple_value_type tuple_type;
        union {
                int ival;
                struct {
                        u_int array_len;
                        char *array_val;
                } array;
        } tuple_val_t_u;
};
typedef struct tuple_val_t tuple_val_t;

struct tuple_t {
        u_int tuple_ID;
        struct tuple_val tuple_val;
};
typedef struct tuple_t tuple_t;
```

The switched union of the specification in Program 15.2 is replaced by a structure containing an ordinary union in Example 15.16. Notice that MAX_BUF does not appear explicitly in these declarations. Be careful not to exceed this limit in the array-valued tuples because the client and server stubs may use this limit in allocating temporary buffer space.

Convert the local tuple-space implementation to a remote server accessed by remote procedure calls. The conversion process should be straightforward if the local version conforms to the specification. Once the remote server is working correctly, implement the following programs to perform error-free, in-order communication through tuple space.

- Write a sender program that reads from standard input and inserts each data block into tuple space by calling out with a tuple ID value of `commun_ID`. Assign `commun_ID` arbitrarily to some preagreed upon value much like well-known ports for sockets. The `sender` program uses an `ARRAY` tuple type for the transmission. When `sender` encounters an end-of-file on standard input, call a final `out` of a tuple of type `INTEGER`. Pass the value of `commun_ID` as a command-line argument to `sender`.

- Write a `receiver` program that performs `in` operations to retrieve tuples with tuple ID `commun_ID` from the tuple space. If a tuple has a type `ARRAY`, the `receiver` writes the retrieved data to standard output. If a tuple has type `INTEGER`, the `receiver` outputs a message to standard error and exits. Pass the value of `commun_ID` as a command-line argument to `receiver`. Be sure to retry failed `in` operations since they are nonblocking.

- Test the tuple-space implementation by using the `sender` and `receiver` programs to transfer a file through tuple space. For example, to transfer the file `my.in` using tuple ID `348` as a communication port, use

```
sender 348 <my.in
receiver 348 >my.out
diff my.in my.out
```

The `sender` and `receiver` each take the `commun_ID` value as a command-line argument. Run the `sender` and `receiver` on different machines, or at least in different windows. When the processes finish, execute the `diff` to verify that the transfer completes correctly. Try running several sender-receiver pairs simultaneously. Each pair will have a distinct `commun_fd`.

As a second test, implement a Richard barrier. Test the barrier using at least ten dummy clients.

15.4 Blackboards: A Tuple Space Application

In a natural community or social system, members interact, compete for resources, and cooperate to solve problems. Researchers have applied the analogy of cooperative agents to systems of distributed processes working on difficult problems such as heuristic searches [39]. Huberman [40] has shown that under appropriate conditions, there can be a nonlinear increase in performance of the overall system if agents cooperate. (A linear dependence means that a plot of performance versus number of agents has a curve with a positive constant slope. Huberman argues that it is possible for the curve to have a positive, increasing slope.) Furthermore, increasing the diversity of the agents improves the chances of achieving an outstanding solution.

To understand how this type of problem solving works, consider the situation in which a group of people is participating in a brainstorming session to solve a problem. A group leader stands at a blackboard and transcribes ideas as participants shout out. The benefit of interaction comes when the ideas of one person trigger an unexpected line of inquiry by other participants. If the group leader directs the discussion or starts with hints about possible approaches, the ideas tend to be more focused. A less-directed discussion leads to more "off-the-wall" ideas, but it may also introduce more creative approaches to solving the problem.

In more quantitative terms, the directed discussion leads most participants to similar solutions, and the distribution of the quality of the solutions appears to have a narrow peak. In the case of a more diverse and unstructured approach, the distribution of solutions should be broader. Some members might have very bad solutions, but there could also be some outstanding solutions. Since only one solution is needed, an outstanding solution is more likely in the latter case. The key elements in this approach are

- A problem in which partial results from one agent can guide the computation of another agent.

- Sufficient diversity so that "off-the-wall" problem solving can occur.

- Sufficient complexity of the agents so that they can make progress without consulting the blackboard too often.

Cooperative problem-solving techniques share some common features with genetic algorithms.

This section develops a cooperative approach to solving the *n*-queens and related optimization problems using a blackboard that is implemented as a tuple space. Programs called *agents* retrieve promising configurations from a central blackboard and use randomized backtracking to attempt to compute solutions. The agents also deposit partial solutions in the blackboard so that other agents have an opportunity to extend them. Figure 15.2 shows the layout of the blackboard server. The agents use *out* to deposit partial solutions and *in* or *rd* to retrieve partial solutions. The agents do not have to be identical, and cooperative problem-solving algorithms often work best with a diverse collection of agents.

15.4.1 The *n*-Queens Problem

In chess, a queen *threatens* another piece if the piece is in the same row or column or on the same diagonal as the queen and there are no intervening pieces. The classic *eight queens (8-queens) problem* is to find a placement of eight queens on an 8×8 chess board so that no queen threatens another. Since each queen must appear exactly once in each row and each column, the possible solutions are permutations of the integers from 0 to 7. The number of permutations of the integers from 0 to 7 is $8! = 40,320$, so it is easy

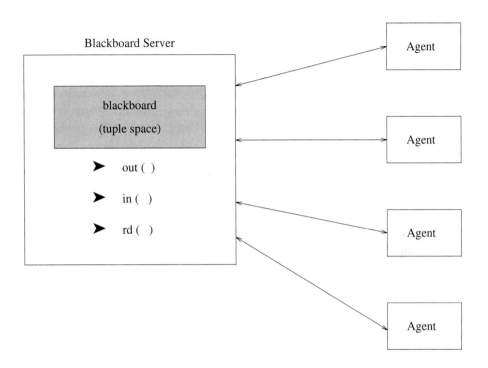

Blackboard Server

blackboard

(tuple space)

➤   out ( )

➤   in ( )

➤   rd ( )

Agent

Agent

Agent

Agent

Figure 15.2: A central blackboard with remote agents.

to find all ninety-two solutions simply by testing each permutation to see whether any queens are on the same diagonals.

Example 15.17

The permutation $(3, 5, 7, 1, 6, 0, 2, 4)$ *is a solution to the 8-queens problem. Here the rows and columns are integers between* 0 *and* 7. *The permutation corresponds to the following placement of queens.*

Row	Column
0	3
1	5
2	7
3	1
4	6
5	0
6	2
7	4

The more general problem of placing n queens on an $n \times n$ chess board is more difficult. Even when n is twenty, the prospect of testing all $20! = 2,432,902,008,176,640,000$ of the permutations of n is daunting. Probabilistic algorithms have proven successful in finding solutions when n is large. Instead of starting with a systematic search, many probabilistic algorithms place some queens at random, and then apply a deterministic algorithm such as backtracking or greedy selection [13].

In this project, agents cooperate in performing a probabilistic search. A cooperative strategy requires a method by which an agent working on the problem can convey useful information to other agents. Here the agents announce the best promising configurations that they compute. A *promising* configuration is a placement of k queens $(0 < k \le n)$ on the board so that no queen threatens another. Represent a promising configuration by a one-dimensional *placement array*. An entry, j, in the ith position in the array corresponds to a placement of a queen in the ith row and jth column on the board. Row positions not in the promising configuration contain -1's.

Example 15.18

The configuration $(3, -1, 7, 2, 6, -1, -1, -1)$ is a nonthreatening placement of four queens on an 8×8 board. It is a promising configuration. Figure 15.3 shows this configuration.

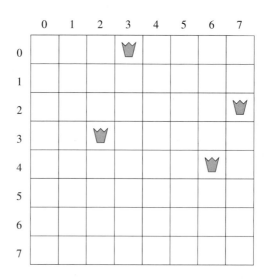

Figure 15.3: The promising configuration $(3, -1, 7, 2, 6, -1, -1, -1)$.

Not all permutations of n are solutions of the n-queens problem. Similarly, there is no guarantee that an arbitrary subset of a permutation is a promising configuration. The one-dimensional array representation of a promising configuration guarantees that no two pieces are in the same row or column, but this representation does not place any restriction that the pieces be on different diagonals.

Example 15.19

The configuration $(0, 1, 2, 3, 4, -1, -1, 7)$ *represents a placement of six queens along the main board diagonal in the 8-queens problem. The configuration is not promising.*

Row i of the board is unoccupied if the ith entry of the placement array contains -1. Similarly a column j of the board is unoccupied if the value j does not appear in the placement array. The diagonal occupancy information is not directly available from the placement array.

The diagonals parallel to the main diagonal are called *forward diagonals*. On a given forward diagonal, the difference between the row and column number is constant. Queens placed at positions (i_1, j_1) and (i_2, j_2) occupy the same forward diagonal when

$$(i_1 - j_1 + n - 1) = (i_2 - j_2 + n - 1)$$

The value $n - 1$ is added to each difference so that the result is in the interval $[0, 2n - 2]$.

The *back diagonals*, which are perpendicular to the main diagonal, are characterized by a constant value of $i + j$. These values are also in the interval $[0, 2n - 2]$. Queens placed at positions (i_1, j_1) and (i_2, j_2) occupy the same back diagonal when

$$(i_1 + j_1) = (i_2 + j_2)$$

An *occupancy array* conveniently conveys information about whether a position is occupied. Each entry represents a position. An entry value of 1 indicates that the position is occupied, and a -1 indicates that the position is unoccupied. The placement's row and column occupancies can be represented by arrays of size n, and its forward-diagonal and back-diagonal occupancies by arrays of size $2n - 1$.

Example 15.20

The promising configuration $(3, -1, 7, 2, 6, -1, -1, -1)$ *has the following occupancy arrays.*

row	$(1, -1, 1, 1, 1, -1, -1, -1)$
column:	$(-1, -1, 1, 1, -1, -1, 1, 1)$
forward diagonal:	$(-1, -1, 1, -1, 1, 1, -1, -1, 1, -1, -1, -1, -1, -1)$
back diagonal:	$(-1, -1, -1, 1, -1, 1, -1, -1, -1, 1, 1, -1, -1, -1).$

Obtain the row-occupancy array from the placement array by replacing all positive entries in the placement array by 1. Notice that for a promising configuration, each occupancy array contains a number of ones equal to the number of queens in the configuration. Represent promising configurations by a structure of the following type:

```
typedef struct promising_type {
    int numberfixed;
    int boardsize;
    int values[MAXCHESSBOARDSIZE];
    int columns[MAXCHESSBOARDSIZE];
    int for_diagonals[2*MAXCHESSBOARDSIZE-1];
    int back_diagonals[2*MAXCHESSBOARDSIZE-1];
} promising_t;
```

MAXCHESSBOARDSIZE is a constant defining the maximum allowed size of the board. The boardsize member defines the size of the problem. It is 8 for the 8-queens problem. The numberfixed member corresponds to the number of queens that are placed in nonthreatening positions. The values member represents the placement, while columns, for_diagonals, and back_diagonals represent occupancy arrays.

The add_if_promising function of Program 15.3 adds a queen at position (i, j) to a promising configuration *rp if the resulting configuration is still promising. It returns 1 if the queen is added and 0 otherwise.

Program 15.3: Add a queen to a promising configuration.

```
int add_if_promising(promising_t *rp, int i, int j)
{
    int f, b;

    f = (i - j + rp->boardsize - 1);
    b = (i + j);
    if ((rp ->values[i] == -1) && (rp ->columns[j] == -1) &&
        (rp->for_diagonals[f] == -1) &&
        (rp->back_diagonals[b] == -1)) {
        rp->columns[j] = 1;
        rp->for_diagonals[f] = 1;
        rp->back_diagonals[b] = 1;
        rp->values[i] = j;
        (rp->numberfixed)++;
        return 1;
    }
    return 0;
}
```

_____ **Program 15.3** _____

15.4.2 Greedy Backtracking

Greedy algorithms try to maximize the improvement at each step without looking ahead for negative future consequences. A greedy algorithm for the n-queens problem is

- Pick an unfilled row at random.
- Try to add a nonthreatening queen in that row by examining all unfilled column positions starting at a random unfilled column.
- Repeat until either the placement represents a full solution or it is impossible to add a queen in the row selected.

Greedy algorithms can dead-end without reaching a solution, so backtracking is often used to improve the probability of reaching a solution. Greedy backtracking proceeds by obtaining a promising solution, removing a certain number of queens at random, and then attempting to extend the promising solution using a greedy algorithm.

Program 15.4 implements a randomized greedy algorithm for the n-queens problem. The program takes two command-line arguments giving the board size and the number of iterations of the greedy algorithm to be done. The `get_random_promising` function produces a promising configuration by attempting to place queens in randomly selected rows. The `compute_queens` implements the greedy backtracking algorithm described above. The constant `MAXDIVERSITY` controls the level of backtracking that is performed. The `post_promising` function is used later to insert the result into the blackboard in the cooperative implementation, and `print_promising` outputs a promising configuration to the specified file.

Program 15.4: A program that uses a randomized greedy algorithm to search for solutions to the n-queens problem.

```
#include "greedy.h"
#define STARTSEED 400
/* The agent randomizes a hint to obtain a new promising
 * configuration
 */
void main(int argc, char *argv[])
{
    struct promising_type r;
    int diversity;
    int i, iterations;

    if (argc != 4) {
        fprintf(stderr, "Usage: %s boardsize iterations\n", argv[0]);
        exit(1);
    }
    r.boardsize = atoi(argv[1]);
    iterations = atoi(argv[2]);
```

```
/* Later initialize the pseudorandom-number generator using the PID */
   initialize_random(STARTSEED);
   for (i = 0; i < iterations; i++) {
      diversity = random_next(MAXDIVERSITY);
      get_random_promising(&r);
      compute_queens(&r, diversity);
      post_promising(r);
      if (r.numberfixed == r.boardsize) {
         fprintf(stdout, "\nA solution is: \n");
         print_promising(stdout, r);
      }
   }
}
```

_____ **Program 15.4** _____

Develop and debug the greedy backtracking algorithm in a nondistributed setting.
Obtain promising configurations by random placement of queens. Write the following
functions referred to in the main program of Program 15.4. Place their prototypes in a
header file called greedy.h.

- The initialize_random function initializes a pseudorandom-number
  generator by calling srand48. Its prototype is

      void initialize_random(int seed);

- The random_next function generates pseudorandom numbers in the range
  0 to upper - 1. Its prototype is

      int random_next(int upper);

  The random_next calls drand48 to generate a double and then converts it to an int in the appropriate range.

- The get_random_promising function constructs a random promising
  configuration. Its prototype is

      void get_random_promising(promising_t *rp);

  Here rp points to the resulting random promising configuration. Pick
  the number of entries to fix in the configuration at random, but do
  not allow this value to be too large relative to the size of the board or
  get_random_promising ends up performing an exhaustive search of the
  solution space.

- The compute_queens function modifies a promising configuration using
  the backtracked greedy algorithm. Its prototype is

      void compute_queens(promising_t *rp, int diversity);

Here `rp` is a pointer to the promising configuration. Randomize this configuration by removing `diversity` entries, and extend the configuration as far as possible using the greedy method. The modified promising configuration is a solution if `rp->numberfixed` equals `rp->boardsize`.

- The `post_promising` is just a stub at this point.

- The `print_promising` function outputs a promising configuration to the indicated file. Its prototype is

  ```
  void print_promising(FILE *f, promising_t r);
  ```

Test the program on several different board sizes and numbers of iterations. Check to make sure that the program computes the promising configurations correctly. Replace the `STARTSEED` used to initialize the pseudorandom-number generator in the main program with a call to `getpid` in order to introduce variation into the tests. Plot the number of solutions found versus board size for $10,000$ iterations as the board size varies from 4 to 32 in multiples of 4.

15.4.3 Blackboards and Agents

A *blackboard* is a depository for information that can be read from or written to by agents. It is a controlled method for communication among agents. Blackboards have been used to organize the solution of many knowledge-based artificial-intelligence problems. More recently blackboards have appeared as a general process communication mechanism. The Blackboard Technology Group [14], for example, has implemented a distributed application support layer in which each node of a network maintains a blackboard. Workgroup computing and conferencing are other related interactive problem-solving techniques that have recently been popularized [56].

Blackboards are often implemented with complicated tree data structures in order to organize large amounts of related information efficiently. This project represents a blackboard using a tuple space. Agents post promising configurations and request promising configurations to randomize and to extend.

Add a blackboard that keeps a set of promising configurations for use by the greedy n-queens program. Implement the blackboard as a tuple space by extending the allowable tuples of Section 15.3 to include placement arrays. Implement the following functions:

- The `get_hint` function obtains a promising configuration from the blackboard. Its prototype is

  ```
  promising_t get_hint(void);
  ```

  Use `in` to get a random promising configuration from the blackboard and convert the placement array representation of the promising configuration into a `promising_t`. The `get_hint` returns a promising configuration containing no queens if the `in` fails to return a placement array.

- The `post_promising` function adds a promising configuration to the tuple space by calling `out`. Its prototype is

```
int post_promising(promising_t s);
```

Extract a placement array from the promising configuration `s`, convert it to a tuple, and call `out` to place it in the tuple space. The `post_promising` operation returns 0 if the operation is successful and −1 otherwise.

Replace the call to `get_random_promising` in the main program of Program 15.4 with a call to `get_hint`. Add code to the main program to add a specified number of random promising configurations to tuple space before beginning the greedy algorithm.

Test the program using `STARTSEED` as the initial value of the pseudorandom-number generator. After debugging the program, replace the `STARTSEED` with a call to `getpid`. Run the program for different board sizes, diversities, and numbers of iterations. Make a plot of the number of solutions found as a function of diversity for different board sizes.

Try running the system with a collection of agents executing on different machines. Instrument the agents so that they keep track of their running time for searching a specified number of promising configurations. Plot the average running time versus number of agents when each agent executes on a different machine. Compare the results with running time when all of the agents are on the same machine but the tuple-space server is on a different machine. Also compare the results when the server and all of the agents are on the same machine.

15.5 Active Tuples in Richard

Linda uses active tuples for function evaluation. The active tuple applies a specified function to its arguments and inserts the result into the tuple space. Linda `eval` semantics is not convenient to implement without compiler support. It is also not convenient for implementing a UNIX-like distributed system. This section explores some aspects of active tuples under Richard semantics starting with the simplest active tuple implementation.

15.5.1 Simplified Design

Incorporate a simple `eval` function into Richard as follows. The `eval` function forks a child to `execvp` a specified command line. The `eval` function has the prototype

```
unsigned int eval(struct tuple_t val);
```

The `eval` function returns 1 if the `fork` is successful or 0 if there is an error. It does not check for a successful `execvp` or insert results into the tuple space. The `eval` function should call `waitpid` with the `WNOHANG` option in a loop to clean up any unwaited for children created on previous executions of `eval`.

Program 15.5 shows the declaration for `struct tuple_val_t` that includes a function tuple type. The function tuple value is just a character string giving the command line to be `exec`'d. The maximum length of the string is `MAX_STR`.

Program 15.5: The tuple declarations for a local implementation of Richard with an `eval` function.

```
#define MAX_BUF 1024
#define MAX_STR 256
enum tuple_value_type {
    INTEGER = 0,
    ARRAY = 1,
    FUNCTION = 2
};

struct array_t {
    unsigned int array_len;
    char *array_val;
};

struct tuple_val_t {
    enum tuple_value_type   tuple_type;
    union {
        int     ival;
        struct array_t array;
        char   *func;
    } tuple_val_u;
};

struct tuple_t {
    unsigned int tuple_ID;
    struct tuple_val_t tuple_val;
};
```

_____ **Program 15.5** _____

Example 15.21

The following C code segment calls `eval` *to execute the command* `ls -l`.

```
char *cmd = "ls -l";
struct tuple_t val;
```

```
val.tuple_ID = 0;
val.tuple_val.tuple_type = FUNCTION;
val.tuple_val.tuple_val_u.func = cmd;
if (!eval(val))
    fprintf(stderr, "The eval of %s failed\n", cmd);
```

Call the `eval` function with several standard utilities such as `ls` and `cat` as commands. Convert to a remote server using a specification file such as the one shown in Program 15.6. Use a version number of 2 for the new Richard service.

Program 15.6: Specification for Richard server with an `eval` service.

```
/*          richard.x - version 2              */
/*          RPC Specification Language.    This is not C.    */

const MAX_BUF = 1024;
const MAX_STR = 256;
enum tuple_value_type {
    INTEGER = 0,
    ARRAY = 1,
    FUNCTION = 2
};

union tuple_val_t switch(enum tuple_value_type tuple_type) {
    case INTEGER:
        int ival;
    case ARRAY:
        char array<MAX_BUF>;
    case FUNCTION:
        string func<MAX_STR>;
};

struct tuple_t {
    unsigned int tuple_ID;
    struct tuple_val_t tuple_val;
};


program RICHPROG {
    version RICHVERS {
        unsigned int OUT(tuple_t) = 1;
        tuple_t IN(tuple_t) = 2;
        tuple_t RD(tuple_t) = 3;
        unsigned int EVAL(tuple_t) = 4;
    } = 2;
} = 0x31234566;
```
—————————————— **Program 15.6** ——————————————

When the remote server executes `eval`, the `exec`'d commands output their results to the server's standard output and wait for input from the server's standard input. If the server executes several commands in rapid succession, their input and output are interspersed much like the process chain of Program 2.12. Another problem with the simple `eval` implementation is that the executed commands inherit their environment and working directory from the tuple server.

15.5.2 Communication with `eval`

To avoid the problems with the simple `eval` implementation, the server can fork an intermediate child to redirect standard input, standard output, and standard error through the tuple space. The intermediate child is called the `Control`, and the grandchild that executes the command is called `Command`. The `Command`'s standard input comes from one set of string tuples, and its standard output and standard error come from two other sets of string tuples. The approach shares some characteristics of shells and background processes, and a review of Chapter 7 may be useful in implementing this phase.

Figure 15.4 illustrates the intermediate child approach. `Control` calls in 348 to fetch input from the tuple space. `Control` writes this data to `Command`'s standard input. Similarly `Control` reads data from `Command`'s standard output and standard error and calls `out` to insert this data in the tuple space under tuple IDs 349 and 350, respectively. The 348 tuple ID is called the `base_ID`.

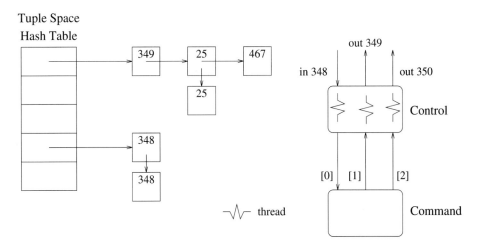

Figure 15.4: The `Control` provides the interface for `Command` to the tuple space. It uses tuple ID 348 for standard input, 349 for standard output, and 350 for standard error.

Write an `eval` function that assigns three consecutive tuple IDs (`base_ID`, `base_ID + 1`, and `base_ID + 2`) to the execution, forks a `Control` process, and returns the `base_ID` to the caller or −1 if the `fork` fails. Specifically, the algorithm for the `eval` function is

- Set `base_ID` to `largest_ID + 1` and increment `largest_ID` by 3.
- Fork a child to execute the `Control` program.
- Call `waitpid` with the `WNOHANG` option to clean up any previously forked children.
- Return the `base_ID` if the `fork` is successful or −1 if the `fork` fails.

As in the first implementation, the prototype of `eval` is

```
int eval(struct tuple_t val);
```

and `val.tuple_val.tuple_type` must be `FUNCTION`.

The `Control` process creates three pipes and forks a child (the grandchild of the tuple-space server) to execute the `Command` program. Specifically, the algorithm for `Control` is

- Create pipes `pipe0`, `pipe1`, and `pipe2`.
- Fork a child to act as the `Command` process.
- Close `pipe0[0]`, `pipe1[1]`, and `pipe2[1]`.
- Create three threads `handle_in`, `handle_out`, and `handle_error`. Each thread creates a handle to the RPC tuple-space server. These RPC handles are local to their threads.
  * The `handle_in` thread is responsible for transferring input information from the tuple space to the `Command`. Specifically, `handle_in` performs an `in` on tuples with ID `base_ID` and writes the information to `pipe0[1]`. Normally information is transferred by tuples of type `ARRAY`. If `handle_in` encounters a `base_ID` tuple of type `INTEGER`, it assumes that an end-of-file has been encountered, closes `pipe0[1]`, destroys its RPC handle, and returns. Since Richard does not have a blocking `in`, the `handle_in` is hard to implement without busy waiting. Devise a scheme for backing off. That is, if `in` fails, the `handle_in` waits for a period of time before trying again.
  * The `handle_out` thread is responsible for transferring output information from the standard output of `Command` to the tuple space under tuple ID `base_ID + 1`. Specifically, `handle_out` reads information from `pipe1[0]` and performs an `out` of an `ARRAY` type tuple containing the data under the tuple ID `base_ID + 1`. If

>   `handle_out` encounters an end-of-file, it closes `pipe1[0]`, per-
> forms an `out` of a tuple with type `INTEGER` and tuple ID `base_ID`
> `+ 1`, destroys its RPC handle, and returns.

* The `handle_error` is similar to `handle_out` except that it transfers information from `pipe2[0]` to the tuple space under tuple ID
  `base_ID + 2`. When `handle_error` encounters an end-of-file on
  `pipe2[0]`, it closes the `pipe2[0]` descriptor and performs a `wait`
  for the `Command` process to complete. The `handle_error` then performs an `out` of a tuple of type `INTEGER` with tuple ID `base_ID`
  `+ 2`. This tuple's value is the status returned by the `wait`. Finally,
  `handle_error` destroys the RPC handle and returns.

- The main thread joins with the three threads it created and then exits.

The structure of the `Control` child allows any process to communicate with
`Command` through tuple space. Furthermore, the server can run ordinary UNIX executables as `Command` programs. The calling process obtains the status of the child by
performing an `in` on ID `base_ID + 2` until it encounters an `INTEGER` type tuple.

    The `Command` process sets up the communication before calling `execvp`. Specif-
ically, the algorithm for `Command` is

- Redirect standard input to `pipe0[0]`.
- Redirect standard output to `pipe1[1]`.
- Redirect standard error to `pipe2[1]`.
- Close `pipe0[0]`, `pipe0[1]`, `pipe1[0]`, `pipe1[1]`, `pipe2[0]`, and
  `pipe2[1]`.
- Call `makeargv` of Figure 1.2 to construct an argument array for the com-
  mand.
- Call `execvp` for the command.

    After the `eval` works, implement the `ring` program of Figure 4.1 using tuple
spaces and `eval` instead of pipes with `execvp`.

15.6 Tuple Spaces as Tuples in Richard

This section describes an extension of Richard to allow tuple-space-valued tuples. Figure 15.5 shows a schematic for the tuple spaces on a given host. Each host has a default
tuple space when Richard starts. The default tuple space acts as a name server for other
tuple spaces that reside on the host. The default tuple space can also contain ordinary
tuples. The *unlinked list* contains tuples that are not in any tuple space. A tuple space
can be deleted or moved only if it is in the unlinked list.

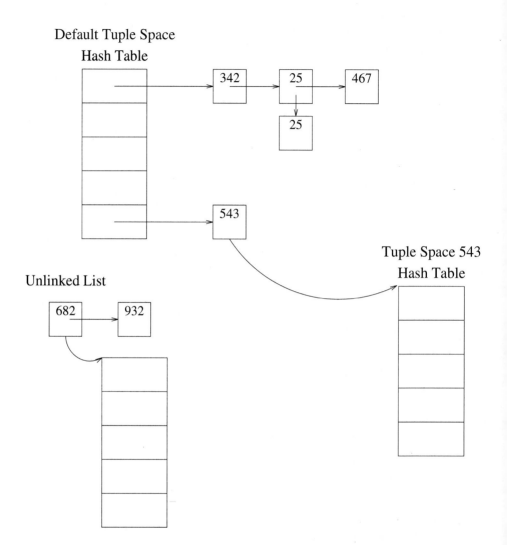

Figure 15.5: Tuple 543 has a tuple-space value. The tuple contains the starting address of the hash table representing the tuple space.

Each tuple space consists of a hash table. Access the tuple space by presenting the tuple server on a given host with the starting address of the tuple-space hash table. The server performs operations relative to the specified hash table. If a call does not give a hash-table address, the server uses the default table.

Program 15.7 shows the tuple declarations for a local implementation of tuple-space-valued tuples. Develop and test all of the functions locally before converting them to remote calls.

Program 15.7: Tuple declarations extended to allow tuple-space values in a local implementation.

```
#define MAX_BUF 1024
#define MAX_STR 256

enum tuple_value_type {
    INTEGER = 0,
    ARRAY = 1,
    FUNCTION = 2,
    TUPLE_SPACE = 3
};

struct array_t {
    unsigned int array_len;
    char *array_val;
};

struct space_t {
    void *start_hash;
    int table_size;
};

struct tuple_val_t {
    enum tuple_value_type  tuple_type;
    union {
        int     ival;
        struct array_t array;
        char   *func;
        struct space_t space;
    } tuple_val_u;
};

struct tuple_t {
    unsigned int tuple_ID;
    unsigned int creator_key;
    unsigned int access_key;
    struct tuple_val_t tuple_val;
};
```

_____ **Program 15.7** _____

Each tuple now has two keys associated with it—the `creator_key` and the `access_key`. In order to access the information contained in a tuple, a request must contain a correct `access_key`. A request to delete the tuple or change its permissions or accessibility must contain a correct `creator_key`. A key value is an `unsigned`

int. A zero `access_key` value is a universal key. If a tuple has an `access_key`
of zero, it is available for all requests except deletion or changing the permissions. If
a tuple has a positive `access_key` value, each request must contain the appropriate
matching access key. The `creator_key` value can never be zero. This key conveys
ownership rights.

15.6.1 Tuple Operations

The Richard tuple-space operations are complicated by the existence of multiple tuple
spaces. The prototypes for the tuple operations are

```
struct tuple_t out(struct tuple_cmd_t val);
struct tuple_t in(struct tuple_cmd_t val);
struct tuple_t rd(struct tuple_cmd_t val);
struct tuple_t eval(struct tuple_cmd_t val);
struct tuple_t mod(struct tuple_cmd_t val);
```

Each function takes a `struct tuple_cmd_t` parameter rather than one of type
`struct tuple_t`. The `mod` operation performs special operations such as changing
permissions. The `struct tuple_cmd_t` is

```
struct tuple_cmd_t {
    void *index_addr;
    unsigned int index_access_key;
    struct tuple_t tuple;
    enum mod_flag modify;
};
```

Each host or server starts with a default tuple space that acts like an index. The
`index_addr` member specifies the starting address of the hash table to be used for the
operation. If `index_addr` is `NULL`, the tuple operation refers to the default tuple
space for the server. If the `index_addr` is not `NULL`, it points to the tuple space used
for the operation. In this case, the `index_access_key` must match the `access_key`
of the tuple space or the operation cannot proceed.

An `out` operation inserts a new tuple in the specified tuple space. If the
`val.tuple.tuple_val.tuple_type` is `TUPLE_SPACE`, the server creates a
new tuple space that is pointed to by the new tuple. When an `out` operation creates a
new tuple space, it generates two random unsigned integers for the `creator_key` and
`access_key`. The `out` returns these keys, the `tuple_ID`, and the `start_hash`
address for the caller to use as the `index_addr` in subsequent operations. In other
words, the `out` creates a tuple space that can be accessed only by its creator. The
creator is free to change permissions or give other processes the access or creation keys.

Both `rd` and `in` operations return a tuple. The `in` operation removes the tuple from
the tuple space, while `rd` does not. When the tuple is of type `TUPLE_SPACE`, the `in`

operation does not delete the hash table pointed to by the tuple. Instead in removes the tuple from the tuple space and puts it on the `unlinked` list. The `in` operation should atomically allow access to a tuple and prohibit other accesses to that tuple. Since an entire tuple space cannot be retrieved with an `in` operation, a pointer is retrieved (the start address of the hash table), and the tuple space is moved from the tuple space in which it resided to the unlinked list.

The `mod` performs control operations on a tuple. The possible operations are

```
enum mod_flag{
    NOOP = 0,             /* do nothing */
    CHMOD = 1,            /* change access or creator key */
    DELETE = 2,           /* delete from unlinked list */
    INSERT = 3            /* insert in a tuple space */
};
```

The `mod` fails unless the `val.tuple.creator_key` matches the `creator_key` of the tuple. The operations refer to tuple with ID `val.tuple.tuple_ID`. The flag values for the `mod` operation are

CHMOD: Change the `access_key` of the tuple. The new access key be-
         comes `val.tuple.tuple_val.access_key`.
DELETE: Delete the tuple from `unlinked` list.
INSERT: Move the tuple from the `unlinked` list to the tuple space
         `val.index_addr`. The tuple space access key must match
         `val.index_access_key` or the operation fails.

Test the implementation thoroughly. Think about how to design a simple distributed operating system based on the tuple model. (There is quite a bit of machinery here, so this is not as silly as it seems.) Consider issues such as naming, ownership, and communication.

15.7 A Multithreaded Server for Richard

This section considers an extension of the basic Richard system to one in which the server is threaded so that it can handle multiple simultaneous tuple-space requests. The tuple-space server is an ideal candidate for threading to improve performance because its services operate on a large shared data structure. The first step in threading a server is to analyze the interaction among the services. Implement a local threaded server to test the analysis before implementing a remote one.

All of the services share and modify the tuple space hash table which must be protected. One approach is to have a single mutex for accessing the hash table. This effectively serializes access to the hash table and eliminates much of the parallelism achieved by threading. The other extreme is a mutex lock for each element in the hash-table array. If this approach appears reasonable, chances are the previous implementation used small hash tables. A more realistic implementation has hash tables with thousands of entries, and mutex locks for each entry would be prohibitively expensive. An intermediate approach uses region mutex locks for each section of the hash table.

In addition to the size of the hash table, also consider how many simultaneous threads of execution are likely to be accessing the hash table. The Sun `rpcgen` assumes a default maximum of 16. The prospect of sixteen threads waking up and contending for the same mutex lock is not very appealing. The implementation of this section uses a combination of region mutex locks and condition variables.

Consider a tuple-space implementation in which a hash table of size `HASH_SIZE` is associated with an array of size `LOCK_SIZE` containing mutex locks and condition variable pairs. The value of `LOCK_SIZE` satisfies $1 \leq$ `LOCK_SIZE` $\leq$ `HASH_SIZE`. If `LOCK_SIZE` is 1, a single mutex-condition variable pair protects the entire table, while if `LOCK_SIZE` equals `HASH_SIZE`, each hash-table element has its own mutex and condition variable. If `LOCK_SIZE` is an intermediate value, the hash table has region locks.

Example 15.22

Suppose `HASH_SIZE` *is* 1000 *and* `LOCK_SIZE` *is* 100. *Each lock protects ten elements of the hash table. Use a simple mapping such as* `hash % 100` *to determine the lock number from the hash-table index.*

Program 15.8 shows the declarations for the hash tables. Each element of the hash table contains a flag called `accessed` that is 1 if the element is being accessed and 0 otherwise. Define a type, `struct hash_node`, for the hash-table entries. The counts in `struct hash_element` are useful for random search-by-type. Write a hash-table initialization function that allocates the hash table and initializes it appropriately. In the local version, call the initialization function when the main program starts execution. In the remote version, insert a call to this function in the server stub to initialize the default hash table when the server starts execution.

Program 15.8: Type declarations for a protected hash table.

```
struct hash_element {
    int number_ints;
    int number_arrays;
    int number_functions;
    int number_spaces;
    unsigned int accessed;
    struct hash_node *node_ptr;
};
```

```
struct lock_element {
    pthread_mutex_t lockv;
    pthread_cond_t condv;
};

typedef struct hash_table {
    struct hash_element hash[HASH_SIZE];
    struct lock_element lock[LOCK_SIZE];
} hash_t;
```
_____ **Program 15.8** _____

In a threaded server, the main event loop in the server stub monitors input descriptors for remote requests. Each time the server stub reads a request, it creates a new thread to execute the corresponding service (eval, in, out, or rd). Suppose the hash table is pointed to by a variable h of type hash_t. To access the hash-table entry hash_in, each thread should do the following:

- Compute the lock number by

      lock_in = hash_in % LOCK_SIZE;

- Acquire the mutex h->lock[lock_in].lockv.
- If h->hash[hash_in].accessed is 0, set it to 1 and release the lock h->lock[lock_in].lockv.
- Otherwise, if h->hash[hash_in].accessed is 1, perform a condition wait on the condition variable h->lock[lock_in].condv.
- Recheck the flag h->hash[hash_in].accessed when awakened from the condition wait. If it is still 1, resume the condition wait. If it is 0, set it to 1 and release the mutex.

Once a thread acquires access to the hash-table element and performs the necessary operation, it should release the element by doing the following:

- Acquire the mutex h->lock[lock_in].lockv.
- Set h->hash[hash_in].accessed to 0.
- Perform a condition broadcast on h->lock[lock_in].condv.
- Release the mutex h->lock[lock_in].lockv.

Test the local threaded server by writing a main program that generates a significant number of threads to perform simultaneous operations. When the server correctly synchronizes simultaneous accesses, consult Section 14.9 for instructions on converting to a remote server.

After converting to a remote server, run tests on the running time of the cooperative search algorithm of Section 15.4 with multiple agents. Compare running times when the server is threaded versus when it is not threaded.

15.8 Additional Reading

The survey article "How to write parallel programs: a guide to the perplexed" describes the general tuple-space approach to parallel computing [16]. The article "Generative communication in Linda" provides the original development of the Linda framework [32]. The simplified Richard semantics bear some resemblance to Kernel Linda, which is the basis of the QIX operating system [46]. Other articles of interest are [17] and [33]. The article "The Linda alternative to message-passing systems" compares the performance of Linda and PVM [18].

Appendix A

UNIX Fundamentals

UNIX is evolving towards a common standard, but there are still variations among vendors in such matters as the format of online documentation, options for compiling programs, and the location of the system libraries. Unfortunately, these are the very services that a systems programmer needs from day one. It would be impossible to cover in a single appendix everything needed for a user to become a UNIX systems programmer. This appendix focuses on how to access UNIX documentation and how to compile and execute C programs. It provides the minimal information needed to get by (assuming some familiarity with C). The appendix also provides guidelines for figuring out the specifics on a given system.

A.1 Getting Help

Most UNIX systems have online documentation called the *man pages*. Here "man" stands for "manual" as in system manual. Those working with UNIX find access to the man pages helpful. Unfortunately the man pages contain few examples and are hard to fathom unless the user already knows the material. The `man` utility displays pages of the online documentation in a readable format.

Traditionally, the man pages are divided into sections similar to those of Table A.1. Each section has an introduction which summarizes important points about the conventions used in that section. Read the introductions to the first three sections of the man pages if unfamiliar with this facility. The man pages refer to items with the section number in parentheses (e.g., `intro(1)` refers to the introduction to section one).

Section	Contents
1	User commands
2	System calls
3	C library functions
4	Devices and network interfaces
5	File formats
6	Games and demos
7	Environments, tables, and `troff` macros
8	System maintenance

Table A.1: Typical table of contents for the UNIX man pages.

Figure A.1 shows the output of the `man` utility when the command `man whatis` executes on a Sun workstation running Solaris 2.3. (Solaris is the name for Sun Microsystems latest version of the UNIX operating system.) The first line of the man page is the header line giving the name of the command followed in parentheses by the man page section number. The `whatis(1)` in Figure A.1 refers to the `whatis` command described in section one of the man pages. Do not try to execute `whatis(1)`. The `(1)` suffix is not part of the command name but rather, a man page section indicator.

Each man page covers some aspect of UNIX (e.g., a command, a utility, a system call). The individual man pages are organized into sections similar to the way that the `whatis` man page of Figure A.1 is laid out. Some common section titles include

HEADER:	a title for the individual man page.
NAME:	a one-line summary.
SYNOPSIS:	describes usage.
AVAILABILITY:	indicates availability on the system.
DESCRIPTION:	discusses what the command or function does.
RETURN VALUES:	the return values if applicable.
ERRORS:	summarizes `errno` values and conditions for errors.
FILES:	lists the system files that the command or function uses.
SEE ALSO:	lists related commands or additional sections of the manual.
ENVIRONMENT:	lists relevant environment variables (see Section A.7).
NOTES:	provides information on unusual usage or implementation features.
BUGS:	lists known bugs and caveats (always reassuring to have a large section here!).

```
whatis(1)                    User Commands                    whatis(1)

NAME
     whatis - display a one-line summary about a keyword

SYNOPSIS
     whatis command...

AVAILABILITY
     SUNWdoc

DESCRIPTION
     whatis looks up a given command and displays the header line
     from  the  manual section.  You can then run the man(1) com-
     mand  to  get  more  information.   If   the   line   starts
     'name(section)  ...'  you can do 'man -s section name' to get
     the documentation for it.   Try  'whatis ed'  and  then  you
     should do 'man -s 1 ed' to get the manual page for ed(1).

     whatis is actually just the -f option to the man(1) command.

     whatis uses the /usr/share/man/windex database.  This  data-
     base  is  created  by catman(1M).  If this database does not
     exist, whatis will fail.


FILES
     /usr/share/man/windex     table of contents and keyword data-
                               base

SEE ALSO
     apropos(1), man(1), catman(1M)
```

Figure A.1: The Sun Solaris man page listing for the `whatis` command. (Reprinted with permission of SunSoft, Inc. Copyright retained by SunSoft, Inc.)

Exercise A.1

The following command provides online help with the `man` command.

```
man man
```

Execute this command and try to understand the description. (Good luck!) There will probably be a line in the lower left corner of the screen like

```
--More--(41%)
```

The percentage in parentheses indicates how much of the information `man` has already displayed. To get the next screenful, hit the space bar. To scroll just one line, press the return key.

Example A.1

The following command displays information about the introduction to section one of the man pages (e.g., intro(1)*).*

```
man intro
```

When invoked with the `-k` option, `man` summarizes all man page entries that contain a given name. The `-k` option relies on the existence of a *summary-database*. This database is also used by `whatis`. The man page for `whatis` in Figure A.1 indicates that the summary-database for Sun Solaris is `/usr/share/man/windex`.

Example A.2

The man -k intro *command might produce the following output related to the first three sections of the man pages.*

```
Intro   Intro (1)  - introduction to commands and
                       application programs
Intro   Intro (1m)- introduction to maintenance commands and
                       application programs
Intro   Intro (2)  - introduction to system calls and error numbers
Intro   Intro (3)  - introduction to functions and libraries
```

There may be several man page entries for a given command, and `man` displays only the first entry unless specifically requested for a later section or for all entries related to the command in question. Sun Solaris uses the `-a` option to indicate all of the man page entries for a command and the `-s` option to indicate a particular section of the man pages. Other systems use the section number directly after `man`. This appendix follows the Sun Solaris usage.

Example A.3

Sun Solaris uses man -s 2 intro *to display the* intro *section two of the man pages, while certain other systems use* man 2 intro*.*

The command `man write` just provides the man page for `write(1)`. The `write` in section one of the man pages is a command executed from the command line. This `write` is not the one most programmers query the man pages about. Rather, they needed information on the `write` system call used in C programs.

Example A.4

The following command displays all of the man pages related to write*.*

```
man -a write
```

A.1.1 System Calls and C Library Functions

The NAME section of a man page lists the names of the items described on that man page. The man pages contain information about many types of items. The man page on write(1) in the above examples contains information on a command, and write(2) describes a system call. The two writes have completely different purposes. Look at the SYNOPSIS section to determine which is which. The SYNOPSIS section gives a summary of how a command or function is invoked. The SYNOPSIS for C system calls and library functions contains function prototypes along with the required header files. The write(2) is a system call that is described in section two of the man pages and requires a header file. This function is called from a C program in contrast to write(1) which is executed from the command prompt or from a shell script.

Example A.5

The following lines show a man page synopsis for write(2).

```
SYNOPSIS
     #include <unistd.h>
     ssize_t write(int fildes, const void *buf, size_t nbyte);
```

The write(2) function takes three parameters and returns a value of type ssize_t. The synopsis specifies that programs must include the unistd.h header file in order to work properly. The man page says that write outputs nbyte bytes from buf to a file specified by fildes.

I/O at the UNIX system level uses file descriptors rather than the more familiar file pointers from the standard C library. Section 3.3 discusses file representation, but the following two examples give a feeling for the subject.

Example A.6

The following code segment writes the message "hello world" to the screen.

```
#include <unistd.h>
#include <string.h>
#define MYMESG "hello world\n"
int bytes;

bytes = write(STDOUT_FILENO, MYMESG, strlen(MYMESG));
```

STDOUT_FILENO designates the file descriptor for standard output. Standard input has a file descriptor STDIN_FILENO, and standard error has a file descriptor STDERR_FILENO. Traditionally, the numerical values for the file descriptors specifiers STDIN_FILENO, STDOUT_FILENO, and STDERR_FILENO have been 0, 1, and 2, respectively; but now that these named constants have been standardized, be sure to use them.

Example A.7

Compare Example A.6 with the following more familiar `fprintf` *statement.*

```
#include <stdio.h>
fprintf(stdout, "hello world\n");
```

The `fprintf` uses file pointers rather than file descriptors. The `fprintf` is part of the ISO C standard I/O library, while `write` is a UNIX system call. The `write` can output arbitrary data (including binary data) without modification. The `fprintf` provides formatting to produce output in a human-readable format.

Exercise A.2

What happens if the header files for Example A.6 are not in the program?

Answer:

The identifier `STDOUT_FILENO` would be undefined, and the compiler would produce an error message.

One common misinterpretation of the function prototype concerns the declaration of pointers. When a pointer designation appears in a function prototype, the program should usually define a variable of the type it is pointing to and pass a pointer to that variable as the parameter.

Example A.8

The following code segment is likely to give a segmentation error because `mybuf` *is an uninitialized pointer.*

```
#include <unistd.h>

char *mybuf;
size_t nbytes;
write(STDOUT_FILENO, mybuf, nbytes);
```

Example A.9

In the following code segment, `mybuf` *is the address of an actual buffer. (Of course the program initialized* `mybuf` *and* `nbytes` *before calling* `write` *or the statement would output garbage.)*

```
#include <unistd.h>

char mybuf[100];
size_t nbytes;
write(STDOUT_FILENO, mybuf, nbytes);
```

The `write` function returns a value of type `ssize_t`. Always capture that value and test for errors. The `RETURN VALUES` section of the man pages for `write(2)` states that in case of error, `write` returns a −1 and sets `errno` to one of the values in the `ERRORS` section of the man pages. (See Section 1.5 for additional discussion.)

A.1.2 UNIX Commands and Utilities

Commands and UNIX utilities are self-contained programs that do not require compilation. A user can execute them directly from the command-line prompt. The `write(1)` command is used send information from one user to another. This text uses the following format to show a synopsis.

```
SYNOPSIS

   write user [line]
                                                    POSIX.2, Spec 1170
```

The `write(1)` command has a required operand, `user`, and an optional operand, `line`. Since the entry is in section one of the man pages, it does not have header files in its synopsis and `write(1)` is a command executed from the shell. The string in the lower left of the box indicates which standards the synopsis conforms to. The `man` utility does not list the standards in its synopsis.

Exercise A.3

The following command description is given in a `man` page for `write(1)`.

`write copies lines from the terminal to that of another user.`

To send information to a user named `annie`, type the following command.

`write annie`

From this point until an end-of-file (i.e., `ctrl-d`), what is typed at the terminal also appears on `annie`'s screen.

The description for `write(1)` also indicates that the optional argument `line` designates a particular terminal for users logged in more than once. Unfortunately the man pages give no indication of how to find out who is logged in, what terminal each user is on, or how to send an end-of-file.

Exercise A.4

Execute the `who -H` command to find out who is logged in and on which terminal line. (The `who` command is part of Spec 1170 but not part of POSIX.2.)

Exercise A.5

Usually a `ctrl-d` entered at the terminal indicates end-of-file. (Hold the `ctrl` key down and press the `d` key.) Use `stty -a` to verify the terminal end-of-file indicator. (The `stty` command probably uses `^d` to denote `ctrl-d`.)

By convention UNIX commands can have three kinds of command-line arguments: options, option-arguments, and operands. The options consist of hyphens and single letters or digits. Certain options have option-arguments following them. Operands are arguments that follow the options and option-arguments. Square brackets ([ ]'s) enclose optional items, while required arguments have no brackets. POSIX.2 (an IEEE standard for UNIX shells and utilities) provides the following guidelines for specifying command-line arguments to commands:

- An option name consists of a single alphanumeric character.

- All options are preceded by "-".

- Options with no option-arguments may be grouped after a single "-".

- The first option-argument following an option is preceded by a tab or space character. (Some historical utilities violate this.)

- Option-arguments cannot be optional.

- Groups of option-arguments following an option must either be separated by commas or separated by tab or space characters and quoted (-o xxx,z,yy or -o "xxx z yy").

- All options must precede operands on the command line.

- "--" may be used to indicate the end of the options.

- The relative order of the operands may affect their significance in ways determined by the command with which they appear.

- "-" preceded and followed by a space character should only be used to mean standard input.

Use the getopt function to parse options in user-written utilities.

Example A.10
The ls *command lists files. The* man *utility on Sun Solaris 2 gives the following synopsis for* ls.

```
SYNOPSIS
        ls [ -abcCdfFgilLmnopqrRstux1 ] [ names ]
```

Each letter in the first [ ] of Example A.10 represents an option described either in the DESCRIPTION or the OPTIONS section of the man page. Here [names] is an optional operand.

A.1.3 Commands Related to `man`

The `apropos x` command displays the section numbers and names of the man pages whose `NAME` lines contain `x`.

Example A.11
> *The following command lists man page entries that contain the phrase* `wait` *in the* `NAME` *section.*

```
apropos wait
```

The `whatis x` command gives a one-line synopsis of the command `x`. The `which x` command gives the complete pathname of the file named `x` that would be executed if a user entered `x` as a command. The `which` utility uses the shell `PATH` environment variable and other aliases set personally or by a system administrator. Chapter 3 discusses the `PATH` environment variable.

Example A.12
> *The* `which kill` *command might produce the response* `/bin/kill`, *indicating that the* `kill` *command from the* `/bin` *directory is executed when a user types a command such as* `kill %1`.

The `which`, `whatis`, and `apropos` commands are not part of the POSIX or Spec 1170 standards, but most systems have them. The `find` command has many options for locating files with different attributes.

```
SYNOPSIS

    find path... [operand-expression...]
                                              POSIX.2, Spec 1170
```

Example A.13
> *The following command lists all of the files in the current directory tree that have a name ending in* `.c`.

```
find . -name "*.c" -print
```

The first argument of `find` in Example A.13 specifies the directory tree to start the search. The `-name` parameter specifies the pattern to match.

A.2 Compilation

The C compiler, `cc`, translates C source programs into object modules or into executable modules. An *executable module* is ready to be loaded and executed. The compilation process proceeds in stages. In the first stage, a preprocessor expands macros and includes header files. The compiler then makes several passes through the code to translate the code first to the assembly language of the target machine and then into machine code. The result is an *object module* consisting of machine code and tables of unresolved references. The final stage of compilation links a collection of object modules together to form the executable module with all references resolved. The executable contains exactly one `main` function.

Example A.14

The following command compiles `mine.c` *and produces an executable* `mine`.

```
cc -o mine mine.c
```

If the `-o mine` option in Example A.14 is omitted, the C compiler produces an executable called `a.out`. Use the `-o` option to avoid the noninformative default name.

Example A.15

The following `mine.c` *source file contains an undefined reference to the* `serr` *function.*

```
void serr(char *msg);

void main(int argc, char *argv[])
{
    serr("This program does not do much\n");
}
```

When `mine.c` of Example A.15 is compiled as in Example A.14, the C compiler displays a message indicating that `serr` is an unresolved reference and does not produce an executable.

Most programs are not contained in a single source file, requiring that the the sources from multiple files be linked together. All of the source files to be compiled may be specified in a single `cc` command. Alternatively, the user can compile the source into separate object modules and link these object modules to form an executable module in a separate step.

Example A.16

Suppose that the `serr` *function is contained in the source file* `minelib.c`. *The following command compiles the* `mine.c` *source file of Example A.15 with* `minelib.c` *to produce an executable module called* `mine`.

```
cc -o mine mine.c minelib.c
```

The `-c` option of `cc` causes the C compiler to produce an object module rather than an executable. An object module cannot be loaded into memory or executed until it is linked to libraries and other modules to resolve references. A misspelled variable or missing library function may not be detected until that object module is linked into an executable.

Example A.17

The following command produces the object module `mine.o`.

```
cc -c mine.c
```

When the `-c` option is used, the C compiler produces an object module named with a `.o` extension. The `mine.o` produced by the `cc` command of Example A.17 can can later be linked with another object file (e.g., `minelib.o`) to produce an executable.

Example A.18

The following links the object modules `mine.o` *and* `minelib.o` *to produce the executable* `mine`.

```
cc -o mine mine.o minelib.o
```

A.3 Makefiles

The `make` utility allows users to recompile incrementally a collection of program modules. Even for a simple compile, `make` is convenient and helps avoid mistakes.

In order to use `make`, the user must specify dependencies among modules in a *description file*. The default description filenames are `makefile` and `Makefile`. When the user types `make`, the `make` utility looks for `makefile` or `Makefile` in the current directory and checks this description file to see if anything needs updating.

The description file describes the dependency relationships that exist between various program modules. Lines starting with `#` are comments. The dependencies in the description file have the form

```
target:          components
TAB              rule
```

The first line is called a *dependency* and the second line is called a *rule*. The first character on a rule line in a description file must be the TAB character. A dependency may be followed by one or more rule lines.

Example A.19

In Example A.18, the executable `mine` *depends on the object files* `mine.o` *and* `minelib.o`. *The following segment describes that dependency relationship.*

```
mine:    mine.o minelib.o
         cc -o mine mine.o minelib.o
```

The description in Example A.19 says that `mine` depends on `mine.o` and `minelib.o`. If either of these latter two files has been modified since `mine` was last changed, `mine` should be updated by executing `cc -o mine mine.o minelib.o`. If the description is contained in a file is called `makefile`, just type the word `make` to perform the needed updates. (Note: The description lines must start with a TAB, so there is an invisible TAB character before the `cc`.)

In Example A.19 the filename preceding the colon, `mine`, is called a *target*. The target depends on its *components* (e.g., `mine.o` and `minelib.o`). The line following the dependency specification is the *command* or *rule* for updating the target if it is older than any of its components. Thus, if `mine.o` or `minelib.o` change, execute `make` to update `mine`.

Example A.20

In more complicated situations, a given target can depend on components that are themselves targets. The following `makefile` *description file has three targets.*

```
my:      my.o mylib.o
         cc -o my my.o mylib.o

my.o:    my.c myinc.h
         cc -c my.c

mylib.o: mylib.c myinc.h
         cc -c mylib.c
```

Just type `make` *to do the required updates.*

Sometimes it is helpful to visualize the dependences in a description file by a directed graph. Use graph nodes (with no duplicates) to represent the targets and components. Draw a directed arc from node A to node B if target A depends on B. A proper description file's graph should have no cycles. Figure A.2 shows the dependency graph for the description file of Example A.20.

A description file can also contain *macro definitions* of the form

```
NAME = value
```

Whenever `$(NAME)` appears in the description file, `value` is substituted before the phrase is processed. Do not use tabs in macros.

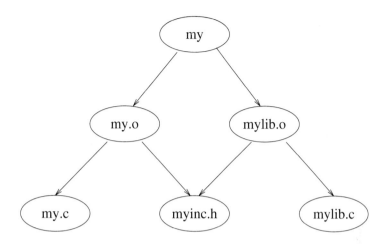

Figure A.2: A dependency graph for the `makefile` of Example A.20.

Example A.21

The following description file uses a macro to represent the compiler options so that compiler options need only be changed in a single place rather than in the entire file.

```
OPTS = -O -H

my:     my.c   my.h
        cc $(OPTS) -o my my.c
```

The `make` command also allows the name of a target to be specified on the command line. In this case `make` updates only the specified target. When developing multiple targets in the same directory (e.g., send and receive programs), use this feature to debug one target at a time. If no targets are explicitly specified on the command line, `make` checks only the first target in the description file. Often a description file has a first target called `all` that depends on all of the other targets. Use the `-f` option with `make` for description files with names other than `makefile` or `Makefile`.

Example A.22

The following command updates the target `target1` *from the description file* `mymake`.

```
make -f mymake target1
```

A.4 Header Files

The C preprocessor copies the header files specified in `#include` statements into the source prior to compilation. By convention, header files have a `.h` extension. Put declarations of constants, types, and functions in header files. *Do not put variable declarations in header files, because this can result in multiply-defined variables.* The next exercise illustrates the difficulties caused by variable declarations placed in header files.

Exercise A.6

What value does the program output if the files `myinc.h`, `my.c`, and `mylib.c` contain the segments specified below? The file `myinc.h` from Example A.20 contains the following segment.

```
#include <stdio.h>
static int num;
void changenum(void);
```

The file `my.c` contains the following main program.

```
#include "myinc.h"
void main (void)
{
    num = 10;
    changenum();
    printf("num is %d\n", num);
    exit(0);
}
```

The file `mylib.c` contains the following function.

```
#include "myinc.h"
void changenum(void)
{
    num = 20;
}
```

Answer:

Both `my.c` and `mylib.c` contain a `num` variable because its definition appears in `myinc.h`. The call by the main program of `changenum` does not affect the value of the variable `num` defined in `my.c`. The program outputs the value `10` rather than the value `20`.

Enclose personal header filenames in double quotes as in

```
#include "myinc.h"
```

The quotes tells the compiler to look for the header file in the directory containing the source file before looking in the standard place. Enclose system-defined header files in angle brackets (as in `#include <stdio.h>`), since the compiler then looks in the standard place. What constitutes the standard place is implementation-dependent, but the man page for `cc` usually describes how the standard search occurs. The `/usr/include` directory holds many of the standard header files. The files in this directory often themselves include other `.h` files from subdirectories beneath `/usr/include`. The `/usr/include/sys` directory is a standard place for many of the `.h` files needed for this book. Be sure to include the header files specified by the man page SYNOPSIS when using system calls or library functions.

Exercise A.7

A program uses the error symbol EAGAIN in conjunction with a call to `write`. The compiler complains that EAGAIN is not defined. Now what?

Answer:

Try the following steps to solve the problem.

- Make sure to include all of the header files mentioned in the synopsis for `write`. The man page specifies the header file `<unistd.h>`.
- Buried somewhere in the man pages is a statement mentioning that `errno.h` must be included in programs that refer to the error symbols. If the program includes `errno.h,` the problem is solved.
- If the `errno.h` statement in the man page escapes notice, look for the symbol EAGAIN directly in the system header files by using

```
cd /usr/include
grep EAGAIN *
```

  The `grep` searches for the string EAGAIN in all of the files in the directory `/usr/include`. Unfortunately, the EAGAIN symbol is not in any of the files in `/usr/include`.
- Change to the `/usr/include/sys` directory and try the `grep` again. The following is a typical response to the `grep`.

```
errno.h:#define EAGAIN 11
errno.h:#define EWOULDBLOCK      EAGAIN
```

  It might be tempting to eliminate the problem by including the file `sys/errno.h` in the source, but what the compiler really wants is `errno.h`. Using `errno.h` directly is better because it includes `sys/errno.h` and also contains additional definitions.

A.5 Linking and Libraries

Just because a program has the right header files does not mean that all troubles are over. A header file gives symbol definitions, and function prototypes, but it does not supply the actual code for the library function or system call.

Exercise A.8

The `mylog.c` source file calculates the logarithm of a value. After including `math.h` in that source file, the user compiles the program and receives an error message that the `log` function could not be found. Why not?

Answer:

The `math.h` header file just tells the C compiler what the form (prototype) of the `log` function is. It does not actually supply the function.

Compilation takes place in two distinct phases. In the first phase the compiler translates each C source file into object code. The `cc -c` option stops at this point. Object code is not ready to execute, because program references to items defined outside of that module have not been resolved. In order for an executable module to be produced, all of the undefined symbols (*unresolved external references*) must be found. The `cc` compiler calls the link editor `ld` to accomplish this task.

Example A.23

The following command compiles the `mylog.c` *source file with the system math library to produce an executable called* `mylog`.

```
cc -o mylog mylog.c -lm
```

In order to use C mathematics library functions put `#include <math.h>` in the source file and also specify that the program should be linked with the math library (`-lm`) when it is compiled.

The names of libraries are specified by the `-l` option. The object files are processed in the order in which they appear on the `cc` command line, so the location of `-l` on the `cc` line is significant. It should come after the object files because only those entries that match unresolved references are loaded. By default the standard C library is automatically searched.

Exercise A.9

Suppose in Example A.23 the math library was linked but the header file `math.h` was not included in the source. What would happen?

Answer:

The program might produce an incorrect answer. For instance, the compiler assumes that `log` has a return value of type `int` rather than `double`. If the program calls the `log` function, the calculation would produce an incorrect numerical result. The compiler might not produce an error or warning messages. However, `lint` (Section A.6) indicates that `log` has been implicitly declared to return `int`.

Example A.24

The following link command processes the object files in the order `my.o,` *the math library, and then* `mylib.o.`

```
cc   -o my my.o -lm mylib.o
```

Only those objects in the library that correspond to unresolved references are included in the executable module. Thus, if `mylib.o` of Example A.24 contains a reference to the math library, that reference is not resolved.

The `-lx` is short for either `libx.a` (a *library archive*) or `libx.so` (a *shared library*). Which one is the default depends on how the system is set up. Specify `-Bstatic -lx` in the `cc` command for a library archive and `-Bdynamic -lx` for a shared library. The compiler scans the *shared libraries* for references but does not actually put the functions in the executable output file. Instead they are loaded at run time using dynamic loading and binding.

There may be several versions of a particular library on a system—at least one for each version of the C compiler. The order in which directories are searched for libraries is system-dependent, but here is a typical strategy:

- `-L` directories,

- Directories indicated by `LD_LIBRARY_PATH`,

- The standard library directories (e.g., `/usr/lib`).

The `-L` option of `cc` is used to specify explicitly pathnames for directories to be searched for libraries. The `LD_LIBRARY_PATH` environment variable can be used to specify default pathnames for searching for load libraries. Generally, it includes pathnames for the directories where the compilers are installed as well as directories such as `/usr/local/lib`. The system administrator has probably set up the `LD_LIBRARY_PATH` variable for using the standard compilers. (See Section A.7.)

A.6 Debugging Aids

The `lint` program finds errors and inconsistencies in C source programs. It is pickier than the C compiler in many areas. It performs stricter type checking, tries to detect unreachable statements, and indicates code that might be wasteful or nonportable. The `lint` utility also detects a variety of common errors, such as using = instead of == or omitting & in arguments of `scanf`. It also checks for inconsistencies between modules. It is wise to lint all programs and pay attention to the resulting warning messages. The C compiler presumes that programs have already been linted and was implemented to be fast rather than fussy.

Exercise A.10

Add the following lines to the description file of Example A.20 to lint the sources.

```
lintall:    my.c mylib.c myinc.h
            lint my.c mylib.c > my.lint
```

Type `make lintall` to lint the programs. The output of `lint` is in `my.lint`.

Exercise A.11

How should the following `lint` message be interpreted?

```
implicitly declared to return int:
    (14) strtok
```

Answer:

This message indicates that the program did not include the `string.h` header file associated with `strtok` appearing on line 14. Lacking information to the contrary, the compiler assumes that `strtok` returns `int`. The lack of header can lead to disastrous results at execution time.

Exercise A.12

How should the following `lint` message be interpreted?

```
(5) warning: variable may be used before set: p
```

Answer:

Suppose the `lint` message refers to the following code segment.

```
char *p;
scanf("%s", p);
```

The pointer `p` is not pointing to an appropriate character buffer. The code compiles fine, but will probably produce a segmentation error when it is executed.

Debuggers are runtime utilities that monitor and control program execution. Common UNIX debuggers include `dbx`, `adb`, `sdb`, and `debug`. Debuggers allow a user to single-step through a program and monitor changes to specified variables. To use a debugger, compile the program with the `-g` option.

Exercise A.13

Compile the program `my.c` with the `-g` option as follows to instrument the executable for debugger control.

```
cc -g -o my my.c
```

Run `my` under the `dbx` debugger by typing

```
dbx my
```

The debugger responds with the following prompt.

```
(dbx)
```

Respond with `help` for a list of commands or `run` to run the program. Set a stopping point with `stop` or turn on tracing when a variable changes with `trace` before typing `run`.

Many programmers find debuggers useful, especially beginning programmers with pointer problems. Some debuggers have graphical user interfaces which make them easy to use. Standard debuggers are less useful in a concurrent environment where processes interact or timing can change the behavior of a program. Thread debuggers are also available on a limited basis. Debuggers may help find a particular execution error, but using a debugger is no substitute for having a program test plan. Good error trapping for system calls is probably the most valuable debugging strategy to follow.

For runtime debugging, the `truss` command is useful. It produces a trace of system calls and signals (discussed in Chapter 5) incurred while a particular process is running. Use the `-f` option with `truss` to trace the calls of all of the children of the process (discussed in Chapter 2). The `truss` command is not part of POSIX or Spec 1170 and is not available on all systems.

Exercise A.14

Suppose a program called `dvips` is installed on a system and this program is unable to locate the file `psfonts.map` that it needs. A copy of `psfonts.map` is available, but `dvips` assumes this file is in a particular directory. How can this problem be corrected?

Answer:

Try executing the following command (from a C shell).

```
truss dvips -f t.dvi |& grep psfonts.map
```

The `|&` causes both the standard output and the standard error of `truss` to be piped to the standard input of `grep`. The output might look as follows.

```
open("./psfonts.map", O_RDONLY, 0666)            Err#2 ENOENT
open("/usr/local/tex/dvips/psfonts.map", O_RDONLY, 0666) Err#2 ENOENT
```

The `truss` program runs the command `dvips -f t.dvi` and grep displays the output lines containing `psfonts.map`. The output indicates that the program first looked for the file in the current directory and then in the directory `/usr/local/tex/dvips`. Running the `dvips` program without the `truss` just produces an `unable to open file` message with no additional information. Copy the `psfonts.map` to `/usr/local/tex/dvips` and everything should be ready to go!

Most C compilers have options for profiling programs. Profilers accumulate statistical information such as execution times for basic blocks and frequency of calls. Consult the man pages for `prof`, `gprof`, `monitor`, `profil`, and `tcov` as well as for `cc` to obtain additional information about profiling.

A.7 User Environment

When a user logs in, a command-line interpreter called a *shell* is executed. The *shell* is a program that outputs a prompt, waits for a command, and executes it. When the prompt appears at the terminal screen, the shell has output its prompt string and is waiting for input.

Three common shells used for UNIX are the C shell (`csh`), the Bourne shell (`sh`), and the KornShell (`ksh`). The C shell executes startup commands from a file called `.cshrc` when it begins execution. The Bourne shell and KornShell take their startup commands from a file called `.profile`. Users can customize their execution environments by putting appropriate commands in their shell startup files. POSIX.2 has standardized certain aspects of shells based on KornShell.

UNIX uses *environment variables* to customize usage and indicate user preference. In a sense, environment variables are global parameters that tell system utilities and applications how things should be done. Common environment variables include:

- `HOME`=home directory
- `SHELL`=shell of the user
- `PATH`=pathnames of directories to be searched when locating commands to be executed
- `LOGNAME`=login name
- `TERM`=terminal type
- `USER`=user name
- `MANPATH`=pathnames of directories to be searched when locating man pages
- `DISPLAY`=display to use for the X Window System

The above environment variables are usually set up when an account is generated. Other environment variables can be defined along the way. The names of environment variables are traditionally in uppercase. Generally a user sets up frequently-used environment variables in the shell startup file so that these variables will be defined at login. The command to list the environment variables and their values for the C shell is `setenv`, while the Bourne shell and the KornShell use `export`.

Exercise A.15

Try `setenv` and `export` to determine whether the current shell is a C shell or a KornShell. If neither of these commands work, contact a system administrator for information on the shell.

Exercise A.16

The environment variable `EDITOR` specifies which editor to use for editing messages when using mail. Insert the following line in `.cshrc` to use `vi` when editing mail under C shell:

```
setenv EDITOR vi
```

Under the Bourne shell or KornShell, insert the following line in .profile:

```
export EDITOR=vi
```

The *environment list* is an array of pointers to *environment strings* of the form *name=value*. The *name* portion is traditionally specified in uppercase, and *value* is a null-terminated string. The env command modifies the current environment and then invokes a specified utility with the modified environment

---

SYNOPSIS

```
env [-i] [name=value]... [utility [argument..]]
```
POSIX.1, Spec 1170

If the utility parameter is omitted, env outputs its current environment list to standard output. The argument parameter is a command-line argument string for utility.

Applications use the environment list to determine useful information about the process environment. A program accesses its environment list through the external variable environ which points to a null-terminated array of pointers to environment strings similar to the argv array.

Example A.25

The following C program prints out the environment list.

```c
#include <stdlib.h>
#include <stdio.h>
extern char **environ;
void main(int argc, char *argv[])
{
    int i;
    for (i = 0; *(environ + i) != NULL; i++)
        printf("%s\n", *(environ + i));
    exit(0);
}
```

The easiest way to get a particular environment variable in a program is with getenv.

SYNOPSIS

```
#include <stdlib.h>

char *getenv(const char *name);
```
POSIX.1, Spec 1170

The `getenv` function returns a pointer to the value associated with `name`, or `NULL` if there is no association.

Example A.26

> *The following segment prints the value of the* `DISPLAY` *environment variable.*

```
#include <stdio.h>
#include <stdlib.h>

char *displayp;
displayp = getenv("DISPLAY");
if (displayp != NULL)
    printf("The DISPLAY variable is %s\n", displayp);
else
    printf("The DISPLAY variable is undefined\n");
```

A.8 Additional Reading

The text *UNIX SYSTEM V: A Practical Guide*, 3rd ed. by Sobell [81] is an up-to-date reference on using the UNIX utilities. The book *UNIX System Administration Handbook*, 2nd ed. by Nemeth et al. [50] is an excellent and readable introduction to many of the configuration issues involved in setting up UNIX systems. O'Reilly Press has individual books on many of the topics in this appendix including `emacs` [15], the libraries [22], `lint` [23], `make` [88], and `vi` [47].

Appendix B

UICI Implementation

This appendix contains source for the three UICI implementations discussed in Chapter 12.

B.1 UICI Prototypes

Program B.1: The file `uici.h` which contains the prototypes of the UICI functions.

```
/******************************** uici.h ************************/
/*    various definitions required for the UICI functions          */
/******************************************************************/
typedef unsigned short u_port_t;
int u_open(u_port_t port);
int u_listen(int fd, char *hostn);
int u_connect(u_port_t port, char *inetp);
int u_close(int fd);
ssize_t u_read(int fd, void *buf, size_t nbyte);
ssize_t u_write(int fd, void *buf, size_t nbyte);
void u_error(char *s);
int u_sync(int fd);
```

--------------------- **Program B.1** ---------------------

B.2 Socket Implementation

Program B.2 is a client program for testing UICI. It takes two command-line arguments, a destination machine and a port number. After making a connection, the client sends whatever comes in from standard input to the remote machine. The client catches the SIGUSR1 and SIGUSR2 signals, demonstrating that the transmission works correctly even when signals are present. The program uses a small block size so that a file transmission results in a large number of transfers even for files of moderate size. The client terminates when an end-of-file is detected on standard input.

Program B.2: A client program for testing the socket and TLI implementations of UICI.

```
#include <stdio.h>
#include <stdlib.h>
#include <unistd.h>
#include <signal.h>
#include <errno.h>
#include <sys/types.h>
#include "uici.h"

#define BLKSIZE   1024

void usr1handler(int s)
{
    fprintf(stderr, "SIGUSR1 signal caught\n");
}

void usr2handler(int s)
{
    fprintf(stderr, "SIGUSR2 signal caught\n");
}


void installusrhandlers()
{
    struct  sigaction  newact;
    newact.sa_handler = usr1handler;        /* set the new usr1 handler */
    sigemptyset(&newact.sa_mask);      /* no additional signals blocked */
    newact.sa_flags = 0;               /* nothing special on the options */
    if (sigaction(SIGUSR1, &newact, (struct sigaction *)NULL) == -1) {
        perror("Could not install SIGUSR1 signal handler");
        return;
    }
    newact.sa_handler = usr2handler;        /* set the new usr2 handler */
    if (sigaction(SIGUSR2, &newact, (struct sigaction *)NULL) == -1) {
        perror("Could not install SIGUSR2 signal handler");
```

```
        return;
    }
    fprintf(stderr,
        "Client process %ld set to use SIGUSR1 and SIGUSR2\n",
        (long)getpid());
}

void main(int argc, char *argv[])
/*
 *  This is a client test of UICI. It opens a connection
 *  to a machine specified by host and a port number.
 *  It reads a file from stdin in blocks of size BLKSIZE
 *  and outputs it to the connection.
 */
{
    unsigned short portnumber;
    int outfd;
    ssize_t bytesread;
    ssize_t byteswritten;
    char buf[BLKSIZE];

    if (argc != 3) {
        fprintf(stderr, "Usage: %s host port\n", argv[0]);
        exit(1);
    }

    installusrhandlers();

    portnumber = (unsigned short)atoi(argv[2]);

    if ((outfd = u_connect(portnumber, argv[1])) < 0) {
        u_error("Unable to establish an Internet connection");
        exit(1);
    }

    fprintf(stderr, "Connection has been made to %s\n", argv[1]);

    for ( ; ; ) {
        bytesread = read(STDIN_FILENO, buf, BLKSIZE);
        if ( (bytesread == -1) && (errno == EINTR) )
            fprintf(stderr, "Client restarting read\n");
        else if (bytesread <= 0) break;
        else {
            byteswritten = u_write(outfd, buf, bytesread);
            if (byteswritten != bytesread) {
                fprintf(stderr,
                    "Error writing %ld bytes, %ld bytes written\n",
                    (long)bytesread, (long)byteswritten);
                break;
```

```
            }
          }
        }
        u_close(outfd);
        exit(0);
}
```

_____ **Program B.2** _____

Program B.3 is a server program for testing UICI. It takes a single command-line argument which is the port to listen on. After a connection, the server reads information from the network and sends it to standard output. The program terminates when it detects an end-of-file from the remote host.

Program B.3: A server program to test the socket and TLI implementations of UICI.

```c
#include <stdio.h>
#include <stdlib.h>
#include <unistd.h>
#include <limits.h>
#include <signal.h>
#include <sys/types.h>
#include <sys/uio.h>
#include "uici.h"

#define BLKSIZE  1024
void usr1handler(int s)
{
    fprintf(stderr, "SIGUSR1 signal caught by server\n");
}

void usr2handler(int s)
{
    fprintf(stderr, "SIGUSR2 signal caught by server\n");
}

void installusrhandlers()
{
    struct  sigaction  newact;
    newact.sa_handler = usr1handler;        /* set the new usr1 handler */
    sigemptyset(&newact.sa_mask);      /* no additional signals blocked */
    newact.sa_flags = 0;              /* nothing special on the options */
    if (sigaction(SIGUSR1, &newact, (struct sigaction *)NULL) == -1) {
       perror("Could not install SIGUSR1 signal handler");
       return;
    }
    newact.sa_handler = usr2handler;        /* set the new usr2 handler */
```

```
    if (sigaction(SIGUSR2, &newact, (struct sigaction *)NULL) == -1) {
        perror("Could not install SIGUSR2 signal handler");
        return;
    }
    fprintf(stderr,
        "Server process %ld set to use SIGUSR1 and SIGUSR2\n",
        (long)getpid());
}

void main(int argc, char *argv[])
/*
 *  This is a server which opens a connection to a
 *  port number and listens for a request.  It then
 *  opens a communication port and reads from the connection
 *  until the connection is terminated.  Each block that is
 *  read is echoed to standard out.
 */
{
    unsigned short portnumber;
    int listenfd;
    int communfd;
    ssize_t bytesread;
    ssize_t byteswritten;
    char buf[BLKSIZE];
    char remote[MAX_CANON];

    if (argc != 2) {
        fprintf(stderr, "Usage: %s port\n", argv[0]);
        exit(1);
    }

    installusrhandlers();

    portnumber = (unsigned short)atoi(argv[1]);

    if ((listenfd = u_open(portnumber)) < 0) {
        u_error("Unable to establish a port connection");
        exit(1);
    }

    if ((communfd = u_listen(listenfd, remote)) < 0) {
        u_error("Failure to listen on server");
        exit(1);
    }
    fprintf(stderr, "Connection has been made to %s\n", remote);

    while( (bytesread = u_read(communfd, buf, BLKSIZE)) > 0) {
        byteswritten = write(STDOUT_FILENO, buf, bytesread);
        if (bytesread != byteswritten) {
```

```
            fprintf(stderr,
                "Error writing %ld bytes, %ld bytes written\n",
                (long)bytesread, (long)byteswritten);
            break;
        }
    }
    u_close(listenfd);
    u_close(communfd);
    exit(0);
}
```

_____ **Program B.3** _____

_____

Program B.4: A complete implementation of UICI in terms of sockets.

```
/* uici.c   sockets implementation */

#include <stdio.h>
#include <unistd.h>
#include <string.h>
#include <netdb.h>
#include <signal.h>
#include <sys/types.h>
#include <sys/socket.h>
#include <netinet/in.h>
#include <netinet/tcp.h>
#include <errno.h>
#include "uici.h"

#define MAXBACKLOG 5

/* return 1 if error, 0 if OK */
int u_ignore_sigpipe()
{
    struct sigaction act;

    if (sigaction(SIGPIPE, (struct sigaction *)NULL, &act) < 0)
        return 1;
    if (act.sa_handler == SIG_DFL) {
        act.sa_handler = SIG_IGN;
        if (sigaction(SIGPIPE, &act, (struct sigaction *)NULL) < 0)
            return 1;
    }
    return 0;
}

/*
```

```
 *                              u_open
 * Return a file descriptor which is bound to the given port.
 *
 * parameter:
 *          s = number of port to bind to
 * returns:  file descriptor if successful and -1 on error
 */
int u_open(u_port_t port)
{
    int sock;
    struct sockaddr_in server;

    if ( (u_ignore_sigpipe() != 0) ||
         ((sock = socket(AF_INET, SOCK_STREAM, 0)) < 0) )
       return -1;

    server.sin_family = AF_INET;
    server.sin_addr.s_addr = INADDR_ANY;
    server.sin_port = htons((short)port);

    if ( (bind(sock, (struct sockaddr *)&server, sizeof(server)) < 0) ||
         (listen(sock, MAXBACKLOG) < 0) )
       return -1;
    return sock;
}


/*
 *                              u_listen
 * Listen for a request from a particular host on a specified port.
 *
 * parameters:
 *          fd = file descriptor previously bound to listening port
 *          hostn = name of host to listen for
 * returns:  communication file descriptor or -1 on error
 *
 * comments: This function is used by the server to listen for
 * communication.  It blocks until a remote request is received
 * from the port bound to the given file descriptor.
 * hostn is filled with an ASCII string containing the remote
 * host name.  It must point to s string which is large enough to
 * hold this name.
 */
int u_listen(int fd, char *hostn)
{
    struct sockaddr_in net_client;
    int len = sizeof(struct sockaddr);
    int retval;
    struct hostent *hostptr;
```

```
   while ( ((retval =
          accept(fd, (struct sockaddr *)(&net_client), &len)) == -1) &&
          (errno == EINTR) )
      ;
   if (retval == -1)
      return retval;
   hostptr =
      gethostbyaddr((char *)&(net_client.sin_addr.s_addr), 4, AF_INET);
   if (hostptr == NULL)
      strcpy(hostn, "unknown");
   else
      strcpy(hostn, (*hostptr).h_name);
   return retval;
}

/*
 *                                u_connect
 * Initiate communication with a remote server.
 *
 * parameters:
 *     port  = well-known port on remote server
 *     inept = character string giving the Internet name of the
 *             remote machine
 * returns: the file descriptor used for communication or -1 if error
 */
int u_connect(u_port_t port, char *hostn)
{
   struct sockaddr_in server;
   struct hostent *hp;
   int sock;
   int retval;

   if ( (u_ignore_sigpipe() != 0) ||
        !(hp = gethostbyname(hostn)) ||
        ((sock = socket(AF_INET, SOCK_STREAM, 0)) < 0) )
      return -1;

   memcpy((char *)&server.sin_addr, hp->h_addr_list[0], hp->h_length);

   server.sin_port = htons((short)port);
   server.sin_family = AF_INET;

   while ( ((retval =
       connect(sock, (struct sockaddr *)&server, sizeof(server))) == -1)
       && (errno == EINTR) )
      ;
   if (retval == -1) {
      close(sock);
      return -1;
```

```
   }
   return sock;
}

/*
 *                        u_close
 * Close communication for the given file descriptor.
 * parameter:
 *         fd = file descriptor of socket connection to be closed
 * returns:
 *         a negative value indicates an error occurred
 */

int u_close(int fd)
{
   return close(fd);
}

/*
 *                        u_read
 *
 * Retrieve information from a file descriptor opened by u_open.
 *
 * parameters:
 *         fd = TLI file descriptor
 *         buf = buffer to be output
 *         nbyte = number of bytes to retrieve
 * returns:
 *         a negative value indicates an error occurred
 *         otherwise the number of bytes read is returned
 */

ssize_t u_read(int fd, void *buf, size_t size)
{
   ssize_t retval;

   while (retval = read(fd, buf, size), retval == -1 && errno == EINTR)
      ;
   return retval;
}

/*
 *                        u_write
 *
 * Send information on a file descriptor opened by u_open.
 *
 * parameters:
 *         fd = TLI file descriptor
 *         buf = buffer to be output
```

```
 *          nbyte = number of bytes to send
 * returns:
 *          a negative value indicates an error occurred
 *          otherwise the number of bytes written is returned
 */

ssize_t u_write(int fd, void *buf, size_t size)
{
    ssize_t retval;

    while (retval = write(fd, buf, size), retval == -1 && errno == EINTR)
        ;
    return retval;
}

/*
 *                              u_error
 *  Display an error message in the manner of perror or t_error.
 *
 *  parameter:
 *           s =  string to be prepended to system error message
 *  returns:    0
 *
 *  algorithm:  Since the only type of error comes from a system call,
 *              we only need to call perror.  This implementation should
 *              be as MT-safe as the underlying sockets.
 */

void u_error(char *s)
{
    perror(s);
}

/*
 *                              u_sync
 *
 * This function must be called after an exec or a dup to attach an
 * opened file descriptor in simple UICI implementations.  It is not
 * needed for sockets.
 *
 */
/*ARGSUSED*/
int u_sync(int fd)
{
/* Not needed for sockets, retained for compatibility */
    return 0;
}
```
_____ **Program B.4** _____

B.3 TLI Implementation

The TLI implementation can use the same client and server test programs as for sockets given in Program B.2 and Program B.3.

Program B.5: A complete implementation of UICI in terms of TLI.

```
/* uici.c TLI implementation */

#include <stdio.h>
#include <unistd.h>
#include <fcntl.h>
#include <netinet/in.h>
#include <sys/socket.h>
#include <netdb.h>
#include <tiuser.h>
#include <errno.h>
#include <string.h>
#include "uici.h"

#define RETRIES 5

/*
 *                          u_open
 * Return a file descriptor which is bound to the given port.
 *
 * parameter:
 *          s = number of port to bind to
 * returns:  file descriptor if successful and -1 on error
 */
int u_open(u_port_t port)
{
    int fd;
    struct t_info info;
    struct t_bind req;
    struct sockaddr_in server;

    fd = t_open("/dev/tcp", O_RDWR, &info);
    if (fd < 0)
        return -1;

    /* Create server with wildcards and bind the socket to port */
    memset(&server, 0, (size_t)sizeof(server));
    server.sin_family = AF_INET;
    server.sin_addr.s_addr = INADDR_ANY;
    server.sin_port = htons((short)port);
```

```
        req.addr.maxlen = sizeof(server);
        req.addr.len = sizeof(server);
        req.addr.buf = (char *)&server;
        req.qlen = 1;

        if (t_bind(fd, &req, NULL) < 0)
            return -1;
        return fd;
}


/*
 *
 *                              u_listen
 * Listen for a request from a particular host on a specified port.
 *
 * parameters:
 *      fd = file descriptor previously bound to listening port
 *      hostn = name of host to listen for
 * returns:  communication file descriptor or -1 on error
 *
 * comments: This function is used by the server to listen for
 * communication.  It blocks until a remote request is received
 * from the port bound to the given file descriptor.
 * hostn is filled in with an ASCII string containing the remote
 * host name.  It must point to s string which is large enough to
 * hold this name.
 */
int u_listen(int fd, char *hostn)
{
    struct t_call *callptr;
    struct sockaddr_in *client;
    struct hostent *hostptr;
    int newfd;
    int tret;

    if ( (callptr =
            (struct t_call *)t_alloc(fd, T_CALL, T_ADDR)) == NULL) {
        return -1;
    }

    while( ((tret = t_listen(fd, callptr)) < 0) &&
            (t_errno == TSYSERR) && (errno == EINTR) )
        ;                               /* t_listen interrupted and restarted */
    if ( (tret < 0) ||
        ((newfd = t_open("/dev/tcp", O_RDWR, NULL)) < 0 ) ||
        (t_bind(newfd, NULL, NULL) < 0 ) ||
        (t_accept(fd, newfd, callptr) < 0) ) {
        t_free((char *)callptr, T_CALL);
        return -1;
    }
```

```
   client = (struct sockaddr_in *)(callptr->addr).buf;
   hostptr =
       gethostbyaddr((char *)&(client->sin_addr.s_addr), 4, AF_INET);
   if (hostptr == NULL)
       strcpy(hostn, "unknown");
   else
       strcpy(hostn, hostptr->h_name);
   t_free((char *)callptr, T_CALL);
   return newfd;
}

/*
 *                              u_connect
 * Initiate communication with a remote server.
 *
 * parameters:
 *      port  = well-known port on remote server
 *      inept = character string giving the Internet name of
 *      the remote machine
 * returns: the file descriptor used for communication or -1 if error
 */
int u_connect(u_port_t port, char *inetp)
{
   struct t_info info;
   struct t_call  *callptr;
   struct sockaddr_in server;
   struct hostent *hp;
   int fd;
   int trynum;
   unsigned int slptime;

   fd = t_open("/dev/tcp", O_RDWR, &info);
   if (fd < 0)
       return -1;

   /* Create TCP addresses for communication with port */
   memset(&server, 0, (size_t)sizeof(server));
   server.sin_family = AF_INET;              /* Internet address family   */
   hp = gethostbyname(inetp);      /* convert name to Internet address */
                                   /* copy Internet address to buffer  */
   if (hp == NULL) {
       fprintf(stderr, "gethostbyname returned NULL\n");
       return -1;
   }
   memcpy(&(server.sin_addr.s_addr), hp->h_addr_list[0],
           (size_t)hp->h_length);
   server.sin_port = htons((short)port);

                              /* set buffer with destination info */
```

```
    if (t_bind(fd, NULL, NULL) < 0)
        return -1;

                                    /* allocate structure for connect    */
    if ( (callptr =
          (struct t_call *)t_alloc(fd, T_CALL, T_ADDR)) == NULL)
        return -1;

    callptr -> addr.maxlen = sizeof(server);
    callptr -> addr.len = sizeof(server);
    callptr -> addr.buf = (char *)&server;
    callptr -> opt.len = 0;
    callptr -> udata.len = 0;

                                /* Keep trying until the server is ready */
    for (trynum=0,slptime=1;
         (trynum < RETRIES) &&
         (t_connect(fd, callptr, NULL) < 0);
         trynum++,slptime=2*slptime) {
       t_rcvdis(fd, NULL);
       sleep(slptime);
    }
    callptr -> addr.buf = NULL;
    t_free((char *)callptr, T_CALL);
    if (trynum >= RETRIES)
        return -1;
    return fd;
}

/*
 *                              u_close
 * Close communication for the given TLI file descriptor.
 * parameter:
 *        fd = file descriptor of TLI connection to be closed
 * returns:
 *        a negative value indicates an error occurred.
 */
int u_close(int fd)
{
   return t_close(fd);
}

/*
 *                               u_read
 *
 * Retrieve information from a file descriptor opened by u_open.
 *
 * parameters:
 *        fd = TLI file descriptor
```

```
 *          buf = buffer to be output
 *          nbyte = number of bytes to retrieve
 * returns:
 *          a negative value indicates an error occurred
 *          otherwise the number of bytes read is returned
 */

ssize_t u_read(int fd, void *buf, size_t nbyte)
{
    int rcvflag;
    ssize_t retval;

    rcvflag = 0;
    while ( ((retval=
             (ssize_t)t_rcv(fd, buf, (unsigned)nbyte, &rcvflag)) == -1) &&
             (t_errno == TSYSERR) && (errno == EINTR) )
        ;
    return retval;
}


/*
 *                          u_write
 *
 * Send information on a file descriptor opened by u_open.
 *
 * parameters:
 *          fd = TLI file descriptor
 *          buf = buffer to be output
 *          nbyte = number of bytes to send
 * returns:
 *          a negative value indicates an error occurred
 *          otherwise the number of bytes written is returned
 */
ssize_t u_write(int fd, void *buf, size_t nbyte)
{
    ssize_t retval;
    while ( ( ( retval =
             (ssize_t)t_snd(fd, buf, (unsigned)nbyte,0)) == -1) &&
             (t_errno == TSYSERR) && (errno == EINTR) )
        ;
    return retval;
}


/*
 *                          u_error
 *  Display an error message in the manner of perror or t_error.
 *
 *  parameter:
 *          s =  string to be prepended to system error message
```

```
*   returns:    0
*
*   algorithm:  Since the only type of error comes from a TLI call,
*               we only need to call t_error.  This implementation
*               should be as MT-safe as the underlying TLI.
*/
void u_error(char *s)
{
    t_error(s);
}


/*
*
*                            u_sync
*
* This routine must be called after an exec or a dup to attach an
* opened file descriptor to the TLI routines
*
* parameter:
*        fd = file descriptor of file to be attached
* returns: -1 on error and something else if successful
*/
int u_sync(int fd)
{
    return t_sync(fd);
}
```

_____ **Program B.5** _____

B.4 Streams Implementation

_____

Program B.6: A client program for testing the streams implementation of UICI.

```
#include <stdio.h>
#include <stdlib.h>
#include <unistd.h>
#include "uici.h"

#define BLKSIZE 1024

void main(int argc, char *argv[])
/*
*
*                       UICI Client
*   Make a UICI connection request to host and port specified
*   as command line arguments.   Read from standard input and
*   write to the UICI communication file descriptor until
*   end-of-file.
```

```
*/
{
    u_port_t portnumber;
    int communfd;
    int bytesread;
    int done = 0;
    char buf[BLKSIZE];

    if (argc != 2) {
        fprintf(stderr, "Usage: %s port\n", argv[0]);
        exit(1);
    }

    portnumber = (u_port_t)atoi(argv[1]);

    if ((communfd = u_connect(portnumber, NULL)) < 0) {
        u_error("Unable to establish a connection");
        exit(1);
    }
    fprintf(stderr, "A connection has been made.\n");

    while (!done) {
        bytesread = read(STDIN_FILENO, buf, BLKSIZE);
        if (bytesread == 0) {
            fprintf(stderr, "Client detected end of file on input.\n");
            done = 1;
        }
        else if (bytesread < 0) {
            fprintf(stderr, "Client read error.\n");
            done = 1;
        }
        else {
            done = (bytesread != u_write(communfd, buf, bytesread));
            if (done)
                u_error("Client write_error");
        }
    }
    u_close(communfd);
    exit(0);
}
```

———————————————————— **Program B.6** ————————————————————

———

Program B.7: A server program for testing the streams implementation of UICI.

```
#include <stdio.h>
#include <stdlib.h>
#include <unistd.h>
```

```c
#include <limits.h>
#include "uici.h"

#define BLKSIZE 1024

void main(int argc, char *argv[])
/*
 *
 *                       UICI Server
 *   Open a UICI port specified as a command line argument
 *   and listen for a  request.  When request
 *   arrives, use the provided communication file descriptor to
 *   read from the UICI connection and echo to standard output
 *   until the connection is terminated.
 */
{
   u_port_t portnumber;
   int listenfd, communfd;
   int bytesread;
   int done = 0;
   char buf[BLKSIZE];
   char client[MAX_CANON];

   if (argc != 2) {
      fprintf(stderr, "Usage: %s port\n", argv[0]);
      exit(1);
   }

   portnumber = (u_port_t)atoi(argv[1]);
   if ((listenfd = u_open(portnumber)) == -1) {
      u_error("Unable to establish a port connection");
      exit(1);
   }

   if ((communfd = u_listen(listenfd, client)) == -1) {
      u_error("Failure to listen on server");
      exit(1);
   }
   fprintf(stderr, "A connection has been made.\n");

   while(!done) {
      bytesread = u_read(communfd, buf, BLKSIZE);
      if (bytesread == 0) {
         fprintf(stderr, "Server detected end of file on input.\n");
         done = 1;
      }
      else if (bytesread < 0) {
         u_error("Server read error");
         done = 1;
      }
```

```
      else {
          done = (bytesread != write(STDOUT_FILENO, buf, bytesread));
          if (done)
             u_error("Server write error");
      }
   }
   u_close(communfd);
   u_close(listenfd);
   exit(0);
}
```

_____ **Program B.7** _____

_____

Program B.8: A streams UICI implementation.

```
/* The UICI functions for the STREAMS implementation */

#include <stdio.h>
#include <stdlib.h>
#include <unistd.h>
#include <errno.h>
#include <sys/conf.h>
#include <sys/types.h>
#include <fcntl.h>
#include <stropts.h>

#include "uici.h"

#define MTMODE 0600

/* this is already in sys/stropts.h without the typedef */
typedef struct strrecvfd1 {
   union {
          struct file *fp;
          int fd;              /* new descriptor */
   } f;
   uid_t   uid;     /* effective user ID of sender */
   uid_t   gid;     /* effective group ID of sender */
   char    fill[8];
} mystrrecvfd;

/*
 *                            u_open
 * Return a file descriptor which is bound to the given port.
 *
 * parameter:
 *         s = number of port to bind to
```

```
 * returns:   file descriptor if successful and -1 on error
 */
int u_open(u_port_t port)
{
    char buffer[MAX_CANON];
    int mtpoint;
    int fd[2];

    sprintf(buffer, "/tmp/streams_uici_%d", (int)port);
    unlink(buffer);
    if ( ((mtpoint = creat(buffer, MTMODE)) != -1) &&
         (close(mtpoint) != -1) &&
         (pipe(fd) != -1) &&
         (ioctl(fd[1], I_PUSH, "connld") != -1) &&
         (fattach(fd[1], buffer) != -1) )
        return fd[0];
    close (fd[0]);
    close (fd[1]);
    return -1;
}


/*
 *
 *                              u_listen
 * Listen for a request from a particular host on a specified port.
 *
 * parameters:
 *      fd = file descriptor previously bound to listening port
 *      hostn = name of host to listen for
 * returns:   communication file descriptor or -1 on error
 *
 * comments: This routine is used by the server to listen for
 * communication.  It blocks until a remote request is received
 * from the port bound to the given file descriptor.
 * hostn is ignored since STREAMS connections cannot use the network.
 */
int u_listen(int fd, char *hostn)
{
    mystrrecvfd conversation_info;
    int retval;

    while ( ((retval =
            ioctl(fd, I_RECVFD, &conversation_info)) == -1) &&
           (errno == EINTR) )
        ;
    if (retval == -1)
        return -1;
    *hostn = 0;
    return conversation_info.f.fd;
}
```

```
/*
 *                           u_connect
 * Initiate communication with a remote server.
 *
 * parameters:
 *      port  = well-known port on remote server
 *      inept = is ignored
 * returns: the file descriptor used for communication or -1 if error
 */
int u_connect(u_port_t port, char *hostn)
{
    char buffer[MAX_CANON];

    sprintf(buffer, "/tmp/streams_uici_%d", (int)port);
    return open(buffer, O_RDWR);
}


/*
 *                           u_close
 * Close communication for the given file descriptor.
 * parameter:
 *        fd = file descriptor of socket connection to be closed
 * returns:
 *        a negative value indicates an error occurred
 */
int u_close(int fd)
{
    return close(fd);
}


/*
 *                           u_read
 *
 * Retrieve information from a file descriptor opened by u_open.
 *
 * parameters:
 *        fd = TLI file descriptor
 *        buf = buffer to be output
 *        nbyte = number of bytes to retrieve
 * returns:
 *        a negative value indicates an error occurred
 *        otherwise the number of bytes read is returned
 */
ssize_t u_read(int fd, void *buf, size_t size)
{
    ssize_t retval;

    while (retval = read(fd, buf, size), retval == -1 && errno == EINTR)
```

```
        ;
    return retval;
}


/*
 *                                  u_write
 *
 * send information on a file descriptor opened by u_open
 *
 * parameters:
 *          fd = TLI file descriptor
 *          buf = buffer to be output
 *          nbyte = number of bytes to send
 * returns:
 *          a negative value indicates an error occurred
 *          otherwise the number of bytes written is returned
 */

ssize_t u_write(int fd, void *buf, size_t size)
{
    ssize_t retval;

    while (retval = write(fd, buf, size), retval == -1 && errno == EINTR)
        ;
    return retval;
}


/*
 *                                  u_error
 *   Display an error message in the manner of perror or t_error.
 *
 *   parameter:
 *            s =  string to be prepended to system error message
 *   returns:    0
 *
 *   algorithm:  Since the only type of error comes from a system call,
 *               we only need to call perror.  This implementation should
 *               be as MT-safe as the underlying TLI.
 */

void u_error(char *s)
{
    perror(s);
}


/*
 *                                  u_sync
 *
 * This routine must be called after an exec or a dup to attach an
```

```
 * opened file descriptor in simple UICI implementations.  It is not
 * needed for sockets.
 *
 */
/*ARGSUSED*/
int u_sync(int fd)
{
/* Not needed for streams, retained for compatibility */
    return 0;
}
```

_____ **Program B.8** _____

B.5 Thread-safe UICI Implementation

The section contains complete source code for a thread-safe UICI implemented with TLI.

_____

Program B.9: The file uici.h which contains the prototypes of the UICI functions for the thread-safe version.

```
/******************************** uici.h ************************/
/*    Various definitions required for the UICI functions.            */
/*    These thread-safe versions return an error number.              */
/******************************************************************/
#define GETHOSTNOERROR     0
#define GETHOSTBYNAMEERROR 1
#define GETHOSTBYADDRERROR 2
#define HOSTBUFFERLENGTH 100
typedef struct {
    int tli_error;
    int syserr;
    int hosterr;
} uerror_t;
int u_open_r(unsigned short port, uerror_t *errorp);
int u_listen_r(int fd, char *hostn, uerror_t *errorp);
int u_connect_r(unsigned short port, char *inetp, uerror_t *errorp);
int u_close_r(int fd, uerror_t *errorp);
ssize_t u_read_r(int fd, void *buf, size_t nbyte, uerror_t *errorp);
ssize_t u_write_r(int fd, void *buf, size_t nbyte, uerror_t *errorp);
void u_error_r(char *s, uerror_t error);
int u_sync_r(int fd, uerror_t *errorp);
```

_____ **Program B.9** _____

Program B.10: A client program similar to Program B.2 which uses the thread-safe version of UICI.

```
#include <stdio.h>
#include <stdlib.h>
#include <unistd.h>
#include <signal.h>
#include <errno.h>
#include <sys/types.h>
#include "uici.h"

#define BLKSIZE   100

void usr1handler(int s)
{
   fprintf(stderr, "SIGUSR1 signal caught\n");
}

void usr2handler(int s)
{
   fprintf(stderr, "SIGUSR2 signal caught\n");
}


void installusrhandlers()
{
    struct  sigaction  newact;
    newact.sa_handler = usr1handler;       /* set the new usr1 handler */
    sigemptyset(&newact.sa_mask);      /* no additional signals blocked */
    newact.sa_flags = 0;                /* nothing special on the options */
    if (sigaction(SIGUSR1, &newact, (struct sigaction *)NULL) == -1) {
       perror("Could not install SIGUSR1 signal handler");
       return;
    }
    newact.sa_handler = usr2handler;       /* set the new usr2 handler */
    if (sigaction(SIGUSR2, &newact, (struct sigaction *)NULL) == -1) {
       perror("Could not install SIGUSR2 signal handler");
       return;
    }
    fprintf(stderr,
       "Client process %ld set to use SIGUSR1 and SIGUSR2\n",
       (long)getpid());
}

void main(int argc, char *argv[])
/*
 *   This is a client test of the UICI. It opens a connection
 *   to a machine specified by host and a port number.
```

```
 *   It reads a file from
 *   stdin in blocks of size BLKSIZE and outputs it to the
 *   connection.
 */
{
    unsigned short portnumber;
    int outfd;
    ssize_t bytesread;
    ssize_t byteswritten;
    char buf[BLKSIZE];
    uerror_t error;

    if (argc != 3) {
        fprintf(stderr, "Usage: %s host port\n", argv[0]);
        exit(1);
    }

    installusrhandlers();

    portnumber = (unsigned short)atoi(argv[2]);

    if ((outfd = u_connect_r(portnumber, argv[1], &error)) < 0) {
        u_error_r("Unable to establish an Internet connection", error);
        exit(1);
    }

    fprintf(stderr, "Connection has been made to %s\n", argv[1]);

    for ( ; ; ) {
        bytesread = read(STDIN_FILENO, buf, BLKSIZE);
        if ( (bytesread == -1) && (errno == EINTR) )
            fprintf(stderr,"Client restarting read\n");
        else if (bytesread <= 0) break;
        else {
            byteswritten =
                u_write_r(outfd, buf, bytesread, (uerror_t *)NULL);
            if (byteswritten != bytesread) {
                fprintf(stderr,
                    "Error writing %ld bytes, %ld bytes written\n",
                    (long)bytesread, (long)byteswritten);
                break;
            }
        }
    }
    u_close_r(outfd, (uerror_t *)NULL);
    exit(0);
}
```

_____ **Program B.10** _____

Program B.11: A server program similar to Program B.3 which uses the thread-safe version of UICI.

```c
#include <stdio.h>
#include <stdlib.h>
#include <unistd.h>
#include <limits.h>
#include <signal.h>
#include <sys/types.h>
#include <sys/unistd.h>
#include <sys/uio.h>
#include "uici.h"

#define BLKSIZE   100
void usr1handler(int s)
{
    fprintf(stderr, "SIGUSR1 signal caught by server\n");
}

void usr2handler(int s)
{
    fprintf(stderr, "SIGUSR2 signal caught by server\n");
}

void installusrhandlers()
{
    struct  sigaction  newact;
    newact.sa_handler = usr1handler;        /* set the usr1 new handler */
    sigemptyset(&newact.sa_mask);      /* no additional signals blocked */
    newact.sa_flags = 0;                /* nothing special on the options */
    if (sigaction(SIGUSR1, &newact, (struct sigaction *)NULL) == -1) {
        perror("Could not install SIGUSR1 signal handler");
        return;
    }
    newact.sa_handler = usr2handler;        /* set the new usr2 handler */
    if (sigaction(SIGUSR2, &newact, (struct sigaction *)NULL) == -1) {
        perror("Could not install SIGUSR2 signal handler");
        return;
    }
    fprintf(stderr,
        "Server process %ld set to use SIGUSR1 and SIGUSR2\n",
        (long)getpid());
}

void main(int argc, char *argv[])
/*
 *   This is a server which opens a connection to a
 *   port number and listens for a request.  It then
```

```
 *   opens a communication port and reads from the connection
 *   until the connection is terminated.    Each block that is
 *   read is echoed to standard output.
 */
{
    unsigned short portnumber;
    int listenfd;
    int communfd;
    ssize_t bytesread;
    ssize_t byteswritten;
    char buf[BLKSIZE];
    char remote[MAX_CANON];
    uerror_t error;

    if (argc != 2) {
        fprintf(stderr, "Usage: %s port\n", argv[0]);
        exit(1);
    }

    installusrhandlers();
    portnumber = (unsigned short)atoi(argv[1]);

    if ((listenfd = u_open_r(portnumber, &error)) < 0) {
        u_error_r("Unable to establish a port connection", error);
        exit(1);
    }

    if ((communfd = u_listen_r(listenfd, remote, &error)) < 0) {
        u_error_r("Failure to listen on server", error);
        exit(1);
    }
    fprintf(stderr, "Connection has been made to %s\n", remote);

    while((bytesread =
           u_read_r(communfd, buf, BLKSIZE, (uerror_t *)NULL)) > 0) {
        byteswritten = write(STDOUT_FILENO, buf, bytesread);
        if (bytesread != byteswritten) {
            fprintf(stderr,
              "Error writing %ld bytes, %ld bytes written\n",
              (long)bytesread, (long)byteswritten);
            break;
        }
    }
    u_close_r(listenfd, (uerror_t *)NULL);
    u_close_r(communfd, (uerror_t *)NULL);
    exit(0);
}
```

_____ **Program B.11** _____

Program B.12: A complete implementation of thread-safe UICI in terms of TLI.

```c
#include <stdio.h>
#include <unistd.h>
#include <fcntl.h>
#include <netinet/in.h>
#include <sys/socket.h>
#include <netdb.h>
#include <tiuser.h>
#include <errno.h>
#include <string.h>
#include "uici.h"

#define RETRIES 5

static void u_set_error(uerror_t *errorp)
{
   if (errorp == NULL)
      return;
   errorp -> hosterr = GETHOSTNOERROR;
   errorp -> tli_error = t_errno;
   if (t_errno == TSYSERR)
      errorp ->syserr = errno;
}

/*
 *
 *                         u_open_r
 * Return a file descriptor which is bound to the given port.
 *
 * parameter:
 *          s = number of port to bind to
 * returns:  file descriptor if successful and -1 on error
 *           on error, the last parameter is set to an error number
 *           if no error occurs, *errnump is not changed
 */
int u_open_r(unsigned short port, uerror_t *errorp)
{
  int fd;
  struct t_info info;
  struct t_bind req,bret;
  struct sockaddr_in server;
  struct sockaddr_in bindinfo;

  fd = t_open("/dev/tcp", O_RDWR, &info);
  if (fd < 0) {
     u_set_error(errorp);
     return -1;
  }
```

```
                /* Create server with wildcards and bind the socket to port */
   memset(&server, 0, (size_t)sizeof(server));
   server.sin_family = AF_INET;
   server.sin_addr.s_addr = htonl(INADDR_ANY);
   server.sin_port = htons((short)port);

   req.addr.maxlen = sizeof(server);
   req.addr.len = sizeof(server);
   req.addr.buf = (char *)&server;
   req.qlen = 1;

   bret.addr.maxlen = sizeof(bindinfo);
   bret.addr.len = sizeof(bindinfo);
   bret.addr.buf = (char *)&bindinfo;

   if (t_bind(fd, &req, &bret) < 0) {
      u_set_error(errorp);
      return -1;
   }
   return fd;
}

/*
 *                          u_listen_r
 * Listen for a request from a particular host on a specified port.
 *
 * parameters:
 *       fd = file descriptor previously bound to listening port
 *       hostn = name of host to listen for
 * returns:  communication file descriptor or -1 on error
 *
 * comments: This function is used by the server to listen for
 * communication.  It blocks until a remote request is received
 * from the port bound to the given file descriptor.
 * hostn is filled in with an ASCII string containing the remote
 * host name.  It must point to s string which is large enough to
 * hold this name.
 */
int u_listen_r(int fd, char *hostn, uerror_t *errorp)
{
   struct t_call *callptr;
   struct sockaddr_in *client;
   struct hostent *hostptr;
   struct hostent hostresult;
   int newfd;
   int tret;
   int herror;
   char hostbuf[HOSTBUFFERLENGTH];
```

```
   if ( (callptr =
         (struct t_call *)t_alloc(fd, T_CALL, T_ADDR)) == NULL) {
      u_set_error(errorp);
      return -1;
   }

   while( ((tret = t_listen(fd, callptr)) < 0) &&
          (t_errno == TSYSERR) && (errno == EINTR) )
          fprintf(stderr, "t_listen interrupted and restarted\n");
   if  ( (tret < 0) ||
         ((newfd = t_open("/dev/tcp", O_RDWR, NULL)) < 0 ) ||
         (t_bind(newfd, NULL, NULL) < 0 ) ||
         (t_accept(fd, newfd, callptr) < 0) ) {
      t_free((char *)callptr, T_CALL);
      u_set_error(errorp);
      return -1;
   }
   client = (struct sockaddr_in *)(callptr->addr).buf;
   hostptr = gethostbyaddr_r((char *)&(client->sin_addr.s_addr), 4,
      AF_INET, &hostresult, hostbuf, HOSTBUFFERLENGTH, &herror);
   if (hostptr == NULL) {
      errorp -> hosterr = GETHOSTBYADDRERROR;
      return -1;
   }
   strcpy(hostn, hostresult.h_name);
   t_free((char *)callptr, T_CALL);
   return newfd;
}


/*
 *                              u_connect_r
 * Initiate communication with a remote server.
 *
 * parameters:
 *     port  = well-known port on remote server
 *     inept = the Internet name of the remote machine
 * returns: the file descriptor used for communication or -1 if error
 */
int u_connect_r(unsigned short port, char *inetp, uerror_t *errorp)
{
   struct t_info info;
   struct t_call *callptr;
   struct sockaddr_in server;
   struct hostent *hp;
   struct hostent hostresult;
   int fd;
   int trynum;
   unsigned int slptime;
   int herror;
```

```
char hostbuf[HOSTBUFFERLENGTH];

fd = t_open("/dev/tcp", O_RDWR, &info);
if (fd < 0) {
    u_set_error(errorp);
    return -1;
}

/* Create TCP addresses for communication with port */
memset(&server, 0, (size_t)sizeof(server));
server.sin_family = AF_INET;              /* Internet address family   */
                              /* convert name to internet address */
hp = gethostbyname_r(inetp, &hostresult, hostbuf, HOSTBUFFERLENGTH,
                     &herror);
if (hp == NULL) {
    errorp -> hosterr = GETHOSTBYNAMEERROR;
    return -1;
}
                              /* copy Internet address to buffer   */
memcpy(&(server.sin_addr.s_addr), hostresult.h_addr_list[0],
    (size_t)hostresult.h_length);
server.sin_port = htons(port);

                              /* set buffer with destination info */
if ( (t_bind(fd, NULL, NULL) < 0) ||
     ((callptr =
         (struct t_call *)t_alloc(fd, T_CALL, T_ADDR)) == NULL) ) {
    u_set_error(errorp);
    return -1;
}

callptr -> addr.maxlen = sizeof(server);
callptr -> addr.len = sizeof(server);
callptr -> addr.buf = (char *)&server;
callptr -> opt.len = 0;
callptr -> udata.len = 0;

                              /* Retry if this fails */
for (trynum = 0, slptime = 1;
     (trynum < RETRIES) &&
         (t_connect(fd, callptr, NULL) < 0);
     trynum++, slptime = 2*slptime) {
    t_rcvdis(fd, NULL);
    sleep(slptime);
}

callptr -> addr.buf = NULL;
t_free((char *)callptr, T_CALL);
if (trynum >= RETRIES) {
```

```
        u_set_error(errorp);
        return -1;
    }
    return fd;
}

/*
 *                              u_close_r
 * Close communication for the given TLI file descriptor
 * parameter:
 *        fd = file descriptor of TLI connection to be closed
 * returns:
 *        a negative value indicates an error occurred
 */
int u_close_r(int fd, uerror_t *errorp)
{
    int retval;
    retval = t_close(fd);
    if (retval < 0)
        u_set_error(errorp);
    return retval;
}

/*
 *                              u_read_r
 *
 * Retrieve information from a file descriptor opened by u_open.
 *
 * parameters:
 *        fd = TLI file descriptor
 *        buf = buffer to be output
 *        nbyte = number of bytes to retrieve
 * returns:
 *        a negative value indicates an error occurred
 */

ssize_t u_read_r(int fd, void *buf, size_t nbyte, uerror_t *errorp)
{
    int rcvflag;
    ssize_t retval;

    rcvflag = 0;
    while ( ( (retval=
            (ssize_t)t_rcv(fd, buf, (unsigned)nbyte, &rcvflag)) == -1) &&
        (t_errno == TSYSERR) && (errno == EINTR) )
        ;                                       /* restarting read */
    if (retval < 0)
        u_set_error(errorp);
    return retval;
}
```

```
}

/*
 *                              u_write_r
 *
 * Send information on a file descriptor opened by u_open.
 *
 * parameters:
 *        fd = TLI file descriptor
 *        buf = buffer to be output
 *        nbyte = number of bytes to send
 * returns:
 *        a negative value indicates an error occurred
 */
ssize_t u_write_r(int fd, void *buf, size_t nbyte, uerror_t *errorp)
{
    ssize_t retval;
    while ( ( (retval =
            (ssize_t)t_snd(fd, buf, (unsigned)nbyte, 0)) == -1) &&
        (t_errno == TSYSERR) && (errno == EINTR) )
        ;                                       /* restarting write */
    if (retval < 0)
        u_set_error(errorp);
    return retval;
}

/*
 *                               u_error_r
 *   Display an error message in the manner of perror or t_error.
 *
 *   parameter:
 *              s =  string to be prepended to system error message
 *   returns:    0
 *
 *   algorithm:  First check for an error in the hosterr field
 *               and print an message if this error is set.I
 *               If this is clear, check the tli_error.  If this is
 *               TSYSERR, print the system error using strerror.
 *               Other print the TLI error from t_errlist.
 */
void u_error_r(char *s, uerror_t error)
{
    if (error.hosterr == GETHOSTBYNAMEERROR)
        fprintf(stderr,"%s: error in getting name of remote host\n", s);
    else if (error.hosterr == GETHOSTBYADDRERROR)
        fprintf(stderr,"%s: error converting host name to address\n", s);
    else if (error.tli_error == TSYSERR)
        fprintf(stderr,"%s: %s\n", s, strerror(error.syserr));
    else
```

```
        fprintf(stderr,"%s: %s\n", s, t_errlist[error.tli_error]);
}

/*
 *
 *                              u_sync_r
 *
 * This function must be called after an exec or a dup to attach an
 * opened file descriptor to the TLI functions.
 *
 * parameter:
 *         fd = file descriptor of file to be attached
 * returns: -1 on error and something else if successful
 */
int u_sync_r(int fd, uerror_t *errorp)
{
    int syncret;
    syncret = t_sync(fd);
    if (syncret == -1)
        u_set_error(errorp);
    return syncret;
}
```

_____ **Program B.12** _____

Bibliography

[1] M. Accetta, R. Baron, D. Golub, R. Rashid, A. Tevanian and M. Young, "Mach: A new kernel foundation for UNIX development," *Proc. Summer 1986 USENIX Conference*, 1986, pp. 93–112.

[2] ANS X3.159-1989, Programming Language C.

[3] T. Anderson, B. Bershad, E. Lazowska and H. Levy, "Scheduler activations: Efficient kernel support for the user-level management of parallelism," *Proc. 13th ACM Symposium on Operating Systems Principles*, 1991, pp. 95–109.

[4] L. J. Arthur, *UNIX Shell Programming*, John Wiley & Sons, 1990.

[5] H. Attiya, M. Snir and M. K. Warmuth, "Computing on an anonymous ring," *Journal of the ACM*, vol. 35, no. 4, 1988, pp. 845–875.

[6] M. J. Bach, *The Design of the UNIX Operating System*, Prentice Hall, 1986.

[7] A. Beguelin, J. Dongarra, A. Geist and V. Sunderam, "Visualization and debugging in a heterogeneous environment," *Computer*, vol. 26, no. 6, 1993, pp. 88–95.

[8] A. D. Birrell and B. J. Nelson, "Implementing remote procedure calls," *ACM Trans. on Computer Systems*, vol. 2, no. 1, 1984, pp. 39–59.

[9] A. Black, N. Hutchinson, E. Jul, H. Levy and L. Carter, "Distribution and abstract types in Emerald," *IEEE Trans. Software Engineering*, vol. SE-13, no. 1, 1987, pp. 65–76.

[10] D. Black, "Scheduling support for concurrency and parallelism in the Mach operating system," *IEEE Computer*, vol. 23, no. 5, 1990, pp. 35–43.

[11] J. Bloomer, *Power Programming with RPC*, O'Reilly & Associates, 1992.

[12] M. I. Bolsky and D. G. Korn, *The New KornShell Command and Programming Language*, 2nd ed., Prentice Hall, 1995.

633

[13] G. Brassard and P. Bratley, *Algorithmics: Theory & Practice*, Prentice Hall, 1988.

[14] Blackboard Technology Group, Inc. Amherst, Mass. as advertised in *Communications of the ACM*, December 1992.

[15] D. Cameron and B. Rosenblatt, *Learning GNU Emacs*, O'Reilly & Associates, 1991.

[16] N. Carriero and D. Gelernter, "How to write parallel programs: A guide to the perplexed," *ACM Computing Surveys*, Sept. 1989, pp. 323-357.

[17] N. Carriero and D. Gelernter, "Linda in context," *Communications of ACM*, vol. 32, no. 4, 1989, pp. 444–458.

[18] N. J. Carriero, D. Gelernter, T. G. Mattson and A. H. Sherman, "The Linda alternative to message-passing systems," *Parallel Computing*, vol. 20, 1994, pp. 633–655.

[19] E. Chang and R. Roberts, "An improved algorithm for decentralized extrema-finding in circular configurations of processes," *Commun. of ACM*, vol. 22, no. 5, 1979, pp. 281–283.

[20] C. Comaford, "Viewpoint: Why people don't succeed with client/server," *IEEE Spectrum*, Jan. 1995, pp. 46–47.

[21] G. Coulouris, J. Dollimore and T. Kindberg, *Distributed Systems: Concept and Design*, 2nd ed., Addison-Wesley, 1994.

[22] D. Curry, *Using C on the UNIX System*, O'Reilly & Associates, 1989.

[23] I. F. Darwin, *Checking C Programs with* lint, O'Reilly & Associates, 1988.

[24] P. Dasgupta, R. J. LeBlanc, Jr., M. Ahamad and U. Ramachandran, "The Clouds distributed operating system," *IEEE Computer*, vol. 24, no. 11, 1991, pp. 34–44.

[25] E. W. Dijkstra, "Co-operating sequential srocesses," in *Programming Languages*, F. Genuys(ed.), Academic Press, 1968, pp. 43–112.

[26] L. Dowdy and C. Lowery, *P.S. to Operating Systems*, Prentice Hall, 1993.

[27] R. P. Draves, B. N. Bershad, R. F. Rashid and R. W. Dean, "Using continuations to implement thread managment and communication in operating systems," *Proc. 13th Symp. on Operating Systems Principles*, 1991, pp. 122–136.

[28] P. DuBois, *Using* csh *and* tsch, O'Reilly & Associates, 1995.

[29] G. A. Geist and V. S. Sunderam, "Experiences with network-based concurrent computing on the PVM system," *Concurrency: Practice and Experience*, vol. 4, no. 4, 1992, pp. 392–311.

[30] B. Furht, D. Kalra, F. L. Kitson, A. A. Rodriguez and W. E. Wall, "Design issues for interactive television systems," *IEEE Computer*, vol. 28, no. 5, 1995, pp. 25–39.

[31] B. Gallmeister, *POSIX.4: Programming for the Real World*, O'Reilly & Associates, 1995.

[32] D. Gelernter, "Generative communication in Linda," *ACM Trans. Prog. Lang Systems*, vol. 7, no. 1, 1985, pp. 80–112.

[33] D. Gelernter, "Getting the job done," *Byte*, vol. 13, no. 11, 1988, pp. 301–308.

[34] D. J. Gemmell, H. M. Vin, D. D. Kandlur, P. V. Rangan and L. A. Rowe, "Multimedia storage servers: A tutorial," *IEEE Computer*, vol. 28, no. 5, 1995, pp. 40–49.

[35] *Lord of the flies*, a novel by William Golding, Faber and Faber, London, 1954.

[36] R. Govindan and D. P. Anderson, "Scheduling and IPC mechanisms for continuous media," *Proc. 13th ACM Symposium on Operating Systems Principles*, 1991 pp. 68–80.

[37] S. P. Harbison and G. L. Steele, Jr., *C: A Reference Manual*, 4th ed., Prentice Hall, 1995.

[38] G. Held, *Data Communications Networking Devices*, 2nd ed., John Wiley & Sons, 1989.

[39] B. A. Huberman and T. Hogg, "The behavior of computational ecologies," *The Ecology of Computation*, ed. B. A. Huberman, North-Holland, Amsterdam, 1988, pp. 71–115.

[40] B. A. Huberman, "The performance of cooperative processes," *Physica*, vol. 42D, 1990, pp. 38–47.

[41] ISO/IEC 9899: 1990, Programming Languages—C.

[42] A. Itai and M. Rodeh, "Symmetry breaking in distributive networks," *Proc. Twenty-Second Annual IEEE Symposium on the Foundations of Computer Science*, 1981, pp. 150–158.

[43] A. Jones and A. Hopper, "Handling audio and video streams in a distributed environment," *Proc. Fourteenth ACM Symposium on Operating Systems Principles*, 1993, pp. 231–243.

[44] S. Kleiman, D. Shah and B. Smaalders, *Programming with Threads*, Prentice Hall, forthcoming.

[45] V. Kumar, A. Grama, A. Gupta and G. Karypis, *Introduction to Parallel Computing: Design and Analysis of Algorithms*, Benjamin-Cummings, 1994.

[46] W. Leler, "Linda meets UNIX," *Computer*, Feb. 1990, pp. 43–54.

[47] L. Lamb, *Learning the* vi *Editor*, 5th ed., O'Reilly & Associates, 1990.

[48] B. Marsh, M. Scott, T. LeBlanc and E. Markatos, "First-class user-level threads," *Proc. Thirteenth ACM Symposium on Operating Systems Principles*, 1991, pp. 110–121.

[49] K. Nahrstedt and R. Steinmetz, "Resource management in networked multimedia systems," *IEEE Computer*, vol. 28, no. 5, 1995, pp. 52–63.

[50] E. Nemeth, G. Snyder, S. Seebass and T. R. Hein, *UNIX System Administration Handbook*, 2nd ed., Prentice Hall, 1995.

[51] S. Nishio, K. F. Li and E. G. Manning, "A resilient mutual exclusion algorithm for computer networks," *IEEE Transactions on Parallel and Distributed Systems*, vol. 1, no. 3, 1990, pp. 344–355.

[52] *IEEE Standard for Information Technology. Portable Operating System Interface (POSIX). Part 1: System Application Program Interface (API) [C Language]*, ISO/IEC 9945-1, IEEE std. 1003.1, 1990.

[53] *IEEE Standard for Information Technology. Portable Operating System Interface (POSIX). Part 1: System Application Program Interface (API)-Amendment 2: Realtime Extension [C Language]*, IEEE std. 1003.1b, 1993.

[54] "Draft Standard for Information Technology Portable Operating System Interface (POSIX) Part 1: System Application Program Interface (API)-Amendment 2: Threads Extension [C Language]", P1003.1c, IEEE DS5314, Draft 10, September 1994.

[55] *IEEE Standard for Information Technology Portable Operating System Interface (POSIX) Part 2: Shells and Utilities*, IEEE std. 1003.2, 1992.

[56] H. Ishii and N. Miyake, "Toward an open shared workspace: Computer and video fusion approach of teamworkstation," *Communications of the ACM*, vol. 34, no. 12, 1991, pp. 37–50.

[57] S. Khanna, M. Sebree and John Zolnowsky, "Realtime scheduling in SunOS 5.0," SunSoft Incorporated, reprint, 1992.

[58] B. W. Kernighan and D. M. Ritchie, *The C Programming Language, 2nd Ed.*, Prentice Hall, 1988

[59] S. J. Leffler, M. K. McKusick, M. J. Karels and J. S. Quarterman, *The Design and Implementation of the 4.3 BSD UNIX Operating System*, Addison-Wesley, 1989.

[60] T. G. Lewis, "Where is computing heading?" *Computer*, vol. 27, no. 8, 1994, pp. 59–63.

[61] "Chapter 2: Lightweight Processes," *SunOS 4.1.2 Programming Utilities and Libraries*, Sun Microsystems.

[62] B. Liskow, "Distributed programming in Argus," *Communications of the ACM*, vol. 31, no. 3, 1988, pp. 300–312.

[63] M. R. Macedonia and D. P. Brutzman, "MBone provides audio and video across the Internet," *Computer*, vol. 27, no. 4, 1994, pp. 30–36.

[64] M. Maekawa, A. E. Oldehoeft and R. R. Oldehoeft, *Operating Systems: Advanced Concepts*, Benjamin/Cummings, 1987.

[65] *Webster's Third New International Dictionary of the English Language Unabridged*, Merriam-Webster Inc, Springfield, Mass., 1981.

[66] "SunOS 5.0 multithread architecture," *Sun Microsystems White Paper*, 1991.

[67] A. Oram and S. Talbott, *Managing Projects with* make, 2nd ed., O'Reilly & Associates, 1991.

[68] *UNIX in a Nutshell: A Desktop Quick Reference for System V*, O'Reilly & Associates, 1987.

[69] R. Perlman, *Interconnections: Bridges and Routers*, Addison-Wesley, 1992.

[70] P. J. Plauger, *The Standard C Library*, Prentice Hall, 1992.

[71] S. A. Rago, *UNIX System V Network Programming*, Addison-Wesley, 1993.

[72] K. A. Robbins, N. R. Wagner and D. J. Wenzel, "Virtual rings: An introduction to concurrency," SIGCSE, vol. 21, 1989, pp. 23–28.

[73] A. A. Rodriguez and L. A. Rowe, "Multimedia systems and applications," *IEEE Computer*, vol. 28, no. 5, 1995, pp. 20–22.

[74] B. Rosenblatt, *Learning the Korn Shell*, O'Reilly & Associates, 1993.

[75] R. Rybacki, K. Robbins and S. Robbins, "Ethercom: A study of audio processes and synchronization," *Proc. Twenty-Fourth SIGCSE Technical Symp. on Computer Science Education*, 1993, pp. 218–222.

[76] R. Sandberg, "The SUN network file system: Design, implementation, and experience," Sun Microsystems White Paper, 1989.

[77] C. Schimmel, *UNIX Systems for Modern Architectures: Symmetric Multiprocessing and Caching for Kernel Programmers*, Addison-Wesley, 1994.

[78] S. Shrivastava, G. N. Dixon and G. D. Parrington, "An overview of the Arjuna distributed programming system," *IEEE Software*, January 1991, pp. 66–73.

[79] R. W. Sevick, "Viewpoint: For commercial multiprocessing the choice is SMP," *IEEE Spectrum*, January 1995, pp. 50.

[80] A. Silberschatz and P. B. Galvin, *Operating Systems Concepts*, 4th ed., Addison-Wesley Publishing, 1994.

[81] M. G. Sobell, *UNIX System V: A Practical Guide*, 3rd ed., Benjamin/Cummings. 1995.

[82] M. G. Sobell, *A Practical Guide to the UNIX System*, 3rd ed., Benjamin/Cummings, 1995.

[83] *Sun OS5.3 Writing Device Drivers*, SunSoft Incorporated, 1993.

[84] W. Stallings, *Local and Metropolitan Area Networks*, 4th ed., Macmillan, 1993.

[85] W. R. Stevens, *UNIX Network Programming*, Prentice Hall, 1990.

[86] W. R. Stevens, *Advanced Programming in the UNIX Environment*, Addison-Wesley, 1992.

[87] V. S. Sunderam, "PVM: A framework for parallel distributed computing," *J. of Concurrency: Practice and Experience*, vol. 2, no. 4, 1990, pp. 315–339.

[88] S. Talbott, *Managing Projects with* make, O'Reilly & Associates, 1991.

[89] A. S. Tanenbaum, *Operating Systems: Design and Implementation*, Prentice Hall, 1987.

[90] A. S. Tanenbaum, *Computer Networks*, Prentice Hall, 1989.

[91] A. S. Tanenbaum, R. van Renesse, H. van Staveren, G. Sharp, S. Mullender, J. Jansen and G. van Rossum, "Experiences with the Amoeba distributed operating system," *Communications of the ACM*, vol. 33, no. 12, 1990, pp. 46–63.

[92] A. S. Tanenbaum, *Modern Operating Systems*, Prentice Hall, 1992.

[93] A. S. Tanenbaum, *Distributed Operating Systems*, Prentice Hall, 1995.

[94] D. B. Terry and D. C. Swinehart, "Managing stored voice in the Etherphone system," *ACM Transactions on Computer Systems*, vol. 6, 1988, pp. 3–27.

[95] G. Varghese and T. Lauck, "Hashed and hierarchical timing wheels: Data structures for efficient implementation of a Timer Facility," *Proc. Eleventh ACM Symp. on OS Principles*, 1987, pp. 25–38.

[96] *X/Open CAE Specification: System Interface Definitions*, Issue 4, Version 2, X/Open Company Ltd., 1994.

[97] *X/Open CAE Specification: System Interfaces and Headers*, Issue 4, Version 2, X/Open Company Ltd., 1994.

[98] *X/Open CAE Specification: Commands and Utilities*, Issue 4, Version 2, X/Open Company Ltd., 1994.

[99] *X/Open CAE Specification: Networking Services*, Issue 4, X/Open Company Ltd., 1994.

[100] *Solaris Multithreaded Programming Guide*, SunSoft Incorporated, 1995.

Index

Entries refer to page numbers in the text. **Boldface** is used for the most important references.

641